Teacher's Edition

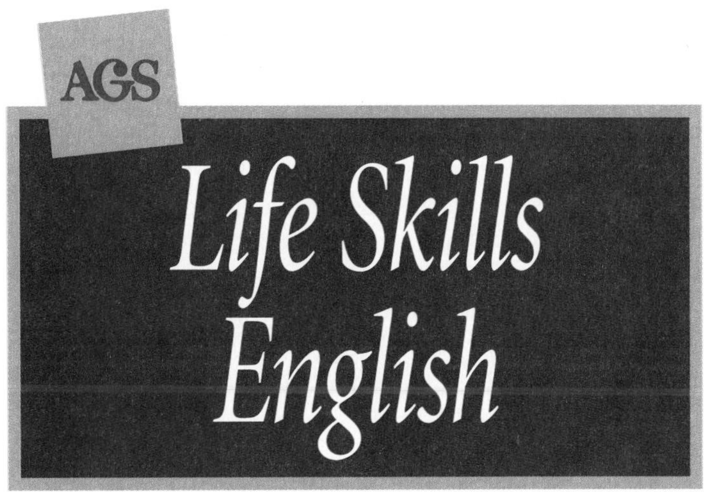

by

Bonnie L. Walker

AGS®
American Guidance Service, Inc.
Circle Pines, Minnesota 55014-1796
800-328-2560

About the Author

Bonnie L. Walker taught for sixteen years in secondary schools and college. She holds a Ph.D. in curriculum theory and instructional design from the University of Maryland, an M.Ed. in secondary education, and a B.A. in English. She studied psycholinguistics at the University of Illinois Graduate School, and was a curriculum developer at the Model Secondary School for the Deaf at Gallaudet University. She is the author of *Basic English Grammar, Basic English Composition,* and numerous workbooks, learning packages, and sound filmstrips in written expression, grammar, and usage. She was a member of Project EduTech, which investigated promising technologies to improve the delivery of special education services. Dr. Walker has written several papers on the applications of personal computers, video technology, and cable television in education. She has been the director for research and development projects funded by the U.S. Department of Education, the U.S. Department of Agriculture, and the Administration on Youth, Children, and Families. Since 1986, Dr. Walker has been president of a research and development company specializing in development of training and educational materials for special populations.

The publisher wishes to thank the following educators for their helpful comments during the review process for *Life Skills English.* Their assistance has been invaluable.

Jeanette D. Pulliam
Reading Supervisor K-12
Curriculum and Staff Development
St. Louis Public Schools
St. Louis, MO

Gayle Boroughs
Special Education Teacher
Oak Ridge High School
Oak Ridge, TN

Diane De Vito
Supervisor of DH/SLD Programs
Warren City Schools, East Instructional Center
Warren, OH

Pamela Kinzler
Special Education Teacher
Penn Hills High School
Pittsburgh, PA

Dr. Bessie Watson Hampton
Coordinator, Family and Consumer Sciences
Kansas City Missouri District
Kansas City, MO

Ruth Greider
Special Education Coordinator
Wichita Public Schools
Wichita, KS

Joyce von Ehrenkrook
Special Education Coordinator
Wichita Public Schools
Wichita, KS

Bill Michel
Manager, Research and Development
Ramsey County Library
Shoreview, MN

Melanie Eick
Disabilities Specialist
Oklahoma Department of Vocational and Technical Education
Stillwater, OK

Geraldine Dumas
Consultant
Bibb County School System
Macon, GA

Caril Baker
Librarian
Selby Public Library
Sarasota County Library System
Sarasota, FL

Printed in the United States of America
ISBN 0-7854-2275-7 (Previously ISBN 0-7854-0511-9) Product Number 91462
A 0 9 8 7 6 5 4 3 2 1

Table of Contents

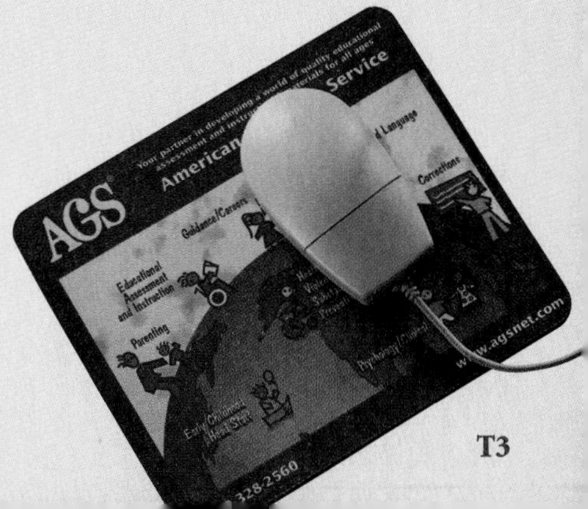

The major goal of **LIFE SKILLS ENGLISH** is to develop language skills that young people and adults need in their everyday lives. The development of this textbook is based on a series of interviews with teachers, supervisors, and students from across the country. Topics included in the text are based on these findings.

The primary focus of *Life Skills English* is seeking and evaluating information. The text first emphasizes the skills needed to find information. Students learn how information is organized and how to use reference tools to locate information. The text teaches students how to use and develop skills that they will apply in other subjects and everyday life.

To motivate students, both the sentence structure and the vocabulary are controlled throughout the text, including the directions, examples, and exercises. This allows students to concentrate on content mastery. Chapter openers, examples, and exercises focus on relevant and practical applications. For example, students are taught how to read a food label, read the yellow pages, follow recipe directions, and read the want ads.

Short, concise lessons help students focus on single concepts. Each topic has been subdivided so that students are introduced to one rule or new concept at a time. Language skills such as spelling, punctuation, and capitalization are presented within the context of the situation in which they are ordinarily used. Instruction is included on using a dictionary and the steps involved in locating words.

The ability to find information is an essential life skill. In *Life Skills English* students are taught to gather information using books, magazines, newspapers, radio, television, computers, and experts. Up-to-date resources are included to help prepare students to meet the challenges of technology.

Whom do you call for an eye exam? Where can you go to have your muffler replaced? Students explore different professions as they search for experts in given areas. Because a practical situation is always presented before a new skill is introduced, your students are motivated to learn more about each area. Students see the relevance of what they are learning.

In addition, *Life Skills English* teaches filling out job applications, financial forms, and order forms. This is the perfect text to prepare students and young adults to become responsible and independent citizens.

AGS Worktexts

CHECK OUT AGS WORKTEXTS! AGS offers additional language arts materials to help you tailor instruction to meet the diverse needs of your students. Each worktext contains 96 pages of up-to-date information and motivating skill lessons with lots of opportunities for practice and reinforcement. These may be used to accompany a basal program or as the core instructional tool.

AGS Grammar and Composition Skills

AGS Practical English Skills

For more information on AGS Worktexts, call 1-800-328-2560.

AGS English Textbooks

Basic English Grammar

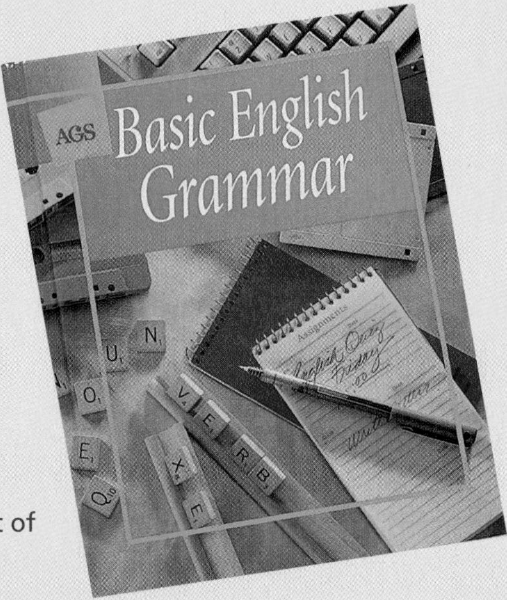

Basic English Grammar is designed to meet the needs of secondary students and adults who read well below grade level. Prior to the book being written, a series of interviews was conducted with teachers, supervisors, and students across the United States. A need was identified for a textbook that would present grammatical rules and concepts one at a time and provide sufficient opportunities for appropriate practice.

All aspects of the text are carefully controlled, including instructions, examples, directions, and exercises. The sentence structure and vocabulary are clear and straightforward, which helps reluctant readers access the material more easily than they could with traditional grammar textbooks. In addition, the high interest content of the activities appeals to older students.

Reading Level: 3.2 Spache
Interest Level: Grades 6-12, ABE, ESL

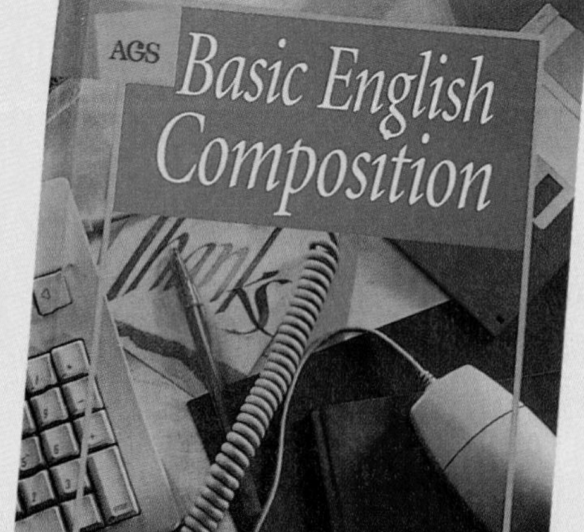

Basic English Composition

Basic English Composition is designed to help secondary students and adults develop practical writing skills. Throughout the text, comprehension is enhanced through the use of simple sentence structure and low-level vocabulary. To add motivational interest, the instruction and activities revolve around a group of high school students experiencing a typical school year.

Prior to development of this text, the author conducted a series of interviews with teachers, curriculum supervisors, and students across the country. As a result, *Basic English Composition* reflects these needs by emphasizing writing sentences, then paragraphs, followed by reports and other projects. All are identified as important skills to be taught.

Reading Level: 3.8 Spache
Interest Level: Grades 6-12, ABE, ESL

For more information on AGS Textbooks, call 1-800-328-2560.

English for the World of Work

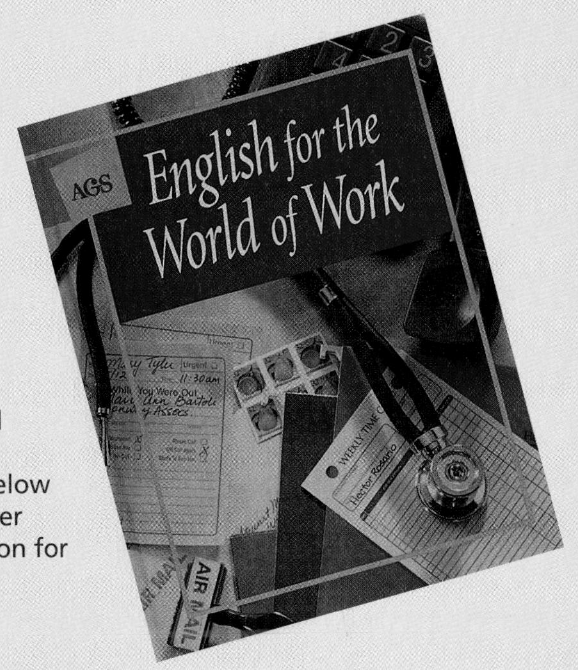

English for the World of Work develops communication skills that are essential for deciding upon a career, obtaining a job, keeping a job, and being prepared for promotions. Students prepare a career portfolio that can be used later during their job searches. This textbook is intended for secondary students and adults who are planning to enter the world of work soon after the course.

This text is designed to be practical and relevant. Activities and exercises are patterned after situations in the working world and are designed to develop better reading, writing, speaking, and listening skills. Effort has been made to keep the reading level below the fourth grade. Some concepts are dealt with at a slightly higher level than others. Suggestions are provided in the Teacher's Edition for directing the students' reading to help them achieve full comprehension.

Reading Level: 3.6 Spache
Interest Level: Grades 6-12, ABE, ESL

English to Use

English to Use is designed to meet the communication needs of secondary students and adults who are reading below grade level or learning English as a second language. Grammar and usage are integrated into each lesson to facilitate an understanding of rules and their practical application to the patterns of written and spoken English. Students practice and apply each language skill in a variety of settings, from identification and classification to evaluative thinking and application.

The instructions, examples, directions, and exercises are presented in a systematic, discrete manner. Particular attention is given to organizing the instruction so that only a single rule or a single concept is presented at one time. Numerous exercises allow the teacher frequent review of students' understanding. Lessons build upon each other throughout the book.

Sign language is featured throughout *English to Use.* By including these illustrations, we hope to connect the spoken word and signing. It is not the intention of this text to provide a total program in signing—only an awareness.

Reading Level: 3.3 Spache
Interest Level: Grades 6-12, ABE, ESL

Student Text Highlights

The student texts are designed to motivate even the most reluctant learner. Concise, targeted lessons allow students to focus on a single concept and experience success. Students will demonstrate increased comprehension with the text written at 3.2 reading level.

- Each chapter opens with a colorful photo that relates the chapter content to real-life application.
- Background information is provided to set the stage for learning and to make the material relevant for students.
- *Goals for Learning* are identified at the beginning of each chapter to help students understand the main ideas they will be learning.

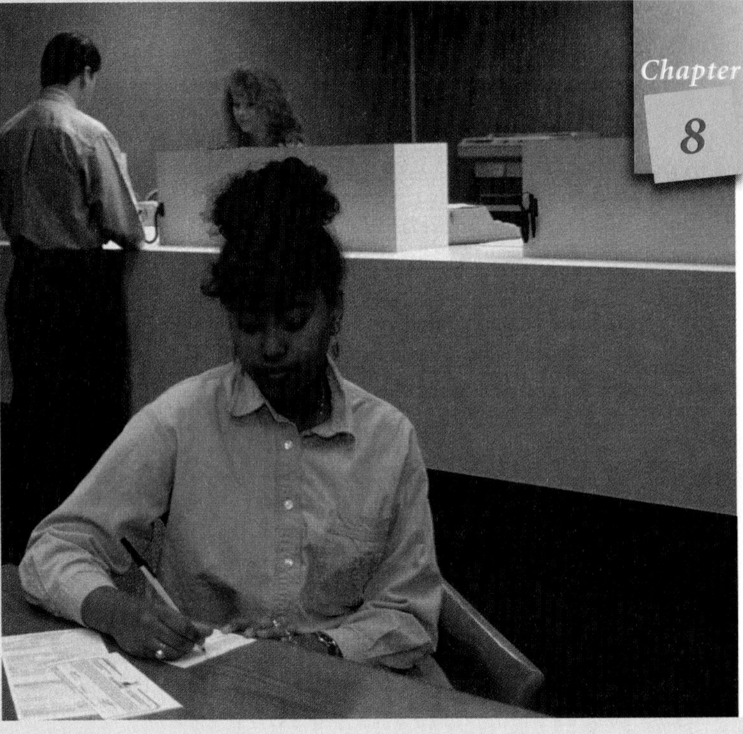

Chapter 8

Completing Applications and Other Forms

Throughout your life, you will be asked to fill out forms. You may have to fill out a form to apply for a job, to obtain a driver's license, to rent an apartment, to open a checking account, or to travel to another country. A form is a printed or typed document with spaces to fill in information about you or someone else.

In Chapter 8, you will learn about completing different types of applications and forms. Each lesson focuses on the kinds of information you have to know to fill out forms and the different kinds of forms you may have to fill out.

Goals for Learning

- To learn how to fill out applications and other forms correctly and completely
- To learn about the kinds of personal information asked for on applications and forms
- To learn how to answer questions on job applications
- To learn about questions and vocabulary related to loans, credit, and financial forms

219

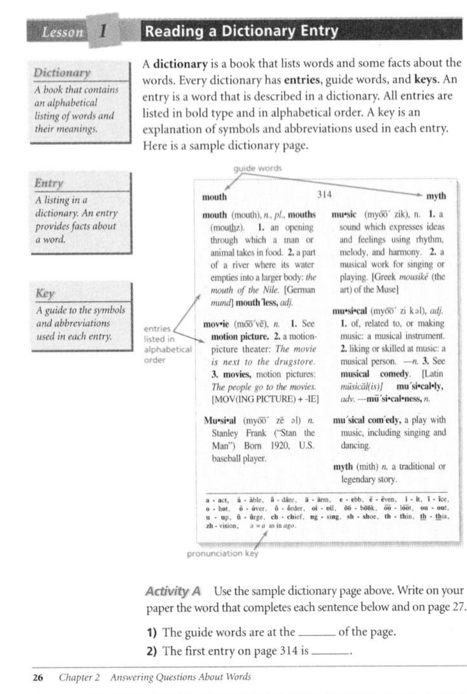

Lesson 1

Reading a Dictionary Entry

Dictionary
A book that contains an alphabetical listing of words and their meanings.

Entry
A listing in a dictionary. An entry provides facts about a word.

Key
A guide to the symbols and abbreviations used in each entry.

A **dictionary** is a book that lists words and some facts about the words. Every dictionary has **entries**, guide words, and **keys**. An entry is a word that is described in a dictionary. All entries are listed in bold type and in alphabetical order. A key is an explanation of symbols and abbreviations used in each entry. Here is a sample dictionary page.

mouth 314 **myth**

mouth (mouth), *n., pl.,* **mouths** (mouthz). **1.** an opening through which a man or animal takes in food. **2.** a part of a river where its water empties into a larger body: *the mouth of the Nile.* [German *mund*] **mouth´less,** *adj.*

mov•ie (mōō´vē), *n.* **1.** See **motion picture. 2.** a motion-picture theater: *The movie is next to the drugstore.* **3. movies,** motion pictures: *The people go to the movies.* [MOV(ING PICTURE) + -IE]

Mu•si•al (myōō´ zē əl) *n.* Stanley Frank ("Stan the Man") Born 1920, U.S. baseball player.

mu•sic (myōō´ zik), n. **1.** a sound which expresses ideas and feelings using rhythm, melody, and harmony. **2.** a musical work for singing or playing. [Greek *mousikē* (the art) of the Muse]

mu•si•cal (myōō´ zi kəl), *adj.* **1.** of, related to, or making music: a musical instrument. **2.** liking or skilled at music: a musical person. —*n.* **3.** See **musical comedy**. [Latin *mūsicāl(is)*] **mu´si•cal•ly,** *adv.* —**mū´si•cal•ness,** *n.*

mu´sical com´edy, a play with music, including singing and dancing.

myth (mith) *n.* a traditional or legendary story.

a - act, ā - āble, â - dâre, ä - ärm, e - ebb, ē - ēven, i - it, ī - īce, o - hot, ō - ōver, ô - ôrder, oi - oil, ŏŏ - bŏŏk, ōō - lōōt, ou - out, u - up, û - ûrge, ch - chief, ng - sing, sh - shoe, th - thin, th - this, zh - vision, ə = *a* as in *ago*.

Activity A Use the sample dictionary page above. Write on your paper the word that completes each sentence below and on page 27.

1) The guide words are at the _____ of the page.
2) The first entry on page 314 is _____.

26 *Chapter 2 Answering Questions About Words*

3) The last entry on the page is _____.
4) The pronunciation key is at the _____ of the page.
5) There are _____ entries on page 314.

Most dictionary entries contain the same basic features. The entries below provide examples of these features.

phonetic spellings to use with pronunciation key to help you pronounce the word
part of speech
numbered definitions, or meanings
syllables, or parts of the word, shown with dots
sample sentence or phrase
synonyms
different forms of the word
cross-reference

wan•der (wän´dər), *v.i.* **1.** to walk around without a purpose or reason: *to wander around town.* **2.** to think about many topics without conscious control: *His attention wandered as the teacher spoke.* —*v.t.* **3.** to travel about, on, or through: *He wandered the streets.* —**wan´der•er,** *n.*

want (wont), *v.t.* **1.** to feel a need for or wish for: *want some dinner; wanting something different.* —*v.i.* **2.** to wish or to like: *We can stay home if you want to.* —*n.* **3.** a need or a necessity: *Her wants are few.* —**Syn.** require, need. See **wish.**

want´ ad´ See **classified ad.**

Activity B Use the sample entries and pronunciation key to answer the questions. Write your answers on your paper.

1) How many meanings are given for *wander*?
2) What are two synonyms for *want*?
3) What is another form of the verb *wander*?
4) Does the *a* in *wander* have the same sound as the *a* in *want*?
5) Which two entries have cross-references?

Answering Questions About Words Chapter 2 27

- Each lesson is clearly labeled to help students focus on main ideas.
- Graphs and charts present concepts visually to reinforce and clarify instruction.
- Glossary words are boldfaced the first time they appear in the text. In addition to being defined in context, they are also defined in a special vocabulary box in the side column. This provides a quick review for students.

Lesson 2 Review

Part A Use the sample classroom map on page 68 to answer these questions. Write the answers on your paper.

1) If you are sitting at the teacher's desk facing the classroom, what direction are you facing?
2) How many windows does the classroom have?
3) How wide (in feet) is each window?
4) What classroom object is located between the two doors?
5) If you are looking out one of the windows, what direction are you facing?
6) What is directly behind the teacher's desk?

Part B Create a gazetteer on your paper for the classroom map on page 68. Include the items listed below. Remember that the items in a gazetteer are listed in alphabetical order.

Example Bulletin board F-4, 5, 6

1) West door
2) East door
3) Middle window
4) Teacher's desk
5) Chalkboard
6) Table

Part C Write on your paper the name of the place found at each of these locations on the grid map below.

1) C-4
2) A-2
3) B-1
4) D-1
5) D-5
6) C-2
7) A-4
8) D-3

Lesson 3 Encyclopedias

Encyclopedia
A book or set of books with a collection of articles and facts on many subjects, organized in alphabetical order.

Volume
A single book, or one book in a set of books.

A very useful type of reference book is an **encyclopedia**. An encyclopedia is a book or set of books with facts on many subjects. It is usually a collection of articles in alphabetical order.

Some encyclopedias are only one book, or **volume**. Others are a set of books, or volumes. *The World Book Encyclopedia*, the *Encyclopædia Brittanica*, and *Compton's Encyclopedia* all have many volumes. Most sets of encyclopedias have similar features, as shown in the diagram below. These features can help you find the information you need quickly.

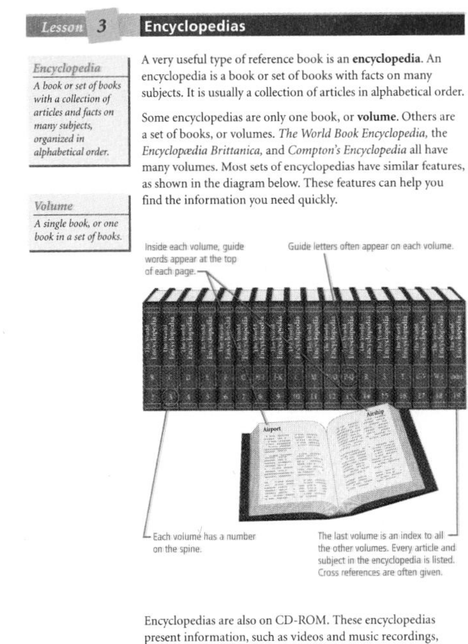
Inside each volume, guide words appear at the top of each page.
Guide letters often appear on each volume.
Airport
Airship
Each volume has a number on the spine.
The last volume is an index to all the other volumes. Every article and subject in the encyclopedia is listed. Cross references are often given.

Encyclopedias are also on CD-ROM. These encyclopedias present information, such as videos and music recordings, in a way that cannot be presented in books.

■ Examples are clearly labeled and illustrate new skills.

■ Frequent exercises offer teachers opportunities to check students' understanding.

■ Exercises focus on practical, real-life applications.

■ *Chapter Reviews* appear in the student text and allow students and teachers to check skill mastery.

■ The *Chapter Reviews* directly reflect the chapter *Goals for Learning.*

Chapter 3 Review

Part A Write the answers to the following questions on your paper.

1) What is the main information in a farmer's almanac?
2) Why would a mariner read a farmer's almanac?
3) Name one general information almanac.
4) Where is the index found in most almanacs?
5) Are you likely to find the answers to the following questions in an almanac—*Yes* or *No*?
   a) Has Denzel Washington ever won an Academy Award?
   b) How do you prepare Mexican Cole Slaw?
   c) Who holds the record for the most home runs?

Part B Use this map to answer the questions below. Write your answers on your paper.

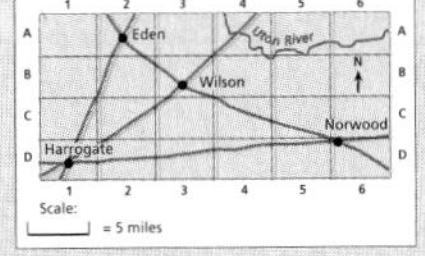
Eden
Uton River
Wilson
Norwood
Harrogate
Scale:
= 5 miles

1) What two cities are southeast of Eden?
2) What city is located at D-1?
3) Is the Uton River north or south of Wilson?
4) What city is northwest of Wilson?
5) How many miles is it from Wilson to Norwood?

Part C Write the answers to the following questions on your paper.

1) How are the articles in an encyclopedia arranged?
2) What is one book in a set of encyclopedias called?
3) What is a "desk" encyclopedia?
4) What would the guide letter be on volume one of *The World Book Encyclopedia*?
5) What would you expect to find at the top of each page of an encyclopedia?

Part D Use the recipe below to answer the questions that follow. Write your answers on your paper.

Corn Pudding

1 17-oz. can creamed corn	1 small can evaporated milk
10 soda crackers, crushed	1 egg, beaten
salt	pepper

Grease a one-quart casserole dish. Pour in creamed corn. Add crushed soda crackers, evaporated milk, and egg. Add salt and pepper to taste. Mix well. Bake at 400°F until brown on top and bubbling (about 20-30 minutes).
Serves 4.

1) What steps should you follow to be sure the recipe turns out right?
2) What abbreviations are in this recipe and what do they mean?
3) What ingredients will you need to prepare this recipe?
4) What utensils will you need?
5) What directions must you follow to prepare this recipe? Write them in order.

Part E Write the answer to these questions on your paper.

1) What kind of magazine has summaries of articles from other magazines?
2) Which magazine is published more often—a biannual or a semiannual?
3) Which of these reference books is a periodical—*The World Book Encyclopedia, Time Magazine, Betty Crocker's Picture Cookbook*?
4) What periodical helps you find articles in other periodicals?
5) Where can you look to learn what articles are in a magazine?

Test Taking Tip When taking a true-false test, read each statement carefully. Write *true* only when the statement is true all of the time. Write *false* if any part or all of the statement is false.

■ Each *Chapter Review* includes a *Test Taking Tip.* These tips will help students prepare to take tests of all types.

Test Taking Tip When taking a true-false test, read each statement carefully. Write *true* only when the statement is true all of the time. Write *false* if any part or all of the statement is false.

Teacher's Edition Highlights

The comprehensive, wraparound teacher's edition provides instructional strategies at point of use. Everything from preparation guidelines to teaching tips and strategies are included in an easy-to-use format. Activities are featured at point of use for teacher convenience.

- Quick overview of the lesson saves time.
- Lesson objectives are listed for easy reference.
- Page references are provided for convenience.
- Instructional resources are clearly identified.
- Reading vocabulary classified above fourth grade level is listed on each page. Grade levels are shown in parentheses. Nongraded words show no number.
- An introductory discussion or activity opens each lesson by activating prior knowledge and setting the stage for learning.
- Suggestions are given for introducing and teaching the activities.
- Teachers are given suggestions for reviewing skills needed for success in the lesson.
- *Application:* There are three kinds of applications—At Home, Career Connection, and In the Community. Relating lessons to the world outside of the classroom helps motivate students and makes learning relevant.

Lesson at a Glance

Chapter 1 Lesson 2

Overview This lesson explains guide words and how to use them to locate information in a reference source.

Objective

- To determine what topics appear on a page with specific guide words.

Student Pages 6–12

Teacher's Resource Library

Activity 3

Workbook Activity 5

Reading Vocabulary

atlas (7)	reference (6)
guide words	

Teaching Suggestions

- **Introducing the Lesson** Discuss the definition of guide words, the different types of reference books that have guide words, and the example shown on the page. If possible, display actual examples of the types of books listed in the box. Invite volunteers to take turns opening to random pages in one of the books and reading the guide words at the top of the page. Then have them read several of the items listed on that page.
- **Reviewing Skills** Review the rules of alphabetizing.

Application

At Home

Encourage students to look through reference books at home to see how many have guide words. Suggest that, once students feel comfortable using guide words, they explain to a family member the process of using guide words to find information quickly.

6 Chapter 1 *What's There and How to Find It*

Lesson 2 **Using Guide Words**

Guide words

Words at the top of a page of information given in alphabetical order. All words that come in alphabetical order between the two guide words can be found on that page.

Guide words help you find information given in alphabetical order. You will find guide words at the top of the page in many reference books. Use the guide words to help you find the page with the information you need. The first guide word is the first word on the page. The second guide word is the last word on the page. The other words on the page come in alphabetical order between these words.

Some books that have guide words are:

telephone books	atlases
dictionaries	encyclopedias

Example

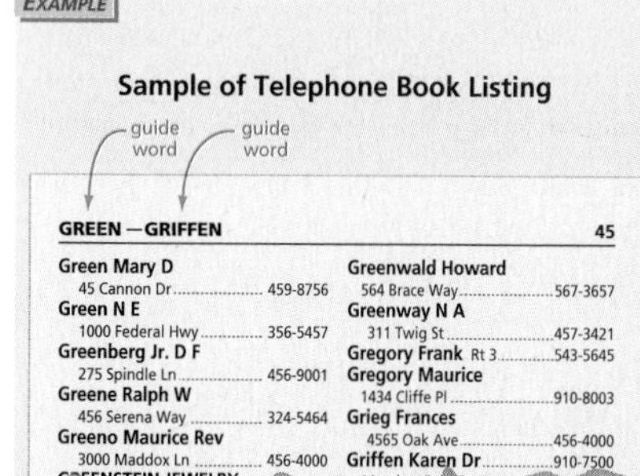

Sample of Telephone Book Listing

GREEN—GRIFFEN 45

Green Mary D 45 Cannon Dr 459-8756	**Greenwald Howard** 564 Brace Way 567-3657
Green N E 1000 Federal Hwy 356-5457	**Greenway N A** 311 Twig St 457-3421
Greenberg Jr. D F 275 Spindle Ln 456-9001	**Gregory Frank** Rt 3 543-5645
Greene Ralph W 456 Serena Way 324-5464	**Gregory Maurice** 1434 Cliffe Pl 910-8003
Greeno Maurice Rev 3000 Maddox Ln 456-4000	**Grieg Frances** 4565 Oak Ave 456-4000
	Griffen Karen Dr 910-7500

6 Chapter 1 *What's There and How to Find It*

Activity A Each set of guide words below is followed by three words. Write on your paper the letters of the words that would appear on the page with each set of guide words.

Example Guide Words: address—April
a) add **b)** American **c)** appear
Answer: b, c

1) mad—map
a) main **b)** maze **c)** manage

2) sad—scream
a) safe **b)** sand **c)** scratch

3) raise—remember
a) rapidly **b)** remain **c)** reason

4) want ad—warp
a) wander **b)** wart **c)** ward

5) fellow—fur
a) frame **b)** Friday **c)** February

6) early—else
a) east **b)** each **c)** elves

Activity B Which of the names listed below would appear between the guide words shown? Write your answers on your paper.

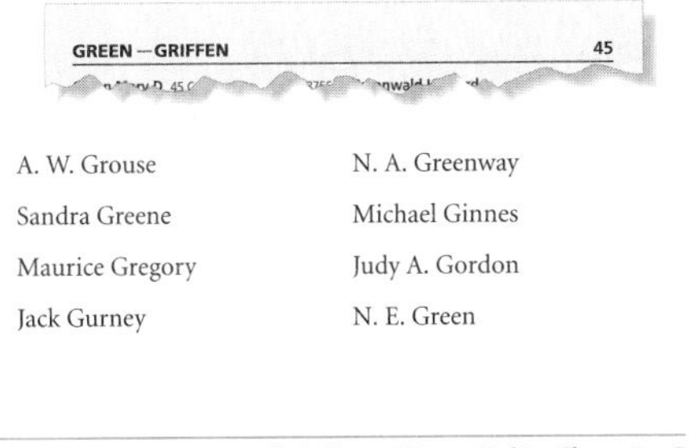

A. W. Grouse
Sandra Greene
Maurice Gregory
Jack Gurney
N. A. Greenway
Michael Ginnes
Judy A. Gordon
N. E. Green

Reading Vocabulary

maze (8) warp (7)
ward (6) wart (6)

■ Presenting Activity A

Discuss the example provided for Activity A, making sure students understand what they are to do. Then do item 1 on the board with students before asking them to complete Activity A on their own.

Activity A Answers
1) a, c 2) a, b, c 3) a, b, c
4) c 5) a, b 6) a

■ Presenting Activity B

Draw the top of a page on the board and print these guide words at the top: *Lewis—Lyons.* Then have students whose last names begin with L decide whether their names would appear on this page. Invite these students to write their last names in alphabetical order under the guide words. Ask the class to check that all the names belong on that page. Repeat this process as often as necessary to confirm that students understand the concept. Use a different initial letter and guide words each time. Then have students complete Activity B on their own. You may wish to have students list their responses in alphabetical order.

Activity B Answers
N. E. Green, Sandra Greene, N. A. Greenway, Maurice Gregory

Using Guide Words

Activity 3

Using Guide Words

Workbook Activity 5

■ Answers are provided in the teacher's edition for all exercises in the student text.

■ The *Global Connection* features will help students connect the lesson to the world community at large. Multicultural issues are emphasized as students view the world as a community.

■ Special helps will assist ESL students with lesson content.

■ Community participation and environmental awareness are encouraged with activities in the teacher's edition as extensions of various lessons.

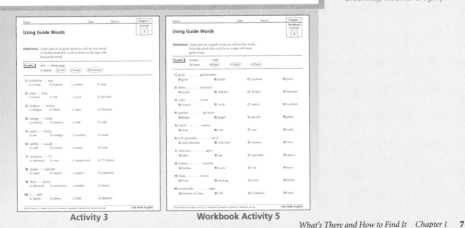

■ Activity and Workbook Activity pages are shown at point of use. The Teacher's Resource Library contains all reproducible activities. Emphasis is placed on including learning activities for reaching a diverse range of learning styles. A variety of teaching and student activities are included at the point of use.

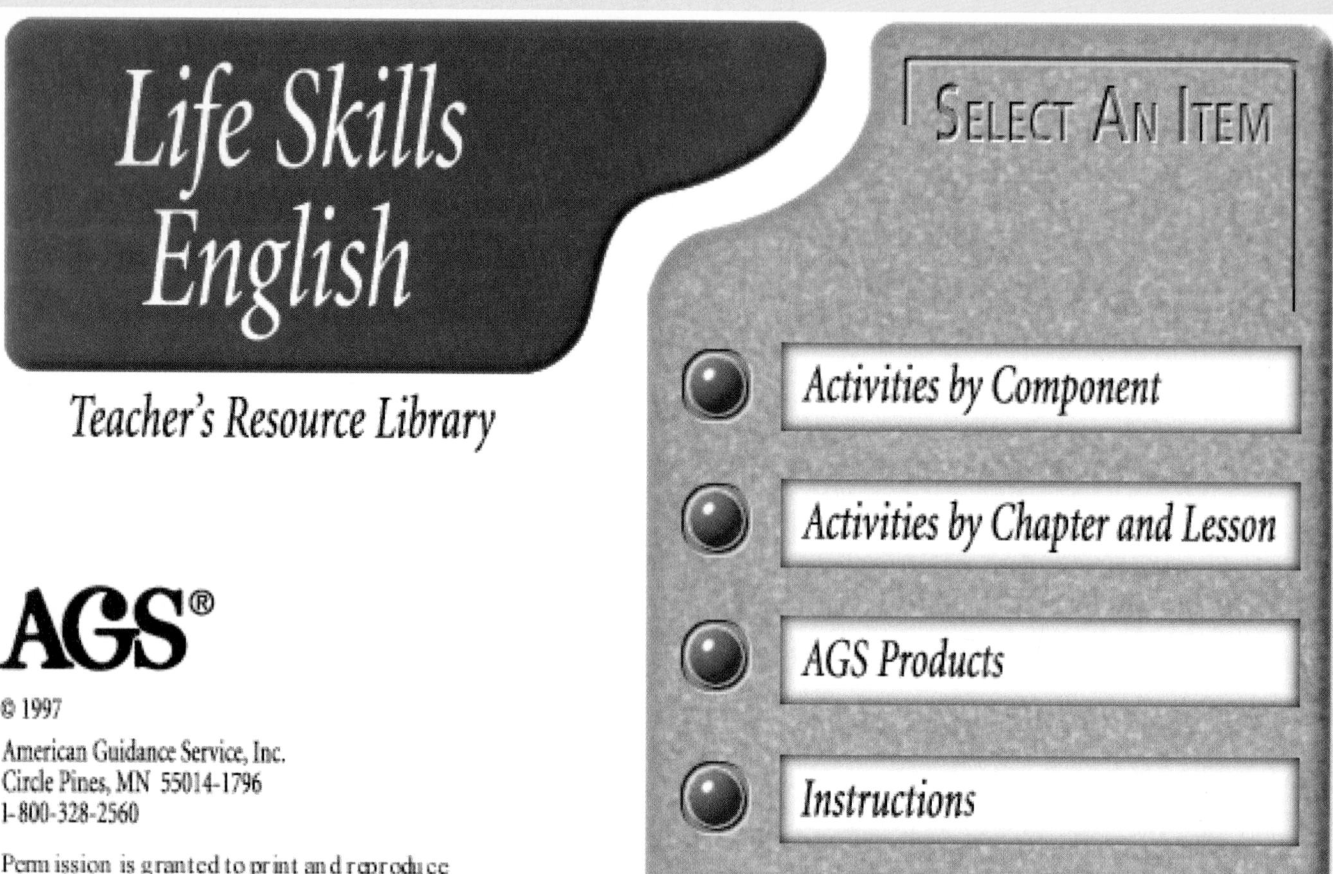

TRL All of the activities you'll need to reinforce and extend the text are conveniently located on the AGS Teacher's Resource Library (TRL) CD-ROM. The reproducible activities featured in the Teacher's Edition are ready to review, select, and print. Additionally, you can preview other materials by directly linking to the AGS web site.

Activities

Lesson activities reinforce the concepts taught in the lesson. Activities are designed to help students see the relevance of the skills being taught. A variety of activities provide additional motivation.

Workbook Activities

Workbook activities may be reproduced as added reinforcement and practice for lessons. These activities are also available in a workbook format.

Putting It Together

Putting It Together activities help students learn to connect the basic communication skills with real-life situations. This helps students see the practical aspects of the skills being taught.

Community Connections

Relevant activities help students apply their new knowledge in the community and reinforce concepts covered in class.

Self-Study Guide

Assignment guides with student/teacher contracts are provided for the entire text. These are suggested lesson plans from the text and workbook. This provides teachers with the flexibility of individualized instruction or independent study.

Mastery Tests

Chapter, midterm, and final mastery tests are conveniently referenced as assessment options.

Self-Study Guide

Assignment guides with student/teacher contracts are provided for the entire text. These guides outline suggested lessons from the text and workbook. This provides teachers with the flexibility of individualized instruction or independent study.

SELF-STUDY GUIDE

Name __________

CHAPTER 2: Answering Questions About Words

Goal 2.1 *To identify the different parts of a dictionary entry*

Date	Assignment	Score
_____	1: Read pages 25-26. Complete Activity A on pages 26-27. Read page 27. Complete Activity B on page 27.	_____

Comments:

Goal 2.2 *To understand how a dictionary is organized*

Date	Assignment	Score
_____	2: Read pages 28-29. Complete Activity C on page 29.	_____
_____	3: Read pages 30-31. Complete Activity D on page 32.	_____
_____	4: Complete the Lesson 1 Review, Parts A-C on page 33.	_____
_____	5: Complete Workbook Activity 9.	_____

Comments:

Goal 2.3 *To use a dictionary to find word meanings*

Date	Assignment	Score
_____	6: Read pages 34-35. Complete Activity A on page 35. Read page 36. Complete Activity B on page 36.	
_____	7: Complete Workbook Activity 10.	
_____	8: Read page 37. Complete Activity C on page 38. Read page 38. Complete Activity D on page 38.	
_____	9: Complete Workbook Activity 11.	

Tests

Teachers are provided with a complete testing program. Tests are provided for each chapter, forms A and B. A midterm and final test provide additional assessment options.

Name Date Period | *Chapter 8 Mastery Test A page 1*

Chapter 8 Mastery Test A

Part A Complete each sentence using a word from the box.

form	maiden	card	document	name
full	Social Security	United States	information	birth

1) Facts about yourself is called personal __________.
2) A __________ is a paper that gives information to another person.
3) A person's whole legal name is called a __________ name.
4) A document saying when and where you were born is called a __________ certificate.
5) The __________ of a person written by that person is called a signature.
6) Most applications ask for your __________ number.
7) A woman's last name before she marries is her __________ name.
8) If you were born in the __________, you are a United States citizen.
9) A green __________ is an official document that allows aliens to work legally in the United States.
10) A printed or typed document with spaces to fill in information is called a __________.

Part B Read the following statements. If the statement is true, write *True* on the line. If the statement is not true, write *False*.

Life Skills English

Name Date Period | *Chapter 4 Activity 14*

Finding Information in the White Pages

Directions: Given below is a sample directory for Frankfort County, U.S.A. (This is not a real place.) Read this directory. The area code is 555. Use the facts in the sample to answer the following questions.

136	Lambros–Laurel
LAMBROS Scott & Becky	LAPIERE Gwenda 1299 L St....334-8754
13226 D Frances Dr....334-9802	LARGO COMMUNITY CHURCH
LANCASTER Carl T atty	12100 West Avenue....334-6500
Ofc 8000 Main St....599-0976	LARGO Mary 12300 Main St....599-6501
Fred M. 4503 Tabor Ln....334-8700	James J. Maj
Jay G & Laura T 2141 Lois Ln....599-8762	700 Larson Blvd....261-8761
LANE B 3421 Wood St....334-8761	LARSON HEALTH ASSOCIATES
B L 12655 Harold St....599-9000	2000 West Street....334-1756
D A 2341 North St....261-8761	LAURA's UPHOLSTERY
Dennis M 100 Western Ave....599-9123	4500 Main St....599-6000

1) On what street does Dennis Lane live?
2) What is Carl Lancaster's profession?
3) What is Gwenda Lapiere's phone number?
4) If you wanted to have your furniture upholstered, what phone number could you call?
5) Name the three exchanges in this town.
6) What is the Largo Community Church's phone number?
7) James J. Largo is in the military ... rank?
8) What is D A Lane's address?
9) What telephone number could ... health care?

©AGS® American Guidance Service, Inc. Permission is granted to reproduce for classroom use only.

Activities

These activities will help you reinforce the concepts taught in the lesson. Many of these activities contain facsimiles of actual forms students will encounter in the workplace.

Activities are designed to help students see the relevance of the skills being taught. A variety of activities will provide additional motivation.

Name Date Period | *Chapter 3 Workbook Activity 17*

Reading the Information on Food Labels

Directions: Read the information on these two labels. Then answer the questions.

Granola Bars — Orchard Blend — Nutrition Facts

Chicken Broth — Nutrition Facts

1) What is the main ingredient in granola bars?
2) What is the second largest ingredient in chicken broth?
3) Which food has more protein—the granola bars or the chicken broth?
4) Which food has less fat?
5) Which food has more carbohydrates?
6) Which food contains less than 4% of the Daily Value of iron?
7) Which food has more calories per serving?
8) Which item under nutritional information is measured in milligrams?

©AGS® American Guidance Service, Inc. Permission is granted to reproduce for classroom use only. Life Skills English

Workbook Activities

Students are encouraged to practice skills and apply knowledge in relevant and real-life situations.

Skills Chart

Life Skills English

	Chapter								
Vocabulary Skills									
Alphabetizing	1			4	5				
Definitions	1	2	3	4	5	6	7	8	9
Synonyms	1								
Dictionary Use		2							
Pronunciation		2							
Abbreviations		2				6	7	8	
Etymology		2							
Homonyms		2							
Parts of Speech		2							
Syllabication		2							
Technical Terms and Jargon						6			
Writing Skills									
Spelling	1	2	3	4					
Letter of Application								8	
Letter of Complaint									9
Filling Out Application Forms								8	
Filling Out Order Forms									9
Filling Out a Subscription Form			3						
Writing Your Address								8	9
Critical Thinking Skills									
Applying Information	1	2	3	4	5	6	7	8	9
Classifying and Categorizing	1	2	3	4	5				
Organizing Information					5				
Separating Fact and Opinion							7		
Recognizing Propaganda Techniques							7		
Making Generalizations					5				9
Drawing Conclusions		2				6			9
Making Predictions			3	4	5	6			9

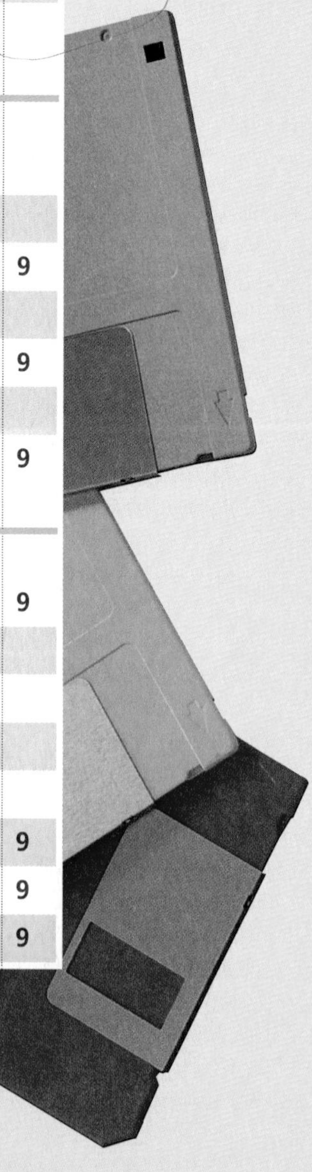

	Chapter								
Practical Skills									
Using the Telephone Book	1			4		6			
Following Recipes			3						
Reading Food Labels			3						
Classified Advertisements							7		
Filling Out Forms			3					8	9
Understanding Job Application Forms								8	
Subscribing to Magazines			3						
Map Reading			3						
Catalog Shopping									9
Understanding Advertisements				4			7		
Establishing Credit								8	
Understanding the Media							7		
Evaluating Expert Information						6			
Research and Library Skills									
Finding Relevant Information	1	2	3	4	5	6	7	8	9
Table of Contents	1		3						
Guide Words	1	2		4					
Index Use	1		3	4			7		9
Cross-referencing	1	2	3	4	5				
Using Reference Books	1	2	3	4	5				
Finding Materials in the Library					5				
Using the Library Catalog					5				
Encyclopedias			3		5				
Almanacs, Atlases, Gazetteers			3		5				
Finding Information in Newspapers							7		
Vertical File					5				
Study Skills									
Using Parts of a Book	1		3	4	5				
Using Reference Books	1	2	3	4	5	6	7		
Finding Relevant Data		2	3		5		7		
Understanding Instructions			3	4	5		7	8	9
Following Written Instructions				4			7	8	9

Adapting Activities for Diverse Learning Styles

The learning style activities in the *Life Skills English* Teacher's Edition provide activities to help students with special needs understand the lesson. These activities focus on the following learning styles: Visual/Spatial, Auditory/Verbal, Body/Kinesthetic, Logical/ Mathematical, Interpersonal/Group Learning, LEP/ESL. These styles reflect Howard Gardner's theory of multiple intelligences. The writing activities suggested in this student text are appropriate for students who fit Gardner's description of Verbal/Linguistic Intelligence.

The activities are designed to help teachers capitalize on students' individual strengths and dominant learning styles. The activities reinforce the lesson by teaching or expanding upon the content in a different way.

Following are examples of activities featured in the *Life Skills English* Teacher's Edition:

Interpersonal/Group learners benefit from working with at least one other person on activities that involve a process and an end product.

Learning Styles

Interpersonal/ Group Learning
Divide the class into groups of five. Give each group a magazine picture. Ask each group to examine its picture to find five broad topics. (For a picture of a new car in the desert, the group might list Automobile, Desert, Environment, Plants, Animals.) Ask each group to exchange its picture and list of broad topics with another group. Have the second group narrow the topics. (Ford, Sahara, Pollution, Cactus, Gila Monster.) Continue doing this until the groups seem to have exhausted possible narrow topics. (Note: Keep the pictures for use with the Learning Styles activity on page 71.)

Body/Kinesthetic learners benefit from activities that include physical movement or tactile experiences.

Learning Styles

Body/Kinesthetic
On the board, make two columns and label them "Regular Verbs" and "Irregular Verbs." Invite volunteers—one by one—to pantomime an action. Encourage the class to guess the action. Ask a volunteer to write the pantomimed action word in the correct column and then to add its past and past participle tenses. Ask other volunteers to check the spellings in a dictionary. Encourage the volunteers to pantomime as many irregular verbs they can think of.

Logical/Mathematical students learn by using logical/mathematical thinking in relation to the lesson content.

Learning Styles

Logical/Mathematical
Before class, ask a librarian at the local public library for help finding children's nonfiction books—grades 1 through 3—that have no index or table of contents. Check out one book for each group of three students in your class. Give each group of three a children's nonfiction book. Ask each group to read its book and to create an index or a table of contents for it. Afterward, have the groups exchange their work and their books and discuss what they learned about the exchanged book from the newly-written index or table of contents.

Auditory/Verbal students benefit from having someone read the text aloud or listening to the text on audiocassette. Musical activities appropriate for the lesson may help auditory learners.

Learning Styles

Auditory/Verbal
Call on volunteers to read aloud the dictionary entries on pages 34 through 40. This can be an opportunity to check that the students understand the various abbreviations and symbols a dictionary uses in its word entries. Print these abbreviations and symbols on the board. Then ask other volunteers to use a class dictionary to find an entry that uses some of these abbreviations and symbols, and to read the entry to the class. Encourage the class to say aloud which abbreviations and symbols the volunteer is probably encountering in the entry.

Visual/Spatial students benefit from seeing illustrations or demonstrations beyond what is in the text.

Learning Styles

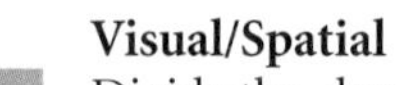

Visual/Spatial
Divide the class into pairs. Give each pair a colorful magazine picture. Ask each pair to look at its picture and to write down, in random order, twenty nouns—persons, places, things—they see. Afterward, ask the pairs to exchange their lists. Have each pair alphabetize the list it received. Once again, have the pairs exchange lists and have each pair check the alphabetizing on the list it received. Afterward, discuss any problems the pairs had with alphabetizing. (Note: Keep the pictures for use with the Learning Styles activity on page 17.)

LEP/ESL students benefit from activities that promote English language acquisition and interaction with English-speaking peers.

Learning Styles

LEP/ESL
Ask students for whom English is a second language to bring in maps of the country from which their families immigrated. Encourage them to use these maps to teach something about their homeland to the rest of the students. Encourage them to talk about the symbols used on their maps. Then ask them to use their maps to make up activities like Activity A on page 64 and Activities C–E on page 67. Ask the English-speaking students to use the maps to complete these activities.

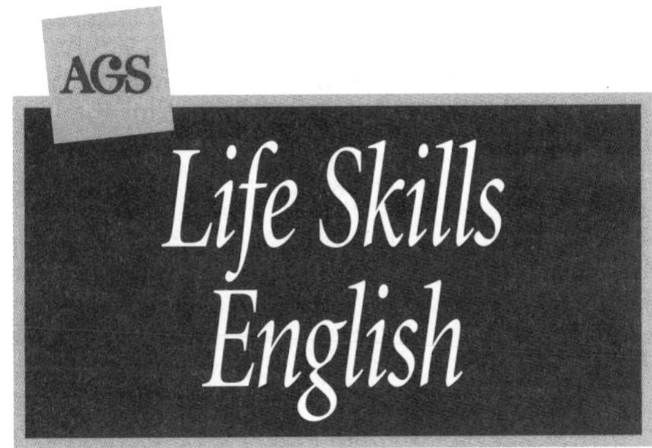

by
Bonnie L. Walker

AGS®
American Guidance Service, Inc.
Circle Pines, Minnesota 55014-1796
800-328-2560

About the Author

Bonnie L. Walker taught for sixteen years in secondary schools and college. She holds a Ph.D. in curriculum theory and instructional design from the University of Maryland, an M.Ed. in secondary education, and a B.A. in English. She studied psycholinguistics at the University of Illinois Graduate School, and was a curriculum developer at the Model Secondary School for the Deaf at Gallaudet University. She is the author of *Basic English Grammar, Basic English Composition,* and numerous workbooks, learning packages, and sound filmstrips in written expression, grammar, and usage. She was a member of Project EduTech, which investigated promising technologies to improve the delivery of special education services. Dr. Walker has written several papers on the applications of personal computers, video technology, and cable television in education. She has been the director for research and development projects funded by the U.S. Department of Education, the U.S. Department of Agriculture, and the Administration on Youth, Children, and Families. Since 1986, Dr. Walker has been president of a research and development company specializing in development of training and educational materials for special populations.

Photo Credits: p. vi—Richard Nowitz/FPG International; pp. 24, 56, 124, 178, 209, 218—Butch Housman; p. 50—Mark Lewis/Tony Stone Images; pp. 100, 223, 246—Jim and Mary Whitmer; p. 128—Farrell Grehan/FPG International; p. 130—Jon Ortner/Tony Stone Images; p. 148—David Young-Wolff/PhotoEdit; p. 156—Kevin Horan/Tony Stone Images; pp. 161, 162—Superstock; p. 172—Michelle Bridwell/PhotoEdit; p. 230—Don Smetzer/Tony Stone Images

Printed in the United States of America

ISBN 0-7854-2324-9 (Previously ISBN 0-7854-0509-7)
Product Number 91460

A 0 9 8 7 6 5 4 3 2 1

Contents

Life Skills English Contents **iii**

iv *Contents Life Skills English*

Life Skills English Contents v

Chapter 1

Planning Guide

What's There and How to Find It

	Student Text Lesson			
	Student Pages	Vocabulary	Practice Exercises	Lesson Review
Lesson 1 Alphabetical Order	2-5	✔	✔	✔
Lesson 2 Using Guide Words	6-12	✔	✔	✔
Lesson 3 Knowing What to Look Up	13-17	✔	✔	✔
Lesson 4 Using Parts of a Book to Find Information	18-21	✔	✔	✔

Chapter Activities

Teacher's Resource Library

Putting It Together 1: Information Crossword Puzzle

Community Connection1: Find the Alphabetical Orders

Assessment Options

Student Text

Chapter 1 Review

Teacher's Resource Library

Chapter 1 Mastery Tests A and B

Teaching Strategies						Language Skills			Learning Styles						Teacher's Resource Library		
Reviewing Skills	Teacher Alert	Career Application	Home Application	Global Connection	Community Application	Identification Skills	Writing Skills	Punctuation Skills	Visual/Spatial	Auditory/Verbal	Body/Kinesthetic	Logical/Mathematical	Group Learning	LEP/ESL	Activities	Workbook Activities	Self-Study Guide
2				5		✔	✔	✔	3						1-2	1-4	✔
6	8, 10-11		6		9	✔	✔	✔			8				3	5	✔
13		16				✔	✔	✔					17		4	6-7	✔
18						✔	✔	✔				21				8	✔

Chapter at a Glance

Chapter 1: What's There and How to Find It pages 1–23

(Answer Keys for the Teacher's Resource Library begin on page 282 of this Teacher's Edition.)

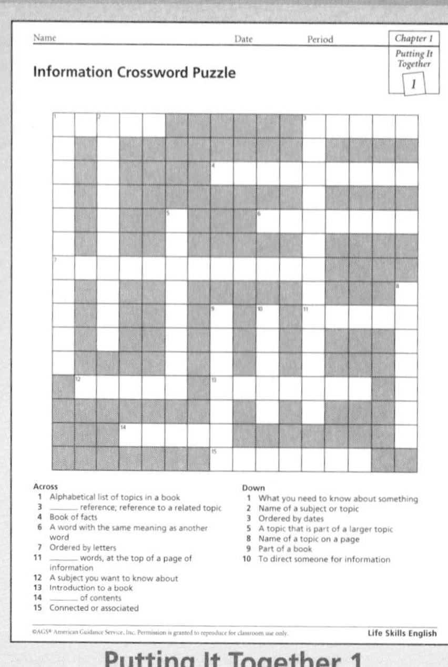

Name Date Period Chapter 1 Putting It Together 1

Information Crossword Puzzle

Across

1 Alphabetical list of topics in a book
3 ______ reference; reference to a related topic
4 Book of facts
6 A word with the same meaning as another word
7 Ordered by letters
11 ______ words, at the top of a page of information
12 A subject you want to know about
13 Introduction to a book
14 ______ of contents
15 Connected or associated

Down

1 What you need to know about something
2 Name of a subject or topic
3 Ordered by dates
5 A topic that is part of a larger topic
8 Name of a topic on a page
9 Part of a book
10 To direct someone for information

 Life Skills English

Putting It Together 1

Name Date Period Chapter 1 Community Connection 1

Find the Alphabetical Orders

Information is often arranged in alphabetical order. When you need to find information quickly, alphabetical order helps. You studied about alphabetical order in Chapter 1. You learned about some places where items are arranged alphabetically. You also can find information in alphabetical order in many places in your community. Follow these steps to find some of those places.

Step 1. Get a pencil and pad of paper.

Step 2. Team up with another person. Brainstorm with your partner places in your community where you might find alphabetical listings. Think of big buildings as well as things you can hold. For example, a building directory may be in alphabetical order by businesses or doctors. An apartment building may have an alphabetical list of residents. Airports and bus stations may list arrivals and departures alphabetically by city. Think of what is in a phone booth.

Step 3. Go out into your community with your partner. Look for places that may have alphabetical listings for different purposes. For example, pick an area with business buildings and offices.

Step 4. Use the chart below to write in all of the places where you find alphabetical listings. Under *Kind of List*, write what is in the list. For example, you might write *inhabitants* for an apartment building.

	Place	Kind of List
1)		
2)		
3)		
4)		
5)		
6)		
7)		
8)		
9)		
10)		

 Life Skills English

Community Connection 1

Chapter 1 What's There and How to Find It

We are living in the "Age of Information." Television news shows and on-line computer services give us up-to-date information instantly. News shows, however, focus on current events, and not everyone has a computer available.

Where, then, can you look to find the information you need? A variety of print resources puts all kinds of information at your fingertips. Print resources include books, newspapers, magazines, catalogues, brochures, pamphlets, and even bulletin board displays.

In this book, you will learn what kinds of print resources are available to you and where to find them. You will learn the kinds of information each resource contains and how that information is arranged. Then you will be able to find the information you need quickly.

Chapter 1 provides general guidelines for finding information in print.

Goals for Learning

- To understand and use alphabetical order
- To use guide words, headings, and book divisions to find information quickly
- To identify key words
- To learn how to find information on a specific topic by using related words and topics
- To use the parts of a book to find information

1

Reading Vocabulary

alphabetical (6)	fingertip
available (6)	focus (7)
brochure	guideline
bulletin (6)	identify (6)
catalog (6)	pamphlet (7)
computer (8)	resource (8)
display (6)	specific (8)
division (5)	variety (6)

Introducing the Chapter

Engage students in a discussion about the variety of print resources that are available to them on a daily basis and that they are already familiar with. Ask students to look around the classroom and identify books and other printed materials that they can use to find information. Invite volunteers to explain what kinds of information each of these resources provides and to give a brief demonstration of how to use the individual resources. Point out to students that they will be able to learn how to use reference materials even more efficiently by the end of this chapter.

SELF-STUDY GUIDE

Name ______

CHAPTER 1: What's There and How to Find It

Goal 1.1 *To understand and use alphabetical order*

Date	Assignment	Score
______	1: Read pages 1-2. Complete Activity A on page 2 and Activities B-C on page 3.	______
______	2: Read page 4. Complete Activities D-E on page 4.	______
______	3: Complete Workbook Activity 1.	______
______	4: Complete the Lesson 1 Review, Parts A-B on page 5.	______
______	5: Complete Workbook Activity 2	______
______	6: Complete Workbook Activity 3.	______
______	7: Complete Workbook Activity 4.	______

Comments:

Goal 1.2 *To use guide words, headings, and book divisions to find information quickly*

Date	Assignment	Score
______	8: Read page 6. Complete Activities A-B on page 7.	______
______	9: Complete Workbook Activity 5.	______
______	10: Read page 8. Complete Activity C on page 8.	______
______	11: Read page 9. Complete Activity D on page 9.	______
______	12: Read page 10. Complete Activity E on page 10 and Activities F-G on page 11.	______
______	13: Complete the Lesson 2 Review, Parts A-B on page 12.	______

Comments:

 Life Skills English

SELF-STUDY GUIDE

Name ______

CHAPTER 1 What's There and How to Find It, continued

Goal 1.3 *To identify key words*

Date	Assignment	Score
______	14: Read page 13. Complete Activity A on page 13.	______
______	15: Read page 14. Complete Activities B-C on page 14.	______
______	16: Complete Workbook Activity 6.	______
______	17: Read page 15. Complete Activity D on page 15.	______
______	18: Complete Workbook Activity 7.	______

Comments:

Goal 1.4 *To learn how to find information on a specific topic by using related words and topics*

Date	Assignment	Score
______	19: Read page 16. Complete Activity E on page 16.	______
______	20: Complete the Lesson 3 Review, Parts A-B on page 17.	______

Comments:

Goal 1.5 *To use the parts of a book to find information*

Date	Assignment	Score
______	21: Read page 18. Complete Activity A on pages 18-19.	______
______	22: Read page 19. Complete Activity B on page 19.	______
______	23: Complete Workbook Activity 8.	______
______	24: Read page 20. Complete Activities C-D on page 20.	______
______	25: Complete the Lesson 4 Review on page 21.	______
______	26: Complete the Chapter 1 Review, Parts A-E on pages 22-23.	______

Comments:

Student's Signature ______ Date ______

Instructor's Signature ______ Date ______

 Life Skills English

Chapter 1 Self-Study Guide

Lesson at a Glance

Chapter 1 Lesson 1

Overview This lesson presents rules for alphabetizing.

Objective

- To alphabetize lists of words.

Student Pages 2–5

Teacher's Resource Library

Activities 1–2

Workbook Activities 1–4

Reading Vocabulary

alphabetical order
cardinal
concert (5)
file (5)
golf (5)
hockey (5)
monitor (6)
software
tennis (5)

Teaching Suggestions

Introducing the Lesson

Discuss the definition of alphabetical order. Be sure students understand alphabetizing to the first letter before moving on to more complex situations.

Reviewing Skills Review the order of letters in the alphabet.

Presenting Activity A List the words in item 1 on the board. Then help students alphabetize the list. If you are sure students understand simple alphabetizing, have them complete Activity A on their own. Otherwise, do all of Activity A together as a class.

Activity A Answers

1) concert, movie, opera, sports, theater **2)** blue jay, cardinal, robin, starling, wren **3)** Charles, Doris, Marie, Nancy, Rosa **4)** computer, joystick, monitor, printer, software **5)** chair, lamp, piano, sofa, table **6)** baseball, football, golf, hockey, tennis

Lesson 1 Alphabetical Order

Alphabetical order
The order of letters of the alphabet.

Words in **alphabetical order** are arranged according to the letters in the alphabet. Information in telephone books, indexes, and office files is arranged in alphabetical order. Knowing how to use alphabetical order can help you find information in these resources quickly.

1. Arrange words in order according to the first letter of the word.

EXAMPLE

ant	elephant
chicken	kangaroo

Activity A Write each list in alphabetical order on your paper.

1) theater
concert
opera
movie
sports

2) robin
cardinal
starling
blue jay
wren

3) Marie
Nancy
Charles
Rosa
Doris

4) computer
monitor
printer
joystick
software

5) sofa
chair
table
lamp
piano

6) baseball
golf
tennis
hockey
football

2. When two words begin with the same letter, alphabetize by the second letter.

EXAMPLE	Marie	Milton
	Melvin	Monroe

Activity B Write each list in alphabetical order on your paper.

1)	2)	3)
prune	beef	fur
plum	biscuit	fruit
pomegranate	brown	fox
pineapple	blueberry	flame
peach	bacon	farmer

3. When the first two letters of words are the same, alphabetize by the third letter.

EXAMPLE	cab	cash
	car	cat

When the first three or more letters of words are the same, go to the next letter.

EXAMPLE	beard	beast

Activity C Write these words in alphabetical order on your paper.

kangaroo	necklace	stuff	sixty	shirt
ship	keeper	known	stump	knight
weak	shore	sixteen	neat	stuck
knife	weather	size	show	week

Reading Vocabulary

biscuit (6) pomegranate
pineapple (5) prune (6)

Presenting Activity B

Write this list of words on the board: *desk, dish, drum, daisy, dust.* Have students explain in their own words what they have to do to alphabetize this list of words. Then underline the second letter in each word and help students alphabetize the list. Following this activity, students should be ready to complete Activity B on their own.

Activity B Answers

1) peach, pineapple, plum, pomegranate, prune 2) bacon, beef, biscuit, blueberry, brown 3) farmer, flame, fox, fruit, fur

Presenting Activity C

Before having students complete Activity C, be sure that they understand alphabetizing to the third and fourth letters. Provide additional examples, if necessary. Then, depending on the ability of your class, have students work independently or with partners to complete Activity C. Be sure students understand that they are to alphabetize all the words in the list and not each column.

Activity C Answers

kangaroo, keeper, knife, knight, known, neat, necklace, ship, shirt, shore, show, sixteen, sixty, size, stuck, stuff, stump, weak, weather, week

Learning Styles

Visual/Spatial

Divide the class into pairs. Give each pair a colorful magazine picture. Ask each pair to look at its picture and to write down, in random order, twenty nouns—persons, places, things—they see. Afterward, ask the pairs to exchange their lists. Have each pair alphabetize the list it received. Once again, have the pairs exchange lists and have each pair check the alphabetizing on the list it received. Afterward, discuss any problems the pairs had with alphabetizing. (Note: Keep the pictures for use with the Learning Styles activity on page 17.)

Reading Vocabulary

annual (6)
apostrophe
bond (6)
bookmark
bookmobile
ignore (5)
itch (5)
item (6)
thorough (6)

■ Presenting Activity D

Write item 1 on the board and elicit from students what rules they must use to alphabetize the words in this list. Then invite a volunteer to write the words in alphabetical order, having the class point out any errors. Following this, ask students to complete Activity D on their own.

Activity D Answers

1) you, young, your, you're, yo-yo
2) the, their, these, they, they're
3) an, animal, annual, ant, any

■ Presenting Activity E

Before having students complete Activity E, you may wish to review the rules that have been presented in the lesson. Then divide the class into teams and have each team work together to alphabetize each list. Ask team representatives to raise their hands when they have finished.

Activity E Answers

1) third, thirsty, thirteen, thirty, thread **2)** receive, record, rob, robber, root **3)** haven, haven't, heart, heaven, heavenly **4)** bond, bone, book, bookmark, bookmobile **5)** it, Italy, itch, item, its **6)** thorough, though, thought, thoughtful, thoughtless

4. When all the letters of a word are the same as the beginning letters of a longer word, the shorter word comes first.

EXAMPLE am amaze

If one of the words has an apostrophe, ignore the apostrophe.

EXAMPLE your you're

Activity D Write each list in alphabetical order on your paper.

1) you're	**2)** they're	**3)** any
your	their	an
you	these	animal
young	they	ant
yo-yo	the	annual

Activity E Use all of the rules that you have learned. Write each of these lists in alphabetical order on your paper.

1) thirty	**2)** record	**3)** haven
thirteen	receive	haven't
third	root	heaven
thirsty	robber	heavenly
thread	rob	heart

4) bookmobile	**5)** itch	**6)** thought
book	its	thorough
bond	item	though
bone	it	thoughtful
bookmark	Italy	thoughtless

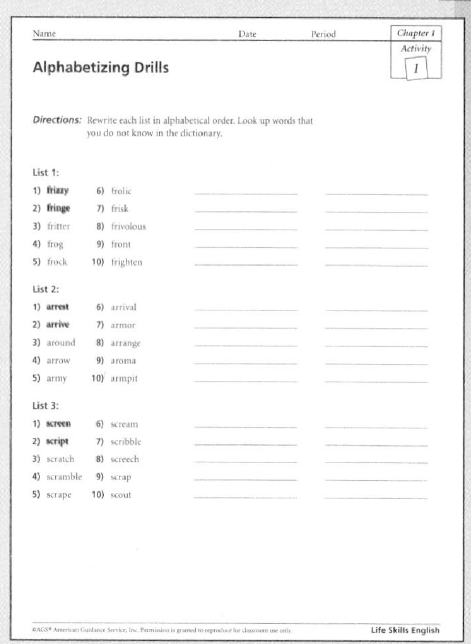

Name Date Period Chapter 1 Activity 1

Alphabetizing Drills

Directions: Rewrite each list in alphabetical order. Look up words that you do not know in the dictionary.

List 1:

1) **frizzy**	6) frolic	______	______
2) **fringe**	7) frisk	______	______
3) fritter	8) frivolous	______	______
4) frog	9) front	______	______
5) frock	10) frighten	______	______

List 2:

1) **arrest**	6) arrival	______	______
2) **arrive**	7) armor	______	______
3) around	8) arrange	______	______
4) arrow	9) aroma	______	______
5) army	10) armpit	______	______

List 3:

1) **screen**	6) scream	______	______
2) **script**	7) scribble	______	______
3) scratch	8) screech	______	______
4) scramble	9) scrap	______	______
5) scrape	10) scout	______	______

 Life Skills English

Activity 1

Name Date Period Chapter 1 Workbook Activity 1

Alphabetizing Drills

Directions: Rewrite each list in alphabetical order.
HINT: Ignore hyphens and apostrophes when you alphabetize.
TIP: Look up the words you do not know in your dictionary.

A.

1) whereas	______	6) whatever	______
2) wheat	______	7) wheel	______
3) when	______	8) wharf	______
4) whatsoever	______	9) whatnot	______
5) wheelchair	______	10) what	______

B.

1) canon	______	6) cannon	______
2) can't	______	7) canyon	______
3) can	______	8) candle	______
4) canning	______	9) candlestick	______
5) canvas	______	10) canned	______

C.

1) do-it-yourself	______	6) does	______
2) dodge	______	7) doe	______
3) do	______	8) door	______
4) done	______	9) donor	______
5) don't	______	10) dome	______

 Life Skills English

Workbook Activity 1

Name Date Period Chapter 1 Activity 2

Alphabetizing Place Names

Part A: **European Countries**

Rewrite this list in alphabetical order. Work as fast as possible.

Time Begun: ______ **Time Ended:** ______

1) Italy ______
2) France ______
3) Iceland ______
4) Greece ______
5) Portugal ______
6) Romania ______
7) Sweden ______
8) Bulgaria ______
9) Switzerland ______
10) Denmark ______

Part B: **World Capitals**

Rewrite this list in alphabetical order. Work as fast as possible.
Beside each name, write the country in which that city is located.

Time Begun: ______ **Time Ended:** ______

	World Capital	Country
1) Sofia	______	______
2) Copenhagen	______	______
3) Lisbon	______	______
4) Reykjavik	______	______
5) Paris	______	______
6) Rome	______	______
7) Bucharest	______	______
8) Bern	______	______
9) Athens	______	______
10) Stockholm	______	______

 Life Skills English

Activity 2

Lesson 1 Review

Part A Write each list in alphabetical order on your paper.

1)	2)	3)
tank	diamond	sweet
stage	desert	sweat
sold	difference	swam
possible	dessert	swallow
taste	direction	sweep
hall	drive	swift
fog	doctor	switch
garage	door	swimming
forty	do	swim
quite	doesn't	swing
jelly	dive	swish
plate	divide	switching
foggy	dime	swept
nail	dine	sword
beyond	dirt	swung

Part B Follow the directions below. Write all your answers on your paper. Use a dictionary to check your spelling.

1) Make a list of at least ten sports.
2) List ten of the United States.
3) List the first names of ten people you know.
4) List ten kinds of animals.
5) Now go back and rewrite each of your lists in alphabetical order.

Reading Vocabulary

rewrite sweat (5)

Lesson Review

Part A Answers

1) beyond, fog, foggy, forty, garage, hall, jelly, nail, plate, possible, quite, sold, stage, tank, taste **2)** desert, dessert, diamond, difference, dime, dine, direction, dirt, dive, divide, do, doctor, doesn't, door, drive **3)** swallow, swam, sweat, sweep, sweet, swept, swift, swim, swimming, swing, swish, switch, switching, sword, swung

Part B Answers

Answers will vary. Be sure lists are rewritten in alphabetical order in the final step.

Global Connection

Not all alphabets have the same number or all of the same letters as the English alphabet. The Hawaiian alphabet, for example, has fewer letters than the English alphabet; the Spanish alphabet has more, with *ch*, *ll*, and other symbols as part of the alphabet. Have students compare the English alphabet to the alphabets of other languages, such as Spanish, Italian, Hawaiian, and so on. Invite students who speak these languages to pronounce the letters. If possible, display the different alphabets for students to see.

Name Date Period *Chapter 1* *Workbook Activity* 2

Alphabetical Order

Directions: Rewrite each list in alphabetical order.

A. Common Last Names
1) Howard
2) Harrison
3) Hewitt
4) Henry
5) Hammel
6) Hamelton
7) Hamilton
8) Harding
9) Harris
10) Hardy

B. Budget Items
1) Groceries
2) Rent
3) Utilities
4) Taxes
5) Clothing
6) Furniture
7) Insurance
8) Gasoline
9) Entertainment
10) Savings

C. Baseball Hall of Famers
Alphabetize these names last name first.
1) Home Run Baker
2) Sandy Koufax
3) Early Wynn
4) Satchel Paige
5) Stan Musial
6) Babe Ruth
7) Cy Young
8) Casey Stengel
9) Lou Gehrig
10) Goose Goslin

 Life Skills English

Workbook Activity 2

Name Date Period *Chapter 1* *Workbook Activity* 3

Alphabetizing Place Names

A. Directions: Alphabetize this list of state names.

1) Maryland
2) Texas
3) Nevada
4) Alabama
5) Alaska
6) Wisconsin
7) Wyoming
8) New Hampshire
9) Arizona
10) New York

B. Directions: Alphabetize this list of capital cities. Then write the name of the state in which each is located.

	Alphabetical Order	States
1) Albany		
2) Phoenix		
3) Juneau		
4) Annapolis		
5) Madison		
6) Carson City		
7) Austin		
8) Montgomery		
9) Boston		
10) Cheyenne		

 Life Skills English

Workbook Activity 3

Name Date Period *Chapter 1* *Workbook Activity* 4

Putting Titles in Order

A. Directions: Alphabetize these famous novels. Put any beginning "articles" at the end.

EXAMPLE Red Pony, The

1) *Gone With the Wind*
2) *Robinson Crusoe*
3) *The Outsiders*
4) *The Lord of the Rings*
5) *Lonesome Dove*
6) *The Call of the Wild*
7) *Treasure Island*
8) *Watership Down*
9) *The Pathfinder*
10) *Show Boat*

B. Directions: Alphabetize these ten Oscar-winning movies. Then write them in chronological order.

Out of Africa (1985)
Going My Way (1944)
Shindler's List (1994)
Kramer vs Kramer (1979)
Gandhi (1983)
Rain Man (1988)
Ben-Hur (1959)
Lawrence of Arabia (1962)
Chariots of Fire (1981)
The French Connection (1971)

Alphabetical Order **Chronological Order**

 Life Skills English

Workbook Activity 4

Lesson at a Glance

Chapter 1 Lesson 2

Overview This lesson explains guide words and how to use them to locate information in a reference source.

Objective

- To determine what topics appear on a page with specific guide words.

Student Pages 6–12

Teacher's Resource Library

Activity 3

Workbook Activity 5

Reading Vocabulary

atlas (7) reference (6)
guide words

Teaching Suggestions

■ Introducing the Lesson

Discuss the definition of guide words, the different types of reference books that have guide words, and the example shown on the page. If possible, display actual examples of the types of books listed in the box. Invite volunteers to take turns opening to random pages in one of the books and reading the guide words at the top of the page. Then have them read several of the items listed on that page.

■ Reviewing Skills

Review the rules of alphabetizing.

Application

At Home

Encourage students to look through reference books at home to see how many have guide words. Suggest that, once students feel comfortable using guide words, they explain to a family member the process of using guide words to find information quickly.

Lesson 2 Using Guide Words

Guide words

Words at the top of a page of information given in alphabetical order. All words that come in alphabetical order between the two guide words can be found on that page.

Guide words help you find information given in alphabetical order. You will find guide words at the top of the page in many reference books. Use the guide words to help you find the page with the information you need. The first guide word is the first word on the page. The second guide word is the last word on the page. The other words on the page come in alphabetical order between these words.

Some books that have guide words are:

telephone books	atlases
dictionaries	encyclopedias

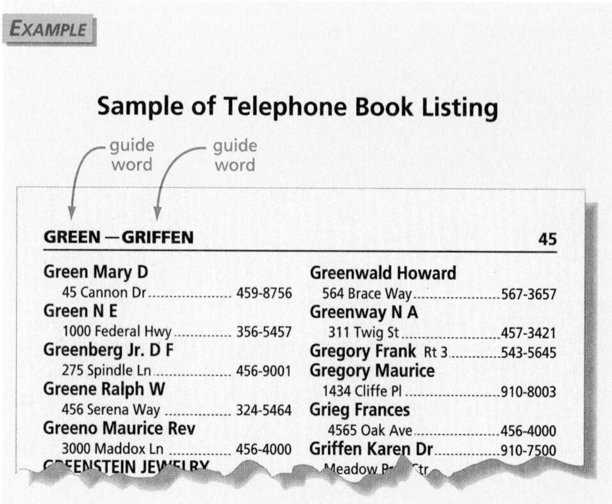

EXAMPLE

Sample of Telephone Book Listing

guide word — guide word

GREEN—GRIFFEN 45

Green Mary D	**Greenwald Howard**
45 Cannon Dr.................... 459-8756	564 Brace Way......................567-3657
Green N E	**Greenway N A**
1000 Federal Hwy.............. 356-5457	311 Twig St..........................457-3421
Greenberg Jr. D F	**Gregory Frank** Rt 3............543-5645
275 Spindle Ln.................. 456-9001	**Gregory Maurice**
Greene Ralph W	1434 Cliffe Pl.......................910-8003
456 Serena Way 324-5464	**Grieg Frances**
Greeno Maurice Rev	4565 Oak Ave.......................456-4000
3000 Maddox Ln 456-4000	**Griffen Karen Dr**...............910-7500

Activity A Each set of guide words below is followed by three words. Write on your paper the letters of the words that would appear on the page with each set of guide words.

Example Guide Words: address—April
a) add **b)** American **c)** appear
Answer: b, c

1) mad—map
a) main **b)** maze **c)** manage

2) sad—scream
a) safe **b)** sand **c)** scratch

3) raise—remember
a) rapidly **b)** remain **c)** reason

4) want ad—warp
a) wander **b)** wart **c)** ward

5) fellow—fur
a) frame **b)** Friday **c)** February

6) early—else
a) east **b)** each **c)** elves

Activity B Which of the names listed below would appear between the guide words shown? Write your answers on your paper.

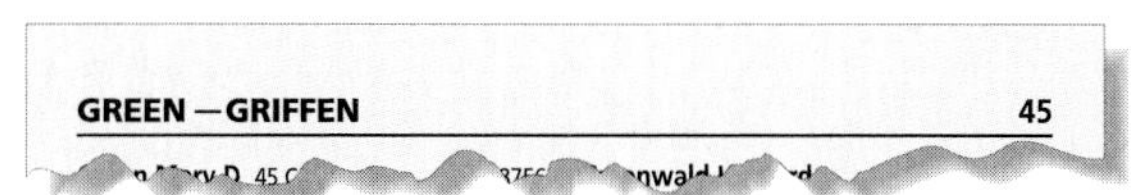

A. W. Grouse	N. A. Greenway
Sandra Greene	Michael Ginnes
Maurice Gregory	Judy A. Gordon
Jack Gurney	N. E. Green

Reading Vocabulary

maze (8) warp (7)
ward (6) wart (6)

Presenting Activity A

Discuss the example provided for Activity A, making sure students understand what they are to do. Then do item 1 on the board with students before asking them to complete Activity A on their own.

Activity A Answers

1) a, c **2)** a, b, c **3)** a, b, c
4) c **5)** a, b **6)** a

Presenting Activity B

Draw the top of a page on the board and print these guide words at the top: *Lewis—Lyons.* Then have students whose last names begin with L decide whether their names would appear on this page. Invite these students to write their last names in alphabetical order under the guide words. Ask the class to check that all the names belong on that page. Repeat this process as often as necessary to confirm that students understand the concept. Use a different initial letter and guide words each time. Then have students complete Activity B on their own. You may wish to have students list their responses in alphabetical order.

Activity B Answers

N. E. Green, Sandra Greene, N. A. Greenway, Maurice Gregory

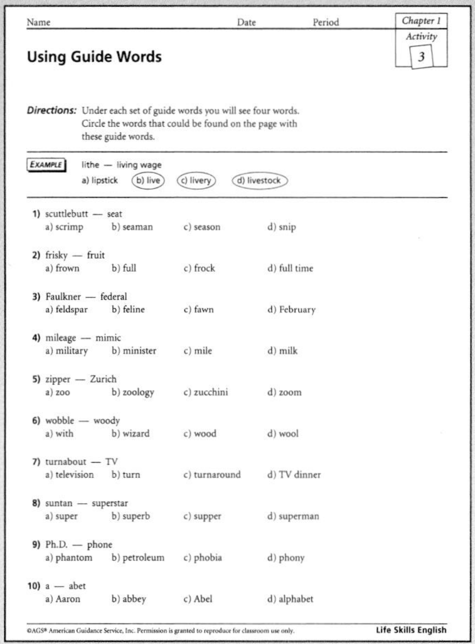
Name Date Period *Chapter 1 Activity 3*

Using Guide Words

Directions: Under each set of guide words you will see four words. Circle the words that could be found on the page with these guide words.

EXAMPLE lithe — living wage
a) lipstick b) live c) livery d) livestock

1) scuttlebutt — seat
a) scrimp b) seaman c) season d) snip

2) frisky — fruit
a) frown b) full c) frock d) full time

3) Faulkner — federal
a) feldspar b) feline c) fawn d) February

4) mileage — mimic
a) military b) minister c) mile d) milk

5) zipper — Zurich
a) zoo b) zoology c) zucchini d) zoom

6) wobble — woody
a) with b) wizard c) wood d) wool

7) turnabout — TV
a) television b) turn c) turnaround d) TV dinner

8) suntan — superstar
a) super b) superb c) supper d) superman

9) Ph.D. — phone
a) phantom b) petroleum c) phobia d) phony

10) a — abet
a) Aaron b) abbey c) Abel d) alphabet

 Life Skills English

Activity 3

Name Date Period *Chapter 1 Workbook Activity 5*

Using Guide Words

Directions: Under each set of guide words you will see four words. Circle the words that could be on a page with those guide words.

EXAMPLE hockey .... holly
A) home B) hoe C) holly D) hole

1) grade .... grandmother
A) grate **B)** graph **C)** graduate **D)** grain

2) dollar .... dooryard
A) docile **B)** dolphin **C)** donkey **D)** doormat

3) script .... scuttle
A) seaport **B)** scrub **C)** search **D)** sculpture

4) giantess .... girl scout
A) ginger **B)** giggle **C)** gerund **D)** ghost

5) match .... mature
A) mate **B)** mat **C)** may **D)** math

6) well-grounded .... we've
A) well-informed **B)** well-read **C)** western **D)** we're

7) afternoon .... agree
A) after **B)** age **C)** agreeable **D)** agency

8) busboy .... butterfat
A) bureau **B)** butter **C)** but **D)** busy

9) frisky .... frozen
A) fruit **B)** frosting **C)** front **D)** frizzle

10) newsworthy .... night
A) Newton, Sir Isaac **B)** NH **C)** nickname **D)** niece

 Life Skills English

Workbook Activity 5

What's There and How to Find It Chapter 1 7

Reading Vocabulary

almanac (7) sample (5)
population (5)

■ Presenting Activity C

Before having students complete Activity C, discuss the example shown. Read through the sample page and point out the different kinds of information listed. Then do Activity C as a class, having students explain how they found the answer to each item.

Activity C Answers

1) 57–58, 457 **2)** 45 **3)** 305, 280 **4)** ambassadors, petroleum production **5)** 563 **6)** States, U.S. **7)** No **8)** Wichita, Kansas City, Knoxville

Teacher Alert

Some students may be unfamiliar with the organization of an index. If necessary, point out that an index is an alphabetical listing of topics covered in a book.

Learning Styles

Body/Kinesthetic

Before class, prepare and post a set of guide-word cards into which all the last names of your students would fit. (For example, you might have six cards on which you have printed Adams-Byron, Carson-Eliot, Forman-Ino, Jackson-Nelson, Olson-Smith, Tennyson-Xavier.) Ask the students to stand by the card on which their last name would fall. Then have each group of students arrange themselves in alphabetical order. Finally, have the students say their names aloud—last name, then first—in alphabetical order.

Sometimes you will see guide letters instead of guide words.

Example

Sample Page from the Index of an Almanac

33 Ka - Le

Kansas		**Key, Francis Scott**	457
(See States, U.S.)		**Kilowatt hour**	690
Agriculture	356	**Knoxville, TN**	402
Area	356, 567	**Koran**	79
Lakes, rivers	456	**Kuwait**	
Population	563	Ambassadors	305
Wichita	400–401	Petroleum production	280
Kansas City, MO	302	— L —	
Kennedy, John F.	57–58, 457	**Labor Day**	45
Kentucky		**Leap years**	102
(See States, U.S.)		**Lee, Robert E.**	458

Activity C Use the sample page above to answer the following questions. Write your answers on your paper.

1) What pages have information about John F. Kennedy?

2) What page has information about Labor Day?

3) What pages have information about Kuwait?

4) What information about Kuwait will you find?

5) What page has information about the population of Kansas?

6) What other topic would you look up to find information about Kansas and Kentucky?

7) Would you find information about Louisiana on this page?

8) What cities in the United States can you look up from this page?

Guide Words and Headings

Some reference books have headings instead of guide words. The heading names the topic on that page.

EXAMPLE

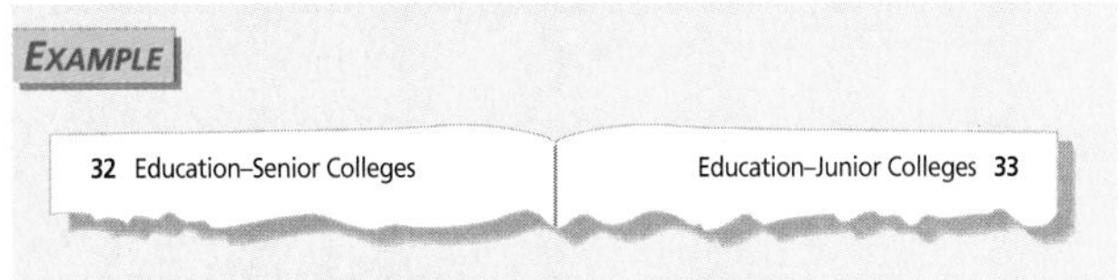

32 Education–Senior Colleges
Education–Junior Colleges 33

Guide letters and a heading may appear on the same page.

EXAMPLE

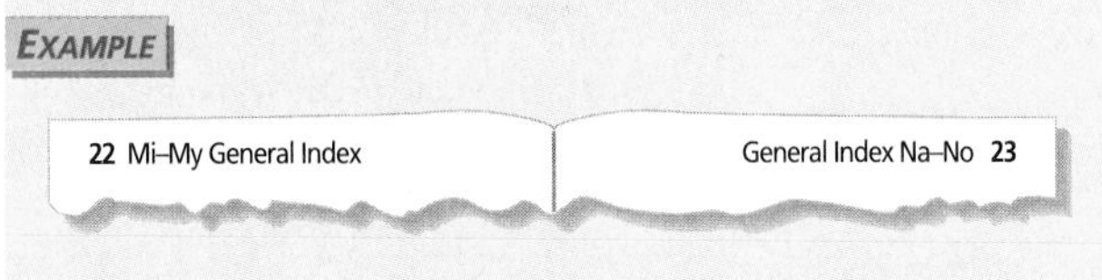

Guide words may be placed close together on one side of the page. In the following example, the first entry on the page is "Connecticut." The last entry is "Connecticut River."

EXAMPLE

Activity D Study the four examples below. Write answers on your paper for each of the questions that follow the examples.

a) 123 COLUMBIA RIVER—COLUMBUS
b) 22 Mi—My General Index
c) 42 Auto Racing
d) 66 La—Ly

1) Which example shows only a heading?
2) Which example shows guide words?
3) Which example shows only guide letters?
4) Which example shows guide letters and a heading?

Reading Vocabulary

college (5) entry (6)
education (5)

Presenting Activity D

Provide several reference books with different styles of guide words for students to look at. Have students identify the book or books that have traditional guide words, headings, guide letters and headings, and guide words close together on one side of the page. Then ask students to complete Activity D on their own.

Activity D Answers

1) c **2)** a **3)** d **4)** b

APPLICATION

In the Community

Many communities have their own telephone directories, community service booklets, and other community-oriented printed materials. These publications are usually available for residents at the library, town or city hall, or other community centers. Encourage students to obtain copies of any such publications in their community to bring to class. Discuss the different types of guide words and headings used in these publications.

Reading Vocabulary

approximately (7)

■ Presenting Activity E

Before asking students to complete Activity E on their own, have them practice following the steps for dividing a dictionary into parts.

Activity E Answers

The following answers are based on the chart on page 10.

1) 1st **2)** 3rd **3)** 4th **4)** 1st **5)** 2nd **6)** 4th **7)** 3rd **8)** 1st **9)** 2nd **10)** 4th

Teacher Alert

Since dictionaries vary in size, some may not open to *M* when divided in half, or to *F* or *S* when divided into quarters. Point out to students that the divide-by-half strategy is meant to help students find the approximate location of a word in the dictionary.

A Quick Way to Find the Word You Want: Dividing by Half

Here is a quick way to find words in a dictionary. First, divide your dictionary into four approximately equal parts. Follow these steps.

Step 1 Divide your dictionary in half. Open it to the middle page. You will probably find that the words begin with the letter *M.*

Step 2 Now divide the first half by half. Find the middle of the first half. You will probably find that the words begin with the letter *F.*

Step 3 Now divide the last half by half. Find the middle of the last half. You will probably find that the words begin with the letter *S.*

Then, before you look up a word, decide which part of the dictionary your word is probably in.

First Half		Last Half	
1st Quarter	2nd Quarter	3rd Quarter	4th Quarter
A B C D E F	**G H I J K L M**	**N O P Q R S**	**T U V W X Y Z**

Activity E In which quarter of the dictionary would you look to find each of the words below? Write each word on your paper. Beside it, write *1st, 2nd, 3rd,* or *4th.* Use a dictionary to check your answers.

1) cheese

2) neighborhood

3) toothpaste

4) animal

5) jelly

6) Thursday

7) potato

8) birthday

9) garden

10) vacation

Activity F Follow the directions below. Write your answers on your paper.

- Find the following words in any dictionary.
- Use the "divide by half" method.
- Write down the time you begin.
- Write down the guide words from each page.
- Write down the time you finish.
- Try to do this in less than five minutes.

1) wisdom	**6)** recognize
2) pleasant	**7)** garage
3) fierce	**8)** flashlight
4) chipmunk	**9)** machine
5) canoe	**10)** blueberry

Activity G Follow the directions below.

- Write the list of words below in alphabetical order on your paper.
- Find the words in a dictionary.
- Use the guide words to help.
- Use the "divide by half" method.
- Time yourself.
- Try to beat five minutes.

1) usually	**6)** meadow
2) perhaps	**7)** harness
3) gnaw	**8)** recognize
4) island	**9)** butcher
5) astonish	**10)** delicious

Reading Vocabulary
method (6)

■ Presenting Activity F

Read through the directions with students and make sure that they understand what they are to do. Then divide students into teams of three or four. Team members can work on their own to complete the activity. When all the members of a team are finished, have them combine their times.

Activity F Answers

Answers will vary depending on the dictionary used.

■ Presenting Activity G

Read through the directions with students and answer any questions they may have about completing the activity. You may also wish to review the rules of alphabetizing before asking students to complete the activity on their own.

Activity G Answers

1) astonish 2) butcher 3) delicious 4) gnaw 5) harness 6) island 7) meadow 8) perhaps 9) recognize 10) usually

Teacher Alert

Some students are intimidated by timed activities and may perform at a slower pace than if the activity were presented routinely. Offer these students an alternative approach that does not require them to complete the activity in a specific amount of time.

Lesson Review

Part A Answers

1) a, d **2)** a, b, c **3)** b, c **4)** b, c
5) a, d **6)** b **7)** a, d **8)** a, b, d
9) a, b, c, d

Part B Answers

Answers will vary depending on the dictionary used.

Lesson 2 Review

Part A Each set of guide words or letters is followed by four words. Write on your paper the letters of the words that would appear on the page with each set of guide words.

1) adventure—belt
   a) among b) brick c) address d) arrange
2) damp—doesn't
   a) danger b) die c) dirt d) don't
3) spider—study
   a) sparkle b) steer c) straw d) stump
4) weather—worry
   a) weak b) welcome c) we're d) worse
5) purple—softly
   a) puzzle b) prove c) softness d) soft
6) va—ye
   a) yellow b) village c) you'll d) year
7) Jackson—Johnson
   a) Jason b) Jones c) Jordon d) Johns
8) Al—Fl
   a) Alaska b) Alabama c) Hawaii d) Arizona
9) Ad—Ar
   a) Adams b) Aiken c) Alcott d) Anders

Part B Use the "divide by half" method to find these words in a dictionary. Write on your paper the guide words from each page.

1) wrap
2) scatter
3) seventy
4) jewel
5) eagle
6) airport
7) passenger
8) holiday
9) Friday
10) quilt

Lesson 3 Knowing What to Look Up

Topic (subject)
What you want to find out about.

Subtopic
A topic that is part of a larger topic.

Key word
A word that names what you want to find out about.

When you don't know the answer to a question, you can often find the answer by looking it up. First, however, you must know what to look up. A **subject** or **topic** is whatever you want to know about. A **subtopic** is a topic that is part of another topic.

The word you look up to find information to answer a question is called a **key word**. A key word can be a topic, a subtopic, or another word related to the question. In the following example, *spider* and *poisonous spider* are key words. Those are the words you might look up to find the answer to the question.

EXAMPLE

Question:	Which spiders are poisonous to humans?
Topic:	spider
Subtopic:	poisonous spider

Activity A Write each pair of key words on your paper. Beside each key word, write *topic* or *subtopic*.

Example tool—**topic** saw—**subtopic**

1) fruit blueberries

2) oak tree plants

3) mosquito insect

4) magazine *Time*

5) game checkers

6) Amy Tan writer

7) plate dishes

8) movie *Apollo 13*

Lesson at a Glance

Chapter 1 Lesson 3

Overview This lesson explains how to find information on a topic using key words, synonyms, and related topics.

Objective

- To identify key words, synonyms, and related topics associated with a specific topic.

Student Pages 13–17

Teacher's Resource Library

Activity 4

Workbook Activities 6–7

Reading Vocabulary

checker (5)
key word
mosquito (5)
poisonous (5)
subtopic
topic (subject) (5)

Teaching Suggestions

■ Introducing the Lesson

Discuss the information and example presented in the text.

■ Reviewing Skills

Review how to use guide words to find information in alphabetical listings.

■ Presenting Activity A

Discuss the example given. Ask students for other examples of subtopics for the topic *tool*. Then have students complete Activity A on their own.

Activity A Answers

1) fruit—topic, blueberries—subtopic **2)** oak tree—subtopic, plants—topic **3)** mosquito—subtopic, insect—topic **4)** magazine—topic, *Time*—subtopic **5)** game—topic, checkers—subtopic **6)** Amy Tan—subtopic, writer—topic **7)** plate—subtopic, dishes—topic **8)** movie—topic, *Apollo 13*—subtopic

Reading Vocabulary

agriculture (5)
banquet (6)
media
physician (6)
similar (6)
synonym (5)

■ Presenting Activity B

Write these words on the board: *fog—wind, rain, haze.* Ask students to find the synonym for *fog.* Remind students that synonyms have the same or nearly the same meaning. Then do item 1 in Activity B with students before having them work on their own to complete the activity.

Activity B Answers

1) c 2) a 3) b 4) a 5) c

• Presenting Activity C

Invite volunteers to take turns saying synonyms for the first three items in Activity C. Then ask students to complete Activity C independently.

Activity C Answers

Answers will vary. Possible answers are given.

1) trains 2) snowstorms 3) farming 4) library 5) meal 6) pop 7) supper 8) doctor 9) insect 10) melodies

What to Do When You Can't Find Your Topic

Use Synonyms

Even when you know what topic to look up, you may not find it listed. When that happens, try to think of another name for your topic. A word that has the same or a similar meaning as another word is a **synonym**. Try thinking of a synonym for your topic. Then look up that word.

> *Synonym*
> *A word with the same or nearly the same meaning as another word.*

EXAMPLES

Key Word	Synonym
insect	bug
nations	countries
author	writer

Activity B Write on your paper the letter of the word that is a synonym for the word given.

1) lady
a) person **b)** Whoopi Goldberg **c)** woman

2) stairs
a) steps **b)** elevator **c)** building

3) dinner
a) meal **b)** supper **c)** food

4) country
a) nation **b)** United States **c)** place

5) movie
a) theater **b)** *Star Wars* **c)** film

Activity C Write a synonym on your paper for each topic below. You may use a dictionary.

1) railroads
2) blizzards
3) agriculture
4) media center
5) banquet
6) soda
7) dinner
8) physician
9) bug
10) songs

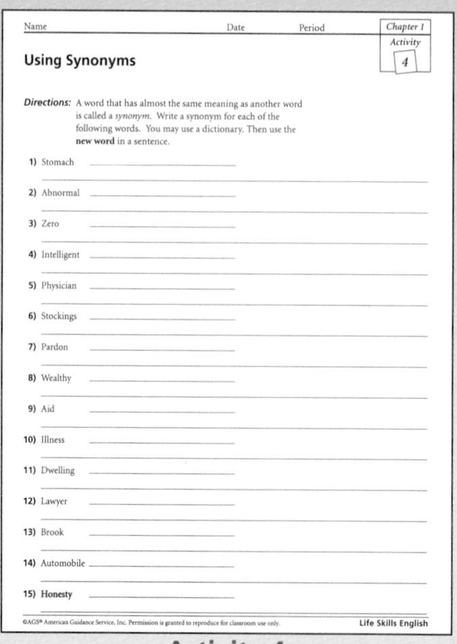

Name Date Period — Chapter 1 Activity 4

Using Synonyms

Directions: A word that has almost the same meaning as another word is called a *synonym.* Write a synonym for each of the following words. You may use a dictionary. Then use the **new word** in a sentence.

1) Stomach
2) Abnormal
3) Zero
4) Intelligent
5) Physician
6) Stockings
7) Pardon
8) Wealthy
9) Aid
10) Illness
11) Dwelling
12) Lawyer
13) Brook
14) Automobile
15) Honesty

 Life Skills English

Activity 4

Name Date Period — Chapter 1 Workbook Activity 6

The Name's the Same

The English language is very rich. Almost every person, place, thing, or idea has more than one name. A word that has almost the same meaning is a synonym.

Directions: Write a synonym for each of the following words. You may use a dictionary.

1) Precipitation
2) Doctor
3) Supervisor
4) Town
5) Stream
6) Supper
7) Woman
8) Sofa
9) Soft drink
10) Popular
11) Tall
12) Thin
13) Swimming
14) Dog
15) Topic

 Life Skills English

Workbook Activity 6

Look for Broad and Narrow Topics

You may not find your topic listed because it is too narrow. Then you should look for a broader topic.

EXAMPLES

Narrow Topic	Broad Topic
collies	dogs
tornadoes	weather

Sometimes your topic may be too broad. Then you should look for a narrower topic.

EXAMPLES

Broad Topic	Narrow Topic
ships	*Constitution*
transportation	trains
patriotic songs	"America the Beautiful"

Activity D Write another word on your paper that you might look up for each topic listed below. Use a dictionary to help identify synonyms as well as broader and narrower topics.

Examples	
coffee	**beverages**
metropolitan areas in the U.S.	**U.S. cities**
higher education in Canada	**Canadian colleges**

1) Miami
2) Cars
3) Mars
4) Lawyers
5) Doctors
6) Kings
7) France
8) Football
9) Highways
10) Thanksgiving
11) Famous writers
12) Famous singers
13) Famous teachers
14) High schools
15) African history
16) Cities with harbors
17) Poodles
18) "The Star-Spangled Banner"
19) Films
20) Songwriters

USING WHAT YOU HAVE LEARNED

Suppose you want to know what a baby kangaroo is called, but you can't find the word *kangaroo* listed. What other word could you look up?

- Write one or two ideas.
- Then try looking them up.
- Share what you find with a partner.

Reading Vocabulary

beverage (8)
collie (5)
constitution (6)
lawyer (5)
metropolitan
patriotic (6)
spangle (6)
songwriter
tornado (6)
transportation (5)

■ Presenting Activity D

Write these words on the board: *movies, tropical birds, biology.* Help students identify a broader and a narrower topic for each word listed. Then introduce Activity D by reading the directions and discussing the example. If you think students are capable, have them complete Activity D on their own or with a partner. Otherwise, do the activity together as a class.

Activity D Answers

Answers will vary. Possible responses are given.

1) Florida, U.S. cities
2) automobiles, convertibles
3) planet, solar system
4) attorneys, law professionals
5) physicians, healers **6)** royalty, rulers, King George III
7) European countries, Paris
8) sports **9)** roads, turnpikes, Route 66 **10)** holidays, the first Thanksgiving **11)** authors, Alice Walker **12)** entertainers, John Lennon **13)** educators
14) schools, Jefferson High School
15) history, Africa, Underground Railroad **16)** cities, New York, ports **17)** dogs, toy poodles
18) patriotic songs, music
19) entertainment, *Star Wars, Apollo 13* **20)** musicians, Bonnie Raitt, Jim Morrison

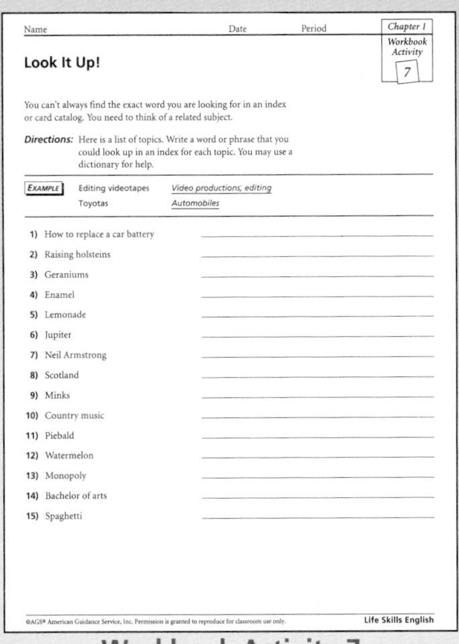

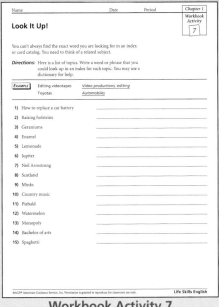

Name Date Period — *Chapter 1 Workbook Activity 7*

Look It Up!

You can't always find the exact word you are looking for in an index or card catalog. You need to think of a related subject.

Directions: Here is a list of topics. Write a word or phrase that you could look up in an index for each topic. You may use a dictionary for help.

EXAMPLE Editing videotapes — *Video productions, editing*
Toyotas — *Automobiles*

1) How to replace a car battery ______
2) Raising holsteins ______
3) Geraniums ______
4) Enamel ______
5) Lemonade ______
6) Jupiter ______
7) Neil Armstrong ______
8) Scotland ______
9) Minks ______
10) Country music ______
11) Piebald ______
12) Watermelon ______
13) Monopoly ______
14) Bachelor of arts ______
15) Spaghetti ______

 Life Skills English

Workbook Activity 7

Reading Vocabulary

associate (7)
bricklaying
license (5)
pizza
practical (5)
process (6)
related topic
sailboating
system (5)
video

■ Presenting Activity E

Begin this activity by asking students for one or two more related topics for the example *Building a fireplace (e.g., hearths, mantles, chimneys)*. Then do Activity E with students. Elicit as many related topics as students can think of for each item and list them on the board.

Activity E Answers

Answers will vary. Possible responses are given.

1) winter sports, snowboarding **2)** agriculture, farming, gardening **3)** pets, dog breeding **4)** computers, business skills **5)** hobbies, model making **6)** musical instruments, stringed instruments **7)** computers, computer games **8)** nursing, medical careers **9)** boating, ships, Coast Guard **10)** transportation, careers in transportation, city transit systems

Application

Career Connection When job-hunting in the classifieds, students should be aware that the same type of position may be listed under different titles. For example, a company looking for a secretary might advertise for an office manager or administrative assistant. Have students scan the help-wanted ads to find different titles for the same type of position. Discuss why a company might use *office manager* rather than *secretary*.

Use Related Words and Topics

If you can't find information on a specific topic, look for **related topics**. A related topic is one that is connected or associated with another topic.

Related topic
A topic connected in some way to another topic.

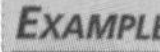

Example If you wanted to open a pizza shop, you might not be able to find any information on pizza shops. Then you might look for information on related topics.

Specific topic: Pizza Shop
Related topics: Italian Cooking
Running a Small Business
Fast Foods

Activity E Write at least one related topic on your paper for each topic listed below. You may use a dictionary.

Example Building a fireplace
Related topics: **bricklaying, heating systems**

1) Skiing
2) Vegetable gardening
3) Raising poodles
4) Learning word processing
5) Making model cars
6) Playing the guitar
7) Video games
8) Becoming a Licensed Practical Nurse (LPN)
9) Sailboating
10) Becoming a bus driver

Lesson 3 Review

Part A Write at least one key word on your paper for each question below.

Example In what years was baseball's World Series not played?
Key words: **baseball, World Series**

1) Who won the Oscar for best actress in 1939?
2) What is the population of Akron, Ohio?
3) What team won the National Basketball Association playoffs in 1994?
4) In what state is Yellowstone National Park?
5) What is the most popular magazine in the United States?

Part B For each question, write at least two key words and a synonym or related topic on your paper. You may use a dictionary for this activity.

Example Who was the president of the United States during World War II?
Key words: **World War II**
U.S. presidents
Synonym: **Leaders**
Related topic: **Wars**

1) Who won the World Series in 1939?
2) What is the weather like in Minneapolis?
3) Who won the Nobel Peace Prize in 1952?
4) What were the names of Henry VIII's six wives?
5) What is the capital city of Mexico?
6) How tall is the Washington Monument?
7) How many students attend Harvard University?
8) What is the closest shoe store?
9) How many strings does a guitar have?
10) Did any volcanoes erupt last year?
11) Which restaurants serve Chinese food?

Reading Vocabulary

actress (6)
association (6)
capital (5)
erupt (7)
monument (6)
playoff
restaurant (5)
series (5)
university (5)

Lesson Review

Part A Answers

Answers may vary. Possible responses are given.

1) Oscar, 1939, actress
2) population, Akron, Ohio
3) National Basketball Association, 1994 playoffs 4) Yellowstone National Park 5) magazine, United States

Part B Answers

Answers may vary. Possible responses are given.

1) World Series, 1939; baseball
2) weather, Minneapolis; U.S. climate 3) Nobel Peace Prize, 1952; awards and prizes 4) Henry VIII, wives; English kings, history of England 5) Mexico, capital city; geography of North America
6) tall, Washington Monument; American landmarks, Washington, D.C. 7) students, Harvard University; American colleges and universities 8) closest, shoe store; department stores, footwear
9) strings, guitar; stringed instruments, musical instruments
10) volcanoes, erupt, last year; natural disasters, earthquakes
11) restaurants, Chinese food; Asian restaurants, dining

Learning Styles

Interpersonal/Group Learning

Divide the class into groups of five. Give each group a magazine picture. Ask each group to examine its picture to find five broad topics. (For a picture of a new car in the desert, the group might list Automobile, Desert, Environment, Plants, Animals.) Ask each group to exchange its picture and list of broad topics with another group. Have the second group narrow the topics. (Ford, Sahara, Pollution, Cactus, Gila Monster.) Continue doing this until the groups seem to have exhausted possible narrow topics. (Note: Keep the pictures for use with the Learning Styles activity on page 71.)

Lesson at a Glance

Chapter 1 Lesson 4

Overview This lesson explains how to use a table of contents and an index to find information in a reference book.

Objective

- To locate information in a sample table of contents and index.

Student Pages 18–21

Teacher's Resource Library

Workbook Activity 8

Reading Vocabulary

chapter (5)	mollusk
emergency (5)	**preface (9)**
finance (8)	**reference book**
index (5)	insurance (7)
section (5)	introduction (6)
table of contents	location (6)
marine (6)	title (5)

Teaching Suggestions

Introducing the Lesson

Discuss the information presented in the text, focusing the discussion on the definitions of *table of contents* and *index.*

Reviewing Skills

Ask students to recall what they have learned so far about finding information quickly in reference sources.

Presenting Activity A

Provide a reference book for pairs or small groups of students to look at together. Ask students to open to the table of contents at the front of the book. Then have students take turns telling one thing they learn about the book from its table of contents. Then have students complete Activity A on their own.

Activity A Answers

1) No 2) Yes

Lesson 4 Using Parts of a Book to Find Information

Chapter
A part of a book.

Index
An alphabetical list of main topics covered in a book.

Preface
An introduction to a book.

Reference book
A book that contains facts about a specific topic or on several topics.

Table of contents
A list of the chapters or sections of a book and the page numbers on which the chapters or sections begin.

When you look up information, you usually look in some type of **reference book.** A reference book is a book of facts. A reference book may contain facts on a single topic or on several topics.

You can usually tell whether a book has the information you need by looking at the book's **table of contents** and its **index.** A table of contents is a list of chapter titles at the beginning of a book. An index is a list of topics in a book, arranged in alphabetical order. An index is usually found at the back of a book.

The Table of Contents

The table of contents is in the front of a book. When you look at the table of contents, you can see at a glance what information the book contains and how it is divided. Some books contain a **preface,** which is an introduction to a book. Many books are divided into **chapters.** A chapter is a part or a section of a book. In a table of contents, the chapter titles are listed in the order that they appear in the book. The page numbers on which the chapters begin are also listed.

EXAMPLES

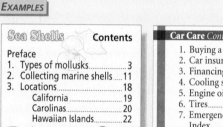

Sea Shells Contents

Car Care *Contents*

Activity A Use the sample tables of contents above to answer the questions below and at the top of the next page. Write your answers on your paper.

1) Is there a chapter in *Car Care* about brakes?

2) You want to collect sea shells in Hawaii. Will the book *Sea Shells* help?

3) On what page does the chapter about tires begin? On what page does that chapter end?
4) Which book has an index?
5) Which book has a preface?
6) Will *Car Care* give you information about buying car insurance?
7) How many chapters does *Car Care* have?

An Index

Almost all reference books and many nonfiction books have an index at the back. An index lists the main topics covered in the book in alphabetical order. Subtopics appear under some of the main topics. The subtopics are also listed in alphabetical order. Page numbers are listed beside each topic and subtopic.

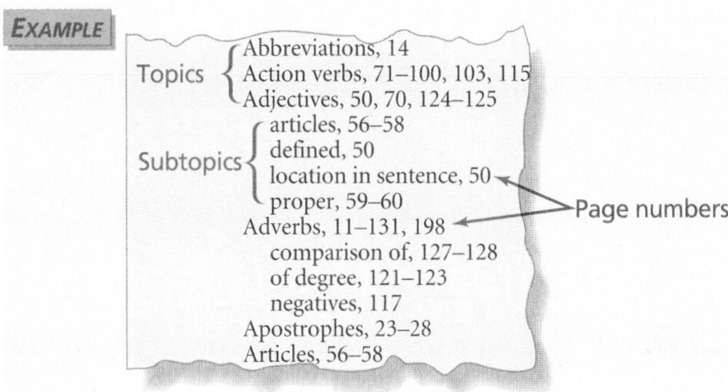

EXAMPLE
Topics
Abbreviations, 14
Action verbs, 71–100, 103, 115
Adjectives, 50, 70, 124–125
Subtopics
articles, 56–58
defined, 50
location in sentence, 50
proper, 59–60
Adverbs, 11–131, 198
comparison of, 127–128
of degree, 121–123
negatives, 117
Apostrophes, 23–28
Articles, 56–58
Page numbers

Activity B Use the sample index above to answer these questions. Write the answers on your paper.

1) Will page 77 tell you about action verbs?
2) Can you find facts about action verbs on page 112?
3) Which pages tell you about apostrophes?
4) Which page has a definition of an adjective?
5) Which pages tell you about articles?
6) To what other topic is "articles" related?
7) Name one subtopic under the main topic "Adverbs."
8) Which pages tell you about adverbs of degree?
9) How many pages tell you about proper adjectives?
10) How many pages tell you about abbreviations?

Reading Vocabulary

abbreviation (8)
adjective
adverb
comparison (6)
define (7)
definition (6)
negative (8)
proper (5)
verb

(Activity A Answers, continued)
3) begins—p. 73; ends—p. 90
4) *Car Care* 5) *Sea Shells*
6) yes/probably 7) seven

Presenting Activity B

You may wish to discuss the sample index further before asking students to complete Activity B. Point out that often, as in this example, main topics are capitalized and subtopics are indented. Page numbers may be provided for any time the topic is mentioned or for when information about the topic is actually given on the referenced page. Elicit any questions students may have about the structure or use of an index. Then have students complete Activity B on their own.

Activity B Answers

1) Yes 2) No 3) 23–28
4) 50 5) 56–58 6) adjectives
7) Students will list one of the following: comparison of, negatives, of degree
8) 121–123 9) two 10) one

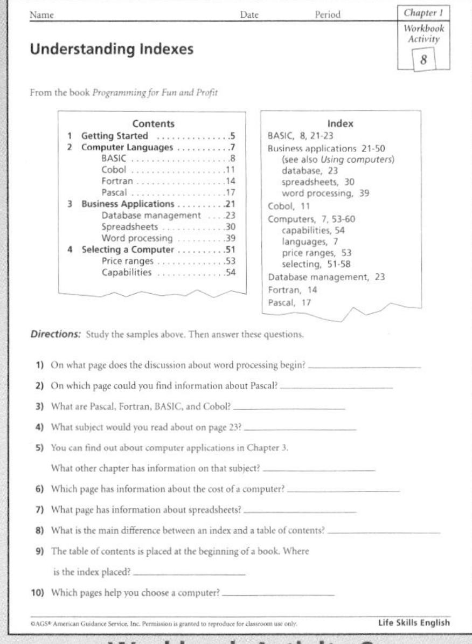

Name ________ Date ________ Period ________

Chapter 1 *Workbook Activity* *8*

Understanding Indexes

From the book *Programming for Fun and Profit*

Contents

Index

Directions: Study the samples above. Then answer these questions.

1) On what page does the discussion about word processing begin? ________
2) On which page could you find information about Pascal? ________
3) What are Pascal, Fortran, BASIC, and Cobol? ________
4) What subject would you read about on page 23? ________
5) You can find out about computer applications in Chapter 3. What other chapter has information on that subject? ________
6) Which page has information about the cost of a computer? ________
7) What page has information about spreadsheets? ________
8) What is the main difference between an index and a table of contents? ________
9) The table of contents is placed at the beginning of a book. Where is the index placed? ________
10) Which pages help you choose a computer? ________

 Life Skills English

Workbook Activity 8

Reading Vocabulary

additional (6) refer (6)
cross reference textbook
homework

■ Presenting Activity C

Write the following on the board: *Mexican Revolution, (See Mexico)/ Ape, 92–110 (For more information on this topic, see Chimpanzee; Gorilla)* Ask students to explain in their own words what the information in each sample index entry tells them. Then ask students to complete Activity C on their own.

Activity C Answers

1) 641, 56, 87 2) States of the U.S. 3) Academy Awards 4) *See also* points out a related topic to look up that will provide additional information on Orlando. *See* means that someone would have to look up Academy Awards to find information on the Oscars instead of actually looking up Oscars.

■ Presenting Activity D

Help students locate the table of contents and the index in their text books. Engage students in a brief discussion about the organization and contents of both the TOC and the index. Then ask students to complete Activity D on their own. After they complete the activity, challenge students to make up other questions to ask the class about the table of contents and the index.

Activity D Answers

1) Yes 2) 71–75,147
3) Chapter 4 4) 261

More About Indexes

To refer means to direct someone for information.

Refer to page 87 for more information on computers.

Cross reference
A related topic you can look up to find additional information on a topic. A cross reference directs you to another part or section of the book.

Many indexes list **cross references.** A cross reference is a related topic that you can refer to. Some cross references tell you where to look to find the information you need. Other cross references tell you where to look to find more information on your topic.

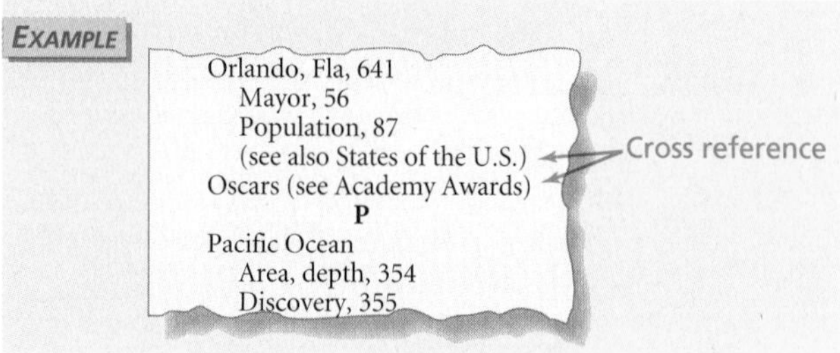

Activity C Use the sample index above to answer these questions. Write your answers on your paper.

1) Name three pages with facts about Orlando, Florida.
2) What other subject can you look up to find facts about Orlando, Florida?
3) What topic must you look up to find out who has won an Oscar?
4) Look carefully at the example above. There are two kinds of cross references. What is the difference between "see also" and "see"?

Using What You Have Learned
- Look at the tables of contents in your other textbooks. What topics are covered in each book?
- Look in the back of each book. Which books have an index?
- Use the index to help you find information when you study or do homework.

Activity D Use the table of contents and index of this textbook to write the answers to the following questions.

1) Does this book have a chapter about using a dictionary?
2) Which pages tell you about using an encyclopedia?
3) Which chapter tells you how to use the Yellow Pages?
4) Which page has a sample business letter?

Lesson 4 Review

Lesson Review Study the sample table of contents and index from the two different books. Write the answers to these questions on your paper.

From *Book of Maps*:

Contents

From *Things to Make*:

Index

Book of Maps

1) On what page is there a map of South America?

2) Does the book have a map that shows only Texas?

3) Is there a map that shows only Alaska?

4) Does this book have a preface?

Things to Make

5) What page tells you how to find material?

6) Which pages tell you about using match boxes?

7) You can find out about pot holders on page 80. What other page will help?

Reading Vocabulary

hemisphere (7)

Lesson Review Answers

1) 22 **2)** No **3)** Yes **4)** No
5) 94 **6)** 20–23 **7)** 56

Learning Styles

Logical/Mathematical
Before class, ask a librarian at the local public library for help finding children's nonfiction books—grades 1 through 3— that have no index or table of contents. Check out one book for each group of three students in your class. Give each group of three a children's nonfiction book. Ask each group to read its book and to create an index or a table of contents for it. Afterward, have the groups exchange their work and their books and discuss what they learned about the exchanged book from the newly-written index or table of contents.

Chapter 1 Review

The Teacher's Resource Library includes two parallel forms of the Chapter 1 Mastery Test. The difficulty level of the two forms is equivalent. You may wish to use one form as a pretest and the other form as a posttest.

Reading Vocabulary

monster (5)

Part A Answers

act, action, brook, brooks, elf, elves, English, forest, forget, forgot, loose, lose, mind, mine, puzzle, seven, seventy, shade, we're, write, wrote, you, you're, you've

Part B Answers

1) c **2)** a, b **3)** b **4)** a, b, c **5)** b

Part C Answers

Answers may vary. Possible responses are given. Accept any reasonable response.

1) Tucson; Arizona; population; U.S. Cities **2)** baseball; World Series; sports; championship series **3)** top film; 1994; movies; entertainment **4)** rain; Arizona; climate; U.S. geography **5)** Amazon; rain forest; South America; Brazil; tropical forests

Chapter 1 Review

Part A Rewrite the following list of words in alphabetical order on your paper.

you've	you	shade	brook
seventy	brooks	seven	wrote
forest	forget	act	action
English	elves	forgot	elf
you're	lose	write	puzzle
loose	mind	we're	mine

Part B Three words follow each set of guide words or guide letters. Write the letters of the words that would appear on the page with each set of guide words or guide letters.

1) Grouse—Gurney
  a) Green **b)** Gordon **c)** Guiness

2) mi—mu
  a) monsters **b)** music **c)** meadows

3) package—pickles
  a) pack **b)** passenger **c)** pillows

4) sh—sw
  a) shadow **b)** sleigh **c)** soap

5) Alaska—Colorado
  a) Alabama **b)** Alaska **c)** Connecticut

Part C For each question, write at least two key words and a synonym or related topic on your paper. You may use a dictionary for this activity.

1) How many people live in Tucson, Arizona?

2) Which baseball team won the World Series six years in a row?

3) What was the top film of 1994?

4) What is the average amount of rain each year in Arizona?

5) Where is the Amazon rain forest?

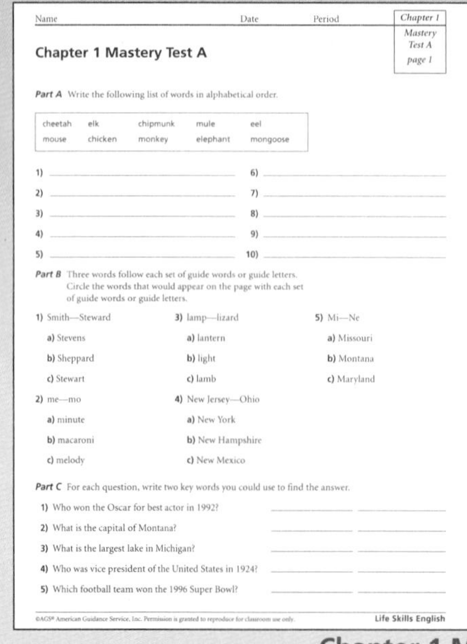

Name Date Period | *Chapter 1 Mastery Test A page 1*

Chapter 1 Mastery Test A

Part A Write the following list of words in alphabetical order.

cheetah	elk	chipmunk	mule	eel
mouse	chicken	monkey	elephant	mongoose

1) ______ 6) ______
2) ______ 7) ______
3) ______ 8) ______
4) ______ 9) ______
5) ______ 10) ______

Part B Three words follow each set of guide words or guide letters. Circle the words that would appear on the page with each set of guide words or guide letters.

1) Smith—Steward
  a) Stevens **b)** Sheppard **c)** Stewart

2) me—mo
  a) minute **b)** macaroni **c)** melody

3) lamp—lizard
  a) lantern **b)** light **c)** lamb

4) New Jersey—Ohio
  a) New York **b)** New Hampshire **c)** New Mexico

5) Mi—Ne
  a) Missouri **b)** Montana **c)** Maryland

Part C For each question, write two key words you could use to find the answer.

1) Who won the Oscar for best actor in 1992? ______ ______

2) What is the capital of Montana? ______ ______

3) What is the largest lake in Michigan? ______ ______

4) Who was vice president of the United States in 1924? ______ ______

5) Which football team won the 1996 Super Bowl? ______ ______

 Life Skills English

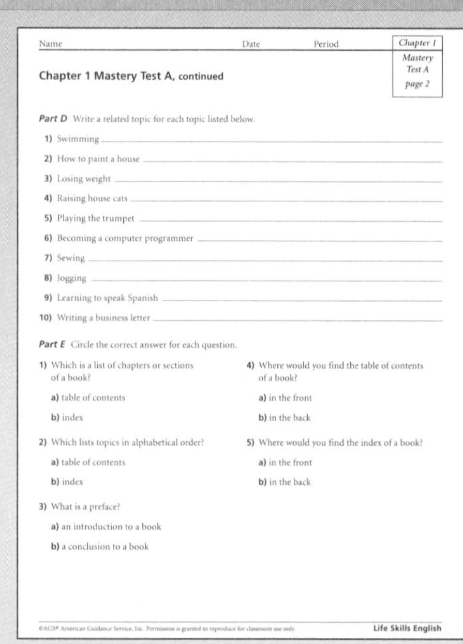

Name Date Period | *Chapter 1 Mastery Test A page 2*

Chapter 1 Mastery Test A, continued

Part D Write a related topic for each topic listed below.

1) Swimming ______

2) How to paint a house ______

3) Losing weight ______

4) Raising house cats ______

5) Playing the trumpet ______

6) Becoming a computer programmer ______

7) Sewing ______

8) Jogging ______

9) Learning to speak Spanish ______

10) Writing a business letter ______

Part E Circle the correct answer for each question.

1) Which is a list of chapters or sections of a book?
  a) table of contents **b)** index

2) Which lists topics in alphabetical order?
  a) table of contents **b)** index

3) What is a preface?
  a) an introduction to a book **b)** a conclusion to a book

4) Where would you find the table of contents of a book?
  a) in the front **b)** in the back

5) Where would you find the index of a book?
  a) in the front **b)** in the back

 Life Skills English

Chapter 1 Mastery Test A

Part D Write the answers to these questions on your paper.

1) Which book part lists topics in alphabetical order—a table of contents or an index?
2) Where in a book do you usually find the index?
3) Where would you look to find the table of contents?
4) Where would you find the preface?
5) If you looked up *skeleton* in the index of your science textbook and saw the following, what would you learn?

   Skeleton (see Human Body)

Part E Use the table of contents and the index of this book to answer the following questions. Write your answers on your paper.

1) Which chapter tells you about using a library?
2) Which page tells about the chamber of commerce?
3) On which page do you find out how to place a classified ad?
4) How many pages does Chapter 6 have?
5) Which chapter and lesson tells you about cable TV?
6) Can you get help from this book about giving a speech?
7) What is the first page of the chapter about newspapers, television, and radio? What is the last page?
8) On what page does the index begin?
9) Does this book have a preface?
10) Which pages tell you about job application forms?

Test Taking Tip Before you begin an exam, skim through the whole test to find out what is expected of you.

Reading Vocabulary

application (8) classify (8)
chamber (5) commerce (7)

Part D Answers

1) index **2)** at the back **3)** in the front of the book; on the opening pages **4)** in the front **5)** that you would have to look up Human Body to find out where to turn to learn about skeletons

Part E Answers

1) Chapter 5 **2)** 173 **3)** 194 **4)** 22 **5)** Chapter 7, Lesson 5 **6)** probably not **7)** 178, 217 **8)** 271 **9)** No **10)** 226–236

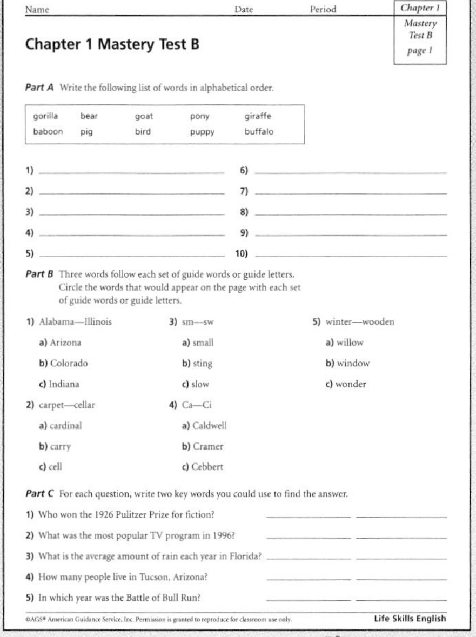

Name Date Period | *Chapter 1 Mastery Test B page 1*

Chapter 1 Mastery Test B

Part A Write the following list of words in alphabetical order.

gorilla	bear	goat	pony	giraffe
baboon	pig	bird	puppy	buffalo

1) ______ 6) ______
2) ______ 7) ______
3) ______ 8) ______
4) ______ 9) ______
5) ______ 10) ______

Part B Three words follow each set of guide words or guide letters. Circle the words that would appear on the page with each set of guide words or guide letters.

1) Alabama—Illinois
   a) Arizona
   b) Colorado
   c) Indiana
2) carpet—cellar
   a) cardinal
   b) carry
   c) cell
3) sm—sw
   a) small
   b) sting
   c) slow
4) Ca—Ci
   a) Caldwell
   b) Cramer
   c) Cebbert
5) winter—wooden
   a) willow
   b) window
   c) wonder

Part C For each question, write two key words you could use to find the answer.

1) Who won the 1926 Pulitzer Prize for fiction? ______ ______
2) What was the most popular TV program in 1996? ______ ______
3) What is the average amount of rain each year in Florida? ______ ______
4) How many people live in Tucson, Arizona? ______ ______
5) In which year was the Battle of Bull Run? ______ ______

 Life Skills English

Name Date Period | *Chapter 1 Mastery Test B page 2*

Chapter 1 Mastery Test B, continued

Part D Write a related topic for each topic listed below.

1) Folk songs ______
2) Learning how to speak French ______
3) Becoming a dentist ______
4) Bird-watching ______
5) Growing herbs ______
6) The Civil War ______
7) Baking chocolate chip cookies ______
8) Playing cards ______
9) Fixing a bicycle ______
10) Fishing ______

Part E Circle the correct answer for each question.

1) What is a table of contents?
   a) list of topics from a book in alphabetical order
   b) list of chapters or sections of a book
2) How does an index list topics?
   a) alphabetical order
   b) the order that they appear in the book
3) What is an introduction to a book called?
   a) preface
   b) table of contents
4) Which would you find at the front of a book?
   a) index
   b) table of contents
5) Which would you find at the back of a book?
   a) index
   b) table of contents

 Life Skills English

Chapter 1 Mastery Test B

Chapter 2

Planning Guide

Answering Questions About Words

	Student Text Lesson			
	Student Pages	Vocabulary	Practice Exercises	Lesson Review
Lesson 1 Reading a Dictionary Entry	26-33	✔	✔	✔
Lesson 2 More About Dictionary Entries	34-41	✔	✔	✔
Lesson 3 Using a Dictionary to Check Spelling	42-48	✔	✔	✔
Lesson 4 Using a Dictionary to Find Facts	49-53	✔	✔	✔

Chapter Activities

Teacher's Resource Library
Putting It Together 2: Dictionary

Community Connection 2:
Look It Up!

Assessment Options

Student Text
Chapter 2 Review

Teacher's Resource Library
Chapter 2 Mastery Tests A and B

Teaching Strategies						Language Skills			Learning Styles						Teacher's Resource Library		
Reviewing Skills	Teacher Alert	Career Application	Home Application	Global Connection	Community Application	Identification Skills	Writing Skills	Punctuation Skills	Visual/Spatial	Auditory/Verbal	Body/Kinesthetic	Logical/Mathematical	Group Learning	LEP/ESL	Activities	Workbook Activities	Self-Study Guide
26	28, 30	30		31		✔	✔	✔						28		9	✔
34	37, 39		41	37		✔	✔	✔		40					5	10-12	✔
42	44				48	✔	✔	✔			44				6-7	13	✔
49	52					✔	✔	✔					52		8	14	✔

Chapter at a Glance

(Answer Keys for the Teacher's Resource Library begin on page 282 of this Teacher's Edition.)

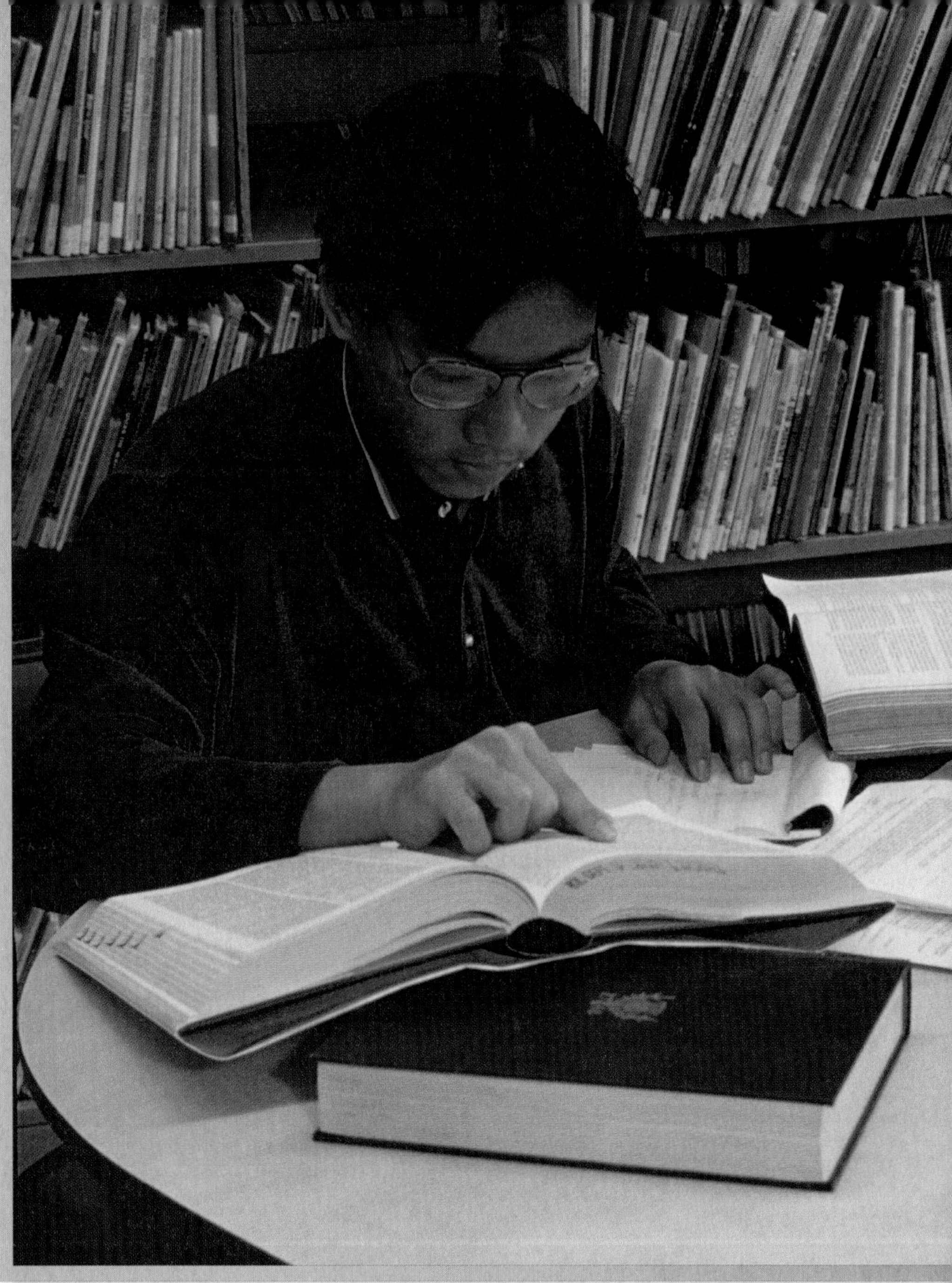

Name ______ Date ______ Period ______ *Chapter 2* *Putting It Together* 2

Dictionary

You can play this game with your class, your friends, or your family. Follow these instructions.

Number of Players:
- Three or more people

You Will Need:
- A dictionary
- Several small sheets of paper. Each player gets a clean paper for each round.
- A pencil for each player

To Play:
1) The Leader chooses a word from the dictionary. It should be a word that he or she thinks no one will know. The Leader says the word aloud and spells it for the other Players.
2) Each Player writes a definition of the word on his or her paper. Players try to make the definition sound correct even if they do not know the meaning of the word.
3) The Leader writes the real definition on his or her paper.
4) Players, including the Leader, write their name on their own paper.
5) Players fold their paper and pass it to the Leader.
6) The Leader shuffles the papers. Then the Leader reads each definition aloud, including the real definition.
7) The Leader reads each definition aloud a second time. This time, Players vote for the meaning they think is correct. The Leader writes the number of votes for each definition on that paper.
8) After everyone has voted, the Leader reads only the real meaning of the word.
9) The Leader adds up the scores.
10) A new person becomes Leader. Play continues like this until each person has a turn to be Leader.
11) The winner is the person with the largest number of points.

To Score:
1) A Player gets one point for each vote for his or her wrong definition.
2) The Leader also gets one point for each vote for a wrong definition.
3) Each Player who chooses the right definition gets two points.

SAMPLE SCORE CARD

	Wrong Definition	Right Definition	Total Points
Player A			
Round 1	1		1
Round 2	2		2
Round 3		2	2
Player B			
Round 1	2		2
Round 2	1		1
Round 3			
Player C			
Round 1	1		1
Round 2			
Round 3	1		1

 Life Skills English

Putting It Together 2

Name ______ Date ______ Period ______ *Chapter 2* *Community Connection* 2

Look It Up!

You see words that are new to you every day. You see them in books or the newspaper. You see them in magazines. You also see them in public places. You can use a dictionary to learn these new words. Follow these directions.

Step 1. Get a pencil. Take the pencil and this paper along with you into your community. Look for places where you see many words. You might see words on or inside buildings. You might see words in directions. You might see words in stores and on packages.

Step 2. Each time you see an unfamiliar word, write it on the chart below. Be sure to spell the word as you see it. You may see familiar words but do not know their meaning. Write those words on the chart, too. Find at least six words.

Step 3. When you have your unfamiliar words, try to guess the meaning of each one. Write your guesses on the chart below.

Step 4. Find a dictionary. Look up each word on your list. If you cannot find each word, go to the unabridged dictionary in the library. Notice the pronunciation of each word. Write the meaning of each word on the chart. Compare the dictionary definitions with your guessed meanings. How many words did you guess correctly?

Step 5. Say the words to a friend or family member. Ask them to tell you what they think each word means. See how well the person knows these words.

Step 6. Keep your list to help you remember these new words you have learned.

	Word	Guessed Meaning	Dictionary Definition
1)	______	______	______
2)	______	______	______
3)	______	______	______
4)	______	______	______
5)	______	______	______
6)	______	______	______

 Life Skills English

Community Connection 2

Chapter 2 Answering Questions About Words

Dictionaries come in all sizes. There are very large dictionaries with hundreds of thousands of words. There are smaller dictionaries that include only the most commonly used words. Every dictionary, however, contains words and information about those words.

No dictionary is ever totally complete. New words and meanings are always being added. Most of the dictionaries that are used in classrooms and homes are abridged, or shortened. This means that some words have been left out of these dictionaries. Unabridged, or complete, dictionaries have not been shortened. They are large books, often in several volumes. Libraries usually have unabridged dictionaries.

In Chapter 2, you will learn about different features of dictionaries and how to use the features.

Goals for Learning

- To understand how a dictionary is organized
- To identify the different parts of a dictionary entry
- To use a dictionary to find word meanings
- To use a dictionary to check spelling
- To use a dictionary as a reference book

Reading Vocabulary

abridged (11)
identify (6)
organize (6)
reference (6)
unabridged
volume (6)

Introducing the Chapter

On the board or on a piece of chart paper, write the word *Dictionary* and draw a circle around it. Then invite students to share what they know about the organization, use, and purpose of a dictionary. Record students' responses in a cluster around *Dictionary,* accepting any reasonable responses. When you have finished, point out that in Chapter 2 students will learn about using a dictionary. Some of what they learn will be familiar while other information may be surprising. Leave the cluster diagram on the board and suggest that students add to the diagram as they learn new and different information about dictionaries.

SELF-STUDY GUIDE

Name ____________

CHAPTER 2: Answering Questions About Words

Goal 2.1 *To identify the different parts of a dictionary entry*

Date	Assignment	Score
______	1: Read pages 25-26. Complete Activity A on pages 26-27. Read page 27. Complete Activity B on page 27.	______

Comments:

Goal 2.2 *To understand how a dictionary is organized*

Date	Assignment	Score
______	2: Read pages 28-29. Complete Activity C on page 29.	______
______	3: Read pages 30-31. Complete Activity D on page 32.	______
______	4: Complete the Lesson 1 Review, Parts A-C on page 33.	______
______	5: Complete Workbook Activity 9.	______

Comments:

Goal 2.3 *To use a dictionary to find word meanings*

Date	Assignment	Score
______	6: Read pages 34-35. Complete Activity A on page 35. Read page 36. Complete Activity B on page 36.	______
______	7: Complete Workbook Activity 10.	______
______	8: Read page 37. Complete Activity C on page 38. Read page 38. Complete Activity D on page 38.	______
______	9: Complete Workbook Activity 11.	______
______	10: Read page 39. Complete Activity E on page 39.	______
______	11: Read page 40. Complete Activity F on page 40.	______
______	12: Complete the Lesson 2 Review on page 41.	______
______	13: Complete Workbook Activity 12.	______

Comments:

 Life Skills English

SELF-STUDY GUIDE

Name ____________

CHAPTER 2 Answering Questions About Words, continued

Goal 2.4 *To use a dictionary to check spellings*

Date	Assignment	Score
______	14: Read page 42. Complete Activity A on page 42. Read page 43. Complete Activity B on page 43.	______
______	15: Read page 44. Complete Activity C on page 44 and Activity D on page 45.	______
______	16: Read page 45. Complete Activity E on page 46.	______
______	17: Read page 46. Complete Activities F-G on page 47.	______
______	18: Complete the Lesson 3 Review, Parts A-B on page 48.	______
______	19: Complete Workbook Activity 13.	______

Comments:

Goal 2.5 *To use a dictionary as a reference book*

Date	Assignment	Score
______	20: Read page 49. Complete Activity A on page 49.	______
______	21: Read page 50. Complete Activity B on page 50.	______
______	22: Complete Activity C on page 51 and Activity D on page 52.	______
______	23: Complete the Lesson 4 Review on page 53.	______
______	24: Complete Workbook Activity 14.	______
______	25: Complete the Chapter 2 Review, Parts A-D on pages 54-55.	______

Comments:

Student's Signature ____________ Date ____________

Instructor's Signature ____________ Date ____________

 Life Skills English

Chapter 2 Self-Study Guide

Lesson at a Glance

Chapter 2 Lesson 1

Overview This lesson explains how a typical dictionary is organized and the parts of a dictionary entry.

Objectives

- To understand the organization of a dictionary.
- To understand common abbreviations used in dictionary entries.
- To demonstrate a basic knowledge of how to use a dictionary.

Student Pages 26–33

Teacher's Resource Library

Workbook Activity 9

Reading Vocabulary

alphabetical (6)	**key (2)**
comedy (7)	musical (5)
dictionary (4)	provide (5)
entry (6)	symbol (5)

Teaching Suggestions

- **Introducing the Lesson** Discuss the information in the text, using the art to illustrate the concepts presented there.

- **Reviewing Skills** Review alphabetical order and guide words.

- **Presenting Activity A** Before doing Activity A, focus students' attention on the sample dictionary page. Invite volunteers to tell one thing that they learn from this page. Then have students complete Activity A on their own.

Activity A Answers

1) top 2) mouth

Lesson 1 Reading a Dictionary Entry

Dictionary
A book that contains an alphabetical listing of words and their meanings.

Entry
A listing in a dictionary. An entry provides facts about a word.

Key
A guide to the symbols and abbreviations used in each entry.

A **dictionary** is a book that lists words and some facts about the words. Every dictionary has **entries**, guide words, and **keys**. An entry is a word that is described in a dictionary. All entries are listed in bold type and in alphabetical order. A key is an explanation of symbols and abbreviations used in each entry. Here is a sample dictionary page.

guide words

mouth 314 **myth**

mouth (mouth), *n., pl.,* **mouths** (mouthz). **1.** an opening through which a human or animal takes in food. **2.** a part of a river where its water empties into a larger body: *the mouth of the Nile.* [German *mund*] **mouth´less,** *adj.*

mov•ie (mo͞o´vē), *n.* **1.** See **motion picture. 2.** a motion-picture theater: *The movie is next to the drugstore.* **3. movies,** motion pictures: *The people go to the movies.*

Mu•si•al (myo͞o´ zē l) *n.* Stanley Frank ("Stan the Man") Born 1920, U.S. baseball player.

mu•sic (myo͞o´ zik), *n.* **1.** a sound which expresses ideas and feelings using rhythm, melody, and harmony. **2.** a musical work for singing or playing. [Greek *mousikē* (the art) of the Muse]

mu•si•cal (myo͞o´ zi kə l), *adj.* **1.** of, related to, or making music: a musical instrument. **2.** liking or skilled at music: a musical person. *—n.* **3.** See **musical comedy.** [Latin *mūsicāl(is)*] **mu´si•cal•ly,** *adv.* **—mū´si•cal•ness,** *n.*

mu´sical com´edy, a play with music, including singing and dancing.

myth (mith) *n.* a traditional or legendary story.

a - act, **ā** - āble, **â** - dâre, **ä** - ärm, **e** - ebb, **ē** - ēven, **i** - it, **ī** - īce, **o** - hot, **ō** - ōver, **ô** - ôrder, **oi** - oil, **o͝o** - bo͝ok, **o͞o** - lo͞ot, **ou** - out, **u** - up, **û** - ûrge, **ch** - chief, **ng** - sing, **sh** - shoe, **th** - thin, **th** - this, **zh** - vision, ə = *a* as in *ago*.

entries listed in alphabetical order

pronunciation key

Activity A Use the sample dictionary page above. Write on your paper the word that completes each sentence below and on page 27.

1) The guide words are at the ______ of the page.

2) The first entry on page 314 is ______.

3) The last entry on the page is ______.

4) The pronunciation key is at the ______ of the page.

5) There are ______ entries on page 314.

Most dictionary entries contain the same basic features. The entries below provide examples of these features.

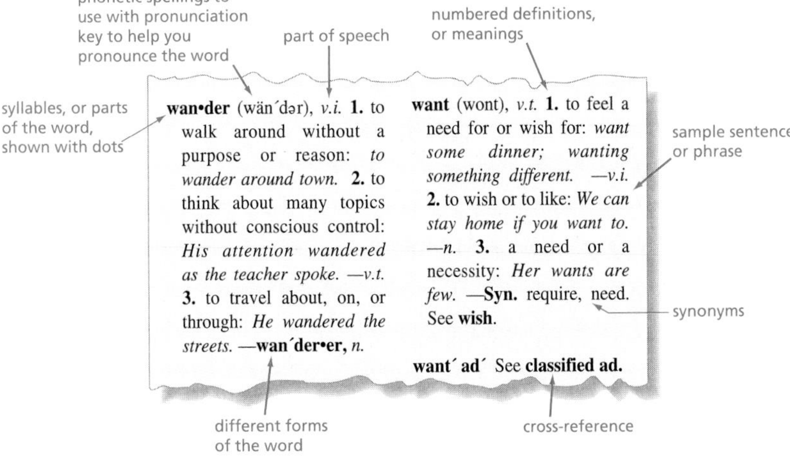

Activity B Use the sample entries and pronunciation key to answer the questions. Write your answers on your paper.

1) How many meanings are given for *wander*?

2) What are two synonyms for *want*?

3) What is another form of the verb *wander*?

4) Does the *a* in *wander* have the same sound as the *a* in *want*?

5) Which two entries have cross-references?

Reading Vocabulary

basic (7)
cross-reference
definition (6)
feature (6)
phonetic
pronunciation (5)
sample (5)
synonym (5)
verb

(Activity A Answers, continued)
3) myth **4)** bottom **5)** seven

■ Presenting Activity B

Before doing Activity B, focus students' attention on the labeled entries. Help them read each label and the part of the entry it identifies. Then work as a class to complete Activity B.

Activity B Answers

1) three **2)** require, need **3)** wanderer **4)** No **5)** want, want ad

Reading Vocabulary

accent mark
emphasis (8)
emphasize (7)
schwa
separate (5)
stress (9)
syllable (4)
unstressed
vowel (6)

Teacher Alert

After discussing the information presented on this page, you may wish to offer students the opportunity to apply these concepts. Randomly select words with two or more syllables from the dictionary. Write each entry word and its phonetic spelling on the board. Then have students answer these questions about each word:

- How many syllables does the word have?
- Which syllable is stressed? How do you know?
- How would you pronounce this word? (Have students use the pronunciation key on page 28.)

Learning Styles

LEP/ESL

On the board, print the following terms: *syllable, accent mark, stress,* and *phonetic spelling.* Then pick a three-syllable word from the dictionary and print it on the board in a way that shows the four terms. Next, call on students for whom English is a second language to choose a three-syllable word from their language and to print it on the board in a way that demonstrates their understanding of the four terms. Discuss any differences between the way an English dictionary handles words and the way a dictionary for another language handles them.

Pronouncing a Word

You may look up a word in a dictionary to find out how it is pronounced. A dictionary entry has three features that can help you pronounce a word.

> *Syllable*
> *A part of a word with one vowel sound.*

> *Accent mark*
> *A mark that shows which part of a word to stress when pronouncing the word.*

> *Stress*
> *To pronounce a syllable with more emphasis than the other syllables in the word.*

1. The word is divided into **syllables** that are separated by dots. A syllable is a part of a word or a unit of speech that has one vowel sound.
2. One of the syllables has an **accent mark** (ˊ). This mark shows which syllable to **stress** when you pronounce the word. When you stress a syllable, you emphasize that syllable more than the other syllables in the word.
3. Each entry gives the phonetic spelling for the word. The pronunciation key can help you understand the phonetic spelling. The key is usually at the bottom of the page. The pronunciation key lists words that you probably know how to say. Match the vowel sound in the word in the pronunciation key with the vowel sound in the entry word. That way you can figure out how to say the word.

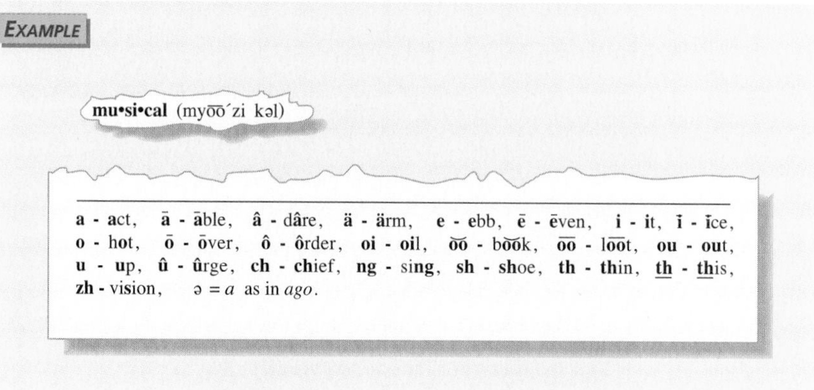

The phonetic spelling of *musical* shows that the vowel sound in the third syllable is the same as the *a* sound in *ago.* This vowel sound is called a schwa. It is shown with the symbol ə. You often hear the schwa vowel sound in unstressed syllables.

Activity C Look at the sample dictionary entry and the pronunciation key below. Write your answers to the questions that follow.

as•sem•bly (ə sem′ blē)

a - act, **ā** - āble, **â** - dâre, **ä** - ärm, **e** - ebb, **ē** - ēven, **i** - it, **ī** - īce,
o - hot, **ō** - ōver, **ô** - ôrder, **oi** - oil, **o͝o** - bo͝ok, **o͞o** - lo͞ot, **ou** - out,
u - up, **û** - ûrge, **ch** - chief, **ng** - sing, **sh** - shoe, **th** - thin, **th** - this,
zh - vision, ə = *a* as in *ago*.

1) How many syllables does *assembly* have? How do you know?
2) Which syllable should you stress when pronouncing *assembly*?
3) How can you tell which syllable to stress?
4) What sound does the vowel in the first syllable have?
5) What sound does the vowel in the last syllable have?

Abbreviation
A shortened form of a written word.

Abbreviations

Some of the features of a dictionary entry are abbreviated. An **abbreviation** is a shortened form of a written word.

You can learn what some common abbreviations stand for in a dictionary entry. Knowing these abbreviations can help you understand the use and meaning of the word you are looking up.

You can see common abbreviations in this dictionary entry.

EXAMPLE

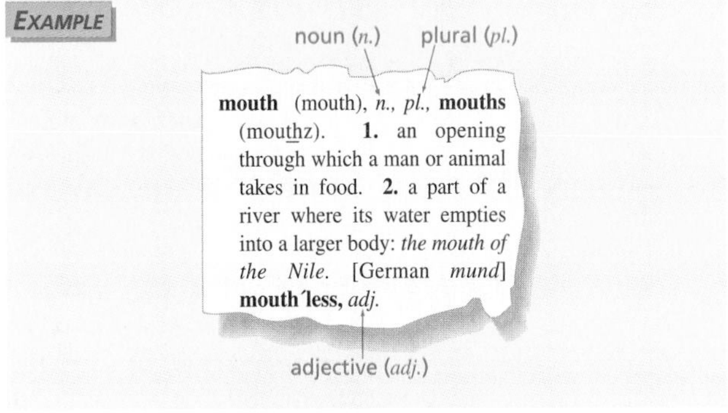

mouth (mouth), *n.*, *pl.*, **mouths** (mouthz). **1.** an opening through which a man or animal takes in food. **2.** a part of a river where its water empties into a larger body: *the mouth of the Nile.* [German *mund*] **mouth′less,** *adj.*

Reading Vocabulary

abbreviate (8)
abbreviation (8)
adjective
assembly (7)
noun
plural (6)

■ Presenting Activity C

Before having students do Activity C on their own, have them study the sample dictionary entry. Then invite volunteers to tell what they learn about the word from the entry.

Activity C Answers

Answers may vary. Probable responses are given.

1) three; the word is divided into three parts by dots **2)** second **3)** The accent mark appears after the second syllable in the phonetic spelling. **4)** schwa; the same vowel sound as the *a* in *ago* **5)** long e; the same vowel sound as the first *e* in *even*

Answering Questions About Words *Chapter 2* **29**

Reading Vocabulary

adverb
conjunction
connect (5)
describe (5)
interjection
intransitive
preposition
pronoun
relationship (6)
replace (6)
transitive

Teacher Alert

Have students refer to the example on the bottom of page 29 as they read the text at the top of page 30.

Application

Career Connection
Employers often ask new employees to read training manuals, pamphlets, and other documents related to company procedures and job benefits. A dictionary can be a useful tool to new employees who may be unfamiliar with important terms and phrases used in these documents. Encourage students to make it a regular practice to use a dictionary whenever they come across unfamiliar words and phrases.

Parts of Speech

In a dictionary entry, abbreviations for parts of speech usually follow the phonetic spelling of the word. This abbreviation tells you what part of speech the word is. Abbreviations for parts of speech may also appear in other parts of the entry if the word can be more than one part of speech.

Here is a list of abbreviations for parts of speech and their meanings.

n.	=	noun: names a person, place, thing, or idea.
pron.	=	pronoun: replaces a noun (he, she, me, that, everyone).
adj.	=	adjective: describes a noun or pronoun.
v.	=	verb: expresses action or a state of being (run, sing, look, become).
adv.	=	adverb: tells how, when, where, or how much (very, slowly, quickly).
prep.	=	preposition: shows a relationship between a noun or pronoun and another part of the sentence (in, above, near).
conj.	=	conjunction: connects sentences or parts of a sentence (and, because, or).
interj.	=	interjection: a word that expresses feelings (Oh! Wow!)

In most dictionary entries, a verb is labeled *v.t.* or *v.i.* rather than just *v.* Some verbs can be both transitive and intransitive.

v.t.	=	verb, transitive: a verb that needs an object to complete its meaning. An object is a noun or a pronoun.
v.i.	=	verb, intransitive: a verb that does not have an object.

Example

Transitive verb: He **throws** the ball. (*Ball* is the direct object.)

Intransitive: He **throws** hard. (*Hard* is an adverb.)

30 Chapter 2 Answering Questions About Words

Singular and Plural

Most words become plural by adding *-s.* If the word you look up forms its plural in a different way, you may see the abbreviation *pl.* followed by the word in its plural form.

sing.	= singular: one person, place, thing, or idea.
pl.	= plural: more than one person, place, thing, or idea.

en•try (en´trē), *n.*, *pl.*, **entries.** **1.** the act of entering: *The army made its entry into the city.* **2.** a statement or item entered in a book. [From Latin *intrāre*, to enter.]

Synonyms

Another abbreviation you might see in a dictionary entry is *Syn.* This stands for the word *synonym.* Synonyms are words with similar meanings. In a dictionary entry, the words that follow the abbreviation *Syn.* are synonyms for the word you looked up.

Syn.	= synonym: a word with the same or nearly the same meaning as another word.

EXAMPLE

cud•dle (kŭd´le), *v.t.* to hold near to keep wárm or to comfort or to show affection. **Syn.** embrace, nestle, snuggle

Reading Vocabulary

singular (8)

Global Connection

Students learning another language will be familiar with bilingual dictionaries. Encourage these students to explain how these dictionaries are organized (e.g., alphabetical Spanish to English/English to Spanish) and how to use them. If possible, provide copies of one or more bilingual dictionaries for students to examine and discuss.

Answering Questions About Words *Chapter 2* **31**

Reading Vocabulary

ivory (5)

■ Presenting Activity D

Before asking students to complete Activity D, review the concepts presented on pages 30 through 32. Then have students work independently to complete Activity D. After reviewing students' answers, challenge them to make up additional questions to ask the class about both sample entries on page 32.

Activity D Answers

1) n.—noun, pl.—plural, adj.—adjective, v.t.—transitive verb, v.i.—intransitive verb, Syn.—synonym, n.—noun **2)** noun and adjective **3)** ivories **4)** It can be both. The abbreviation *v.t.* in the entry means *change* can be transitive; the abbreviation *v.i.* means *change* can also be intransitive. **5)** alter, vary, shift **6)** noun

Activity D Use these sample dictionary entries to answer the questions below. Write your answers on your paper.

i•vo•ry (ī´ və rē, ī´ vrē), *n., pl.* **-ies** [ME < OF *ivurie*] **1.** the hard creamy-white dentine that composes the tusks of the elephant, walrus, etc. **2.** the substance used to make carvings, billiard balls, etc. **3.** a yellowish-white color. **4.** something made of ivory (as dice or piano keys) or of a similar substance. **–ivory** *adj.*

change (chānj), *v.t.* **1.** to cause to be different in some way. **2.** to replace with something else. *v.i.* **1.** to become different in some way. **2.** to go from one stage to another. **Syn.** alter, vary, shift *–n.* **1.** a shift from one thing to another.

1) What abbreviations appear in the two entries? Write the abbreviations and their meanings in order.

2) What two parts of speech can *ivory* be?

3) What is the plural spelling of *ivory*?

4) Is *change* a transitive or intransitive verb? How do you know?

5) What are three synonyms for *change?*

6) What other part of speech can *change* be?

Lesson 1 Review

Part A Number your paper from 1 to 8. Write the letter of the correct matching definition beside the number of the term.

Example **1)** c

1) dictionary
2) entry words
3) guide words
4) pronunciation key
5) abbreviation
6) synonym
7) cross-reference
8) plural

a) A related entry
b) More than one
c) A book that lists words
d) Explanation of symbols used in phonetic spelling
e) Words listed in a dictionary
f) Words at the top of a dictionary page showing the first and last entries on that page
g) A word that has almost the same meaning as another word
h) A shortened form of a written word

Part B Write on your paper the full word or words for each abbreviation.

1) pl.
2) n.
3) syn.
4) adj.
5) prep.
6) v.i.
7) v.t.
8) adv.
9) conj.
10) pron.

Part C Write the answers to these questions on your paper.

1) Where are the guide words in a dictionary?
2) How are syllables separated in a dictionary entry?
3) What does an accent mark tell you?
4) Where is the pronunciation key usually found?

Reading Vocabulary

relate (6)

Part A Answers

1) c **2)** e **3)** f **4)** d **5)** h **6)** g **7)** a **8)** b

Part B Answers

1) plural **2)** noun **3)** synonym **4)** adjective **5)** preposition **6)** verb, intransitive **7)** verb, transitive **8)** adverb **9)** conjunction **10)** pronoun

Part C Answers

1) Guide words are usually at the top of the page. **2)** Dots separate the syllables. **3)** An accent mark tells which syllable to stress or emphasize when saying the word aloud. **4)** The pronunciation key is usually at the bottom of the page.

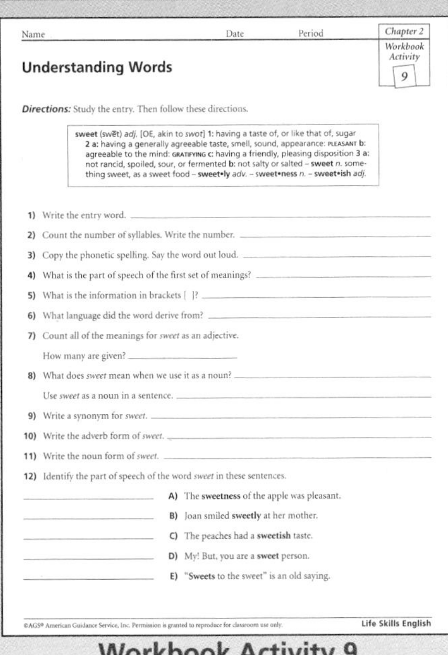

Name ______ Date ______ Period ______

Chapter 2 Workbook Activity 9

Understanding Words

Directions: Study the entry. Then follow these directions.

sweet (swēt) *adj.* [OE, akin to *swot*] **1:** having a taste of, or like that of, sugar **2 a:** having a generally agreeable taste, smell, sound, appearance: PLEASANT **b:** agreeable to the mind: GRATIFYING **c:** having a friendly, pleasing disposition **3 a:** not rancid, spoiled, sour, or fermented **b:** not salty or salted – **sweet** *n.* something sweet, as a sweet food – **sweet•ly** *adv.* – **sweet•ness** *n.* – **sweet•ish** *adj.*

1) Write the entry word. ______
2) Count the number of syllables. Write the number. ______
3) Copy the phonetic spelling. Say the word out loud. ______
4) What is the part of speech of the first set of meanings? ______
5) What is the information in brackets [ ]? ______
6) What language did the word derive from? ______
7) Count all of the meanings for *sweet* as an adjective.
How many are given? ______
8) What does *sweet* mean when we use it as a noun? ______
Use *sweet* as a noun in a sentence. ______
9) Write a synonym for *sweet*. ______
10) Write the adverb form of *sweet*. ______
11) Write the noun form of *sweet*. ______
12) Identify the part of speech of the word *sweet* in these sentences.

______ **A)** The **sweetness** of the apple was pleasant.
______ **B)** Joan smiled **sweetly** at her mother.
______ **C)** The peaches had a **sweetish** taste.
______ **D)** My! But, you are a **sweet** person.
______ **E)** "**Sweets** to the sweet" is an old saying.

 Life Skills English

Workbook Activity 9

Lesson at a Glance

Chapter 2 Lesson 2

Overview This lesson presents additional information about dictionary entries, including word meanings, cross-references, and word origins.

Objective

- To understand and identify the parts of a dictionary entry.

Student Pages 34–41

Teacher's Resource Library

Activity 5

Workbook Activities 10–12

Reading Vocabulary

apply (6)
miner (5)
overcast (8)
parentheses
phrase (6)

Teaching Suggestions

■ Introducing the Lesson

Discuss the information presented in the text. Reinforce the concepts presented in the text by having students look up these words in a dictionary: *fuel, style, safe.* Ask students to share what they learn about each word with a partner or in a small group. Then invite volunteers to make up sentences for the different meanings of each word.

■ Reviewing Skills

Review what students have learned about the different parts of a dictionary entry.

Lesson 2 More About Dictionary Entries

Word Meanings

You may look up a word in a dictionary to find out what the word means. A dictionary entry gives one or more meanings for each word listed. Each meaning is numbered. Sample phrases or sentences are often given for each meaning. If a word can be more than one part of speech, different meanings for each part of speech are also given.

EXAMPLE

o•ver•cast (ō´və r kast), *n.* **1.** a covering, esp. of clouds. **2.** an arch in a mine, supporting an overhead passage. *–adj.* **3.** cloudy; dark; said of the sky or weather. **4.** Sewing made with overcasting. *–v.t.* **-cast´, -cast´ing, 5.** to overcloud; darken. **6.** *Sewing* to sew over an edge of material with long, loose stitches so as to prevent raveling.

If you know how a word is used in a sentence, you can figure out which meaning applies. In the following examples, the word *overcast* is used three different ways. The number in parentheses after each sentence matches the number of the meaning in the dictionary entry above.

EXAMPLE

Because the sky was **overcast**, she grabbed her umbrella. (3)

Our sewing teacher showed us how to **overcast** the edges of the material. (6)

The miners knew the **overcast** would give way in an earthquake. (2)

Activity A Number your paper from 1 to 5. Beside each number write the part of speech and meaning of *overcast* as it is used in the sentence. Copy the meanings from the dictionary entry on page 34.

Example Today will be overcast. (Adjective, cloudy, dark; said of the sky or weather.)

1) The overcast fell down and trapped the miners.
2) Mrs. Gomez overcast the seams in Marie's shirt.
3) The overcast hem would not ravel easily.
4) An overcast sky was expected on Monday.
5) The overcast made everyone feel gloomy.

When you look up a word to find its meaning, the meaning may contain other words that you do not know. When that happens, you will have to look up the unfamiliar words. This can take several steps.

Here is an example of what might happen when you want to find out a word's meaning.

EXAMPLE

You are reading an article about your favorite baseball team in the sports section of the newspaper. You come to this sentence:

"The Cubs will play a twin bill Sunday afternoon against the Mets."

You think you know what *twin bill* means, but you decide to check its meaning in the dictionary. When you look up *twin bill,* what you find is below.

> **twin bill** *n.* same as **1.** DOUBLE FEATURE. **2.** DOUBLEHEADER (sense 2)

Words in capital letters are synonyms and cross references for the entry word. Therefore, you look up both *double feature* and *doubleheader.* When you look up *doubleheader,* what you find is below.

> **dou•ble•head•er** (dub əl hed´ər), *n.* **1.** a train pulled by two locomotives. **2.** two games played on the same day between two teams in succession.

Reading Vocabulary

capital (5)
double (5)
doubleheader
ravel
section (5)
unfamiliar

■ Presenting Activity A

Discuss the example provided for Activity A, making sure students know where the information in parentheses came from. Then do Activity A together as a class or have students complete the activity on their own.

Activity A Answers

1) Noun, an arch in a mine, supporting an overhead passage **2)** Verb, transitive, to sew over an edge of material with long, loose stitches so as to prevent raveling **3)** Adjective, sewing made with overcasting **4)** Adjective, cloudy; dark; said of the sky or weather **5)** Noun, a covering, esp. of clouds

Reading Vocabulary

attorney (8) spangle (6)
mature (6) succession (7)

■ Presenting Activity B

Read the directions for Activity B with students to be sure that they understand what they are to do. Then depending on the ability of your students, have them complete Activity B on their own or do the activity together as a class.

Activity B Answers

Sentences will vary. Possible responses are given.

1) The Williams family spent their summer vacation at a place people go for relaxation or recreation. **2)** "I'm inspecting the area to gather information," said the police officer. **3)** Marie does not look like her twin sister Michelle in any way. **4)** Chris said that O. Henry wrote under a fictitious name that authors sometime assume. **5)** "O'er the high embankment built around a guarded place we watched," is a line from "The Star-Spangled Banner." **6)** John works for Anita Valdez, an attorney with an honorable reputation. **7)** After their long journey on foot, Al and Justin were extremely hungry. **8)** The house was under enforced isolation to prevent the spread of a highly contagious disease characterized by coughing and wheezing spells. **9)** The coach hoped that the first-year player would be a valuable item to the team.

EXAMPLE The cross-reference for *doubleheader* tells you to look at "sense 2." When you look at meaning 2, you learn that a doubleheader means that two games are played on the same day in succession. To understand exactly what that means, you also look up *succession.*

> **suc•ces•sion** (sək sesh′ ən), *n.* the coming of one person or thing after another in order.

Finally, you know what the sentence in the article means:

On Sunday afternoon, the Cubs will play two games against the Mets. The second game will be played right after the first one.

Activity B Use a dictionary to find the meanings of the words in bold. Look up any words that you do not know. Then rewrite each sentence on your paper. Replace the words in bold with their meanings. You may have to add some words so that the sentence makes sense.

Example Mr. Gomez realized that his son Eddie was **precocious**.
Mr. Gomez realized that his son Eddie was extremely mature for his age.

1) The Williams family spent their summer vacation at a **resort**.
2) "I'm doing some **reconnaissance** work," said the police officer.
3) Marie does not **resemble** her twin sister Michelle in any way.
4) Chris said that O. Henry wrote under a **pseudonym**.
5) "O'er the **ramparts** we watched," is a line from the "The Star-Spangled Banner."
6) John works for Anita Valdez, a **reputable** attorney.
7) After their long **trek,** Al and Justin were **ravenous**.
8) The house was under **quarantine** because someone had **whooping cough**.
9) The coach hoped that the **rookie** would be an **asset** to the team.

Name Date Period | *Chapter 2 Workbook Activity 10*

Dictionary Search

Directions: Use a dictionary to find the answers to these questions. Write the number of the page where you found the answer.

1) What would you do with a lobster thermidor?
2) Was Robin Hood a real person?
3) What is the first name of the Rockefeller who was vice president of the United States?
4) Where would you expect to find a mudskipper?
5) Everyone says that Frances is munificent. Is that a compliment?
6) What could you do with a four-o'clock?
7) Karl weighs 130 pounds. Can he box as a featherweight?
8) Lance received a fedora for his birthday. What could he do with it?
9) Juan is a bibliophile. How can his friends tell?
10) Ralph's family is going to a cantata. What should Ralph expect?

 Life Skills English

Workbook Activity 10

Word Origins

Etymology
The study of the history of a word.

Origin
The beginning of something.

Derived
To come from. (Many English words are derived from other languages.)

You may look up a word to learn its history, or **etymology**. Over time, a word can change its spelling, its pronunciation, and its meaning. All of these changes are part of the history of the word.

When you look up a word to learn its **origin**, you may see the symbol <. This symbol means "**derived** from," or "comes from." The information that follows the symbol < explains the word's history. Some dictionaries use the word *from* or the abbreviation *fr* instead of the symbol <. Here are some other abbreviations you may see when you look up a word's history. They stand for the languages in which the words were first used.

OE = Old English	ME = Middle English	L = Latin
G = German	Gk = Greek	It = Italian
OF = Old French	F = French	S = Spanish

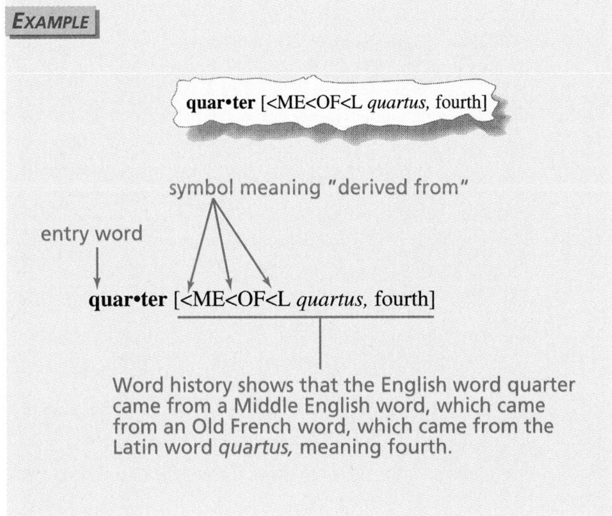

EXAMPLE
quar•ter [<ME<OF<L quartus, fourth]
symbol meaning "derived from"
entry word
quar•ter [<ME<OF<L quartus, fourth]
Word history shows that the English word quarter came from a Middle English word, which came from an Old French word, which came from the Latin word quartus, meaning fourth.

Reading Vocabulary

derived (8) **origin (6)**
etymology

Teacher Alert

Some students may be intimidated by the word *etymology* and, as a result, fail to grasp the concepts presented here. Help students understand that when they look up a word in a dictionary, they will find information that explains how that word came into the English language.

Global Connection

Point out to students that many words in the English language have been borrowed directly from other languages. Some examples of borrowed words are *squash* (Native American), *ballet* (French), and *stampede* (Spanish). Challenge students to identify other English words that have been borrowed directly from other languages and to share what they learn about these words with the class.

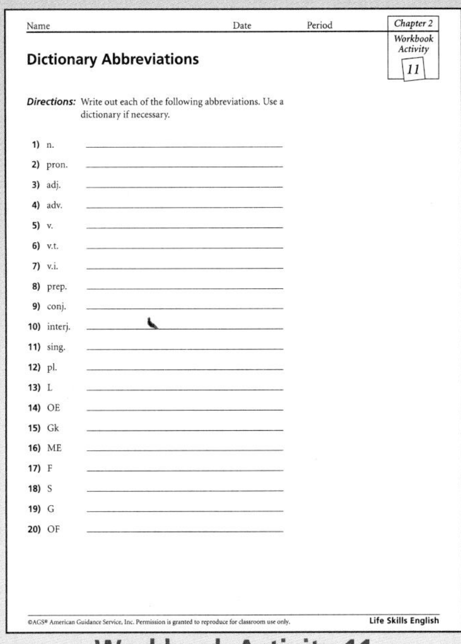

Name Date Period

Chapter 2 Workbook Activity 11

Dictionary Abbreviations

Directions: Write out each of the following abbreviations. Use a dictionary if necessary.

1) n. ________
2) pron. ________
3) adj. ________
4) adv. ________
5) v. ________
6) v.t. ________
7) v.i. ________
8) prep. ________
9) conj. ________
10) interj. ________
11) sing. ________
12) pl. ________
13) L ________
14) OE ________
15) Gk ________
16) ME ________
17) F ________
18) S ________
19) G ________
20) OF ________

 Life Skills English

Workbook Activity 11

Answering Questions About Words Chapter 2 **37**

Reading Vocabulary

embarrass (5) query (11)

■ Presenting Activity C

Before having students do Activity C, have them look up the origins of the following words in a dictionary: *sister, love, breakfast, January, calendar.* After discussing the origins of each word, have students complete Activity C on their own or with partners. Students can look at the chart on page 37 for the meanings of the language abbreviations.

Activity C Answers

1) [ ] or brackets **2)** Middle English **3)** Latin **4)** fourth **5)** ask

■ Presenting Activity D

Have students review the list of abbreviations for parts of speech and their meanings on page 30. Then have students identify the different forms of the entry word given in the entries for *overcast* on page 34 and *query* on page 38. Following this, have students complete Activity D on their own.

Activity D Answers

1) embarrass **2)** embarrassing **3)** embarrassment **4)** Sentences will vary.

Activity C Find the etymology of the two entry words in the two sample entries below. Write your answers to the questions on your paper.

> **quar•ter** (kwôr´ tər), *n.* [<ME<OF<L *quartus,* fourth] **1.** a fourth of something. **2.** a fourth of a year. **3.** one fourth of an hour. **4.** one fourth of a dollar, 25¢.
>
> **que•ry** (kwēr´ ē), *n.* [<L *quaerere,* ask] **1.** a question, inquiry. **2.** a question mark. –*v.t.* **que´ried, que´ry•ing** to question.

1) What marks are around the etymology of a word?
2) What was the most recent origin of the word *quarter?* (The name of the language is abbreviated.)
3) In what language did the word *query* begin?
4) What does the Latin word *quartus* mean?
5) What does the Latin word *quaerere* mean?

Other Forms

A dictionary often gives other forms of the entry word followed by their parts of speech.

EXAMPLE

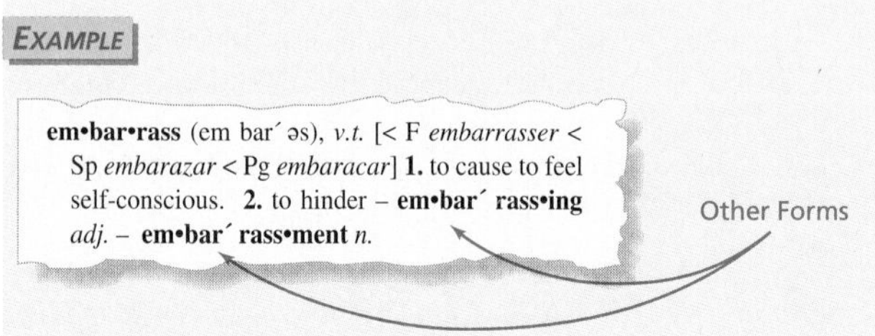

em•bar•rass (em bar´ əs), *v.t.* [< F *embarrasser* < Sp *embarazar* < Pg *embaracar*] **1.** to cause to feel self-conscious. **2.** to hinder – **em•bar´ rass•ing** *adj.* – **em•bar´ rass•ment** *n.*

Activity D Use the sample entry to complete the following. Write your answers on your paper. Use a dictionary for help if you need it.

1) Write the word *embarrass* on your paper.
2) Write the adjective form of *embarrass.*
3) Write the noun form of *embarrass.*
4) Write a sentence for each of the two meanings of *embarrass.*

Differences in Dictionary Entries

No two dictionaries are exactly alike. An entry for the same word in different dictionaries may contain different information.

Here are examples of entries for the word *home run* from four different dictionaries. Each entry presents the definition in a slightly different way.

EXAMPLE

This word in italic, or slanted type, explains that *home run* is a baseball term.

This symbol means that the word is an Americanism. It is used in American speech and writing.

A

home run *Baseball* a hit that allows the batter to touch all bases and score a run; also (Colloq.) **hom´er** *n.*

B

***home run** *Baseball* a safe hit that allows the batter to touch all bases and score a run.

C

home run *n*: a hit in baseball that enables the batter to make a circuit of the bases and score a run.

D

home´ run´ *Baseball,* a hit that enables a batter, without the aid of a fielding error, to score a run by making a nonstop circuit of the bases.

This abbreviation stands for *colloquial.* It means that we use the word in informal speech.

Activity E Use the sample entries to answer these questions. Write your answers on your paper.

1) Which of the entries is the simplest to understand—A, B, C, or D? Why?

2) Which entry gives extra information? What is that information?

3) What is another term for *home run?*

4) Which entries give the part of speech? What part of speech is *home run?*

Reading Vocabulary

Americanism
colloquial (12)
italic (6)
slightly

■ Presenting Activity E

Before doing Activity E, encourage students to discuss the differences that they notice on their own in each of the entries. Then do Activity E together as a class.

Activity E Answers

1) Students will probably say that B is the simplest because it uses the simplest language and is the most straightforward of the definitions. **2)** D; without the aid of a fielding error **3)** homer **4)** A, C; noun

TEACHER ALERT

Some students may not understand the difference between formal and informal language. Point out that formal language is more appropriate to writing, while informal language is more appropriate for speaking than writing. Suggest that they use their newly acquired dictionary skills to look up both *formal* and *informal* in the dictionary.

Reading Vocabulary

chart (5) introduction (6)
hockey (5)

■ Presenting Activity F

Have students take turns looking up the word *sport* in the dictionary. Ask each student to tell one new thing that they learn about the word *sport* from the entry. Then have students complete Activity F on their own.

Activity F Answers

1) probably Old French
2) hockie (Some students may say *hoquet.*) **3)** B, hockey. See ice hockey; see field hockey. **4)** Ice hockey is played on ice. Field hockey is played on a field.

Learning Styles

Auditory/Verbal

Call on volunteers to read aloud the dictionary entries on pages 34 through 40. This can be an opportunity to check that the students understand the various abbreviations and symbols a dictionary uses in its word entries. Print these abbreviations and symbols on the board. Then ask other volunteers to use a class dictionary to find an entry that uses some of these abbreviations and symbols, and to read the entry to the class. Encourage the class to say aloud which abbreviations and symbols the volunteer is probably encountering in the entry.

Most dictionaries give the same basic information for a word. Some dictionaries give more information, and some give less. Different dictionaries may also give information in a different order.

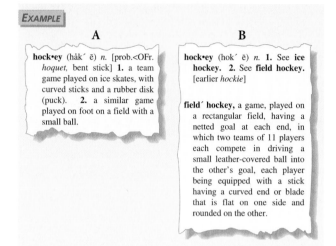

Example

A

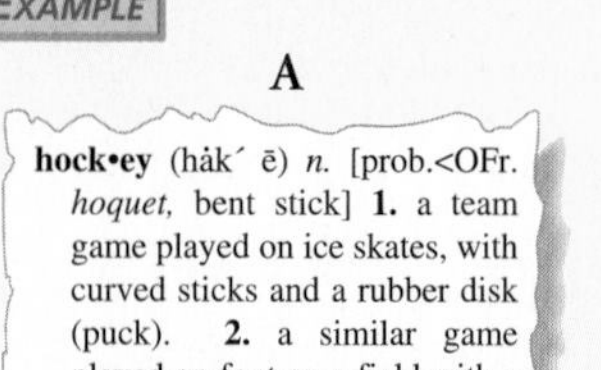

hock•ey (hȧk´ ē) *n.* [prob.<OFr. *hoquet,* bent stick] **1.** a team game played on ice skates, with curved sticks and a rubber disk (puck). **2.** a similar game played on foot on a field with a small ball.

B

hock•ey (hok´ ē) *n.* **1.** See **ice hockey.** **2.** See **field hockey.** [earlier *hockie*]

field´ hockey, a game, played on a rectangular field, having a netted goal at each end, in which two teams of 11 players each compete in driving a small leather-covered ball into the other's goal, each player being equipped with a stick having a curved end or blade that is flat on one side and rounded on the other.

Activity F Use the information in the sample entries to answer these questions. Write your answers on your paper.

1) What is the origin of *hockey*?

2) How was *hockey* probably spelled in the past?

3) Under which letter—A or B—are cross-references given? Which entry word has the cross-references and what are they?

4) What is the difference between the playing surfaces in the two kinds of hockey?

A dictionary entry may include symbols and abbreviations that have not been covered in this lesson. The introduction in dictionaries explains the symbols and abbreviations used in the entries. Most dictionaries have a chart that explains every possible part of a dictionary entry. Look at the notes and chart in the introduction to help you understand parts of an entry.

Lesson Review Read each entry carefully. Write on your paper the answers to the questions.

con•fet•ti (kən fet´ ē) *n.* [It. pl. of *confetto,* sweetmeat] bits of colored paper or ribbon for throwing around at celebrations.

1) How many syllables does the word *confetti* have?
2) What vowel sound do you hear in the first syllable?
3) What part of speech is the word *confetti*?
4) What country is the word from?
5) What would you do with confetti?

in•voice (in´vois), *n.* [prob. <MF *envois* messages] a list of goods shipped to a buyer stating prices. – *v.t.* **in•voiced, invoic•ing** to present an invoice for goods sold or services provided to someone.

6) Can *invoice* be used as a verb?
7) What did the word *invoice* mean in Middle French? How was it spelled?
8) When would you expect to get an invoice?

e•mo•tion•al (i mō´shən əl), *adj.* [< L *e-* out + *movere* to move] **1.** showing strong feeling. **2.** appealing to the emotions. – **e•mo•tion•al•ly** *adv.*

9) What is the meaning of the word *emotional* in these sentences—meaning 1 or meaning 2?
   a) That music is very emotional.
   b) Marie gets emotional at sad movies.
10) From what language is the word *emotional* derived?
11) How many syllables are in the word *emotional*?
12) What is the adverb form of the word *emotional*?

Reading Vocabulary

confetti (8) invoice (11)
emotional

Lesson Review Answers

Wording of some answers may vary.

1) three 2) schwa or *a* as in *ago* 3) noun 4) Italy 5) Throw it at a celebration. 6) Yes 7) The word *envois* meant "messages." 8) after being shipped goods from a company 9a) 2 9b) 1 10) Latin 11) four 12) emotionally

Application

At Home

Students may enjoy creating a word-of-the-day calendar at home. Suggest that each day they find a new word in a book, magazine, or newspaper. They can write that word on a piece of paper with the day and the date and then display the word in a prominent place, such as on the refrigerator door. Students can challenge family members to look up the word in a dictionary and then use the word correctly in a sentence or tell something interesting they learned about the word.

Name Date Period | *Chapter 2* *Activity* 5

Dictionary Entries

Directions: Answer these questions about the entry word *employ.*

em • ploy *vt.* [< L. *in -*, in + *plicare,* to fold] **1.** to use, **2.** to keep busy or occupied, **3.** to engage the services of; hire — *n.* **employment**

1) How many syllables does *employ* have? ______
2) How many meanings does *employ* have? ______
3) What part of speech is *employ*? ______
4) What is a synonym for *employ*? ______
5) Write the noun form of this word. ______
6) From what language did *employ* come? ______
7) What did *employ* originally mean? ______

Directions: Answer these questions about the entry word *employer.*

em • ploy • er *n.* one who employs others for wages or a salary

8) What part of speech is *employer*? ______
9) How many syllables does *employer* have? ______
10) How many meanings does this word have? ______

Directions: Answer these questions about the entry word *empower.*

em • pow • er *vt.* **1.** to give power to; authorize, **2.** to enable

11) How many syllables does this word have? ______
12) What part of speech is *empower*? ______
13) How many meanings does this word have? ______
14) Write a synonym for *empower.* ______

 Life Skills English

Activity 5

Name Date Period | *Chapter 2* *Workbook Activity* 12

The Meaning of a Word

Directions: Read the entry below. Then follow the directions.

eat (´ēt) *v.* **ate** (´āt, *chiefly Brit or substand* ´et); **eat•en** (´e-tᵊn); **eat•ing** [OE *etan*] *vt.* **1:** to take in through the mouth as food: ingest, chew, and swallow in turn **2:** to destroy, consume, or waste by or as if by eating: DEVOUR (operating expenses *ate* up the profits) **3 a:** to consume gradually: CORRODE **b:** to consume with vexation: BOTHER (what's *-ing* her now) —*vi.* **1:** to take food or a meal **2:** to affect something by gradual destruction or consumption – usu. used with *into, away,* or *at* – **eat•er** *n.*

1) Fill in the blanks with the correct form of *eat.*
   a) Don't disturb the dog while he is ______ .
   b) Yesterday I ______ chicken for dinner.
   c) Mary has ______ all of her lunch.
   d) Mother said the baby was a good ______ .
   e) Be sure to ______ your spinach!
2) What language did *eat* derive from? ______
3) Write the root form of the word *eat.* ______
4) Which meaning of *eat* is used in the following sentences? Write the number (and letter if necessary) of each meaning on the line.
   ______ a) The rust **ate** up the iron fence.
   ______ b) The moths **ate** a hole in my wool coat.
   ______ c) **Eat** your dinner.
   ______ d) You look upset. Is something **eating** you, Harry?
   ______ e) The locusts **ate** up the crops.
5) What part of speech is *eat*? ______
6) Which of the following sentences illustrates *eat* as an intransitive verb (vi.)? Circle the letter of the correct answer.
   a) I am **eating** my dinner.
   b) I am **eating** slowly.
7) Write the noun form of the verb *eat.* ______

 Life Skills English

Workbook Activity 12

Answering Questions About Words Chapter 2 41

Lesson at a Glance

Chapter 2 Lesson 3

Overview This lesson explains how to use a dictionary to find the correct spelling of words.

Objective

- To use a dictionary to find the correct spelling of words.

Student Pages 42–48

Teacher's Resource Library

Activities 6–7

Workbook Activity 13

Teaching Suggestions

■ Introducing the Lesson

Ask students what types of spelling problems give them the most trouble. Then use the information in the text to help students understand how helpful the dictionary can be with common spelling problems.

■ Reviewing Skills

Review the parts of a dictionary entry.

■ Presenting Activity A

Write these words on the board: *horse, box, goose, glass, donkey,* and *bunny.* Ask students to identify the words that follow the *-s* or *-es* plural rule and the ones that don't. Then have volunteers check the plural spelling of each word in a dictionary to verify students' responses. After this activity, have students complete Activity A on their own.

Activity A Answers

1) dictionaries—No 2) umbrellas—Yes 3) men—No 4) shelves—No 5) moose—No 6) guesses—Yes 7) puppies—No 8) keys—Yes

Lesson 3 Using a Dictionary to Check Spelling

Even the best spellers need to check the spelling of a word now and then. The dictionary is a useful tool when you want to find out how a word is spelled. You may wonder how you can look up a word if you can't spell it. In this lesson, you will learn some general spelling rules that will help you spell words. You can use the dictionary to check that you have spelled the words correctly.

Spelling the Plurals of Nouns

Form the plural of most nouns by adding *-s* or *-es.*

EXAMPLES

house—houses	shoe—shoes
boy—boys	watch—watches

If a noun does not follow the *-s* or *-es* rule for forming its plural, look at the dictionary entry to find its plural form.

EXAMPLE

child (child) *n. pl.* **chil•dren** [ME>OE *cild*] **1.** a young girl or boy between the age of infancy and teens. *adj.* childlike.

Here are some other nouns that do not follow the *-s* or *-es* rule.

EXAMPLES

mouse—mice	woman—women
city—cities	deer—deer

Activity A Look up each of the words below in a dictionary. Write the plural form on your paper. Beside each word, write *Yes* if the word follows the *-s* or *-es* rule. Write *No* if it does not.

1) dictionary
2) umbrella
3) man
4) shelf
5) moose
6) guess
7) puppy
8) key

Adding Endings to Words

Double the final consonant of some words before adding an ending. If you are not sure whether to double the final consonant before adding an ending, check your dictionary.

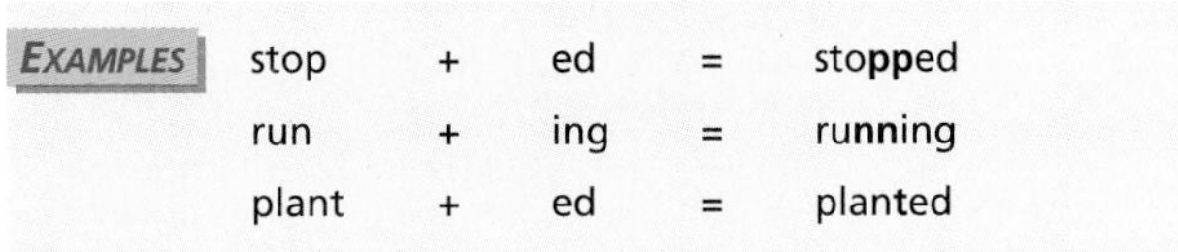

EXAMPLES
stop + ed = stopped
run + ing = running
plant + ed = planted

For some words that end with a silent *e*, drop the *e* before adding an ending. If you are not sure whether to drop the final *e*, check your dictionary.

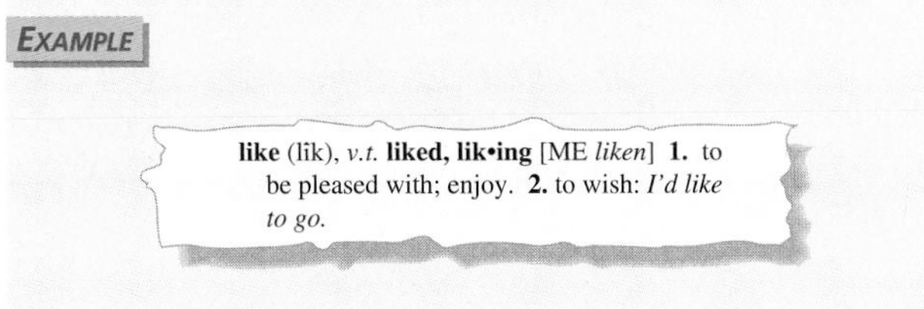
EXAMPLE

like (lik), *v.t.* **liked, lik•ing** [ME *liken*] **1.** to be pleased with; enjoy. **2.** to wish: *I'd like to go.*

Activity B Add the endings in parentheses to these words. Write the words with the endings on your paper. Then use a dictionary to check your spelling.

1) bake (ed)

2) charge (ing)

3) use (ful)

4) safe (ty)

5) write (er)

6) step (ing)

7) tall (est)

8) plan (ed)

9) hum (ing)

10) drop (ed)

Reading Vocabulary

consonant

■ Presenting Activity B

Write the following on the board: *hop (ed), love (ing), pretty (est), drive (en), operate (or), hope (ful).* Invite volunteers to write on the board each word with the ending added. Then have the class check the spelling of each word in a dictionary and correct any mistakes. Then repeat this process using the list of words from Activity B or have students complete Activity B independently.

Activity B Answers

1) baked **2)** charging **3)** useful **4)** safety **5)** writer **6)** stepping **7)** tallest **8)** planned **9)** humming **10)** dropped

Reading Vocabulary

irregular (7) participle

■ **Presenting Activity C** Ask volunteers to look up these verbs in a dictionary and write their past and past participle forms on the board: *break, write, begin, burst, receive.* Have students point out the irregular verbs. Then ask them to complete Activity C on their own.

Activity C Answers

1) enjoy—no other verb forms are shown **2)** cost **3)** draw **4)** crept

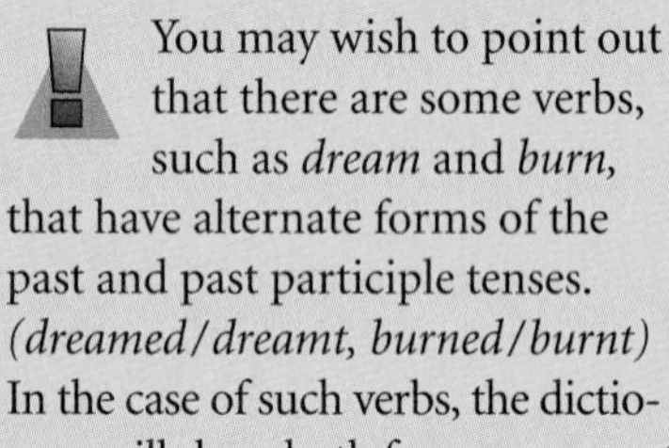

TEACHER ALERT

You may wish to point out that there are some verbs, such as *dream* and *burn,* that have alternate forms of the past and past participle tenses. *(dreamed/dreamt, burned/burnt)* In the case of such verbs, the dictionary will show both forms as correct.

LEARNING STYLES

Body/Kinesthetic

On the board, make two columns and label them "Regular Verbs" and "Irregular Verbs." Invite volunteers—one by one—to pantomime an action. Encourage the class to guess the action. Ask a volunteer to write the pantomimed action word in the correct column and then to add its past and past participle tenses. Ask other volunteers to check the spellings in a dictionary. Encourage the volunteers to pantomime as many irregular verbs they can think of.

Spelling Verbs

Add *-ed* to the end of regular verbs to make their past or past participle forms.

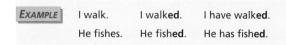

EXAMPLE	I walk.	I walk**ed**.	I have walk**ed**.
	He fishes.	He fish**ed**.	He has fish**ed**.

Form the past or past participle of irregular verbs in other ways. The dictionary entry will show you the past and, sometimes, the past participle for irregular verb forms, along with the present participle. Study the example.

EXAMPLE

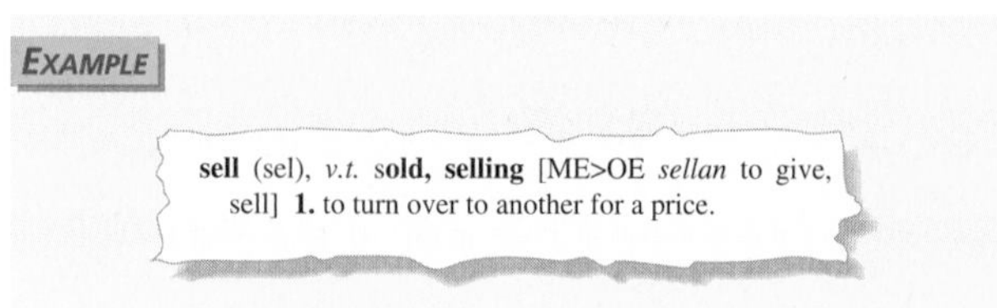

sell (sel), *v.t.* **sold, selling** [ME>OE *sellan* to give, sell] **1.** to turn over to another for a price.

Activity C Write on your paper the answers to the questions about the entries below.

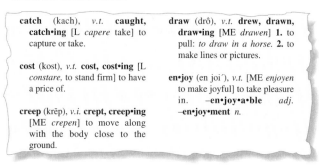

catch (kach), *v.t.* **caught, catch•ing** [L *capere* take] to capture or take.

cost (kost), *v.t.* **cost, cost•ing** [L *constare,* to stand firm] to have a price of.

creep (krēp), *v.i.* **crept, creep•ing** [ME *crepen*] to move along with the body close to the ground.

draw (drô), *v.t.* **drew, drawn, draw•ing** [ME *drawen*] **1.** to pull: *to draw in a horse.* **2.** to make lines or pictures.

en•joy (en joi′), *v.t.* [ME *enjoyen* to make joyful] to take pleasure in. **–en•joy•a•ble** *adj.* **–en•joy•ment** *n.*

1) Which verb forms its past form in a regular way? How do you know?

2) Which verb does not add an ending to make the past form?

3) Which entry shows four different forms for the verb?

4) Write the past form of *creep.*

Activity D Write on your paper the past form of the verb in parentheses. Then check your spelling in the entries on page 44.

1) Eddie (draw) a picture in art class.

2) The turtle (creep) across the road.

3) That car (cost) them a lot!

4) Lisa (enjoy) the movie.

Homonyms and Sound-Alike Words

Homonym
A word that sounds exactly like another word but is spelled differently and has a different meaning.

Homonyms are words that sound exactly alike but are spelled differently and have different meanings. To be sure you have used the correct homonym in a sentence, check its meaning and spelling in a dictionary.

EXAMPLES there their they're
There is my house. (adverb)
Their vacation starts soon. (pronoun)
They're my best friends. (They are)

Words that sound almost alike can also cause spelling problems. To be sure you have used the correct word in a sentence, look up both words in the dictionary. Read the meanings to find out which word you need.

EXAMPLES probable probably
It is **probable** that it will rain today. (adjective)
It will **probably** rain today. (adverb)

accept except
I am pleased to **accept** this award. (verb)
Everyone was surprised **except** me! (preposition)

Reading Vocabulary

award (5) probable (7)
homonym (13)

■ **Presenting Activity D** Ask students to write sentences using the past forms of each of these words listed on the board: *break, write, begin, burst, receive.* Then ask students to complete Activity D on their own.

Activity D Answers

1) drew **2)** crept **3)** cost **4)** enjoyed

Reading Vocabulary

height (5) science (5)
recommend (6) thorough (6)

■ Presenting Activity E

Write *your* and *you're* on the board. Ask students to look up each of these words in a dictionary. Then write these sentences on the board: *Where did you put ______ coat?/I hope ______ right.* Ask students to tell which word—*you're* or *your*—completes each sentence correctly.

Activity E Answers

1) its 2) It's 3) its 4) It's

Activity E Write on your paper the word that completes each sentence correctly. Use the dictionary entries to be sure you have used the correct word.

> **its** (its) *pron.* of or relating to it. (used as an adjective)
>
> **it's** (its) **1.** a contraction of *it is.* **2.** a contraction of *it has.*

1) Here is my book. Have you seen ______ cover?

2) ______ been a nice day today.

3) I wonder what ______ name is.

4) ______ a quarter past two.

Other Troublesome Words to Spell

Some words are harder to spell than other words. It may take more than one try to check the spelling of these words in a dictionary.

EXAMPLES

Words with the letters *ei* and *ie* can be tricky.
reins science believe friend

Words with double consonants are often hard to spell.
committee recommend different

Some words have letters that are not pronounced.
knowledge thorough Wednesday

Some words are pronounced incorrectly and then spelled the way they are pronounced.
interesting height across

Some words are not spelled the way they sound.
scissors necessary

Some words sound as if they could begin with different letters.
eighty imagine invite

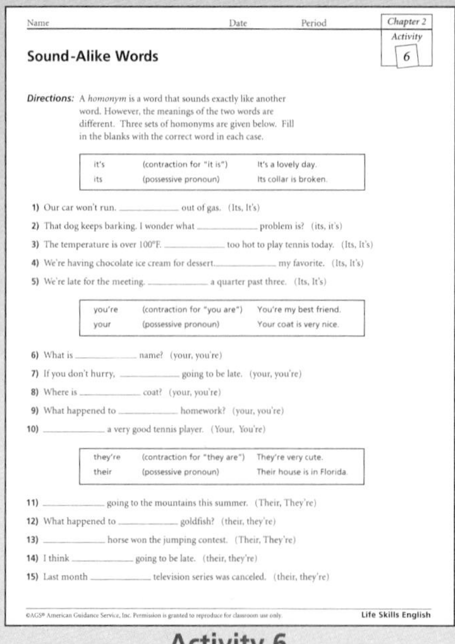

Name Date Period — Chapter 2 Activity 6

Sound-Alike Words

Directions: A *homonym* is a word that sounds exactly like another word. However, the meanings of the two words are different. Three sets of homonyms are given below. Fill in the blanks with the correct word in each case.

it's	(contraction for "it is")	It's a lovely day.
its	(possessive pronoun)	Its collar is broken.

1) Our car won't run. ______ out of gas. (Its, It's)
2) That dog keeps barking. I wonder what ______ problem is? (its, it's)
3) The temperature is over 100°F. ______ too hot to play tennis today. (Its, It's)
4) We're having chocolate ice cream for dessert. ______ my favorite. (Its, It's)
5) We're late for the meeting. ______ a quarter past three. (Its, It's)

you're	(contraction for "you are")	You're my best friend.
your	(possessive pronoun)	Your coat is very nice.

6) What is ______ name? (your, you're)
7) If you don't hurry, ______ going to be late. (your, you're)
8) Where is ______ coat? (your, you're)
9) What happened to ______ homework? (your, you're)
10) ______ a very good tennis player. (Your, You're)

they're	(contraction for "they are")	They're very cute.
their	(possessive pronoun)	Their house is in Florida.

11) ______ going to the mountains this summer. (Their, They're)
12) What happened to ______ goldfish? (their, they're)
13) ______ horse won the jumping contest. (Their, They're)
14) I think ______ going to be late. (their, they're)
15) Last month ______ television series was canceled. (their, they're)

 Life Skills English

Activity 6

Activity F Write on your paper the word that names each picture below. Check the spelling of each word in a dictionary.

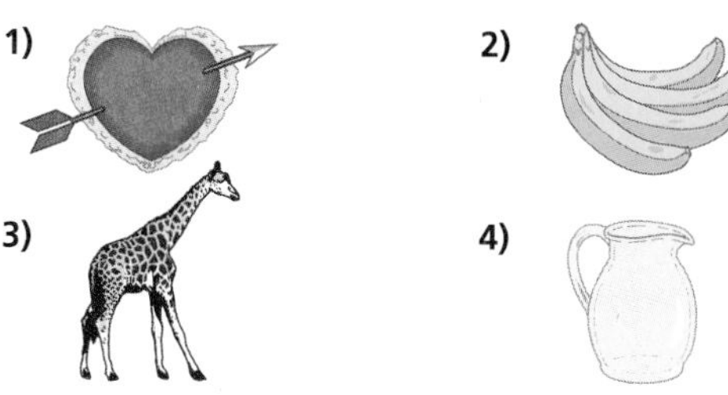

Activity G Use a dictionary to help you find five spelling errors in the paragraph below. Write the correct spellings on your paper.

> Next Munday, I'll call my freind after school. I'll invite him to visit me and my fammily for the weekend. We always find the same things intresting, witch is why we like each other's company.

■ **Presenting Activity F** In preparation for Activity F, draw or cut out pictures of objects from old magazines and newspapers. Try to select objects whose names might create spelling problems, such as an envelope, mask, crayon, luggage, calendar, and so on. Display the pictures on poster paper and have students identify each object and write its name beside or beneath the object. Encourage students to check the spelling of each word in a dictionary. Following this activity, have students complete Activity F on their own.

Activity F Answers

1) heart (or valentine)
2) bananas **3)** giraffe
4) pitcher

■ **Presenting Activity G** Read the passage with students. Rather than have students check every word in the passage, suggest that first they write down any words that they think are misspelled and check those words in a dictionary. If they don't identify all five misspelled words this way, they can then go back and check the spelling of the other words.

Activity G Answers

1) Monday **2)** friend **3)** family
4) interesting **5)** which

Answering Questions About Words Chapter 2 **47**

Reading Vocabulary

incorrectly misspelled

Part A Answers

1) Baseball 2) dedicated 3) museum 4) organized 5) holy

Part B Answers

1) foremen, Wednesday 2) calves 3) planned, Thanksgiving 4) necessary 5) too, commotion 6) no misspelled word 7) no misspelled word 8) believes, succeed

Application

In the Community Some dictionaries are published on CD-ROM; others are available through on-line computer services. Community libraries may provide access to these electronic dictionaries through their computer systems and computer networks. Encourage students to investigate these electronic dictionaries. Invite them to share what they learn about their ease of use and content with the class. Then engage students in a discussion of the benefits and disadvantages of electronic versus book-bound dictionaries.

Lesson 3 Review

Part A The words in bold in the paragraph below are spelled incorrectly. Use a dictionary to find each correct spelling. Write the paragraph on your paper with all of the words spelled correctly.

> The **Basball** Hall of Fame is in Cooperstown, New York. It was **dedecated** in 1939. People like to visit the **musuem**. The Hall of Fame is called "The shrine of **orgonized** baseball." A shrine is a **wholly** place!

Part B Ten of the words in bold below are misspelled. Check the spelling of all the bold words in a dictionary. Write the misspelled words correctly on your paper.

1) The **foremans** on Robert's job have a meeting every **Wensday**.
2) A friend of mine has two **calfs** for sale.
3) Maria's club **planed** the **Thanxsgiving** party.
4) "Is all that noise **nessessary**?" asked Mr. Williams.
5) "I'm **to** tired for this **comotion**!" he said.
6) Chris would rather see a movie **than** watch TV.
7) "Where is **your** homework?" asked the teacher.
8) He **beleives** that everyone deserves a chance to **suceed**.

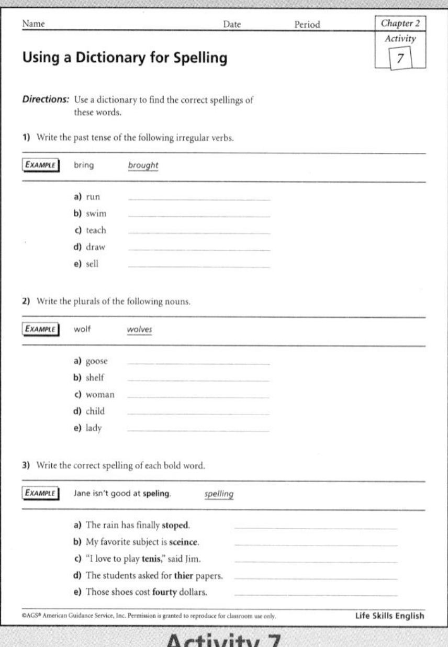

Name Date Period — Chapter 2 Activity 7

Using a Dictionary for Spelling

Directions: Use a dictionary to find the correct spellings of these words.

1) Write the past tense of the following irregular verbs.

EXAMPLE bring *brought*

a) run ______
b) swim ______
c) teach ______
d) draw ______
e) sell ______

2) Write the plurals of the following nouns.

EXAMPLE wolf *wolves*

a) goose ______
b) shelf ______
c) woman ______
d) child ______
e) lady ______

3) Write the correct spelling of each bold word.

EXAMPLE Jane isn't good at **speling**. *spelling*

a) The rain has finally **stoped**. ______
b) My favorite subject is **sceince**. ______
c) "I love to play **tenis**," said Jim. ______
d) The students asked for **thier** papers. ______
e) Those shoes cost **fourty** dollars. ______

 Life Skills English

Activity 7

Name Date Period — Chapter 2 Workbook Activity 13

Dictionary Entries

Directions: Study each sample entry below. Then follow the directions given for each entry.

A. **ici•cle** ('ī-,si-kəl) *n.* [OE *is* ice + *gicel*, piece of ice] : a tapering, pointed, hanging piece of ice, formed by the freezing of dripping or falling water

1) What part of speech is *icicle*? ______
2) How many syllables does this word have? ______
3) From what language did this word come? ______
4) What are the two root words from which *icicle* was derived? What did they originally mean?

Root word	Meaning
______	______
______	______

5) What is an *icicle*? ______
6) How is an *icicle* formed? ______
7) Write the plural form of the word *icicle*. ______

B. **i•cy** ('ī-sē) *adj.* **ic•i•er; ic•i•est 1:** having much ice: full of or covered with ice **2:** of ice **3:** like ice; specif. **a:** slippery **b:** very cold: FRIGID **4:** cold in manner or attitude: UNFRIENDLY – **ic•i•ly** *adv.* – **ic•i•ness** *n.*

1) Write the noun form of the word *icy*. ______
2) Write a synonym for *icy*. ______
3) How many syllables does *icy* have? ______
4) Fill in the blanks with the correct form of the word:
   A) The streets will become ______ after dark.
   B) She stared at him ______.
   C) He sensed the ______ in her attitude.
5) Which meaning of the word is used in the following sentences? Write the number of each meaning on the line.
   ______ A) He gave her an **icy** look to show his displeasure.
   ______ B) The streets were **icy**.
   ______ C) Pour me an **icy** drink.

 Life Skills English

Workbook Activity 13

Lesson 4

Using a Dictionary to Find Facts

You can use a dictionary to find out interesting and important facts. Here are some kinds of facts you might find in a dictionary.

- Facts about real people
- Facts about fictional characters
- Facts about cities, rivers, states, and countries
- The meaning of foreign words

EXAMPLE

> **Columbus, Christopher.** 1451–1506. Italian, served Spain as an explorer. First European to discover America (1492) in an attempt to sail to Asia from Europe.

Activity A Look up the following words in a dictionary. Write on your paper one fact you learn about each item. If your dictionary does not contain an entry for a word, write *no entry* on your paper. Later, look up the word in a different dictionary.

1) hors d'oeuvres

2) Dakota

3) Marconi

4) Robinson Crusoe

5) impressionism

6) pomegranate

7) otter

8) Nike

9) NASA

10) O'Keeffe

Lesson at a Glance

Chapter 2 Lesson 4

Overview This lesson explains how to use a dictionary to find facts.

Objective

- To use sample dictionary entries to find facts.

Student Pages 49–53

Teacher's Resource Library

Activity 8

Workbook Activity 14

Reading Vocabulary

fictional	impressionism
foreign (5)	otter
hors d'oeuvres	pomegranate

Teaching Suggestions

Introducing the Lesson

As you discuss the text, point out that specialized dictionaries, such as a dictionary of science or a dictionary of literature, can be used to find facts on a specific subject.

Reviewing Skills

Review how to use alphabetical order to look up words and names in a dictionary.

Presenting Activity A

Before asking students to complete Activity A on their own, focus students' attention on the entry for Christopher Columbus. Have volunteers take turns telling one fact they learn about Columbus from this entry.

Activity A Answers

Answers will vary. Answers should contain at least one fact about each word.

Reading Vocabulary

antonyms
biographical dictionary
geographical dictionary

■ **Presenting Activity B** If possible before assigning Activity B to students, provide them with copies of a geographical dictionary, a biographical dictionary, and a dictionary of synonyms and antonyms to examine. Remind students that regular dictionaries also provide synonyms and antonyms for certain entries. Then write the words *happy* and *great* on the board. Ask students to use a dictionary of synonyms and antonyms or a regular dictionary to find synonyms and antonyms for both words. Have students list the words they find on the board under *happy* or *great* and label the synonyms with an *S* and the antonyms with an *A*. Then have students complete Activity B on their own.

Activity B Answers

1) geographical **2)** synonyms and antonyms **3)** biographical **4)** synonyms and antonyms **5)** biographical **6)** geographical

Different Kinds of Dictionaries

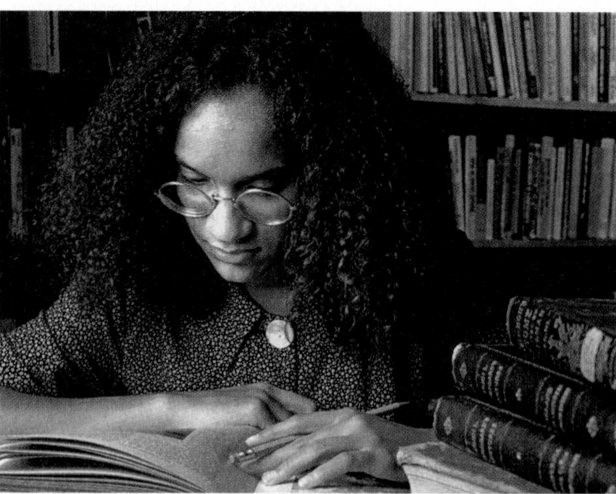

Most libraries have many different types of dictionaries in the reference section.

Some dictionaries provide special information.

> ***Geographical dictionary***
> *A reference book with a list of rivers, mountains, cities, and other features.*

A **geographical dictionary** has a list of rivers, mountains, cities, and other geographical features of the world. A **biographical dictionary** has a list of famous people and some facts about their lives.

A dictionary of synonyms and **antonyms** has a list of words with other words that have the same meanings and words that have opposite meanings.

> ***Biographical dictionary***
> *A reference book that lists famous people and facts about their lives.*

> ***Antonym***
> *A word that means the opposite of another word.*

Activity B Write on your paper the type of dictionary that would probably have the information listed in each item below. Write *geographical, biographical,* or *synonyms and antonyms.*

1) Information about your town or city

2) A word that means the same as *nice*

3) The date that Calvin Coolidge became president

4) A word that means the opposite of *large*

5) A list of some of the inventions of Thomas Edison

6) The height of Mount Everest

50 *Chapter 2 Answering Questions About Words*

Using What You Have Learned

Find the answers to these questions in a dictionary.

1. What color is a topaz?
2. Where would you be likely to see a llama?
3. Was Hercules a real person?
4. Marie's teacher said that Marie was loquacious. What other word might the teacher have used to describe Marie?
5. Where is the Mojave Desert?
6. What would you do with a glockenspiel?
7. When did people do the jitterbug?

Activity C Use the information in the entries below to complete this activity. Write your answers on your paper.

au gra•tin (ō grät´ən), *adj.* [F *with scrapings*] made with a crust of bread crumbs and cheese.

Ba•con (bā´kən), *n.* **Francis,** 1561–1626, English philosopher and writer.

ba•gel (bā´ gəl), *n.* [Yiddish] a hard bread roll shaped like a small doughnut.

Bagh•dad (bag´ dad), *n.* capital city of Iraq; pop. about 1,000,000. also **Bagdad**.

ban•shee (ban´ shē), *n.* (in Irish folklore) a female spirit whose loud screams warn of a coming death.

bant•am•weight (bant´əm wāt), *n.* a boxer or wrestler weighing 113 to 118 pounds.

Bar•num (bär´ nəm), *n.* **P(hineas) T(aylor)**, 1810–91, U.S. showman and circus owner.

chop su•ey (chop sōō´ ē), *n.* a Chinese-American dish of meat, bean sprouts, etc., served with rice.

C.O.D. *abbr.* **1.** cash on delivery. **2.** collect on delivery.

dè•já vu (dā zhä vyōō), *n.* [F already seen] the feeling that one has previously had an experience that is actually new.

Doyle (doil), *n.* **Sir Arthur Conan** (kō´nə n), 1859–1930, British physician and novelist: known for his Sherlock Holmes stories.

flib•ber•ti•gib•bet (flib´ ər tə jib´ it), *n.* an irresponsible flighty person.

leap year *n.* a year of 366 days, occurring every fourth year; the extra day is on February 29: a leap year is a year whose number can be divided by 4.

L.P.N. *abbr.* licensed practical nurse.

Mickey Mouse *adj.* [a tradename for a cartoon character created by Walt Disney] lacking importance, unrelated to reality: *a Mickey Mouse course.*

pop. (pop) *abbr.* **1.** popular. **2.** population.

R.N. *abbr.* **1.** registered nurse. **2.** Royal Navy.

Sher•lock Holmes (shûr´ lok hōmz´), *n.* a fictional British detective with great powers of deduction, the main character in many stories by A. Conan Doyle.

Yo•sem•i•te Falls (yō sem´ə tē), *n.* [AmInd name of the Valley Indians, lit. *grizzly bears, killers*] series of waterfalls in Yosemite National Park in California: upper falls, 1,430 ft.; lower falls, 320 ft.; total drop: 2,526 ft.

a - act, **ā** - āble, **â** - dâre, **ä** - ärm, **e** - ebb, **ē** - ēven, **i** - it, **ī** - īce, **o** - hot, **ō** - ōver, **ô** - ôrder, **oi** - oil, **o͝o** - bo͝ok, **ōō** - lōōt, **ou** - out, **u** - up, **û** - ûrge, **ch** - chief, **ng** - sing, **sh** - shoe, **th** - thin, **th** - this, **zh** - vision, ə = *a* as in *ago*.

1) List the entries that are foreign words.

2) List the names of real people.

3) List the fictional characters.

4) List the entries that are abbreviations. Write what they mean.

5) List the geographical locations.

Reading Vocabulary

au gratin, bagel, banshee, bantamweight, dèjá vu, flibbertigibbet, glockenspiel, jitterbug, llama (5), location (6), loquacious (13), topaz

■ **Presenting Activity C** Ask students to look at the sample entries and take turns telling one fact they learn from these entries. Then ask students to complete Activity C on their own.

Activity C Answers

1) au gratin, banshee (possible), déjà vu **2)** Francis Bacon, Phineas Taylor Barnum, Sir Arthur Conan Doyle **3)** banshee (possible), Mickey Mouse, Sherlock Holmes **4)** C.O.D.—cash on delivery; L.P.N.—licensed practical nurse; pop.—popular or population; R.N.—Registered Nurse or Royal Navy **5)** Baghdad, Yosemite Falls

Using What You Have Learned

You may wish to have students complete this activity on their own or with partners. Wording of some of the answers may vary. Accept any reasonable responses.

Answers

1) yellow, pink, brown, blue, or colorless **2)** in South America **3)** No, Hercules was a mythological character. **4)** chatty, talkative, garrulous, gabby **5)** in southern California, southeast of the Sierra Nevada **6)** play it; it's a percussion instrument **7)** 1940s

Reading Vocabulary

spinach (5) wrestle (5)
translation

- **Presenting Activity D** Do item 1 together as a class. After discussing how students found the answer, suggest that they complete Activity D with partners. When they have finished, invite students to share and discuss their answers with the class.

Activity D Answers

1) No, he is one pound over the upper limit. **2)** The L stands for licensed. **3)** No, Mickey Mouse is fictional. **4)** The cook put on bread crumbs and cheese. **5)** Arthur Conan Doyle was the real person. **6)** The name means grizzly bears or killers. **7)** The city is spelled Baghdad or Bagdad. **8)** A bagel is a round hard bread roll similar to a doughnut. **9)** Eddie was probably acting irresponsible and flighty. **10)** She had to pay cash when it was delivered.

Teacher Alert

Remind students that as in most references sources, dictionaries list the names of real people alphabetically last name first. Fictional characters are usually listed alphabetically by their name in its usual order, for example, *Mickey Mouse.*

Activity D Use the information in the entries on page 51 to answer these questions. Write the answers in complete sentences on your paper.

1) Burt weighs 119 pounds. Can he wrestle as a bantamweight?

2) Chris wants to become an L.P.N. What does the *L* stand for?

3) The movie the children saw starred Mickey Mouse. Was the leading character in the movie real?

4) Aunt Margaret ordered spinach au gratin. What did the cook put on the spinach?

5) Who is the real person—Sherlock Holmes or Arthur Conan Doyle?

6) What is the translation of *Yosemite*?

7) What are two ways to spell the name of the capital of Iraq?

8) Describe a bagel.

9) "Stop being a flibbertigibbet!" Aunt Margaret said to Eddie. Why would Eddie's aunt say this?

10) Mrs. Gomez received a package C.O.D. What did she have to do?

Learning Styles

Interpersonal/Group Learning

Divide the class into pairs. Give each pair a dictionary. Invite each pair to use its dictionary to prepare a five-question quiz on facts they find in it. Then have the pairs exchange their quizzes. (Have students exchange dictionaries if the dictionaries the students are using differ.) Ask each pair to find the answers to the quiz. Afterward, invite the students to discuss what they learned from the dictionaries.

Lesson 4 Review

Lesson Review Use the entries to answer the questions that follow. Write the answers on your paper.

Ak•ron (ak´ rən), *n.* a city in N.E. Ohio: pop. 275,425.

Al•ex•an•der the Great (al´ig zan´ dər), 356–323 B.C.; king of Macedonia, 336–323; conqueror.

an•cient (ān´ shənt), *adj.* [< L *ante* before] **1.** of times long past. **2.** very old.

At•lan•tis (at lan´ tis), *n.* a mythical island in the Atlantic Ocean west of Gibralter, and that was swallowed up by the sea.

B.C. *abbr.* **1.** bachelor of commerce. **2.** before Christ. **3.** British Columbia.

e•qui•nox (ē´ kwə noks´), *n.* [< L *aequus* equal + *nox* night] the time when the sun crosses the equator, making night and day an equal length in all parts of the earth.

Leip•zig (līp´ sig), *n.* a city in Germany; pop. 596,000.

N. *abbr.* **1.** north. **2.** northern.

1) Which city has more people—Akron or Leipzig?
2) Was Alexander the Great a real person? How do you know?
3) Twice each year, day and night are equal in Norway. Are they equal on these same days where you live?
4) When Vanessa's brother graduates from college, he will receive a B.C. degree. What do those letters mean?
5) Lynda's parents live in B.C. What is the full name of that place?
6) How old was Alexander the Great when he became king of Macedonia?
7) Can tourists visit the island of Atlantis?

Reading Vocabulary

college (5) graduate (6)
equinox tourist (5)

Lesson Review Answers

1) Leipzig has more people.
2) Yes; the entry says he lived from 356–323 B.C. and that he was a king.
3) Yes **4)** bachelor of commerce
5) British Columbia **6)** twenty
7) No; it's a mythical place.

Name Date Period — *Chapter 2 Activity 8*

Words About Words

Part A: Unscramble these words. Then use them to fill in the missing words in the sentences in Part B.

Scrambled Words	Unscrambled Words
1) RLALUP	________
2) NFOIICT	________
3) TIONABEVIABR	________
4) YPHAGRIOB	________
5) ASYBLELL	________
6) TAYMNONS	________
7) MMNHOYOS	________
8) YSONYNM	________
9) OEVWSL	________

Part B: Complete these sentences. Use the words you unscrambled in Part A.

1) A person's life story is called a ________.
2) A ________ is more than one.
3) A ________ is a part of a word with one vowel sound.
4) A ________ is a word that means the same as another word.
5) A shortened form of a word is an ________.
6) The letters *a*, *e*, *i*, *o*, and *u* are ________.
7) Two words that sound alike but have different meanings are ________.
8) The words *hot* and *cold* are ________.
9) A story that is not true is ________.

 Life Skills English

Activity 8

Name Date Period — *Chapter 2 Workbook Activity 14*

The Dictionary as a Reference Tool

Directions: Use the entries below to answer the questions that follow.

Mao Tse-tung ('maù-(') (d)zə dùŋ) 1893-1976 Chinese communist leader

mar•a•thon ('mar-ə -,thän) *n.* [*Marathon*, Greece, site of a victory of Greeks over Persians in 490 B.C., the news of which was carried to Athens by a long-distance runner] **1:** a foot race of 26 miles, 385 yards **2:** any long-distance or endurance contest

Mar•di Gras ('mär-dē-,grä) *n.* [Fr, lit., fat Tuesday] **1:** Shrove Tuesday, the last day before Lent **2:** a day of merrymaking and carnival (as in New Orleans) of marking the climax of a carnival period

Marie An•toi•nette (,an-twə-'net, -tə -), 1755-1793 wife of Louis XVI; queen of France (1774-1792): guillotined

Mars ('märz) *n.* **1:** *Rom. Myth.* the god of war — identified with the Greek Ares **2:** a personification of war **3:** a planet of the solar system

1) How old was Mao Tse-tung when he died? ________
2) Of what country was Mao Tse-tung the leader? ________
3) Jack is running in a marathon next month. How many miles must he run to finish the race? ________
4) In what country was the ancient city of Marathon? ________
5) What does *Mardi Gras* mean in French? ________
6) When is *Mardi Gras* each year? ________
7) In which city is the most famous *Mardi Gras* celebration in the United States? ________
8) To whom was Marie Antoinette married? ________
9) How old was she when she died? ________
10) How did Marie Antoinette die? ________
11) How old was Mao Tse-tung when Marie Antoinette died? ________
12) What planet is named after the Roman god of war? ________

 Life Skills English

Workbook Activity 14

Chapter 2 Review

The Teacher's Resource Library includes two parallel forms of the Chapter 2 Mastery Test. The difficulty level of the two forms is equivalent. You may wish to use one form as a pretest and the other form as a posttest.

Reading Vocabulary

compassion (11) fashion (5)

Part A Answers

1) top of the page **2a)** fancy **2b)** fashion **2c)** No **3)** bottom of a dictionary page **4)** phonetic spelling **5a)** verb, intransitive **5b)** popular or population **5c)** adjective **5d)** derived from **5e)** plural **5f)** Latin

Part B Answers

1) three **2)** noun **3)** Middle English from Latin **4)** patient **5)** Yes

Chapter 2 Review

Part A Write the answers to these questions on your paper.

1) Where are the guide words found in a dictionary?
2) Here are two guide words: fancy—fashion
   a) What is the first entry on this page?
   b) What is the last entry on this page?
   c) Would you find the entry *family* on this page?
3) Where do you usually find a pronunciation key?
4) Which part of the entry does the pronunciation key explain?
5) What does each of these abbreviations or symbols mean?
   a) v.i. c) adj. e) pl.
   b) pop. d) < f) L

Part B Use the entry below to answer the questions that follow. Write the answers on your paper.

> **com•pas•sion** (kəm păsh´ ən), *n.* [ME>L. *compati,* to suffer, bear pain. See PATIENT.] **1.** the feeling of another's pain or sorrow. **Syn.** pity, concern

1) How many syllables does *compassion* have?
2) What part of speech is *compassion*?
3) What is the origin of *compassion*?
4) What other word could you look up to find information about the origin of *compassion*?
5) Do people with *compassion* care about others' feelings?

Name Date Period | *Chapter 2 Mastery Test A page 1*

Chapter 2 Mastery Test A

Part A Find the correct definition for each term. Write the letter of the definition on the line.

_____ 1) entry word

_____ 2) pronunciation key

_____ 3) guide words

_____ 4) abbreviation

_____ 5) dictionary

a) a shortened form of a written word

b) book that has alphabetical listings of words and their meanings

c) word listed in a dictionary

d) words at the top of a dictionary page that show the first and last entries on the page

e) explanation of symbols used in phonetic spelling

Part B Use the entry below to answer the questions.

trag•e•dy \'tra-jə-dē\ *n, pl* **-dies** [ME *tragedie,* fr. MF, fr. L *tragoedia,* fr Gk tragōidia, fr. *tragos* goat (akin to Gk *trōgein* to gnaw) + *aeidein* to sing—more at TROGLODYTE, ODE] (14c) **1 a :** a medieval narrative poem or tale typically describing the downfall of a great man **b :** a serious drama typically describing a conflict between the protagonist and a superior force (as destiny) and having a sorrowful or disastrous conclusion that excites pity or terror **c :** the literary genre of tragic dramas **2 a :** a disastrous event : CALAMITY **b :** MISFORTUNE **3 :** tragic quality or element

1) How many syllables does tragedy have? _____
2) What part of speech is tragedy? _____
3) What is the plural spelling of tragedy? _____
4) How many definitions are given for tragedy? _____
5) If someone says that an event is disastrous, would it also be correct to call the event a tragedy? _____

 Life Skills English

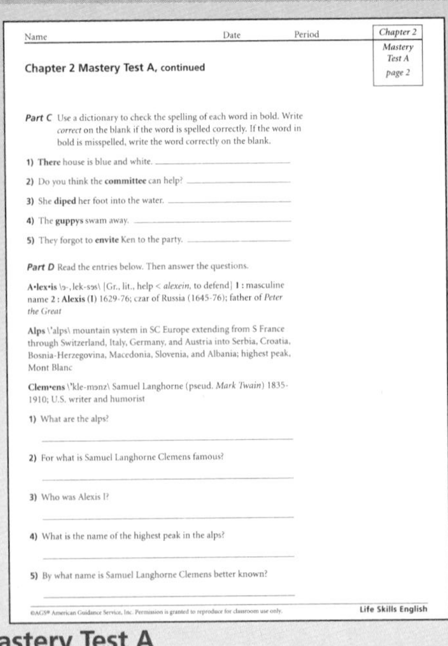

Name Date Period | *Chapter 2 Mastery Test A page 2*

Chapter 2 Mastery Test A, continued

Part C Use a dictionary to check the spelling of each word in bold. Write *correct* on the blank if the word is spelled correctly. If the word in bold is misspelled, write the word correctly on the blank.

1) **There** house is blue and white. _____
2) Do you think the **committee** can help? _____
3) She **diped** her foot into the water. _____
4) The **guppys** swam away. _____
5) They forgot to **envite** Ken to the party. _____

Part D Read the entries below. Then answer the questions.

A•lex•is \ə-,lek-səs\ [Gr., lit., help < *alexein,* to defend] **1 :** masculine name **2 : Alexis (I)** 1629-76; czar of Russia (1645-76); father of *Peter the Great*

Alps \'alps\ mountain system in SC Europe extending from S France through Switzerland, Italy, Germany, and Austria into Serbia, Croatia, Bosnia-Herzegovina, Macedonia, Slovenia, and Albania; highest peak, Mont Blanc

Clem•ens \'kle-mənz\ Samuel Langhorne (pseud. *Mark Twain*) 1835-1910; U.S. writer and humorist

1) What are the alps?
_____
2) For what is Samuel Langhorne Clemens famous?
_____
3) Who was Alexis I?
_____
4) What is the name of the highest peak in the alps?
_____
5) By what name is Samuel Langhorne Clemens better known?
_____

 Life Skills English

Chapter 2 Mastery Test A

Part C Check the spelling of each word in bold in a dictionary. Then number your paper from 1 to 5. Beside each number, copy the word if it is spelled correctly. If the word in bold is misspelled, write the word correctly.

1) I **beleive** that he has lived in five different **citys**.
2) The **safety** of the **childrens** was her biggest concern.
3) She **catched** the ball for the final out, and **evryone** cheered.
4) My sisters are coming, but **there probably** going to be late.
5) It was **nessessary** for the winner to **except** the prize in person.

Part D Use the entries below to answer the questions that follow. Write the answers on your paper.

John•son (jon´sən), *n.* **1. Andrew** 1808-75; 17th president of the U.S. 1865-69. **2. James Weldon** (wel´ dən), 1871-1938; U.S. writer. **3. Lyn•don Baines** (lin´ dən bānz), 1908-73; 36th U.S. president 1963-69. **4. Samuel** 1709-84; Eng. lexicographer and writer.

lex•i•cog•ra•pher (lek´ sə kog´ rə fər), *n.* a person who writes a dictionary.

Lou•is (lo͞o´ is), **Joe** (born *Joseph Louis Barrow*) 1914-81; U.S. boxer: world heavyweight champion 1937-49.

Lou•is•ville (lo͞o´ ē vil´), *n.* (after Louis XVI) city in Northern Kentucky on the Ohio river: pop. 361,958.

par•a•dise (par´ ə dīs´), *n.* [< Gk *paradeisos* garden] **1.** the garden of Eden. **2.** heaven. **3.** any place of great happiness.

1) How many U.S. presidents were named Johnson?
2) Who was James Weldon Johnson?
3) What kind of book does a lexicographer write?
4) Who was the city of Louisville named after?
5) What are two meanings of *paradise?*

Test Taking Tip Use a marker to highlight important facts and terms in your notes. Review the highlighted areas before the test.

Reading Vocabulary

highlight paradise (6)
lexicographer

Part C Answers

1) believe, cities **2)** safety, children **3)** caught, everyone **4)** they're, probably **5)** necessary, accept

Part D Answers

1) two **2)** an American writer **3)** dictionary **4)** Louis XVI **5)** *accept any two responses:* garden of Eden; heaven; any place of great happiness

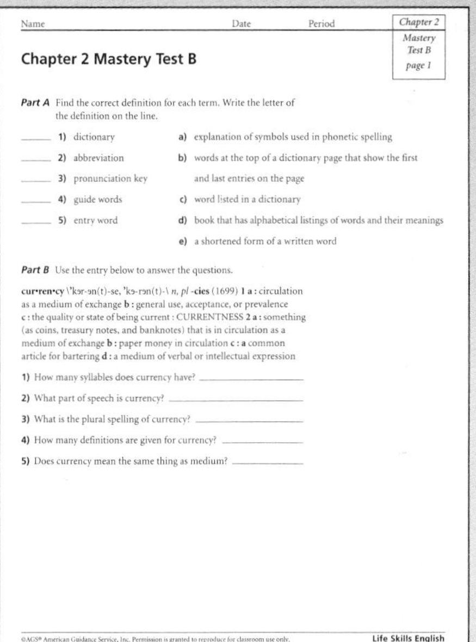

Name Date Period | *Chapter 2 Mastery Test B page 1*

Chapter 2 Mastery Test B

Part A Find the correct definition for each term. Write the letter of the definition on the line.

_____ **1)** dictionary
_____ **2)** abbreviation
_____ **3)** pronunciation key
_____ **4)** guide words
_____ **5)** entry word

a) explanation of symbols used in phonetic spelling
b) words at the top of a dictionary page that show the first and last entries on the page
c) word listed in a dictionary
d) book that has alphabetical listings of words and their meanings
e) a shortened form of a written word

Part B Use the entry below to answer the questions.

cur•ren•cy \'kər-ən(t)-se, 'kə-rən(t)-\ *n, pl* **-cies** (1699) **1 a :** circulation as a medium of exchange **b :** general use, acceptance, or prevalence **c :** the quality or state of being current : CURRENTNESS **2 a :** something (as coins, treasury notes, and banknotes) that is in circulation as a medium of exchange **b :** paper money in circulation **c : a** common article for bartering **d :** a medium of verbal or intellectual expression

1) How many syllables does currency have? _____
2) What part of speech is currency? _____
3) What is the plural spelling of currency? _____
4) How many definitions are given for currency? _____
5) Does currency mean the same thing as medium? _____

 Life Skills English

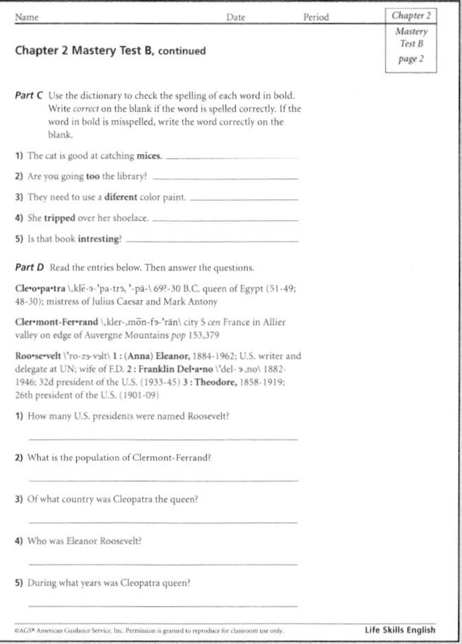

Name Date Period | *Chapter 2 Mastery Test B page 2*

Chapter 2 Mastery Test B, continued

Part C Use the dictionary to check the spelling of each word in bold. Write *correct* on the blank if the word is spelled correctly. If the word in bold is misspelled, write the word correctly on the blank.

1) The cat is good at catching **mices**. _____
2) Are you going **too** the library? _____
3) They need to use a **diferent** color paint. _____
4) She **tripped** over her shoelace. _____
5) Is that book **intresting**? _____

Part D Read the entries below. Then answer the questions.

Cle•o•pa•tra \,klē-ə-'pa-trə, '-pä-\ 69?-30 B.C. queen of Egypt (51-49; 48-30); mistress of Julius Caesar and Mark Antony

Cler•mont-Fer•rand \,kler-,mōn-fə-'rän\ city S *cen* France in Allier valley on edge of Auvergne Mountains *pop* 153,379

Roo•se•velt \'ro-zə-vəlt\ **1 : (Anna) Eleanor,** 1884-1962; U.S. writer and delegate at UN; wife of F.D. **2 : Franklin Del•a•no** \'del-ə,no\ 1882-1946; 32d president of the U.S. (1933-45) **3 : Theodore,** 1858-1919; 26th president of the U.S. (1901-09)

1) How many U.S. presidents were named Roosevelt? _____
2) What is the population of Clermont-Ferrand? _____
3) Of what country was Cleopatra the queen? _____
4) Who was Eleanor Roosevelt? _____
5) During what years was Cleopatra queen? _____

 Life Skills English

Chapter 2 Mastery Test B

Chapter 3

Planning Guide

Some Everyday References

	Student Text Lesson			
	Student Pages	Vocabulary	Practice Exercises	Lesson Review
Lesson 1 What's in an Almanac?	58-62	✔	✔	✔
Lesson 2 Atlases and Gazetteers	63-70	✔	✔	✔
Lesson 3 Encyclopedias	71-75	✔	✔	✔
Lesson 4 References for Cooks	76-86	✔	✔	✔
Lesson 5 Using Information in How-To Books	87-90	✔	✔	✔
Lesson 6 Magazines for Facts and Fun	91-97	✔	✔	✔

Chapter Activities

Teacher's Resource Library

Putting It Together 3: Reference Book Botticelli

Community Connection 2: Draw a Grid Map

Assessment Options

Student Text

Chapter 3 Review

Teacher's Resource Library

Chapter 3 Mastery Tests A and B

Teaching Strategies						Language Skills			Learning Styles						Teacher's Resource Library		
Reviewing Skills	Teacher Alert	Career Application	Home Application	Global Connection	Community Application	Identification Skills	Writing Skills	Punctuation Skills	Visual/Spatial	Auditory/Verbal	Body/Kinesthetic	Logical/Mathematical	Group Learning	LEP/ESL	Activities	Workbook Activities	Self-Study Guide
58		60				✔	✔	✔				61					✔
63	67, 69				66	✔	✔	✔						70		15	✔
71					74	✔	✔	✔	71								✔
76	78	81	79	77	84	✔	✔	✔		77					9-10	16-17	✔
87				88		✔	✔	✔		90							✔
91			95			✔	✔	✔							11-12	18-20	✔

Chapter at a Glance

Chapter 3: Some Everyday References

pages 56–99

(Answer Keys for the Teacher's Resource Library begin on page 282 of this Teacher's Edition.)

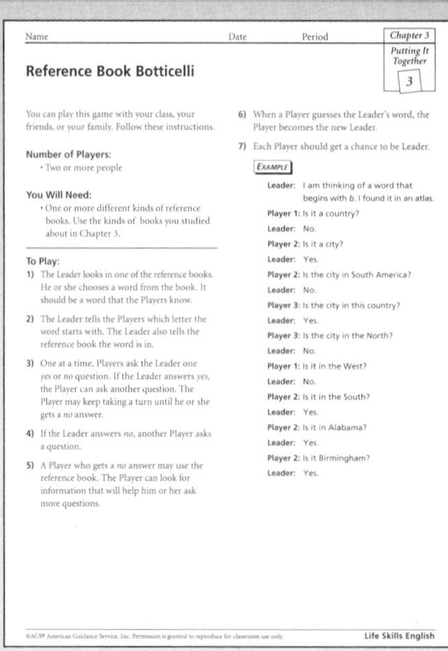

Name ______ Date ______ Period ______

Chapter 3 *Putting It Together* 3

Reference Book Botticelli

You can play this game with your class, your friends, or your family. Follow these instructions.

Number of Players:

- Two or more people

You Will Need:

- One or more different kinds of reference books. Use the kinds of books you studied about in Chapter 3.

To Play:

1) The Leader looks in one of the reference books. He or she chooses a word from the book. It should be a word that the Players know.
2) The Leader tells the Players which letter the word starts with. The Leader also tells the reference book the word is in.
3) One at a time, Players ask the Leader one *yes* or *no* question. If the Leader answers *yes*, the Player can ask another question. The Player may keep taking a turn until he or she gets a *no* answer.
4) If the Leader answers *no*, another Player asks a question.
5) A Player who gets a *no* answer may use the reference book. The Player can look for information that will help him or her ask more questions.
6) When a Player guesses the Leader's word, the Player becomes the new Leader.
7) Each Player should get a chance to be Leader.

EXAMPLE

Leader: I am thinking of a word that begins with *b*. I found it in an atlas.
Player 1: Is it a country?
Leader: No.
Player 2: Is it a city?
Leader: Yes.
Player 2: Is the city in South America?
Leader: No.
Player 3: Is the city in this country?
Leader: Yes.
Player 3: Is the city in the North?
Leader: No.
Player 1: Is it in the West?
Leader: No.
Player 2: Is it in the South?
Leader: Yes.
Player 2: Is it in Alabama?
Leader: Yes.
Player 2: Is it Birmingham?
Leader: Yes.

 Life Skills English

Putting It Together 3

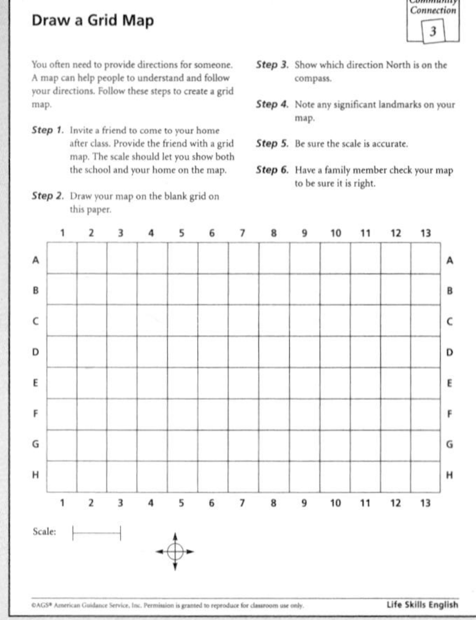

Name ______ Date ______ Period ______

Chapter 3 *Community Connection* 3

Draw a Grid Map

You often need to provide directions for someone. A map can help people to understand and follow your directions. Follow these steps to create a grid map.

Step 1. Invite a friend to come to your home after class. Provide the friend with a grid map. The scale should let you show both the school and your home on the map.

Step 2. Draw your map on the blank grid on this paper.

Step 3. Show which direction North is on the compass.

Step 4. Note any significant landmarks on your map.

Step 5. Be sure the scale is accurate.

Step 6. Have a family member check your map to be sure it is right.

	1	2	3	4	5	6	7	8	9	10	11	12	13	
A														A
B														B
C														C
D														D
E														E
F														F
G														G
H														H
	1	2	3	4	5	6	7	8	9	10	11	12	13	

Scale:

 Life Skills English

Community Connection 3

Chapter 3 Some Everyday References

Have you ever needed to know how to fix a leaky faucet? Make a special dessert? Or get to a place you wanted to visit? Books, magazines, and other references can help you find the answers you are looking for. You just need to know which reference has the information you need and where to find the reference. Then you need to know how to use the information you found.

In Chapter 3, you will learn how to find and use everyday references.

Goals for Learning

- To discover the kinds of information in an almanac
- To understand and use the contents of an atlas
- To locate information in an encyclopedia
- To follow directions in a recipe
- To follow directions in a how-to book
- To recognize and find different kinds of information in magazines

57

Reading Vocabulary

reference (6)

Introducing the Chapter

Display copies of each type of reference book covered in this chapter, including farmer's almanacs, general information almanacs, atlases, encyclopedia volumes, cookbooks, how-to-books, and magazines. Then list each type of book in a chart on the board. Ask students what type of information they would expect to find in each of these books. Write all reasonable responses, without comment, in the chart. Explain that in Chapter 3, students will learn more about these reference books, what they contain, and how to use them efficiently to find information. Then as you complete each lesson in the chapter, have students refer back to the information in the chart to revise it or add to it.

SELF-STUDY GUIDE

Name ______

CHAPTER 3: Some Everyday References

Goal 3.1 *To discover the kinds of information in an almanac*

Date	Assignment	Score
______	1: Read pages 57-58. Complete Activity A on page 58. Read page 59. Complete Activity B on page 59.	______
______	2: Read page 60. Complete Activity C on page 61.	______
______	3: Complete the Lesson 1 Review, Parts A-B on page 62.	______

Comments:

Goal 3.2 *To understand and use the contents of an atlas*

Date	Assignment	Score
______	4: Read page 63. Complete Activity A on page 64.	______
______	5: Complete Workbook Activity 15.	______
______	6: Read page 65. Complete Activity B on page 65.	______
______	7: Read page 66. Complete Activities C-E on page 67.	______
______	8: Read page 68. Complete Activity F on page 68. Read page 69. Complete Activity G on page 69	______
______	9: Complete the Lesson 2 Review, Parts A-C on page 70.	______

Comments:

Goal 3.3 *To locate information in an encyclopedia*

Date	Assignment	Score
______	10: Read page 71. Complete Activity A on page 72.	______
______	11: Read page 72. Complete Activities B-C on page 73.	______
______	12: Read page 74. Complete Activity D on page 74.	______
______	13: Complete the Lesson 3 Review, Parts A-B on page 75.	______

Comments:

 Life Skills English

SELF-STUDY GUIDE

Name ______

CHAPTER 3 Some Everyday References, continued

Goal 3.4 *To follow directions in a recipe*

Date	Assignment	Score
______	14: Read page 76. Complete Activity A on page 76.	______
______	15: Read page 77. Complete Activities B-C on page 78.	______
______	16: Complete Workbook Activity 16.	______
______	17: Read page 79. Complete Activity D on page 80. Read page 81. Complete Activity E on page 81.	______
______	18: Read page 82. Complete Activity F on page 82. Read page 83. Complete Activity G on page 83.	______
______	19: Read page 84. Complete Activity H on page 85.	______
______	20: Complete Workbook Activity 17.	______
______	21: Complete the Lesson 4 Review, Parts A-C on page 86.	______

Comments:

Goal 3.5 *To follow directions in a how-to book*

Date	Assignment	Score
______	22: Read page 87. Complete Activity A on page 87.	______
______	23: Read pages 88-89. Complete Activities B-D on page 89.	______
______	24: Complete the Lesson 5 Review, Parts A-B on page 90.	______

Comments:

Goal 3.6 *To recognize and find different kinds of information in magazines*

Date	Assignment	Score
______	25: Read pages 91-92. Complete Activity A on pages 92-93.	______
______	26: Read page 93. Complete Activities B-C on page 93.	______
______	27: Complete Workbook Activity 18.	______
______	28: Read page 94. Complete Activity D on page 94. Read pages 95-96. Complete Activities E-F on page 96.	______
______	29: Complete Workbook Activity 19.	______
______	30: Complete the Lesson 6 Review on page 97.	______
______	31: Complete Workbook Activity 20.	______
______	32: Complete the Chapter 3 Review, Parts A-E on pages 98-99.	______

Comments:

Student's Signature ______ Date ______

Instructor's Signature ______ Date ______

 Life Skills English

Chapter 3 Self-Study Guide

Lesson at a Glance

Chapter 3 Lesson 1

Overview This lesson describes two types of almanacs—the farmer's almanac and the general information almanac.

Objectives

- To identify the kind of information found in an almanac.
- To distinguish between information found in a farmer's almanac and in a general information almanac.

Student Pages 58–62

Reading Vocabulary

annual (6)
astronomical
astronomy (7)
CD-ROM
compact (5)
computer (8)
determine (5)
disc
farmer's almanac
forecast (6)
mariner
memory (5)
navigator (6)
phase (7)
prediction

Teaching Suggestions

Introducing the Lesson

Discuss the information in the text. If possible, provide farmer's almanacs and general information almanacs for students to examine.

Reviewing Skills

Review using an index.

Presenting Activity A

Read Activity A together as a class. Call attention to item 2 and briefly discuss what a ship's navigator does. Then have students complete the activity on their own.

Activity A Answers

1) Yes **2)** The phases of the moon affect the tides.
3) Almanacs contain facts about the weather and facts about astronomy.

Using What You Have Learned

Students can complete this activity on their own or with partners. The Latin word for *moon* means *month.*

Lesson 1 What's in an Almanac?

CD-ROM
A computer science term that stands for compact disc read-only memory.

Farmer's almanac
An annual calendar of days, weeks, and months with weather predictions and astronomical facts.

An almanac is a book of facts published once a year. Two kinds of almanacs are farmer's almanacs and general information almanacs. Some almanacs are published on **CD-ROM**. CD-ROM stands for compact disc read-only memory. You use a computer to find the information in almanacs on CD-ROM.

Farmer's Almanacs

A **farmer's almanac** is a yearly calendar of days, weeks, and months with weather forecasts and facts about astronomy. The weather forecasts help farmers decide when to plant or harvest crops. Because the moon affects tides, mariners use the astronomy information in farmer's almanacs to determine when the tide will be high or low. Farmer's almanacs provide other information helpful for farm and home management.

Phases of the Moon

New Moon

First Quarter

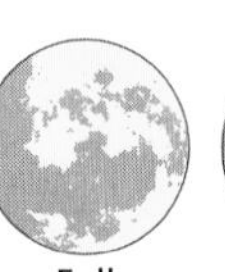
Full Moon

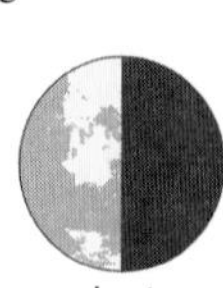
Last Quarter

Using What You Have Learned

1. Find a farmer's almanac in a library and study it.
2. Look up *new moon* and *full moon* in a dictionary.
3. The Latin word for *moon* has another meaning. Can you guess what it is? Check a dictionary.

Activity A Write the answers to these questions on your paper.

1) Would you expect to find a calendar in a farmer's almanac?

2) Why would a ship's navigator want to know about the phases of the moon?

3) Name two kinds of information that are in farmer's almanacs.

General Information Almanacs

General information almanac

An almanac that contains facts and figures about a variety of subjects from the previous year and from the past.

A **general information almanac** has facts and figures about many subjects from the most recent year and from the past. Most general information almanacs are published once a year. Two popular general information almanacs are *The World Almanac and Book of Facts* and *The Information Please Almanac.* To discover what topics an almanac covers, look in the index. Unlike most other reference books, the index of an almanac is usually in the front of the book.

Here are some topics you might find in a general information almanac:

Biographies of U.S. presidents	Agricultural facts
Facts about the United States	Awards and prizes
Facts about other countries	Events of the last year
Facts about Social Security	History of the world
Number of calories in foods	Income tax information
Populations of U.S. cities	Names of U.S. colleges
Supreme Court decisions	People in Congress
ZIP codes and area codes	Sports facts

Activity B Write complete sentences on your paper to answer these questions.

1) How is the index in an almanac different from indexes in other reference works?

2) What are three types of facts you might find in a general information almanac?

3) A statistic is a numerical fact. Write three statistics from this almanac account:

> William Henry Harrison was the ninth president of the United States. He was president only 31 days. He got pneumonia during the inauguration and died on April 4, 1841.

Reading Vocabulary

agricultural
award (5)
biography (7)
calorie (8)
code (5)
college (5)
congress (5)
general information almanac
inauguration
income (6)
index (5)
numerical
pneumonia (8)
population (5)
previous (6)
social (5)
security (8)
statistics (11)
subject (5)
supreme (6)
tax (5)
topic (5)
variety (6)

■ Presenting Activity B

Before having students complete Activity B on their own, have them generate a list of other topics besides those listed in the box on page 59 that they might find in a general information almanac. Write all reasonable suggestions on the board. Then review the list with students and have them explain why they think these topics are likely to be in a general information almanac. After students complete Activity B, invite volunteers to look in an almanac to find each topic listed on the board. (Most libraries will have a current general information almanac in the reference section.) Have students make check marks next to the topics that they found listed.

Activity B Answers

Wording of students' responses will vary. Some answers may vary. Possible responses are given.

1) An index in an almanac is usually at the front. Other reference books have the index in the back. **2)** An almanac may contain facts about the United States, other countries, and sports. **3)** Harrison was the *ninth* president. He was president for *31* days. He died on *April 4, 1841*.

Reading Vocabulary

career (6)
diet (6)
expand (5)
instance
issue (6)
nutrition
product (5)
publication (7)
purchase (5)
university (5)

APPLICATION

Career Connection
General information almanacs, such as *The World Almanac and Book of Facts,* provide facts and statistics about a variety of topics related to employment. Divide students who are interested into small groups, and have each group prepare an oral report on employment in the United States today. Encourage students to consult a variety of reference sources, including a general information almanac. Students who wish can illustrate their reports with graphs, diagrams, and other visual aids. When they are ready, invite students to share their reports with the class.

An almanac can be very useful in your everyday life; for example:

- if you are on a special diet, you can find facts about calories and nutrition.
- if you want information about a college, you can find the names, addresses, number of students, and number of teachers in most of the colleges and universities in the United States.
- if you are interested in sports, you can find facts about nearly every sport and sporting event.
- if you are writing a letter, most almanacs list the ZIP codes for each area of the United States.
- if you have purchased a product that doesn't work, you can find the addresses of many large companies.
- if you are interested in choosing a career with plenty of job openings, almanacs list the most rapidly expanding careers.
- if you want information about recent world events, almanacs list that information.

An almanac has facts about the year *before* its title date. For example, the 1997 almanac includes facts about 1996. To learn facts about 1997, you would have to read the 1998 almanac.

To find information that is more current, use a publication that is issued more often. For instance, magazines come out every week or every month. The most up-to-date facts are in the daily newspaper.

60 *Chapter 3 Some Everyday References*

Activity C Use these facts from an almanac published in 1995 to answer the questions that follow. Write your answers on your paper.

1995 Almanac

Awards — Medals — Prizes

1994 Nobel Prize Winners	
Physics	Bertram N. Brockhouse, Canada Clifford G. Shull, U.S.
Chemistry	George A. Olah, U.S.
Physiology/Medicine	Alfred G. Golman, U.S. Martin Rodbell, U.S.
1994 Nobel Prize Winners	
Literature	Kenzaburo Oe, Japan
Peace	Yasir Arafat, Palestine Shimon Peres, Israel Yitzhak Rabin, Israel
Pulitzer Prize in Journalism, Letters, & Music	
Journalism	
1995	Virgin Islands Daily News, St. Thomas
1994	Akron Beacon Journal
1993	Miami Herald
Miss America Winners	
1996	Shawntel Smith, Muldrow, Oklahoma
1995	Heather Whitestone, Birmingham, Alabama
1994	Kimberly Aiken, Columbia, South Carolina
Academy Awards 1994	
Best Picture	*Forrest Gump*
Best Actor	Tom Hanks, *Forrest Gump*
Best Actress	Jessica Lange, *Blue Sky*
Best Director	Robert Zemeckis, *Forrest Gump*

123

1) Where did the winner of the 1994 Nobel Prize in literature come from? What was that person's name?

2) What countries were represented by the 1994 Nobel Peace Prize winners?

3) What was the top picture of 1994? How do you know that?

4) Who is Heather Whitestone?

5) What newspaper won the Pulitzer Prize in Journalism in 1995?

Reading Vocabulary

academy (5)
actress (6)
chemistry (5)
director (7)
journal (5)
journalism
literature (6)
physics (8)
physiology (11)

■ Presenting Activity C

Before having students complete Activity C on their own, have them take turns pointing out facts that they glean on their own from the sample almanac. As a follow-up to Activity C, you might have students look in a current general information almanac to find out the most recent years' winners of the awards and prizes listed in the sample almanac.

Activity C Answers

1) Japan, Kenzaburo Oe **2)** Palestine and Israel **3)** *Forrest Gump*—It won the 1994 Academy Award for Best Picture. **4)** 1995 Miss America **5)** Virgin Islands Daily News, St. Thomas

LEARNING STYLES

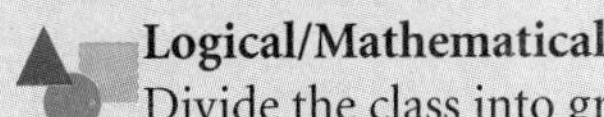

Logical/Mathematical
Divide the class into groups of three. Give each group several pages from a newspaper. (The newspapers need not be today's.) Ask each group to read its newspaper pages and to find three facts that might be put in an almanac for this calendar year. Challenge each group to list these facts under the heading the almanac publisher might use. Afterward, invite each group to explain its selections.

Reading Vocabulary

series (5)

Part A Answers

Wording of students' responses may vary. Possible responses are given.

1) A farmer's almanac contains information about weather and astronomy. **2)** A general information almanac has (descriptive) facts and figures (statistics). Examples are population of U.S. cities and major events of the last year. **3)** A popular almanac is *The World Almanac and Book of Facts* or *The Information Please Almanac.* **4)** Most almanacs are published once a year. **5)** You would first look in the index. **6)** A statistic is a numerical fact.

Part B Answers

1) FA **2)** FA **3)** GIA **4)** FA **5)** GIA **6)** GIA **7)** GIA **8)** FA

Lesson 1 Review

Part A Write complete sentences on your paper to answer these questions.

1) What are two kinds of information given in a farmer's almanac?
2) What kinds of facts would you find in a general information almanac? Give two examples.
3) Name one popular general information almanac.
4) How often are most almanacs published?
5) Where would you look first to find out if an almanac has information about a certain country?
6) What is a statistic?

Part B Number your paper from 1 to 8. Beside each number write *FA* if you can find the answer to the question in a farmer's almanac or *GIA* if you can find the answer to the question in a general information almanac.

1) When will the next full moon be?
2) Suppose that the fish are biting best at high tide. What time should you go fishing?
3) Who won the World Series in 1950?
4) When should I set out my tomato plants this year?
5) Who won the Oscar for best actor in 1993?
6) What is the ZIP code for Boise, Idaho?
7) Which team won the Super Bowl in 1995?
8) What would be the best day to plant my garden this year?

62 *Chapter 3 Some Everyday References*

Lesson 2 Atlases and Gazetteers

Atlas

A book of maps and geographical facts.

Gazetteer

A dictionary of geographical place names.

Scale

The relationship shown between distances on the map and actual distances.

Symbol

A sign or mark that stands for something else.

An **atlas** is a book of maps. A **gazetteer** is a dictionary of geographical place names. Both of these reference sources can also be found on CD-ROM.

In Greek mythology, there was a Titan named Atlas. Titans were a family of giants who wanted to rule the heavens. When Zeus defeated the Titans, Zeus punished Atlas by making him hold the Earth and sky on his shoulders forever. For hundreds of years, books of maps have shown a drawing of Atlas holding up the earth. As a result, people began to call any book of maps an "atlas."

Reading a Map

To use an atlas, you must be able to read a map. To read a map, you must understand its symbols. A **symbol** is something that represents something else. The key, or legend, on a map explains the symbols used on the map.

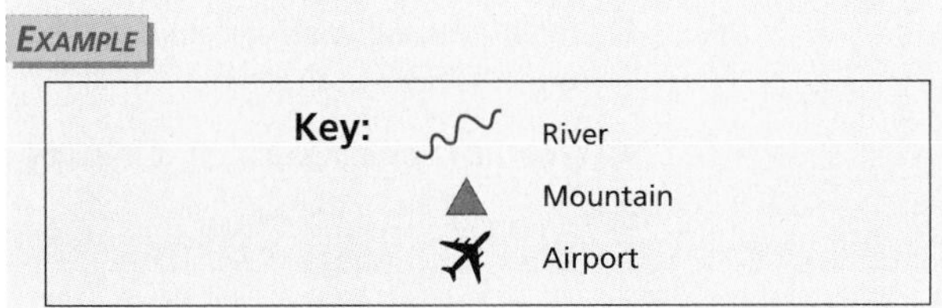

Maps are drawn to **scale**. You can use the scale to find the actual distances shown on the map.

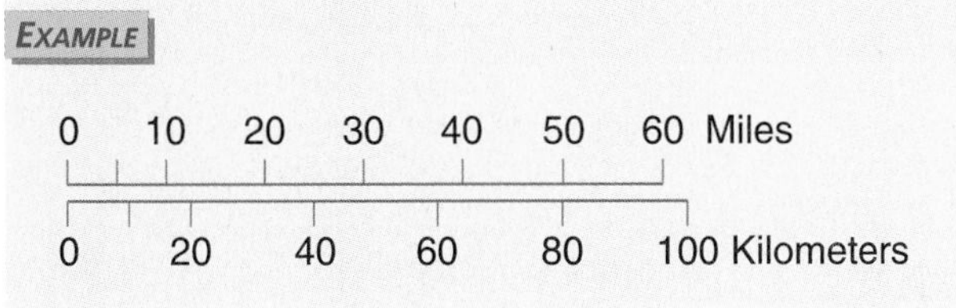

Lesson at a Glance

Chapter 3 Lesson 2

Overview This lesson explains how to read a map and how to use a gazetteer.

Objectives

- To interpret information on a map.
- To create a gazetteer.

Student Pages 63–70

Teacher's Resource Library

Workbook Activity 15

Reading Vocabulary

actual (7)	mythology (8)
atlas (7)	relationship (6)
gazetteer	**scale (4)**
geographical	**symbol (5)**
kilometer	

Teaching Suggestions

- **Introducing the Lesson** Discuss the information and the graphics presented in the text. If possible, provide an atlas and a gazetteer for students to examine. Then ask students to describe opportunities they have had to use a map, how they learned to read a map, and why they think knowing how to read a map is important.

- **Reviewing Skills** Review the different types of reference sources students have learned about so far, including dictionaries and almanacs.

Reading Vocabulary

capital (5)

Presenting Activity A

Display a section of a state or county map that shows several cities and towns. Use an overhead projector if possible. Have students identify particular places on the map, using the map's legend. Then have them use the map's scale to calculate distances between specific cities and towns shown on the map. Ask students what else they learn from this map. Then have them complete Activity A on their own.

Activity A Answers

1) approximately 16 miles 2) Princeton 3) approximately 68 miles (4.25 × 16) 4) Ralston 5) Newton

Activity A Use the map below to answer the questions that follow. Write the answers on your paper.

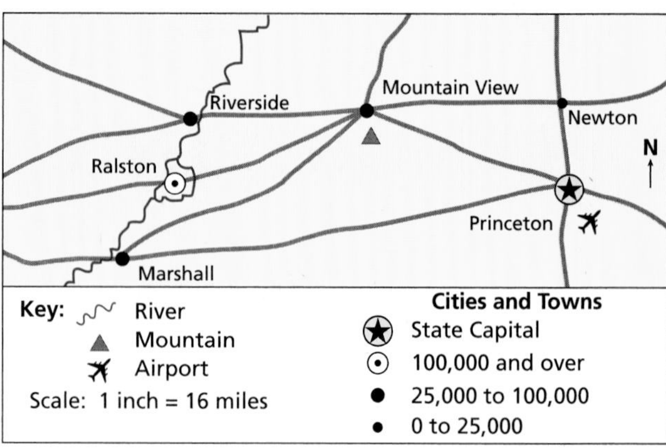

1) How far is the mountain from the river?

2) Which city is the capital?

3) If this map shows all of Gilbert County, how wide is the county from east to west?

4) What city has a population of 100,000 or more?

5) What town has fewer than 25,000 people?

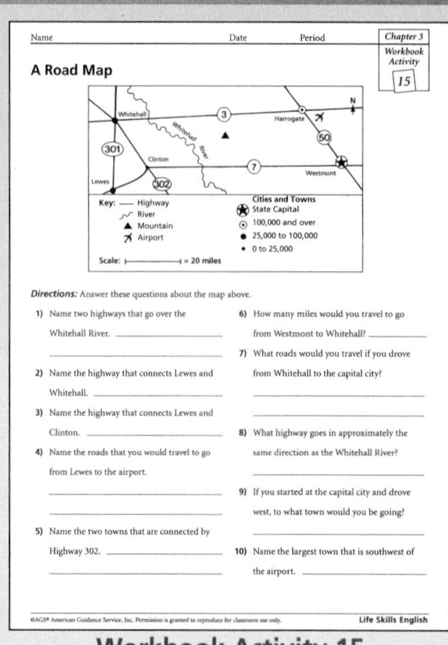

Name ____ Date ____ Period ____

Chapter 3 Workbook Activity 15

A Road Map

Directions: Answer these questions about the map above.

1) Name two highways that go over the Whitehall River. ____

2) Name the highway that connects Lewes and Whitehall. ____

3) Name the highway that connects Lewes and Clinton. ____

4) Name the roads that you would travel to go from Lewes to the airport. ____

5) Name the two towns that are connected by Highway 302. ____

6) How many miles would you travel to go from Westmont to Whitehall? ____

7) What roads would you travel if you drove from Whitehall to the capital city? ____

8) What highway goes in approximately the same direction as the Whitehall River? ____

9) If you started at the capital city and drove west, to what town would you be going? ____

10) Name the largest town that is southwest of the airport. ____

 Life Skills English

Workbook Activity 15

Kinds of Maps

There are many different kinds of maps with different features and purposes. Here are some kinds of maps.

Road map:	Shows roads, highways, towns, and other information helpful to a traveler.
Political map:	Shows the boundaries of states and countries clearly. Usually each state or country is in a different color.
Physical map:	Shows the roughness of the earth's surface. Mountains and hills can be seen, along with rivers.
Globe:	A model of the earth. It shows the placement of the continents, islands, and oceans as they actually are.
Product map:	Uses symbols to show where goods are grown or produced.

Globe

A model of the earth. It shows the actual placement of the continents, islands, and oceans.

Physical map

A map that shows the roughness of the earth's surface.

Political map

A map that shows the boundaries of states and countries clearly.

Product map

A map that has symbols that show where goods are grown or produced.

Road map

A map that shows roads, highways, towns, and other useful travel information.

Activity B Match each of the maps below to one of the descriptions above. Then number your paper from 1–4. Beside each number, write the kind of map shown.

1)

2)

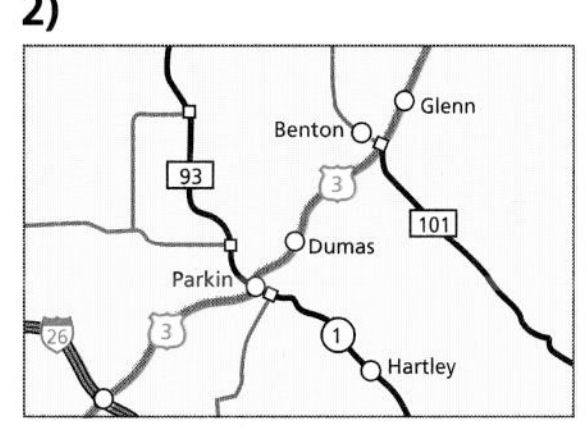

3)

4)

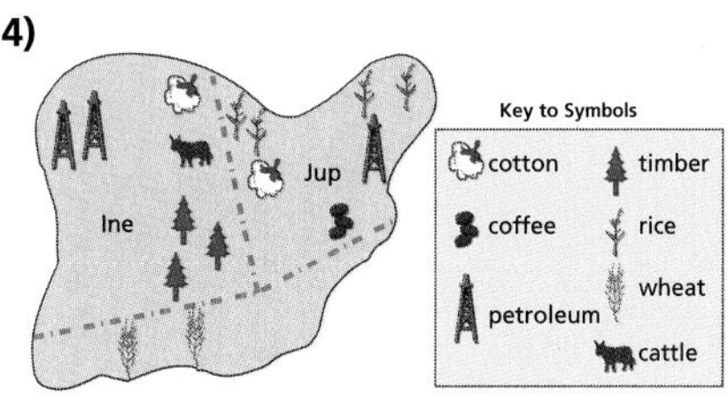

Reading Vocabulary

boundary (6)
feature (6)
globe (5)
physical map
political map
produce (5)
product map
road map
roughness

■ **Presenting Activity B** As an additional challenge after students complete Activity B, divide the class into five groups. Assign each group one of the types of maps listed on page 65 and have them create that type of map for their own geographical region. Have students display their completed maps for classmates to examine and discuss.

Activity B Answers

1) political map **2)** road map **3)** globe **4)** product map

Some Everyday References *Chapter 3* **65**

Reading Vocabulary

alphabetical (6)
grid
grid map
horizontal (7)
network
specific (8)
vertical (6)

Application

In the Community

Encourage students to work together to compile a book of maps of their city or town, county, and state, as well as maps of parks, hiking trails, and other outdoor recreational facilities in the region. Students can write to the local and state chambers of commerce to request maps for their project. Once students have collected the maps, have them devise a way to assemble all of the maps that allows easy access to each map. For example, they might store the maps in plastic sleeves in a three-ring binder with an index at the front that lists the maps in alphabetical order. Students can then donate their "atlas" to the school or town library for others to use and enjoy.

How to Use a Gazetteer

A gazetteer is a dictionary of geographical place names. It is like an index. It lists the names of all the places shown on the maps in the atlas in alphabetical order.

Grid

A network of lines on a map that makes it possible to locate specific places.

Grid map

A map with grid lines.

Horizontal

A word that means going across.

Vertical

A word that means going up and down.

A **grid** is a network of lines on a map that helps to locate certain places. The lines go across (**horizontal**) and up and down (**vertical**). A **grid map** is a map with grid lines. The spaces between the vertical lines on a grid map have numbers. The spaces between the horizontal lines have letters.

The letter and number beside a place name in the gazetteer tells you exactly where to look on the map to locate that place.

Example If you were to look up Etonville in the gazetteer of the atlas for this map, you might see:

Etonville B-4

To locate Etonville on the map, first find the B down the left or right side of the map. Then find the 4 across the top or bottom of the map. Run your finger across the map from the B to the space under the 4. Etonville is located in the square beside the B and under the 4.

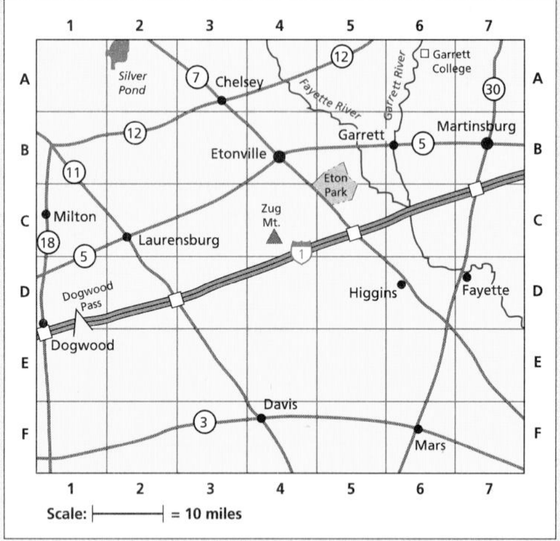

66 Chapter 3 Some Everyday References

Activity C Locate each place listed in the gazetteer below on the map on page 66.

Dogwood D-1
Fayette River A-4, B-5, C-6, D-7
Laurensburg C-2
Martinsburg B-7
Zug Mountain C-4
Mars F-6

Activity D Locate each of these places on the map on page 66. On your paper, write the letter and number of their location on the grid.

1) Milton
2) Garrett River
3) Dogwood Pass
4) Higgins
5) Chelsey
6) Eton Park
7) Silver Pond
8) Garrett College
9) Fayette
10) Davis

Activity E Use the map on page 66 to answer these questions. Write the answers on your paper.

1) What road connects Milton and Dogwood?
2) How far is it from Silver Pond to Chelsey?
3) Which town is closer to Zug Mountain—Laurensburg or Etonville?
4) How far is Martinsburg from Garrett College?
5) What town is next to the Garrett River?
6) What towns are located along Route 7?

Reading Vocabulary

connect (5) location (6)

■ Presenting Activity C

Do Activity C as a whole class activity. Have volunteers demonstrate how to locate each place listed, using a similar process as the one described for locating Etonville on page 66.

Activity C Answers

No written responses are required.

■ Presenting Activity D

Students might enjoy completing this activity in teams of two or three.

Activity D Answers

1) C-1 **2)** A-6, B-6, & C-6 **3)** D-1 **4)** D-6 **5)** A-3 **6)** B-5 & C-5 **7)** A-2 **8)** A-6 **9)** D-7 **10)** F-4

■ Presenting Activity E

After students complete Activity E, have them make up additional questions based on the map on page 66 to ask their classmates.

Activity E Answers

1) Route 18 **2)** about 14 miles **3)** Etonville **4)** about 15 miles **5)** Garrett **6)** Chelsey, Etonville, and Higgins

Teacher Alert

As students complete Activity D, stress that they should look at where the dot for a city or town is located and not where the name of the city or town is printed to identify its location on the grid.

Reading Vocabulary

bulletin (6)
chalkboard
create (6)
horizontally
imaginary (5)
indicate (6)
latitude lines
longitude lines
mapmaker
student (5)
vertically

■ Presenting Activity F

Before having students draw their own maps, discuss the sample classroom map. Have students take turns using the key to point out different elements on the map. Students might also enjoy working together to develop a series of symbols that they can use to create their map keys. Invite students with drawing skills to draw the symbols on the board or chart paper as students suggest them.

Activity F Answers

Students' classroom maps and map keys will vary.

Study this sample classroom map. Then complete the activity below.

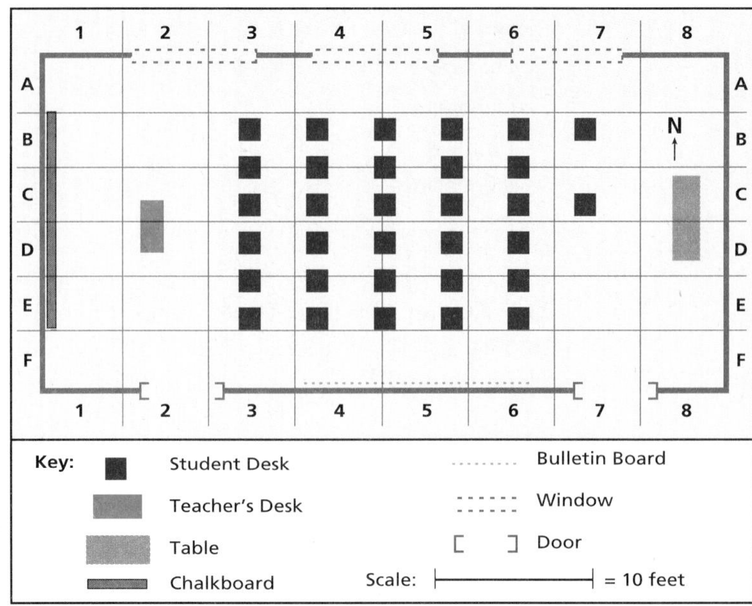

Activity F Draw a grid map of your classroom on your paper. Create a map key. Use the symbols shown in the sample map above or make up some of your own.

Longitude and Latitude

> ***Longitude lines***
> *The vertical lines on a map that indicate north to south.*

> ***Latitude lines***
> *The horizontal lines on a map that indicate east to west.*

A globe is a model of the earth. Like the earth, a globe is a round object. Mapmakers have divided the surface of the globe into parts. They use imaginary lines called longitude and latitude.

Longitude lines go from north to south (vertically) on a map. They are used to measure the distance from east to west. **Latitude lines** go from east to west (horizontally) on a map. They are used to measure the distance from north to south.

Equator

An imaginary line that circles the center of the earth.

The **equator** is an imaginary line of latitude. It runs from east to west around the center of the earth. All other lines of latitude are measured from the equator.

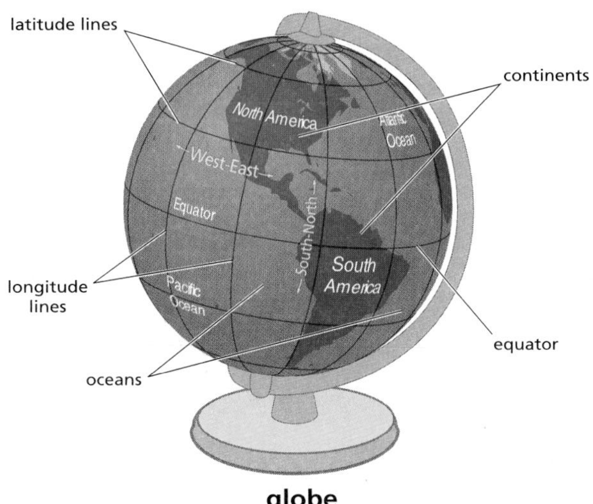

globe

Activity G Use the view of the globe above to answer these questions. Write the answers on your paper.

1) What is the name of the latitude line in the center of the globe?

2) What two continents are shown on the globe?

3) Which continent is mostly south of the equator?

4) What two bodies of water are shown on the globe?

5) Which body of water is west of the two continents?

Reading Vocabulary

equator (4)

■ Presenting Activity G

If possible, have students use a real globe to answer the questions in Activity G. Give each student or pairs of students the opportunity to locate all of the continents and major bodies of water on the globe. If a real globe is not available in the classroom, encourage students to visit another classroom or a library that does have a globe to get actual hands-on experience using a globe. Then stimulate a discussion among students of the differences between a globe and a map and the benefits of each.

Activity G Answers

1) equator **2)** North America and South America
3) South America **4)** Pacific Ocean and Atlantic Ocean
5) Pacific Ocean

Teacher Alert

For some students, it may be necessary to define the terms *continent* (one of the seven main masses of land of the earth, including North America, South America, Australia, Africa, Asia, Antarctica) and *ocean* (principal bodies of water of the earth, including Atlantic, Pacific, Indian, and Arctic Oceans).

Reading Vocabulary

include (5) item (6)

Part A Answers

1) east 2) three 3) approximately 6–7 feet 4) bulletin board 5) north 6) chalkboard

Part B Answers

Students' responses should appear in alphabetical order as shown here.

Chalkboard	B-1, C-1, D-1, E-1
East door	F-7, F-8
Middle window	A-4, A-5
Table	C-8, D-8
Teacher's desk	C-2, D-2
West door	F-2, F-3

Part C Answers

1) Crockett 2) Boone 3) Flora 4) Bass State Park 5) Hilary 6) Fern Lake 7) Timber Mountains 8) Grand

Learning Styles

LEP/ESL

Ask students for whom English is a second language to bring in maps of the country from which their families immigrated. Encourage them to use these maps to teach something about their homeland to the rest of the students. Encourage them to talk about the symbols used on their maps. Then ask them to use their maps to make up activities like Activity A on page 64 and Activities C–E on page 67. Ask the English-speaking students to use the maps to complete these activities.

Lesson 2 Review

Part A Use the sample classroom map on page 68 to answer these questions. Write the answers on your paper.

1) If you are sitting at the teacher's desk facing the classroom, what direction are you facing?
2) How many windows does the classroom have?
3) How wide (in feet) is each window?
4) What classroom object is located between the two doors?
5) If you are looking out one of the windows, what direction are you facing?
6) What is directly behind the teacher's desk?

Part B Create a gazetteer on your paper for the classroom map on page 68. Include the items listed below. Remember that the items in a gazetteer are listed in alphabetical order.

Example Bulletin board F-4, 5, 6

1) West door
2) East door
3) Middle window
4) Teacher's desk
5) Chalkboard
6) Table

Part C Write on your paper the name of the place found at each of these locations on the grid map below.

1) C-4
2) A-2
3) B-1
4) D-1
5) D-5
6) C-2
7) A-4
8) D-3

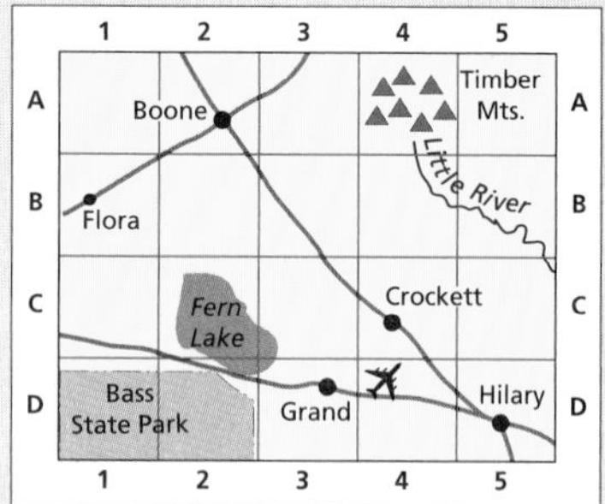

70 Chapter 3 Some Everyday References

Lesson 3 Encyclopedias

Encyclopedia
A book or set of books with a collection of articles and facts on many subjects, organized in alphabetical order.

Volume
A single book, or one book in a set of books.

A very useful type of reference book is an **encyclopedia**. An encyclopedia is a book or set of books with facts on many subjects. It is usually a collection of articles in alphabetical order.

Some encyclopedias are only one book, or **volume**. Others are a set of books, or volumes. *The World Book Encyclopedia,* the *Encyclopædia Brittanica,* and *Compton's Encyclopedia* all have many volumes. Most sets of encyclopedias have similar features, as shown in the diagram below. These features can help you find the information you need quickly.

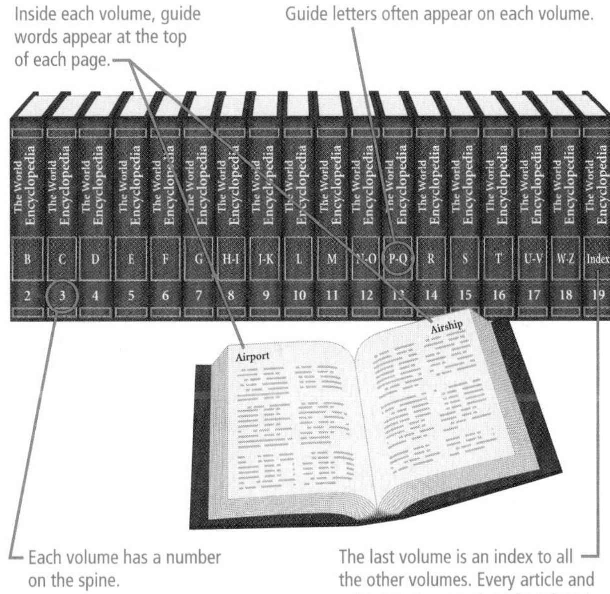

Inside each volume, guide words appear at the top of each page.
Guide letters often appear on each volume.
The World Encyclopedia
B C D E F G H-I J-K L M N-O P-Q R S T U-V W-Z Index
2 3 4 5 6 7 8 9 10 11 12 13 14 15 16 17 18 19
Airport
Airship
Each volume has a number on the spine.
The last volume is an index to all the other volumes. Every article and subject in the encyclopedia is listed. Cross references are often given.

Encyclopedias are also on CD-ROM. These encyclopedias present information, such as videos and music recordings, in a way that cannot be presented in books.

Lesson at a Glance

Chapter 3 Lesson 3

Overview This lesson describes multivolume and single-set encyclopedias. It explains how they are organized and how to use them to find information.

Objectives

- To answer questions about the organization of encyclopedias.
- To match topic to volume number in a pictured multi-volume encyclopedia.

Student Pages 71–75

Reading Vocabulary

cross-reference
diagram (6)
encyclopedia (4)
organize (6)
similar (6)
video
volume (6)

Teaching Suggestions

■ **Introducing the Lesson**
Discuss the text and the accompanying illustrations. Ask students to describe their experiences with finding information in an encyclopedia. Use the following questions to stimulate students' responses: *When do you tend to use the encyclopedia? Do you have trouble locating the information you need quickly? What aids does the encyclopedia you use provide to help you find information quickly within an article (e.g., heads, subheads, outlines; photographs and other visuals)?*

■ **Reviewing Skills** Review alphabetical order, using an index, and cross-references.

Learning Styles

Visual/Spatial
Divide the class into groups of three and give each group a magazine picture. Invite each group to use the picture to create seven questions it might look up in an encyclopedia. (For example, a picture of an Olympic athlete might bring forth questions about the Olympics, famous gold medal winners in a specific sport, places the Olympics have been held, and so on.) If possible, have the groups use encyclopedias to find the answers to their questions. Afterward, invite sharing.

Reading Vocabulary

honeysuckle refer (6)
nectar relate (6)

■ Presenting Activity A

After reviewing the example given for Activity A, write item 1 on the board. (*History of Argentina*) Ask students to identify the most obvious topic to look up for this item. (*Argentina*) Next, work with students to develop one or two other possible topics to look up. (e.g., *South America*) Then have students identify the matching volume numbers for these topics. Depending on the ability of your students, you may wish to continue this process to complete Activity A, or you might divide the class into groups of two or three students. Have them work together to complete the activity.

Activity A Answers

Some answers will vary. Possible responses are given.

1) Vol. 1—Argentina, Vol. 15—South America **2)** Vol. 6—fish, Vol. 12—North America **3)** Vol. 1—Amazon wildlife, Vol. 14—rain forest **4)** Vol. 17—United States, Vol. 1—America **5)** Vol. 2—basketball, Vol. 15—sports **6)** Vol. 11—Mexico, Vol. 8—International trade, Vol. 16—Trade **7)** Vol. 6—Franklin, Benjamin, Vol. 8—Inventors, Inventions **8)** Vol. 14—Robin Hood **9)** Vol. 15—Supreme Court, Vol. 17—United States Government, Vol. 10—Law

Activity A Which volume of the encyclopedia pictured on page 71 would you look in to find facts about each topic listed below? Since some topics may suggest more than one idea, write the volume number or numbers on your paper. Beside each number, write the subject you would look up.

Example Honeysuckle plants
Vol. 8—honeysuckle
Vol. 13—plants

1) History of Argentina

2) Fish of North America

3) Animals of the Amazon rain forest

4) United States history

5) Basketball

6) Products of Mexico

7) Benjamin Franklin's inventions

8) Robin Hood

9) The Supreme Court

Related Topics and Cross-References

When you read about a topic in an encyclopedia, you may find that the article names another related topic. Some articles also give a specific cross-reference to another related topic. If you look up these related topics, you will find more information about your subject.

HONEY PLANTS, a group of plants that furnish the nectar from which bees make honey — often also called bee plants.

NECTAR is a sugary liquid produced by many flowers. Besides being the main source of honey, it is also very important in cross-pollination. *See also* **Pollination**. G.W.K.

When you use a CD-ROM encyclopedia, you click on a part of the computer screen to see cross-references. When you use books, you may have to refer to another volume of the encyclopedia.

Activity B Use the encyclopedia entries on page 72 to answer these questions. Write the answers on your paper.

1) What is the related topic named in the entry about honey plants?

2) If you were to look up this topic, what guide letter would appear on the correct volume?

3) What is the cross-reference named in the article on nectar?

4) What do you think the letters G. W. K. refer to at the end of the entry on nectar?

5) Where might you look to find out what those letters mean?

6) What is another name for honey plants?

7) What guide letter would appear on the volume containing the article about pollination?

8) Would the article about honey plants be on a page with these guide words: Harrisburg—Honduras?

Activity C Use the examples below to answer the questions that follow. Write the answers on your paper.

Example 1

... Boundary arguments with Guatemala were settled in 1933. For Bibliography, *See* **Costa Rica** (History).

Example 2

HONDURAS, BRITISH. *See* Belize (History).
HONDURAS BARK is the bitter bark from a small tropical American shrub, used as a medicine. Also called Cascarilla Bark.

1) What two specific cross-references are named in the examples above?

2) What related topic would you look up to learn more about Honduras bark?

3) What is a bibliography? Use a dictionary if you need to.

4) The article in *Example 1* has a bibliography. What topic must you look up to find it?

5) Explain what Costa Rica (History) means.

6) What will be the guide letter on the volume that contains the articles in *Example 2*?

7) What will be the guide letter on the volume that has a related article about British Honduras?

Reading Vocabulary

bibliography (9) pollination
entry (6)

■ Presenting Activity B

Have students create a list of questions that they would want to answer in a report on bees. For example, *How many different species of bees are there? What is the difference between honey bees and bumble bees? How do bees make honey?* and so on. Then have students explain how they could use an encyclopedia to find the answers to these questions.

Activity B Answers

1) nectar **2)** N **3)** Pollination **4)** These could be the initials of the author of the article, Pollination. **5)** Look at the introductory material in the front of the encyclopedia or perhaps in the index. **6)** bee plants **7)** P **8)** No

■ Presenting Activity C

Invite volunteers to point out facts and details that they glean on their own from the sample entries.

Activity C Answers

1) Costa Rica (History); Belize (History) **2)** Cascarilla Bark **3)** A bibliography is a list of reference sources used by an author to prepare a work. **4)** Costa Rica (History) **5)** Look under the subhead *History* in the article on Costa Rica. **6)** H **7)** B

Reading Vocabulary

author (6) medical (6)
detail (5) provide (5)

■ Presenting Activity D

Have students discuss the advantages and disadvantages of multivolume encyclopedias and desk encyclopedias. When would they anticipate using one over the other?

Activity D Answers

1) articles **2)** alphabetical **3)** index **4)** alphabetical **5)** atlas **6)** one **7)** volume **8)** cross-reference **9)** initials

APPLICATION

In the Community Because of the lack of available funds, many schools and some small community libraries have outdated encyclopedias and other reference materials. Encourage students to investigate the current status of its schools' reference libraries. Students may find that some reference materials are outdated. Engage students in a discussion of what might be done to improve this situation. Are there ways that students can think of to get the whole community involved in solving this problem? Perhaps, students might be willing to initiate a campaign to raise money for the purchase of new and current reference materials for their libraries.

Encyclopedias About Special Subjects

You are probably most familiar with the large sets of encyclopedias. However, there are many other kinds of encyclopedias. One-volume general encyclopedias have short articles about many different subjects. They are sometimes called "desk" encyclopedias. One example is the *Columbia Encyclopedia.*

There are also encyclopedias about just one subject. In these encyclopedias, all the articles provide details about that subject. For example, a home medical encyclopedia includes only information related to medical topics.

Activity D Write the word on your paper that completes each sentence correctly.

1) An encyclopedia is a collection of ______ on many subjects.

2) The subjects in an encyclopedia are arranged in ______ order.

3) The last volume of a set of encyclopedias is often an ______.

4) The topics in an index are arranged in ______ order.

5) An index is to an encyclopedia as a gazetteer is to an ______.

6) A desk encyclopedia has ______ volume.

7) A ______ is one in a set of books.

8) A ______ tells where to look to find information on a related topic.

9) You may find the author's ______ at the end of an article in an encyclopedia.

Lesson 3 Review

Part A Write the answer to these questions on your paper.

1) What is one way that dictionaries and encyclopedias are alike?
2) What is one way that almanacs and encyclopedias are alike?
3) What is one difference between a desk encyclopedia and *The World Book Encyclopedia?*
4) Encyclopedia sets have guide letters on the spine of each volume. What else may appear there to help you find the right volume?
5) What do the guide words on each page tell you?

Part B Study the encyclopedia in the picture. In which volume would you look to find each topic below? Write the number and the guide letters of the volume on your paper.

1) President Franklin Roosevelt
2) The History of France
3) The Solar System
4) Football (History)
5) Cities of Saudi Arabia
6) Wildlife of Australia
7) Alexander the Great
8) Zebras

Reading Vocabulary

solar (6) wildlife
system (5) zebra

Part A Answers

1) The information in both is arranged in alphabetical order.
2) They have information on many topics. They have a subject index arranged in alphabetical order.
3) A desk encyclopedia has one volume; *The World Book Encyclopedia* has many volumes.
4) There may also be numbers.
5) Guide words tell you the first and last entry that appear on a page alphabetically between the guide words.

Part B Answers

1) 14—R **2)** 6—F **3)** 15—S
4) 6—F **5)** 15—S **6)** 1—A
7) 1—A **8)** 18—Z

Lesson at a Glance

Chapter 3 Lesson 4

Overview This lesson defines terms and abbreviations used in recipes and explains the purpose of certain kitchen equipment.

Objectives

- To identify abbreviations found in recipes.
- To explain how to follow a recipe.
- To demonstrate an understanding of cooking terms.

Student Pages 76–86

Teacher's Resource Library

Activities 9–10

Workbook Activities 16–17

Reading Vocabulary

advice (5)
housekeeping
ingredient (7)
specialty
suggestion (5)
vitamin (7)
wok

Teaching Suggestions

Introducing the Lesson

Display several cookbooks and recipes for students to examine. Ask students to select a recipe that appeals to them and explain why. Does the recipe seem easy to prepare? Do they understand all the terms used in the recipe? Could they follow this recipe?

Reviewing Skills

Review the importance of following directions in order.

Presenting Activity A

Do Activity A as a class. Then challenge students to find the answers to the questions in Activity A in cookbooks in class, at home, or at the library.

Activity A Answers

1) Yes 2) Yes 3) No 4) Yes 5) Yes 6) Yes 7) Yes 8) Yes 9) No 10) Yes

Lesson 4 References for Cooks

Cookbooks

A cookbook is a reference book about food. Most cookbooks contain some of the following information:

- Facts about storing foods
- Meal planning help
- How to carve meat
- Food shopping advice
- Nutrition facts
- Calorie charts
- Suggestions for a low-fat diet
- How to measure ingredients

There are general cookbooks, such as *Betty Crocker's Picture Cookbook* or the *Good Housekeeping Cookbook.* There are specialty cookbooks like *Cooking With a Wok* or *Simple and Healthy Cooking.*

Activity A Write *Yes* or *No* on your paper to tell whether a cookbook would have the answer to these questions.

1) How many calories are in a baked potato?
2) How do you carve a turkey?
3) Which store in your town has the best fresh fruit?
4) How can you tell if a watermelon is ripe?
5) What foods are good for breakfast?
6) What should you eat to be sure you get enough vitamins?
7) How do you store fresh vegetables?
8) How can you cook pork chops?
9) How much do blueberries cost?
10) How long should you roast a 15-pound turkey?

Recipe
A list of ingredients and directions for the preparation of a specific food.

A **recipe** is a set of directions a cook uses to prepare each part of a meal. Recipes use many specialized terms and abbreviations.

Most cookbooks give the meanings of recipe terms and abbreviations in the front or back of the book. These meanings do not appear in the actual recipe. Here are some of the most common cooking terms and abbreviations.

Terms Used in Cooking	
baste	To brush melted butter or drippings over a food that is cooking.
beat	To mix ingredients until smooth.
blend	To combine two or more ingredients well.
boil	To cook in bubbling hot liquid; 212°F.
braise	To brown meat in hot fat on all sides; then to add liquid, cover, and simmer until tender.
broil	To cook under the heat of a broiler, or directly over hot coals.
cream	To mix sugar and shortening until completely mixed and creamy.
cut into	To use two knives or a pastry blender to cut shortening into dry ingredients until the fat particles are tiny.
dice	To cut into very small cubes.
dissolve	To mix a dry ingredient with liquid until the dry particles disappear.
drain	To pour off the liquid.
ingredient	One of the items that is used in a food mixture.
marinate	To soak a food in a liquid mixture to improve its flavor.
mince	To chop fine.
peel	To cut off the skin from a food, such as a potato or apple.
sauté	To fry a food in a small amount of fat.
shortening	Fat, such as margarine, butter, or lard.
simmer	To cook at a temperature just below boiling.
tender	Easily chewed.
uniform	All the same.

Reading Vocabulary

abbreviation (8)
baste (9)
braise
broil (6)
broiler
combine (6)
cube (6)
dice (6)
dissolve (6)
drain (5)
lard (6)
margarine
marinate
mince
particle (7)
pastry (7)
recipe (6)
sauté
shortening
simmer
specialize

Global Connection

Cookbooks that focus on the food of one country often contain text that provides background information on the culture and traditions associated with the food of that country. Ask students to look through any international cookbooks that they might have at home to find information about the cultural traditions associated with the food of different countries. Invite students to share what they learn with the class.

Students whose families maintain the cooking traditions of their cultural heritage might enjoy sharing these traditions with the class. These students might also like to bring in an old family recipe to share. Students can compare the terms used in the family recipes with those used in modern American recipes.

Learning Styles

Auditory/Verbal
Invite volunteers to read aloud the cooking terms and definitions on page 77. After each term is read, invite the volunteer to give an example of a term—such as *ingredient;* or to demonstrate the meaning of a word—such as *tender*—by using it in a sentence. If time permits, invite the students to think of other categories of books for which a reader needs a specialized vocabulary—for example, books on auto mechanics, computers, gardening, crafts, and so on.

Reading Vocabulary

gram	tablespoon
ounce (6)	teaspoon
pint (6)	term (5)

■ Presenting Activity B

Encourage pairs of students to quiz each other on the cooking terms shown on page 77. Students can say a term and have their partners define it or give a definition and have partners identify the term.

Activity B Answers

1) Marinate 2) drain 3) Cream 4) simmer

■ Presenting Activity C

Suggest that students create a bookmark of cooking terms and abbreviations. On one side, they can list cooking terms and their definitions. On the other side, they can list cooking abbreviations and their meanings. Students can refer to their bookmarks as they do the activities in this lesson and when they cook.

Activity C Answers

1) oz.—ounce 2) drained—pour off liquid 3) diced—cut into small cubes 4) c.—cup 5) minced—chopped fine 6) T.—tablespoon 7) t.—teaspoon 8) tsp.—teaspoon 9) blend—combine two or more ingredients well 10) ingredients—items used in a food mixture 11) min.—minutes

Teacher Alert

The recipes in this lesson use standard measurements based on the U.S. Customary System. Students should, however, be aware of the metric system, which is used throughout the world and is gaining acceptance in the U.S.

Activity B Choose the word in parentheses that completes each cooking instruction correctly. Write the word on your paper.

1) (Marinate, Mince) the meat in French dressing for one hour.
2) Boil the carrots for half an hour; then (boil, drain) the water.
3) (Baste, Cream) the sugar and butter in a bowl.
4) Partly cover and (dissolve, simmer) the soup for an hour.

Here are some abbreviations that are used in recipes.

Abbreviations Used in Recipes			
lb.	= pound	min.	= minute
oz.	= ounce	hr.	= hour
doz.	= dozen	pt.	= pint
pkg.	= package	qt.	= quart
tsp.	= teaspoon	F	= Fahrenheit
t.	= teaspoon	g	= gram
tbsp.	= tablespoon	c.	= cup
T.	= tablespoon	sq.	= square

Activity C Write each underlined term and abbreviation in the recipe below on your paper. Beside each term and abbreviation, write its meaning.

Salsa Cruda

1 16-oz. can of drained and chopped tomatoes
1 4-oz. can of green chili drained, seeded, and diced
1/2 c. of onion, minced
1 T. of vinegar
1 t. of sugar
1/8 tsp. of salt

Blend the following ingredients in a bowl: tomatoes, green chili, and onion. Add vinegar, sugar, and salt to tomato mixture. Keep at room temperature for 30 min. Serve with tacos and enchiladas.

Name Date Period

Chapter 3 Workbook Activity 16

Abbreviations in Cookbooks

Abbreviation:	Stands for:	Equivalent to:
c.	cup	8 ounces
doz.	dozen	12 units
F.	Fahrenheit (a measure of heat)	
g.	gram	1/28 of an ounce
hr.	hour	60 minutes
L.	liter (basic unit in the metric system for measuring liquids; about one quart)	
lb.	pound	16 dry ounces
min.	minute	60 seconds
oz.	ounce	1/16 of a pound; 1/8 of a cup
pkg.	package (container)	
pt.	pint	16 ounces
qt.	quart	32 fluid ounces
t., tsp.	teaspoon (a unit of liquid or dry measure)	1/3 of a tablespoon
T., tbsp.	tablespoon (a unit of liquid or dry measure)	3 teaspoons

1) How many pints do you need to make a quart? ______
2) Write two ways to abbreviate *teaspoon.* ______
3) What is the abbreviation for *pound*? ______
4) How many cups are in a pint? ______
5) What measurement unit is almost the same as a quart? ______
6) What is the abbreviation for *ounce*? ______
7) A cake is to bake at 350° F. What does *F.* mean? ______
8) How many teaspoons equal one tablespoon? ______
9) A recipe calls for 1/2 dozen eggs. How many eggs do you need? ______
10) The stew should simmer for one hour and a half. How many minutes does that equal? ______
11) How much larger than a gram is an ounce? ______
12) Which is larger—a pint or a cup? ______
13) Which is smaller—a teaspoon or a tablespoon? ______
14) Which is larger—a quart or a pint? ______
15) How many ounces make up a pint? ______
16) How many ounces make up a quart? ______
17) How many ounces make up a cup? ______

 Life Skills English

Workbook Activity 16

Kitchen Tools

After listing ingredients, most recipes tell you how to prepare those ingredients. For example, a recipe might say "beat 2 eggs well." To follow this instruction, it would be helpful for you to know what kitchen tool you should use to beat eggs.

Here are some common kitchen tools, or utensils, and their uses.

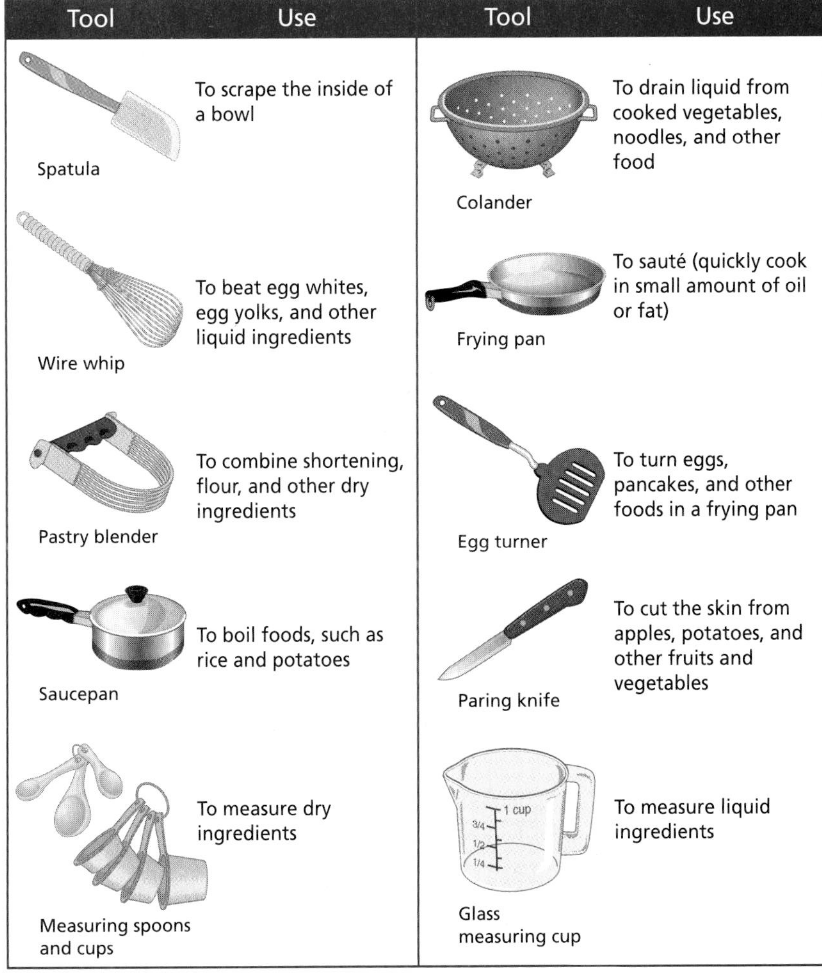

Tool	Use	Tool	Use
Spatula	To scrape the inside of a bowl	Colander	To drain liquid from cooked vegetables, noodles, and other food
Wire whip	To beat egg whites, egg yolks, and other liquid ingredients	Frying pan	To sauté (quickly cook in small amount of oil or fat)
Pastry blender	To combine shortening, flour, and other dry ingredients	Egg turner	To turn eggs, pancakes, and other foods in a frying pan
Saucepan	To boil foods, such as rice and potatoes	Paring knife	To cut the skin from apples, potatoes, and other fruits and vegetables
Measuring spoons and cups	To measure dry ingredients	Glass measuring cup	To measure liquid ingredients

Reading Vocabulary

colander
instruction (5)
noodle
paring
saucepan
scrape (5)
spatula
utensil (6)
yolk (6)

APPLICATION

At Home
Ask students to check their family kitchens for the items pictured on this page. If any of the items are missing, have students find out what alternative tools are used to do that item's job on a regular basis in the kitchen. For example, instead of using a pastry blender to combine shortening and flour, some cooks "cut" the shortening into the flour with two forks or butter knives, using a back and forth, crisscross motion.

Some Everyday References *Chapter 3* **79**

Reading Vocabulary

crust (5)	olive (5)
double (5)	oregano
dough (5)	puree
garlic (8)	spaghetti (5)
occasionally	sprinkle (6)

■ Presenting Activity D

To make this activity more enjoyable, invite volunteers to mime the preparation of each recipe. Have a variety of kitchen utensils available for students to use in their mimes. Ask other students to watch carefully and to let the student volunteer know if he or she makes a mistake by clapping their hands twice.

Activity D Answers

Some answers may vary. Possible responses are given.

Double-Crust Pie Dough

1) bowl—to hold the ingredients **2)** measuring cups and measuring spoons—to measure the ingredients **3)** pastry blender—to blend the flour, salt, and shortening **4)** tablespoon—to sprinkle water over flour mixture **5)** knife—to cut dough into two halves **6)** rolling pin—to roll out dough **7)** pastry sheet—to roll dough on

Spaghetti With Tomato Sauce

8) frying pan—to sauté garlic in olive oil **9)** 2-quart saucepan (or larger)—for cooking the sauce **10)** 4-quart pan (or larger) —to boil water for cooking spaghetti **11)** measuring spoons—to measure spices and oil; glass measuring cup to measure tomatoes **12)** knife—to peel and slice garlic **13)** long spoon—to stir sauce **14)** colander—to drain spaghetti **15)** ladle—to spoon sauce over spaghetti

Activity D Read each recipe below. Then write on your paper the name of the kitchen utensils you could use to prepare each recipe. Beside the name of each utensil, explain how you would use it.

Double-Crust Pie Dough

2 cups all-purpose flour
1 tsp. salt
2/3 cup shortening
5 to 8 tbsp. cold water

Blend together flour and salt. Cut shortening into flour mixture until pea-sized pieces form. Sprinkle with cold water, adding 1 tbsp. at a time. Toss after each tablespoon water is added. When mixture sticks together, shape into a ball. Cut ball into two halves. Roll out each ball to 1/8 inch thickness on lightly floured surface or pastry sheet.

Spaghetti With Tomato Sauce

3 large cloves of garlic
2 tbsp. olive oil
1 can (3 1/3 c.) Italian tomato puree
2 tsp. oregano
salt / pepper
1 lb. spaghetti

Peel and slice garlic. Sauté garlic in olive oil over medium to high heat. Remove garlic. Add tomato puree and oregano. Cook over medium heat for 15 to 20 minutes, stirring occasionally. Add salt and pepper to taste. Meanwhile, bring 4 qts. of water to boil. Add spaghetti and cook according to package directions. Drain cooked spaghetti and serve topped with sauce.

80 *Chapter 3 Some Everyday References*

Following a Recipe

Here are some important steps you should follow to be sure that the recipes you prepare turn out right.

Step 1	Read the whole recipe.
Step 2	Assemble all of the ingredients called for in the recipe.
Step 3	Gather all of the utensils you will need.
Step 4	Follow the directions in order.

Activity E Read the recipe below. Then write on your paper the answers to the questions that follow.

Mashed Vegetables

1 lb. medium potatoes
3 large carrots
2 cloves garlic

butter
salt / black pepper
paprika

Peel and slice potatoes. Trim and peel carrots. Cut carrots into chunks. Boil potatoes and carrots with peeled garlic until soft in enough water to cover the vegetables. Drain cooked vegetables. Mash the vegetables with a hand-masher or in a food processor. Add butter, salt, and black pepper to taste. Sprinkle with paprika before serving.

1) What ingredients will you need to prepare this recipe?

2) What utensils will you need?

3) After gathering ingredients and utensils, what is the next thing you must do?

4) What should you do before serving this recipe?

Reading Vocabulary

assemble (6) processor
paprika

■ Presenting Activity E

Even when cooks follow directions, recipes do not always turn out right. Before having students complete Activity E, invite them to share their favorite cooking stories about a time when they or someone they know met with "disaster" in the kitchen. You might start the discussion by sharing your own kitchen disaster story. Following the discussion, be sure to point out that disasters are sure to occur if cooks do not follow recipes carefully.

Activity E Answers

1) 1 pound of potatoes, 3 large carrots, 2 cloves of garlic, butter, salt, black pepper, and paprika **2)** paring knife, knife for cutting, pan, colander, masher or food processor **3)** You should prepare the vegetables: peel and slice the potatoes; trim, peel, and cut the carrots; peel the garlic; place them all in a pan of water; and then boil. **4)** Add butter, salt, and pepper to taste. Sprinkle with paprika.

Application

Career Connection
Students may enjoy hearing about the different career opportunities in the food industry. Invite local chefs, restaurant managers, nutritionists, and restaurant reviewers to speak to the class about their jobs. Encourage students to prepare a list of questions to ask the speakers.

Reading Vocabulary

desire (5) plastic (6)
macaroni (6) tenderness

■ Presenting Activity F

Display several examples of packaged foods, such as gelatin, dry and canned soups, stuffing mix, and so on. Invite volunteers to study the directions on the packages. Then ask them to "teach" the class how to prepare these foods. Students should be sure to identify the ingredients and utensils needed to prepare these foods in their presentations.

Activity F Answers

1) water, salt, margarine, and milk **2)** saucepan, $\frac{1}{4}$ cup measuring cups (regular and glass), 1 tsp. measuring spoon, colander, and spoon for stirring and mixing **3)** Put 6 cups of water in a pan and boil. **4)** 7 to 10 minutes **5)** a colander **6)** Add margarine, milk, and cheese sauce and mix. **7)** 1 cup

Following Directions on a Package

Packaged foods come in cans, boxes, and sealed plastic bags. Some packaged foods are stored at room temperature. Some are frozen. Packaged foods are convenient. Almost anyone who can read can prepare them. Simple and easy-to-follow recipes are printed on the packages. Use what you have learned about following a recipe to prepare packaged foods.

Activity F Read these directions from a package of macaroni and cheese. Then write on your paper the answers to the questions that follow.

Directions

Add macaroni and 1 tsp. salt to 6 c. boiling water. Stir. Boil rapidly, stirring occasionally, 7 to 10 minutes or to desired tenderness. Drain. Add 1/4 c. margarine, 1/4 c. milk, and the cheese sauce mix; mix well. Makes 4 1/2 cup servings.

1) Dry macaroni and an envelope of cheese sauce mix were in the box. What other ingredients would you need to prepare this meal?

2) What utensils would you need?

3) What is the first thing you would do if you were following the directions correctly?

4) How long would you cook the macaroni?

5) What would you use to drain the macaroni?

6) What would you do after you drained the macaroni?

7) How large would the servings be if only two people ate this meal?

Preparing Frozen Foods

Frozen vegetables are easy to cook, and they taste good. Freezing keeps more of the vegetable's fresh flavor and nutritional value. Like other packaged food, directions for preparing frozen vegetables are printed on the package.

Activity G Read these directions from a package of frozen broccoli cuts. Then write on your paper the answers to the questions that follow.

BROCCOLI CUTS

Store in freezer at 0°F.
Keep frozen until ready to use. Do not refreeze.

Microwave: Combine vegetable and 2 tablespoons water in a microwave-safe container. Microwave on high 7-11 minutes, or to desired tenderness, stirring halfway through cooking time. Drain and season to taste.

Stovetop: Bring 1/2 cup water to boiling in saucepan. Add desired amount of frozen vegetable. Bring to second boil. Stir; cover and reduce heat. Simmer 3-6 minutes, or to desired tenderness, stirring occasionally. Drain and season to taste.

Makes 5 servings.

1) Where would you store the package of broccoli?

2) Where would be the best place to store the package if it were to thaw before you were ready to use it?

3) What other ingredients besides broccoli and water would you need to prepare the vegetable?

4) What utensils would you use for each method of cooking?

5) What is the first step of the directions for each method of cooking?

6) Which is the fastest method of cooking the broccoli?

7) How many servings does one package make?

Reading Vocabulary

broccoli
halfway
method (6)
microwave
nutritional
thaw (5)

■ Presenting Activity G

Display pictures of fresh, canned, dried, and frozen vegetables. For example, you might show a bunch of carrots, a can of peas, a bag of dried beans, a box of dehydrated potatoes (instant mashed), and an empty package of frozen broccoli. Ask students to share what they know about the preparation, storage, and nutritional value of the different foods.

Activity G Answers

1) freezer **2)** refrigerator **3)** None, but you might wish to add salt and pepper. **4)** For microwaving, you would need a tablespoon to measure the water, a microwave-safe container to cook in, and a spoon to stir with. For stovetop preparation, you would need a glass measuring cup for the water, a saucepan to cook in, and a spoon to stir with. **5)** For microwaving, combine broccoli with 2 tablespoons of water. For stovetop preparation, boil $\frac{1}{2}$ cup of water. **6)** stovetop **7)** five

Reading Vocabulary

frequent (6) **predominance**
label (6) quantity (6)

Application

In the Community

Community suppers, Meals-On-Wheels, and other programs that serve the elderly, sick, disabled, homeless, and poorer members of the community are often in need of canned goods, packaged foods, and other nonperishable products. Encourage students to find out what the current and most essential needs of these programs are. Discuss with students what they as individuals and the school as a whole might do to help.

Predominance

Being most frequent or common.

Food Labels

The label on a food package lists all of the package's ingredients in order of **predominance**. That means that the ingredient of the greatest quantity is listed first. The ingredient with the smallest amount is listed last. Labels also give nutrition information per serving.

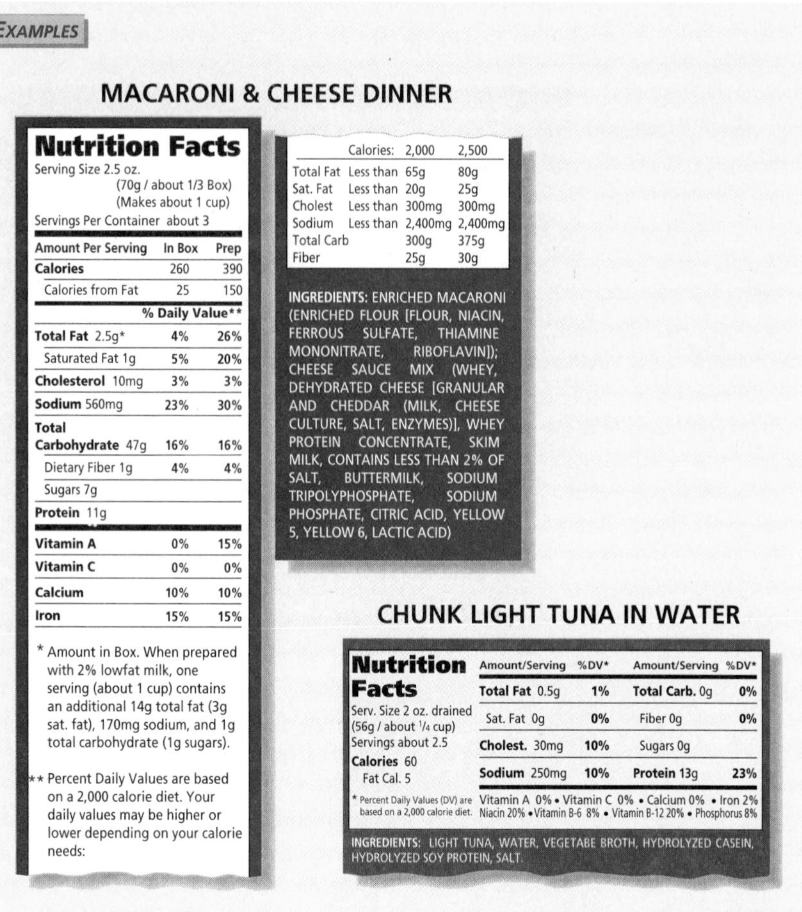

Examples

MACARONI & CHEESE DINNER

Nutrition Facts

Serving Size 2.5 oz.
(70g / about 1/3 Box)
(Makes about 1 cup)
Servings Per Container about 3

Amount Per Serving	In Box	Prep
Calories	260	390
Calories from Fat	25	150
	% Daily Value**	
Total Fat 2.5g*	4%	26%
Saturated Fat 1g	5%	20%
Cholesterol 10mg	3%	3%
Sodium 560mg	23%	30%
Total Carbohydrate 47g	16%	16%
Dietary Fiber 1g	4%	4%
Sugars 7g		
Protein 11g		
Vitamin A	0%	15%
Vitamin C	0%	0%
Calcium	10%	10%
Iron	15%	15%

* Amount in Box. When prepared with 2% lowfat milk, one serving (about 1 cup) contains an additional 14g total fat (3g sat. fat), 170mg sodium, and 1g total carbohydrate (1g sugars).

** Percent Daily Values are based on a 2,000 calorie diet. Your daily values may be higher or lower depending on your calorie needs:

	Calories:	2,000	2,500
Total Fat	Less than	65g	80g
Sat. Fat	Less than	20g	25g
Cholest	Less than	300mg	300mg
Sodium	Less than	2,400mg	2,400mg
Total Carb		300g	375g
Fiber		25g	30g

INGREDIENTS: ENRICHED MACARONI (ENRICHED FLOUR [FLOUR, NIACIN, FERROUS SULFATE, THIAMINE MONONITRATE, RIBOFLAVIN]); CHEESE SAUCE MIX (WHEY, DEHYDRATED CHEESE [GRANULAR AND CHEDDAR (MILK, CHEESE CULTURE, SALT, ENZYMES)], WHEY PROTEIN CONCENTRATE, SKIM MILK, CONTAINS LESS THAN 2% OF SALT, BUTTERMILK, SODIUM TRIPOLYPHOSPHATE, SODIUM PHOSPHATE, CITRIC ACID, YELLOW 5, YELLOW 6, LACTIC ACID)

CHUNK LIGHT TUNA IN WATER

Nutrition Facts

Serv. Size 2 oz. drained (56g / about ¼ cup)
Servings about 2.5
Calories 60
Fat Cal. 5

Amount/Serving	%DV*	Amount/Serving	%DV*
Total Fat 0.5g	1%	**Total Carb.** 0g	0%
Sat. Fat 0g	0%	Fiber 0g	0%
Cholest. 30mg	10%	Sugars 0g	
Sodium 250mg	10%	**Protein** 13g	23%

* Percent Daily Values (DV) are based on a 2,000 calorie diet.

Vitamin A 0% • Vitamin C 0% • Calcium 0% • Iron 2%
Niacin 20% • Vitamin B-6 8% • Vitamin B-12 20% • Phosphorus 8%

INGREDIENTS: LIGHT TUNA, WATER, VEGETABE BROTH, HYDROLYZED CASEIN, HYDROLYZED SOY PROTEIN, SALT.

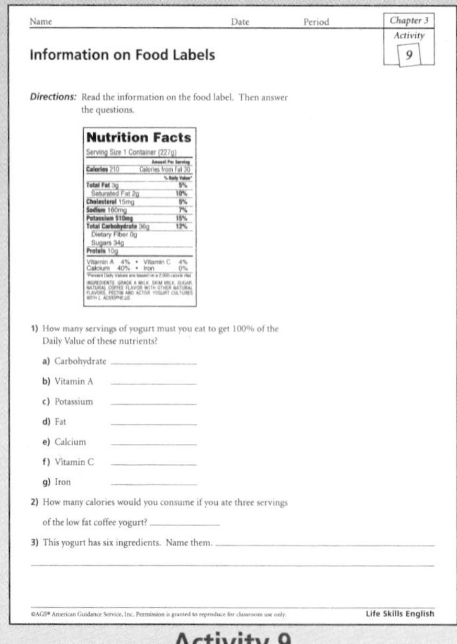

Name Date Period *Chapter 3 Activity* 9

Information on Food Labels

Directions: Read the information on the food label. Then answer the questions.

Nutrition Facts

Serving Size 1 Container (227g)

	Amount Per Serving
Calories 210	Calories from Fat 30
	% Daily Value*
Total Fat 3g	5%
Saturated Fat 2g	10%
Cholesterol 15mg	5%
Sodium 160mg	7%
Potassium 510mg	15%
Total Carbohydrate 36g	12%
Dietary Fiber 0g	
Sugars 34g	
Protein 10g	

Vitamin A 4% • Vitamin C 4%
Calcium 40% • Iron 0%

1) How many servings of yogurt must you eat to get 100% of the Daily Value of these nutrients?

a) Carbohydrate ________

b) Vitamin A ________

c) Potassium ________

d) Fat ________

e) Calcium ________

f) Vitamin C ________

g) Iron ________

2) How many calories would you consume if you ate three servings of the low fat coffee yogurt? ________

3) This yogurt has six ingredients. Name them. ________

 Life Skills English

Activity 9

Using What You Have Learned

1. Look up these words in a dictionary: *sodium phosphate, artificial citric acid, lactic acid, whey.*
2. Look up any other words from the labels you do not know. If one of the words is not in your dictionary, how could you find out what it means?
3. How would you define "processed" foods? How do processed foods differ from natural foods?
4. Which course in school would help people understand more about processed and natural foods?

Activity H Study the two food labels on page 84. Write the answers to the following questions on your paper.

1) What is the main ingredient in the macaroni?

2) What is the main ingredient in the cheese sauce mix?

3) What is the main ingredient in the can of tuna fish?

4) Which food has more calories per serving?

5) What does the abbreviation *DV* mean?

6) Which food has been enriched?

7) How many servings are in one can of tuna fish?

8) How many servings are in the macaroni and cheese?

9) Which food has the most protein?

10) Which food has the most fat?

11) What happens to the fat content when 2% milk is used to prepare the macaroni and cheese?

12) What percentage of the daily value of vitamin B-12 would you get from a serving of the tuna fish?

Name Date Period

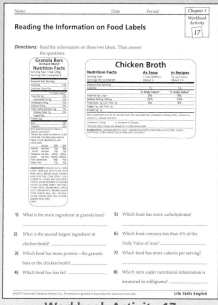

Chapter 3 Workbook Activity 17

Reading the Information on Food Labels

Directions: Read the information on these two labels. Then answer the questions.

Granola Bars
Orchard Blend
Nutrition Facts

Chicken Broth
Nutrition Facts

1) What is the main ingredient in granola bars? ____________

2) What is the second largest ingredient in chicken broth? ____________

3) Which food has more protein—the granola bars or the chicken broth? ____________

4) Which food has less fat? ____________

5) Which food has more carbohydrates? ____________

6) Which food contains less than 4% of the Daily Value of iron? ____________

7) Which food has more calories per serving? ____________

8) Which item under nutritional information is measured in milligrams? ____________

 Life Skills English

Workbook Activity 17

Reading Vocabulary

define (7)	percentage
differ (6)	processed (6)
enrich (8)	protein

■ Presenting Activity H

Before having students complete Activity H, distribute copies of food labels cut from packaged foods to small groups of students. Have each group discuss the ingredients and nutritional values for each food, based on the information in the labels.

Activity H Answers

1) enriched macaroni **2)** whey **3)** light tuna **4)** macaroni and cheese **5)** Daily Value **6)** macaroni and cheese **7)** about 2.5 **8)** about 3 **9)** tuna **10)** macaroni and cheese **11)** With 2% milk, one serving contains an additional 14g total fat. **12)** 20%

Using What You Have Learned

Students can provide oral or written responses to the questions in this activity.

Answers

1) Dictionary definitions will vary. **2)** Answers will vary. Students might look in a cookbook or food-related dictionary to find words. **3)** A processed food has been cooked, frozen, or packaged in some way. Natural foods have no artificial additives but still may be packaged and processed in some way. **4)** Life Management, Home Economics, Chemistry

Reading Vocabulary

optional slaw
screwtop

Part A Answers

1) 18 grams 2) 2 ounces
3) 1 pint 4) 450 degrees Fahrenheit
5) $\frac{1}{2}$ package 6) 2 tablespoons
7) $\frac{1}{2}$ teaspoon 8) Daily Value
9) one pound

Part B Answers

Ingredients needed: 1 head of purple cabbage, 3 large carrots, olive oil, lemon or lime, ground black pepper, water, onion powder, salt, brown sugar, liquid hot sauce (optional)

Utensils: measuring cups and spoons, juicer, paring knife, grater, large bowl, 2 cup jar with lid, plastic wrap or other cover for bowl, spoon (for tossing)

1) Gather equipment and ingredients. 2) Peel carrots; then shred cabbage and carrots into a large bowl. 3) Measure and combine in jar: olive oil, lemon (lime) juice, liquid hot sauce, pepper, water, onion powder, salt, and brown sugar. 4) Cover and shake mixture in jar. 5) Pour liquid mixture over vegetables. 6) Toss, cover, and set aside until serving. 7) Toss again before serving.

Part C Answers

1) sauté 2) meat that isn't tender
3) chop it up in small pieces

Lesson 4 Review

Part A Write out the meaning of each of these terms on your paper.

1) 18 g	4) 450°F	7) $\frac{1}{2}$ tsp.
2) 2 oz.	5) $\frac{1}{2}$ pkg.	8) DV
3) 1 pt.	6) 2 T.	9) one lb.

Part B On your paper, explain step-by-step what you would do to prepare the recipe below. Be sure to include a list of all the ingredients and utensils you will need.

Mexican Cole Slaw

Shred finely one head purple cabbage and three large peeled carrots into large bowl. Set aside. In a 2-cup screwtop jar combine:

2/3 c. olive oil	1/3 c. water
juice of one lemon or lime	2 tsp. onion powder
2 tsp. ground black pepper	1 tsp. salt or to taste
2 T. liquid hot sauce (optional)	1/4 c. brown sugar

Shake together in jar until well mixed. Pour liquid over cabbage and carrots. Toss well. Cover and set aside until serving time. Toss lightly before serving.

Part C Write the word or words on your paper that best complete each sentence.

1) To cook food quickly in a small amount of fat, ______ it.
   a) broil b) sauté c) simmer
2) A cook usually braises ______ .
   a) a T-bone steak b) meat that isn't tender c) frozen vegetables
3) To *mince* an onion, ______ .
   a) chop it up in small pieces b) cook it until it is tender c) pull off the skin

Name ______ Date ______ Period ______ Chapter 3 Activity 10

Finding Information in Reference Books

Directions: Given below is a list of reference books. Which book or books would you use to find the answers to these questions? Write your answers on the lines provided.

Roget's Thesaurus of Words and Phrases
The World Almanac and Book of Facts
Hammond Contemporary World Atlas
The Telephone Book
Webster's New World Dictionary
Julia Child's Home Cooking Cookbook
The Handyman's Encyclopedia
The World Book Encyclopedia

1) What time does The Golden Star Restaurant close? ______
2) What is the meaning of "southpaw"? ______
3) How many people were born in Pennsylvania in 1969? ______
4) What is a synonym for "broken"? ______
5) How do you make chocolate chip cookies? ______
6) What happened when John F. Kennedy was president? ______
7) How can I install a new kitchen sink? ______
8) Where is Afghanistan located? ______
9) Where can I find an automobile mechanic? ______
10) Who was Susan B. Anthony? ______

 Life Skills English

Activity 10

Lesson 5 Using Information in How-To Books

Do It Yourself With How-To Books

How-to books
Reference books that provide detailed instructions for how to complete specific tasks.

How-to books tell you how to do something. You can probably find a how-to book to help you do anything you want to do. Some subjects of how-to books include:

All About Stamp Collecting	Be Your Own Lawyer
Introduction to the Guitar	How to Design and Sew Your Own Clothing
How to Make a Speech	Getting Started in Computing
Pay Fewer Taxes—Legally!	Improve Your Vocabulary
Teach Yourself to Type	Easy Home Repairs

Internet
The largest computer network in the world. It allows people from all over the world to use computers to interact with one another and to get information on a wide variety of topics.

Many how-to books are available on CD-ROM. You can also find how-to information on the **Internet.** The Internet is a large computer network. The Internet allows people from all over the world to use their computers to get information on a wide variety of topics. How-to information is also available on videocassettes that you can get at the library or a video store.

Activity A Decide which of the following books probably tell you how to do something. Write their titles on your paper.

1) *Setting Up a Tropical Fish Tank*

2) *Do-It-Yourself Home Decorating*

3) *Building a Model Ship*

4) *The Red Pony*

5) *How to Care for Your Automobile*

6) *Two Dozen Wooden Toys to Make for Children*

7) *The History of the World*

8) *Complete Guide to Flower Gardening*

Lesson at a Glance

Chapter 3 Lesson 5

Overview This lesson presents how-to information in print and other media. It also explains how to follow directions in how-to books.

Objectives

- To interpret information in a sample set of instructions.
- To follow instructions.

Student Pages 87–90

Reading Vocabulary

available (6)	legally
how-to books	network
interact	variety (6)
Internet	videocassette
lawyer (5)	vocabulary (7)

Teaching Suggestions

- **Introducing the Lesson** Ask students if they ever used a how-to book to build something, do a craft project, or fix something. Then encourage students who are familiar with using the Internet to explain how they would use the on-line service to find out how to build a birdhouse, for example.

- **Reviewing Skills** Review how to follow directions in a recipe.

- **Presenting Activity A** Do Activity A as an oral activity. Read and discuss each title and the probable content of that book.

Activity A Answers
1) Setting Up a Tropical Fish Tank 2) Do-It-Yourself Home Decorating 3) Building a Model Ship 4) How to Care for Your Automobile 5) Two Dozen Wooden Toys to Make for Children 6) Complete Guide to Flower Gardening

Reading Vocabulary

appropriate (6)
bind (5)
glue (5)
photograph (6)
punch (5)
relative (5)
task (5)
theme (6)
yarn (5)

Global Connection

Birthday calendars are a Dutch tradition that have grown in popularity in the United States in recent years. The piñata, a traditional sight at birthday parties of Mexican children, has also become a familiar sight in the United States. Discuss the birthday and holiday traditions of other countries and cultures. Have students research how traditions and objects associated with these cultural celebrations have been assimilated into the American culture. Some students may wish to use a how-to book to create one of these objects, such as a piñata.

Following Directions

A how-to book provides step-by-step instructions that explain how to do or make something. Any materials that you will need to complete the task are listed. Photographs or drawings of the finished product are often shown.

EXAMPLE

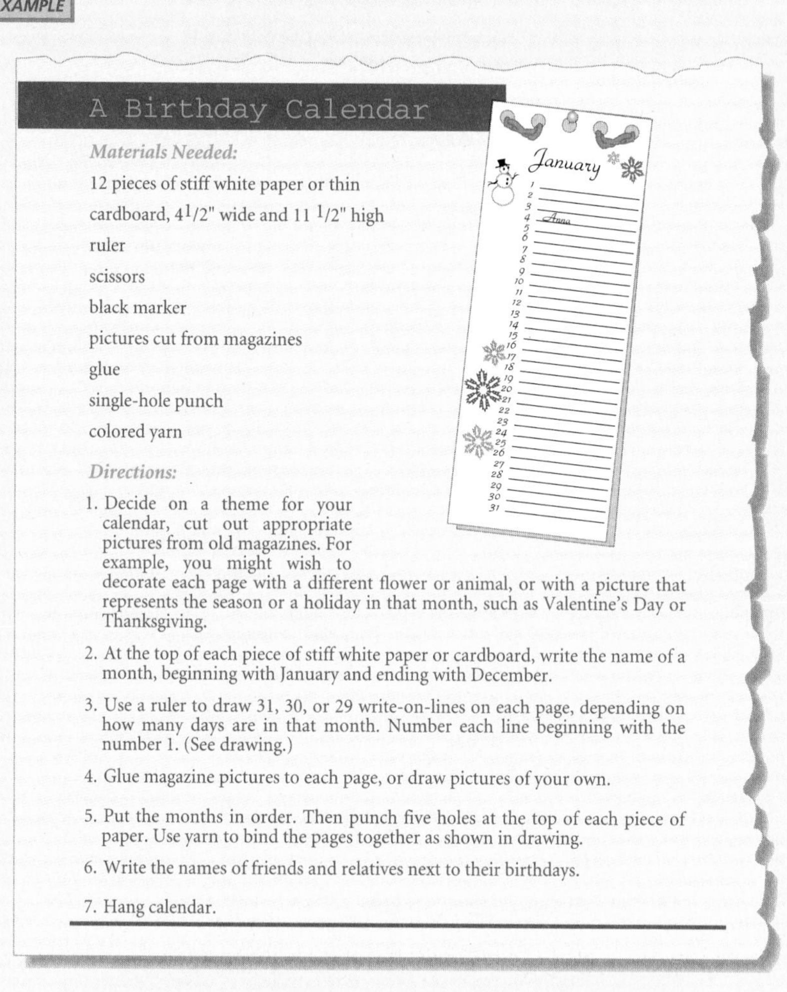

A Birthday Calendar

Materials Needed:

12 pieces of stiff white paper or thin cardboard, 4 1/2" wide and 11 1/2" high
ruler
scissors
black marker
pictures cut from magazines
glue
single-hole punch
colored yarn

Directions:

1. Decide on a theme for your calendar, cut out appropriate pictures from old magazines. For example, you might wish to decorate each page with a different flower or animal, or with a picture that represents the season or a holiday in that month, such as Valentine's Day or Thanksgiving.
2. At the top of each piece of stiff white paper or cardboard, write the name of a month, beginning with January and ending with December.
3. Use a ruler to draw 31, 30, or 29 write-on-lines on each page, depending on how many days are in that month. Number each line beginning with the number 1. (See drawing.)
4. Glue magazine pictures to each page, or draw pictures of your own.
5. Put the months in order. Then punch five holes at the top of each piece of paper. Use yarn to bind the pages together as shown in drawing.
6. Write the names of friends and relatives next to their birthdays.
7. Hang calendar.

USING WHAT YOU HAVE LEARNED

Design and make your own Birthday Calendar. Follow the directions on page 88.

Activity B Use the directions on page 88 to answer these questions. Write your answers on your paper.

1) What materials do you need to make the calendar?
2) What are the different tools that you will need?
3) What will you need the tools for?
4) How many pieces of paper do you need? Why?
5) Why should you decide on a theme before beginning?
6) What are the lines on each page for?
7) What is the purpose of the holes at the top of each page?

In some how-to books, the directions are written in paragraph form rather than listed step-by-step. The materials you will need to complete a project are included within the directions.

Activity C Use these directions to answer the questions. Write your answers on your paper.

Setting Up an Aquarium

People have set up aquariums for thousands of years. The first aquarium would be as old as the ancient pyramids. In America, raising tropical fish is one of the most popular hobbies.

You will need a fish tank, some lights, a heater and thermometer, a pump, and a filter. You will need some glass wool and charcoal for the filter. On the bottom, you will put some gravel. For cleaning the tank, get an algae scraper and a dip tube. A nylon fish net will be useful. Try some guppies for your first fish. They are very hardy.

1) What do the directions tell you how to do?
2) What materials will you need to buy or borrow to complete this project?
3) What instructions must you follow to complete this project? List the steps in order.

Activity D List three things you would like to learn how to make or do. Take your list to the library and try to find at least one how-to book for each project.

USING WHAT YOU HAVE LEARNED

Have students share their finished calendars with the class.

Reading Vocabulary

algae
filter (7)
gravel (5)
guppies
hardy (7)
nylon (6)
pyramid (7)
scraper
thermometer (6)

■ Presenting Activity B

Discuss the importance of reading the directions completely before trying to follow them. How can illustrations help?

Activity B Answers

1) 12 pieces of paper or cardboard; ruler; marker; magazine pictures; glue; hole punch; yarn; [also, tack or a nail for hanging calendar] **2)** ruler, hole punch, scissors, marker **3)** You will need the ruler to measure the pages and to draw lines; the scissors to cut out pictures and the pages; the hole punch to make holes on top of pages; the marker to write months, draw lines, and write names. **4)** You need 12 because there are 12 months. **5)** It will help you choose pictures. **6)** They are for dates and names of people with birthdays on that date. **7)** The two holes on each side are for binding the calendar; the middle one is for hanging it.

■ Presenting Activity C

Discuss which type of instructions are easier for students to follow—step-by-step or paragraph form.

Activity C Answers

1) set up aquarium **2)** tank, lights, heater, thermometer, pump, filter, glass wool and charcoal, gravel, algae scraper, dip tube, nylon fish net, guppies or other fish **3)** (1) Gather materials. (2) Assemble the tank and put gravel on bottom. (3) Fill the tank and put in fish.

■ Presenting Activity D

Have students first discuss their ideas with partners.

Activity D Answers

Answers will vary.

Reading Vocabulary

cement (5) roughen
project (5) sandpaper

Part A Answers

Wording of answers may vary. Possible responses are given.

1) It explains how to hang a mirror on a door. **2)** You will need: sandpaper, rubber cement, mirror, a tool to spread and smooth rubber cement, and a ruler or tape measure. **3)** If necessary, you must first roughen the door with sandpaper. Probably, the next thing you should do is measure $\frac{1}{2}$ inch from each of the four door edges. Next, you must spread rubber cement on the back of the mirror. Finally, you press the mirror on the door and allow 24 hours to set.

Part B Answers

Answers will vary depending on the project students choose.

Learning Styles

Auditory/Verbal

Invite the students to think of things they do that require following a series of steps: using the Internet, baking bread, making a pizza, taking an order at a fast-food restaurant, sewing an article of clothing, making a bird-house, training a dog, and so on. Ask each student to prepare a three-minute talk on how to do something. Afterward, provide time for the students' presentations. Conclude by having the students write their how-to presentation in numbered steps. Collect their papers and use them to make a class "how-to" booklet.

Lesson 5 Review

Part A Read the paragraph below. Then write on your paper answers to the questions that follow.

Hanging a Mirror on a Door

If the door is very smooth, roughen it with sandpaper. Spread rubber cement on the back of the mirror. Put it about $\frac{1}{2}$ inch from the 4 edges. Press the mirror firmly on the door. Allow 24 hours for the cement to set.

1) What does the paragraph tell you how to do?
2) What materials will you need to complete this project?
3) What instructions must you follow to complete this project? List the steps in order.

Part B Follow the instructions below. Write your answers on your paper.

1) Think of a project you have done in the past.
2) Make a drawing of the completed project.
3) Write a list of the materials you used.
4) Write the directions you followed in order.

90 Chapter 3 Some Everyday References

Lesson 6 Magazines for Facts and Fun

Magazine
A paperback publication with stories and articles on a variety of topics by different writers.

Periodical
A magazine published at regular intervals, such as daily, weekly, or monthly.

Interval
The space of time between events.

A **magazine** is a paperback publication. It has stories and articles by several writers. It usually has illustrations and advertisements. **Periodical** is another name for a magazine. A periodical comes out at regular **intervals**, such as daily, weekly, or monthly. An interval is a space of time between events. Some magazines are on CD-ROM. Some are also available through on-line computer services, including the Internet.

Kinds of Magazines

There are hundreds of different kinds of magazines to choose from. Most magazines have stories and articles for people with special interests.

News and Business
- *Time*
- *Newsweek*
- *U.S. News and World Report*

Entertainment
- *TV Guide*
- *Soap Opera Digest*
- *Rolling Stone*
- *Stereo Review*
- *People*

Magazines for Women
- *Martha Stewart Living*
- *Redbook*
- *Good Housekeeping*
- *Ladies' Home Journal*

Magazines for Men
- *Men's Health*
- *Men's Fitness*
- *Men's Journal*
- *Men Talk*

Sports
- *Sports Illustrated*
- *Sport*
- *Golf Digest*
- *World Tennis*
- *Outdoor Life*
- *Field and Stream*
- *Triathlete*

Hobbies and Special Interests
- *Hot Rod*
- *Apartment Life*
- *Compute*
- *Computer User*
- *Byte*
- *PC Magazine*
- *Scouting*
- *Modern Photography*
- *National Geographic*
- *Quilting Today*
- *Astronomy*

Lesson at a Glance

Chapter 3 Lesson 6

Overview This lesson describes different types of magazines and explains how to subscribe to them and find information in them. It also introduces *The Readers' Guide to Periodical Literature.*

Objective
- To understand concepts related to magazines.

Student Pages 91–97

Teacher's Resource Library
- Activities 11–12
- Workbook Activities 18–20

Reading Vocabulary

advertisement (6)
daily (10)
entertainment (5)
illustration (6)
intervals (5)
magazine (4)
periodical (8)

Teaching Suggestions

Introducing the Lesson
After discussing the information in the text, ask students to name their favorite magazines and explain the kinds of articles the magazine contains and why they enjoy these magazines.

Reviewing Skills
Review how to use a table of contents.

Reading Vocabulary

condensed (5)	refresh (8)
digest (7)	summary (8)
newsstand	title (5)
original (5)	version (7)

Presenting Activity A

Before students complete Activity A, write the subject heads from page 91 on the board and have students name from memory magazines that fit each category.

Activity A Answers

Answers will vary.

Digest

A magazine that contains summaries or condensed articles from other magazines.

Condensed

A shorter version of an article but with the same main idea.

Digests

Most people don't have time to read a lot of magazines. That is why digests are so popular. A **digest** is a periodical that has summaries of articles from other magazines. *Reader's Digest* is one of the most widely read magazines in the world. It was first published in 1922.

Many digests contain **condensed** articles from other publications. An article that is condensed is shortened but keeps the main ideas.

Below are some examples of popular digests. They have condensed articles from other publications, summaries of other publications, or very short original articles.

EXAMPLE *Golf Digest* *Soap Opera Digest*
Book Digest *Reader's Digest*

Activity A Follow the directions below. Write your answers on your paper.

1) Write a list of all the magazines that you have read or know about. Visit the library or a newsstand to refresh your memory.

2) Beside each title, write the general subject of the magazine. Use the bold subject heads on page 91 as a guide.

3) Put a circle around the magazines you subscribe to or read regularly.

4) Share your list with your class.

5) Bring old issues of magazines to class to share if possible.

Publication Cycles

Publish
To print and distribute magazines, books, newspapers, or other reading materials.

Cycle
The period of time between events, such as the publishing of a magazine.

To **publish** means to print and distribute magazines, books, newspapers, or other materials. Most magazines are published monthly. A few magazines are published weekly. Some are published less often. This is referred to as the publication **cycle**. A cycle is the period of time needed for a certain event to repeat itself.

Activity B Match each numbered word on the left with its correct meaning on the right. Write each word and its meaning on your paper. Use a dictionary to help you.

1) daily	a) twice a month
2) weekly	b) twice a year
3) monthly	c) every day
4) annually	d) every other year
5) bimonthly	e) every other month
6) semimonthly	f) once a month
7) biannually	g) once a week
8) semiannually	h) once a year

Activity C Write the answers to these questions on your paper. You may have to visit a library or newsstand to answer some of these questions.

1) Name a magazine that is published weekly.

2) Name a magazine that is published monthly.

3) What type of publication appears daily?

4) If a book is published once, is it a periodical?

5) Is an almanac a periodical? Explain why or why not.

6) Is an encyclopedia a periodical? Explain why or why not.

Reading Vocabulary

cycle (6) distribute (6) **publish (6)** subscribe (7)

(Activity A Answers, continued)
Answers will vary.

■ Presenting Activity B

Discuss other events that occur in cycles, such as elections, Olympic Games, and distribution of grades. List each event on the board and its cycle. After completing Activity B, have students match the cycles listed on the board with the words in the first column. If there is no match, suggest that students look in a dictionary to see if there is a word for that cycle.

Activity B Answers

1) daily—every day **2)** weekly—once a week **3)** monthly—once a month **4)** annually—once a year **5)** bimonthly—every other month **6)** semimonthly—twice a month **7)** biannually—every other year **8)** semiannually—twice a year

■ Presenting Activity C

Point out to students that they can usually tell how often a magazine is published by looking at its cover. If, for example, the date on the cover says *Jan./Feb. 1997,* it's a bimonthly publication; if it says *Spring 1997,* it's a quarterly; and so on.

Activity C Answers

1–2) Answers will vary.
3) newspaper **4)** No
5) Yes. Almanacs are yearly publications. **6)** No. Although new editions are published periodically, the information in them is updated rather than new or different.

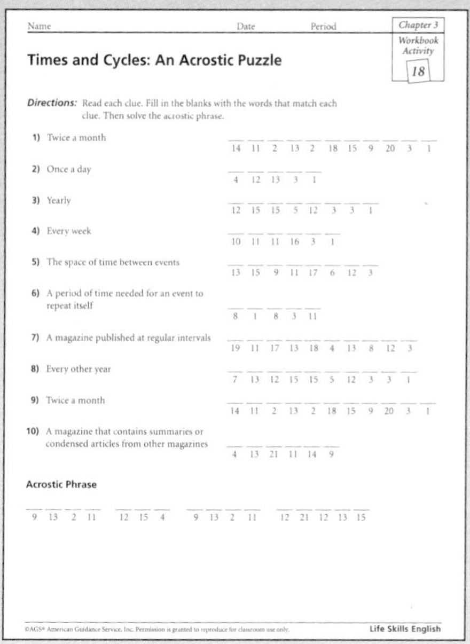

Name Date Period *Chapter 3 Workbook Activity 18*

Times and Cycles: An Acrostic Puzzle

Directions: Read each clue. Fill in the blanks with the words that match each clue. Then solve the acrostic phrase.

1) Twice a month ___ ___ ___ ___ ___ ___ ___ ___ ___ ___ ___ (14 11 2 13 2 18 15 9 20 3 1)

2) Once a day ___ ___ ___ ___ ___ (4 12 13 3 1)

3) Yearly ___ ___ ___ ___ ___ ___ ___ ___ (12 15 15 5 12 3 3 1)

4) Every week ___ ___ ___ ___ ___ ___ (10 11 11 16 3 1)

5) The space of time between events ___ ___ ___ ___ ___ ___ ___ ___ (13 15 9 11 17 6 12 3)

6) A period of time needed for an event to repeat itself ___ ___ ___ ___ ___ (8 1 8 3 11)

7) A magazine published at regular intervals ___ ___ ___ ___ ___ ___ ___ ___ ___ ___ (19 11 17 13 18 4 13 8 12 3)

8) Every other year ___ ___ ___ ___ ___ ___ ___ ___ ___ ___ (7 13 12 15 15 5 12 3 3 1)

9) Twice a month ___ ___ ___ ___ ___ ___ ___ ___ ___ ___ ___ (14 11 2 13 2 18 15 9 20 3 1)

10) A magazine that contains summaries or condensed articles from other magazines ___ ___ ___ ___ ___ ___ (4 13 21 11 14 9)

Acrostic Phrase

___ ___ ___ ___ (9 13 2 11) ___ ___ ___ (12 15 4) ___ ___ ___ ___ (9 13 2 11) ___ ___ ___ ___ ___ (12 21 12 13 15)

 Life Skills English

Workbook Activity 18

Reading Vocabulary

advertising (6)
payment (7)
rate (6)
recommend (6)
subscription (7)

■ Presenting Activity D

Copy or create samples of different magazine subscription order forms and distribute them to small groups of students. Have each group discuss the similarities and differences among the forms and practice filling them in.

Activity D Answers

1) $1.25 **2)** once a month/monthly **3)** It cost less by subscription. **4)** You can probably read it at the library or perhaps borrow it from a friend.

Using What You Have Learned

Provide time for students to share what they learn about magazines with their classmates.

Subscription
A regular order for a magazine, newspaper, or other publication.

Using What You Have Learned

Go to a library or a newsstand. Find an interesting magazine. Read it. Tell your class about the magazine. If possible, bring the magazine to class to show the others. Here are some questions to think about.

1. How much does it cost? How often is it published?
2. Who is this magazine for? Who would be interested in the articles?
3. How many pages does it have? How much of the magazine is advertising?
4. What are some of its special departments or regular features?
5. Would you recommend this magazine to others?

How to Get a Magazine

You can get a magazine in several ways:

- You can read one at the library.
- You can buy one at a newsstand.
- You can subscribe to one.

When you subscribe to a magazine, you fill out an order form to have the magazine sent to you by mail. You may enclose the payment for the **subscription** with the order form, or you may receive a bill later. The subscription rate is often lower than the newsstand rate.

Here is an example of a subscription order form.

Sports Car Digest

One-year subscription (12 issues): $15.00
Two-year subscription (24 issures): $27.00

SAVE 30% OVER THE NEWSSTAND RATE!

☐ Payment enclosed. ☑ Bill me later.

Name Chris Williams
Address 31 E. Ralston Place
City/State/Zip Wilton, Delaware 19999
Signature Chris Williams

Activity D Use the order form above to answer these questions. Write your answers on your paper.

1) How much does each issue of the *Sports Car Digest* cost with a one-year subscription?

2) How often is this magazine published?

3) Does the magazine cost less at the newsstand or by subscription?

4) Where might you get this magazine to read at no cost?

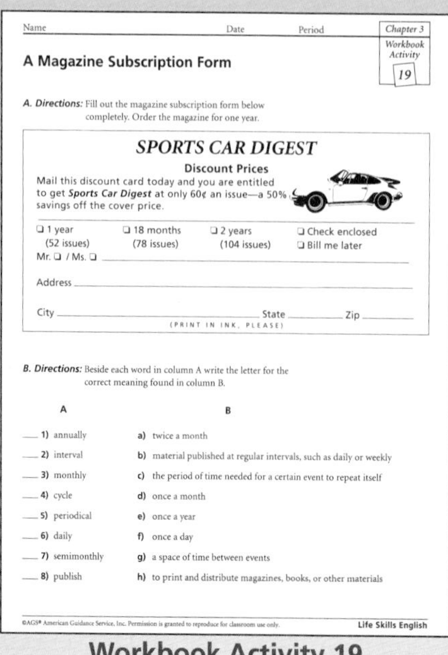

Name Date Period *Chapter 3 Workbook Activity 19*

A Magazine Subscription Form

A. Directions: Fill out the magazine subscription form below completely. Order the magazine for one year.

SPORTS CAR DIGEST

Discount Prices

Mail this discount card today and you are entitled to get ***Sports Car Digest*** at only 60¢ an issue—a 50% savings off the cover price.

❑ 1 year (52 issues) ❑ 18 months (78 issues) ❑ 2 years (104 issues) ❑ Check enclosed ❑ Bill me later

Mr. ❑ / Ms. ❑ ____

Address ____

City ____ State ____ Zip ____

(PRINT IN INK, PLEASE)

B. Directions: Beside each word in column A write the letter for the correct meaning found in column B.

A	B
___ **1)** annually	**a)** twice a month
___ **2)** interval	**b)** material published at regular intervals, such as daily or weekly
___ **3)** monthly	**c)** the period of time needed for a certain event to repeat itself
___ **4)** cycle	**d)** once a month
___ **5)** periodical	**e)** once a year
___ **6)** daily	**f)** once a day
___ **7)** semimonthly	**g)** a space of time between events
___ **8)** publish	**h)** to print and distribute magazines, books, or other materials

 Life Skills English

Workbook Activity 19

Finding Articles in Magazines

To learn what kinds of articles are in a magazine, look in the magazine's table of contents. The table of contents is usually near the front of the magazine. In some magazines, several pages of advertisements may come before the table of contents. In other magazines, the table of contents may appear on the cover as in the sample cover below.

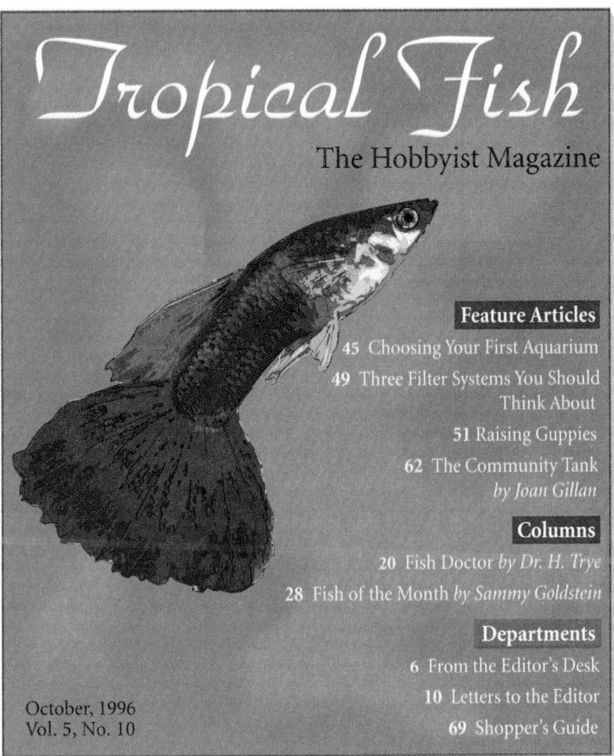

Tropical Fish
The Hobbyist Magazine
Feature Articles
45 Choosing Your First Aquarium
49 Three Filter Systems You Should Think About
51 Raising Guppies
62 The Community Tank by Joan Gillan
Columns
20 Fish Doctor by Dr. H. Trye
28 Fish of the Month by Sammy Goldstein
Departments
6 From the Editor's Desk
10 Letters to the Editor
69 Shopper's Guide
October, 1996
Vol. 5, No. 10

Reading Vocabulary

contents

Application

At Home
Encourage students to ask family members and friends about the magazines they like to read and those they do not. Have them consider what a person's magazine likes and dislikes say about the interests of that person.

Some Everyday References *Chapter 3* **95**

Reading Vocabulary
abbreviate (8)
crisis (6)
The Readers' Guide to Periodical Literature

■ Presenting Activity E
Display several magazine covers for students to examine. Ask students to tell what they learn about each magazine from its cover. Then have students complete Activity E on their own or with partners.

Activity E Answers
1) tropical fish 2) people who have tropical fish; people interested in tropical fish as a hobby 3) October, 1996 4) four 5) page 10 6) two

■ Presenting Activity F
Do Activity F together as a class. If possible, provide an opportunity for the class to visit the library to use *The Readers' Guide.* Give each student or pairs of students a topic to look up.

Activity F Answers
1) Auto Week 2) "Three Small Cars" and "Exploring the Andes" 3) John Hernandez 4) Business Reports, "New from Japan"

Activity E Use the sample magazine cover on page 95 to answer these questions. Write your answers on your paper.

1) What is the theme of this magazine?
2) Who is likely to read this magazine?
3) When was this issue of the magazine published?
4) How many feature articles are in this issue?
5) On what page do the letters to the editor begin?
6) If you had a one-year subscription to this magazine, how many more issues would you expect to get in 1996?

The Readers' Guide to Periodical Literature
A magazine found in the library that lists articles from many other magazines.

You can use ***The Readers' Guide to Periodical Literature*** to find a specific magazine article. *The Readers' Guide* is a periodical. You can find it in the library. It lists articles from many magazines. The articles are listed by subject, title, and author. Here are some sample entries from *The Readers' Guide.*

COMPACT CARS
Choosing a new car. Y. Jones. Auto Week 15:56-61 Ap 8 '98
New from Japan K.L. Sukato. Business Reports 17:62 Mr '99
Three small cars. il New Car Digest 5:89-93 Mr '97
COMPTON, Howard E.
Exploring the Andes. il Explorers Magazine 81:126-134+ Ap '96
CRISIS in the family. John Hernandez. Short Story Digest 8:23-31 Mr '99

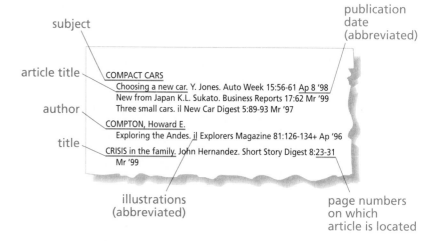

Activity F Use the sample from *The Readers' Guide* to answer these questions. Write your answers on your paper.

1) Which magazine is published weekly?
2) Which articles have pictures?
3) Who wrote the article "Crisis in the Family"?
4) Which magazine has an article by K. L. Sukato? What is the title of the article?

Lesson 6 Review

Lesson Review Write your answers to the following questions on your paper.

1) What is a periodical?
2) What are some different kinds of magazines? List at least three kinds and give one title for each kind. If necessary, look at the list on page 91.
3) Why might someone want to read a condensed version of an original article?
4) Give three examples of a publication cycle.
5) What is the most common interval for magazine publication?
6) Which magazine is published more often—a bimonthly or a semimonthly?
7) Which magazine is published more often—a semiannual or a biannual?
8) Where can you read magazines at no cost?
9) Which is usually less expensive—buying a magazine at a newsstand or having a subscription?
10) Is it possible that you would find an article from *Woman's Day* in *The Reader's Digest?*
11) Which magazine can help you locate an article—*The Reader's Digest* or *The Readers' Guide?*

Lesson Review Answers

Some answers will vary. Possible responses are given.

1) A periodical is a magazine or newspaper that is published at regular intervals. **2)** News and Business: *Time;* Entertainment: *TV Guide;* Magazines for Women: *Redbook* **3)** They may be interested in the topic but might not have time to read the whole article. **4)** Three examples are: annually, bimonthly, weekly. **5)** Most magazines are published on a monthly basis. **6)** A semimonthly magazine is published more often—twice a month. **7)** A semiannual magazine is published more often—twice a year. **8)** You can read magazines for free at the library. **9)** A subscription usually costs less. **10)** Yes. The article will probably be condensed. **11)** *The Readers' Guide* can help you find an article.

Name ____ Date ____ Period ____ *Chapter 3 Activity 11*

Building Vocabulary

Directions: Match the words in the first column with the meanings in the second column. Write the correct letters on the lines provided. Use a dictionary to check your answers.

	Words	Meanings
____	**1)** article	**A)** a list of books on a subject
____	**2)** author	**B)** picture
____	**3)** bibliography	**C)** subject
____	**4)** collection	**D)** an example
____	**5)** illustration	**E)** a piece of writing
____	**6)** reference	**F)** the exact words someone said
____	**7)** related	**G)** the person who wrote a book or article
____	**8)** sample	**H)** items gathered together
____	**9)** topic	**I)** a small fact
____	**10)** quotation	**J)** not specific
____	**11)** detail	**K)** one book in a set
____	**12)** seldom	**L)** connected together
____	**13)** system	**M)** a way of doing something
____	**14)** volume	**N)** not very often
____	**15)** general	**O)** the source of information

 Life Skills English

Activity 11

Name ____ Date ____ Period ____ *Chapter 3 Activity 12*

Reference Book Word Search

Part A: Find the names of 9 reference books in the puzzle. Words are UP, DOWN, ACROSS, BACKWARD, and DIAGONAL.

E	B	N	O	N	N	I	E	S	A	M	E
E	N	D	I	C	T	I	O	N	A	R	Y
Z	X	C	M	O	U	S	E	C	A	R	L
A	R	E	Y	K	O	O	B	K	O	O	C
M	S	M	V	C	B	O	B	T	T	I	L
C	A	N	A	M	L	A	W	W	S	S	S
P	L	G	Q	G	U	O	Y	J	E	H	Y
W	T	T	A	A	H	H	P	P	G	L	M
W	A	C	V	Z	X	Z	R	E	I	Q	W
R	S	X	Z	C	I	E	I	K	D	S	A
W	A	L	K	E	R	N	S	N	B	I	W
I	G	A	Z	E	T	T	E	E	R	P	A

Part B: Write the correct reference word beside each definition given below.

1) A book of facts and figures ____
2) A book of maps ____
3) A list of geographical place names ____
4) A set of books with facts on many subjects ____
5) A paperback publication published at regular intervals ____
6) A book of recipes ____
7) A book of facts about words ____
8) Summaries of articles from other publications ____
9) Book of instructions ____

 Life Skills English

Activity 12

Name ____ Date ____ Period ____ *Chapter 3 Workbook Activity 20*

Reference Puzzle

Directions: Read each description carefully. Write the word on the line that best fits each description. Then find each word in the puzzle below. The words go across, down, and diagonally.

1) A book of facts ____
2) A life story ____
3) Topics in alphabetical order ____
4) A numerical fact ____
5) A model of the earth ____
6) A book of maps ____
7) A list of geographical place names ____
8) A part of a circle ____
9) A set of books with facts on many subjects ____
10) A single book or one of a set of books ____
11) A periodical ____
12) Summaries of articles from other magazines ____
13) Directions for preparing food ____
14) A reference book about food ____
15) A network of lines on a map ____
16) The name of the story or book ____
17) An imaginary story ____

N	O	W	D	I	S	T	H	E	R	E	C	I	P	E
T	C	I	T	S	I	T	A	T	S	R	A	L	N	L
I	R	M	E	N	F	O	S	N	O	I	T	C	I	F
G	R	G	D	O	O	A	D	M	P	E	Y	O	P	L
C	E	E	T	A	L	M	A	N	A	C	O	C	O	M
O	X	E	E	T	T	G	V	O	L	T	E	A	I	D
O	E	O	A	T	A	B	I	O	G	R	A	P	H	Y
K	E	F	T	Z	T	H	P	H	L	L	E	I	R	C
B	R	O	I	U	N	E	T	R	Y	U	O	M	B	O
O	G	N	N	N	D	I	Z	E	W	A	M	B	L	K
O	E	E	T	I	T	L	E	A	I	L	W	E	E	X
K	D	R	A	A	P	R	D	I	G	E	S	T	A	L

 Life Skills English

Workbook Activity 20

Chapter 3 Review

The Teacher's Resource Library includes two parallel forms of the Chapter 3 Mastery Test. The difficulty level of the two forms is equivalent. You may wish to use one form as a pretest and the other form as a posttest.

Part A Answers

1) weather facts and astronomy facts **2)** to find out about the tides and the weather on a particular day or night **3)** *The World Almanac and Book of Facts* **4)** at the front **5a)** Yes **5b)** No **5c)** Yes

Part B Answers

1) Wilson and Norwood **2)** Harrogate **3)** North **4)** Eden **5)** approximately 12.5 miles

Part C Answers

1) alphabetically by topic **2)** volume **3)** a one-volume encyclopedia **4)** A **5)** guide words

Chapter 3 Review

Part A Write the answers to the following questions on your paper.

1) What is the main information in a farmer's almanac?

2) Why would a mariner read a farmer's almanac?

3) Name one general information almanac.

4) Where is the index found in most almanacs?

5) Are you likely to find the answers to the following questions in an almanac—*Yes* or *No*?

- **a)** Has Denzel Washington ever won an Academy Award?
- **b)** How do you prepare Mexican Cole Slaw?
- **c)** Who holds the record for the most home runs?

Part B Use this map to answer the questions below. Write your answers on your paper.

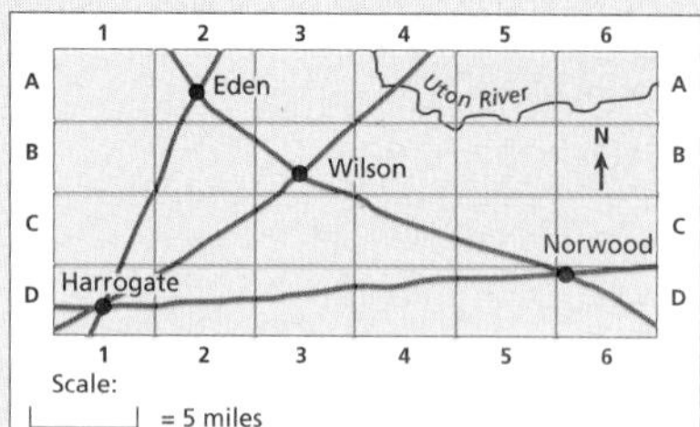

1) What two cities are southeast of Eden?

2) What city is located at D-1?

3) Is the Uton River north or south of Wilson?

4) What city is northwest of Wilson?

5) How many miles is it from Wilson to Norwood?

Part C Write the answers to the following questions on your paper.

1) How are the articles in an encyclopedia arranged?

2) What is one book in a set of encyclopedias called?

3) What is a "desk" encyclopedia?

4) What would the guide letter be on volume one of *The World Book Encyclopedia?*

5) What would you expect to find at the top of each page of an encyclopedia?

Name ______ Date ______ Period ______ *Chapter 3 Mastery Test A page 1*

Chapter 3 Mastery Test A

Part A Read the following statements. If the statement is true, write *True* on the line. If the statement is not true, write *False*.

_____ **1)** Farmer's almanacs contain information about the weather.

_____ **2)** *The World Almanac and Book of Facts* is the same as a Farmer's almanac.

_____ **3)** The index in most almanacs is found in the front.

_____ **4)** A digest is a magazine that contains summaries or condensed articles.

_____ **5)** The table of contents in most magazines is found in the back.

Part B Study this map. Then answer the questions.

1) Name the city northeast of Sole. ______

2) What are the names of the rivers? ______

3) How many miles is it from Rio to Sole? ______

4) You live in Rio. Which is the closest river? ______

5) What city is located in C-3? ______

1 2 3 4 5 6 / A B C D / Wasco River / Meran River / Evan / Sole / Rio / N / Scale = 5 miles

Part C Circle the correct answer for each question.

1) An encyclopedia is a book ______.
- **a)** or set of books of facts
- **b)** or set of books of facts about one subject
- **c)** containing weather forecasts

2) One book in a set of encyclopedias is called a ______.
- **a)** set **b)** collection **c)** volume

3) How many volumes does a desk encyclopedia generally have?
- **a)** 1 **b)** 5 **c)** 10

4) What would the guide letter be on Volume Two of the *World Book Encyclopedia*?
- **a)** A **b)** B **c)** C

5) An encyclopedia is most commonly arranged like ______.
- **a)** an almanac **b)** a dictionary **c)** a magazine

 Life Skills English

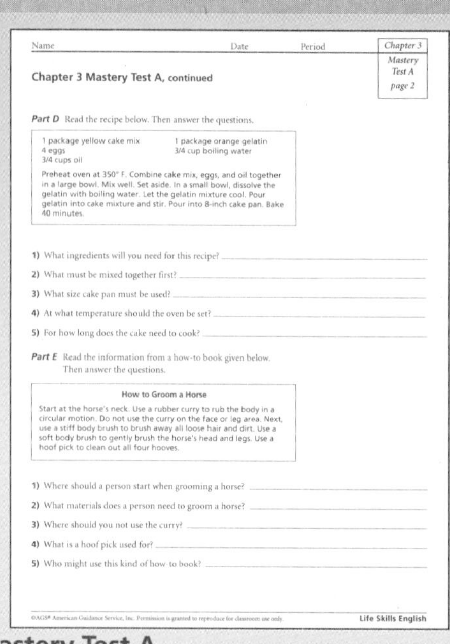

Name ______ Date ______ Period ______ *Chapter 3 Mastery Test A page 2*

Chapter 3 Mastery Test A, continued

Part D Read the recipe below. Then answer the questions.

1 package yellow cake mix
4 eggs
3/4 cups oil
1 package orange gelatin
3/4 cup boiling water

Preheat oven at 350° F. Combine cake mix, eggs, and oil together in a large bowl. Mix well. Set aside. In a small bowl, dissolve the gelatin with boiling water. Let the gelatin mixture cool. Pour gelatin into cake mixture and stir. Pour into 8-inch cake pan. Bake 40 minutes.

1) What ingredients will you need for this recipe? ______

2) What must be mixed together first? ______

3) What size cake pan must be used? ______

4) At what temperature should the oven be set? ______

5) For how long does the cake need to cook? ______

Part E Read the information from a how-to book given below. Then answer the questions.

How to Groom a Horse

Start at the horse's neck. Use a rubber curry to rub the body in a circular motion. Do not use the curry on the face or leg area. Next, use a stiff body brush to brush away all loose hair and dirt. Use a soft body brush to gently brush the horse's head and legs. Use a hoof pick to clean out all four hooves.

1) Where should a person start when grooming a horse? ______

2) What materials does a person need to groom a horse? ______

3) Where should you not use the curry? ______

4) What is a hoof pick used for? ______

5) Who might use this kind of how-to book? ______

 Life Skills English

Chapter 3 Mastery Test A

Part D Use the recipe below to answer the questions that follow. Write your answers on your paper.

Corn Pudding

1 17-oz. can creamed corn	1 small can evaporated milk
10 soda crackers, crushed	1 egg, beaten
salt	pepper

Grease a one-quart casserole dish. Pour in creamed corn. Add crushed soda crackers, evaporated milk, and egg. Add salt and pepper to taste. Mix well. Bake at 400°F until brown on top and bubbling (about 20-30 minutes).
Serves 4.

1) What steps should you follow to be sure the recipe turns out right?
2) What abbreviations are in this recipe and what do they mean?
3) What ingredients will you need to prepare this recipe?
4) What utensils will you need?
5) What directions must you follow to prepare this recipe? Write them in order.

Part E Write the answer to these questions on your paper.

1) What kind of magazine has summaries of articles from other magazines?
2) Which magazine is published more often—a biannual or a semiannual?
3) Which of these reference books is a periodical—*The World Book Encyclopedia, Time Magazine, Betty Crocker's Picture Cookbook?*
4) What periodical helps you find articles in other periodicals?
5) Where can you look to learn what articles are in a magazine?

Test Taking Tip

When taking a true-false test, read each statement carefully. Write *true* only when the statement is true all of the time. Write *false* if any part or all of the statement is false.

Reading Vocabulary

casserole (8) evaporate (6) crush (5)

Part D Answers

1) (1) Read the whole recipe. (2) Assemble all of the ingredients called for in this recipe (3) Gather all of the utensils you will need. (4) Follow the directions in order **2)** oz—ounce, 400°F—400 degrees Fahrenheit **3)** creamed corn, soda crackers, salt, evaporated milk, one egg, pepper **4)** one quart casserole dish, can opener, wire whip, small mixing bowl, spoon for mixing, pot holder **5)** (1) Grease casserole dish. (2) Pour in can of creamed corn. (3) Add crushed soda crackers. (4) Add evaporated milk. (5) Beat egg. (6) Add beaten egg. (7) Add salt and pepper. (8) Mix well. (9) Bake at 400° until brown on top and bubbling (about 20–30 minutes).

Part E Answers

1) a digest **2)** semiannual **3)** *Time Magazine* **4)** *The Readers' Guide to Periodical Literature* **5)** table of contents

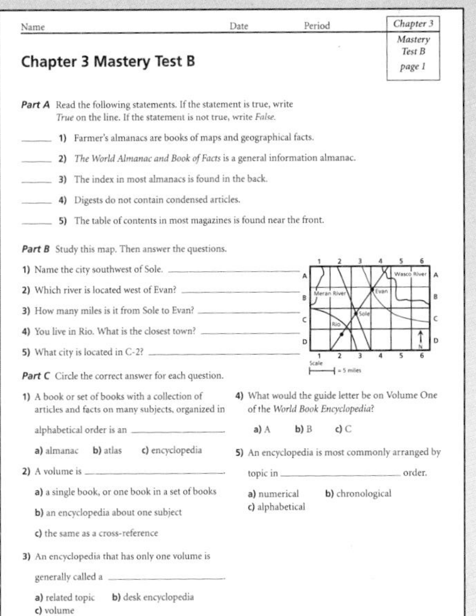

Name Date Period *Chapter 3 Mastery Test B page 1*

Chapter 3 Mastery Test B

Part A Read the following statements. If the statement is true, write *True* on the line. If the statement is not true, write *False.*

_____ 1) Farmer's almanacs are books of maps and geographical facts.
_____ 2) *The World Almanac and Book of Facts* is a general information almanac.
_____ 3) The index in most almanacs is found in the back.
_____ 4) Digests do not contain condensed articles.
_____ 5) The table of contents in most magazines is found near the front.

Part B Study this map. Then answer the questions.

1) Name the city southwest of Sole. _____
2) Which river is located west of Evan? _____
3) How many miles is it from Sole to Evan? _____
4) You live in Rio. What is the closest town? _____
5) What city is located in C-2? _____

Part C Circle the correct answer for each question.

1) A book or set of books with a collection of articles and facts on many subjects, organized in alphabetical order is an _____.
   a) almanac b) atlas c) encyclopedia
2) A volume is _____.
   a) a single book, or one book in a set of books
   b) an encyclopedia about one subject
   c) the same as a cross-reference
3) An encyclopedia that has only one volume is generally called a _____.
   a) related topic b) desk encyclopedia c) volume
4) What would the guide letter be on Volume One of the *World Book Encyclopedia?*
   a) A b) B c) C
5) An encyclopedia is most commonly arranged by topic in _____ order.
   a) numerical b) chronological c) alphabetical

 Life Skills English

Name Date Period *Chapter 3 Mastery Test B page 2*

Chapter 3 Mastery Test B, continued

Part D Read the recipe below. Then answer the questions.

1 package blueberry muffin mix
3 eggs
1 cup oil

Preheat oven at 375° F. Combine muffin mix, eggs, and oil together in a large bowl. Mix well. Pour into greased muffin pan.
Bake 20 minutes.

1) What ingredients will you need for this recipe? _____
2) What must be mixed together? _____
3) What is used to cook the muffins in? _____
4) At what temperature should the oven be set? _____
5) How long do the muffins need to cook? _____

Part E Read the information from a how-to book given below. Then answer the questions.

How to Use a Fax Machine

To send a fax, first insert your document into the tray face down and top end first. Slide it in until the automatic feed pulls the page. Dial the fax number for where you would like the fax to be sent. (If you are sending the fax long distance, press 1, dial the area code, then dial the number.) Press start. The document will feed through automatically. You will hear a beep when the document has been sent.

1) Should the document be face up or face down when sending a fax? _____
2) What must you do to send a fax long distance? _____
3) What must you do after dialing the fax number? _____
4) How do you know when the fax has been sent? _____
5) What will the fax machine do automatically? _____

 Life Skills English

Chapter 3 Mastery Test B

Chapter 4

Planning Guide

The Telephone Book

	Student Text Lesson			
	Student Pages	Vocabulary	Practice Exercises	Lesson Review
Lesson 1 The White Pages	102-111	✔	✔	✔
Lesson 2 The Yellow Pages	112-119	✔	✔	✔
Lesson 3 The Blue Pages	120-121	✔	✔	✔

Chapter Activities

Teacher's Resource Library

Putting It Together 4: Telephone Book Jeopardy

Community Connection 4: Find Help in the Yellow Pages

Assessment Options

Student Text

Chapter 4 Review

Teacher's Resource Library

Chapter 4 Mastery Tests A and B

Midterm Mastery Test

Teaching Strategies						Language Skills			Learning Styles						Teacher's Resource Library		
Reviewing Skills	Teacher Alert	Career Application	Home Application	Global Connection	Community Application	Identification Skills	Writing Skills	Punctuation Skills	Visual/Spatial	Auditory/Verbal	Body/Kinesthetic	Logical/Mathematical	Group Learning	LEP/ESL	Activities	Workbook Activities	Self-Study Guide
102	102		107	107	103	✔	✔	✔						110	13-14	21-24	✔
112		113				✔	✔	✔	114						15	25-27	✔
120						✔	✔	✔					121		16		✔

Chapter at a Glance

(Answer Keys for the Teacher's Resource Library begin on page 282 of this Teacher's Edition.)

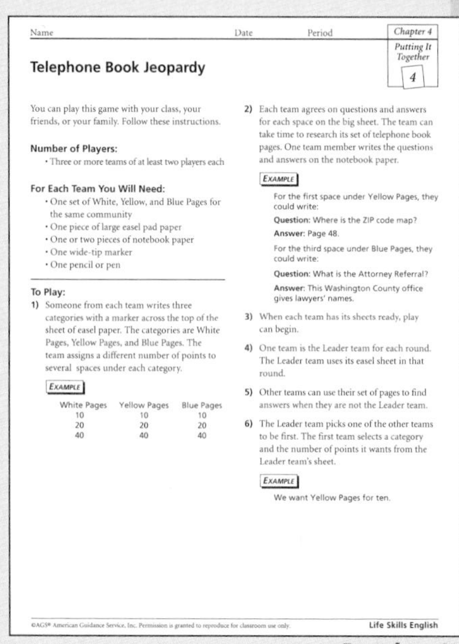

Name Date Period | Chapter 4 Putting It Together 4

Telephone Book Jeopardy

You can play this game with your class, your friends, or your family. Follow these instructions.

Number of Players:
- Three or more teams of at least two players each

For Each Team You Will Need:
- One set of White, Yellow, and Blue Pages for the same community
- One piece of large easel pad paper
- One or two pieces of notebook paper
- One wide-tip marker
- One pencil or pen

To Play:

1) Someone from each team writes three categories with a marker across the top of the sheet of easel paper. The categories are White Pages, Yellow Pages, and Blue Pages. The team assigns a different number of points to several spaces under each category.

EXAMPLE

White Pages	Yellow Pages	Blue Pages
10	10	10
20	20	20
40	40	40

2) Each team agrees on questions and answers for each space on the big sheet. The team can take time to research its set of telephone book pages. One team member writes the questions and answers on the notebook paper.

EXAMPLE

For the first space under Yellow Pages, they could write:

Question: Where is the ZIP code map?

Answer: Page 48.

For the third space under Blue Pages, they could write:

Question: What is the Attorney Referral?

Answer: This Washington County office gives lawyers' names.

3) When each team has its sheets ready, play can begin.

4) One team is the Leader team for each round. The Leader team uses its easel sheet in that round.

5) Other teams can use their set of pages to find answers when they are not the Leader team.

6) The Leader team picks one of the other teams to be first. The first team selects a category and the number of points it wants from the Leader team's sheet.

EXAMPLE

We want Yellow Pages for ten.

 Life Skills English

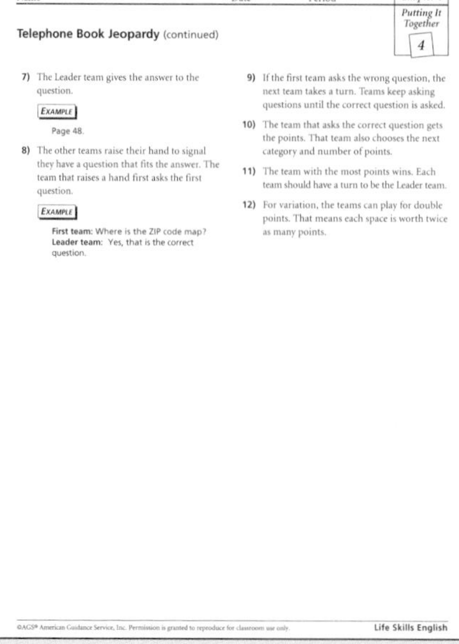

Name Date Period | Chapter 4 Putting It Together 4

Telephone Book Jeopardy (continued)

7) The Leader team gives the answer to the question.

EXAMPLE

Page 48.

8) The other teams raise their hand to signal they have a question that fits the answer. The team that raises a hand first asks the first question.

EXAMPLE

First team: Where is the ZIP code map?
Leader team: Yes, that is the correct question.

9) If the first team asks the wrong question, the next team takes a turn. Teams keep asking questions until the correct question is asked.

10) The team that asks the correct question gets the points. That team also chooses the next category and number of points.

11) The team with the most points wins. Each team should have a turn to be the Leader team.

12) For variation, the teams can play for double points. That means each space is worth twice as many points.

 Life Skills English

Putting It Together 4

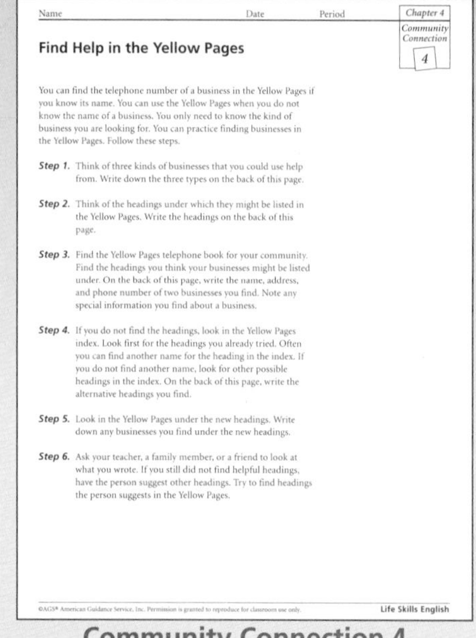

Name Date Period | Chapter 4 Community Connection 4

Find Help in the Yellow Pages

You can find the telephone number of a business in the Yellow Pages if you know its name. You can use the Yellow Pages when you do not know the name of a business. You only need to know the kind of business you are looking for. You can practice finding businesses in the Yellow Pages. Follow these steps.

Step 1. Think of three kinds of businesses that you could use help from. Write down the three types on the back of this page.

Step 2. Think of the headings under which they might be listed in the Yellow Pages. Write the headings on the back of this page.

Step 3. Find the Yellow Pages telephone book for your community. Find the headings you think your businesses might be listed under. On the back of this page, write the name, address, and phone number of two businesses you find. Note any special information you find about a business.

Step 4. If you do not find the headings, look in the Yellow Pages index. Look first for the headings you already tried. Often you can find another name for the heading in the index. If you do not find another name, look for other possible headings in the index. On the back of this page, write the alternative headings you find.

Step 5. Look in the Yellow Pages under the new headings. Write down any businesses you find under the new headings.

Step 6. Ask your teacher, a family member, or a friend to look at what you wrote. If you still did not find helpful headings, have the person suggest other headings. Try to find headings the person suggests in the Yellow Pages.

 Life Skills English

Community Connection 4

- The directory uses many abbreviations without punctuation.

EXAMPLES

Jos	=	Joseph	Jr	=	Junior
Chas	=	Charles	Ret	=	Retired
Geo	=	George	&	=	and
St	=	Saint	MD	=	Medical Doctor

- The directory lists names the way people want them listed.

EXAMPLES

Williams H Chas	Suarez Emelio & Anita E
Wing B W atty	Kostas Omar Mrs
Blackhorse John H	Sina G J MD

- A name that is listed with an initial comes before a first name that begins with the same letter.

EXAMPLES Waters D
Waters David

- Some abbreviations are alphabetized as if they were spelled out. Notice that *St James* is alphabetized as if it were *Saint James.*

EXAMPLES Sabato Isabella
St James Peter
Sanford Lance

- The telephone company usually publishes a new directory once a year. You may get a number that has not been published yet by calling Directory Assistance.

Reading Vocabulary

abbreviation (8) alphabetize assistance (6) initial (6) junior (5) medical (6) publish (6) punctuation (7) retire (6)

APPLICATION

In the Community
Community organizations often publish small telephone directories that usually list only the numbers of residents, businesses, and public services of a particular community. These small directories serve a dual purpose: they allow the organizations that publish them to raise money through advertisements placed in the directories by local businesses and services; and they provide a quick, convenient way for residents to find local numbers. Have students find out if such a directory is published in their community and by whom.

Reading Vocabulary

alphabetically	highlight
apostrophe	organize (6)
electrical	sample (5)

■ **Presenting Activity A** Do Activity A as a whole class activity. When appropriate, as in items 1, 2, and 5, have volunteers write the answers on the board.

Activity A Answers

1) Mendes Charles
Mong Raymond
Mulkern Maria

2) B. Hogan **3)** It would be helpful to know the person's first name and address. **4)** You could call Directory Assistance. **5)** Answers will vary. Responses should reflect information about directory listings presented on pages 102–103.

Activity A Write your answers to the following questions on your paper.

1) In what order would these names be listed in the telephone book—Raymond Mong, Charles Mendes, Maria Mulkern? Write the names as they would appear.

2) Which of these names would be listed first in the telephone book—Bonnie Hogan or B. Hogan?

3) Besides a person's last name, what are two other helpful things to know when you are looking up a person's number?

4) How would you get the telephone number of someone who has just moved to town?

5) How would you have your name listed in the telephone book? Give two different ways.

Business Listings

Businesses are sometimes listed in a special section of the White Pages and also in the **Yellow Pages**. In the White Pages, business names are listed alphabetically by the first word of the name of the business.

Yellow Pages
A part of the telephone book with business listings that are organized under subject headings arranged in alphabetical order.

Examples Bob Wilsons Fine Foods
Jiffy Cleaners

More About Business Listings

- To find the telephone number of a business, you need the name of the business. It also helps to know the address.
- Businesses may ask to have their listing highlighted in bold, in extra-large letters, or some other way. There is usually a fee for this service.
- In business listings, the apostrophe (') may be left out. See the sample listing below for Jack Gillan's Electrical Service.

Examples Jack Gillans Electrical Service
Jack Gillan Electrical Service

104 *Chapter 4 The Telephone Book*

- Business names that are all capital letters, such as radio stations, are listed at the beginning of each letter section.

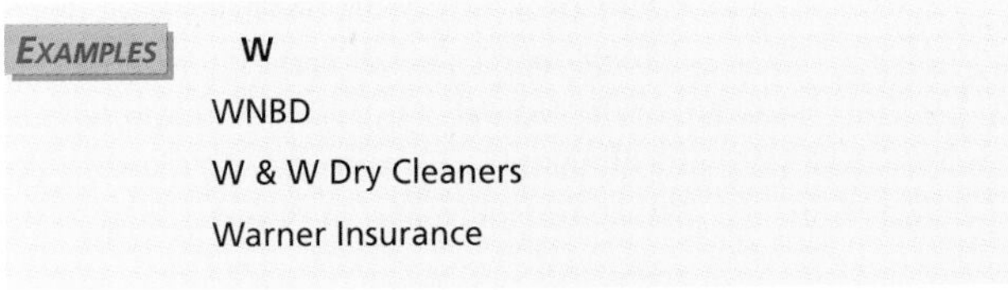

EXAMPLES

W

WNBD

W & W Dry Cleaners

Warner Insurance

- When *the* begins a business name, it usually follows the name. The name is alphabetized according to the first word after *the.*

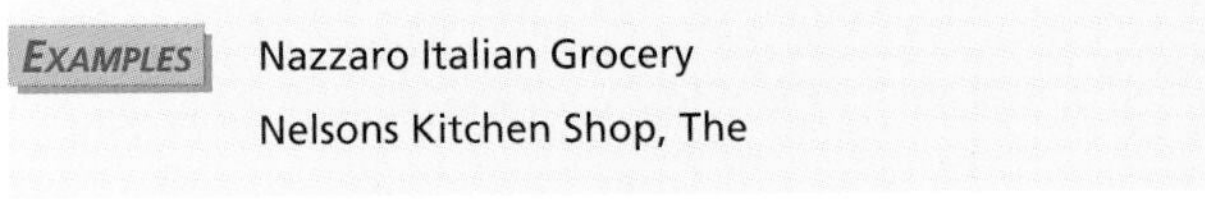

EXAMPLES

Nazzaro Italian Grocery

Nelsons Kitchen Shop, The

Activity B Write on your paper your answers to the following questions.

1) In which two sections of the directory could you look to find the number for Video Clips, a video store in your town?

2) Under what letter would you look to find the number for The Fancy Flounder Fish Market?

3) In what order would the business names below appear in the White Pages of the telephone book? Write the names as they would be printed.

WDMS-AM 1500

The Jacksons' Sport Center

WDMS-TV 5

George Jones Office Supplies

W & A Clothing

Jackson's Plumbing Supplies

Reading Vocabulary

capital (5)
flounder (8)
insurance (7)
plumbing
video

■ Presenting Activity B

Ask students to name three or four local businesses. For example, they might name a convenience store, a movie theater, a book store, and a fast-food restaurant. List the names on the board and ask students what letter they would look under in the White Pages to find each business. Write the letter beside the name of the business. Then have volunteers look in a local directory to find each business under the suggested letter. If a student can't find the business listed under that letter, help students figure out what other letter the business is probably listed under. Once the student finds the business listing, ask him or her to write it on the board exactly as it appears in the directory. Then discuss each listing and any idiosyncrasies associated with it. Be sure to discuss a business listing that has an ampersand, such as L & S Pizza. The ampersand should be overlooked when looking for alphabetical order. Following this activity, encourage students to complete Activity B on their own.

Activity B Answers

1) business listings of the White Pages and in the Yellow Pages
2) F
3) George Jones Office Supplies
Jacksons Plumbing Supplies
Jacksons Sport Center, The
W & A Clothing
WDMS-AM 1500
WDMS-TV 5

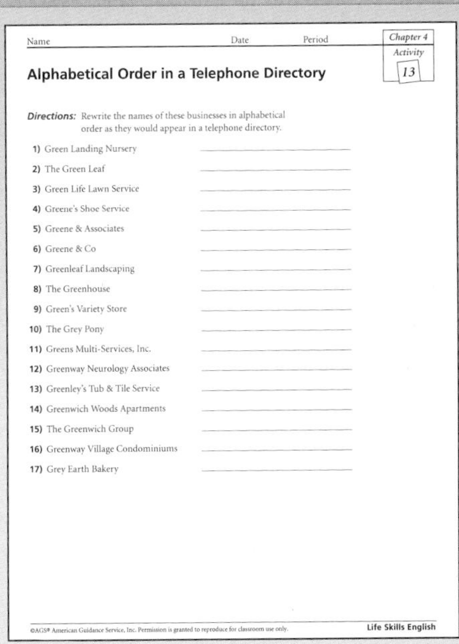

Name Date Period

Chapter 4 Activity 13

Alphabetical Order in a Telephone Directory

Directions: Rewrite the names of these businesses in alphabetical order as they would appear in a telephone directory.

1) Green Landing Nursery
2) The Green Leaf
3) Green Life Lawn Service
4) Greene's Shoe Service
5) Greene & Associates
6) Greene & Co
7) Greenleaf Landscaping
8) The Greenhouse
9) Green's Variety Store
10) The Grey Pony
11) Greens Multi-Services, Inc.
12) Greenway Neurology Associates
13) Greenley's Tub & Tile Service
14) Greenwich Woods Apartments
15) The Greenwich Group
16) Greenway Village Condominiums
17) Grey Earth Bakery

 Life Skills English

Activity 13

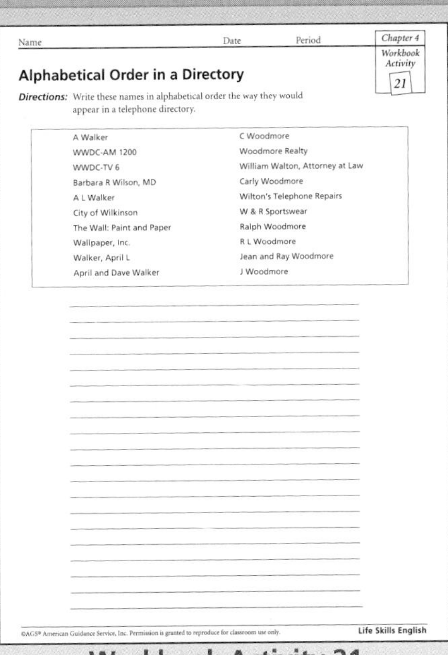

Name Date Period

Chapter 4 Workbook Activity 21

Alphabetical Order in a Directory

Directions: Write these names in alphabetical order the way they would appear in a telephone directory.

A Walker	C Woodmore
WWDC-AM 1200	Woodmore Realty
WWDC-TV 6	William Walton, Attorney at Law
Barbara R Wilson, MD	Carly Woodmore
A L Walker	Wilton's Telephone Repairs
City of Wilkinson	W & R Sportswear
The Wall: Paint and Paper	Ralph Woodmore
Wallpaper, Inc.	R L Woodmore
Walker, April L	Jean and Ray Woodmore
April and Dave Walker	J Woodmore

 Life Skills English

Workbook Activity 21

Reading Vocabulary

code (5)
dial (5)
local (6)
prefix (9)
require (6)

■ Presenting Activity C

Have students name area codes, other than their own, that they know and use often. What city and state does this area code cover? Then have students find the page in local directories that lists area codes across the country. (If it is not possible to provide a directory for teams of students, have students take turns doing this.) What state has the most number of area codes? Which states have only one area code?

Activity C Answers

1) 555 **2)** Answer will vary.
3) Answers may vary. Possible response: You could call Directory Assistance or look in the local directory.

Using Area Codes

Each part of the United States has its own area code. Your area code usually appears on the front of your directory. The directory also has a map that shows the area codes for each part of the United States. To call people who are not in your local calling area, you must dial their area code and then their telephone number. In most places, you must dial a 1 before the area code.

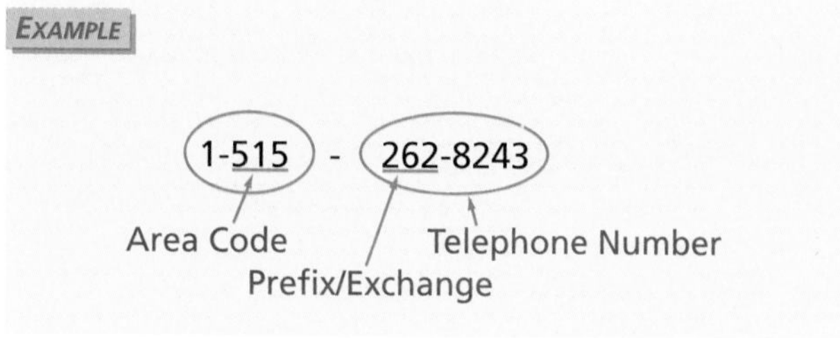

You may have to dial the area code to make some local calls. Check your directory to find out which local calls require an area code.

Activity C Write on your paper your answer to these questions.

1) Which part of the following telephone number is the area code: 1-555-284-7890?

2) What is your area code? Write your telephone number with the area code.

3) How could you find out if you have to dial the area code to call towns or cities in your local calling area?

106 *Chapter 4 The Telephone Book*

Directory Assistance

When you know someone's number, dial it directly. When you do not know the number, look for it in the directory. If the person or the business is not listed in your directory, you may call Directory Assistance. However, if a person has requested an unlisted number, Directory Assistance will not give out the number.

For local information, dial 411 for Directory Assistance. For long-distance information, dial: 1 + area code + 555-1212. If you do not know the area code, dial: 555-1212 or 1-555-1212. An operator will help you find the information you need. There is usually a charge for these services.

Toll-Free Numbers (800 Numbers)

Toll-free

A long-distance number with an 800 area code.

Many businesses have **toll-free** numbers. A toll-free number is a long-distance number with an 800 area code. Although the call is long distance, you do not have to pay for the call. The people you are calling pay for the call. To call an 800 number, dial 1-800 and then the number.

You may ask Directory Assistance for a toll-free number by dialing 1-800-555-1212.

International Calling

The telephone directory has directions for making international calls. It also lists calling codes for countries and cities around the world. You can dial foreign countries directly if you know the number.

EXAMPLES

	International Access Code		Country Code		City Code	
London	011	+	44	+	1	+ Local Number
Cairo	011	+	20	+	2	+ Local Number

Reading Vocabulary

access (8)
foreign (5)
international (6)
operator (5)
toll-free

Application

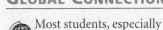

At Home

The widespread use of fax machines, computer modems, and cellular telephones around the country and the world has contributed to the need for additional area codes within a state so that telephone companies can provide enough different telephone numbers for all of this equipment. Whereas in the past people might have one telephone number with one or two extension phones using that same number, today it is not unusual for one person to have two, three, or more telephone numbers for several telephones as well as other communication equipment. Have students peruse local telephone directories to see the number of households that list more than one telephone number.

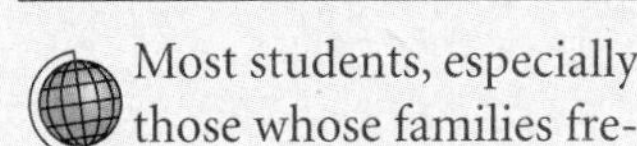

Global Connection

Most students, especially those whose families frequently make international calls, will be aware of the ease (for the most part) with which these calls are made today. Encourage students to talk with parents, grandparents, and other older relatives and friends who recall the difficulty and expense of placing international calls in the past. Invite students to share what they learn with the class. Students may also enjoy doing research to discover how the cost of international phone calls have dropped in the last five decades.

Reading Vocabulary

cafe (5)

■ Presenting Activity D

Before having students do Activity D, review the material presented so far in the lesson, eliciting any questions students might have. Then, depending on the needs of your students and their grasp of the information, have them complete Activity D on their own or in small groups.

Activity D Answers

1) 800 **2)** at the beginning of the W section under WSDE **3)** D.L. Turner **4)** Early **5)** Call Directory Assistance and give the operator Fred's full name and address. **6)** Dial 1 plus the area code of the state plus 555-1212. **7)** address and, possibly, his middle initial **8)** telephone book **9)** 345 **10a)** 411 **10b)** 1 + [state's area code] + 555 + 1212 **10c)** 1-800-555-1212

Activity D Use the information you've learned so far in this lesson. Answer each question. Write your answers on your paper.

1) What is the area code for toll-free numbers?

2) Where would you look in the directory to find the phone number for WSDE, a local radio station?

3) Which person would be listed first in the directory—D. L. Turner or Dwayne Turner?

4) What word would you look up to find the number for The Early Bird Cafe?

5) Fred Hernandez is new in town and not yet listed in the directory. How can you find out his number?

6) How can you find out the number for a business that is located in another state?

7) There are ten Robert Jacksons listed in the directory. What information will help you find the number for the Robert Jackson you wish to call?

8) What is another name for the telephone directory?

9) What is the area code in this telephone number: 1-345-564-6700?

10) What number would you call to get:

- **a)** local information?
- **b)** long-distance information?
- **c)** toll-free information?

108 *Chapter 4 The Telephone Book*

Alternative Spellings for Names

> *Alternative*
> *A choice between two or more possibilities.*

Some names may be spelled in different, or **alternative**, ways. An alternative offers a choice between two or more possibilities. If you cannot find a name listed one way, think of another way the name may be spelled. Then look up the alternative spelling. Some directories provide cross-references for names with alternative spellings.

EXAMPLE

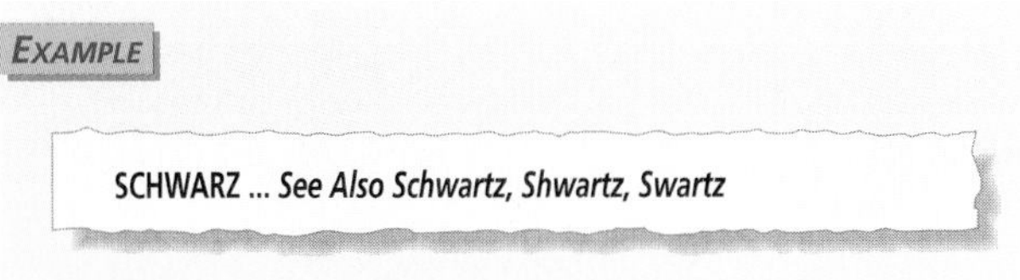

> USING WHAT YOU HAVE LEARNED
>
> Publish a classroom telephone directory. Prepare the directory like the white pages. Some people might prefer to have an unlisted number.

Activity E Match the names in List 1 with their alternative spellings. Write each pair of names on your paper.

List 1	Alternative Spellings
1) Adkins	**a)** Louis
2) Smith	**b)** Miers
3) Jackman	**c)** More
4) Johnson	**d)** Atkins
5) Myers	**e)** Schaeffer
6) Michaelson	**f)** Bernsten
7) Johnston	**g)** Freedman
8) Bryan	**h)** Morgen
9) Berry	**i)** Allen
10) Bernstein	**j)** Johnstone
11) Thomas	**k)** Saunders
12) Stephens	**l)** Jackmon
13) Morgan	**m)** Brian
14) Moore	**n)** Tailor
15) Lewis	**o)** Stevens
16) Taylor	**p)** Barry
17) Allan	**q)** Jonson
18) Sanders	**r)** Smythe
19) Schaffer	**s)** Tomas
20) Friedman	**t)** Mickelson

Reading Vocabulary

alternative
choice (5)
cross-reference
possibility (8)
prefer (6)
provide (5)

■ Presenting Activity E

Write your last name and the last names of all the students in the class on the board in a column. Help students figure out alternative spellings for as many of their last names as possible. Ask students to write the alternative spellings beside their last names. Then have students complete Activity E on their own or with a partner. After, ask students if they can come up with a second alternative spelling for any of the names in List 1. If necessary, they can look in a directory.

Activity E Answers

1) Adkins—Atkins **2)** Smith—Smythe **3)** Jackman—Jackmon **4)** Johnson—Jonson **5)** Myers—Miers **6)** Michaelson—Mickelson **7)** Johnston—Johnstone **8)** Bryan—Brian **9)** Berry—Barry **10)** Bernstein—Bernsten **11)** Thomas—Tomas **12)** Stephens—Stevens **13)** Morgan—Morgen **14)** Moore—More **15)** Lewis—Louis **16)** Taylor—Tailor **17)** Allan—Allen **18)** Sanders—Saunders **19)** Schaffer—Schaeffer **20)** Friedman—Freedman

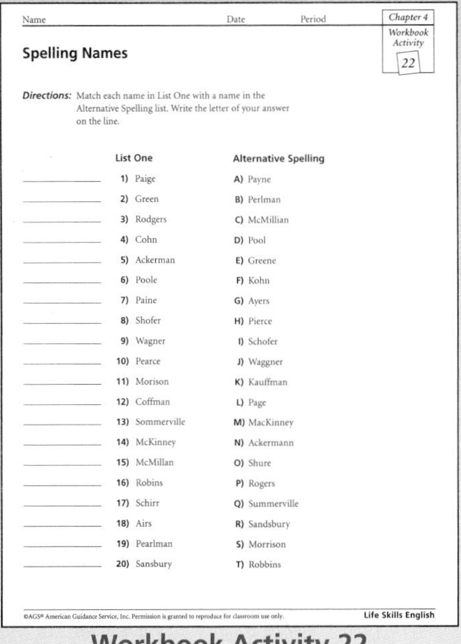

Name ____ Date ____ Period ____ *Chapter 4* *Workbook Activity* *22*

Spelling Names

Directions: Match each name in List One with a name in the Alternative Spelling list. Write the letter of your answer on the line.

	List One	Alternative Spelling
____	**1)** Paige	**A)** Payne
____	**2)** Green	**B)** Perlman
____	**3)** Rodgers	**C)** McMillian
____	**4)** Cohn	**D)** Pool
____	**5)** Ackerman	**E)** Greene
____	**6)** Poole	**F)** Kohn
____	**7)** Paine	**G)** Ayers
____	**8)** Shofer	**H)** Pierce
____	**9)** Wagner	**I)** Schofer
____	**10)** Pearce	**J)** Waggner
____	**11)** Morison	**K)** Kauffman
____	**12)** Coffman	**L)** Page
____	**13)** Sommerville	**M)** MacKinney
____	**14)** McKinney	**N)** Ackermann
____	**15)** McMillan	**O)** Shure
____	**16)** Robins	**P)** Rogers
____	**17)** Schirr	**Q)** Summerville
____	**18)** Airs	**R)** Sandsbury
____	**19)** Pearlman	**S)** Morrison
____	**20)** Sansbury	**T)** Robbins

 Life Skills English

Workbook Activity 22

Reading Vocabulary

itemized (9) separate (5)
payment (7)

■ Presenting Activity F

Most telephone directories include a foreword section that discusses the telephone company's billing policies as well as a description of its bills. If possible, use an overhead projector to display this section in a local directory, or have pairs or small groups of students turn to this section in individual copies of the directory. After having students skim the information presented in this section, ask them if they learned anything new or surprising about billing policies and telephone use.

Activity F Answers

1) (701) 555-1234 2) (701) 555-3000 3) $30.23 4) $2.68

Learning Styles

LEP/ESL

On the board, make two columns. In Column #1, print the following eight terms used in this chapter: *residential listing, fee, business listing, area code, directory assistance, toll-free number, international calling,* and *alternative spellings.* Call on ESL students to translate these terms into their primary language and to write the translations in Column #2. Ask them to give examples of each term. If they have difficulty with this, ask students for whom English is a primary language to explain the terms by using examples from their own life experience.

Telephone Bills

Itemized
Listed one by one.

Telephone companies charge fees for telephone services. Long distance calls cost more than local calls. Each long-distance call is **itemized**, or listed one by one, on a separate page of the bill. A bill is a request for payment of services. Here is a sample telephone bill.

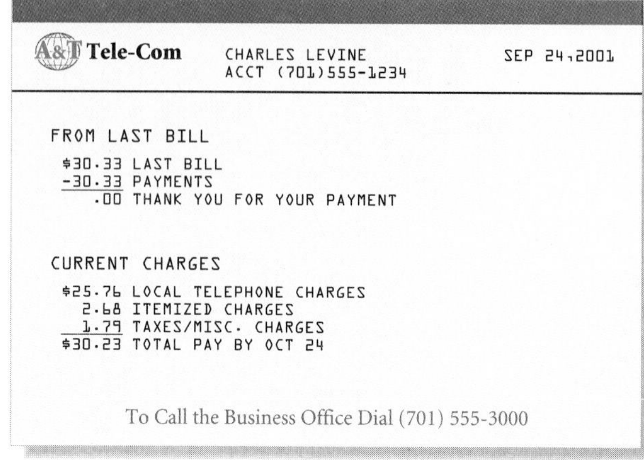

A&T Tele-Com CHARLES LEVINE SEP 24,2001
ACCT (701)555-1234

FROM LAST BILL
$30.33 LAST BILL
-30.33 PAYMENTS
.00 THANK YOU FOR YOUR PAYMENT

CURRENT CHARGES
$25.76 LOCAL TELEPHONE CHARGES
2.68 ITEMIZED CHARGES
1.79 TAXES/MISC. CHARGES
$30.23 TOTAL PAY BY OCT 24

To Call the Business Office Dial (701) 555-3000

Activity F Use the sample telephone bill above to answer these questions. Write your answers on your paper.

1) What is Mr. Levine's telephone number?

2) What number should he call if he has questions about the charges on his bill?

3) How much does Mr. Levine owe for this month?

4) How much were the charges for long-distance calls?

Lesson 1 Review

Part A Use the information in the sample directory listings to answer the questions below. Write your answers on your paper.

VYSKOCIL Thomas A 58 Gale Pl Norwood	**368-8900**	**WILMINGTON Grace** atty	
Thomas J 4800 48th Pl Westport	**456-8765**	54 Rand Ter Westport	**456-9000**
		WINE A E MD	
W		15 Durham St Suite 10 Southview	**359-6000**
		Answering Service	**359-5609**
WAAS Anne Jones Rt 1 Norwood	**369-8700**	**Arnold Edward MD** 5601 56th Pl Westport	**456-6859**

1) What is the phone number of the attorney listed?

2) What is Dr. Wine's home phone number?

3) What number can you call if Dr. Wine is not at home or in his office?

4) How could you find out the area code for the towns listed in this directory?

5) What is the last name of Thomas J of 4800 48th Place?

WBQ TV REPAIR INC		**WINE & CHEESE SHOP** 48 Sand Ln Norwood	**369-4000**
54 Rand Ter Westport	**456-9005**		
WEBB Broadcasting Station		**Wine Insurance Co**	
5617 Webb Road Westport	**457-5600**	34 Water Blvd Southview	**359-7650**

6) Why is WEBB listed after WBQ TV Repair?

7) What has been left out of the name of the business located on Sand Lane in Norwood?

8) How could someone from out of the local area code find out if Wine Insurance Company has a toll-free number?

Part B Write the answer to these questions on your paper.

1) What are two reasons for calling Directory Assistance?

2) What calls are itemized on your monthly telephone bill?

Reading Vocabulary

attorney (8)

Part A Answers

1) 456-9000 **2)** 456-6859 **3)** 359-5609 (Answering Service) **4)** Answers may vary. Possible answers include: look at the information on the cover of the directory; look at the introductory material in the directory; call Directory Assistance. **5)** Vyskocil **6)** The initials WEBB come after the initials WBQ. **7)** The period after the abbreviation *Ln* is missing. **8)** Call 1-800-555-1212.

Part B Answers

1) Answers may vary. Possible responses are: to get the number of someone not yet listed in the directory; to get the area code for town, city, or state. **2)** long-distance calls

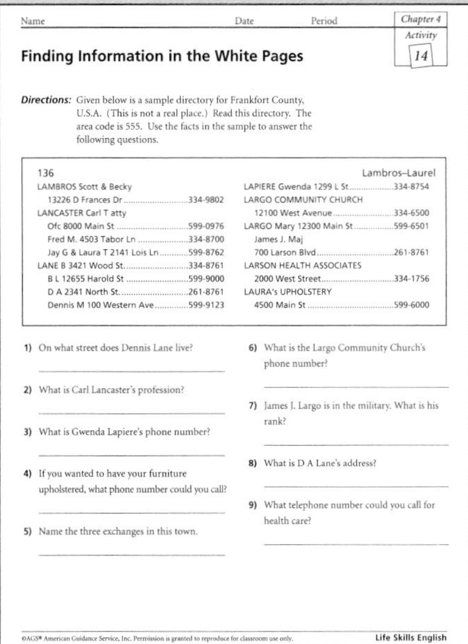

Name ______ Date ______ Period ______ *Chapter 4 Activity 14*

Finding Information in the White Pages

Directions: Given below is a sample directory for Frankfort County, U.S.A. (This is not a real place.) Read this directory. The area code is 555. Use the facts in the sample to answer the following questions.

136		Lambros–Laurel	
LAMBROS Scott & Becky		LAPIERE Gwenda 1299 L St	334-8754
13226 D Frances Dr	334-9802	LARGO COMMUNITY CHURCH	
LANCASTER Carl T atty		12100 West Avenue	334-6500
Ofc 8000 Main St	599-0976	LARGO Mary 12300 Main St	599-6501
Fred M. 4503 Tabor Ln	334-8700	James J. Maj	
Jay G & Laura T 2141 Lois Ln	599-8762	700 Larson Blvd	261-8761
LANE B 3421 Wood St.	334-8761	LARSON HEALTH ASSOCIATES	
B L 12655 Harold St	599-9000	2000 West Street	334-1756
D A 2341 North St.	261-8761	LAURA's UPHOLSTERY	
Dennis M 100 Western Ave	599-9123	4500 Main St	599-6000

1) On what street does Dennis Lane live?

2) What is Carl Lancaster's profession?

3) What is Gwenda Lapiere's phone number?

4) If you wanted to have your furniture upholstered, what phone number could you call?

5) Name the three exchanges in this town.

6) What is the Largo Community Church's phone number?

7) James J. Largo is in the military. What is his rank?

8) What is D A Lane's address?

9) What telephone number could you call for health care?

 Life Skills English

Activity 14

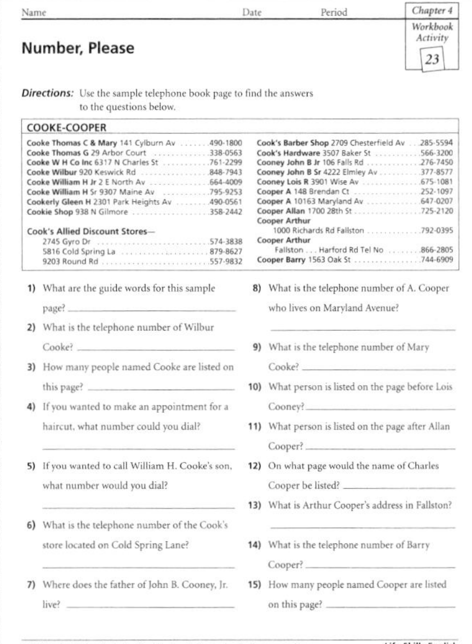

Name ______ Date ______ Period ______ *Chapter 4 Workbook Activity 23*

Number, Please

Directions: Use the sample telephone book page to find the answers to the questions below.

COOKE-COOPER			
Cooke Thomas C & Mary 141 Cylburn Av	490-1800	**Cook's Barber Shop** 2709 Chesterfield Av	285-5594
Cooke Thomas G 29 Arbor Court	338-0563	**Cook's Hardware** 3507 Baker St	566-3200
Cooke W H Co Inc 6317 N Charles St	761-2299	**Cooney John B Jr** 106 Falls Rd	276-7450
Cooke Wilbur 920 Keswick Rd	848-7943	**Cooney John B Sr** 4222 Elmley Av	377-8577
Cooke William H Jr 2 E North Av	664-4009	**Cooney Lois R** 3901 Wise Av	675-1081
Cooke William H Sr 9307 Maine Av	795-9253	**Cooper A** 148 Brendan Ct	252-1097
Cookerly Gleen H 2301 Park Heights Av	490-0561	**Cooper A** 10163 Maryland Av	647-0207
Cookie Shop 938 N Gilmore	358-2442	**Cooper Allan** 1700 28th St	725-2120
		Cooper Arthur	
Cook's Allied Discount Stores—		1000 Richards Rd Fallston	792-0395
2745 Gyro Dr	574-3838	**Cooper Arthur**	
5816 Cold Spring La	879-8627	Fallston . . . Harford Rd Tel No	866-2805
9203 Round Rd	557-9832	**Cooper Barry** 1563 Oak St	744-6909

1) What are the guide words for this sample page? ______

2) What is the telephone number of Wilbur Cooke? ______

3) How many people named Cooke are listed on this page? ______

4) If you wanted to make an appointment for a haircut, what number could you dial? ______

5) If you wanted to call William H. Cooke's son, what number would you dial? ______

6) What is the telephone number of the Cook's store located on Cold Spring Lane? ______

7) Where does the father of John B. Cooney, Jr. live? ______

8) What is the telephone number of A. Cooper who lives on Maryland Avenue? ______

9) What is the telephone number of Mary Cooke? ______

10) What person is listed on the page before Lois Cooney? ______

11) What person is listed on the page after Allan Cooper? ______

12) On what page would the name of Charles Cooper be listed? ______

13) What is Arthur Cooper's address in Fallston? ______

14) What is the telephone number of Barry Cooper? ______

15) How many people named Cooper are listed on this page? ______

 Life Skills English

Workbook Activity 23

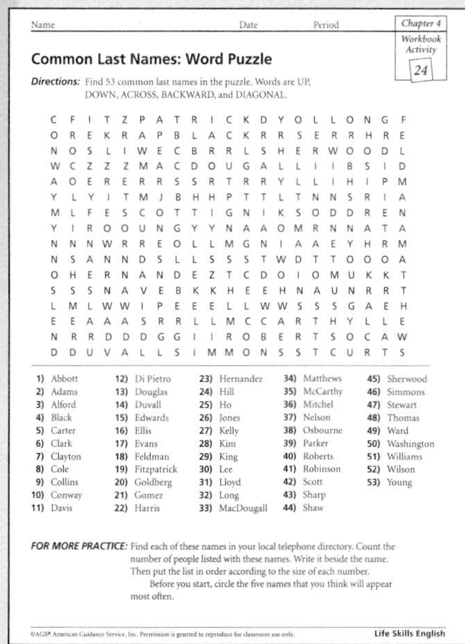

Name ______ Date ______ Period ______ *Chapter 4 Workbook Activity 24*

Common Last Names: Word Puzzle

Directions: Find 53 common last names in the puzzle. Words are UP, DOWN, ACROSS, BACKWARD, and DIAGONAL.

```
C F I T Z P A T R I C K D Y O L L O N G F
O R E K R A P B L A C K R R S E R R H R E
N O S L I W E C B R R L S H E R W O O D L
W C Z Z Z M A C D O U G A L L I I B S I D
A O E R E R R S S R T R R Y L L I H I P M
Y L Y I T M J B H H P T T L T N N S R I A
M L F E S C O T T I G N I K S O D D R E N
Y I R O O U N G Y Y N A A O M R N N A T A
N N N W R R E O L L M G N I A A E Y H R M
N S A N N D S L L S S S T W D T T O O O A
O H E R N A N D E Z T C D O I O M U K K T
S S S N A V E B K K H E E H N A U N R R T
L M L W W I P E E E L L W W S S S G A E H
E E A A A S R R L L M C C A R T H Y L L E
N R R D D D G G I I R O B E R T S O C A W
D D U V A L L S I M M O N S S T C U R T S
```

1) Abbott 2) Adams 3) Alford 4) Black 5) Carter 6) Clark 7) Clayton 8) Cole 9) Collins 10) Conway 11) Davis 12) Di Pietro 13) Douglas 14) Duvall 15) Edwards 16) Ellis 17) Evans 18) Feldman 19) Fitzpatrick 20) Goldberg 21) Gomez 22) Harris 23) Hernandez 24) Hill 25) Ho 26) Jones 27) Kelly 28) Kim 29) King 30) Lee 31) Lloyd 32) Long 33) MacDougall 34) Matthews 35) McCarthy 36) Mitchel 37) Nelson 38) Osbourne 39) Parker 40) Roberts 41) Robinson 42) Scott 43) Sharp 44) Shaw 45) Sherwood 46) Simmons 47) Stewart 48) Thomas 49) Ward 50) Washington 51) Williams 52) Wilson 53) Young

FOR MORE PRACTICE: Find each of these names in your local telephone directory. Count the number of people listed with these names. Write it beside the name. Then put the list in order according to the size of each number.

Before you start, circle the five names that you think will appear most often.

 Life Skills English

Workbook Activity 24

The Telephone Book Chapter 4 **111**

Lesson at a Glance

Chapter 4 Lesson 2

Overview This lesson explains the organization of the Yellow Pages and how to find numbers in the Yellow Pages.

Objectives

- To identify situations in which to use the Yellow Pages.
- To answer questions about the Yellow Pages.

Student Pages 112–119

Teacher's Resource Library

Activity 15

Workbook Activities 25–27

Reading Vocabulary

agent (5)
bureau (6)
classified
consumer (7)
emergency (5)
individual (6)
installation (8)
musical (5)
products (5)
retail (8)
service (4)
specific (8)
storage (6)

Teaching Suggestions

Introducing the Lesson

Ask students what they think of when they hear the words, "The Yellow Pages." Then have students raise their hands if they have ever used the Yellow Pages. Ask students to describe the occasions they had for looking in the Yellow Pages. Following this discussion, focus students' attention on the text.

Reviewing Skills Review how to use the White Pages.

Presenting Activity A Do Activity A as a class. Discuss each item and help students decide whether the subject heading indicates a product or a service.

Activity A Answers

1) service 2) service
3) service 4) product
5) product 6) service

Lesson 2 The Yellow Pages

Products
Goods that you can buy.

Services
What a business or individual can do for you.

Products and Services

The Yellow Pages is a classified telephone directory that lists businesses, **products**, and **services** for a city or town and its surrounding area. Products are goods that you can buy. A service is something that a business or individual does for you.

EXAMPLES

Products:	Automobiles, Carpet, Musical Instruments
Services:	Automobile Repair, Carpet Installation, Music Lessons

Activity A Number your paper from 1 to 6. Beside each number, write whether the subject heading is a *product* or a *service.*

1) Travel Agents & Bureaus

2) Pianos—Tuning & Repair

3) Automobile Body Repairing

4) Pianos

5) Dolls—Retail

6) Moving & Storage

When you do not know the name of a business, use the Yellow Pages. To find a number in the Yellow Pages, you only need to know the type of business you are looking for.

You can also use the Yellow Pages to look up the telephone number of a specific business if you know its name.

The Yellow Pages also provides other useful information. In your Yellow Pages Directory you can find emergency numbers, an emergency medical guide, consumer information, local places of interest, a local ZIP code map, and a local road map.

Subject Listings

The classified listings in the Yellow Pages are arranged alphabetically by subject. Under each subject the individual businesses or professionals are also listed alphabetically.

EXAMPLE

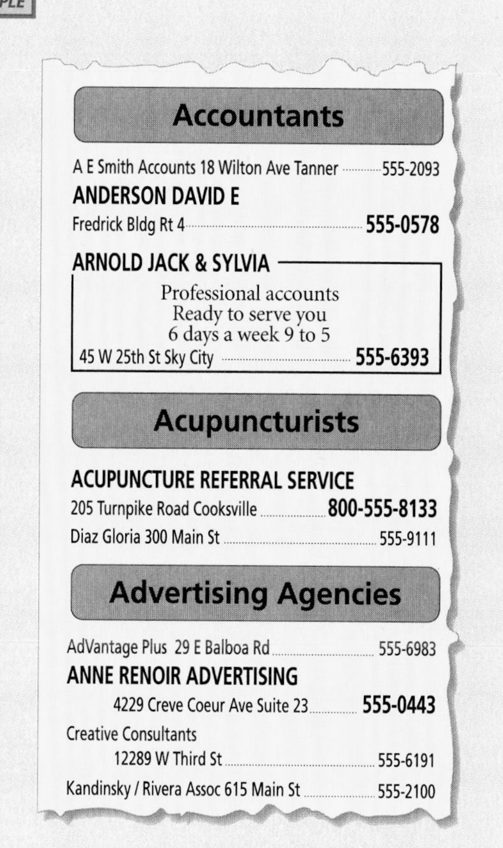

Accountants

A E Smith Accounts 18 Wilton Ave Tanner 555-2093
ANDERSON DAVID E
Fredrick Bldg Rt 4 .... **555-0578**
ARNOLD JACK & SYLVIA
Professional accounts
Ready to serve you
6 days a week 9 to 5
45 W 25th St Sky City **555-6393**

Acupuncturists

ACUPUNCTURE REFERRAL SERVICE
205 Turnpike Road Cooksville **800-555-8133**
Diaz Gloria 300 Main St 555-9111

Advertising Agencies

AdVantage Plus 29 E Balboa Rd 555-6983
ANNE RENOIR ADVERTISING
4229 Creve Coeur Ave Suite 23 .... **555-0443**
Creative Consultants
12289 W Third St 555-6191
Kandinsky / Rivera Assoc 615 Main St 555-2100

Reading Vocabulary

account (5)
accountant
acupuncture
acupuncturist
professional (6)
referral

APPLICATION

Career Connection

The Yellow Pages can be a useful tool as students consider different career paths. Subheadings listed under a main subject heading can provide clues to the variety of jobs associated with a particular field. If, for example, a student were interested in a career in landscaping, he or she might look up *Landscaping* in the Yellow Pages and find these subheadings: *Landscape Architects, Landscape Contractors, Landscape Designers,* and *Landscape Lighting.* The student could then investigate the jobs related to each of these areas and proceed toward a career with a more focused, positive attitude. Have students choose a general career area and find the subheadings that are listed under it in the Yellow Pages.

The Telephone Book Chapter 4 **113**

Reading Vocabulary

dealer (7)
equipment (5)
rebuilt
subject (5)
subtopic
system (5)
topic (5)

■ Presenting Activity B

Before students complete Activity B on their own, have them turn to the sample Yellow Pages listing on page 113. Have students take turns telling what they learn from these entries.

Activity B Answers

1) They are all accountants. **2)** It tells when they are open for business. **3)** They would be listed alphabetically as follows:

Anderson David E
Arnold Jack and Sylvia
Smith A E

4) No. The 800 number indicates that the call is toll-free. **5)** She's an acupuncturist, so you might call to make an appointment.

Learning Styles

Visual/Spatial

Divide the class into pairs. Provide each pair with a page from the Yellow Pages of an old telephone book. Ask each pair to use its page to create a ten-question quiz like the one in Activity B on page 114. Afterward, invite the pairs to exchange their sample pages and their quizzes. Provide time for the pairs to answer the quiz questions and have them checked. Then invite the students to share what they learned from their work with the Yellow Pages.

Activity B Use the sample Yellow Pages on page 113 to answer these questions. Write your answers on your paper.

1) What do A. E. Smith, David E. Anderson, and Jack and Sylvia Arnold have in common?
2) What information does the Arnolds' listing provide that the other two listings do not?
3) How would these three names be listed in the White Pages? Write them as they would appear.
4) Is there a long-distance charge for calling the Acupuncture Referral Service? How do you know?
5) Why might you call Gloria Diaz?

More About Subject Listings

Many subjects have several subtopics. These subtopics are also listed in alphabetical order. Notice that the following list of automobile topics are alphabetized by the word that follows *Automobile.*

Example
Automobile Air Conditioning Equipment
Automobile Body Repairing & Painting
Automobile Dealers – New Cars
Automobile Dealers – Used Cars
Automobile Electric Service
Automobile Parts & Supplies – New
Automobile Parts & Supplies – Used & Rebuilt
Automobile Radios & Stereo Systems

114 *Chapter 4 The Telephone Book*

Activity C Rewrite each list in alphabetical order on your paper.

List 1

Pianos
Pianos—Tuning & Repair
Piano & Organ Moving

List 2

Party Supplies—Renting
Party Planning Service
Party Supplies

List 3

Lawn Mowers
Lawn Maintenance
Lawn Mowers—Sharpening & Repairing

List 4

Dolls—Retail
Dolls—Repairing
Doll Houses & Accessories

Cross-References

Some subjects in the Yellow Pages have cross-references. See the example below.

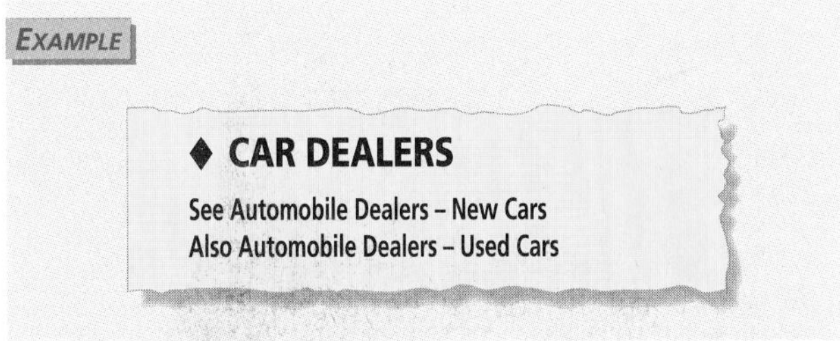

EXAMPLE
♦ CAR DEALERS
See Automobile Dealers – New Cars
Also Automobile Dealers – Used Cars

Look in the index of this textbook to find out more about cross-references.

Reading Vocabulary

accessory (8)
index (5)
maintenance (8)
mower
sharpening
textbook

■ Presenting Activity C

Write List 1 on the board and help students rewrite the list in alphabetical order. Have them explain why *Pianos* is listed after *Piano & Organ Moving* but before *Pianos—Tuning and Repairing.* If you believe students can complete Activity C on their own, have them do so. Otherwise, complete the activity together following a similar procedure to the one described above for List 1.

Activity C Answers

List 1: Piano & Organ Moving
Pianos
Pianos—Tuning & Repairing

List 2: Party Planning Service
Party Supplies
Party Supplies—Renting

List 3: Lawn Maintenance
Lawn Mowers
Lawn Mowers—Sharpening and Repairing

List 4: Doll Houses & Accessories
Dolls—Repairing
Dolls—Retail

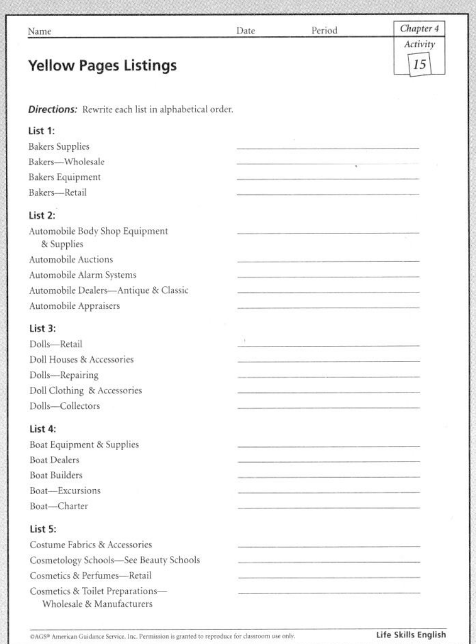
Name Date Period — *Chapter 4* *Activity* *15*

Yellow Pages Listings

Directions: Rewrite each list in alphabetical order.

List 1:
Bakers Supplies
Bakers—Wholesale
Bakers Equipment
Bakers—Retail

List 2:
Automobile Body Shop Equipment & Supplies
Automobile Auctions
Automobile Alarm Systems
Automobile Dealers—Antique & Classic
Automobile Appraisers

List 3:
Dolls—Retail
Doll Houses & Accessories
Dolls—Repairing
Doll Clothing & Accessories
Dolls—Collectors

List 4:
Boat Equipment & Supplies
Boat Dealers
Boat Builders
Boat—Excursions
Boat—Charter

List 5:
Costume Fabrics & Accessories
Cosmetology Schools—See Beauty Schools
Cosmetics & Perfumes—Retail
Cosmetics & Toilet Preparations—Wholesale & Manufacturers

 Life Skills English

Activity 15

Name Date Period — *Chapter 4* *Workbook Activity* *25*

Alphabetical Lists

Directions: Rewrite each list in alphabetical order.

List 1:
Florists
Floral Arrangements
Flowers — See Florists
Florists — Weddings

List 2:
Dancing Supplies
Dancing Schools
Dancing — Clothing
Dance Instruction — See Dancing Schools

List 3:
Day Nurseries & Schools
Day Care
Baby-Sitting — See Day Care
Child Care — See Day Care

List 4:
Physicians — Dermatology
Physicians — Allergy
Physicians Clinics & Medical Groups
Physical Therapists
Physicians — Family Practice

List 5:
Rental Services
Realtors — See Real Estate
Rental Management
Real Estate

 Life Skills English

Workbook Activity 25

Reading Vocabulary

academic (8)
amateur (6)
architect (6)
athlete (6)
landscaper
physician (6)
profession (6)
professional (6)

■ **Presenting Activity D** Ask students to name professions they hope to have some day. List these on the board. Then read through the list of professions one by one and have students tell what training they believe each profession requires and what service a person who follows this profession provides. If students are unsure of any answers, provide time for them to find the appropriate responses after they complete Activity D.

Activity D Answers

1) Wording of answers will vary. Possible responses are given. Teacher—educates others; Architect—designs buildings; Accountant—keeps, inspects financial records; Attorney—provides legal advice and legal representation to others; Landscaper—arranges grounds; Registered Nurse—cares for the sick and disabled; Pharmacist—prepares and dispenses drugs for prescriptions; Physician—treats illnesses; Optometrist—examines eyes, diagnoses eye problems 2) Answers will vary. 3) amateur 4) to get business

Using What You Have Learned

Answers

Answers will vary.

Professional Listings

Profession
A job that requires special information and training.

Professional
Someone who works at a specific profession.

A **profession** is a job, or occupation, that requires special information and often long academic training. A **professional** is someone who has a profession. Professionals provide a service to people.

EXAMPLES	Teacher	Attorney	Physician
	Architect	Accountant	Landscaper

Athletes and actors who receive pay for their work are also called professionals. The opposite of a professional athlete or actor is an amateur. An amateur is a person who does something for fun and is not paid.

Activity D Write the answers to these questions on your paper.

1) What service does each of these professionals provide? Use a dictionary if necessary.

teacher
architect
accountant
attorney
landscaper
registered nurse
pharmacist
physician
optometrist

2) What are three other professions? What service do they provide for others?

3) Maria plays on a baseball team for fun. Is she a professional or an amateur?

4) Why do you think a professional would pay to have his or her name listed in the Yellow Pages?

Using What You Have Learned

Look in the Yellow Pages to find the name of a professional who could help you with each problem below. Write the name and number on your paper.

a) Your faucet is leaking. You need a plumber.
b) You have a toothache. You want a dentist near your home.
c) There has been a snowstorm. You need someone to remove the snow from your driveway.

Advertisements in the Yellow Pages

Each business pays a fee to be listed in the Yellow Pages. The size of the fee depends on how the business wishes to be listed. Display ads and special listings cost more than regular listings. The size of the ad or listing also increases the fee. When a business chooses to have a display ad, the business name also appears in the regular listings.

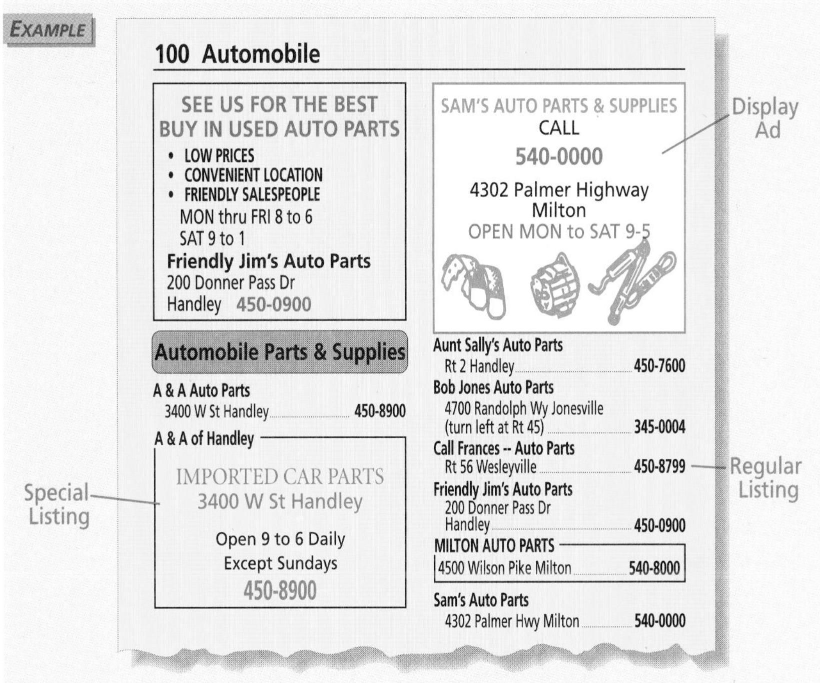

Activity E Use the sample Yellow Pages listings above to answer these questions. Write your answers on your paper.

1) Which two companies have display ads and regular listings?

2) Which two companies have special listings?

3) Which businesses are open every day but Sunday?

4) Where is Bob Jones Auto Parts located?

5) What is the telephone number for A & A of Handley?

Reading Vocabulary

advertisement (6) location (6) display (6) salespeople increase (5)

■ Presenting Activity E

Divide students into small groups. Give each group a local directory, and have them open to the same page in the Yellow Pages. After allowing time for students to look at the page, engage them in a discussion about the various sizes and styles of the ads and listings on the page. Which ads do students think are most effective? Why would they call one business listed on this page over another? Following the discussion, have the members of each group work together to complete Activity E.

Activity E Answers

1) Friendly Jim's Auto Parts and Sam's Auto Parts **2)** A & A of Handley and Milton Auto Parts **3)** Friendly Jim's Auto Parts, A & A of Handley, and Sam's Auto Parts & Supplies **4)** 4700 Randolph Way, Jonesville **5)** 450-8900

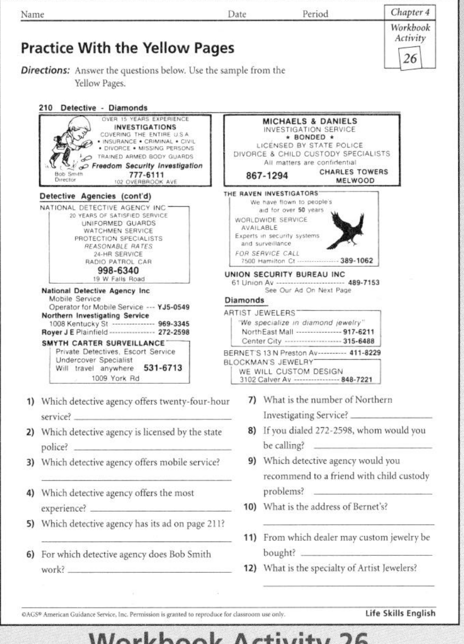

Name Date Period | *Chapter 4* *Workbook Activity* *26*

Practice With the Yellow Pages

Directions: Answer the questions below. Use the sample from the Yellow Pages.

1) Which detective agency offers twenty-four-hour service? ____________

2) Which detective agency is licensed by the state police? ____________

3) Which detective agency offers mobile service? ____________

4) Which detective agency offers the most experience? ____________

5) Which detective agency has its ad on page 211? ____________

6) For which detective agency does Bob Smith work? ____________

7) What is the number of Northern Investigating Service? ____________

8) If you dialed 272-2598, whom would you be calling? ____________

9) Which detective agency would you recommend to a friend with child custody problems? ____________

10) What is the address of Bernet's? ____________

11) From which dealer may custom jewelry be bought? ____________

12) What is the specialty of Artist Jewelers? ____________

 Life Skills English

Workbook Activity 26

Reading Vocabulary

apparel (8) vocabulary (7)
archery (7) volume (6)
beverage (8)

■ Presenting Activity F

Help students recall what they have learned about using an index. Point out that the same basic principals apply to the organization and use of a Yellow Pages index as to the indexes of other reference books. If possible, provide a Yellow Pages index for students to examine. You might suggest that they skim through the index to find examples of cross references. Following this activity, have students complete Activity F on their own.

Activity F Answers

1) Dogs—Pets **2)** Drinks—Beverages **3)** Doctors—Physicians **4)** Attorneys—Lawyers **5)** Cars—Automobiles **6)** Clothing—Apparel **7)** Film—Motion picture **8)** Kayaks—Boats **9)** Dishes—Chinaware

The Index of the Yellow Pages

The Yellow Pages directories for big cities are very large. Some come in two volumes. Subjects may be listed under several different topics. Many of these large directories provide an index. Using the index is often the quickest way to find the business you need.

EXAMPLE

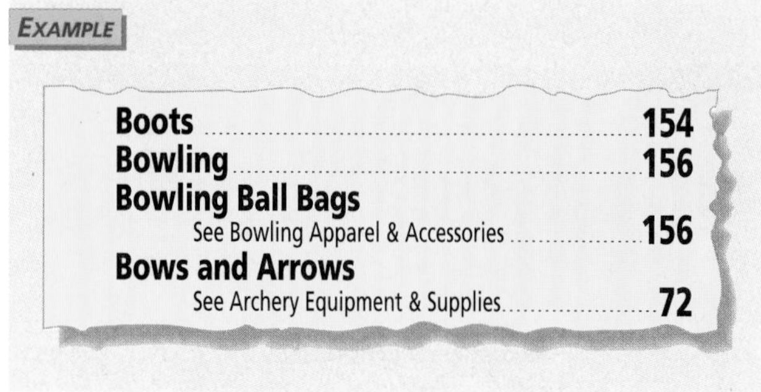

Boots 154
Bowling 156
Bowling Ball Bags
See Bowling Apparel & Accessories 156
Bows and Arrows
See Archery Equipment & Supplies 72

Activity F The following vocabulary exercise can help you find topics in the Yellow Pages. Number your paper from 1 to 9. Beside each number write a topic from Column 1. Beside each topic write the word from Column 2 that you might look up as a cross-reference for the topic.

Example **1)** Dogs—Pets

Column 1	Column 2
1) Dogs	**a)** Physicians
2) Drinks	**b)** Apparel
3) Doctors	**c)** Boats
4) Attorneys	**d)** Beverages
5) Cars	**e)** Pets
6) Clothing	**f)** Chinaware
7) Film	**g)** Lawyers
8) Kayaks	**h)** Automobiles
9) Dishes	**i)** Motion picture

Lesson 2 Review

Part A For which of the following situations would the Yellow Pages be most helpful? Choose only one item from each group. Write the letter of your choice on your paper.

1) a) You want to call Dr. Simon Vilas.
- **b)** You need the telephone number of the Franklin Drug Store.
- **c)** You want to call several stores to find out the price of a new television set.

2) a) You need the area code for Dallas, Texas.
- **b)** You need the ZIP code for a town in your state.
- **c)** You want to call the Handley Movie Theater to find out when the next show begins.

3) a) You have a question about your phone bill.
- **b)** You need to call a dentist.
- **c)** You lost your best friend's phone number.

4) a) You want to find a school that teaches computer science.
- **b)** You want the number of your high school.
- **c)** You need to call your aunt Rebecca.

Part B Write the answer to these questions on your paper.

1) How are listings in the Yellow Pages different from those in the White Pages?
2) How are listings organized in the Yellow Pages?
3) Will you find residential listings in the Yellow Pages?
4) What is one product and one service that might be listed in the Yellow Pages?
5) What are two kinds of professionals who might be listed in the Yellow Pages?

Reading Vocabulary

computer (8) situation (5) item (6)

Part A Answers

1) c **2)** b **3)** b **4)** a

Part B Answers

1) The Yellow Pages lists products and services; the White Pages lists names. **2)** The Yellow Pages is organized according to subjects, with subject headings and subheadings. **3)** No **4)** Answers will vary. An example of a product is *Carpets and Rugs—Retail;* an example of a service is *Carpet and Rug Cleaners.* **5)** Answers will vary. Examples are: attorneys, physicians, accountants, jewelers.

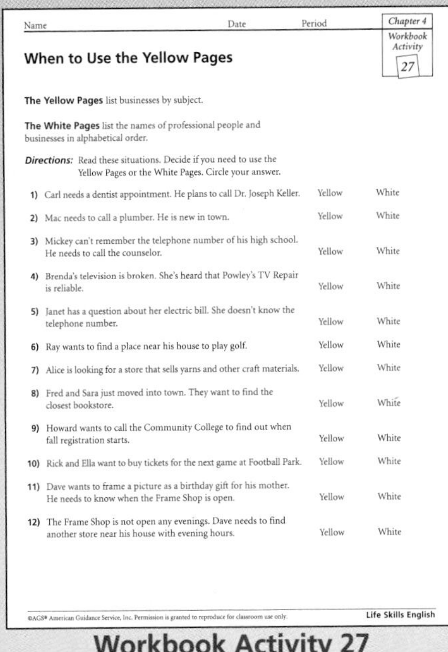

Name Date Period — *Chapter 4 Workbook Activity 27*

When to Use the Yellow Pages

The Yellow Pages list businesses by subject.

The White Pages list the names of professional people and businesses in alphabetical order.

Directions: Read these situations. Decide if you need to use the Yellow Pages or the White Pages. Circle your answer.

1)	Carl needs a dentist appointment. He plans to call Dr. Joseph Keller.	Yellow	White
2)	Mac needs to call a plumber. He is new in town.	Yellow	White
3)	Mickey can't remember the telephone number of his high school. He needs to call the counselor.	Yellow	White
4)	Brenda's television is broken. She's heard that Powley's TV Repair is reliable.	Yellow	White
5)	Janet has a question about her electric bill. She doesn't know the telephone number.	Yellow	White
6)	Ray wants to find a place near his house to play golf.	Yellow	White
7)	Alice is looking for a store that sells yarns and other craft materials.	Yellow	White
8)	Fred and Sara just moved into town. They want to find the closest bookstore.	Yellow	White
9)	Howard wants to call the Community College to find out when fall registration starts.	Yellow	White
10)	Rick and Ella want to buy tickets for the next game at Football Park.	Yellow	White
11)	Dave wants to frame a picture as a birthday gift for his mother. He needs to know when the Frame Shop is open.	Yellow	White
12)	The Frame Shop is not open any evenings. Dave needs to find another store near his house with evening hours.	Yellow	White

 Life Skills English

Workbook Activity 27

Lesson at a Glance

Chapter 4 Lesson 3

Overview This lesson describes the purpose of the Blue Pages in a telephone directory.

Objectives

- To distinguish among the listings found in the different sections of a telephone directory.
- To answer questions about the listings in the Blue Pages.

Student Pages 120–121

Teacher's Resource Library

Activity 16

Reading Vocabulary

administration (7)
Blue Pages
circuit (8)
civil (5)
crime (5)
development (7)
domestic (7)
economic
environmental
federal (6)
impair (8)
internal (8)
official (5)
process (6)
relation (6)
revenue (8)
security (8)
social (5)
sewer (7)
tax (5)
vehicle (5)
veteran (7)
warrant (7)

Teaching Suggestions

■ Introducing the Lesson
As you present this lesson, point out to students that not all directories have Blue Pages. Instead, to find government listings, they may have to look in the Business Listings of the White Pages under the name of their city, county, or state or under such headings as *United States Government.*

■ Reviewing Skills Review the White Pages and Yellow Pages.

■ Presenting Activity A Do Activity A together as a class.

Activity A Answers

1) 800-325-0778; no charge
2) state official 800-772-9801
3) 222-1000 4) 255-4002

Lesson 3 The Blue Pages

> ***Blue Pages***
> *A part of the telephone book that lists the numbers of government agencies.*

Some telephone books have a separate section called the **Blue Pages** that lists government agencies. The Blue Pages lists numbers for the city, county, state, and federal governments.

EXAMPLE

GOVERNMENT OFFICES

GOVERNMENT – CITY

GALESVILLE - CITY OF –	
City Clerk's Office	255-7942
Economic Development	255-6000
Fire Dept	
Emergency calls Dial 9-1-1	
or	255-9865
Mayor's Office	255-8740
Police Dept	255-4000
Crime Solvers	255-4002
Drug Hot Line	255-4001
Emergency calls Dial 9-1-1	
Public Information	255-6859

GOVERNMENT – COUNTY

GALES - COUNTY OF –	
Aging, Department of	222-2222
Toll Free	800-555-2222
Finance Department	222-9810
Property Tax	222-1000
Water & Sewer	222-1001
Information	222-5000
Sheriff	
Civil Court Process	222-3000
Warrant	222-4000
Circuit Court	222-1600
Domestic Relations	222-9000

GOVERNMENT – STATE

Attorney General	800-772-9801
Dept of Motor Vehicles	800-772-9900

GOVERNMENT – FEDERAL

Environmental	
Protection Agency	202-562-2090
Internal Revenue Service	202-829-1040
Social Security Administration	
Toll Free	800-772-1213
Hearing Impaired—TDD Only	
Toll Free	800-325-0778
Veterans Administration	800-827-1000

The Blue Pages of the telephone book may be on blue paper, or they may have a blue outer edge.

> **USING WHAT YOU HAVE LEARNED**
> Look in the Blue Pages in your telephone directory. Find these numbers.
> a) Your sheriff
> b) The department of motor vehicles
> c) The library

Activity A Use the sample Blue Pages above to answer these questions. Write your answers on your paper.

1) What number would you use to contact the Social Security Administration if you were hearing impaired? Is there a charge for this call?
2) Is the Attorney General a city, state, or federal official? What is the Attorney General's number?
3) What number would a person in Gales County call with questions about his or her property tax?
4) What number should a person in Galesville call with information about a crime?

USING WHAT YOU HAVE LEARNED

Answers

Answers will vary.

Lesson 3 Review

Part A On your paper, write the section or sections of the telephone book you would look in to find the telephone numbers for each of the following. Write on your paper *WP* for White Pages, *YP* for Yellow Pages, or *BP* for Blue Pages.

Examples	Michelle DeFalco—**WP**	a dentist—**YP**
	Whitehorse Art Studios—**WP, YP**	the sheriff—**BP**

1) The fire department
2) A piano tuner
3) John's Auto Repair
4) Roberto Martinez
5) An attorney
6) The Social Security Administration
7) Rosa's Pizza
8) Derek C. Jones
9) Department of Aging
10) A lawn mower repairer

Part B Write on your paper the answer to these questions about the Blue Pages.

1) What are the four levels of government agencies usually listed in the Blue Pages?
2) What type of agency is the Social Security Administration?
3) How are the agencies listed under each level of government?

Reading Vocabulary

studio (6)

Part A Answers

1) BP or WP 2) YP 3) WP, YP 4) WP 5) YP 6) BP or WP 7) WP, YP 8) WP 9) BP or WP 10) YP

Part B Answers

1) city, county, state, and federal 2) federal 3) alphabetical order

Learning Styles

Interpersonal/Group Learning

Explain to the students that they are going to create their own small town with homes, businesses, and government. Stress that all these places will have telephone numbers. Divide the class into three groups. Assign Group #1 the White Pages for the town. Assign Group #2 the Yellow Pages for the town. Assign Group #3 the Blue Pages. Invite the groups to create a telephone book for their imaginary town. Encourage them to be creative!

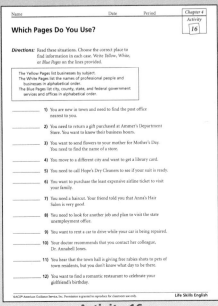

Name Date Period

Chapter 4 *Activity* *16*

Which Pages Do You Use?

Directions: Read these situations. Choose the correct place to find information in each case. Write *Yellow*, *White*, or *Blue Pages* on the lines provided.

> The Yellow Pages list businesses by subject.
> The White Pages list the names of professional people and businesses in alphabetical order.
> The Blue Pages list city, county, state, and federal government services and offices in alphabetical order.

________ **1)** You are new in town and need to find the post office nearest to you.

________ **2)** You need to return a gift purchased at Ammer's Department Store. You want to know their business hours.

________ **3)** You want to send flowers to your mother for Mother's Day. You need to find the name of a store.

________ **4)** You move to a different city and want to get a library card.

________ **5)** You need to call Hope's Dry Cleaners to see if your suit is ready.

________ **6)** You want to purchase the least expensive airline ticket to visit your family.

________ **7)** You need a haircut. Your friend told you that Anna's Hair Salon is very good.

________ **8)** You need to look for another job and plan to visit the state unemployment office.

________ **9)** You want to rent a car to drive while your car is being repaired.

________ **10)** Your doctor recommends that you contact her colleague, Dr. Annabell Jones.

________ **11)** You hear that the town hall is giving free rabies shots to pets of town residents, but you don't know what day to be there.

________ **12)** You want to find a romantic restaurant to celebrate your girlfriend's birthday.

 Life Skills English

Activity 16

Chapter 4 Review

The Teacher's Resource Library includes two parallel forms of the Chapter 4 Mastery Test. The difficulty level of the two forms is equivalent. You may wish to use one form as a pretest and the other form as a posttest.

Chapters 1–4 Midterm Mastery Test

The Teacher's Resource Library includes the Midterm Mastery Test. The Midterm Mastery Test assesses the major learning objectives for Chapters 1–4.

Reading Vocabulary

contractor

Part A Answers

1) Selby, Jackson, Denton **2)** (222) 349-0837 **3)** Doctor; the initials MD, the abbreviation for Medical Doctor, follow his name. **4)** Yes. (222) 343-8700 **5)** EJ's Pizza, E Smith Inc., Edison M K MD, Edison Inc. Contractors, Edwards C Attorney

Chapter 4 Review

Part A Use the facts in the sample directory page below to answer the following questions. Write your answers in complete sentences on your paper.

119 D'ZMURA – EHRLICK

D'ZMURA T 15 Eaton Ln Denton 450-4321
DZWONCHYK Martha Rt 4 Selby 343-7654

E

EJ's Pizza Rt 4 Selby 343-8700
E Smith Inc 601 Rouse Way Jackson 349-0837
EDDY R Frank 39 Wither Av Denton 450-0426
EDGE Wm C 80 W St Jackson 349-0837
EDGERION John & Susan 24 Tulip Dr Denton 450-3410
EDISON M K MD 3 Howard Plaza Selby 342-5400
If no answer call 342-1740
EDISON Inc. contractors
140 Town Hwy Jackson 349-9090
EDWARDS C Attorney 4 Howard Plaza Selby 342-4000

1) What towns does this directory cover?

2) What is Bill Edge's telephone number?

3) What is M. K. Edison's profession? How can you tell?

4) Would Frank Eddy have to use an area code to order a pizza from EJ's? Write the number as he would have to dial it.

5) Which of the listings on this page would probably also be found in the Yellow Pages?

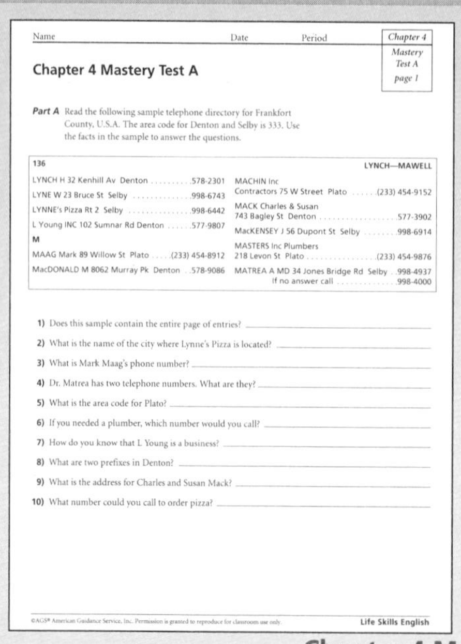

Name Date Period *Chapter 4 Mastery Test A page 1*

Chapter 4 Mastery Test A

Part A Read the following sample telephone directory for Frankfort County, U.S.A. The area code for Denton and Selby is 333. Use the facts in the sample to answer the questions.

136 LYNCH—MAWELL

LYNCH H 32 Kenhill Av Denton 578-2301
LYNE W 23 Bruce St Selby 998-6743
LYNNE's Pizza Rt 2 Selby 998-6442
L Young INC 102 Sumnar Rd Denton 577-9807
M
MAAG Mark 89 Willow St Plato .... (233) 454-8912
MacDONALD M 8062 Murray Pk Denton 578-9086
MACHIN Inc
Contractors 75 W Street Plato .... (233) 454-9152
MACK Charles & Susan
743 Bagley St Denton 577-3902
MacKENSEY J 56 Dupont St Selby 998-6914
MASTERS Inc Plumbers
218 Levon St Plato .... (233) 454-9876
MATREA A MD 34 Jones Bridge Rd Selby 998-4937
If no answer call 998-4000

1) Does this sample contain the entire page of entries? ______

2) What is the name of the city where Lynne's Pizza is located? ______

3) What is Mark Maag's phone number? ______

4) Dr. Matrea has two telephone numbers. What are they? ______

5) What is the area code for Plato? ______

6) If you needed a plumber, which number would you call? ______

7) How do you know that L Young is a business? ______

8) What are two prefixes in Denton? ______

9) What is the address for Charles and Susan Mack? ______

10) What number could you call to order pizza? ______

 Life Skills English

Name Date Period *Chapter 4 Mastery Test A page 2*

Chapter 4 Mastery Test A, continued

Part B Read each pair of situations below. From each pair, choose the situation in which you would need the Yellow Pages. Circle the letter of the correct answer.

1) a) Frank needs to find someone to paint his house.
b) Georgette wants new paneling for her living room. Her best friend Diane recommends Shilling Paneling, Inc.

2) a) Mr. Kuono plans to take his wife out to a nice Chinese restaurant for their anniversary. He doesn't know of any Chinese restaurants in the area.
b) Mrs. Foskey needs to order a cake from Susie's Bakery.

3) a) The Ryan's air conditioner isn't working. They want to get it fixed.
b) Connie wants to call her friend, but she forgot the number.

4) a) Mr. Winters needs to hire a lawyer. His neighbor recommends Babcock & Associates.
b) Sandra wants to buy a violin. She's not sure where to go.

5) a) Alonzo wants to see what time the Pineville Public Library opens.
b) Mrs. O'Conner needs to find a new insurance agency.

Part C Read the following statements. If the statement is true, write *True* on the line. If the statement is not true, write *False*.

______ **1)** If you are looking for a business, but you don't know its name, you should look it up in the White Pages.

______ **2)** Residential listings in the White Pages are listed alphabetically by last name.

______ **3)** The area code for toll-free numbers is 600.

______ **4)** The Yellow Pages has residential listings.

______ **5)** Many larger Yellow Pages have an index.

______ **6)** The Yellow Pages lists professionals that provide services.

______ **7)** The Blue Pages has residential listings.

______ **8)** The Blue Pages lists city, county, state, and federal government telephone numbers.

______ **9)** You could find your local sheriff by looking in the Blue Pages.

______ **10)** The Blue Pages lists phone numbers of private businesses.

 Life Skills English

Chapter 4 Mastery Test A

Part B From each pair of situations that follow, choose the one in which the person would be most likely to use the Yellow Pages. Write the letter of your choice on your paper.

1) a) Elena Wong needs a plumber. Her sister Dolores recommends John J. Rowlands, Inc.

b) John Williams has a toothache. He needs to call a dentist.

2) a) Maria Sanchez needs to call the Walton Library.

b) Nancy Gillan wonders where she can buy computer supplies.

3) a) Margaret wants to find an Italian restaurant near her office.

b) Mr. Wilson needs to call Erlickson Dry Cleaning Company.

4) a) Robert forgot his friend Lamar's phone number.

b) Chris needs to find a company that sells nursing uniforms.

5) a) Mrs. Simone wants to buy five large pizza pans.

b) Doris Williams wants to call Wilson Department Store.

Part C Write answers to the following questions.

1) What is listed in the White Pages? the Yellow Pages?

2) What kinds of listings are in the Blue Pages?

3) Would you find a number for the School Department in the Blue Pages? Why or why not?

4) In which section of the directory would you look to find the telephone numbers for City Hall? for an auto supply store?

5) These federal agencies are listed in the Blue Pages: Interior, Department of; Medicare; Consumer Products Safety Commission. Write the listings in the order in which they appear.

Test Taking Tip

When taking a multiple-choice test, cross out any answers that you know for sure are incorrect. From the remaining answers, choose the one that seems most correct.

Reading Vocabulary

commission (6) plumber (6)
interior (6) restaurant (5)
multiple (8) toothache

Part B Answers

1) b **2)** b **3)** a **4)** b **5)** a

Part C Answers

1) White Pages—names of residents; Yellow Pages—products and services **2)** city, county, state, and federal government agencies **3)** Yes. The School Department is a city (or town) agency. **4)** City Hall—Blue Pages or Business Listings of White Pages; auto supply store—Yellow Pages **5)** Consumer Products Safety Commission; Interior, Department of; Medicare

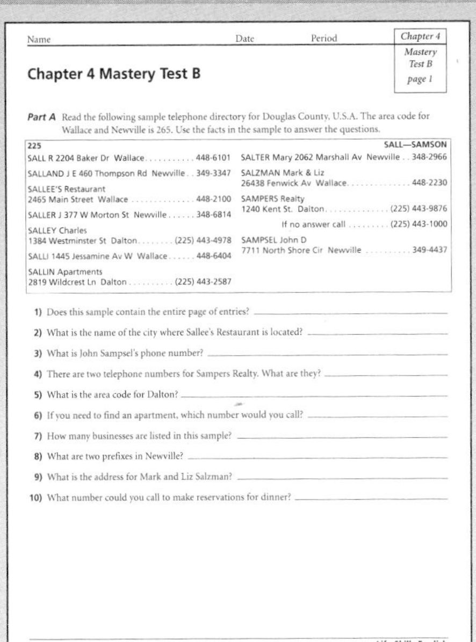

Name Date Period *Chapter 4 Mastery Test B page 1*

Chapter 4 Mastery Test B

Part A Read the following sample telephone directory for Douglas County, U.S.A. The area code for Wallace and Newville is 265. Use the facts in the sample to answer the questions.

225	SALL—SAMSON
SALL R 2204 Baker Dr Wallace 448-6101	SALTER Mary 2062 Marshall Av Newville . . 348-2966
SALLAND J E 460 Thompson Rd Newville . . 349-3347	SALZMAN Mark & Liz 26438 Fenwick Av Wallace 448-2230
SALLEE'S Restaurant 2465 Main Street Wallace 448-2100	SAMPERS Realty 1240 Kent St. Dalton . . . . . (225) 443-9876
SALLER J 377 W Morton St Newville 348-6814	If no answer call . . . . . (225) 443-1000
SALLEY Charles 1384 Westminster St Dalton . . . . . (225) 443-4978	SAMPSEL John D 7711 North Shore Cir Newville 349-4437
SALLI 1445 Jessamine Av W Wallace 448-6404	
SALLIN Apartments 2819 Wildcrest Ln Dalton . . . . . (225) 443-2587	

1) Does this sample contain the entire page of entries? ________

2) What is the name of the city where Sallee's Restaurant is located? ________

3) What is John Sampsel's phone number? ________

4) There are two telephone numbers for Sampers Realty. What are they? ________

5) What is the area code for Dalton? ________

6) If you need to find an apartment, which number would you call? ________

7) How many businesses are listed in this sample? ________

8) What are two prefixes in Newville? ________

9) What is the address for Mark and Liz Salzman? ________

10) What number could you call to make reservations for dinner? ________

 Life Skills English

Name Date Period *Chapter 4 Mastery Test B page 2*

Chapter 4 Mastery Test B, continued

Part B Read each pair of situations below. From each pair, choose the situation in which you would need the Yellow Pages. Circle the correct letter in each case.

1) a) Wanda wants to buy a new pair of shoes. She's not sure where the nearest shoe store is.
b) Tony plans to buy a catcher's mitt for the upcoming season. He needs the phone number for Johnston Sports Store.

2) a) Tanya forgot her mother's work number.
b) Paul wants to buy a bike. He wants the best price possible.

3) a) Suzette wants to get her hair cut. She wants to try a new hair stylist.
b) Mrs. Taylor needs to call Rugs Unlimited to get her carpet cleaned.

4) a) Paul doesn't feel well. He needs to call Dr. Monroe's office, but he doesn't remember the number.
b) The Mulrooneys are looking for a new house. They need to find a real estate agent.

5) a) Doctor Mendoza needs to call Joe's pharmacy. He doesn't have the phone number.
b) Tuan wants to see a movie, but he doesn't know what's showing. He doesn't know the name of any movie theaters in the area.

Part C Read the following statements. If the statement is true, write *True* on the line. If the statement is not true, write *False*.

______ **1)** If you are looking for a business, but you don't know its name, you should look it up in the Yellow Pages.

______ **2)** Residential listings in the White Pages are listed alphabetically by first name.

______ **3)** The area code for toll-free numbers is 800.

______ **4)** The Yellow Pages lists businesses, products, and services.

______ **5)** The Yellow Pages does not have indexes.

______ **6)** The White Pages lists professionals under subject headings.

______ **7)** The Blue Pages has residential listings.

______ **8)** The Blue Pages lists government agencies.

______ **9)** If you wanted to find your uncle's phone number, you could find it by looking in the Blue Pages.

______ **10)** The Blue Pages does not list phone numbers of private businesses.

 Life Skills English

Chapter 4 Mastery Test B

The Telephone Book Chapter 4 **123**

Chapter 5

Planning Guide

Using a Library to Find Information

	Student Text Lesson			
	Student Pages	Vocabulary	Practice Exercises	Lesson Review
Lesson 1 What's in a Library?	126-131	✔	✔	✔
Lesson 2 Fiction and Nonfiction Books	132-136	✔	✔	✔
Lesson 3 Nonfiction Books and the Dewey Decimal System	137-142	✔	✔	✔
Lesson 4 Finding Information in a Library	143-153	✔	✔	✔

Chapter Activities

Teacher's Resource Library

Putting It Together 5: Library Treasure Hunt

Community Connection 5: Know Your Library

Assessment Options

Student Text

Chapter 5 Review

Teacher's Resource Library

Chapter 5 Mastery Tests A and B

Teaching Strategies						Language Skills			Learning Styles						Teacher's Resource Library		
Reviewing Skills	Teacher Alert	Career Application	Home Application	Global Connection	Community Application	Identification Skills	Writing Skills	Punctuation Skills	Visual/Spatial	Auditory/Verbal	Body/Kinesthetic	Logical/Mathematical	Group Learning	LEP/ESL	Activities	Workbook Activities	Self-Study Guide
126	130			129	128	✔	✔	✔				131			17		✔
132						✔	✔	✔			136				18	28	✔
137	139			138		✔	✔	✔		139					19	29-30	✔
143	149	144	146		148	✔	✔	✔				144			20	31-33	✔

Chapter at a Glance

Name ______ Date ______ Period ______ *Chapter 5* *Putting It Together* *5*

Library Treasure Hunt

You can play this game in teams with your class.

Number of Players:
- Two or more teams of two players each

For Each Team You Will Need:
- Several small pieces of paper
- Pencils or pens

To Play:

1) Each team decides on a "treasure" in the library for the other teams to find. They can have one treasure for each team. Examples of treasures are a novel, a video, a magazine, or an entry in an encyclopedia. Each team should have enough time in the library to decide on their treasures and how to find them.

2) Each team writes a series of four or five clues that will lead the other teams to the treasure. The clues should be mysterious but not too hard. The team writes each clue on a separate piece of paper. They fold the clue papers in half and write the number of the clue on the outside.

3) The Leader team gives one series of clues to one member of each team. The member opens the clues one at a time. For example, after a team finds the first clue, the member opens the second clue. When the team finds the second clue, the member opens the third clue. The teams figure out each clue until they find the treasure.

4) The team that finds their treasure first is the next Leader team. Each team should have a turn to be the Leader team.

EXAMPLE

Clue 1:
At the library door, take 10 steps forward. Turn right. Take 15 steps forward. Turn left. Take three steps forward. [The clue leads the team to the computer for the library catalog.]

Clue 2:
Sit at the keyboard. [Include any instruction that is needed.]

[The rest of the clue might tell what to enter in the computer. The next clue might be more mysterious. The team might have to decide which entry is the right choice. The last clue could lead to the shelf or part of the library where the treasure is kept.]

 Life Skills English

Putting It Together 5

Name ______ Date ______ Period ______ *Chapter 5* *Community Connection* *5*

Know Your Library

Every library is organized somewhat differently. Each library may have a different kind of catalog. Still, you can find almost any information you want in most libraries. Becoming familiar with your library can help you to find information quickly. Follow these steps to become familiar with your library.

Step 1. Find out where the library nearest your home is. Go there. Spend at least an hour becoming familiar with the library.

Step 2. Ask one of the librarians to point out where things are. Find out where the library catalog, books, references, and periodicals are. Find out where the audiovisual materials are.

Step 3. Spend some time with the library catalog. Learn how to use it. Ask a librarian to help you if necessary. Find at least two of each of the three kinds of records. The three records are author, title, and subject.

Step 4. Write down the title and Dewey Decimal Number of two books you find in the catalog. If your library has its catalog on computer, you can tell whether the books are checked out. Find two books that are not checked out. Pick one fiction and one nonfiction book.

Step 5. Next, go the shelves where the books are. Try to find the two books you wrote down. Ask a librarian for help if you need it. Notice how the books are organized on the shelf.

Step 6. Then go to the reference section. Look at the different kinds of references. Think of something you would like to know about. See if you can find a reference that will help you. Ask a librarian for help if you need it.

Step 7. Next go to the periodical section. Find *The Readers' Guide to Periodical Literature*. Study it. Choose a periodical that interests you. Try to find that periodical in the library. Ask a librarian for help if you need it.

Step 8. Then go to the audiovisual section or sections. Study the library's video catalog. Ask to listen to a cassette or CD that you like.

Step 9. Before you leave the library, ask how to get a library card. Follow the necessary steps to get one. Then check out at least one item from your library.

Step 10. Finally, write a one-page report on how your library is organized. Have your teacher or a family member read your report. Ask if they understand from your report how your library is organized.

 Life Skills English

Community Connection 5

Chapter 5

Using a Library to Find Information

The library is the best place to look for information. Nowhere else is so much information on so many different subjects in one place. At first glance, you may think that the library is too big and has too much information. How will you ever find what you are looking for? All libraries, big and small, follow a similar plan for arranging books and other resources. You can understand that plan. It will help you find the information you are looking for.

In Chapter 5, you will learn about libraries. You will understand the kinds of resources libraries have. You will learn how those resources are organized. You will learn how to find the information you need.

Goals for Learning

- To learn how to find information in a library
- To learn about the types of materials available in a library
- To learn to recognize and find fiction materials
- To learn how to find nonfiction books using the Dewey Decimal System

125

Reading Vocabulary

available (6) similar (6)
organize (6) subject (5)
resource (8)

Introducing the Chapter

Explain to students that they are going to help you make up a survey that they can then use to test their own library knowledge. Then elicit a series of questions to include in the survey. Write each question on the board. Some example questions are: *How often do you use the library in a week, month, year? Where is the closest public library? What are examples of books in the library's reference section? Have you ever asked a librarian for help in finding information? Are you familiar with any of the following: card catalog, computer catalog, microfiche, The Readers' Guide?* Allow time for students to answer each question on their own paper, and help them devise a scale to rate their own library knowledge. Explain to students that in Chapter 5, they are going to learn about libraries and the information they contain. When they have finished the chapter, they can take the survey again to see how much they have improved their knowledge about libraries.

SELF-STUDY GUIDE

Name ____________

CHAPTER 5: Using a Library to Find Information

Goal 5.1 *To learn about the types of materials available in a library*

Date	Assignment	Score
______	1: Read pages 125-126. Complete Activity A on page 127.	______
______	2: Read pages 127-129. Complete Activity B on page 129.	______
______	3: Read page 130. Complete Activity C on page 130.	______
______	4: Complete the Lesson 1 Review, Parts A-B on page 131.	______

Comments:

Goal 5.2 *To learn to recognize and find fiction materials*

Date	Assignment	Score
______	5: Read pages 132-133. Complete Activity A on page 133.	______
______	6: Read page 134. Complete Activity B on page 134.	______
______	7: Complete Workbook Activity 28.	______
______	8: Read page 135. Complete Activity C on page 135.	______
______	9: Complete the Lesson 2 Review, Parts A-B on page 136.	______

Comments:

Goal 5.3 *To learn how to find nonfiction books using the Dewey Decimal System*

Date	Assignment	Score
______	10: Read pages 137-140. Complete Activity A on page 140 and Activity B on page 141.	______
______	11: Complete the Lesson 3 Review on page 142.	______
______	12: Complete Workbook Activity 29.	______
______	13: Complete Workbook Activity 30.	______

Comments:

 Life Skills English

SELF-STUDY GUIDE

Name ____________

CHAPTER 5 Using a Library to Find Information, continued

Goal 5.4 *To learn how to find information in a library*

Date	Assignment	Score
______	14: Read pages 143-145. Complete Activities A-B on page 145.	______
______	15: Complete Workbook Activity 31.	______
______	16: Read pages 146-147. Complete Activities C-D on page 147.	______
______	17: Read page 148. Complete Activity E on page 149.	______
______	18: Complete Workbook Activity 32.	______
______	19: Read pages 149-150. Complete Activity F on page 150.	______
______	20: Read page 151. Complete Activity G on page 151 and Activity H on page 152.	______
______	21: Read page 152. Complete Activity I on page 152.	______
______	22: Complete the Lesson 4 Review, Parts A-B on page 153.	______
______	23: Complete Workbook Activity 33.	______
______	24: Complete the Chapter 5 Review, Parts A-C on pages 154-155.	______

Comments:

Student's Signature ____________ Date ____________

Instructor's Signature ____________ Date ____________

©AGS® American Guidance Service, Inc. Permission is granted to reproduce for classroom use only. Life Skills English

Chapter 5 Self-Study Guide

Lesson at a Glance

Chapter 5 Lesson 1

Overview This lesson describes the variety of print and electronic materials found in today's libraries and how to access that material.

Objectives

- To answer questions about what is in a library.
- To understand the purpose of different library materials and equipment.

Student Pages 126–131

Teacher's Resource Library

Activity 17

Reading Vocabulary

atlas (7)
audiovisual
college (5)
display (6)
equipment (5)
handbook
hardback
hardcover
issue (6)
media
paperback
reference (6)
requirement (8)
section (5)
separate (5)
softcover
subscribe (7)
variety (6)
vocational

Teaching Suggestions

Introducing the Lesson

Discuss the text, focusing students' attention on the descriptions of the different print materials and equipment found in a library today.

Reviewing Skills Help students recall the type of facts and information found in a dictionary, encyclopedia, almanac, atlas, and magazine.

Lesson 1 What's in a Library?

When people think about libraries, they usually think about books. Today, however, libraries are about more than books. Today, libraries have a wide variety of print materials as well as audiovisual materials and equipment. Because of this, some libraries today are called media centers.

Print Materials in a Library

Here are some of the print materials you will find in most libraries.

Hardback books	Books in hardcover include fiction and nonfiction. You can check out most of these books.
Paperback books	Most libraries have collections of paperback, or softcover, books that can be checked out.
Reference books	The reference section has encyclopedias, atlases, and other books. You usually cannot check out books in the reference section. You must use these books in the library.
Magazines	Libraries subscribe to many kinds of magazines. The most recent issues are usually displayed on a rack. Old issues are kept on separate shelves. You often have to ask the librarian to get them for you.
Newspapers	Most libraries subscribe to all the local newspapers. Some get newspapers from other cities. The library keeps old issues on file. Ask your librarian for help.
Telephone books	You can find local telephone books in your library. Some libraries have copies of telephone books from other cities.
Guides	Libraries have many kinds of guides and handbooks. You can look in guides to colleges and vocational schools to find out about their programs and requirements.

Activity A What kind of print material would you look for in the library for each situation? Write your answers on your paper.

1) You are moving to a new city and plan to rent an apartment. You need the number of a service in that city to help you.

2) You plan to go to the community college in the fall and want to know if it offers courses in electronics.

3) You want to read an article in last February's *The Reader's Digest.*

4) You want to find a part-time job.

5) You want to look at a map of Chile.

Audiovisual Materials in a Library

Here are some of the audiovisual materials you will find in most libraries.

Videotapes	Videotape cassettes store motion pictures on tape. These may be movies, nonfiction documentaries, training programs, or other productions. Videotapes are often stored on the shelves alongside books. Videotapes are played on VCRs.
Compact discs (CDs)	CDs store music. Computer information is stored on CD-ROMs. (ROM stands for "Read Only Memory.") One CD-ROM can hold an entire encyclopedia with color photographs, video, sound, and text. You need a CD player to play music CDs. You need a computer with a CD-ROM drive to access information on a CD-ROM.
Videodiscs	A videodisc is similar to a CD. Videodiscs can store print and motion pictures. Some libraries have movies and encyclopedias stored on videodisc. You need a videodisc player and a television or a computer monitor to view the information on a videodisc.
Other materials	Libraries may also have other items that you can check out or use in the library. These may include copy machines, personal computers and software, videocassette recorders, videodisc players, televisions, filmstrips, audiocassettes, and records. Ask the librarian for available resources.

Reading Vocabulary

access (8)	memory (5)
audiocassette	monitor (6)
cassette	photograph (6)
community (5)	production (6)
compact (5)	projector (8)
computer (8)	recorder (8)
digest (7)	situation (5)
disc	software
documentary	text (6)
electronic (5)	video
film (6)	videocassette
filmstrip	videodisc
format	videotape

Presenting Activity A

Do Activity A together as a class. Briefly discuss each situation before asking students to respond. Point out that some situations may have more than one correct response. After you have completed the activity, ask students to make up new situations modeled on those in Activity A or use situations from their own experience. Invite volunteers to present the situation to the class and have the class identify the kind of print material they would consult at the library for each situation.

Activity A Answers

Some answers may vary. Possible responses are given with the most probable response listed first. Accept all reasonable responses.

1) telephone book, newspaper
2) college guide or handbook
3) magazine (back issue)
4) newspaper **5)** atlas, encyclopedia, nonfiction book about Chile

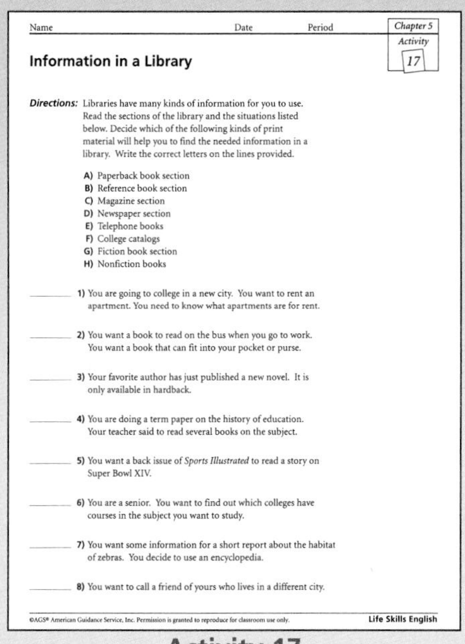

Name ______ Date ______ Period ______ *Chapter 5 Activity 17*

Information in a Library

Directions: Libraries have many kinds of information for you to use. Read the sections of the library and the situations listed below. Decide which of the following kinds of print material will help you to find the needed information in a library. Write the correct letters on the lines provided.

A) Paperback book section
B) Reference book section
C) Magazine section
D) Newspaper section
E) Telephone books
F) College catalogs
G) Fiction book section
H) Nonfiction books

______ **1)** You are going to college in a new city. You want to rent an apartment. You need to know what apartments are for rent.

______ **2)** You want a book to read on the bus when you go to work. You want a book that can fit into your pocket or purse.

______ **3)** Your favorite author has just published a new novel. It is only available in hardback.

______ **4)** You are doing a term paper on the history of education. Your teacher said to read several books on the subject.

______ **5)** You want a back issue of *Sports Illustrated* to read a story on Super Bowl XIV.

______ **6)** You are a senior. You want to find out which colleges have courses in the subject you want to study.

______ **7)** You want some information for a short report about the habitat of zebras. You decide to use an encyclopedia.

______ **8)** You want to call a friend of yours who lives in a different city.

 Life Skills English

Activity 17

Reading Vocabulary

adult (6)	operate (5)
application (8)	public (5)
branch (2)	resident (7)
connect (5)	security (8)
county (5)	social (5)
license (5)	sponsor (8)
local (6)	system (5)

Using What You Have Learned

As students research the library's resources, suggest that they also take the time to speak to the research librarian who can point out the location of specific equipment and how to use it. The research librarian can also provide information about the library's future plans for acquiring additional reference materials and equipment. After students have finished their investigation, invite volunteers to share their findings with the class. On a scale of 1 to 10, with 10 being the highest rating, how would students rate their library on availability and accessibility of print materials and audiovisual equipment?

Application

In the Community
Point out to students that there are probably many people in their community who would enjoy taking advantage of the library's resources, but because of disabilities, poor health, advanced age, or lack of transportation, these people cannot get to the library themselves. Suggest that students ask the librarian if he or she knows of anyone in the community for whom students can act as library "gofers," checking out books and doing any necessary research.

Other Libraries

To borrow books from a public library, you usually need a library card. In some cities and towns, you must be a resident to get a library card. In other places, you must only be a resident of the state. You can get a library card by filling out a simple application. You may be asked for a Social Security number, your driver's license, or some other form of identification. If you do not have one of these, you may need an adult who already has a card to sponsor you.

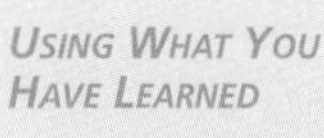

Branch
One of the libraries in a system of libraries.

In most places, the city or county government operates the local public library. Depending on where you live, your county library may have one branch or many branches. A **branch** is one of the libraries in a system. If your library is part of a system, you can use your card to borrow books and other materials from any of the branches in the system.

Using What You Have Learned

Make a list of the equipment and materials that you read about in this lesson. Go to your school library or your public library. Find out what is available in your area. The next time you want information, don't overlook these resources.

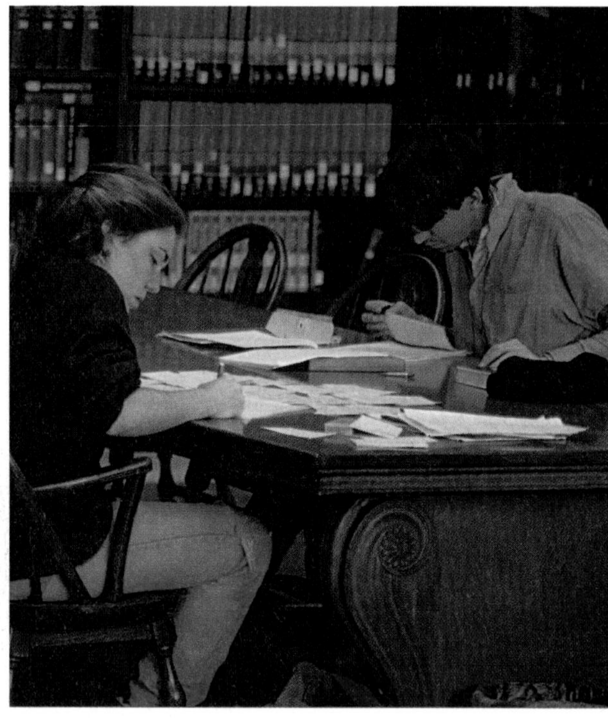

Students find libraries useful for doing research and studying for classes.

128 Chapter 5 Using a Library to Find Information

Finding Material in a Library

Libraries have thousands and sometimes millions of different books and other materials. To make these materials easy to find, libraries list them in **catalogs.** Here are some kinds of catalogs in a library.

Catalog
Any list of information.

Library catalog
A catalog that lists most of the materials in a library. There are three types of listings: title, author, and subject.

Magazine catalog
A catalog that lists all the magazines a library subscribes to and identifies the issues the library has.

Microfiche
A film card on which many pages of reduced copy are stored.

Video catalog
A catalog that lists films or videotapes that a library owns by title or subject.

Library catalog	A **library catalog** lists most of the materials in a library. It may be printed on index cards or stored on a computer or on **microfiche.** The materials may include fiction and nonfiction books, videotapes, and other types of materials. There are three types of listings: title, author, and subject. Newspapers are not usually included in the main library catalog.
Magazine catalog	A **magazine catalog** lists all the magazines a library subscribes to. It identifies the issues the library has.
Newspapers	A library has a list of the newspapers it subscribes to and all of the old issues it has. The old issues of some newspapers may be stored on microfilm or microfiche.
Video catalog	A **video catalog** lists all the films and videotapes a library owns by title or subject.

Activity B For each item, decide which catalog each person should look at. Write your answers on your paper.

1) Ramon wants to find a nonfiction book about volcanoes.

2) Chan wants to know if the library has a copy of the December 1994 issue of *Personal Computing.*

3) Mary wants to know if the library has the movie *Dances With Wolves.*

4) Mr. Jackson wants to know if the library has any books of Jack London's short stories.

5) Chris would like to read an article in the sports section of the September 25, 1995, issue of *Fieldstone Daily News.*

Reading Vocabulary

author (6)
catalog (6)
identify (6)
item (6)
library catalog
magazine catalog
microfiche
microfilm
personal (6)
title (5)
video catalog

■ Presenting Activity B

Before having students do Activity B, have them take turns describing the different catalogs in their own words.

Activity B Answers

1) library catalog **2)** magazine catalog **3)** video catalog **4)** library catalog **5)** newspapers

Global Connection

Today's libraries serve both English and non-English speaking patrons. Ask students to find out what programs their library has in place to serve its non-English speaking patrons. Questions they might try to answer include:

- Do any of the librarians speak a second or third language?
- Are any library pamphlets or brochures written in languages other than English?
- What effort does the library make to help non-English speaking residents become acquainted with the library's resources?
- Does the library subscribe to any foreign language newspapers or magazines? What are they?

Reading Vocabulary

agencies
congress (5)
Library of Congress
original (5)
pamphlet (7)
periodical (8)
scholar (5)
volume (6)

■ Presenting Activity C

Invite students who have been to the Library of Congress to describe their experiences. Ask them to describe it and tell how it compares to other libraries they have visited. If possible, display photographs and pictures of the inside of the Library of Congress for students to see. As a class, write the Library of Congress for information about our national library.

Activity C Answers

1) Washington, D.C. **2)** Thomas Jefferson **3)** over 80 million **4)** Students may choose any three: pamphlets, periodicals, films, videocassettes, CDs, photographs, music, and maps **5)** anyone

Teacher Alert

You may wish to point out to students who are unfamiliar with American history that Thomas Jefferson was the third President of the United States from 1801–1809. Before becoming president, Jefferson drafted the Declaration of Independence in 1776 during the second Continental Congress.

The Library of Congress

Library of Congress
The national library of the United States.

The **Library of Congress** is in Washington, D.C. It serves as the national library of the United States. Congress started the library in 1800 for its members. Now the Library of Congress also serves other government agencies, scholars, other libraries, and the general public.

In 1815, Congress bought Thomas Jefferson's library, which had 6,000 volumes. Today, the library has over 80 million items in 470 languages. The library has books, pamphlets, periodicals, films, videocassettes, CDs, photographs, music, and maps.

For more information about our national library, write:

Library of Congress
101 Independence Avenue SE
Washington, DC 20540

Activity C Answer on your paper these questions about the Library of Congress.

1) Where is the Library of Congress?
2) Who owned the original 6,000 volumes in the Library of Congress?
3) About how many items does the Library of Congress own today?
4) Besides books, what are three other kinds of materials found in the Library of Congress?
5) Who can use the Library of Congress?

130 Chapter 5 Using a Library to Find Information

Lesson 1 Review

Part A Write the answers to these items on your paper.

1) Because of the kinds of materials they have, what are libraries sometimes called today?
2) Name at least two types of print materials other than books that you would find in most libraries.
3) Name two types of audiovisual materials that many libraries have today.
4) Name two other kinds of equipment that you might find in a library.
5) What is the name for lists of materials in libraries?

Part B For each of the following items, decide what kind of material each person should look for at the library. Write your answers on your paper.

1) Ruby wants the telephone number of an organization in another city.
2) Ben wants to use an encyclopedia on computer.
3) Elena would like to watch the movie *Forrest Gump.*
4) Ossie needs extra help learning Spanish. It would help if he could hear the correct pronunciation of words.
5) Kimi wants to know the entrance requirements at the local community college.
6) Richard is interested in finding out about a major earthquake that occurred a year ago.

Reading Vocabulary

major (6) organization (7)
occur (6) pronunciation (5)

Part A Answers

Some answers may vary. Possible responses are given.

1) media centers **2)** magazines and newspapers **3)** videotapes and CDs **4)** computer, copy machine **5)** catalog

Part B Answers

1) telephone book **2)** CD **3)** videocassette **4)** audiocassette (language tape) **5)** college guide/handbook **6)** newspaper or news magazine (back issues)

Learning Styles

Logical/Mathematical
Divide the class into pairs. Invite each pair to create a nonverbal chart for a library that will tell people what the library contains. Suggest that the pairs use symbols, icons, drawing, pictures, or code to illustrate the information in the boxes on pages 126, 127, and 129. Afterward, invite the pairs to share their work. Discuss the most helpful aspect of each chart.

Lesson at a Glance

Chapter 5 Lesson 2

Overview This lesson presents different types of fiction and nonfiction books and explains how fiction books are arranged in a library.

Objectives

- To answer questions about fiction books in a library.
- To match types of books with their descriptions.

Student Pages 132–136

Teacher's Resource Library

Activity 18

Workbook Activity 28

Reading Vocabulary

account (5)
actual (7)
autobiography (9)
biographical novel
biography (7)
combine (6)
complex (9)
conversation (5)
dialogue (7)
fiction (7)
historical novel
history (3)
imaginary (5)
literature (6)
nonfiction
novel (7)
novella
outcome
short story

Teaching Suggestions

- **Introducing the Lesson** Discuss the information presented in the text. Be sure students understand the distinction between fiction and nonfiction and the characteristics of the different types of fiction and nonfiction listed.

- **Reviewing Skills** Review the different kinds of books found in a library.

Lesson 2 Fiction and Nonfiction Books

Autobiography *A story of a real person's life written by that person.*

Biographical novel *A fictional account of a real person's life.*

Biography *A nonfiction book about a real person written by someone other than that person.*

Dialogue *Conversation.*

Fiction *An imaginary story.*

Historical novel *A fictional story about real people and events.*

History *A nonfiction book about real people and events of the past.*

Nonfiction *Based on facts.*

Novel *A long, complex story.*

Short story *A story that can usually be read in one sitting.*

Fiction is an imaginary story. **Nonfiction** is based on facts.

Novels and short stories are two kinds of fiction. A **novel** is a long story with many characters and events. Usually, the story has several twists and turns before the final outcome. Most novels are several hundred pages long. Some, such as *Gone With the Wind* by Margaret Mitchell, may be more than 1,000 pages. Others, such as *The Red Pony* by John Steinbeck, have fewer than 100 pages. Short novels are sometimes called novellas.

A **short story** may be only one or two pages long. It may also be as long as several dozen pages. Many short stories are first printed in magazines. You may also find collections of short stories in a book. Literature textbooks often have short stories.

Most fiction is about imaginary people and events. Sometimes, however, authors include real people and events in their stories. They might use actual words that the people said. Sometimes authors make up words for people to say. Authors also combine facts and imagination to write about the way events may have happened.

Here are five kinds of fiction and nonfiction books.

Biography	A book about a real person written by someone else. All of the events actually happened. If there is **dialogue,** or conversation, it is the exact words that someone said.
Autobiography	A story about a real person written by that person. If you write a story about your own life, it is an autobiography.
Biographical novel	A story about a real person. The author adds imaginary dialogue and imaginary events.
History	A nonfiction book about real people and events of the past.
Historical novel	A story about real people and events. The author adds imaginary dialogue and events.

If you are not sure whether a book is fiction or nonfiction:

- Look for the word *novel* or *short story* on the cover or title page.
- Check to see if the book is marked with an *F* or *FIC* for fiction. If it is, it is stored in the fiction section of the library.

Activity A Make two columns on your paper. Write *Fiction* at the top of one column and *Nonfiction* at the top of the other. Look over the five kinds of books described on page 132. List them in the correct columns. Beside each type of book, write a title of a real book that is an example of that type. You may need to go to your school library to complete this activity.

How Fiction Books Are Arranged in the Library

All libraries arrange fiction books in alphabetical order according to the authors' last names. Some authors have written many books. Their books will be grouped together and arranged in alphabetical order by title. The words *the, a,* or *an* are not used to alphabetize titles.

EXAMPLE These books by John Steinbeck would be arranged in the following order:

Cannery Row
The Grapes of Wrath
Of Mice and Men
The Red Pony

Reading Vocabulary

alphabetical (6)
alphabetize
cannery
column (5)
describe (5)
wrath (6)

■ Presenting Activity A

Display an example of each type of book listed on page 132 for students to see. Write *Fiction* and *Nonfiction* at the top of two columns on the board. Then hold up one of the books at a time, read its title, and briefly describe what it's about. Help students determine the type of book that it is and whether it belongs in the *Fiction* or *Nonfiction* column on the board. Write the type of book and the book title in the appropriate column. Following this activity, encourage students to complete Activity A on their own or with partners.

Activity A Answers

Book titles will vary. Fiction—biographical novel, historical novel; Nonfiction—biography, autobiography, history.

Using a Library to Find Information *Chapter 5* **133**

Reading Vocabulary

best-seller	romance (7)
fang (6)	science (5)
height (5)	topic (5)
kidnap (7)	wrestling

■ Presenting Activity B

Place eight to ten fiction books by a variety of authors on a flat surface. Invite a volunteer to arrange the books in the order that the books would appear on a library shelf. Then read aloud to the class the titles with the authors' names in the order they have been arranged. If necessary, spell an author's last name or write it on the board so that students can determine if the books are in the correct order.

Activity B Answers

1) *Watership Down* by Richard Adams **2)** *Superfudge* by Judy Blume **3)** *Jane Eyre* by Charlotte Brontë **4)** *Wuthering Heights* by Emily Brontë **5)** *Seventeenth Summer* by Maureen Daly **6)** *The Wrestling Match* by Buchi Emecheta **7)** *The Outsiders* by S. E. Hinton **8)** *That Was Then, This Is Now* by S. E. Hinton **9)** *Call of the Wild* by Jack London **10)** *White Fang* by Jack London **11)** *Dragonsong* by Anne McCaffrey **12)** *Hawaii* by James Michener **13)** *Kidnapped* by Robert Louis Stevenson **14)** *Treasure Island* by Robert Louis Stevenson **15)** *Huckleberry Finn* by Mark Twain

If two authors share the same last name, the books are arranged in alphabetical order according to the authors' first names.

EXAMPLE *The Count of Monte Cristo* by Alexandre Dumas
Jonoah and the Green Stone by Henry Dumas

> ***Using What You Have Learned***
>
> Look in your Sunday newspaper this week. Find out what the best-sellers are in hardcover and paperback fiction and nonfiction.
>
> Make a list of the topics that people like to read about. Here are some examples.
>
> *Fiction:*
> Spy stories
> Romance
>
> *Nonfiction:*
> Biographies
> How to make money

Some libraries group certain types of fiction books together. For example, they might put all the mystery books in one section. They might put all the science fiction books in another section. As with other fiction books, these books will be arranged in alphabetical order. The order will be according to the authors' last names within that section.

Activity B Arrange these fiction books in the order that they would appear on a shelf in a library. Write the books in order on your paper.

1) *The Outsiders* by S. E. Hinton
2) *White Fang* by Jack London
3) *Hawaii* by James Michener
4) *That Was Then, This Is Now* by S. E. Hinton
5) *Seventeenth Summer* by Maureen Daly
6) *Call of the Wild* by Jack London
7) *Huckleberry Finn* by Mark Twain
8) *Wuthering Heights* by Emily Brontë
9) *Jane Eyre* by Charlotte Brontë
10) *Treasure Island* by Robert Louis Stevenson
11) *Watership Down* by Richard Adams
12) *Superfudge* by Judy Blume
13) *The Wrestling Match* by Buchi Emecheta
14) *Dragonsong* by Anne McCaffrey
15) *Kidnapped* by Robert Louis Stevenson

Name Date Period — *Chapter 5 Activity 18*

Arranging Books in a Library

Directions: Arrange these fiction books in the order that they would appear on a shelf in the library. Write the authors (last name first) and the titles in correct order on the lines given below.

Marjorie Morningstar by Herman Wouk
The Maltese Falcon by Dashiell Hammett
Catch-22 by Joseph Heller
The Good Earth by Pearl Buck
Ragtime by E. L. Doctorow
Pride and Prejudice by Jane Austen
Little Women by Louisa May Alcott
Look Homeward, Angel by Thomas Wolfe
Jane Eyre by Charlotte Brontë
Ethan Frome by Edith Wharton
Treasure Island by Robert Louis Stevenson
Main Street by Sinclair Lewis
Jazz by Toni Morrison
Moby Dick by Herman Melville
The Great Gatsby by F. Scott Fitzgerald

	Author	Title
1)		
2)		
3)		
4)		
5)		
6)		
7)		
8)		
9)		
10)		
11)		
12)		
13)		
14)		
15)		

 Life Skills English

Activity 18

Name Date Period — *Chapter 5 Workbook Activity 28*

Arranging Books in a Library

Directions: Arrange these fiction books in the order that they would appear on a shelf in a library.

1) *Tom Sawyer* by Mark Twain
2) *The Outsiders* by S. E. Hinton
3) *Watership Down* by Richard Adams
4) *Robinson Crusoe* by Daniel Defoe
5) *The Clan of the Cave Bear* by Jean Auel
6) *The Valley of the Horses* by Jean Auel
7) *Bleak House* by Charles Dickens
8) *A Tale of Two Cities* by Charles Dickens
9) *Penrod* by Booth Tarkington
10) *Exodus* by Leon Uris
11) *Book of Lights* by Chaim Potok
12) *Rebecca of Sunnybrook Farm* by Kate Douglas Wiggins
13) *Show Boat* by Edna Ferber
14) *Murder at the Vicarage* by Agatha Christie
15) *The Living Reed* by Pearl Buck

 Life Skills English

Workbook Activity 28

Finding a Fiction Book in a Library

Finding a fiction book in the library can be easy if you remember the following guidelines:

- To find a fiction book on the library shelf, you need to know the author's last name and the title of the book.
- To find a fiction book when you know the title but not the author's name, use the library catalog. The library catalog has records for each book. Each book has an author record and a title record. Some fiction books have subject records. If you look up the title or the subject of the book, you will find the author's name.
- If you search for a book on a computer catalog, you can type the author's name, the title, or the subject. The computer catalog will list all of the books that were written by that author. It will also list the books that have that title or are about that subject.

Activity C Decide if you would look up the title record, author record, or subject record for each item in the library catalog. Write on your paper *A* for author, *T* for title, or *S* for subject.

1) *Gone With the Wind*

2) Margaret Mitchell

3) the Civil War

4) *Huckleberry Finn*

5) Mark Twain

6) adventure and adventurers

7) sailing

8) *Moby Dick*

9) Herman Melville

10) ocean travel

Reading Vocabulary

civil (5) guideline

■ Presenting Activity C

Have pairs of students role-play the parts of a librarian and a student looking for a particular book, a book by a particular author, or a book on a specific topic. The student should explain what he or she is looking for, and the librarian can explain how to find the book. Students playing the role of the librarian can use the bulleted information on page 135 for their explanations. Students playing the role of students can use the items listed in Activity C, or you can provide other titles, authors, and subjects.

Activity C Answers

1) T 2) A 3) S 4) T 5) A 6) S 7) S 8) T 9) A 10) S

Reading Vocabulary
ceremony (5)

Part A Answers
1 a) short story **b)** novel **c)** short story **2)** *Ceremony* by Leslie Marmon Silko *The Grapes of Wrath* by John Steinbeck *The Joy Luck Club* by Amy Tan *The Kitchen God's Wife* by Amy Tan **3)** Students may choose any two of the following responses: They are in the fiction section. They are marked with an *F* or *FIC*. They have only call letters, no numbers. They may have the words *novel* or *short stories* on the cover. **4)** First, you need to know the author's last name; if there is more than one book by that author, you need to know the title.

Part B Answers
1) e **2)** d **3)** b **4)** c **5)** a

Learning Styles

Body/Kinesthetic
Write the title and the author of a book on a slip of paper for each student in your class. (Note that the Sunday paper provides the titles of best-selling books.) Label each slip as fiction or nonfiction. Next, designate one area of the classroom as fiction and another as nonfiction. Then give each student a slip and ask the students to congregate in the area in which their book title fits. Finally, ask them to arrange themselves in alphabetical order according to the author's name on their slip of paper.

Lesson 2 Review

Part A Write the answers to the following questions on your paper.

1) Here are some famous fiction stories. Are they novels or short stories?
   a) "The Tell-Tale Heart" by Edgar Allan Poe. (9 pages)
   b) *20,000 Leagues Under the Sea* by Jules Verne. (447 pages)
   c) "The Most Dangerous Game" by Richard Connell. (13 pages)
2) Write the following book titles in the order that they would appear on a shelf in the fiction section of the library.
   The Kitchen God's Wife by Amy Tan
   The Grapes of Wrath by John Steinbeck
   The Joy Luck Club by Amy Tan
   Ceremony by Leslie Marmon Silko
3) What are two ways that you can recognize a fiction book in a library?
4) What do you need to know to find a fiction book on a library shelf?

Part B Match each type of book with its description. Write the item number and the matching letter on your paper.

1) Historical novel	a) A book about someone's life written by that person
2) History	b) A book about a real person written by someone else
3) Biography	c) A fictional story about a real person
4) Biographical novel	d) A book about real people and events of the past
5) Autobiography	e) A fictional story about real people and events of the past

Nonfiction Books and the Dewey Decimal System

What is a nonfiction book?

A nonfiction book is about real people, real events, facts, or people's ideas.

How can I recognize a nonfiction book?

Bibliography
A list of books and articles an author has used as references to write a book. Bibliographies usually appear in the back of the book.

Nonfiction books often have a reference list or **bibliography.** These are the books and articles the author consulted when writing the book. Look for the references in the back of the book.

Nonfiction books often have indexes. An index is an alphabetical list of the topics included in the book. Look at the index at the end of this book.

In a library, a nonfiction book has a number on the binding. Under the number are the first one or two letters of the author's last name.

Who was Dewey?

Dewey Decimal System
A system that libraries use to classify and organize books.

Melvil Dewey was a librarian who lived from 1851 to 1931. In 1876, he invented a system for arranging books in a library. Today, this system is called the **Dewey Decimal System.** Dewey also started the first school for training librarians. He taught his system to his students.

What is a decimal system?

Call number
The numbers and letters assigned to a library book. The call number determines where the book will be placed on the shelf.

Decimals are based on the number ten. Dewey divided the information in nonfiction books into ten main subject areas. He used the numbers from 000 to 999 to cover the fields of general knowledge. He used decimals and letters to fit special subjects within each group. The **call number** on the spine of a book shows these numbers and letters.

Each book has three numbers before the decimal point. It may have several numbers after the decimal point. Several books with the same number are alphabetized by author's last name.

Lesson at a Glance

Chapter 5 Lesson 3

Overview This lesson explains how to use the Dewey Decimal System to find nonfiction books in the library.

Objective

- To classify books according to the Dewey Decimal System.

Student Pages 137–142

Teacher's Resource Library

Activity 19

Workbook Activities 29–30

Reading Vocabulary

assign (6)	determine (5)
bibliography (9)	**Dewey Decimal System**
binding	include (5)
call number	index (5)
classify (8)	librarian (5)
consult (5)	
decimal (6)	

Teaching Suggestions

- **Introducing the Lesson**
To enliven the presentation of the Dewey Decimal System, you may wish to use the question and answer format of the text to stage a panel discussion. Select three or four students to be expert panel members and ten students to ask the questions. Panel members can decide which questions they will answer beforehand, using the text as their guide. Students asking questions should ask the questions in the order that they appear in the text.

- **Reviewing Skills** Review how fiction books are arranged in the library.

Reading Vocabulary

classification (8) memorize (6)
initial (6)

Global Connection

Although many libraries in the United States use the Dewey Decimal System, there are two other classification systems that are widely used in the United States and around the world. One is the Universal Decimal Classification system which is a European adaptation of the Dewey Decimal System. The second is a classification system created and used by the Library of Congress.

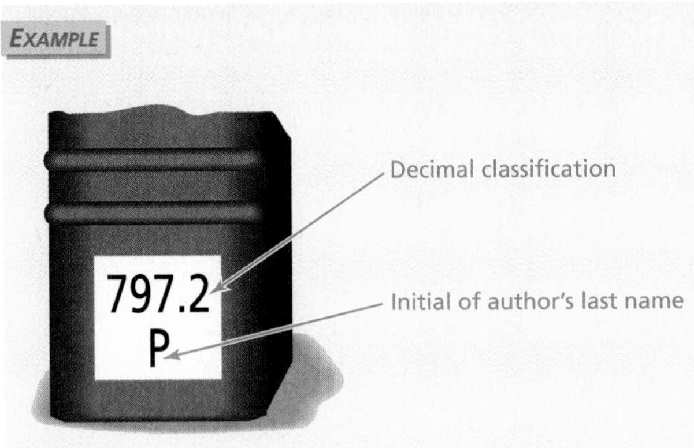

How can the Dewey Decimal System help me?

To find a book in the library catalog, you use one of these three things:

- the title
- the author's name
- the subject

The record in the catalog gives the Dewey Decimal numbers, or call number. Suppose a book has the call number 797.2/P. First find the 700 shelves in the nonfiction section of the library. Skim the shelves, looking for the 790s. Then find the books with 797.2. Finally, look for the books with the letter *P.*

What if the book I want isn't there?

All of the books with the same number are about the same subject. If you know the number that matches your subject, you can find other books on that subject.

Do I need to memorize the whole Dewey Decimal System?

Since the call numbers are on the catalog records, it is not necessary to memorize the numbers. However, it is helpful to know the system's ten main groups.

138 *Chapter 5 Using a Library to Find Information*

What are the ten main categories of the Dewey Decimal System?

Numbers	Subjects and Subtopics
000–099	General Works *Encyclopedias, periodicals, library facts*
100–199	Philosophy and Psychology *Logic, mental health*
200–299	Religion *Mythology*
300–399	Social Sciences *Government, education, economics*
400–499	Language *Dictionaries, foreign languages, grammar*
500–599	Pure Sciences *Biology, mathematics, botany, chemistry*
600–699	Technology (Applied Sciences) *Engineering, aviation, home economics*
700–799	Arts and Recreation *Fine art, music, sports, architecture*
800–899	Literature *Poetry, plays, speeches, humor*
900–999	History and Geography *Travel, biography*

How are main topics divided?

Each main topic is divided into subtopics.

EXAMPLE

History and Geography	900–999	900–909	General History
		910–919	Travel
		920–929	Biography and Autobiography

Reading Vocabulary

apply (6)
architecture (6)
aviation (6)
biology (10)
botany (11)
category (9)
chemistry (5)
economics (6)
education (5)
foreign (5)
geography (5)
grammar (5)
humor (5)
logic (8)
mathematics (6)
mental (6)
mythology (8)
philosophy (11)
poetry (6)
psychology (10)
pure (5)
recreation (6)
religion (6)
technology

TEACHER ALERT

Although it is certainly helpful for students to know the Dewey Decimal System's main categories and their subtopics, emphasize once more that students do not need to memorize the system. Point out that in fact, usually only librarians and people studying library science actually memorize these numbers. For library patrons, most libraries provide a detailed map that shows where each numbered category of books is located in the library, along with a map key that explains the topics and subtopics for each group of numbers.

LEARNING STYLES

Auditory/Verbal
Invite volunteers to read aloud the ten main categories of the Dewey Decimal System that are listed in the box on page 139. After each category is read, invite other volunteers to name any nonfiction book they have read or know about that would fit into the category. If your room has any nonfiction books in it, distribute these to the students and ask them to name the category in which these books would fit in Dewey's system.

Reading Vocabulary

advance (5) region (5)
exception (7)

■ **Presenting Activity A** In preparation for Activity A, ask a volunteer to copy the chart on page 139 onto the board or onto a large piece of chart paper. Then as you do Activity A together, encourage students to refer to the chart to determine which topic heading and numbers applies to each item.

Activity A Answers

1) Religion—200–299 **2)** Technology (Applied Sciences)—600–699 **3)** History and Geography—900–999 **4)** Literature—800–899 **5)** Arts and Recreation—700–799 **6)** Philosophy and Psychology—100–199 **7)** General Works—000–099 **8)** Language—400–499 **9)** Pure Sciences—500–599 **10)** Social Sciences—300–399

How are nonfiction books arranged on the shelf?

Nonfiction books are arranged by number first. Then they are put in order by the author's last name. Study these examples closely:

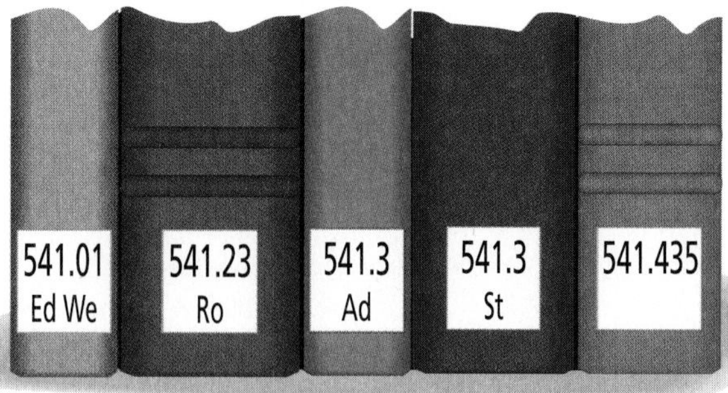

Are there any exceptions to the Dewey Decimal System that I should know about?

The purpose of the system is to help people find books. With biographies, you are more interested in the subject than in the author. Biographies are arranged alphabetically according to the person whom the book is about. For example, *My Life* by Golda Meir, an autobiography, would come before *Adlai Stevenson of Illinois* by John Bartlow Martin. Alphabetically, *Meir* comes before *Stevenson.*

Activity A Write the main topic heading and numbers of the Dewey Decimal System for each type of book listed below. Write your answers on your paper.

1) Greek mythology
2) Computer science
3) Southwest region
4) Poetry
5) Sports
6) Mental health care
7) Library science
8) English grammar
9) Advanced math
10) Education in the United States

Activity B Use the facts on pages 137–140 to answer these questions. Write your answers on your paper.

1) You see the number 920 on a book. What subject is it about?

a) Travel

b) Geography

c) Biography

2) You want to read *The Babe Ruth Story* by Howard Smith. Should you look for *Smith* or *Ruth* alphabetically on the shelf?

3) Who invented the system that most libraries use to arrange books?

a) Melvil Dewey

b) Thomas Jefferson

4) Will you find the letter *N* or a call number on nonfiction books at the library?

5) You need to know at least one of three things to find a nonfiction book in the library catalog. What are these three things?

6) In which category would you expect to find an encyclopedia?

a) Pure Sciences

b) General Works

c) History

7) Which of these books would come first on the shelf?

USING WHAT YOU HAVE LEARNED

- Write down five subjects that you would like to know more about.
- Take your list to the library.
- Look up your subjects in the library catalog.
- Write down the complete Dewey Decimal number for a book on that subject.
- Find that book on the library shelves.

■ Presenting Activity B

Before asking students to complete Activity B on their own, review the information presented on pages 137 through 140. Elicit any questions that students might still have about nonfiction books and the Dewey Decimal System.

Activity B Answers

1) (c) Biography **2)** Ruth **3)** (a) Melvil Dewey **4)** call number **5)** title, author, or subject **6)** (b) General Works **7)** 793.961/M (second book from the left)

USING WHAT YOU HAVE LEARNED

After students complete this activity, ask them to share their experiences with the class.

Reading Vocabulary

almanac (7)   geometry (8)

Lesson Review Answers

1) Pure Sciences—500–599 2) Literature—800–899 3) Literature—800–899 4) Religion—200–299 5) Philosophy and Psychology—100–199 6) General Works—000–099 7) General Works—000–099 8) Technology (Applied Sciences)—600–699 9) Technology (Applied Sciences)—600–699 10) Arts and Recreation—700–799 11) Arts and Recreation—700–799 12) Technology (Applied Sciences)—600–699 13) History and Geography—900–999 14) Literature—800–899 15) History and Geography—900–999 16) Pure Sciences—500–599 17) Pure Sciences—500–599 18) Language—400–499 19) General Works—000–099 20) General Works—000–099

Lesson 3 Review

The Dewey Decimal System
- Main Headings -

000–099	General Works
100–199	Philosophy and Psychology
200–299	Religion
300–399	Social Sciences
400–499	Language
500–599	Pure Sciences
600–699	Applied Sciences
700–799	Arts and Recreation
800–899	Literature
900–999	History and Geography

Lesson Review Write the main heading and numbers that would be used to classify a book on each of the subjects listed below. Use the information above and on page 139. Write your answers on your paper.

Example A book about modern art—**Arts and Recreation, 700s**

1) A math book
2) A poetry book
3) Shakespeare's plays
4) A Bible
5) Psychology
6) An atlas
7) A book about the Dewey Decimal System
8) A cookbook
9) How to build a ship
10) Famous paintings
11) Football rules
12) How to build a computer
13) Traveling in Europe
14) O. Henry's short stories
15) Life story of Hank Aaron
16) Growing vegetables
17) A geometry book
18) *Life Skills English*
19) World Almanac
20) A dictionary

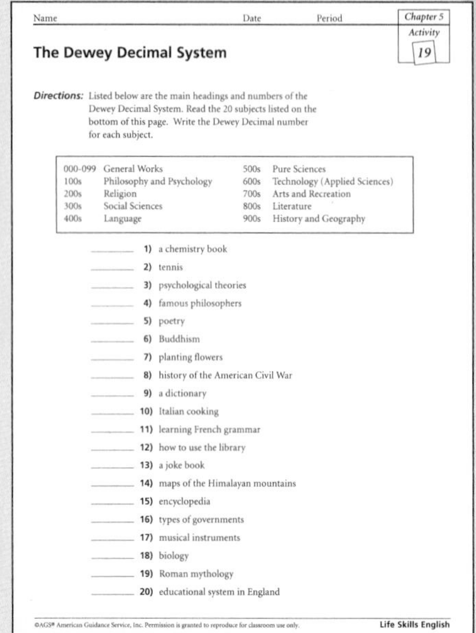
Name Date Period — Chapter 5 Activity 19

The Dewey Decimal System

Directions: Listed below are the main headings and numbers of the Dewey Decimal System. Read the 20 subjects listed on the bottom of this page. Write the Dewey Decimal number for each subject.

000-099	General Works	500s	Pure Sciences
100s	Philosophy and Psychology	600s	Technology (Applied Sciences)
200s	Religion	700s	Arts and Recreation
300s	Social Sciences	800s	Literature
400s	Language	900s	History and Geography

_____ 1) a chemistry book
_____ 2) tennis
_____ 3) psychological theories
_____ 4) famous philosophers
_____ 5) poetry
_____ 6) Buddhism
_____ 7) planting flowers
_____ 8) history of the American Civil War
_____ 9) a dictionary
_____ 10) Italian cooking
_____ 11) learning French grammar
_____ 12) how to use the library
_____ 13) a joke book
_____ 14) maps of the Himalayan mountains
_____ 15) encyclopedia
_____ 16) types of governments
_____ 17) musical instruments
_____ 18) biology
_____ 19) Roman mythology
_____ 20) educational system in England

 Life Skills English

Activity 19

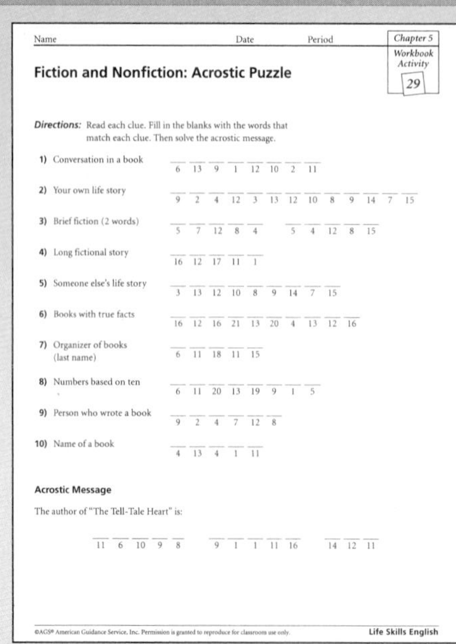
Name Date Period — Chapter 5 Workbook Activity 29

Fiction and Nonfiction: Acrostic Puzzle

Directions: Read each clue. Fill in the blanks with the words that match each clue. Then solve the acrostic message.

1) Conversation in a book — 6 13 9 1 12 10 2 11
2) Your own life story — 9 2 4 12 3 13 12 10 8 9 14 7 15
3) Brief fiction (2 words) — 5 7 12 8 4 / 5 4 12 8 15
4) Long fictional story — 16 12 17 11 1
5) Someone else's life story — 3 13 12 10 8 9 14 7 15
6) Books with true facts — 16 12 16 21 13 20 4 13 12 16
7) Organizer of books (last name) — 6 11 18 11 15
8) Numbers based on ten — 6 11 20 13 19 9 1 5
9) Person who wrote a book — 9 2 4 7 12 8
10) Name of a book — 4 13 4 1 11

Acrostic Message

The author of "The Tell-Tale Heart" is:

11 6 10 9 8 / 9 1 1 11 16 / 14 12 11

 Life Skills English

Workbook Activity 29

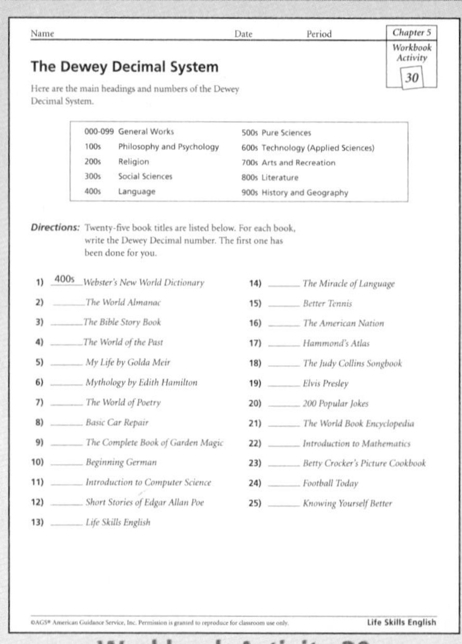
Name Date Period — Chapter 5 Workbook Activity 30

The Dewey Decimal System

Here are the main headings and numbers of the Dewey Decimal System.

000-099	General Works	500s	Pure Sciences
100s	Philosophy and Psychology	600s	Technology (Applied Sciences)
200s	Religion	700s	Arts and Recreation
300s	Social Sciences	800s	Literature
400s	Language	900s	History and Geography

Directions: Twenty-five book titles are listed below. For each book, write the Dewey Decimal number. The first one has been done for you.

1) 400s *Webster's New World Dictionary*
2) _____ *The World Almanac*
3) _____ *The Bible Story Book*
4) _____ *The World of the Past*
5) _____ *My Life by Golda Meir*
6) _____ *Mythology by Edith Hamilton*
7) _____ *The World of Poetry*
8) _____ *Basic Car Repair*
9) _____ *The Complete Book of Garden Magic*
10) _____ *Beginning German*
11) _____ *Introduction to Computer Science*
12) _____ *Short Stories of Edgar Allan Poe*
13) _____ *Life Skills English*
14) _____ *The Miracle of Language*
15) _____ *Better Tennis*
16) _____ *The American Nation*
17) _____ *Hammond's Atlas*
18) _____ *The Judy Collins Songbook*
19) _____ *Elvis Presley*
20) _____ *200 Popular Jokes*
21) _____ *The World Book Encyclopedia*
22) _____ *Introduction to Mathematics*
23) _____ *Betty Crocker's Picture Cookbook*
24) _____ *Football Today*
25) _____ *Knowing Yourself Better*

 Life Skills English

Workbook Activity 30

Lesson 4

Finding Information in a Library

Finding information in a library can be easy as long as you follow some simple guidelines. At times you may follow these guidelines and still cannot find what you need. If this happens, do not hesitate to ask a librarian for help.

How to Find What You Need

Here's how to find a book in the library using either the computer or the card catalog.

Step 1 Find the entry for the book you want. Use either the title record, author record, or subject record.

Step 2 Copy the complete call number for nonfiction books on a piece of paper. For a fiction book, you only need the author's name and title.

Step 3 Find the section of the library that has the book you want. If you are not familiar with the library layout, check with the librarian. Many libraries post a map of the library layout near the checkout desk.

Step 4 Use the call number to find the book on the shelf.

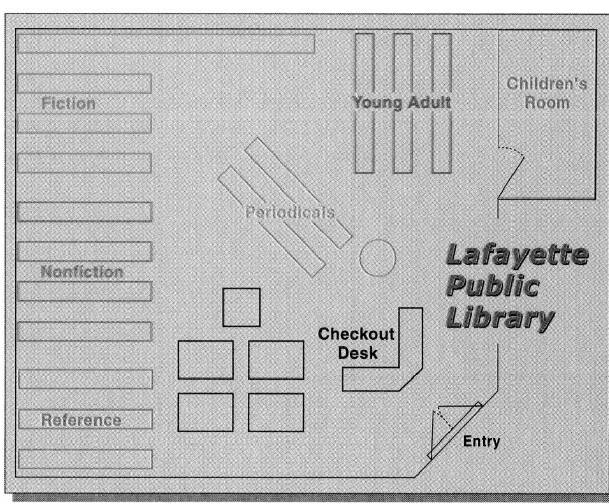

Lesson at a Glance

Chapter 5 Lesson 4

Overview This lesson explains how to use the library's catalogs to find information.

Objectives

- To understand how information is organized in the library catalog.
- To answer questions about the library's different catalogs.

Student Pages 143–153

Teacher's Resource Library

Activity 20

Workbook Activities 31–33

Reading Vocabulary

checkout
layout
entry (6)

Teaching Suggestions

- **Introducing the Lesson** Discuss the steps for finding information using the library catalog—card and computer. If possible, after the entire lesson has been presented, arrange a library field trip during which time students can apply what they have learned in this lesson. Following the field trip, encourage students to assess their ability to use the library's different catalogs to find information. Provide additional support to students who need it.

- **Reviewing Skills** Review the organization of fiction and nonfiction books in the library.

Reading Vocabulary

cross-reference   juvenile (8)

Application

Career Connection

As part of a Careers Day program, invite a librarian to speak to students about the required training and responsibilities of a librarian. If possible, also invite an older or retired librarian and ask the two to discuss how libraries have changed because of technology. Students might wish to know what skills are required today that weren't required fifty or even twenty-five years ago. The librarians can also discuss how funding affects the services that a library can offer to a community and what materials and equipment the ideal library should have.

Application

Career Connection

Local employers often post notices for job openings on the library bulletin board. Encourage students seeking work to consider this resource. Suggest that some students look at what is posted on the bulletin board and report their findings to the class.

Learning Styles

Logical/Mathematical

Divide the class into groups of three. Give each group three note cards and a nonfiction book. Ask each group to create the three cards—author, title, subject—that this book would have in a library's card catalog drawer. As the groups prepare their cards, direct the students to study the sample cards on page 144. Afterward, collect the cards and invite the class to work together as a group to create a card catalog drawer in which they alphabetize all the cards.

Understanding Call Numbers

The Dewey Decimal number appears on the back of each nonfiction book. You may see other letters before the number:

R = Reference   *Y* or *YA* = Young Adult   *J* = Juvenile

An *F* or *FIC* sometimes labels fiction books. A special label may also appear:

M = Mystery   *SS* = Short Story Collection
R = Romance   *SF* = Science Fiction

Records in the Library Catalog

Most libraries have switched from card catalog drawers to a computer catalog. Some smaller libraries and school libraries may still use a card catalog. The three kinds of cards in a card catalog are author card, title card, and subject card. Each card has the same facts arranged differently.

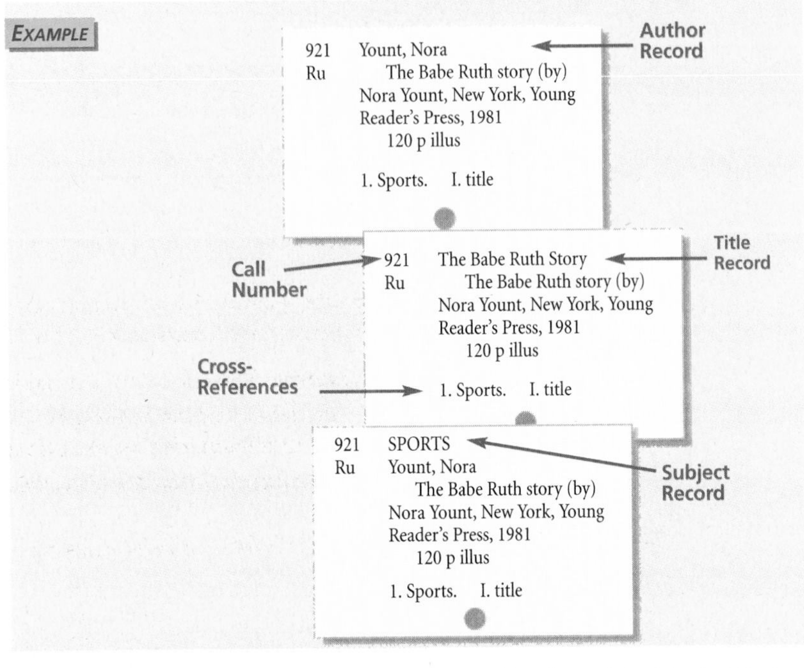

Activity A Use the information on the cards on page 144 to answer these questions. Write your answers on your paper.

1) What is the complete title of the book?

2) Who is the author of the book?

3) Is this book a biography or an autobiography?

4) What is the complete call number?

Other Facts in a Record

The record also provides other useful information about a book, including:

- the place the book was published.
- the publisher's name.
- the copyright date, or what year the book was published. This tells you how current the information and facts in the book are.
- the number of pages in the book.
- whether the book is illustrated.

Activity B Use the information on the cards on page 144 to answer these questions. Write your answers on your paper.

1) Where and when was this book published?

2) Who is the publisher?

3) How many pages does the book have?

4) Does this book have pictures?

Edit

To get written material ready for publication.

You may also see the notation *ed* before or after a person's name in a record. This means that the person has edited the book. To **edit** means to prepare written material for publication.

Reading Vocabulary

copyright (8) notation (11)
edit (8) publication (7)
illustrate (7) publish (6)

■ Presenting Activity A

You may wish to do Activity A as a whole class activity. If possible, make a transparency of the three catalog cards on page 144 and display them on an overhead projector. Discuss the labeled items, making sure students recognize the differences in the way the same information is organized on the three cards. Then have them complete Activity A.

Activity A Answers

1) The Babe Ruth Story **2)** Nora Yount **3)** Biography **4)** 921/RU

■ Presenting Activity B

Ask students whether they think Nora Yount's book would be good to use as the main reference for a paper on Babe Ruth. Encourage students to focus on both the pros and cons of using this book as a main reference source. For example, a positive point is that it is specifically about Babe Ruth. A negative point is that it was published in 1981. A more current biography might provide new or additional information about Babe Ruth that would improve the accuracy of the research paper.

Activity B Answers

1) New York, 1981 **2)** Young Readers Press **3)** 120 pages **4)** Yes

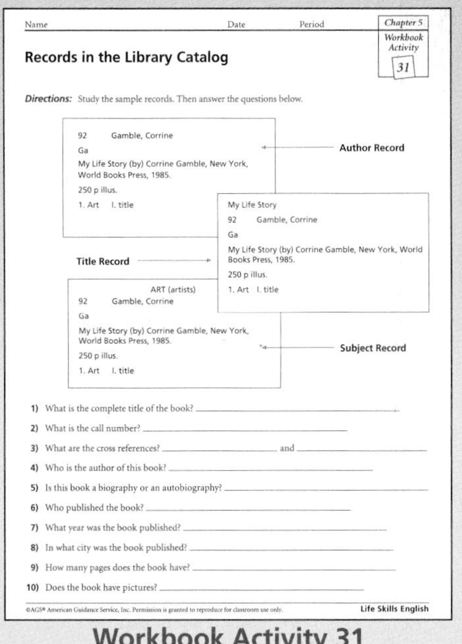
Name Date Period

Chapter 5 Workbook Activity 31

Records in the Library Catalog

Directions: Study the sample records. Then answer the questions below.

Author Record

92 Gamble, Corrine
Ga
My Life Story (by) Corrine Gamble, New York, World Books Press, 1985.
250 p illus.
1. Art I. title

Title Record

My Life Story
92 Gamble, Corrine
Ga
My Life Story (by) Corrine Gamble, New York, World Books Press, 1985.
250 p illus.
1. Art I. title

Subject Record

ART (artists)
92 Gamble, Corrine
Ga
My Life Story (by) Corrine Gamble, New York, World Books Press, 1985.
250 p illus.
1. Art I. title

1) What is the complete title of the book? ______

2) What is the call number? ______

3) What are the cross references? ______ and ______

4) Who is the author of this book? ______

5) Is this book a biography or an autobiography? ______

6) Who published the book? ______

7) What year was the book published? ______

8) In what city was the book published? ______

9) How many pages does the book have? ______

10) Does the book have pictures? ______

 Life Skills English

Workbook Activity 31

Reading Vocabulary

conservation (6) instruction (5)
conservationist

Application

At Home

Many libraries with computer catalog systems, especially those libraries that are part of large networks, provide access to these systems by modem. This means that people can search a library's catalogs from their home if they have a modem and a computer. Some systems require users to type in their library card numbers before they can access the system. Encourage students to find out if this resource is available in their library system and how it works. Students can then use school or home computers to take advantage of this convenient research method.

Using a Computer Catalog

Most libraries today keep their records on a computer.

Example

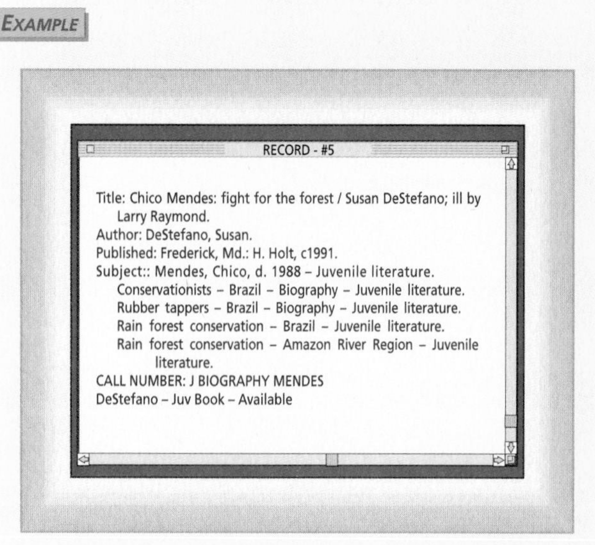

RECORD - #5

Title: Chico Mendes: fight for the forest / Susan DeStefano; ill by Larry Raymond.
Author: DeStefano, Susan.
Published: Frederick, Md.: H. Holt, c1991.
Subject:: Mendes, Chico, d. 1988 – Juvenile literature.
Conservationists – Brazil – Biography – Juvenile literature.
Rubber tappers – Brazil – Biography – Juvenile literature.
Rain forest conservation – Brazil – Juvenile literature.
Rain forest conservation – Amazon River Region – Juvenile literature.
CALL NUMBER: J BIOGRAPHY MENDES
DeStefano – Juv Book – Available

To find a book using a computer catalog, follow the instructions on the screen.

Step 1	Enter the title, author, or subject of the book you want.
Step 2	The computer will probably list several titles. Select the one you want.
Step 3	Read the record to find out if this is the book you want and if the book is available to be checked out.
Step 4	Copy or print out the complete call number for nonfiction books or the author's name and title for fiction books.

Activity C Use the information in the sample computer record on page 146 to answer these questions. Write your answers on your paper.

1) What is the complete title of the book?
2) Who is the author of the book?
3) Is this book fiction or nonfiction?
4) What is the complete call number of this book?
5) Is a copy of this book available to check out of the library?

The Reference Section

To find specific information, use the reference section of the library. Encyclopedias, atlases, and art books are types of reference books you will often find in the reference section.

Circulate
Can be taken out of the library.

The books in the reference section usually do not **circulate.** This means they cannot be checked out. As a result, these books are always available to the people who need to use them.

Sample Record for a Reference Book

R
709
Ja   Art of the western world (ed)
Franco Jackson, Chicago, ArtWorld,
Inc.,
1983
359 p illus

1. Art I.   title   noncirc.

Activity D Use the entry to answer these questions. Write your answers on your paper.

1) What does the *R* on the entry tell you?
2) What was Franco Jackson's job on this book?
3) What is the complete call number for this book?
4) Can you check this book out of the library?

Reading Vocabulary

circulate (7) specific (8)
sample (5)

Presenting Activity C

Some libraries no longer have a card catalog for patrons to use. Smaller libraries have been slower to convert to a computer catalog because of lack of funds and the personnel needed to transfer records. These libraries maintain card catalogs. Invite students to share their experiences using a card catalog and computer catalog. Ask students to compare the ease of use of both catalogs. Although it may take some people a little longer to learn how to use the computer catalog, the advantages of a computer catalog over a card catalog cannot be denied. Ask students to list these advantages.

Activity C Answers

1) Chico Mendes: Fight for the Forest 2) Susan DeStefano 3) nonfiction 4) J BIOGRAPHY MENDES 5) Yes

Presenting Activity D

Before asking students to complete Activity D on their own, invite them to take turns telling one fact they learn from the sample record on page 147. To avoid repetition, list the facts on the board as students suggest them.

Activity D Answers

1) This is a reference book. 2) He edited the book. 3) R/709/Ja 4) No

Reading Vocabulary

back issue recent (6)
current issue recently (5)
interval (5) request (6)

APPLICATION

In the Community
Libraries with limited funding may not be able to subscribe to all of the magazines that they would like. Suggest that students interview the librarian to find out what magazines the library has on its wish list. Residents who subscribe to these magazines may be willing to donate back issues to the library. Notices placed in the newspaper and on community bulletin boards can alert residents to the library's needs.

Finding Magazines in the Library

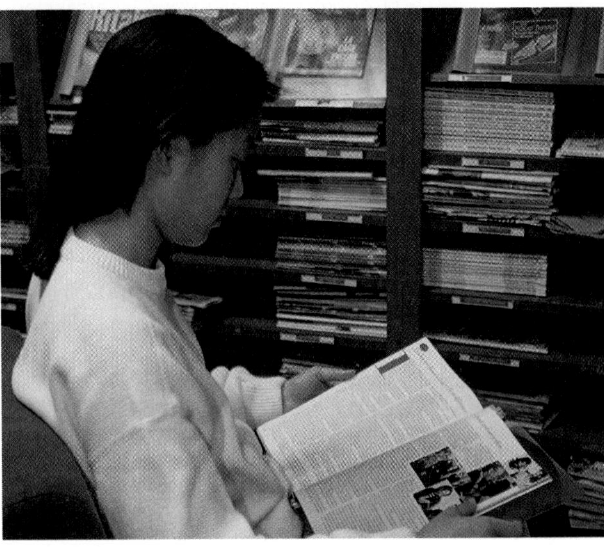

You can find all of the periodicals, or magazines, that your library has in the magazine catalog. A periodical, such as a magazine, is published every week, every month, or at some other regular interval. Each magazine is called an "issue." All of the issues in one year make one "volume."

Current issue
The most recently published issue of a magazine.

Back issue
An issue that was published in the past.

The **current issue** of a magazine is the most recent issue. It is displayed on a library shelf. A **back issue** is a past issue of a magazine. Some back issues may be kept on the shelves. Usually, issues more than six or twelve months old are kept somewhere else in the library. To look at a back issue, you sometimes must put in a written request. Request forms usually ask for the name of the magazine, the publication date, the volume number, and the issue number.

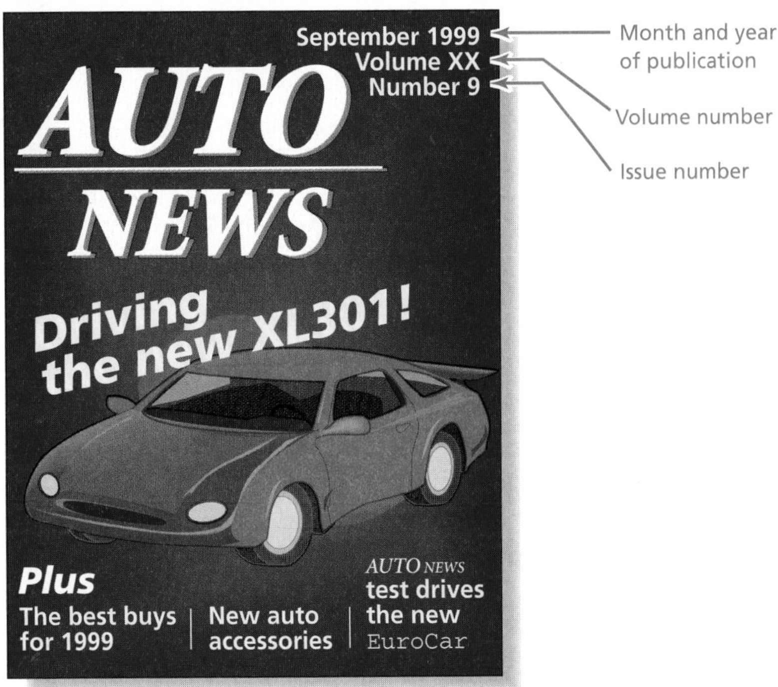

Activity E Use the magazine pictured above to answer these questions. Write your answers on your paper.

1) What is the volume number of this magazine?

2) What is the issue number?

3) What is the name of the magazine?

4) When was it published?

The Readers' Guide to Periodical Literature

When you wish to find magazine articles on a specific subject, you can use *The Readers' Guide to Periodical Literature. The Readers' Guide* lists articles and stories from major general interest magazines. Articles are listed by subject and author. Stories are

Reading Vocabulary

accessory (8)

Teacher Alert

You may wish to provide a brief review of Roman Numerals and their Arabic equivalents before students complete Activity E. Have students complete Workbook Activity 32 before assigning Activity E.

■ Presenting Activity E

Distribute back issues of a variety of magazines to students, giving one magazine to each student or to pairs of students. Ask students questions similar to those in Activity E about their magazines. As students respond to a question, have them point to the place on the cover of their magazine that provides the information to answer that question. Following this activity, have students complete Activity E independently.

Activity E Answers

1) XX (20) **2)** 9 **3)** *Auto News* **4)** September 1999

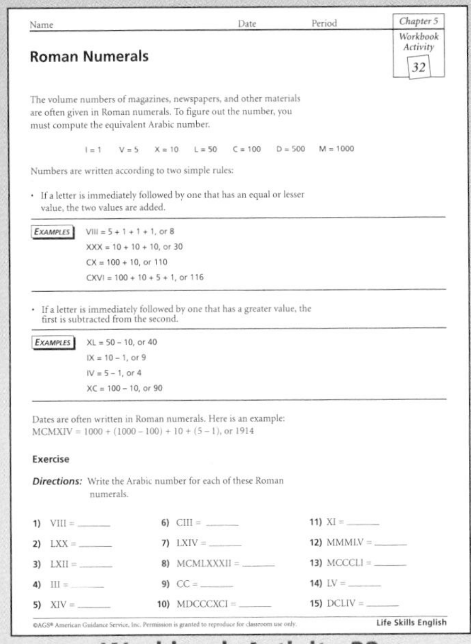

Name Date Period

Chapter 5 Workbook Activity 32

Roman Numerals

The volume numbers of magazines, newspapers, and other materials are often given in Roman numerals. To figure out the number, you must compute the equivalent Arabic number.

I = 1 V = 5 X = 10 L = 50 C = 100 D = 500 M = 1000

Numbers are written according to two simple rules:

- If a letter is immediately followed by one that has an equal or lesser value, the two values are added.

EXAMPLES
VIII = 5 + 1 + 1 + 1, or 8
XXX = 10 + 10 + 10, or 30
CX = 100 + 10, or 110
CXVI = 100 + 10 + 5 + 1, or 116

- If a letter is immediately followed by one that has a greater value, the first is subtracted from the second.

EXAMPLES
XL = 50 – 10, or 40
IX = 10 – 1, or 9
IV = 5 – 1, or 4
XC = 100 – 10, or 90

Dates are often written in Roman numerals. Here is an example:
MCMXIV = 1000 + (1000 – 100) + 10 + (5 – 1), or 1914

Exercise

Directions: Write the Arabic number for each of these Roman numerals.

1) VIII = ______	**6)** CIII = ______	**11)** XI = ______
2) LXX = ______	**7)** LXIV = ______	**12)** MMMLV = ______
3) LXII = ______	**8)** MCMLXXXII = ______	**13)** MCCCLI = ______
4) III = ______	**9)** CC = ______	**14)** LV = ______
5) XIV = ______	**10)** MDCCCXCI = ______	**15)** DCLIV = ______

 Life Skills English

Workbook Activity 32

Using a Library to Find Information Chapter 5 **149**

Presenting Activity F You may wish to have students refer back to page 96 in Chapter 3 to recall what they have already learned about using *The Readers' Guide to Periodical Literature.* Then focus students' attention on the sample entries on page 150. Invite volunteers to relate, in sentences, the facts that each entry provides. Following this process, have students complete Activity F on their own.

Activity F Answers

1) "Air Travel with 50-Foot TV Screens" 2) *News Magazine* 3) 23 (pages 45–67) 4) 123 5) Yes

listed by author and title. *The Readers' Guide* is published every month and bound into a volume each year. Some libraries have a guide to magazine articles on computer.

Here are some sample entries in *The Readers' Guide:*

READER'S GUIDE TO PERIODICAL LITERATURE 1999

TRAVEL
  Air travel with 50-foot TV screens.
    B. Howard. il Video Today 13:6-7 Mr. '99
  Moon trips without cheese.
    J. Lee. Short Story Monthly 45:45-67. Ap. '99
TRAVERS, Janice S.
  The Mad Venusian. Tomorrow's Woman. 123:30-46. Ap. '99
  Tunes from another world. Purplebook. 12:24-25. Mr. '99
VIDEO
  What's new in video? News Mag 24:36 il Ap. 11, '99

Activity F Use the facts in the sample entries above to answer these questions. Write your answers on your paper.

1) What is the title of the article by B. Howard?
2) Which magazine is published weekly?
   a) *Purplebook*
   b) *News Magazine*
   c) *Video Today*
3) How many pages are in the story by J. Lee?
4) What is the volume number of *Tomorrow's Woman* in which Janice Travers's story appears?
5) Does the article "What's New in Video?" have pictures?

150 Chapter 5 Using a Library to Find Information

Video Catalogs

You can learn about many topics by watching a film, a videocassette, or a videodisc. Not many people have 16mm film projectors at home, but many have videocassette recorders (VCRs). Some have videodisc players. Many libraries have videocassette and videodisc collections. You may be able to check these materials out just like a book.

A video catalog is usually in book form or on a computer system. The materials are grouped by subject. Titles are listed alphabetically. The catalog entries provide facts you might wish to know before you check out or view the work.

READER'S GUIDE TO PERIODICAL LITERATURE 1999

PHYSICAL FITNESS

Better health through exercise, 1997, 60 min Color VHS.
(Overnight only.)
The importance of exercise, 1999. 20 min B&W 16 mm film.
Suzy Smith's exercise program. 30 min Color VHS.
You and your health, 1995. 15 min Audiocassette.
(Lesson guide available)
Your health today, 60 min 1998, Color videodisc (CED).
(Library only)

Activity G Use the information on the video catalog page above to answer these questions. Write your answers on your paper.

1) How many programs are available on videocassette?

2) Which program is available on 16mm film? Write the title.

3) What equipment will you need to watch "Your Health Today"?

4) What equipment will you need to use "You and Your Health"?

5) Which program would have to be returned the day after it is checked out?

6) Which program cannot be checked out of the library?

Reading Vocabulary

provide (5)

■ Presenting Activity G

Engage students in a discussion of videos as a reference source. What kind of information might a video provide that a book or a magazine article on the same topic might not provide as well or at all? If possible, show clips from videos on a variety of topics. Encourage students to take advantage of the videos at their library for both entertainment and educational purposes.

Activity G Answers

1) two **2)** "The Importance of Exercise" **3)** videodisc player **4)** tape deck **5)** "Better Health Through Exercise" **6)** "Your Health Today"

Reading Vocabulary

agriculture (5) soccer (6)
association (6) source (6)
diet (6) valuable (5)
embassy (8) **vertical file**
produce (5)

■ Presenting Activity H

Before having students complete Activity H on their own, remind them that a video catalog has a record for each video the library has. Ask students what facts about a film they would expect to find on a film record. How might these facts be helpful?

Activity H Answers

1) Rules for Playing Soccer
2) 20 minutes **3)** 1989

■ Presenting Activity I

In preparation for this part of the lesson, check a variety of items out of your library's vertical file. Allow students time to examine these items to give them a good idea of the kinds of materials available in a typical vertical file.

Activity I Answers

2) a pamphlet on Indiana parks
3) "Growing Vegetables" by the U. S. Department of Agriculture
5) A road map of your state
6) "A Balanced Diet," 20 pages, published by the Dairy Association
7) A copy of a speech by the town mayor

Using What You Have Learned

Encourage students to use the vertical file in their library.

Activity H Write the answers to the following questions.

1) What is the title of the film in the film catalog entry below?

> Sports
> Rules for playing soccer, 1989,
> b&w, 20 min.

2) How long is this film?

3) In what year was the film produced?

Vertical File

Vertical file
A file that contains pamphlets and other materials too small to put on a shelf.

A **vertical file** is a valuable source of information in the library. It has pamphlets and other material too small or too large to put on a shelf. The vertical file sometimes contains the most current material on a subject. These materials come from a variety of sources, including:

- Government agencies
- Embassies
- Colleges
- Businesses
- Museums
- Organizations

Materials in the vertical file are arranged in alphabetical order according to subject.

Using What You Have Learned

When you go to the library, look up a subject in the vertical file. Use the vertical file the next time you do a report.

Activity I Which of these materials might be found in the vertical file? Write your answers on your paper.

1) A world almanac

2) A pamphlet on Indiana parks

3) "Growing Vegetables" by the U.S. Department of Agriculture

4) A biography of Malcolm X

5) A road map of your state

6) "A Balanced Diet," 20 pages, published by the Dairy Association

7) A copy of a speech by the town mayor

Lesson 4 Review

Part A Use the facts on the cards to answer the questions that follow. Write your answers on your paper.

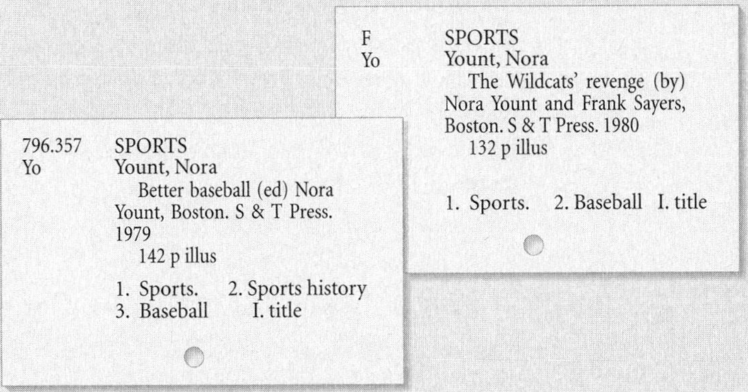

F
Yo
SPORTS
Yount, Nora
The Wildcats' revenge (by)
Nora Yount and Frank Sayers,
Boston. S & T Press. 1980
132 p illus
1. Sports. 2. Baseball I. title
796.357
Yo
SPORTS
Yount, Nora
Better baseball (ed) Nora
Yount, Boston. S & T Press.
1979
142 p illus
1. Sports. 2. Sports history
3. Baseball I. title

1) What kind of cards are shown—subject, title, or author?
2) What is the title of the book that Nora Yount wrote?
3) What is the title of the book that she edited?
4) What is the call number of the fiction book?
5) In which part of the nonfiction section would you find *Better Baseball*? How do you know?
   a) History b) Arts and Recreation c) Biography

Part B Write your answers to the following questions on your paper.

1) What are the three kinds of records in a library catalog?
2) Which issues of magazines might you have to ask to see?
3) Which of these call numbers are nonfiction?

Fr	346.03	92	003.1
F	Ho	Ru	To

4) How are entries in a video catalog usually arranged?
5) Which of these books would be in the reference section?
   a) a literature book b) an almanac c) a mystery novel
6) Where would you look to find a pamphlet about France?

Part A Answers

1) subject cards **2)** *The Wildcats' Revenge* **3)** *Better Baseball* **4)** F/Yo **5)** (b) Arts and Recreation—The call number is 796.357. The call numbers for Arts and Recreation are 700–799.

Part B Answers

1) author, title, and subject **2)** back issues **3)** 346.03/Ho; 003.1/To **4)** alphabetically by title **5)** (b) almanac **6)** vertical file

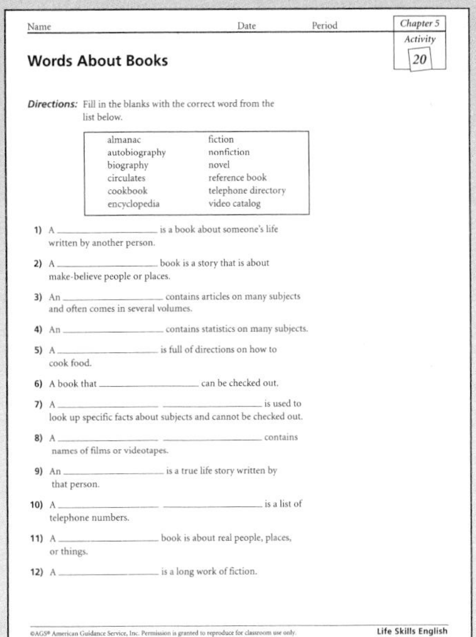

Name Date Period — Chapter 5 Activity 20

Words About Books

Directions: Fill in the blanks with the correct word from the list below.

almanac	fiction
autobiography	nonfiction
biography	novel
circulates	reference book
cookbook	telephone directory
encyclopedia	video catalog

1) A ______ is a book about someone's life written by another person.
2) A ______ book is a story that is about make-believe people or places.
3) An ______ contains articles on many subjects and often comes in several volumes.
4) An ______ contains statistics on many subjects.
5) A ______ is full of directions on how to cook food.
6) A book that ______ can be checked out.
7) A ______ ______ is used to look up specific facts about subjects and cannot be checked out.
8) A ______ ______ contains names of films or videotapes.
9) An ______ is a true life story written by that person.
10) A ______ ______ is a list of telephone numbers.
11) A ______ book is about real people, places, or things.
12) A ______ is a long work of fiction.

 Life Skills English

Activity 20

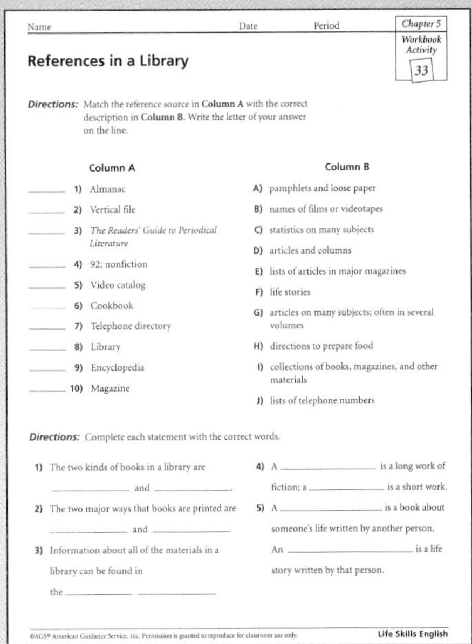

Name Date Period — Chapter 5 Workbook Activity 33

References in a Library

Directions: Match the reference source in **Column A** with the correct description in **Column B**. Write the letter of your answer on the line.

Column A

____ 1) Almanac
____ 2) Vertical file
____ 3) *The Readers' Guide to Periodical Literature*
____ 4) 92; nonfiction
____ 5) Video catalog
____ 6) Cookbook
____ 7) Telephone directory
____ 8) Library
____ 9) Encyclopedia
____ 10) Magazine

Column B

A) pamphlets and loose paper
B) names of films or videotapes
C) statistics on many subjects
D) articles and columns
E) lists of articles in major magazines
F) life stories
G) articles on many subjects; often in several volumes
H) directions to prepare food
I) collections of books, magazines, and other materials
J) lists of telephone numbers

Directions: Complete each statement with the correct words.

1) The two kinds of books in a library are ______ and ______.
2) The two major ways that books are printed are ______ and ______.
3) Information about all of the materials in a library can be found in the ______ ______
4) A ______ is a long work of fiction; a ______ is a short work.
5) A ______ is a book about someone's life written by another person. An ______ is a life story written by that person.

 Life Skills English

Workbook Activity 33

Chapter 5 Review

The Teacher's Resource Library includes two parallel forms of the Chapter 5 Mastery Test. The difficulty level of the two forms is equivalent. You may wish to use one form as a pretest and the other form as a posttest.

Reading Vocabulary

zoology

Part A Answers

1) Library of Congress **2)** Washington D.C. **3)** Answers will vary. Possible responses are given: print material—newspapers and magazines; video equipment—projector and videodisc player; other equipment—copy machine and computer **4)** *Watership Down* by Richard Adams *Robinson Crusoe* by Daniel Defoe *The Outsiders* by S. E. Hinton **5)** Fiction: biographical novel, novel, historical novel, short story; Nonfiction: biography, autobiography, history, article

Part B Answers

1) history **2)** social sciences **3)** recreation **4)** science (Pure Sciences or Applied Sciences) **5)** language

Chapter 5 Review

Part A Write the answer to these questions on your paper.

1) What is the name of our national library?
2) In what city would you find that library?
3) List two kinds of print materials other than books; two kinds of video equipment; and two other kinds of equipment you might find in the library.
4) In what order would these fiction books be arranged on a library shelf? Write them in order.
   a) *Robinson Crusoe* by Daniel Defoe
   b) *The Outsiders* by S. E. Hinton
   c) *Watership Down* by Richard Adams
5) Which of these types of books are fiction? Which are nonfiction? Make two lists on your paper.
   a) Biography
   b) Autobiography
   c) Biographical novel
   d) Novel
   e) History
   f) Historical novel
   g) Short story
   h) Article

Part B Which of the subjects in each group is a main category in the Dewey Decimal system? Write your answers on your paper.

Example poetry humor literature plays
Answer: **Literature**

1) travel	climate	biography	history
2) government	education	social sciences	economics
3) sports	hobbies	recreation	games
4) math	zoology	chemistry	science
5) dictionary	grammar	French	language

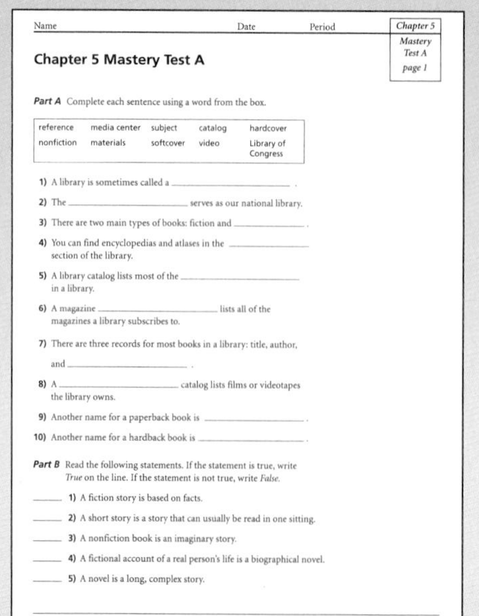

Name Date Period — *Chapter 5 Mastery Test A page 1*

Chapter 5 Mastery Test A

Part A Complete each sentence using a word from the box.

reference	media center	subject	catalog	hardcover
nonfiction	materials	softcover	video	Library of Congress

1) A library is sometimes called a ________ .
2) The ________ serves as our national library.
3) There are two main types of books: fiction and ________ .
4) You can find encyclopedias and atlases in the ________ section of the library.
5) A library catalog lists most of the ________ in a library.
6) A magazine ________ lists all of the magazines a library subscribes to.
7) There are three records for most books in a library: title, author, and ________ .
8) A ________ catalog lists films or videotapes the library owns.
9) Another name for a paperback book is ________ .
10) Another name for a hardback book is ________ .

Part B Read the following statements. If the statement is true, write *True* on the line. If the statement is not true, write *False.*

____ 1) A fiction story is based on facts.
____ 2) A short story is a story that can usually be read in one sitting.
____ 3) A nonfiction book is an imaginary story.
____ 4) A fictional account of a real person's life is a biographical novel.
____ 5) A novel is a long, complex story.

 Life Skills English

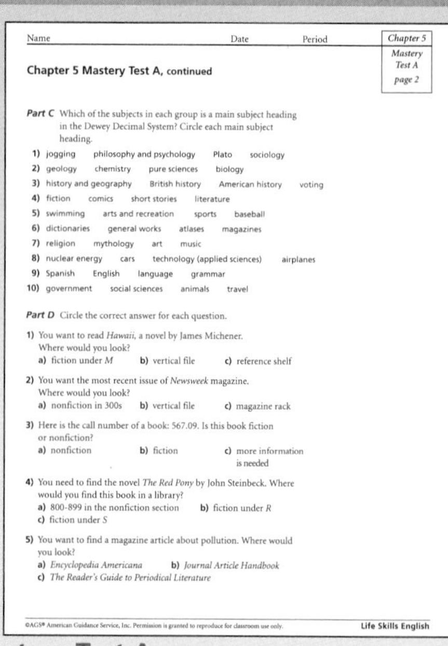

Name Date Period — *Chapter 5 Mastery Test A page 2*

Chapter 5 Mastery Test A, continued

Part C Which of the subjects in each group is a main subject heading in the Dewey Decimal System? Circle each main subject heading.

1) jogging philosophy and psychology Plato sociology
2) geology chemistry pure sciences biology
3) history and geography British history American history voting
4) fiction comics short stories literature
5) swimming arts and recreation sports baseball
6) dictionaries general works atlases magazines
7) religion mythology art music
8) nuclear energy cars technology (applied sciences) airplanes
9) Spanish English language grammar
10) government social sciences animals travel

Part D Circle the correct answer for each question.

1) You want to read *Hawaii,* a novel by James Michener. Where would you look?
   a) fiction under *M* b) vertical file c) reference shelf
2) You want the most recent issue of *Newsweek* magazine. Where would you look?
   a) nonfiction in 300s b) vertical file c) magazine rack
3) Here is the call number of a book: 567.09. Is this book fiction or nonfiction?
   a) nonfiction b) fiction c) more information is needed
4) You need to find the novel *The Red Pony* by John Steinbeck. Where would you find this book in a library?
   a) 800-899 in the nonfiction section b) fiction under *R*
   c) fiction under *S*
5) You want to find a magazine article about pollution. Where would you look?
   a) *Encyclopedia Americana* b) *Journal Article Handbook*
   c) *The Reader's Guide to Periodical Literature*

 Life Skills English

Chapter 5 Mastery Test A

Part C Write the answer to these questions on your paper.

1) In which section of the library would you look to find the novel *Emma* by Jane Austen?
2) Where would you look to find the most recent issue of *Reader's Digest*?
   a) the vertical file b) the nonfiction shelf in 300–399
   c) on the magazine display rack
3) Where would you look for a pamphlet about the Falkland Islands?
   a) the reference shelf b) the vertical file
   c) the nonfiction shelf in 900–999
4) Which of these usually do not circulate in most libraries?
   a) short story collections
   b) books from the reference section
5) What are three kinds of records in the library catalog?
6) According to the call numbers given, is this book fiction or nonfiction? 453.01
Ty
7) Which of these might be the call number of a biography of Thomas Jefferson by R. Hernandez?
   a) 921
Je b) 921
He
8) In what reference book would you look to find a list of magazine articles on a specific subject?
9) Which of these books would probably be in the reference section?
   a) an encyclopedia b) a historical novel
   c) a literature book
10) Besides title, author, and subject, what are two other pieces of information you might find in a library record?

Test Taking Tip

When studying for a test, write your own test questions. Then find a partner and complete each other's tests. Double-check your answers.

Reading Vocabulary

double-check

Part C Answers

1) fiction section **2)** (c) on the magazine display rack **3)** (b) the vertical file **4)** (b) books from the reference section **5)** author, title, subject **6)** nonfiction **7)** (a) 921/Je **8)** *The Readers' Guide to Periodical Literature* **9)** (a) an encyclopedia **10)** Answers may vary. Possible answers: publication place and date; whether the book has illustrations

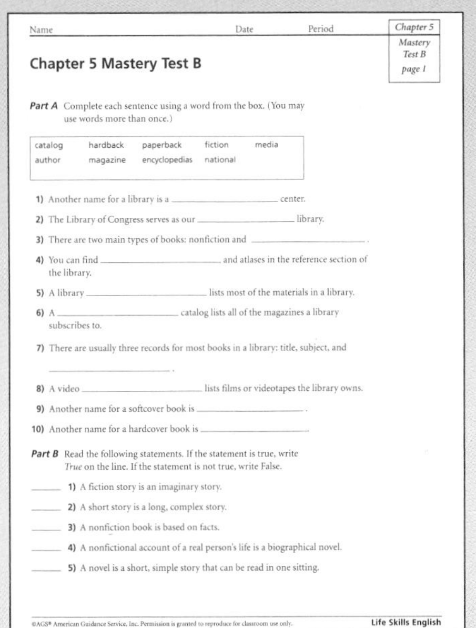

Name Date Period

Chapter 5 Mastery Test B page 1

Chapter 5 Mastery Test B

Part A Complete each sentence using a word from the box. (You may use words more than once.)

catalog	hardback	paperback	fiction	media
author	magazine	encyclopedias	national	

1) Another name for a library is a ____________ center.
2) The Library of Congress serves as our ____________ library.
3) There are two main types of books: nonfiction and ____________.
4) You can find ____________ and atlases in the reference section of the library.
5) A library ____________ lists most of the materials in a library.
6) A ____________ catalog lists all of the magazines a library subscribes to.
7) There are usually three records for most books in a library: title, subject, and ____________.
8) A video ____________ lists films or videotapes the library owns.
9) Another name for a softcover book is ____________.
10) Another name for a hardcover book is ____________.

Part B Read the following statements. If the statement is true, write *True* on the line. If the statement is not true, write False.

_____ 1) A fiction story is an imaginary story.
_____ 2) A short story is a long, complex story.
_____ 3) A nonfiction book is based on facts.
_____ 4) A nonfictional account of a real person's life is a biographical novel.
_____ 5) A novel is a short, simple story that can be read in one sitting.

 Life Skills English

Name Date Period

Chapter 5 Mastery Test B page 2

Chapter 5 Mastery Test B, continued

Part C Which of the subjects in each group is a main subject heading in the Dewey Decimal System? Circle each main subject heading.

1) how-to books general works library facts periodicals
2) pure sciences mathematics plants doctors
3) sociology religion health laws
4) education people economics social sciences
5) sports arts and recreation movies buildings
6) French language Japanese German
7) short stories French Revolution Civil War history and geography
8) technology (applied sciences) home economics cooking sports
9) gardening philosophy and psychology police health
10) poetry movies music literature

Part D Circle the correct answer for each question.

1) You want to read *Women of Brewster Place*, a novel by Gloria Naylor. Where would you look?
   a) reference shelf b) fiction under *N* c) vertical file
2) You want the most recent issue of *Time* magazine. Where would you look?
   a) reference section b) magazine rack c) fiction section under *T*
3) A book's call number is 122.49. Is this book fiction or nonfiction?
   a) fiction b) more information is needed c) nonfiction
4) You need to find the book *Jane Eyre* by Charlotte Brontë. Where would you find this book in a library?
   a) fiction under *J* b) 200-299 in the nonfiction section c) fiction under *B*
5) You want to find a magazine article about cancer. Where would you look?
   a) *The Reader's Guide to Periodical Literature*
   b) vertical file
   c) the nonfiction section under medicine

 Life Skills English

Chapter 5 Mastery Test B

Chapter 6

Planning Guide

Finding Expert Help

	Student Pages	Vocabulary	Practice Exercises	Lesson Review
	Student Text Lesson			
Lesson 1 How to Recognize a Professional	158-165	✔	✔	✔
Lesson 2 Help From Other Experts	166-170	✔	✔	✔
Lesson 3 Using Organizations	171-175	✔	✔	✔

Chapter Activities

Teacher's Resource Library

Putting It Together 6: What's My Line?

Community Connection 6: Get Information From an Organization

Assessment Options

Student Text

Chapter 6 Review

Teacher's Resource Library

Chapter 6 Mastery Tests A and B

Teaching Strategies						Language Skills			Learning Styles						Teacher's Resource Library		
Reviewing Skills	Teacher Alert	Career Application	Home Application	Global Connection	Community Application	Identification Skills	Writing Skills	Punctuation Skills	Visual/Spatial	Auditory/Verbal	Body/Kinesthetic	Logical/Mathematical	Group Learning	LEP/ESL	Activities	Workbook Activities	Self-Study Guide
158	158	161			164	✔	✔	✔					162			34	✔
166			170	167		✔	✔	✔						167	21-23	35-37	✔
171				173	172	✔	✔	✔	173							38-39	✔

Chapter at a Glance

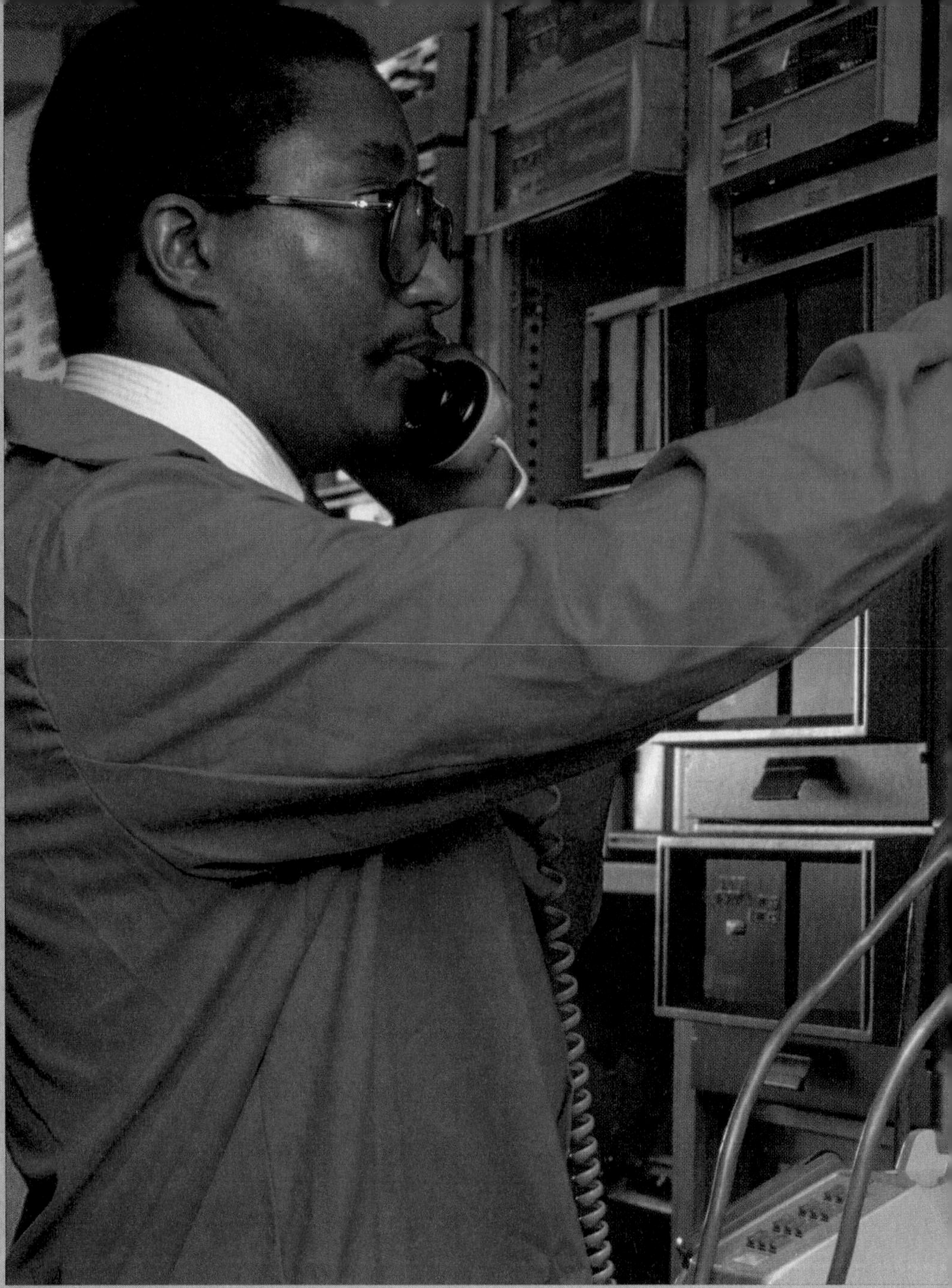

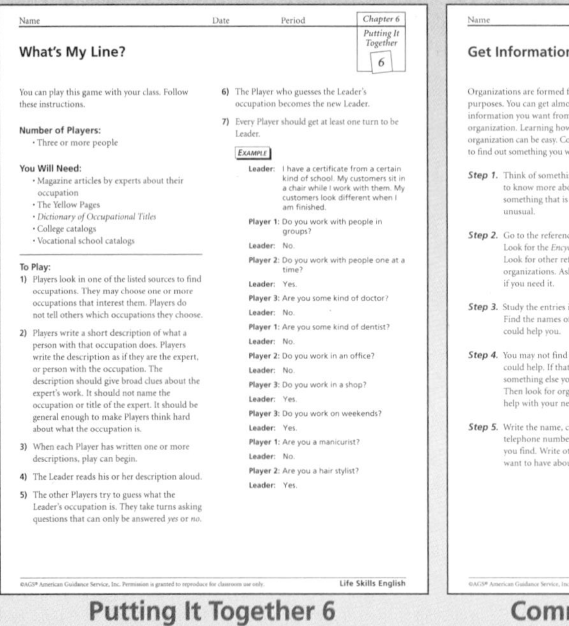

Chapter 6: Finding Expert Help

Teacher's Resource Library

Activities 21–23

Workbook Activities 34–39

Putting It Together 6

Community Connection 6

Chapter 6 Self-Study Guide

Chapter 6 Mastery Tests A and B

(Answer Keys for the Teacher's Resource Library begin on page 282 of this Teacher's Edition.)

Name Date Period

Chapter 6 *Putting It Together* 6

What's My Line?

You can play this game with your class. Follow these instructions.

Number of Players:
- Three or more people

You Will Need:
- Magazine articles by experts about their occupation
- The Yellow Pages
- *Dictionary of Occupational Titles*
- College catalogs
- Vocational school catalogs

To Play:

1) Players look in one of the listed sources to find occupations. They may choose one or more occupations that interest them. Players do not tell others which occupations they choose.

2) Players write a short description of what a person with that occupation does. Players write the description as if they are the expert, or person with the occupation. The description should give broad clues about the expert's work. It should not name the occupation or title of the expert. It should be general enough to make Players think hard about what the occupation is.

3) When each Player has written one or more descriptions, play can begin.

4) The Leader reads his or her description aloud.

5) The other Players try to guess what the Leader's occupation is. They take turns asking questions that can only be answered *yes* or *no*.

6) The Player who guesses the Leader's occupation becomes the new Leader.

7) Every Player should get at least one turn to be Leader.

EXAMPLE

Leader: I have a certificate from a certain kind of school. My customers sit in a chair while I work with them. My customers look different when I am finished.

Player 1: Do you work with people in groups?

Leader: No.

Player 2: Do you work with people one at a time?

Leader: Yes.

Player 3: Are you some kind of doctor?

Leader: No.

Player 1: Are you some kind of dentist?

Leader: No.

Player 2: Do you work in an office?

Leader: No.

Player 3: Do you work in a shop?

Leader: Yes.

Player 3: Do you work on weekends?

Leader: Yes.

Player 1: Are you a manicurist?

Leader: No.

Player 2: Are you a hair stylist?

Leader: Yes.

 Life Skills English

Putting It Together 6

Name Date Period

Chapter 6 *Community Connection* 6

Get Information From an Organization

Organizations are formed for many different purposes. You can get almost any kind of information you want from the right organization. Learning how to find the right organization can be easy. Complete the steps below to find out something you want to know.

Step 1. Think of something that you would like to know more about. Try to think of something that is different but not too unusual.

Step 2. Go to the reference section of a library. Look for the *Encyclopedia of Associations*. Look for other references that list organizations. Ask the librarian for help if you need it.

Step 3. Study the entries in these references. Find the names of organizations that could help you.

Step 4. You may not find organizations that could help. If that happens, think of something else you want to know about. Then look for organizations that might help with your new interest.

Step 5. Write the name, complete address, and telephone number of two organizations you find. Write other information you want to have about the organization.

Step 6. Next, write a letter to one of the organizations. Use a word processor if you can. Write neatly if you cannot use a computer.

Step 7. Ask the organization to send you its printed material on what you want to know. Ask the organization to send a catalog if it has one. Ask where else you can find helpful information. Include your name, address, city and state, and zip code. Sign your letter.

Step 8. Proofread your letter. Make sure your meaning is clear. Check that you spelled every word correctly.

Step 9. Have your teacher, a family member, or a friend read your letter. Ask the person to make sure your letter is clear and readable. Ask the person if he or she understands what you want. If not, ask for hints on how to improve your letter.

Step 10. Make any improvements the person suggested. Have the person check your letter again.

 Life Skills English

Community Connection 6

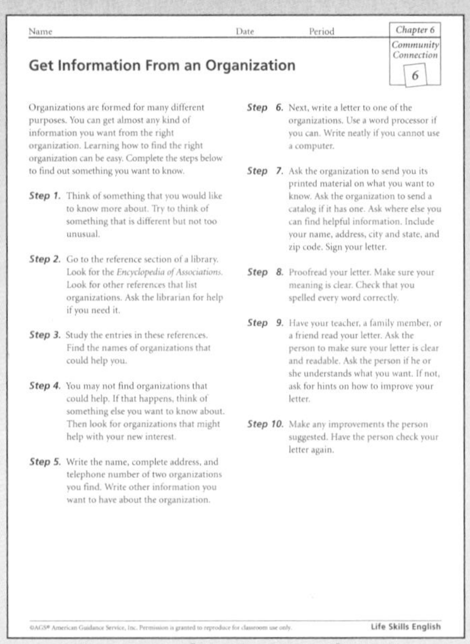

Chapter 6 Finding Expert Help

What is an expert? An expert is a person who has training and knowledge about a certain subject. An expert may be able to perform a special service for you. For example, an electrician is an expert on electrical wiring. An electrician can install or repair an electrical system.

An expert can also give you advice. For example, an attorney is an expert on matters related to the law. An attorney can give you legal advice or speak for you in a court of law.

In Chapter 6, you will learn how to find expert help. Each lesson will help you know where to go and whom to ask for expert help.

Goals for Learning

- To learn how to find expert help when you need it
- To learn about nonprofessional experts and how they can help you
- To identify organizations that can help you find skilled workers

Reading Vocabulary

advice (5)	legal (6)
attorney (8)	nonprofessional
electrician	organization (7)
identify (6)	subject (5)
install (6)	system (5)

Introducing the Chapter

Play this game with students to prepare them for Chapter 6. Distribute pieces of paper with the names of a variety of professions and occupations. If necessary, have students look in a dictionary to find out what a person in that profession or occupation does. Then have each student play the role of a person in that profession or occupation, saying something like the following: "I'm an expert. You'd call me if your car's engine started sputtering. Who am I?" Students can give as many details as they wish to help the class guess the profession or occupation. Then explain to students that in this chapter they will learn what kind of expert help is available to them and how to find that help.

SELF-STUDY GUIDE

Name ____________

CHAPTER 6: Finding Expert Help

Goal 6.1 *To learn how to find expert help when you need it*

Date	Assignment	Score
______	1: Read pages 157–159. Complete Activities A–B on page 159.	______
______	2: Read page 160. Complete Activity C on page 160.	______
______	3: Read page 161. Complete Activities D–E on page 162.	______
______	4: Read page 163. Complete Activity F on page 163.	______
______	5: Read page 164. Complete Activity G on page 164.	______
______	6: Complete Workbook Activity 34.	______
______	7: Complete the Lesson 1 Review, Parts A–B on page 165.	______

Comments:

Goal 6.2 *To learn about nonprofessional experts and how they can help you*

Date	Assignment	Score
______	8: Read page 166. Complete Activity A on page 166.	______
______	9: Read page 167. Complete Activity B on page 168, Activity C on pages 168–169, and Activity D on page 169.	______
______	10: Complete Workbook Activity 35.	______
______	11: Complete Workbook Activity 36.	______
______	12: Complete the Lesson 2 Review, Parts A–B on page 170.	______
______	13: Complete Workbook Activity 37.	______

Comments:

 Life Skills English

SELF-STUDY GUIDE

Name ____________

CHAPTER 6 Finding Expert Help, continued

Goal 6.3 *To identify organizations that can help you find skilled workers*

Date	Assignment	Score
______	14: Read pages 171–173. Complete Activity A on page 174.	______
______	15: Complete Workbook Activity 38.	______
______	16: Complete the Lesson 3 Review on page 175.	______
______	17: Complete Workbook Activity 39.	______
______	18: Complete the Chapter 6 Review, Parts A–C on pages 176–177.	______

Comments:

Student's Signature ____________ Date ____________

Instructor's Signature ____________ Date ____________

 Life Skills English

Chapter 6 Self-Study Guide

Lesson at a Glance

Chapter 6 Lesson 1

Overview This lesson explains what an expert is and how to recognize an expert's credentials.

Objectives

- To recognize the credentials of experts.
- To match the needs of an individual with the right professional.

Student Pages 158–165

Teacher's Resource Library

Workbook Activity 34

Reading Vocabulary

acknowledge (7)
architect (6)
associate's degree
bachelor's degree
certificate (5)
college (5)
community (5)
consider (5)
credentials (10)
expert (4)
individual (6)
license (5)
occupation (6)
pharmacist
physician (6)
profession (6)
professional (6)
reference (6)
require (6)
science (5)
specific (8)
university (5)

Teaching Suggestions

Introducing the Lesson

As you discuss the information in the text, you might describe your own credentials as a teacher.

Reviewing Skills

Review how to use a dictionary.

Lesson 1 How to Recognize a Professional

Associate's degree A degree from a two-year college or a community college.

Bachelor's degree A degree from a four-year college or university.

Credentials Proof that a person is an expert in a certain area of work.

Expert A person with training and knowledge about a specific subject.

Occupation The regular work or business a person does.

You can find expert help when you need it. An **expert** is a person who has training and knowledge about a certain subject. An expert has a profession. A profession is a job that requires special information and often long training. Examples of professionals are architects, engineers, physicians, attorneys, and pharmacists.

A person who is considered to be an expert has certain professional **credentials**. Credentials are proof that a person is an expert in a certain **occupation**. An occupation is the regular work or business of an individual.

A person's credentials may include these things:

- A college degree in a certain field
- A degree from a professional school
- A license or certificate
- Experience or references

Understanding College Degrees

Colleges and universities offer different degrees which acknowledge that a person has studied in a particular subject area, such as math or science. Various degrees require different numbers of years of study.

Associate's Degree: A degree from a two-year college or a community college. For example:

A.A.—Associate in Arts

Bachelor's Degree: A degree from a four-year college or university. Many professional occupations require this degree. The most common of these degrees are

B.A.—Bachelor of Arts

B.S.—Bachelor of Science

Teacher Alert

Throughout this chapter, students will encounter words that name professions and professionals. If students are unsure of the meaning of any of these words, encourage them to look up the words in a dictionary. You may also wish to point out at this time that some professional titles, such as *physician* and *doctor* or *attorney* and *lawyer*, are interchangeable.

Master's degree

An advanced degree, beyond a bachelor's degree, from a graduate school or university.

Doctoral degree

The highest degree awarded by a university or professional school.

Master's Degree: A degree from a graduate school or a university. This degree means that the person has had advanced training after a bachelor's degree. Some examples are

M.Ed.—Master of Education

M.B.A.—Master of Business Administration

M.S.—Master of Science

Doctoral Degree: The highest degree that a university or professional school may award. Many medical professionals must have this degree. Many professors in colleges and universities have this degree. Some examples are

M.D.—Doctor of Medicine

Ph.D.—Doctor of Philosophy

D.V.M.—Doctor of Veterinary Medicine

Activity A Match the degree with the best definition. Write each number and matching letter on your paper.

1) Associate degree	**a)** Awarded by four-year colleges or universities
2) Bachelor's degree	**b)** The highest degree a person can receive in a field
3) Master's degree	**c)** Awarded by community colleges
4) Doctoral degree	**d)** Awarded by graduate schools

Activity B Here are some abbreviations of credentials. Use a dictionary to find out what each abbreviation means. Write their meanings on your paper.

1) M.A.	**6)** B.F.A.
2) J.D.	**7)** L.L.B.
3) R.N.	**8)** L.P.N.
4) C.P.A.	**9)** Ed.D.
5) D.D.S.	**10)** D.V.M.

Reading Vocabulary

abbreviation (8)
administration (7)
advance (5)
award (5)
definition (6)
doctoral degree
education (5)
graduate (6)
master's degree
philosophy (11)
veterinary (9)

■ Presenting Activity A

Before having students complete Activity A on their own, review the definitions of the different degrees described on pages 158 and 159. Then invite students to describe their own professional goals and the degrees they plan to obtain in the pursuit of these goals.

Activity A Answers

1) c **2)** a **3)** d **4)** b

■ Presenting Activity B

Point out that many dictionaries have a separate abbreviations section that is usually after the main entries section. Students should look at the abbreviations section to complete Activity B.

Activity B Answers

1) Master of Arts **2)** Juris Doctor/Doctor of Jurisprudence (Law degree) **3)** Registered Nurse **4)** Certified Public Accountant **5)** Doctor of Dental Surgery (dentist) **6)** Bachelor of Fine Arts **7)** Bachelor of Laws **8)** Licensed Practical Nurse **9)** Doctor of Education **10)** Doctor of Veterinary Medicine

Reading Vocabulary

attend (5)
lawyer (5)
medical (6)
supervision
undergraduate

■ Presenting Activity C

You may wish to do Activity C together as a class. Have students discuss and decide the order of the steps. Then invite a volunteer to write the steps in order on a large piece of chart paper. Students may also wish to create a title for the list such as "Five Steps to a Profession." Display the list as a part of a career planning exhibit.

Activity C Answers

Graduate from high school. **(4)**
Attend a four-year college or university. **(5)**
Graduate from a professional school. **(3)**
Get experience under the supervision of another expert. **(1)**
Pass a state board examination. **(2)**

Professional Schools

Professional schools provide training for certain occupations. For example, a lawyer must graduate from a law school, and a doctor must graduate from a medical school. Often these schools are part of a large university. Most students receive a bachelor's degree before they attend professional schools.

Becoming a Professional

Professionals usually graduate from a college or a professional school and sometimes from both. Then they must get experience. Finally, they must take an examination. State governments give these exams. They are called State Board Examinations. A person who passes the examination receives a license to practice the profession.

On the wall in your physician's office you may see several degrees to show his or her credentials. They probably include:

- An undergraduate degree from a college or university.
- A degree from a medical school.
- A license to practice medicine in the state where the physician practices.

Activity C A person must do the following things to become a professional. Arrange the steps in the order they are usually done. Write them in order on your paper.

1) Get experience under the supervision of another expert.

2) Pass a state board examination.

3) Graduate from a professional school.

4) Graduate from high school.

5) Attend a four-year college or university.

Business and Financial Experts

There are many experts you may go to for advice and service in business and financial matters. Here are some examples:

Bankers loan people money for automobiles, houses, and other purchases. Many bankers have college degrees and years of experience working at various jobs in banking.

Real estate agents and brokers help people buy, sell, and rent property. Agents and brokers must have a license. A broker has more training and experience than an agent. Agents and brokers must pass state examinations.

Accountants prepare financial reports for businesses. They help people with their taxes. They check financial reports to be sure they are correct. Most accountants have college degrees. Some accountants become certified public accountants or C.P.A.s. An accountant must have experience and pass a state examination to become a C.P.A.

Attorneys, or lawyers, graduate from law school. Then they must take a state examination called a bar exam. After they pass this exam, attorneys may practice law in a court and represent other people in court. They can draw up legal papers such as wills and contracts and give advice to people about the law.

Architects graduate from college. Then they must get experience. Finally, they can take a state examination to become certified. Architects design homes and other buildings.

Architects must study math, design, and engineering to do their jobs well.

Reading Vocabulary

accountant
agent (5)
broker (8)
certify (8)
contract (6)
estate (6)
financial (8)
public (5)
purchase (5)
various (5)

Application

Career Connection

The material in this chapter presents a perfect opportunity to discuss career goals and the requirements for achieving those goals. Invite a panel of experts—specifically those in fields in which students have expressed interest—to share their professional stories with students. Beforehand, encourage students to prepare a list of questions that they would like to ask panel members about their work and their credentials.

Reading Vocabulary

aspect (8)
consult (5)
corporation (8)
location (6)
restaurant (5)
tax (5)

Presenting Activity D

Use questions such as the following to stimulate a discussion about the professions discussed on page 161:

- Which of these professions appeals most to you?
- Which professions do you think would be the most demanding?
- Which sounds most creative?

Have students explain their answers. Following the discussion, ask students to complete Activity D on their own.

Activity D Answers

1) Certified Public Accountant 2) bar exam 3) real estate broker 4) banker 5) yes

Presenting Activity E

Ask students to imagine the kinds of problems that a restaurant owner might encounter. List the problems on the board. Then invite students to name an expert that could help the restaurant owner solve each problem.

Activity E Answers

1) banker 2) accountant or C.P.A. 3) real estate agent or broker 4) architect 5) attorney (lawyer)

Activity D Use the information on page 161 to answer these questions. Write your answers on your paper.

1) What does C.P.A. stand for?
2) What is the name of the examination attorneys must pass?
3) Which person has more training and experience—a real estate agent or a real estate broker?
4) What kind of professional helps you borrow money for a car or house?
5) Does an architect need a license or certificate to practice his or her profession?

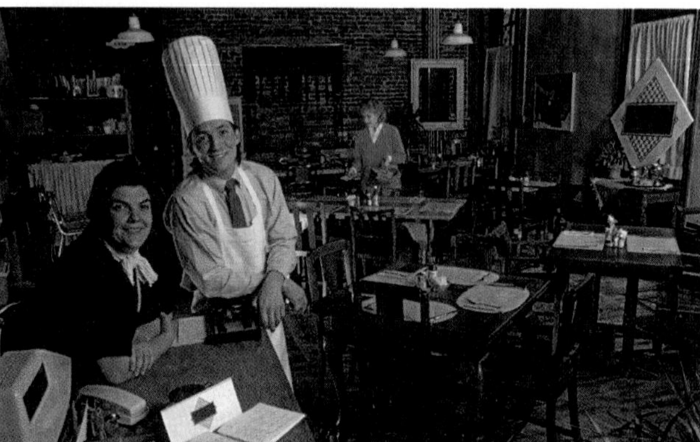

As Mrs. Sabatino's business grows, she consults different professionals to help her with banking, taxes, and buying a second restaurant.

Activity E Mrs. Rose Sabatino owns a pizza restaurant. On your paper, write the kind of professional who can help Mrs. Sabatino with each of the problems described below.

1) Mrs. Sabatino has been selling a lot of pizzas. She needs a bigger kitchen. She would like to borrow some money.
2) Mrs. Sabatino thinks she is paying too much in taxes every year.
3) Mrs. Sabatino has been thinking about opening another restaurant. She has found a location but would like to know more about the area.
4) Mrs. Sabatino's son suggested that she have a second restaurant built. She would like to see some designs before making a decision.
5) Mrs. Sabatino would like to know about the legal aspects of becoming a corporation.

Learning Styles

Interpersonal/Group Learning

Divide the class into groups of three. Ask each group to pick a profession in which they have some interest. Then ask each group to prepare a series of five questions to ask someone who works in this profession. If the groups need help with this, direct them to Activity E on page 162 and brainstorm questions the class might ask Mrs. Sabatino to learn about her profession. Afterward, encourage the groups to complete their own interview questions. Provide time for the groups to read their questions to the class. Encourage volunteers to add additional questions to each interview.

Physicians and Surgeons

There are many kinds of physicians, or medical doctors. Some of these physicians are general practitioners, or family doctors. Other physicians are specialists in certain areas.

EXAMPLES

Name of Specialist	Area of Special Training
Allergist	Allergies
Cardiologist	Heart
Dermatologist	Skin disorders
Internist	Diseases that do not require surgery
Obstetrician	Pregnancy and childbirth
Oncologist	Cancer
Ophthalmologist	Eyes
Orthopedist	Bones, joints, and muscles
Otolaryngologist	Ear, nose, and throat
Pediatrician	Infants and children
Psychiatrist	Nervous or mental disorders
Radiologist	High-energy radiation (X-rays)
Surgeon	Surgery (operations)

Activity F Which kind of specialist could help with each of these problems? Write your answers on your paper.

1) Mr. Lopez hurt his eye.

2) Jim has a skin rash.

3) Marta has an earache.

4) Mrs. Rosen starts sneezing every time she is near a cat.

5) Mrs. Tsao is pregnant.

6) Leon sprained his ankle playing basketball.

7) Mr. Franklin is depressed and cannot sleep.

8) Ted has to have his appendix removed.

9) Mr. and Mrs. Ashike's baby has a fever.

10) Liz needs a complete physical examination for college.

Reading Vocabulary

allergist
allergy
ankle (5)
appendix (7)
cancer (7)
cardiologist
childbirth
depress (8)
dermatologist
disorder (7)
earache
fever (5)
joint (6)
infant (6)
internist
mental (6)
muscle (5)
obstetrician
oncologist
operation (6)
ophthalmologist
orthopedist
otolaryngologist
pediatrician
physical (5)
practitioner
pregnancy
pregnant (10)
psychiatrist
radiation
radiologist
rash (7)
specialist (9)
sprain (5)
surgeon (8)
surgery (8)
X-ray (6)

■ Presenting Activity F

Invite volunteers to list some common physical ailments and diseases on the board. Through discussion, have the class eliminate items that would not require medical attention by a physician. Then have students identify the type of specialist they might see for the remaining items. Following this activity, ask students to complete Activity F with partners. Encourage partners to discuss each item before deciding on an answer.

Activity F Answers

1) opthamologist
2) dermatologist
3) otolaryngologist **4)** allergist
5) obstetrician **6)** orthopedist
7) psychiatrist **8)** surgeon
9) pediatrician **10)** internist

Reading Vocabulary

chiropractor
column (5)
diet (6)
ingrown
manipulate (10)
pharmacy (8)
podiatric
podiatrist
prescribe (8)
prescription (8)
specialize
spinal
veterinarian

■ Presenting Activity G

Focus students' attention on the text that precedes Activity G and discuss each medical professional listed. After students complete Activity G, invite them to take turns creating scenarios in which people might consult one of the medical professionals listed on page 164. Suggest that they model their scenarios on those in Activity G.

Activity G Answers

1) dentist 2) veterinarian 3) pharmacist 4) optometrist 5) chiropractor 6) podiatrist

APPLICATION

In the Community

Students who are interested may wish to interview medical professionals in the community about their duties and responsibilities. Suggest that students consult the Yellow Pages for names and numbers of medical professionals, or they can contact their own family physicians. Because of the intense schedules of many medical professionals, students may wish to write their interview questions in a letter. The professionals can then respond at their convenience.

Other Medical Professionals

Many medical professionals have degrees from a professional school. However, they are not medical doctors. Each of these professionals must pass a state examination to receive a license to practice.

Podiatrists are doctors of podiatric medicine. They specialize in problems related to feet.

Pharmacists fill prescriptions that medical doctors write. They work in drug stores and pharmacies. A doctoral degree is not required for this job.

Dentists are doctors of dental surgery. They treat teeth and gums. They may write prescriptions.

Chiropractors treat people by manipulating the spinal column. They prescribe diet, exercise, and rest. They do not write prescriptions or perform surgery.

Optometrists examine eyes and write prescriptions for glasses. They do not treat injuries or perform surgery.

Veterinarians treat animals and perform surgery if needed. They also can prescribe medicines for animals.

Activity G Which kind of medical professional could help with each of these problems? Write your answers on your paper.

1) Della's gums are sore.

2) Carolyn's cat won't eat.

3) Aunt Julia needs a prescription filled.

4) Joey is having trouble seeing the blackboard from his seat in the back of the classroom.

5) Mr. Williams's back is aching.

6) Steve has an ingrown toenail.

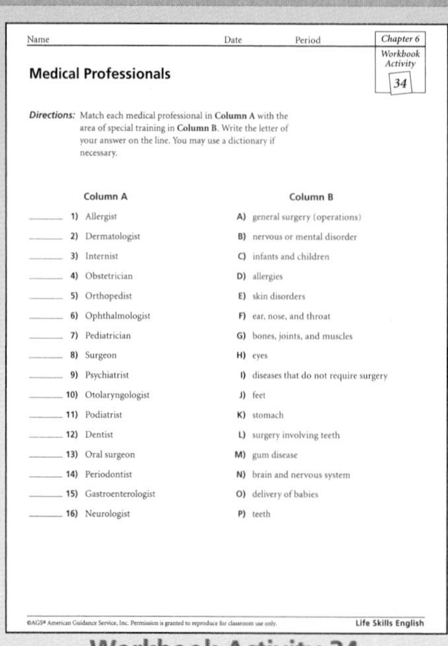

Name Date Period *Chapter 6 Workbook Activity 34*

Medical Professionals

Directions: Match each medical professional in **Column A** with the area of special training in **Column B**. Write the letter of your answer on the line. You may use a dictionary if necessary.

Column A	Column B
______ **1)** Allergist	**A)** general surgery (operations)
______ **2)** Dermatologist	**B)** nervous or mental disorder
______ **3)** Internist	**C)** infants and children
______ **4)** Obstetrician	**D)** allergies
______ **5)** Orthopedist	**E)** skin disorders
______ **6)** Ophthalmologist	**F)** ear, nose, and throat
______ **7)** Pediatrician	**G)** bones, joints, and muscles
______ **8)** Surgeon	**H)** eyes
______ **9)** Psychiatrist	**I)** diseases that do not require surgery
______ **10)** Otolaryngologist	**J)** feet
______ **11)** Podiatrist	**K)** stomach
______ **12)** Dentist	**L)** surgery involving teeth
______ **13)** Oral surgeon	**M)** gum disease
______ **14)** Periodontist	**N)** brain and nervous system
______ **15)** Gastroenterologist	**O)** delivery of babies
______ **16)** Neurologist	**P)** teeth

 Life Skills English

Workbook Activity 34

Lesson 1 Review

Part A Write the answers to these questions on your paper.

1) Which of these degrees does a community college give?
   a) bachelor's b) associate's c) master's
2) What is the highest degree a college or university can give?
   a) bachelor's b) master's c) doctoral
3) What type of professional worker can receive a C.P.A.?
   a) banker b) accountant c) attorney
4) Which of these health professionals is a medical doctor?
   a) chiropractor b) podiatrist c) allergist
5) What kind of examination does a lawyer take?
   a) C.P.A. exam b) bar exam c) medical exam

Part B Which professional does the person in each situation need? Write the letter of the correct answer on your paper.

1) Mr. and Mrs. Weber want to draw up a will.
   a) attorney b) accountant c) podiatrist
2) Aunt Lynn needs to have a filling replaced.
   a) allergist b) chiropractor c) dentist
3) Alan Fowler's hamster is sick.
   a) pediatrician b) veterinarian c) pharmacist
4) Paul Carter wants to start a business. He needs a loan.
   a) banker b) accountant c) real estate agent
5) Anna Walters needs help with her taxes.
   a) attorney b) accountant c) real estate broker
6) Aunt Harriet broke her arm.
   a) orthopedist b) podiatrist c) dermatologist
7) Susanna Choy needs a chest x-ray.
   a) radiologist b) cardiologist c) surgeon

Reading Vocabulary

hamster situation (5)
loan (5)

Part A Answers

1) b 2) c 3) b 4) c 5) b

Part B Answers

1) a 2) c 3) b 4) a 5) b
6) a 7) a

Lesson at a Glance

Chapter 6 Lesson 2

Overview This lesson focuses on experts other than professionals and the credentials of these experts.

Objectives

- To identify credentials of people in different trades.
- To list the steps for becoming an expert in a trade.

Student Pages 166–170

Teacher's Resource Library

Activities 21–23

Workbook Activities 35–37

Reading Vocabulary

apply (6)	plumber (6)
apprenticeship	practical (5)
combination (6)	recent (6)
intern (11)	supervise (7)
oral (6)	technical (6)
participate (7)	vocational

Teaching Suggestions

Introducing the Lesson

Focus a discussion on the steps required to become an expert in a trade.

Reviewing Skills

Review the definition of a professional.

Presenting Activity A

Ask students to give definitions orally in their own words.

Activity A Answers

1) person learning a trade under the supervision of an expert in that trade 2) a recent medical school graduate practicing under the supervision of an experienced doctor 3) a person with great knowledge or skill in a subject 4) a person lacking the knowledge and skills of a professional 5) a person with training and knowledge about a specific subject

Lesson 2 Help From Other Experts

Experts learn their skills in many different ways. They may attend technical or vocational schools, or they may go to business schools. They may participate in apprenticeship programs or get on-the-job training.

Becoming an Expert

Skilled workers develop skills through a combination of training and experience.

1. They go to school to learn facts about the work.
2. They get experience on the job where they are carefully supervised by an experienced person. This applies to both professionals and nonprofessionals.

Examples An intern is a recent medical school graduate who practices medicine under the supervision of an experienced doctor.

An apprentice is someone who is learning a trade, such as plumbing, under the supervision of a licensed plumber.

3. After the training period, workers usually take an examination. The exam may be written, oral, or practical.
4. Workers are then allowed to do their jobs on their own. They still have a boss, but they are not closely supervised.

Activity A Write a definition for each of the following on your paper.

1) apprentice

2) intern

3) professional

4) nonprofessional

5) expert

Apprentice
A worker being trained by an experienced and skilled person.

Contractor
A person who agrees to perform work or to provide supplies for a job.

Foreman
A supervisor or boss.

Independent contractors
People in business for themselves.

Journeyman
A worker who has completed an apprenticeship and passed a test.

Master's level
A worker who has more experience than a journeyman and has passed another test. This worker has earned a master's license.

Trade
An occupation that requires manual or mechanical skill.

Choosing an Expert

There is more than one way to get a job done. You can do it yourself. You can find a friend to help you. You can hire an expert. People often hire other experts to do work for them, such as cutting hair or fixing a television set. When you hire an expert to do a job, you have the right to expect expert work. To ensure that you receive expert work, be sure to check the person's credentials. Remember that credentials are proof that the person has been trained to do the job.

Credentials can include these things:

- A license issued by your state government
- A certificate or degree from a school
- Recommendations from other people
- A written guarantee from the worker

Experts in the Trades

A **trade** is an occupation that requires manual or mechanical skill. Examples are plumber, electrician, carpenter, auto mechanic, and printer.

An **apprentice** is a worker who is learning from an experienced and skilled person.

A **journeyman** has completed an apprenticeship and passed a test.

A **master's level** worker has more experience than a journeyman and has passed another test. This worker has a master's license.

A **foreman** is a supervisor or boss.

A **contractor** agrees to perform work or to provide supplies. Contractors may not be skilled workers themselves, but they hire other people with skills.

Independent contractors are people in business for themselves. They do not work for just one company or corporation.

Reading Vocabulary

apprentice (5)
boss (5)
contractor
corporation (8)
ensure
foreman (6)
guarantee (7)
independent contractors
journeyman
manual (6)
master's level
mechanical (6)
recommendation (8)
supervisor (7)
trade (3)

Global Connection

There is tendency, especially in the United States, to diminish the accomplishments of people in the trades while valuing the skills of physicians and other such professionals more. Engage students in a discussion of how these contrasting attitudes might have developed and how students feel about these attitudes. Invite students from different backgrounds to describe the attitudes toward tradespersons in their cultures and societies.

Learning Styles

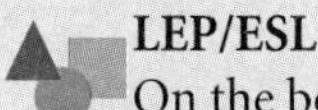

LEP/ESL

On the board, make two columns. In Column #1, print the following five words: *apprentice, intern, professional, nonprofessional,* and *expert.* Ask students for whom English is a second language to translate each of these five words into their primary language. Have them write their translations in Column #2. Then ask the ESL students to name any differences between what the terms mean in the United States and what they mean in other countries and cultures. Use any differences as an opportunity for class discussion.

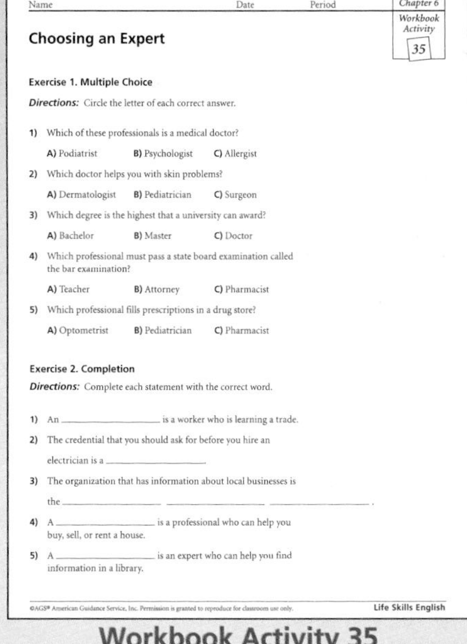

Name ________ Date ________ Period ________

Chapter 6 Workbook Activity 35

Choosing an Expert

Exercise 1. Multiple Choice

Directions: Circle the letter of each correct answer.

1) Which of these professionals is a medical doctor?
   A) Podiatrist B) Psychologist C) Allergist
2) Which doctor helps you with skin problems?
   A) Dermatologist B) Pediatrician C) Surgeon
3) Which degree is the highest that a university can award?
   A) Bachelor B) Master C) Doctor
4) Which professional must pass a state board examination called the bar examination?
   A) Teacher B) Attorney C) Pharmacist
5) Which professional fills prescriptions in a drug store?
   A) Optometrist B) Pediatrician C) Pharmacist

Exercise 2. Completion

Directions: Complete each statement with the correct word.

1) An ________ is a worker who is learning a trade.
2) The credential that you should ask for before you hire an electrician is a ________.
3) The organization that has information about local businesses is the ________ ________ ________.
4) A ________ is a professional who can help you buy, sell, or rent a house.
5) A ________ is an expert who can help you find information in a library.

 Life Skills English

Workbook Activity 35

Reading Vocabulary

alter (5) squad (7)
appliance (8) technician
emergency (5)

■ Presenting Activity B

Do Activity B together as an oral activity. Help students locate the answer to each item in the text on page 167. After students have completed the activity, encourage them to create additional sentences based on the information on page 167 for their classmates to complete.

Activity B Answers

1) trade 2) apprentice
3) work 4) supervisor, boss
5) journeyman 6) master's

■ Presenting Activity C

Read through each of the scenarios with students before asking them to complete Activity C on their own.

USING WHAT YOU HAVE LEARNED

After student have completed their lists, invite them to share their lists with the class. You may also wish to have students work in small groups to compile their lists.

USING WHAT YOU HAVE LEARNED

Think about the skilled people who have helped you. List the names of their occupations and what they did. Share your list with your classmates. Do not list professional workers such as doctors.

Example

Tailor: Altered my new suit.

Activity B Write on your paper the missing words to complete these sentences. Refer to page 167.

1) A plumber, a printer, and a carpenter each have a ______ .
2) An ______ is a worker who is learning a skill from someone with more experience or credentials.
3) Contractors agree to perform ______ .
4) A foreman is a ______ or ______ .
5) A worker who has completed an apprenticeship is a ______ .
6) A journeyman must take another test to receive a ______ license.

Activity C Read about these workers. Then write on your paper the answers to the questions on page 169.

a) Mr. Johnson repairs appliances such as washing machines and stoves. He goes to people's houses to do his work. He has an apprentice who helps him.
b) The Franklin Appliance Company sells appliances. You can also hire the company to fix appliances. Skilled workers and apprentices work there.
c) Ralph Attaway is a piano tuner. He was an apprentice at the Fine Music Store for four years. Now he is in business for himself. He will come to your house to tune or repair your piano.
d) Carlotta Rios is an emergency medical technician. She works for the fire department. You can get her help by calling for the Rescue Squad. Her training included special medical emergency courses and many hours of experience.
e) Fred Collins works for Mac's Service Station. He is an auto mechanic. He was an apprentice to an auto dealer for four years. Now he is a head mechanic. There are two part-time workers who help him.
f) Andrea Brown is an air conditioning specialist. She works for Young's Heating and Air Conditioning, Inc. Her company sent her to evening classes for several years. Now she trains new workers.

168 *Chapter 6 Finding Expert Help*

1) Which worker does not charge a fee for services?

2) Which workers are independent contractors?

3) If you hire Fred Collins to repair your car, who is actually responsible for his work—Fred or Mac's Service Station?

4) Where did Ralph Attaway work as an apprentice?

5) Andrea Brown trains new workers. What is the name for these workers?

Activity D Choo[illegible] problem described [illegible]

auto mechanic
beautician
roofer
travel agent
locksmith

1) Sandy wants [illegible]

2) Harold Willi[illegible] dented. He n[illegible] repair work.

3) Lyn wants to fly to Chicago. [illegible] or she could call someone to make reservations for her.

4) Jane Anderson wants to order a wedding cake.

5) Mrs. West bought a ring that is too small. She needs to have it made larger.

6) Mr. Cosby locked his keys inside his car and cannot get them out.

7) Kim Williams admired her sister's tile floor. Now Kim wants new flooring in her bathroom.

8) The Andersons' roof is leaking.

9) The Rosen family found a lot of land they really like. Before they buy it, they must find a worker who can measure the land and mark the boundaries.

10) The Garcias want to hire a good dance band for their daughter's wedding.

Reading Vocabulary

airline
barber (6)
beautician
boundary (6)
dent (5)
describe (5)
fender (6)
firefighter
ironworker
jeweler
locksmith
responsible (6)
surveyor
tilesetter
watchmaker

Activity C Answers

1) Carlotta Rios, emergency medical technician
2) Mr. Johnson, Ralph Attaway
3) Mac's Service Station
4) Fine Music Store
5) apprentices

Presenting Activity D

Before having students complete Activity D on their own, ask them to tell what they know about the duties and responsibilities of each expert listed. Then invite students to provide an example of a situation in which they might need each of these experts.

Activity D Answers

1) beautician 2) auto body mechanic 3) travel agent 4) baker 5) jeweler 6) locksmith 7) tilesetter 8) roofer 9) surveyor 10) musician

Name Date Period — *Chapter 6 Activity 21*

Selecting Experts

Directions: Read the following situations. Select the correct expert for each situation. Choose from the following list of experts. Use each person only once. Use a dictionary if needed. Write your answers on the lines provided.

career counselor	horticulturist	school guidance counselor
dentist	nutritionist	social worker
dermatologist	optometrist	
florist	realtor	

_______ 1) You want to sell your house. You would like to get advice about the price you should ask for the house.

_______ 2) You are having trouble reading the signs when you drive. You may need eyeglasses.

_______ 3) You are planning a dinner party. You would like to buy some flower arrangements for a table centerpiece.

_______ 4) Your family has been having problems communicating with each other. You would like to talk to someone about this.

_______ 5) You are not sure what classes you should be taking in high school to prepare for college. You need some advice.

_______ 6) You wake up with a very bad toothache. You don't think that it will just go away.

_______ 7) You need a special diet. You want to be sure it will help your problem.

_______ 8) You will be graduating from college soon. You would like information about job opportunities in your field.

_______ 9) You would like to plant a flower bed in your yard. You need to know what flowers are best suited for your area.

_______ 10) There is a rash on your face and hands. You don't know what is causing it.

 Life Skills English

Activity 21

Name Date Period — *Chapter 6 Workbook Activity 36*

Select an Expert

Directions: Read each situation. Choose the expert from the list that you would contact for each situation. Write the name of the expert on the line.

Plumber	Electrician	Banker	Pharmacist
Attorney	Architect	Cabinetmaker	Librarian
Veterinarian	Accountant		

1) You want to make a will. You want someone to advise you and to write the will.
You could consult the _______.

2) The tax laws have changed again. You are having problems trying to prepare your income taxes.
You could consult the _______.

3) In your kitchen you have wooden cupboards. One of the doors needs to be replaced. You cannot find one that matches exactly at the hardware store.
You could consult the _______.

4) Your dog isn't eating. He lies around whimpering all day. You think he might be sick.
You could consult the _______.

5) You are putting in a rock garden. You'd like a book that tells you all about the best kinds of flowers and plants to use.
You could consult the _______.

6) You decide to add a porch to your house. You need someone to draw up the plans.
You could consult the _______.

7) The porch costs more money than you thought. You don't have enough money, and decide to get a loan.
You could consult the _______.

8) Your pipes are leaking. Your drains are clogged. Your faucets are dripping.
You could consult the _______.

9) You decide to put in an additional outlet in your kitchen to use for your new microwave oven.
You could consult the _______.

10) Your doctor prescribed a medication. You think it is making you sick to your stomach. You need to know about the drug's side effects.
You could consult the _______.

 Life Skills English

Workbook Activity 36

Reading Vocabulary

consider (5)
craftsperson
insurance (7)
item (6)
response (6)

Part A Answers

1) b 2) b 3) d 4) b 5) d 6) a

Part B Answers

1) Students can choose any two of the following: a license; a certificate or degree; recommendation from another person; written guarantee
2) Become an apprentice.
Become a journeyman.
Get a master's license.

Application

At Home
Older family members can offer support, encouragement, and advice to students who are interested in a particular trade or profession. Encourage students to share their career goals with family members. Together, they can make a plan that will help students achieve their professional goals.

Lesson 2 Review

Part A Choose the best answer for each item. Write the letter of your answer on your paper.

1) A plumber who is learning the trade is
   a) a journeyman. b) an apprentice. c) an intern.
2) The most skilled craftsperson is a
   a) journeyman. b) master craftsworker. c) contractor.
3) Which of the following can be considered credentials?
   a) a license c) a written guarantee
   b) a recommendation d) all of the above
4) Which worker can help you plan a trip?
   a) a jeweler b) a travel agent c) a locksmith
5) Which worker must go to college to learn the job?
   a) an insurance agent c) a jeweler
   b) a travel agent d) none of the above
6) What is true about independent contractors?
   a) They work for more than one company.
   b) They have more experience than other contractors.
   c) They do not need a special license.

Part B Write your responses to each item.

1) Name at least two ways that you can identify an expert.
2) Here is a list of the steps needed to become an expert in a trade. Write these steps in order on your paper.
   - Become a journeyman.
   - Get a master's license.
   - Become an apprentice.

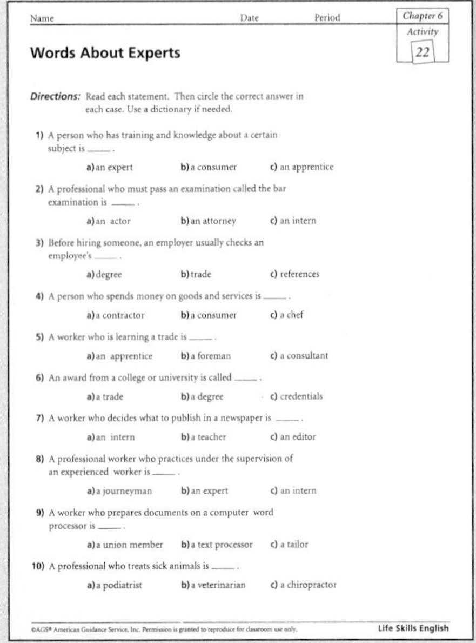
Name Date Period Chapter 6 Activity 22

Words About Experts

Directions: Read each statement. Then circle the correct answer in each case. Use a dictionary if needed.

1) A person who has training and knowledge about a certain subject is ____ .
   a) an expert b) a consumer c) an apprentice
2) A professional who must pass an examination called the bar examination is ____ .
   a) an actor b) an attorney c) an intern
3) Before hiring someone, an employer usually checks an employee's ____ .
   a) degree b) trade c) references
4) A person who spends money on goods and services is ____ .
   a) a contractor b) a consumer c) a chef
5) A worker who is learning a trade is ____ .
   a) an apprentice b) a foreman c) a consultant
6) An award from a college or university is called ____ .
   a) a trade b) a degree c) credentials
7) A worker who decides what to publish in a newspaper is ____ .
   a) an intern b) a teacher c) an editor
8) A professional worker who practices under the supervision of an experienced worker is ____ .
   a) a journeyman b) an expert c) an intern
9) A worker who prepares documents on a computer word processor is ____ .
   a) a union member b) a text processor c) a tailor
10) A professional who treats sick animals is ____ .
   a) a podiatrist b) a veterinarian c) a chiropractor

 Life Skills English

Activity 22

Name Date Period Chapter 6 Activity 23

Occupational Sentence Completion

Directions: Fill in the blanks by choosing the correct occupation from the word list. Use a dictionary to look up the meanings of words you do not know.

accountant	dental hygienist	pharmacist
allergist	florist	plumber
architect	horticulturist	psychiatrist
attorney	nutritionist	real estate agent
barber	obstetrician	tailor
chef	pediatrician	travel agent
chiropractor	periodontist	

1) The ____________ delivers babies.
2) The ____________ sews, repairs, or alters clothing.
3) The ____________ treats people by manipulating the spinal column.
4) The ____________ treats people who have hay fever.
5) The ____________ helps prepare wills and represents people in law courts.
6) The ____________ treats ill children.
7) The ____________ fixes leaky pipes and dripping faucets.
8) The ____________ treats nervous or mental disorders.
9) The ____________ prepares food and creates recipes.
10) The ____________ cleans teeth.
11) The ____________ treats people with gum disease.
12) The ____________ cuts and styles hair.
13) The ____________ plans diets and special menus.
14) The ____________ helps do tax returns and prepares financial statements.
15) The ____________ designs buildings.
16) The ____________ prepares flower arrangements.
17) The ____________ sells and rents homes.
18) The ____________ helps people plan vacation or business trips.
19) The ____________ grows flowers, shrubs, fruits, and vegetables.
20) The ____________ fills prescriptions written by medical doctors.

 Life Skills English

Activity 23

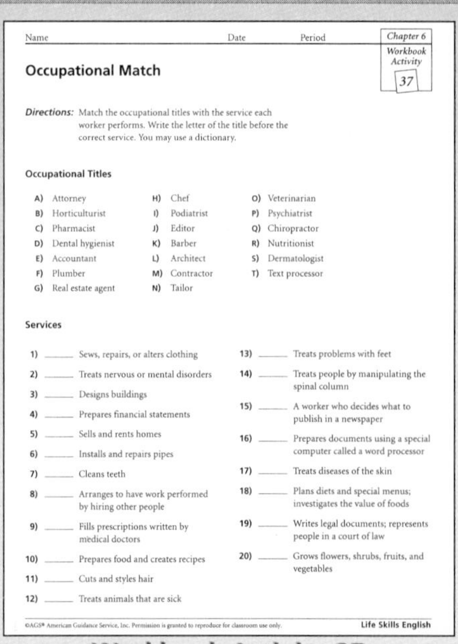
Name Date Period Chapter 6 Workbook Activity 37

Occupational Match

Directions: Match the occupational titles with the service each worker performs. Write the letter of the title before the correct service. You may use a dictionary.

Occupational Titles

A) Attorney	H) Chef	O) Veterinarian
B) Horticulturist	I) Podiatrist	P) Psychiatrist
C) Pharmacist	J) Editor	Q) Chiropractor
D) Dental hygienist	K) Barber	R) Nutritionist
E) Accountant	L) Architect	S) Dermatologist
F) Plumber	M) Contractor	T) Text processor
G) Real estate agent	N) Tailor	

Services

1) ____ Sews, repairs, or alters clothing
2) ____ Treats nervous or mental disorders
3) ____ Designs buildings
4) ____ Prepares financial statements
5) ____ Sells and rents homes
6) ____ Installs and repairs pipes
7) ____ Cleans teeth
8) ____ Arranges to have work performed by hiring other people
9) ____ Fills prescriptions written by medical doctors
10) ____ Prepares food and creates recipes
11) ____ Cuts and styles hair
12) ____ Treats animals that are sick
13) ____ Treats problems with feet
14) ____ Treats people by manipulating the spinal column
15) ____ A worker who decides what to publish in a newspaper
16) ____ Prepares documents using a special computer called a word processor
17) ____ Treats diseases of the skin
18) ____ Plans diets and special menus; investigates the value of foods
19) ____ Writes legal documents; represents people in a court of law
20) ____ Grows flowers, shrubs, fruits, and vegetables

 Life Skills English

Workbook Activity 37

Lesson 3

Using Organizations

You already have learned one important skill to help you find expert help. You can use the Yellow Pages of your telephone directory. You have also learned ways to check for the credentials experts should have.

Organization

A group of people united for a common cause.

There is another way to check the credentials of people you wish to hire. You can get help from **organizations** or **bureaus**. An organization is a group of people united for a common cause. A bureau is a specialized group or department that focuses on one main topic.

Bureau

A specialized group or department that focuses on one area or one main topic.

Look at the following list of organizations and bureaus. You or a member of your family may have received help from one or more of them sometime in the past.

The Medical Bureau
The Better Business Bureau
Welcome Wagon
The Chamber of Commerce
Travelers Aid Society
The Legal Aid Society
The Consumers Union

Organizations and How They Can Help

1. **The Medical Bureau or the Medical Society**

   If you need a doctor, this group can help. Representatives can give names of doctors near your home who are taking new patients.

Lesson at a Glance

Chapter 6 Lesson 3

Overview This lesson explains how specific organizations can help people identify experts.

Objective

- To match an individual's needs with an organization that can help identify an expert to meet those needs.

Student Pages 171–175

Teacher's Resource Library

Workbook Activities 38–39

Reading Vocabulary

aid (5)	**organization (7)**
bureau (6)	representative (6)
chamber (5)	society (5)
commerce (7)	topic (5)
directory (7)	unite (7)
focus (7)	

Teaching Suggestions

- **Introducing the Lesson** Discuss the information provided in the text. Encourage students to share any personal experiences that they or members of their families may have had with the organizations listed on page 171.

- **Reviewing Skills** Review how to use the telephone directory and Yellow Pages to find information.

Reading Vocabulary

complaint (6) judgment (6)

APPLICATION

In the Community

You might encourage students to find out what specific services the organizations described on pages 171–173 provide for non-English speaking members of the community. Students who are bilingual might consider becoming volunteers for these organizations.

2. **The Better Business Bureau**

   People at the Better Business Bureau can help by giving you information about the services and service record of a certain company. You can use your own judgment about whether to use the company or not. You can find the telephone number of the Better Business Bureau in the telephone directory.

BETTER BUSINESS BUREAU OF YOUR CITY	
General Information 1223 Main St	**454-9000**
Complaint Service 1223 Main St	**454-9020**

3. **Welcome Wagon or Welcome, Neighbor**

   If you are new in town, you can call a group that welcomes people to the community. Local businesses support these groups. Groups like the Welcome Wagon give facts about shopping, schools, hospitals, and doctors in your town.

Your neighbors can also help you settle into a new home.

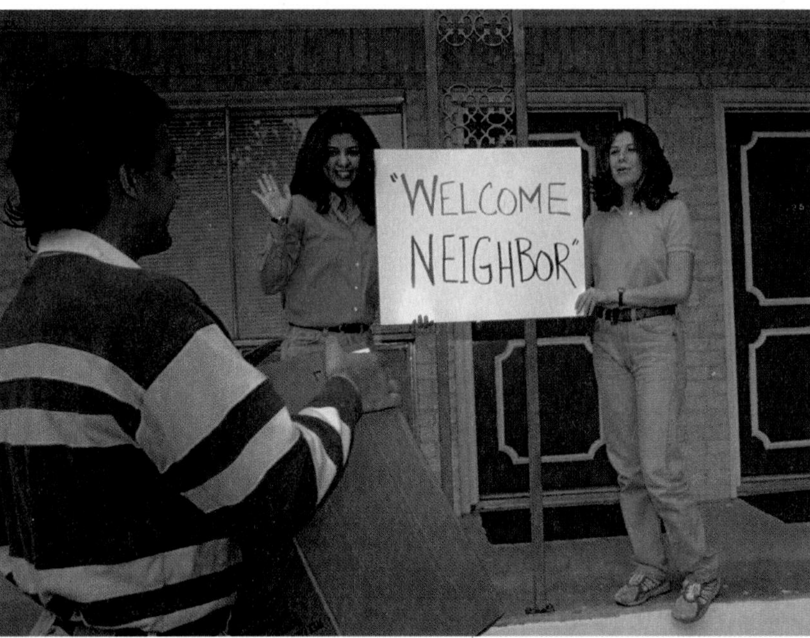

172 Chapter 6 Finding Expert Help

4. **The Chamber of Commerce**

Business people from the community belong to this organization. You can write to the Chamber of Commerce of any city or town in the United States to request information about places to visit, hotels, restaurants, and other businesses in the city or town.

5. **Travelers Aid or Travelers Assistance**

If you are visiting a new place and need help with a problem, you can call this group. For example, if you lose your wallet or need to find a doctor, this kind of group may be able to help. However, a group such as Travelers Aid is not a travel agent. Look for this organization in the telephone book or call the operator for help.

6. **The Legal Aid Society**

Attorneys at the Legal Aid Society will answer your questions on the telephone. They will agree to see you in person for a fee. They may also recommend another attorney who can help you with your problem.

7. **The Consumers Union**

Consumer

Someone who buys and uses goods and services.

A **consumer** is a person who buys and uses goods and services. The **Consumers Union** is an organization that tests products and investigates businesses. It publishes the results in a magazine called *Consumer Reports.* You can find this magazine in most libraries.

Consumers Union

A group that tests products and investigates businesses. The Consumers Union publishes the results of its tests in a magazine called Consumer Reports.

Your town or city may also have a consumers' group. This group would report about businesses in your area. You may find the name and telephone number in your directory. Your librarian should know about consumer groups.

Reading Vocabulary

assistance (6)
consumer (7)
Consumer's Union
investigate (6)
librarian (5)
operator (5)
product (5)
publish (6)
request (6)
wallet (6)

Global Connection

Many organizations provide brochures and pamphlets that are written in two or more languages. Provide samples of such materials for students to examine. Discuss with students how certain languages are chosen for brochures and pamphlets. Do students agree with the choices? Why or why not?

Learning Styles

Visual/Spatial

Divide the class into groups of three. Ask each group to make a chart that presents the information on the seven organizations listed on pages 171– 173. Suggest that they simply list the groups or use key words, symbols, icons, pictures, drawings, or code to present their information. Afterward, discuss the most helpful aspects of each chart.

Reading Vocabulary

athletic (5)
available (6)
brand (5)
comparison (6)
computer (8)
nutritious (11)
personal (6)

■ Presenting Activity A

Review the descriptions of each organization described on pages 171–173. Ask students to provide actual or made-up examples of situations when they or family members might call one of these groups.

Activity A Answers

1) Medical Bureau or Medical Society **2)** Better Business Bureau **3)** Travelers Aid or Travelers Assistance **4)** Legal Aid Society **5)** Welcome Wagon or Welcome, Neighbor **6)** Chamber of Commerce

Using What You Have Learned

Encourage students to find the local telephone numbers and addresses of all the organizations listed on pages 171–173. Suggest that students then write, call, or visit the headquarters of each organization to request copies of pamphlets and brochures about the organization in English. Students can then collect all the information they gather into an "How to Find Expert Help" file for the school or community library.

Using What You Have Learned

Find the telephone number for one of the groups listed on pages 171–173. Call the group and ask for information. Ask the person who answers to send you whatever printed information is available. Prepare a report about the group for your class.

Activity A Use the information on pages 171–173 to answer these questions. Write your answers on your paper.

1) Which group would you call for the name of a pediatrician in your town?

2) Which group would you call to ask if there have been any complaints about Mac's Service Station?

3) What organization could help if you were traveling in a new city and had a problem?

4) What organization would you call for legal advice?

5) What is a group that gives information to people who are new in town?

6) What organization helps businesses in the community?

Name Date Period *Chapter 6 Workbook Activity 38*

Organizations That Can Help

Directions: Read each situation. Choose the organization from the list that you could contact for each situation. Write the name of the organization on the line.

A) The Medical Bureau or Medical Society
B) The Better Business Bureau
C) Welcome Wagon, or Welcome, Neighbor
D) The Chamber of Commerce
E) Travelers Assistance or Travelers Aid
F) The Legal Aid Society

1) You arrive in a strange city. You need a hotel room, but you do not know where to go.

You could call ____________.

2) You want to start a business. You decide to form your own corporation. You need advice.

You could call ____________.

3) You just moved into Happy Villa. You don't know where any stores or doctors are. You need information about this new town.

You could call ____________.

4) You've been thinking about visiting Houston, Texas. You want the names of hotels, restaurants, and places to visit.

You could write ____________.

5) You want to roof your house. You've chosen a roofer. You want to know something about the roofer's service record.

You could call ____________.

6) You broke a bone. You are in a lot of pain. You are new in town, and don't know a doctor.

You could call ____________.

 Life Skills English

Workbook Activity 38

174 *Chapter 6 Finding Expert Help*

Lesson 3 Review

Lesson Review Number your paper 1 to 10. Read about each person's problem and write the name of the group or organization that might help solve that problem. There may be more than one right answer for each question.

1) Justin wants a new car. He would like to know the price of compact cars. He also wants to know some facts about each one.

2) Mrs. Okada needs an attorney to help her with business.

3) Nick's doctor retired. Nick would like to find a new doctor. Nick wants the office to be near his house.

4) The Sanapaws are new in town. They would like information about the community.

5) Jack Bevan is planning a trip to Los Angeles, California. He would like to know about interesting places to visit while he is there.

6) Trisha Earle wants to have her washing machine repaired. John's Small Appliance Store is listed in the Yellow Pages. Trisha wants to find out if that business is reliable.

7) Uncle Jonathan needs new glasses. He wants the name of an optometrist.

8) Sam Young went to Wilkinsburg on business. He lost his wallet.

9) Mary Franklin is buying a vacuum cleaner. She wants to know which is the most reliable model.

10) The Home Improvement Company has called Mrs. Condelli. The company wants to sell her new storm doors and windows. She wants to check on their reputation.

Reading Vocabulary

compact (5) retire (6) reliable (7) vacuum (5) reputation (5)

Lesson Review Answers

1) Consumers Union **2)** Legal Aid Society **3)** Medical Bureau or Medical Society **4)** Welcome Wagon or Welcome, Neighbor **5)** Chamber of Commerce **6)** Better Business Bureau **7)** Medical Bureau or Welcome Wagon **8)** Travelers Aid or Travelers Assistance **9)** Consumers Union **10)** Better Business Bureau

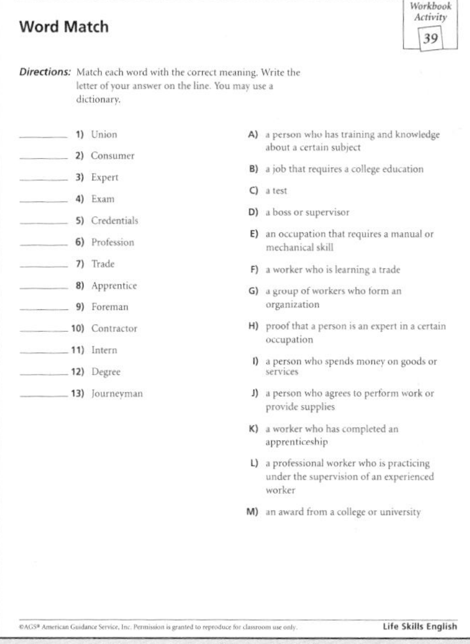
Name Date Period

Chapter 6 Workbook Activity 39

Word Match

Directions: Match each word with the correct meaning. Write the letter of your answer on the line. You may use a dictionary.

_____ **1)** Union
_____ **2)** Consumer
_____ **3)** Expert
_____ **4)** Exam
_____ **5)** Credentials
_____ **6)** Profession
_____ **7)** Trade
_____ **8)** Apprentice
_____ **9)** Foreman
_____ **10)** Contractor
_____ **11)** Intern
_____ **12)** Degree
_____ **13)** Journeyman

A) a person who has training and knowledge about a certain subject
B) a job that requires a college education
C) a test
D) a boss or supervisor
E) an occupation that requires a manual or mechanical skill
F) a worker who is learning a trade
G) a group of workers who form an organization
H) proof that a person is an expert in a certain occupation
I) a person who spends money on goods or services
J) a person who agrees to perform work or provide supplies
K) a worker who has completed an apprenticeship
L) a professional worker who is practicing under the supervision of an experienced worker
M) an award from a college or university

 Life Skills English

Workbook Activity 39

Finding Expert Help Chapter 6 **175**

Chapter 6 Review

The Teacher's Resource Library includes two parallel forms of the Chapter 6 Mastery Test. The difficulty level of the two forms is equivalent. You may wish to use one form as a pretest and the other form as a posttest.

Part A Answers

1) c 2) b 3) b 4) c 5) b 6) b
7) a 8) b 9) b 10) a

Chapter 6 Review

Part A Choose the letter of the correct answer. Write it on your paper.

1) Which of these professionals is a medical doctor?
   a) optometrist b) pharmacist c) pediatrician
2) Which expert will help you find information on any subject?
   a) lawyer b) librarian c) accountant
3) Which degree is the highest that a university can award?
   a) A.A. b) Ph.D. c) C.P.A.
4) Which professional must pass a state board examination?
   a) accountant b) librarian c) attorney
5) Which professional can help you buy, sell, or rent a house?
   a) plumber b) real estate broker c) lawyer
6) Which credential should a nonprofessional worker have?
   a) a college degree b) proof of skills or training
7) What is the name of a worker who is learning a trade?
   a) apprentice b) journeyman c) foreman
8) Which worker will help you plan a trip?
   a) pharmacist b) travel agent c) intern
9) Which of these is a credential?
   a) a big ad b) recommendation c) a bright sign
10) Which worker may not have special skills for a job but hires other workers who do have the skills?
    a) contractor b) apprentice c) journeyman

Name Date Period — *Chapter 6 Mastery Test A page 1*

Chapter 6 Mastery Test A

Part A Circle the correct answer for each question.

1) A person with knowledge and training about a specific subject is an ______________ .
   a) occupation b) expert c) allergist
2) Which degree could you get from a four-year college or university?
   a) bachelor's degree b) doctoral degree c) associate's degree
3) Which describes a doctoral degree?
   a) degree from a four-year college or university
   b) highest degree awarded by a university or professional school
   c) degree from a two-year college or community college
4) What does an attorney do?
   a) prepares financial reports for businesses
   b) helps people get loans
   c) represents people in court and gives legal advice
5) Joe wants to buy a house. Which professional should he call?
   a) internest
   b) real estate agent
   c) certified public accountant
6) What does an architect do?
   a) designs houses and buildings
   b) loans people money
   c) represents people in court and gives legal advice
7) Mrs. Mooney's infant son Tim has been running a fever. Which medical professional should she take him to?
   a) pediatrician b) obstetrician c) radiologist
8) Which medical professional performs operations?
   a) oncologist b) surgeon c) radiologist
9) Where would someone go if they have a sick pet?
   a) veterinarian b) podiatrist c) chiropractor
10) What does a pharmacist do?
    a) specializes in problems related to feet
    b) treats people by manipulating the spinal column
    c) fills prescriptions that medical doctors write

 Life Skills English

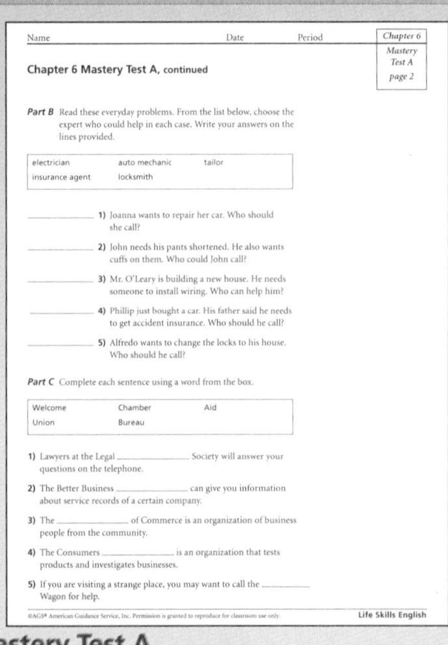

Name Date Period — *Chapter 6 Mastery Test A page 2*

Chapter 6 Mastery Test A, continued

Part B Read these everyday problems. From the list below, choose the expert who could help in each case. Write your answers on the lines provided.

electrician	auto mechanic	tailor
insurance agent	locksmith	

______________ 1) Joanna wants to repair her car. Who should she call?

______________ 2) John needs his pants shortened. He also wants cuffs on them. Who could John call?

______________ 3) Mr. O'Leary is building a new house. He needs someone to install wiring. Who can help him?

______________ 4) Phillip just bought a car. His father said he needs to get accident insurance. Who should he call?

______________ 5) Alfredo wants to change the locks to his house. Who should he call?

Part C Complete each sentence using a word from the box.

Welcome	Chamber	Aid
Union	Bureau	

1) Lawyers at the Legal ______________ Society will answer your questions on the telephone.
2) The Better Business ______________ can give you information about service records of a certain company.
3) The ______________ of Commerce is an organization of business people from the community.
4) The Consumers ______________ is an organization that tests products and investigates businesses.
5) If you are visiting a strange place, you may want to call the ______________ Wagon for help.

 Life Skills English

Chapter 6 Mastery Test A

Part B When you have a problem, you need to know the kind of expert that can help. Number your paper 1 to 5. Write the kind of expert that can help with each problem. Use the *Experts* list below.

Problems	Experts
1) Sal's car is making a funny noise.	librarian
2) Donna's cat, Larson, needs his annual shots.	pharmacist
3) Robert wonders if there is a book about repairing air conditioners.	mechanic
4) Floyd has a stain on his new suit.	dry cleaner
5) Kenesha needs some medicine for poison ivy.	veterinarian

Part C Write on your paper your answers to these questions.

1) Which organization can give you legal advice?
2) Which organization helps people who are new to a city?
3) Which organization publishes a magazine that reports on products and services?
4) Which organization can tell you if a company has been reliable in the past?
5) If you needed a doctor, which group could you call?

Test Taking Tip

If you know you will have to define certain terms on a test, write the term on one side of a card. Write its definition on the other side. Use the cards to test yourself, or work with a partner.

Reading Vocabulary

annual (6) ivy (6)
define (7) stain (5)

Part B Answers

1) mechanic 2) veterinarian 3) librarian 4) dry cleaner 5) pharmacist

Part C Answers

1) Legal Aid Society 2) Welcome Wagon or Welcome, Neighbor 3) Consumers Union 4) Better Business Bureau 5) Medical Bureau or Medical Society

Name Date Period | *Chapter 6 Mastery Test B page 1*

Chapter 6 Mastery Test B

Part A Circle the correct answer for each question.

1) What is an expert?
   a) person with a two-year degree
   b) person with knowledge and training about a specific subject
   c) any person with an occupation
2) What is a bachelor's degree?
   a) degree from a four-year college or university
   b) degree from a two-year college or community college
   c) highest degree awarded by a university or professional school
3) What is the highest degree awarded by a university or professional school?
   a) master's degree b) bachelor's degree c) doctoral degree
4) What is the name of a professional who represents people in court and gives legal advice?
   a) banker b) attorney c) accountant
5) What does a real estate agent do?
   a) helps people buy, sell, or rent property
   b) designs homes and other buildings
   c) prepares financial reports
6) What is a professional who designs houses and buildings called?
   a) accountant b) attorney c) architect
7) Mr. Lee has allergies. Who should he see?
   a) radiologist b) orthopedist c) allergist
8) What does a surgeon do?
   a) performs operations
   b) cures skin disorders
   c) cures allergies
9) What does a veterinarian do?
   a) fills prescriptions b) examines eyes c) treats animals
10) Which medical professional fills prescriptions that medical doctors write?
   a) podiatrist b) pharmacist c) pediatrician

 Life Skills English

Name Date Period | *Chapter 6 Mastery Test B page 2*

Chapter 6 Mastery Test B, continued

Part B Read these everyday problems. Then choose the expert from the box who could help in each case. Write your answers on the lines provided.

locksmith	insurance agent	auto mechanic
tailor	electrician	

_______ 1) Tami wants a lock repaired. Who should she call?

_______ 2) Mr. Luong wants to get insurance for his home. Who should he call?

_______ 3) Tom's suit needs to be altered. Who could he call?

_______ 4) The electrical wiring in Mrs. Willis's house needs to be replaced. Who can help her?

_______ 5) Roberto needs new brakes for his car. Who should he call?

Part C Complete each sentence using a word from the box.

Wagon	Consumers	Legal
Business	Commerce	

1) Lawyers at the _______ Aid Society will answer your questions on the telephone.
2) The Better _______ Bureau can give you service records for a certain company.
3) The Chamber of _______ is an organization of business people from the community.
4) The _______ Union is an organization that tests products and investigates businesses.
5) If you are visiting a strange place, you may want to call the Welcome _______ for help.

 Life Skills English

Chapter 6 Mastery Test B

Chapter 7

Planning Guide

Information From the Media

	Student Text Lesson			
	Student Pages	Vocabulary	Practice Exercises	Lesson Review
Lesson 1 Parts of a Newspaper	180-184	✔	✔	✔
Lesson 2 Reading the Newspaper	185-191	✔	✔	✔
Lesson 3 Classified Ads	192-199	✔	✔	✔
Lesson 4 The Help Wanted Ads	200-205	✔	✔	✔
Lesson 5 Television and Radio	206-215	✔	✔	✔

Chapter Activities

Teacher's Resource Library

Putting It Together 7: Media Jeopardy

Community Connection 7: Find a Job in the Help-Wanted Ads

Assessment Options

Student Text

Chapter 7 Review

Teacher's Resource Library

Chapter 7 Mastery Tests A and B

Teaching Strategies						Language Skills			Learning Styles						Teacher's Resource Library		
Reviewing Skills	Teacher Alert	Career Application	Home Application	Global Connection	Community Application	Identification Skills	Writing Skills	Punctuation Skills	Visual/Spatial	Auditory/Verbal	Body/Kinesthetic	Logical/Mathematical	Group Learning	LEP/ESL	Activities	Workbook Activities	Self-Study Guide
180				180		✔	✔	✔					184			40	✔
185		191	186		187	✔	✔	✔	189							41-42	✔
192	197		197		195	✔	✔	✔		199					24-25		✔
200	203	202				✔	✔	✔				205			26	43-44	✔
206			208	207, 214	210-211	✔	✔	✔			207				27	45	✔

Chapter at a Glance

Name ______ Date ______ Period ______ *Chapter 7 Putting It Together 7*

Media Jeopardy

You can play this game with your class, your friends, or your family. Follow these instructions.

Number of Players:

- Three or more teams of at least two players each

For Each Team You Will Need:

- One piece of large easel pad paper
- One or two pieces of notebook paper
- One wide-tip marker
- One pencil or pen

To Play:

1) Each team thinks of three or more broad categories related to media. Someone writes the categories with a marker across the top of the sheet of easel paper. The team assigns a different number of points to several spaces under each category.

EXAMPLE

Newspaper	Radio	Television
10	10	10
20	20	20
40	40	40

2) Each team agrees on questions and answers for each space on the big sheet. The team can take time to research the media categories and items it chooses. One team member writes the questions and answers on the notebook paper.

EXAMPLE

For the first space under newspaper, they could write:

Question: What is a daily newspaper?

Answer: This newspaper comes out every day.

For the third space under newspaper, they could write:

Question: Who is Dear Abby?

Answer: She writes a daily advice column.

3) When each team has its sheets ready, play can begin.

4) One team is the Leader team for each round. The Leader team uses its easel sheet in that round.

5) The Leader team picks one of the other teams to be first. The first team selects a category and the number of points it wants from the Leader team's sheet.

EXAMPLE

We want Newspaper for forty.

6) The Leader team gives the answer to the question.

EXAMPLE

She writes a daily advice column.

 Life Skills English

Name ______ Date ______ Period ______ *Chapter 7 Putting It Together 7*

Media Jeopardy (continued)

7) The other teams raise their hand to signal they have a question that fits the answer. The team that raises a hand first asks the first question.

EXAMPLE

First team: Who is Ann Landers?

Leader team: No, that is the wrong question.

8) If the first team asks the wrong question, the next team takes a turn. Teams keep asking questions until the correct question is asked.

EXAMPLE

Second team: Who is Dear Abby?

Leader team: Yes, that is the correct question.

9) The team that asks the correct question gets the points. That team also chooses the next category and number of points.

10) The team with the most points wins. Each team should have a turn to be the Leader team.

11) For variation, the teams can play for double points. That means each space is worth twice as many points.

 Life Skills English

Putting It Together 7

Name ______ Date ______ Period ______ *Chapter 7 Community Connection 7*

Find a Job in the Help-Wanted Ads

Help-wanted ads are important when you look for a job. You have studied help-wanted ads in Chapter 7 Lesson 4. You learned about the abbreviations used in these ads. You learned words you need to know when reading the ads. You learned that similar jobs can have different titles. You can learn about jobs that interest you by studying the help-wanted ads. Follow these steps.

Step 1. Get the classified section of your favorite Sunday newspaper. Sunday editions usually have the most job listings each week.

Step 2. Think of a kind of job that interests you.

Step 3. Find three ads that match the kind of job you chose. Cut out or copy each ad. Remember, jobs that are nearly the same may have different position titles.

Step 4. Use the ads you found to fill out the chart below. Write out completely any abbreviated words from the ads. You may not be able to fill in every column for each job. Some ads do not list all of the information on the chart.

Step 5. Give a teacher or a family member the chart and your ads. Ask the person to check if you have entered information in the right column.

	Ad #1	Ad #2	Ad #3
Guide Words on the Page			
Job Title			
Name of Company			
Qualifications			
Experience			
Education			
Salary			
Hours			
Benefits			

 Life Skills English

Community Connection 7

Chapter 7 Information From the Media

When someone has a message for one or two people, a letter or a telephone call is the best means of communication. When someone has a message for the general public, the best means of communication is mass media. Mass media, which includes television, radio, newspapers, and magazines, reaches the most people at one time.

In Chapter 7, you will learn about three types of media: newspapers, television, and radio. Each lesson focuses on the characteristics of the different types of media and how you can use them to find information.

Goals for Learning

- To learn about information from three types of media: newspapers, television, and radio
- To learn about the parts of a newspaper
- To learn about reading a newspaper for information
- To learn how to use the classified advertising section
- To learn how to use the help wanted section of the classified ads
- To learn how to use television and radio for information

Reading Vocabulary

characteristic (6)
communication (6)
focus (7)
public (5)
section (5)

Introducing the Chapter

To stimulate students' interest in the chapter topic, ask the following questions:

- What is your primary purpose for watching television, listening to the radio, and reading the newspaper?
- Why else might you turn to these three forms of mass media?
- How does each of these media sources deliver factual information?
- How might you use these media sources to communicate with the general public?

Explain to students that when they complete Chapter 7, they will know how to use the media to find the information they need.

SELF-STUDY GUIDE

Name ________

CHAPTER 7: Information From the Media

Goal 7.1 *To learn about information from three types of media: newspapers, television, and radio*

Date	Assignment	Score
____	1: Read page 179.	____

Comments:

Goal 7.2 *To learn about the parts of a newspaper*

Date	Assignment	Score
____	2: Read pages 180-181. Complete Activity A on page 181.	____
____	3: Read page 182. Complete Activity B on page 182. Read page 183. Complete Activity C on page 183.	____
____	4: Complete Workbook Activity 40.	____
____	5: Complete the Lesson 1 Review, Parts A-B on page 184.	____

Comments:

Goal 7.3 *To learn about reading a newspaper for information*

Date	Assignment	Score
____	6: Read page 185. Complete Activity A on page 185 and Activity B on page 186.	____
____	7: Complete Workbook Activity 41.	____
____	8: Read pages 186-187. Complete Activity C on page 187 and Activity D on page 188.	____
____	9: Read page 189. Complete Activity E on page 189. Read page 190. Complete Activity F on page 190.	____
____	10: Complete Workbook Activity 42.	____
____	11: Complete the Lesson 2 Review, Parts A-B on page 191.	____

Comments:

 Life Skills English

SELF-STUDY GUIDE

Name ________

CHAPTER 7 Information From the Media, continued

Goal 7.4 *To learn how to use the classified advertising section*

Date	Assignment	Score
____	12: Read page 192. Complete Activities A-B on page 193.	____
____	13: Read page 194. Complete Activities C-D on page 194.	____
____	14: Read page 195. Complete Activity E on page 196 and Activity F on pages 197-198.	____
____	15: Complete the Lesson 3 Review, Parts A-C on page 199.	____

Comments:

Goal 7.5 *To learn how to use the help wanted section of the classifieds*

Date	Assignment	Score
____	16: Read page 200. Complete Activity A on page 200.	____
____	17: Read page 201. Complete Activity B on page 201.	____
____	18: Complete Workbook Activity 43.	____
____	19: Read page 202. Complete Activity C on page 202.	____
____	20: Read page 203. Complete Activity D on page 203 and Activity E on page 204.	____
____	21: Complete Workbook Activity 44.	____
____	22: Complete the Lesson 4 Review, Parts A-B on page 205.	____

Comments:

Goal 7.6 *To learn how to use television and radio for information*

Date	Assignment	Score
____	23: Read page 206. Complete Activity A on page 206.	____
____	24: Read pages 207-208. Complete Activities B-C on page 209.	____
____	25: Read pages 210-212. Complete Activity D on page 212.	____
____	26: Complete Workbook Activity 45.	____
____	27: Read page 213. Complete Activities E-F on page 213. Read page 214.	____
____	28: Complete the Lesson 5 Review on page 215.	____
____	29: Complete the Chapter 7 Review, Parts A-C on pages 216-217.	____

Comments:

Student's Signature ________ Date ________

Instructor's Signature ________ Date ________

 Life Skills English

Chapter 7 Self-Study Guide

Lesson at a Glance

Chapter 7 Lesson 1

Overview This lesson presents an overview of the different parts of a newspaper.

Objectives

- To locate parts of a newspaper.
- To match newspaper terms with their meanings.

Student Pages 180–184

Teacher's Resource Library

Workbook Activity 40

Reading Vocabulary

communicate (6)	personality (6)
current (4)	publish (6)
daily (5)	recent (6)
distribute (6)	regional
feature (6)	separate (5)
local (6)	similar (6)
mass media	slightly
national (4)	stock (5)
organize (6)	suburb (7)

Teaching Suggestions

Introducing the Lesson

Distribute several copies of newspapers to partners or small groups of students. As you discuss each element or section of the newspaper described in the text, ask students to find that element or section in their copies of the newspaper. Suggest that students then skim that section and share one piece of information they learned.

Reviewing Skills

Review how to use an index.

Global Connection

Provide copies of foreign language newspapers for bilingual students to share. Students can read aloud and translate the names of the different newspaper sections for the class as well as headlines and column titles.

Lesson 1 Parts of a Newspaper

Current
Up to the present.

Daily
Every day.

Local
Having to do with one certain place.

Mass media
A way to communicate with the most people at one time; for example, television, radio, newspapers, and magazines.

National
Having to do with a whole country, or nation.

Newspapers are part of the **mass media**. Everyone who reads a newspaper receives the same information. There are two main kinds of newspapers: **daily** and weekly. Daily newspapers are published and distributed every day. They have the most **current**, or up-to-the-present, news. They usually have more **national** and world news than weekly papers. National news has to do with what's happening in a nation. Generally, daily newspapers have more regular readers than weekly papers. Weekly newspapers often are published in small towns. They usually focus on **local** news. Local news has to do with one certain place.

Parts of a Newspaper and Kinds of News

Newspapers are divided into parts, or sections. Each part has a different kind of news: national and world news, local news, sports news, business news, regular features, and classified advertisements, or ads. Although all newspapers are organized in slightly different ways, many follow a similar plan.

- Articles about national and world news appear in the front section of most large city newspapers. They usually continue to another page or section of the newspaper. Local newspapers that serve suburbs of large cities may not carry national and world news.
- Local news is information about local events of interest. Local news is often placed in a special section of the newspaper. Sometimes it follows the national and world news section. Local news may also be called regional news.
- Sports news is information about sports. Most newspapers have a special sports section. These pages have results from recent sporting events, articles about sports personalities, and general sports news.
- Business news is information about the stock market and events affecting businesses large and small. Many newspapers have a separate section for business news.

Column

A regular newspaper feature about recent events, current political and social issues, and other topics of interest to readers.

Classified advertisements

Short public notices (items for sale, apartments or houses for rent, help wanted).

- Regular features are **columns** and articles with information of interest to the public, such as gardening, health, advice, or celebrities. Comics, television and movie schedules, and announcements about weddings and engagements are included in the regular features of the newspaper.
- **Classified advertisements**, or ads, are short public notices that offer items for sale. This section of the paper includes houses for sale, apartments for rent, and the help wanted ads that announce available jobs. People pay money to place an ad in the classified section of the newspaper. Classified ads are a source of income for the newspaper publishers. Additional money to run the paper comes from newspaper sales and subscriptions and from the sales of advertisements.

Activity A Use the information that begins on page 180 to answer these questions. Write your answers on your paper.

1) Which type of news would you expect to find on the front pages of a big city newspaper?

a) world news **c)** sports news
b) local news **d)** business news

2) Which section of the paper would you check to find the score of last night's basketball game?

a) classified advertisements **c)** front page
b) business news **d)** sports section

3) Which section of the paper would you check for information about used computers for sale?

a) business section **c)** classified advertisements
b) sports section **d)** feature section

4) Which section of the newspaper would you check for information about a company that was sold?

a) business section **c)** national news
b) sports section **d)** regular features

Reading Vocabulary

additional (6)	include (5)
advice (5)	issue (6)
available (6)	item (6)
celebrity (9)	political (6)
classified advertisement	publisher (6)
column (5)	schedule (6)
computer (8)	social (5)
engagement	subscription (7)
	topic (5)

■ Presenting Activity A

Have on hand a large city newspaper and a small suburban newspaper. Invite volunteers to skim the different sections of each paper. Then have them take turns comparing parts of the two papers. For example, they might read the headlines on the front pages, point out the focus of the sports sections, or describe the length of the classified sections. Following this activity, have students complete Activity A on their own.

Activity A Answers

1) a **2)** d **3)** c **4)** a

Reading Vocabulary

columnist (8) photograph (6)
editorial (8) response (6)
directory (7) staff (6)
personal (9)

■ Presenting Activity B

Help students generate a list of current events in local, national, and world news. Write the list on the board. Then have students skim the editorial pages of newspapers to find letters, cartoons, and columns related to any of the events they listed. Invite volunteers to read aloud several of the editorial pieces to the class. Then ask students whether they agree or disagree with the writer's or cartoonist's opinion and explain why.

Activity A Answers

1) the last two pages of the front section of the newspaper
2) letters to the editor, political cartoons, opinion columns
3) to express opinions about current events **4)** people who read the newspaper in response to editorials, feature articles, columns, and photographs
5) recent events, current political and social issues, and other topics of interest to readers

Using What You Have Learned

Before students write their letters, review the correct form of a business letter. Point out to students that as they write their letters, they should present their opinions with conviction and support their ideas with reasons and examples.

Editorial Pages

Editorial
Opinion about an issue or event in the news. Editorials are written by members of the newspaper staff.

The **editorial** section of the paper often appears on the last two pages of the front section of the newspaper. Editorials express opinions about events in the news. The people who write them work for the newspaper. The editorial pages also usually have letters to the editor, political cartoons, and opinion columns.

Letters to the editor are written by people who read the newspaper. Anyone may write a letter to the editor of any newspaper. The letters are often opinions of the readers in response to editorials, feature articles, columns, and even photographs printed in the newspaper.

Political cartoons show an artist's opinion about current events.

Columnist
A person who writes from a personal point of view on events and issues and on how problems can be solved.

A column is a regular newspaper feature. Columns tell about recent events, current political and social issues, and other topics of interest to readers. Columns are written by professional writers called **columnists.** Columnists explain events and issues in the news from their points of view. They often give their opinions about how problems can be solved.

Activity B Use the information given above to answer these questions. Write your answers on your paper.

1) Where will you usually find the editorial pages in a newspaper?

2) What kinds of information will you find in the editorial section of the newspaper?

3) What is the purpose of an editorial?

4) Who writes the letters to the editor and why?

5) What do columnists write about?

Using What You Have Learned

Write a letter to the editor of a newspaper in your area. Express your opinions about a recent event.

Other Parts of a Newspaper

Newspapers contain many other kinds of information. For example, the television programming directory is a feature that lists the names, times, and channels of programs scheduled for viewing that day. The movie section of the newspaper lists all of the movie theaters in the area with the names of current movies

Cartoon
Usually a single drawing that the artist uses to tell a joke or express an idea.

Comic strip
A series of cartoon frames that tell a story.

Death notice
Information about a person's death and details about the funeral arrangements.

Obituary
A short article about someone who has recently died.

and show times. Information about television programs, movies, and other arts and entertainment events is often placed in a separate section of the paper. This section may be titled *Living, Arts & Entertainment,* or simply *Entertainment.*

Obituaries and **death notices** are included in another section. This section may be called *Obituaries* or *Deaths.* An obituary is a brief article about someone who has recently died. A death notice gives information about a person's death and funeral arrangements.

Columns related to fashion, sports, television, new movies, bridge, chess, gardening, or health can be found in different sections of the newspaper. Some columnists give advice to readers about how to improve some aspect of their lives.

Comic strips and **cartoons** can be found in a special section of the newspaper called the comics. A comic strip is a series of cartoons that tell a story. A cartoon is usually a single drawing that the artist uses to tell a joke or express an idea.

Activity C Use the information on page 182 and above to answer these questions. Write your answer on your paper.

1) José wants to see a movie at a local theater. Which part of the newspaper will tell him what time the movie begins?

2) Marie enjoys the reruns of the old television program *M*A*S*H.* What newspaper feature would tell her when it is on?

3) Which part of the paper lists the names of people who have recently died?

4) Eddie enjoys the cartoon characters in "Peanuts." In which section of the paper should he look to read about their latest adventures?

Reading Vocabulary

aspect (8)
brief (6)
cartoon (6)
chess (7)
comic strip
death notice
detail (5)
entertainment (5)
funeral (5)
obituary (10)
relate (6)
series (5)
title (5)

Presenting Activity C

If any members of the class have worked on a school newspaper, invite them to share their experiences with the class. Then ask students to list the parts of a newspaper that they think a school newspaper should have and why. Which section would they most like to work on and why? As an extension of this discussion, divide students into groups and have them create a layout of a school newspaper with the essential parts blocked out and labeled.

Activity C Answers

Answers may vary.

1) Living or Arts & Entertainment
2) Living or Arts & Entertainment
3) Obituaries or Death Notices
4) Comic Strips

Name ______ Date ______ Period ______

Chapter 7
Workbook Activity
40

Media Puzzle

Directions: Write the correct word on the line for each of the following clues. Then find the word in the puzzle. The words go up, down, across, backwards, and diagonally.

Clues

1) Death notice in the newspaper ______
2) Statement of opinions ______
3) Regular feature about topics of interest to readers ______
4) A way to communicate with the most people at one time ______
5) Up to the present ______
6) Every day ______
7) Worker who writes about the news ______
8) People who decide which story to print ______
9) Groups of advertisements in the newspapers ______
10) Short public notice that offers something for sale ______

```
A D V E R T I S E M E N T N G
P A T L D A N H A M W I N R L
B I O M N I I E A O P R E Q T
D L D W V Y T K C D G T D W B
H Y J K C C K O K S R R I R L
J K E D X Y L I R O T R T T W
X V E B Z U K A P I Y P O W C
B O N N M Y Y E S S A N R Y U
N I I N Z E R K K S G L S S R
C R L T Y P D Z Z M I H X B R
A B Y R A U T I B O C F R T E
B O B N N I E W K K N K I Y N
L K E R B A R B R J B C K E T
M A S S M E D I A S T M A S D
```

 Life Skills English

Workbook Activity 40

Reading Vocabulary

term (5)

Part A Answers

No responses required.

Part B Answers

1) j 2) c 3) i 4) a 5) f 6) d 7) b 8) g 9) e 10) h

Learning Styles

Interpersonal/Group Learning

Divide the class into groups of ten. Ask each group to create a newspaper that contains examples of the ten terms in Part B of the review on page 184. Provide large sheets of paper for the groups to make into newspapers. Suggest that they name their paper, draw columns on the pages, and write examples of the ten terms within the columns. Challenge them to create cartoons and comic strips, too. Afterward, have the groups exchange newspapers. Ask each group to point out the examples of the ten terms in the paper it received.

Lesson 1 Review

Part A Use any newspaper for this activity. Find each of the following parts of the newspaper.

1) National and world news
2) Local news
3) Columns
4) Sports news
5) Television and movies
6) Classified ads
7) Comics
8) Editorial page
9) Obituaries
10) Business news

Part B Copy the following list of terms on your paper. Beside each term, write the letter of its meaning.

Terms

1) Editorial
2) Daily
3) Regular feature
4) Mass media
5) Classified ad
6) National news
7) Current event
8) Obituary
9) Local news
10) Columnist

Meanings

a) A way to get information to many people at one time
b) A very recent happening
c) Happening every day
d) An event of interest to people in a whole country
e) An event of interest to people in a certain area
f) A list of automobiles, houses, and other things for sale or rent
g) An article about someone who has just died
h) A writer who gives personal opinions
i) An item that appears in every issue
j) An opinion about a current event or issue

Reading the Newspaper

In Lesson 1, you learned about daily and weekly newspapers. Daily newspapers have the most up-to-date, or current, world, national, and regional news. A weekly paper usually contains more local news that is of interest to a smaller number of people.

Activity A Number your paper 1 to 5. Decide whether you would be more likely to look in a daily paper or a local weekly paper to find the answer to each of the following questions. Write *Daily* or *Local* beside each number on your paper.

1) What time will the high school production of *West Side Story* begin Friday evening?

2) Did the president meet with other world leaders to discuss ways to preserve our environment?

3) Who won the city championship in baseball last week?

4) What are the win-loss records of teams in the National Football Conference?

5) When is the Calverton City Council's next meeting?

The Newspaper Index

Most newspapers have an index on the front page or the second page. You can use the index to quickly locate the pages on which the different sections of the paper begin.

INDEX

Business	C-9	Living	D-1
Classified	C-18	Local	B-1
Comics	B-9	Movies	D-4
Deaths	B-6	Sports	C-1
Editorials	A-26	TV/Radio	D-8
Food	E-1	Weather	B-10

Lesson at a Glance

Chapter 7 Lesson 2

Overview This lesson explains how to use a newspaper index and provides strategies for reading the newspaper.

Objectives

- To answer questions about newspapers, including questions about the organization of a newspaper article.
- To answer questions about newspaper ads.

Student Pages 185–191

Teacher's Resource Library

Workbook Activities 41–42

Reading Vocabulary

championship
conference (6)
environment (7)
index (5)
production (6)

Teaching Suggestions

■ Introducing the Lesson

Be sure to have copies of weekly and daily papers available for students to examine as you present the information in this lesson.

■ Reviewing Skills

Review the main sections of a newspaper.

■ Presenting Activity A

Read aloud a variety of headlines that you have copied beforehand from a small local weekly and a large city daily paper. After you read each headline, ask students if they think the article was more likely to have come from a daily paper or from a local weekly paper.

Activity A Answers

1) Local 2) Daily 3) Local 4) Daily 5) Local

Reading Vocabulary

admission (5)
coupon (6)
election (5)
exhibit (5)
financial (8)
investor
recipe (6)
restaurant (5)
specific (8)

Presenting Activity B

Before having students complete Activity B on their own, give them an opportunity to find the index in an actual newspaper. Have students compare the index entries in the newspaper to the entries in the index on page 185 in their text.

Activity B Answers

1) B-9 **2)** A-26 **3)** C-1 **4)** B-6 **5)** D-1 **6)** D-8 **7)** E-1 **8)** B-1 **9)** C-18 **10)** B-1 **11)** A-26 **12)** D-4 **13)** C-9 **14)** C-18 **15)** B-10

Application

At Home
Everyone has his or her own way of reading the newspaper. Encourage students to take an informal survey of family members and friends to find out what newspaper or newspapers they read regularly, what their primary purpose for reading the paper is, and how they read the paper. Invite students to share their findings with the class.

Activity B Use the index on page 185 to locate the page on which you would find each of these items. Write your answers on your paper.

1) Comic strips

2) A political cartoon

3) Scores of last night's basketball game

4) The time a funeral will be held for someone who recently died

5) "Dear Abby" or "Ann Landers"

6) The time and channel of a TV program

7) Recipes and food store advertisements

8) News about local events

9) A list of used cars for sale

10) The damage caused by yesterday's storm

11) A letter to the editor

12) The movies that are playing at your local movie theater

13) How the stock market did yesterday

14) Apartments for rent

15) What the weather will be like tomorrow across your state.

Choosing What to Read

Some people read the daily newspaper from cover to cover. Others skim the paper, looking for specific articles and information. For example, some people may wish to know the results of yesterday's state elections. Others may want to find the coupon for free admission to the Science Museum's new exhibit. Some may wish to read a review of the new Mexican restaurant on Main Street. Investors may look in the business or financial section of the paper for information on the stock market. Recent high-school and college graduates might turn to the help wanted ads to find out what jobs are available in the area. Sports fans may look in the sports section to find out when the Harlem Globetrotters will be in town.

Name ______ Date ______ Period ______

Chapter 7 Workbook Activity 41

Using a Newspaper Index

Directions: Use the newspaper index to answer the questions below. Write the name of the section, its letter, and the page number on the lines below each question.

1) In which section would you look for a help wanted ad?

2) Which section would have your favorite comic strip?

3) Is a rerun of M*A*S*H showing? Where would you look?

4) Where might you find a recipe for potato salad?

5) Where would you look to find out when a movie begins?

6) Where would you find out the time of a funeral?

7) Which section would have the paper's opinion of an event?

8) Where would you find a report on the president's speech?

9) Where would you find an article about a new park in your town?

10) Where would you find the scores of last night's baseball games?

11) You want to find a used bike. Where would you look?

12) Where would you find a report on an election in another country?

 Life Skills English

Workbook Activity 41

News Stories

Reporter

A person who researches facts and writes stories for a newspaper.

Editor

A person who decides which stories will be reported to the public.

Lead

The first paragraph of a news story; summarizes the most important facts in the story and answers the questions Who? What? Where? *and* When?

News stories are the result of the combined efforts of newspaper **reporters** and their **editors**. A reporter finds facts and writes stories, or articles, for a newspaper. An editor decides which stories will be reported to the public. An editor also may rearrange and correct the information in a reporter's story.

Most news stories begin with a strong first paragraph called a **lead**. The lead is a summary of the most important facts in the story. It answers the questions *Who? What? Where?* and *When?* Other paragraphs in the story explain more about the news event and also answer questions: *Why did the event happen? How did the event happen?*

Reporters arrange facts and details in paragraphs in order of importance. They usually put the least important facts in the last paragraph. Editors know how much space is available for each story. When there is not enough room for the entire story, an editor may cut the last paragraphs.

Activity C Read the news story below. Then write your answers to the questions that follow on your paper.

Sabatino to Open Pizza Parlor

Beginning Wednesday, March 8, you can eat Rosa Sabatino's pizza at a new location. Rosa's Pizza Parlor is opening in the Fairmont Shopping Center. In her announcement, Mrs. Sabatino said that the demand for her pizza had outgrown her original small kitchen and she had to open a larger facility.

1) Who is the story about?

2) What will happen?

3) When will it happen?

4) Why is it happening?

5) Where will the event take place?

Reading Vocabulary

combine (6)	location (6)
detail (5)	original (5)
editor (4)	parlor (5)
effort (5)	pizza
facility (8)	**reporter**
importance (6)	research (6)
lead (3)	summary (8)

■ Presenting Activity C

Have pairs of students select a brief news article from the newspaper to read together. Ask each pair of students to find the answers to these questions as they read:

Who is the story about?

What happened?

Where did this event take place?

When did it happen?

Why or how did it happen?

Following this activity, have partners work together to complete Activity C.

Activity C Answers

1) Rosa Sabatino **2)** She is opening a new pizza place. **3)** Wednesday, March 8 **4)** Her original restaurant was not large enough to meet the demand for her pizza. **5)** Rosa's Pizza Parlor at Fairmont Shopping Center

Application

In the Community Visually impaired members of the community may enjoy having sections of the newspaper read aloud to them. Suggest that students contact nursing homes and senior centers to volunteer their services in this area.

Reading Vocabulary
development (7)

■ Presenting Activity D

Read the news story aloud for students or ask a volunteer to read it. Then work with students to complete Activity D. If possible, make a transparency of the article and display it, using an overhead projector. As students answer each item, have a volunteer use a pointer to indicate the answer in the article.

Activity D Answers

Wording of some answers may vary.

1) "Welcome, Neighbor" will open a new office in the Rolling Hills Mall in Calverton on April 3. The director's phone number is given. **2)** She is the director of "Welcome, Neighbor." **3)** It was needed because of the new townhouse development. **4)** They can call Sharon Imai at 455-0980. **5)** It offers information about schools, churches, businesses, doctors, and hospitals. **6)** at the Rolling Hills Mall **7)** April 3 **8)** Two hundred new families will be moving into town in the next year. People who want to help can call Imai between 9 A.M. and 3 P.M. weekdays.

Activity D Read this news story. Then write on your paper your answers to the questions that follow.

"Welcome, Neighbor" Opens Office

As of April 3, Calverton will have its own "Welcome, Neighbor" with offices in the Rolling Hills Mall. Anyone new to town can call Sharon Imai, director, at 455-0980.

Imai stated that there was a need for a Calverton branch of the group because of the new townhouse development in Calverton. More than 200 new families will be moving into the area during the next year.

"Welcome, Neighbor" offers information about schools, churches, businesses, doctors, and hospitals. Local business people and other groups who wish to help should call Imai weekdays, between 9 A.M. and 3 P.M.

1) What facts are presented in the lead paragraph?

2) Who is Sharon Imai?

3) Why was there a need for a "Welcome, Neighbor" in Calverton?

4) How can someone get help from this group?

5) What does "Welcome, Neighbor" do for people new to town?

6) Where will the Calverton branch of "Welcome, Neighbor" be?

7) When will the branch open?

8) List some other facts or details that are in this story.

188 *Chapter 7 Information From the Media*

Getting Information From Advertisements

Advertisement
A public notice, usually about a product or service for sale.

A newspaper earns money in two ways. First, people buy the newspaper. Second, people pay to have their **advertisements** printed. An advertisement is a public notice, often about something for sale. Newspaper ads also give you information that you might find useful.

Activity E Write on your paper your answers to these questions about the ad for Rosa's Pizza Parlor.

1) How will the advertisement help Rosa's Pizza Parlor?

2) When will Rosa's Pizza Parlor open for business?

3) Where is the Pizza Parlor located?

4) What do you have to do to get a free pizza?

5) When will the coupon offer end?

6) What information about the pizza supreme is missing?

Reading Vocabulary

advertisement (6) supreme (6)
product (5)

■ Presenting Activity E

Encourage each student to clip an advertisement about a business or event from the local newspaper. Have students show the ad they selected to the class and explain what the purpose of the ad is and the facts that it contains. Following each ad presentation, ask students if they think the ad is successful and why or why not.

Activity E Answers

1) It makes people aware of the opening. People will go to Rosa's to take advantage of the coupon. **2)** Wednesday, March 8 **3)** Fairmont Shopping Center **4)** Buy one large pizza supreme at regular price **5)** March 18 **6)** its price

Learning Styles

Visual/Spatial

Ask the students to choose a business for which they could create an ad similar to the one on page 189. Suggest that they look around their classroom for ideas or think of places in their neighborhood that offer products and services. Challenge the students to use interesting lettering and drawings in their ads. Afterward, display the ads in the classroom.

Reading Vocabulary

consumer (7)
gimmick
mislead (8)
organization (7)
phrase (6)
slogan (7)

■ **Presenting Activity F** Do Activity F as an oral activity. After students identify the gimmick in the Auto Center ad, elicit possible outcomes once people come into the store, such as the radials on sale may not be the best ones; sales people may talk customers into buying more expensive, better tires. As an extension to Activity F, divide students into small groups and have them work together to create a new product, such as a cereal, toothpaste, or other everyday item. Each group should name its product, create a slogan for it, and design a newspaper ad. Display the ads and have students vote on the best one.

Activity F Answers

1) The Store for Men **2)** Winter Coat Sale; 100s of coats; $134.95 and up; located in Darby Mall on Main and 5th **3)** Only the lowest price is given. There is no way of knowing how expensive the other coats are. **4)** The place to go for all your auto needs. **5)** Tire Sale; $79 radials for $54; located at 1245 W. Tulip Drive **6)** The other tires for sale may not have good discounts.

Gimmick
An important feature about something that is kept secret.

Slogan
A word or phrase that is repeated over and over again that expresses the main idea of a product, business, political group, or other organization.

Advertisements often have **gimmicks** and **slogans** that can mislead consumers. A gimmick is an important feature about something that is kept secret. It is also called a catch.

A slogan is a word or phrase expressing the main idea of a product, business, political group, or other organization. Businesses repeat their slogans over and over again.

EXAMPLE

USING WHAT YOU HAVE LEARNED

Make a list of familiar products and services. Do their companies use slogans in their ads? Write the ones you know. As you read the newspaper, read some of the advertisements, too. Look for items that you need and that are on sale. Look for facts in the ads. Beware of gimmicks and slogans.

Activity F Study the two ads. Then write on your paper your answers to the following questions.

1) What is the slogan of Dawson's Department Store?

2) List the facts in the Dawson ad.

3) What important piece of information is missing about the price of the coats? Why does this make the ad misleading?

4) What is the slogan of The Auto Center?

5) List the facts in the Auto Center ad.

6) What is a possible gimmick in the Auto Center ad?

USING WHAT YOU HAVE LEARNED

Invite students to share their observations about gimmicks and slogans in newspaper ads.

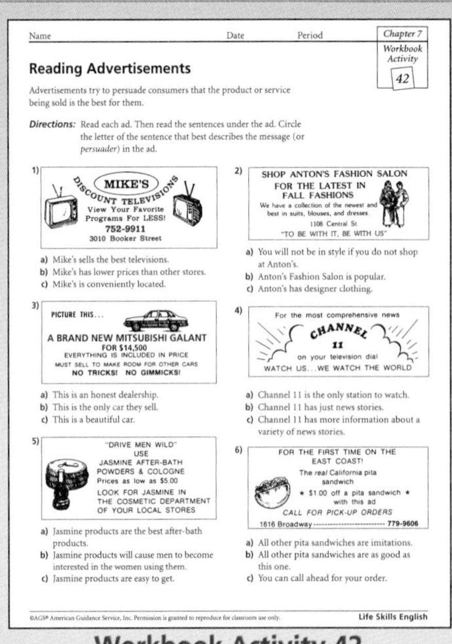

Name Date Period — *Chapter 7 Workbook Activity 42*

Reading Advertisements

Advertisements try to persuade consumers that the product or service being sold is the best for them.

Directions: Read each ad. Then read the sentences under the ad. Circle the letter of the sentence that best describes the message (or *persuader*) in the ad.

1) MIKE'S DISCOUNT TELEVISIONS View Your Favorite Programs For LESS! 752-9911 3010 Booker Street

a) Mike's sells the best televisions.
b) Mike's has lower prices than other stores.
c) Mike's is conveniently located.

2) SHOP ANTON'S FASHION SALON FOR THE LATEST IN FALL FASHIONS We have a collection of the newest and best in suits, blouses, and dresses. 1108 Central St. "TO BE WITH IT, BE WITH US"

a) You will not be in style if you do not shop at Anton's.
b) Anton's Fashion Salon is popular.
c) Anton's has designer clothing.

3) PICTURE THIS... A BRAND NEW MITSUBISHI GALANT FOR $14,500 EVERYTHING IS INCLUDED IN PRICE MUST SELL TO MAKE ROOM FOR OTHER CARS NO TRICKS! NO GIMMICKS!

a) This is an honest dealership.
b) This is the only car they sell.
c) This is a beautiful car.

4) For the most comprehensive news CHANNEL 11 on your television dial WATCH US...WE WATCH THE WORLD

a) Channel 11 is the only station to watch.
b) Channel 11 has just news stories.
c) Channel 11 has more information about a variety of news stories.

5) "DRIVE MEN WILD" USE JASMINE AFTER-BATH POWDERS & COLOGNE Prices as low as $5.00 LOOK FOR JASMINE IN THE COSMETIC DEPARTMENT OF YOUR LOCAL STORES

a) Jasmine products are the best after-bath products.
b) Jasmine products will cause men to become interested in the women using them.
c) Jasmine products are easy to get.

6) FOR THE FIRST TIME ON THE EAST COAST! The *real* California pita sandwich ★ $1.00 off a pita sandwich ★ with this ad CALL FOR PICK-UP ORDERS 1616 Broadway ---------- 779-9606

a) All other pita sandwiches are imitations.
b) All other pita sandwiches are as good as this one.
c) You can call ahead for your order.

 Life Skills English

Workbook Activity 42

Lesson 2 Review

Part A Write on your paper your answers to these questions.

1) What six questions do newspaper stories usually answer?

2) Which newspaper worker is responsible for finding the facts and writing the story?

3) Who decides which stories to print?

4) Which paragraph of the news story tells the main facts?

5) What are some reasons why people usually read the newspaper?

6) How often are local newspapers usually published?

7) How often are large city newspapers usually published?

8) Where could you look to find out on which page the sports section of the newspaper begins?

Part B Write on your paper your answers to these questions.

1) Name two ways that newspapers make money.

2) What is an advertisement?

3) What kind of information do ads contain?

4) How can ads mislead people?

5) Give an example of a slogan. It can be an actual slogan or one you make up.

Reading Vocabulary

actual (7)

Part A Answers

1) Who? What? When? Where? Why? How? **2)** reporter **3)** editor **4)** lead **5)** Answers will vary. Possible responses are: to get an overview of the news; for specific articles and information; to find the results of sports events; to look for a job in the help wanted ads. **6)** weekly **7)** daily **8)** the newspaper index

Part B Answers

1) by selling newspapers; through advertisements **2)** a public notice usually about a product or service for sale **3)** information useful to consumers; products for sale; cost of the item **4)** through gimmicks that keep important facts secret **5)** Answers will vary.

Application

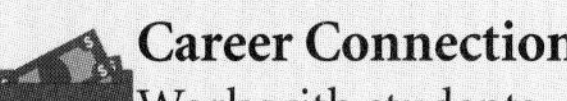

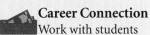

Career Connection Work with students to generate a list of newspaper-related jobs, beginning with *reporter* and *editor.* Encourage students to do research, if necessary, to learn about the different positions available in the newspaper industry. Suggest that students who think they might be interested in one of these jobs investigate further to learn what education, training, and skills are required for the job.

Lesson at a Glance

Chapter 7 Lesson 3

Overview This lesson explains how to find information and how to interpret abbreviations in classified ads.

Objectives

- To locate sections of the classifieds using a sample index.
- To interpret abbreviations in sample ads.
- To write a classified ad.

Student Pages 192–199

Teacher's Resource Library

Activities 24–25

Reading Vocabulary

advertise (6)
broadcast (6)
employment (6)
estate (6)
fee (7)
gourmet
host (6)
instruction (5)
leisure (6)
merchandise (7)
recreation (6)
rental (7)
transportation (5)

Teaching Suggestions

- **Introducing the Lesson** Engage students in a discussion about the goals of advertising, focusing specifically on advertising in the classified section of the newspaper. As you present the information in the text, direct student's attention to the classified directory on page 192. Ask students how this index is different from other indexes they have learned about. Elicit that while other indexes are arranged in alphabetical order, this one is organized according to the order in which each group of ads appears. As you continue through this lesson, have available classified sections of several newspapers for students to examine.

- **Reviewing Skills** Review students' understanding of products and services.

Lesson 3 Classified Ads

Advertise
To announce something to the public through the media.

Large businesses use newspaper ads, television, radio, and magazines to **advertise** their products and services. To advertise means to announce to the public by printed notice or broadcast.

There may be a time when you want to advertise something. You may have something you want to sell, or you may be running a business and looking for help. You can reach a lot of people at one time if you advertise in the classified ads in daily and weekly newspapers. When things are classified, they are divided into groups. In the classified section of the newspaper, short announcements about job openings or items for sale are arranged, or classified, into sections. Often there will be an index at the beginning of the classified ads that lists each section. Usually there will be guide words or numbers or both at the top of each column to help people find what they are looking for quickly.

CLASSIFIED INDEX

100 – 199	Announcements and Notices
200 – 299	Personal and Business Services
300 – 399	Recreation and Leisure
400 – 499	Gourmet and Hosting
500 – 599	Home Repairs and Services
600 – 699	Pets and Animals
700 – 799	Merchandise
800 – 899	Instruction
900 – 999	Employment
1000 – 1099	Rentals
1100 – 1199	Real Estate
1200 – 1299	Business and Business Real Estate
1300 – 1399	Financial
1400 – 1499	Transportation

To advertise in most papers, you will have to pay a fee. The amount of the fee will depend on the size of your ad. Some papers have special programs that charge a fee only after your ad gets results.

Activity A Use the Classified Index on page 192 to answer these questions. Write the numbers and the title of each topic on your paper.

1) Under which classification would you find a truck for sale?

2) Under which classification would you expect to find a house for sale?

3) Where would you expect to find job openings?

4) Where would you look if you wanted to get a cat?

5) If you wanted to take a class, what would you look under?

Activity B Sort the following advertisements into two sections that you might see in the classified ads in the newspaper—*Furniture* and *Business Equipment.* Write *F* on your paper if an item should be listed in the Furniture section or *BE* if the item should be listed in the Business Equipment section.

BEDROOM SET New $1995. Moving; must sacrifice. $650 or best offer. 238-4212.

SOFA Green brushed twill in good condition. $650. Call 345-0984. Ask for Marlene.

CASH REGISTER New in sealed carton, $129. Calvert Cash Register Co. 567-0900.

DESK AND CHAIR Solid wood. Good condition, $450. Call evenings. 399-4039.

COPIERS Reconditioned. All sizes. Like new. Bargain priced $399 and up. Call 320-4835 between 8 and 5.

DINETTE, RECLINER, LAMPS, and more. We're moving south and everything must go. Call 430-9864.

Reading Vocabulary

carton (6)
classification (8)
dinette
equipment (5)
recliner
recondition
register (6)
sacrifice (5)
twill

■ Presenting Activity A

Before asking students to complete Activity A on their own, focus their attention on the Classified Index on page 192. Engage students in a discussion about the kinds of notices they would expect to find under each topic. Then challenge them to think of other topics that might appear in a classified index. Suggest that they look at actual classified sections for ideas.

Activity A Answers

1) 1400–1499 Transportation
2) 1100–1199 Real Estate
3) 900–999 Employment
4) 600–699 Pets and Animals
5) 800–899 Instruction

■ Presenting Activity B

Distribute copies of classified sections to pairs of students. Have each pair select a different topic in the classified and read aloud some of the different items listed under that topic. Following this activity, have each pair of students work together to complete Activity B.

Activity B Answers

Furniture: Bedroom Set, Sofa, Desk and Chair, Dinette, Recliner, Lamps
Business Equipment: Cash Register, Desk and Chair, Copiers

Reading Vocabulary

appropriate (6) income (6)
bracket (7) lend (5)
bricklayer tax (5)
cartridge (7) video
groom (6)

■ Presenting Activity C

Invite students to give suggestions for rewriting the ad. Discuss the merits of the different versions suggested. Then work together to write a final draft.

Activity C Answers

Answers will vary. The most productive ad would probably begin with the words VIDEO-GAME PLAYER or the actual brand name of the player. The ad might be placed in Recreation and Leisure or Merchandise.

■ Presenting Activity D

Do the first two items in Activity D together. Then ask students to complete Activity D independently.

Activity D Answers

Some answers may vary. Possible responses are given.

1) Pets and Animals
2) Financial **3)** Instruction
4) Personal and Business Services
5) Gourmet and Hosting
6) Employment **7)** Home Repairs and Services **8)** Rentals
9) Transportation **10)** Real Estate

Using What You Have Learned

Invite students to share the items they listed with the class. Have them tell which topic the item was listed under and under which topic they think it might also be listed.

Using What You Have Learned

Practice using the index of the classified ads in any newspaper. Select a topic heading in the index and then find that topic in the classified ads. Notice the different items that are listed under that topic. List any items that you think could be listed under a different topic.

Placing Classified Ads

If you place a classified ad in the paper, you want people to find it. You want people to know what you are selling or advertising. The classified ad operator can help you write the ad and place it in the most appropriate section of the classifieds.

Examples

Mr. Sanchez wanted to buy a used piano. He looked under Merchandise (things for sale). First, he looked for the word *Piano*. Then he looked for the words *Musical Instruments.* He found a piano for sale.

Rosa Sabatino wanted to rent a place for a pizza parlor. She looked under Rentals and Real Estate. She only found apartments and houses. Then she looked under Business Property. She found a place to rent in a shopping center.

Activity C Rewrite on your paper the ad below so that someone looking to buy a video game player might find it in the classifieds. In brackets [ ] after the ad, write the section of the classifieds in which you think the ad should be placed.

> **FOR SALE** Cartridge-type computer player. Almost new, with 10 games. $75. Call 340-9800 and ask for Sue.

Activity D Use the classified index on page 192. Write the section where you would probably find these products or services listed.

1) People who groom poodles
2) People who lend money
3) A computer training school
4) Help with income taxes
5) People who plan parties
6) A list of jobs
7) A bricklayer
8) Apartments for rent
9) Automobiles for sale
10) Houses for sale

194 Chapter 7 Information From the Media

Reading Classified Ads

The price of a classified ad is usually determined by the number of lines in the ad. Abbreviations are often used to keep the ad short and the price down. You will have an easier time finding what you want in the classifieds if you know the meaning of some of these abbreviations.

Abbreviations Used in Housing Advertisements

a/c	—	air conditioned
apt.	—	apartment
BA	—	bathroom
bdrm.	—	bedroom
BR	—	bedroom
carp.	—	carpeting
Condo.	—	Condominium
dep.	—	deposit
Effcy.	—	efficiency
EHO	—	Equal Housing Opportunity
elec.	—	electricity
firepl.	—	fireplace
gar.	—	garage
incl.	—	including
kit.	—	kitchen
MBR	—	master bedroom
NS	—	nonsmoker
Rte.	—	route
shpng.	—	shopping
spac.	—	spacious (large and roomy)
TH	—	townhouse
TV	—	television
utils.	—	utilities
w/d	—	washer and dryer

Reading Vocabulary

abbreviation (8)
condominium
determine (5)
deposit (6)
efficiency (8)
opportunity (5)
spacious
townhouse
utility

Application

In the Community

Encourage students to contact the classified department of all the newspapers in the area. Different students can call different papers. Have them find out the newspaper's classified rates and how these rates are established—for example, per word, per line, by the week, by the day, and so forth. Callers should also find out the paper's circulation. Later, students can record their findings in a chart that shows the name of the paper, the cost of the ads, and the paper's circulation. Ask students to then determine which paper would be the best to advertise in based on cost and number of people reached.

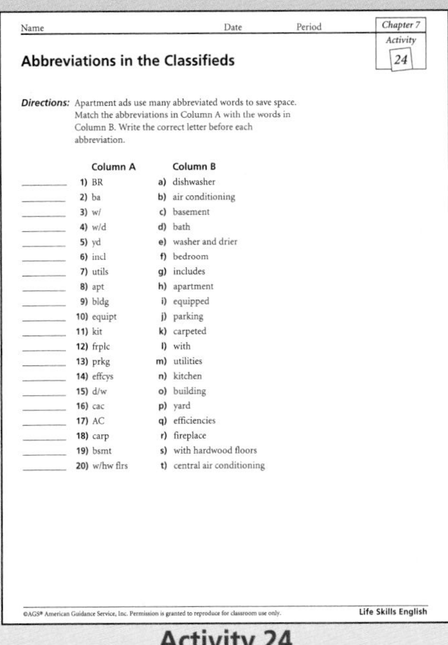

Name ______ Date ______ Period ______ *Chapter 7* *Activity* 24

Abbreviations in the Classifieds

Directions: Apartment ads use many abbreviated words to save space. Match the abbreviations in Column A with the words in Column B. Write the correct letter before each abbreviation.

	Column A	Column B
______	1) BR	a) dishwasher
______	2) ba	b) air conditioning
______	3) w/	c) basement
______	4) w/d	d) bath
______	5) yd	e) washer and drier
______	6) incl	f) bedroom
______	7) utils	g) includes
______	8) apt	h) apartment
______	9) bldg	i) equipped
______	10) equipt	j) parking
______	11) kit	k) carpeted
______	12) frplc	l) with
______	13) prkg	m) utilities
______	14) effcys	n) kitchen
______	15) d/w	o) building
______	16) cac	p) yard
______	17) AC	q) efficiencies
______	18) carp	r) fireplace
______	19) bsmt	s) with hardwood floors
______	20) w/hw flrs	t) central air conditioning

 Life Skills English

Activity 24

Reading Vocabulary

community (5) require (6)
renovate (10) sample (5)

■ Presenting Activity E

Work with students to complete Activity E. Then, invite volunteers to make up other questions about the ads on page 196 to ask the class. You may also wish to have students select apartment rental ads in the classified section of a local paper. Invite them to share the information in these ads with the class.

Activity E Answers

1) Answers may vary. Possible responses are: number of bedrooms, location, price, telephone number to call.
2) Hyatts 2 BR **3)** Utilities: Gaith 1 & 2 BR; Hyatts 2 BR; Hyatts 1 & 2 Brs.; Condo. Electricity: Gaith/Ivy Oak; Wilton **4)** Wilton **5)** Condo; Wilton **6)** Wilton **7)** Hyatts Bsmt. apt.; Condo **8)** Condo **9)** Gaith/Ivy Oak **10)** Gaith/Ivy Oak

Activity E Study the sample apartment ads. Use the information on page 195 to answer the questions that follow. Write your answers on your paper.

GAITH/Ivy Oak 3 BR TH, 1 1/2 BA, covered gar. $800 + elec. 555-900-1092.

GAITH 1 & 2 BR apts. starting at $558, all utils. incl. Call for details, 555-201-2000. EHO.

HYATTS 2 BR, a/c. Pets welcome. $660 incl. utils. 555-188-0910.

HYATTS Bsmt. apt. for NS. 1 BR. New paint/carp/kit. Walk shpng./buses. Avail 3/1. $395/mo. + dep. + utils. 555-091-8990.

HYATTS 1 & 2 BRs. $450 utils incl. 2 wks free rent. 555-982-0001.

LAUREL Small cozy community on Rte. 197, 2 bdrms, convenient to Rte. 1. From $540. EHO. Call 555-099-0111.

CONDO Walking dist. to bus. Effcy. Pool. $570. No pets. Util. incl. 987-320-7400.

WILTON 1 & 2 BR, Newly renovated. With w/d, pool, adults only building. $710 & $875 + elec. 555-420-0910.

1) Name three kinds of information contained in every ad.

2) Which apartment has air conditioning?

3) Which apartments include utilities (heat and electricity)? Which apartment owners require that you pay electricity only?

4) Which apartment includes a washer and dryer?

5) Which apartments might you choose if you like to swim?

6) Which apartments would not be good for someone with children?

7) Which apartments might suit someone without a car?

8) Which apartments would not be good for someone with a dog?

9) Which apartment has a parking garage?

10) Which one of these ads is for a townhouse?

Name Date Period

Chapter 7 Activity 25

Abbreviations in Ads

Directions: Circle the abbreviations in these apartment ads. Then write the complete words on the lines provided.

1) Fabulous 2 BR, 2 ba just remodeled, w/d, porch. Incl some utils. Call 332-4048.

2) Sunny and spacious 1 BR apt w/classic charm, AC. Call 332-8900.

3) 2 BR, $2\frac{1}{2}$ ba in 6-unit bldg; fully equipt kit, frplc, w/d, prkg and patio. 387-6643.

4) Sunny effcys, w/d, d/w, prkg. Short and long term leases. 296-5097.

5) Spacious 2 BR w/hw flrs, cac, w/d and patio. Available immediately. 821-2745.

6) Large 1 BR carp bsmt apt; w/d, all utils incl. Call 544-6894.

 Life Skills English

Activity 25

Abbreviations Used in Automobile Advertisements	
5 spd	— 5-speed transmission
4 dr	— 4 door
6 cyl	— 6 cylinder engine
a/c	— air conditioning
lo mi	— low mileage
int	— interior (refers to upholstery)
inte	— interior
rear defr	— rear window defroster
auto	— automatic transmission
air	— air conditioned
ps	— power steering
pb	— power brakes
pwr	— power
sunrf	— sunroof
eng	— engine
74K	— 74,000 miles
fact. warr.	— factory warranty
am/fm	— AM/FM radio
cass	— cassette tape player
CD	— compact disc player
conv	— convertible
pl	— power locks
4wd	— four-wheel drive
excl/cond	— excellent condition
pw	— power windows

Reading Vocabulary

automatic (5)
brake (5)
cassette
compact (5)
convertible (9)
cylinder (6)
defroster
excellent (5)
interior (6)
mileage (7)
refer (6)
transmission (8)
upholstery
warranty

Teacher Alert

Point out to students that different papers may use different abbreviations in their classified ads. The abbreviations provided on page 197 and elsewhere in the chapter indicate some of the words that are often abbreviated in classified ads and common abbreviations for these words. Suggest that students become familiar with the abbreviations and their meanings used in the classified section of their local papers.

Application

At Home
Students can apply their newly acquired knowledge of classified ads to help family members, relatives, and friends compose classified ads for items they wish to sell and also to help them locate information in the classifieds.

Reading Vocabulary

abbreviate (8) stereo
cabriolet triple (7)
cruise (6)

■ Presenting Activity F

Engage students in a discussion of the kinds of things a consumer should consider when looking for a car in the classified section. Invite students to share any experiences they or people they know have had—both positive and negative—finding and purchasing a car through the classified ads as well as selling a car through the classifieds. Ask students which of the ads on page 198 they might respond to if they wanted to buy a car and why.

Activity F Answers

1) brand and year of car, model name, phone number to call **2)** Ford 94 Tempo **3)** Chevy; Dodge; Ford **4)** 4-speed transmission **5)** 4 door **6)** Porsche, Dodge **7)** Honda, Nissan, Chevy, Ford **8)** automatic transmission **9)** Chevy, Ford **10)** Only the abbreviated words are listed: 1996, power, factory warranty, miles **11)** Honda

Activity F Study the sample classifieds. Use the information on page 197 to answer the questions that follow. Write your answers on your paper.

AUTOMOBILES—IMPORTS (1455)

AUDI '95 4000S. Auto. 4 dr excel. body & int. Needs eng. work. Best offer. 809-555-1021.

HONDA '94 Civic LX, 4 dr coupe. 5 spd, a/c, stereo, pwr windows & sunrf, low miles. LIKE NEW! Call 703-555-0920.

NISSAN '92—240SX GPL, AC, ster., 5 spd, blue met., $10,995. 901-555-1000.

PORSCHE '96, 944S 11 Cabriolet, triple black. Cruise, pwr. top, airbags, alarm, leather. Loaded. Fact. warr. 1 owner. Car phone. Only 3450 mi. Listed for $51,000. Make offer. Save thousands! 809-555-0102.

AUTOMOBILES—DOMESTIC (1460)

CHEVY '92 GEO Storm, 5 spd, AC, PS, PB, AM/FM stereo cass, 61K mi. Call today for special sale price. JACK'S CHEVROLET. 201-555-9800.

DODGE '93 Dynasty, loaded, fact. warr., lo mi. A steal if you buy today. 890-555-8000. Ask for Sam.

FORD '94 Tempo GL, 4 dr auto a/c ps pb, stereo, rear defr. Today's bargain prices. 800-555-9088.

1) Name three kinds of information contained in each ad.

2) Which car has a rear window defroster?

3) Which cars are made by American companies?

4) What does "4 spd" mean?

5) What does "4 dr" mean?

6) Which cars come with a factory warranty?

7) Which cars have air conditioning?

8) What does "auto" mean?

9) Which cars have power steering and power brakes?

10) Write the ad for the Porsche on your paper. Spell out each abbreviated word.

11) Which car has air conditioning and a sunroof?

Lesson 3 Review

Part A Use the classified index on page 192. Write the section on your paper where you would probably find these products or services listed.

1) Used cars for sale
2) Used furniture for sale
3) Apartments for rent
4) Houses for sale
5) Business property to rent

Part B Read these ads. Write on your paper your answers to the questions that follow the ads.

RECREATION AND LEISURE (300)

VACATION in Bermuda! 7 days, 6 nights, air, hotel, meals incl. $1300. Mac's Travel Services, 540-8009.

PETS AND ANIMALS/CATS (610)

KITTEN Free. 10 wks., F. b&w, short hair, litter-trained. Suzy, 565-9849.

MERCHANDISE (700)

DIAMOND RING Perf. cond. Cost $500. Make offer, 450-0982. Ask for Ralph.

1) What color is the kitten? Is it a male or a female?
2) Whom can you call about the diamond ring?
3) How much did the diamond ring originally cost?
4) What is the name of the travel agency that is offering the Bermuda vacation?
5) What is included in the price of the Bermuda vacation?

Activity C Write a classified ad for something that you would like to sell. Limit yourself to three or four lines. Use abbreviations to keep your ad short. Write your ad on your paper.

Reading Vocabulary

agency
female (5)
limit (5)
litter (6)
male (5)

Part A Answers

1) Transportation (1400–1499) **2)** Merchandise (700–799) **3)** Rentals (1000–1099) **4)** Real Estate (1100–1199) **5)** Business and Business Real Estate (1200–1299)

Part B Answers

1) black and white; female **2)** Ralph **3)** $500.00 **4)** Mac's Travel Service **5)** airfare, hotel for 6 nights, meals

Part C Answers

Ads will vary but should indicate an understanding of classified ads and abbreviations used in them. The ads should be only three or four lines long.

Learning Styles

Auditory/Verbal

Invite volunteers to read aloud the lists of abbreviations on pages 195 and 197. After each abbreviation is read, invite questions on its meaning. Then ask the students to use these abbreviations in writing two ads—one to advertise a house for sale or an apartment for rent, and one to advertise a car for sale. Afterward, invite volunteers to read their ads. Ask the students to raise their hands when they hear a word that the volunteer probably abbreviated in the ad.

Lesson at a Glance

Chapter 7 Lesson 4

Overview This lesson explains how to use the help wanted section of the classifieds.

Objectives

- To answer questions about the help wanted ads.
- To interpret abbreviations that appear in sample ads.

Student Pages 200–205

Teacher's Resource Library

Activity 26

Workbook Activities 43–44

Reading Vocabulary

accounting (5)
accurate (6)
administrative
aptitude (9)
assistant (6)
atmosphere (5)
bookkeeper (5)
cashier (7)
chef (7)
clerical (9)
clerk (5)
dental (8)
edit (8)
file (5)
invoice (11)
mechanic (6)
operator (5)
pastry (7)
prefer (6)
refrigeration
require (6)
résumé (8)
security (8)
title (5)
typist

Teaching Suggestions

■ **Introducing the Lesson** Discuss the various ways people look for and find jobs. Invite students to share their personal job-hunting experiences.

■ **Reviewing Skills** Review what students have learned about reading classified ads.

■ **Presenting Activity A** Invite volunteers to select an ad listed on page 200 and tell what information it contains. Ask students to use complete sentences to describe the job discussed in each ad.

Lesson 4 The Help Wanted Ads

Many people read the help wanted section of the classified ads to find jobs. People who run businesses use this section of the classifieds to advertise job openings.

Sunday, October 25 ***The Daily Banner***

CLASSIFIED ADVERTISING

Employment

EMPLOYMENT SERVICES (901)

JOB RESUME
$15 & UP
Writing/Editing/Typing
While You Wait. 484-6916

CAREER TRAINING (903)

THE MEDIC SCHOOL. Train med. dental asst. 821-5222.

HELP WANTED (905)

ACCOUNTING CLERK Part time. Entry level position, incls. invoicing, filing, accurate typing, 45/50 WPM. Permanent position, 20-25 hrs. per wk. Security area. Call bet. 9 & 1, 298-4706.

HELP WANTED (905)

ADMINISTRATIVE SECY. $25,500 fee paid. This top Co. needs polished sect'l. talents! Good skills and figure aptitude. 837-0778.

AIR COND & Heat Pump Mechanic fully exp. only. Call Frosty Refrig. 747-2024.

AUTO SALESPERSON Sell and make big money on cars and trucks. Salary plus comm. Benefits. 466-1320.

BOOKKEEPER With aptitude for computerized bkkp. Dependable. 675-1118

CASHIER/CLERK Some exp. req'd. All shifts avail. Apply 100 S. Broad bet 9 & 12 noon.

HELP WANTED (905)

CHEF PASTRY 4 yrs. exp. required, knowledge of European pastry pref. Send résumé to Box CS 47822.

CLERICAL If you love to type, my firm needs your skills. Excellent Salary & Benefits. Call Lisa 539-5804.

CLERK TYPIST General office work, 5 days, vic. Smallwood St. 566-5806.

COMPUTER OPERATOR To work part time eves. Must love to type. WP exp. pref. Pleasant atmosphere, free parking. Call 9-5 at 358-TYPE.

Activity A Use the sample help wanted ads to answer these questions. Write your answers on your paper.

1) Where can you get training as a dental assistant?

2) What kind of job is open at Frosty Refrigeration?

3) Which jobs require or prefer some experience?

4) What number could you call to get your résumé typed?

5) How are job titles organized in the help wanted section?

Activity A Answers

1) at The Medic School **2)** air conditioning and heat pump mechanic **3)** Administrative Secretary; A/C and Heat Pump mechanic; Cashier/Clerk; Pastry Chef; Computer Operator **4)** 484-6916 **5)** alphabetically

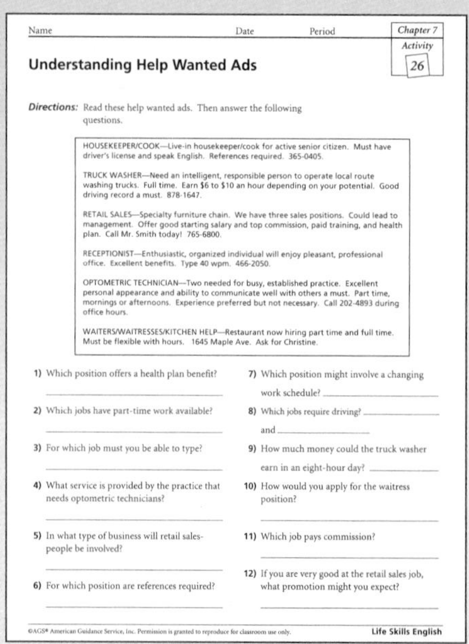

Name Date Period *Chapter 7 Activity 26*

Understanding Help Wanted Ads

Directions: Read these help wanted ads. Then answer the following questions.

HOUSEKEEPER/COOK—Live-in housekeeper/cook for active senior citizen. Must have driver's license and speak English. References required. 365-0405.

TRUCK WASHER—Need an intelligent, responsible person to operate local route washing trucks. Full time. Earn $6 to $10 an hour depending on your potential. Good driving record a must. 878-1647.

RETAIL SALES—Specialty furniture chain. We have three sales positions. Could lead to management. Offer good starting salary and top commission, paid training, and health plan. Call Mr. Smith today! 765-6800.

RECEPTIONIST—Enthusiastic, organized individual will enjoy pleasant, professional office. Excellent benefits. Type 40 wpm. 466-2050.

OPTOMETRIC TECHNICIAN—Two needed for busy, established practice. Excellent personal appearance and ability to communicate well with others a must. Part time, mornings or afternoons. Experience preferred but not necessary. Call 202-4893 during office hours.

WAITERS/WAITRESSES/KITCHEN HELP—Restaurant now hiring part time and full time. Must be flexible with hours. 1645 Maple Ave. Ask for Christine.

1) Which position offers a health plan benefit? ______

2) Which jobs have part-time work available? ______

3) For which job must you be able to type? ______

4) What service is provided by the practice that needs optometric technicians? ______

5) In what type of business will retail salespeople be involved? ______

6) For which position are references required? ______

7) Which position might involve a changing work schedule? ______

8) Which jobs require driving? ______ and ______

9) How much money could the truck washer earn in an eight-hour day? ______

10) How would you apply for the waitress position? ______

11) Which job pays commission? ______

12) If you are very good at the retail sales job, what promotion might you expect? ______

 Life Skills English

Activity 26

Understanding Abbreviations in the Help Wanted Ads

Job titles and other information in the help wanted ads are often abbreviated. The same words may be abbreviated in many different ways.

EXAMPLE

- Admin. Assistant
- Administrative Assist.
- Admin. Asst.

An administrative assistant helps an administrator. An administrator is a supervisor or manager of an office or a company.

Activity B Write on your paper every abbreviation in the following help wanted ads. Beside each abbreviation, write its meaning. Use the words in the list below to help you figure out the meanings of the abbreviations.

ADMIN ASSISTANT Opp'ty w/CPA firm. Typing 60 wpm, control logs, gen. ofc. exper. req. Résumé to WPR, POB 551, Fairmont.

ADMIN. ASSIST. Printing co. needs qual. indiv. immed. Good salary & benefits. Respond to POB 456, Wesleyville.

ADMIN. ASST. Exec. level. Typing & attention to detail req'd. Also Windows 6.1 and Lotus 1-2-3. Excell. sal., benefits. Call Mr. Kim, 560-8000.

with	administrative	Post Office Box	assistance
executive	experience	required	individual
excellent	qualified	words per minute	general
company	and	opportunity	immediately
office	salary	Certified Public Accountant	

Reading Vocabulary

accountant
administrator
assistance (6)
certify (8)
individual (6)
manager (6)
opportunity (5)
qualify (6)
respond (6)
salary (5)
supervisor (7)

■ Presenting Activity B

Do Activity B together, writing the abbreviations and their meanings on the board as students identify them. Then ask students to select several help wanted ads from the classified section of a local paper. Have students identify all the abbreviations in the ads and tell their meanings.

Activity B Answers

1) Admin Assistant: admin—administrative; opp'ty—opportunity; w/—with; CPA—Certified Public Accountant; wpm—words per minute; gen.—general; ofc.—office; exper.—experience; req.—required; POB—Post Office Box **2)** Admin. Assist.: admin.—administrative; assist.—assistant; co.—company; qual.—qualified; indiv.—individual; immed.—immediately; &—and; POB—Post Office Box **3)** Admin. Asst.: admin.—administrative; asst.—assistant; exec.—executive; &—and; req'd.—required; excell.—excellent; sal.—salary

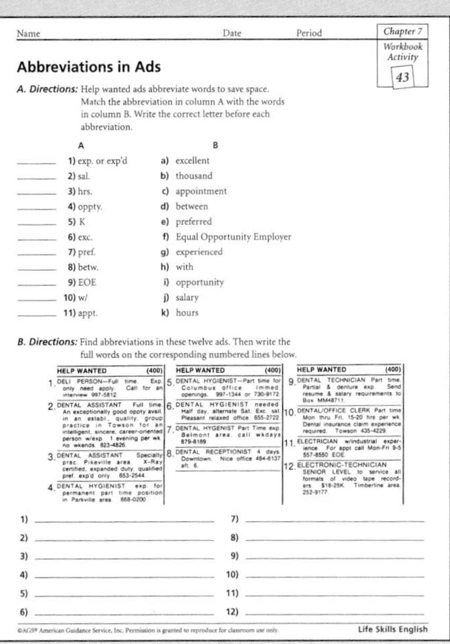
Name Date Period | Chapter 7 Workbook Activity 43

Abbreviations in Ads

A. Directions: Help wanted ads abbreviate words to save space. Match the abbreviation in column A with the words in column B. Write the correct letter before each abbreviation.

	A	B
____	1) exp. or exp'd	a) excellent
____	2) sal.	b) thousand
____	3) hrs.	c) appointment
____	4) oppty.	d) between
____	5) K	e) preferred
____	6) exc.	f) Equal Opportunity Employer
____	7) pref.	g) experienced
____	8) betw.	h) with
____	9) EOE	i) opportunity
____	10) w/	j) salary
____	11) appt.	k) hours

B. Directions: Find abbreviations in these twelve ads. Then write the full words on the corresponding numbered lines below.

HELP WANTED (400)

1. DELI PERSON—Full time. Exp. only need apply. Call for an interview 997-5812.
2. DENTAL ASSISTANT Full time. An exceptionally good oppty avail. in an establ., quality, group practice in Towson for an intelligent, sincere, career-oriented person w/exp. 1 evening per wk. no wkends. 823-4826.
3. DENTAL ASSISTANT Specialty prac. Pikeville area. X-Ray certified, expanded duty, qualified pref. exp'd only. 653-2544.
4. DENTAL HYGIENIST exp. for permanent part time position in Parkville area. 668-0200.
5. DENTAL HYGIENIST—Part time for Columbus office. Immed. openings. 997-1344 or 730-9172.
6. DENTAL HYGIENIST needed. Half day, alternate Sat. Exc. sal. Pleasant relaxed office. 655-2722.
7. DENTAL HYGENIST Part Time exp. Belmont area. call wkdays 879-8189.
8. DENTAL RECEPTIONIST 4 days. Downtown. Nice office 484-6137 aft. 6.
9. DENTAL TECHNICIAN Part time. Partial & denture exp. Send resume & salary requirements to Box MM48711.
10. DENTAL/OFFICE CLERK Part time Mon thru Fri, 15-20 hrs per wk. Dental insurance claim experience required. Towson 435-4229.
11. ELECTRICIAN w/industrial experience. For appt call Mon-Fri 9-5 557-8550 EOE.
12. ELECTRONIC-TECHNICIAN SENIOR LEVEL to service all formats of video tape recorders. $18-25K. Timberline area. 252-9177.

1) ____ 7) ____
2) ____ 8) ____
3) ____ 9) ____
4) ____ 10) ____
5) ____ 11) ____
6) ____ 12) ____

 Life Skills English

Workbook Activity 43

Reading Vocabulary

approximately (7)
benefits (5)
dependable
description (6)
determine (5)
executive (7)
experience (4)
full time
insurance (7)
interview (6)
part time
permanent (6)
qualifications (7)
recommend (6)
references (6)
reliable (7)
requirement (8)
temporary (8)
wages (6)

■ **Presenting Activity C** In preparation for Activity C, ask students to take turns using each of the words in the box on page 202 in a sentence related to looking for or finding a job. Some groups of students might enjoy the challenge of writing a paragraph that uses all of the words.

Activity C Answers

1) temporary 2) reliable
3) experience 4) benefits
5) part time

APPLICATION

Career Connection Students looking for work can use their skills to identify jobs in the classified sections of their local papers that match their qualifications. Suggest that students circle the appropriate ads and follow through by calling or writing about the job. Offer your support in helping students write letters and prepare résumés when required.

Benefits
What workers receive in addition to wages, such as health insurance and vacations.

Executive
A manager, a supervisor, or an administrator.

Experience
The same kind of work that you have done before.

Full time
A job that requires approximately 40 hours per week, or 8 hours a day for 5 days.

Part time
A job that requires less than 40 hours per week.

Permanent
A job that is expected to last a long time.

Qualifications
A description of your skills and work experience.

References
People who know about your work and who will recommend you for a job.

Reliable
A worker who is dependable and does what he or she is expected to do.

Temporary
A job that lasts for a limited amount of time.

Words to Know in the Help Wanted Ads

When looking for a job, there are certain terms you should know. Some of these words describe requirements for specific jobs. Many will appear in the want ads. Others may be used during a job interview. Knowing what these words mean will help you determine if you are qualified for the advertised job.

reliable	dependable; workers who do what they are expected to do
experience	the same kind of work that you have done before
executive	a manager, a supervisor, or an administrator
references	people who know about your work and who will recommend you for a job
qualifications	your skills and work experience
permanent	expected to last a long time
temporary	a limited amount of time
full time	a job that requires approximately 40 hours per week, or 8 hours a day for 5 days
part time	a job that requires less than 40 hours per week
benefits	what workers receive in addition to wages, such as health insurance and vacations

Activity C Use the words from the list to complete these sentences. Write the words on your paper.

1) Ellis Electronics needs a worker for three weeks. This is a ______ position.
2) Rosa Sabatino needs a server who will be at work on time every day. The person must be ______.
3) Rosa wants a server who has worked at a pizza parlor. She wants someone with ______.
4) Rosa will give her workers these ______: full health insurance and a paid vacation.
5) Dan would like a ______ job working evenings and weekends.

Job Titles

The same type of job may have many names. For example, a teacher may be called an instructor or a trainer. Office workers with typing skills have many job titles. They may be called administrative assistants, typists, secretaries, clerk/typists, or word processors.

The way people do their work has changed because of new technology. Job descriptions and titles have also changed. For example, people who type documents today are often called word processors because they use computers and word processing programs. What these workers type has not changed. How they type has.

Activity D Read these job descriptions. Then write your answers to the questions that follow on your paper.

WORD PROCESSING ASSISTANT Must type 75 WPM minimum and be reliable. Full time, permanent position. Knowledge of word processing helpful but not necessary. Salary depends on experience. Send references with résumé to Wilson, Inc., 4500 Westfield St., Kingsport.

ADMINISTRATIVE ASSISTANT Responsibilities include supervision of a small staff of office workers. Experience with WordPerfect and computer spreadsheet programs required. 60 wpm typing required. Call 240-7598 for appointment.

1) What skill does each of these jobs require?

2) Both of these workers will use word processing equipment. Which company will train the worker?

3) Which job requires recommendations from previous employers?

4) Which job would you apply for if you had computer experience?

Reading Vocabulary

appointment (6)
document (6)
employer (6)
instructor (7)
minimum (8)
previous (6)
processor
recommendation (8)
reference (6)
responsibility (6)
spreadsheet
technology

■ Presenting Activity D

Discuss each of the ads shown. If possible, display the ads on an overhead projector. Have students identify any unfamiliar terms and help them figure out their meanings.

Activity D Answers

1) typing **2)** Wilson, Inc. (Word Processing Assistant)
3) Word Processing Assistant
4) Administrative Assistant

Teacher Alert

Although most students will have some familiarity with computers, many may not recognize specific word processing programs; many may not have ever used a spreadsheet program. If the school has computers available, invite knowledgeable students, staff members, or parents to provide a demonstration of the features of well-known word processing and spreadsheet programs.

Reading Vocabulary

apprentice (5)
automate
cabinetmaker
classification (8)
countertop
data (9)
decimal (6)
desirable (7)
education (5)
illustrate (7)
inventory (8)
negotiable
premium (7)
system (5)
various (5)
warehouse (5)

■ Presenting Activity E

After students complete Activity E, suggest that pairs of students take turns role-playing employer and hopeful employee. Have each pair of students select one of the ads listed on page 204 or have them select an ad from the help wanted ads in a local newspaper. Ask each pair to act out the initial interview meeting between the employer and the job seeker. Students can use the information in the ad as well as personal experience in job hunting to prepare their presentation. Allow time for each pair to practice. Then invite them to present their interview to the class.

Activity E Answers

1) Answers will vary depending on students' choices. **2) a)** F/T **b)** perm. **c)** appt. **d)** wpm **e)** sal. **f)** immed. **3)** Alarm installer; Artist; Asst. Office Mgr; Cabinetmakers; Data Entry **4)** Asst. Cataloger; Bookkeeper **5)** Bookkeeper; Data Entry

Activity E Use the information in the help wanted ads below to answer the questions that follow. Write your answers on your paper.

ALARM INSTALLER Trainee position electronics or elec. background. Call 540-5433.

ARTIST Full time job with fast growing advertising agency. 2 yrs exper. req. Must be able to illustrate quickly on Macintosh. Exp. with typesetting machine or willing to learn. Send résumé to Daily Banner, Box 45A.

ASST. CATALOGER Qualifications: Exper. with Dewey Decimal classification system. Degree from 2-yr or 4-yr college highly desirable. Call the Library. 430-9800.

ASST. OFFICE MGR Small but growing Property Mgt. firm on easy-to-learn computer. F/T. Starting salary $25,000. Send résumé to Daily Banner, Box 87D.

BOOKKEEPER 4 yrs exper. in automated accounting data. Accounting degree preferred. 23,000 plus benefits. Send résumé to Daily Banner, Box 35C.

AUTO BODY REPAIR PERSON & HELPER Must have own tools. Ask for Julian. 453-0988.

BAKER, PASTRY CHEF Exper'd for excell. European bakery. Perm. position. Call 459-3210.

CABINETMAKERS Apprentices only. Will train. Countertop shop. Start immed. 345-9870.

CASHIER Full time position for person with one year exper. Good with figures. Call Sue. 432-0983.

CLERICAL Dependable, exper. worker to handle warehouse inventory, shipping and receiving, & various office clerical work. Call 240-8450 bet. 9 & 12 for appt.

DATA ENTRY Immed. opening, 50 wpm, quick learner, phone manners. Sal. negotiable. Free parking and other benefits. Call Ms. Samaki 8 to 12 for appt. 540-9800.

1) Choose four of the positions. List the qualifications required for the jobs.

2) Write the abbreviations that match each of these terms.

a) full time
b) permanent
c) appointment
d) words per minute
e) salary
f) immediately

3) In which jobs will workers receive on-the-job training?

4) Which jobs require education beyond high school?

5) Which jobs will probably cover health care premiums?

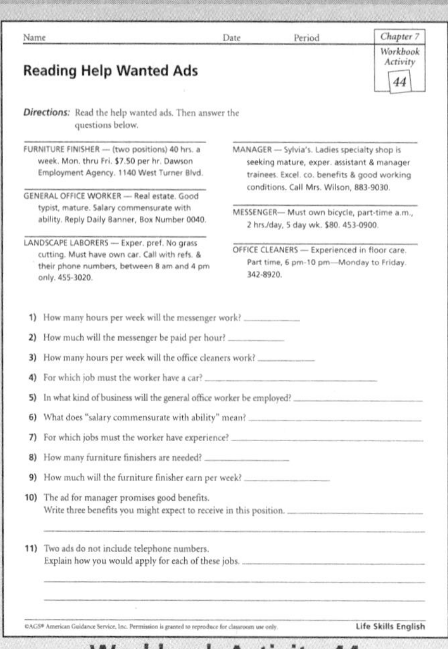

Name Date Period | *Chapter 7 Workbook Activity 44*

Reading Help Wanted Ads

Directions: Read the help wanted ads. Then answer the questions below.

FURNITURE FINISHER — (two positions) 40 hrs. a week. Mon. thru Fri. $7.50 per hr. Dawson Employment Agency. 1140 West Turner Blvd.

GENERAL OFFICE WORKER — Real estate. Good typist, mature. Salary commensurate with ability. Reply Daily Banner, Box Number 0040.

LANDSCAPE LABORERS — Exper. pref. No grass cutting. Must have own car. Call with refs. & their phone numbers, between 8 am and 4 pm only. 455-3020.

MANAGER — Sylvia's. Ladies specialty shop is seeking mature, exper. assistant & manager trainees. Excel. co. benefits & good working conditions. Call Mrs. Wilson, 883-9030.

MESSENGER— Must own bicycle, part-time a.m., 2 hrs./day, 5 day wk. $80. 453-0900.

OFFICE CLEANERS — Experienced in floor care. Part time, 6 pm-10 pm—Monday to Friday. 342-8920.

1) How many hours per week will the messenger work? ______

2) How much will the messenger be paid per hour? ______

3) How many hours per week will the office cleaners work? ______

4) For which job must the worker have a car? ______

5) In what kind of business will the general office worker be employed? ______

6) What does "salary commensurate with ability" mean? ______

7) For which jobs must the worker have experience? ______

8) How many furniture finishers are needed? ______

9) How much will the furniture finisher earn per week? ______

10) The ad for manager promises good benefits. Write three benefits you might expect to receive in this position. ______

11) Two ads do not include telephone numbers. Explain how you would apply for each of these jobs. ______

 Life Skills English

Workbook Activity 44

204 *Chapter 7 Information From the Media*

Lesson 4 Review

Part A Write on your paper the answers to these questions.

1) What word would you look for in the newspaper index to find the help wanted ads?
2) Put these job titles in the order that you would expect to find them in the help wanted ads.
   a) Computer Operator
   b) Machinist
   c) Accountant
3) What does it mean if an ad says that a job is "open"?
4) About how many hours would you expect to work each week in a full time job?
5) Name one of the benefits an employer might offer besides wages.
6) Name one qualification, other than skills and experience, that many employers say they want.

Part B List all of the abbreviations in these ads on your paper. Beside each abbreviation, write the word or words you think the abbreviation stands for.

DATA DISTRIBUTION SPECIALIST Entry level pos. in our mail room. If you have good organizational skills, your own trans., and are able to lift 50 lb., we want to talk to you. Typ. is helpful. Call Mrs. Verney, 450-9800.

BOOKKEEPER/PAYROLL Reliable individual w/exper. working computerized payroll. Needed immed. Good sal. & benefits. Call 321-0984.

CARPET MECHANIC Excellent opp. Must have truck & tools. Apply in person. CarpetTown, 1200 Eastern Avenue, Milton.

BOOK STORE F/T sales/cashier pos. Previous exper. Call 453-0939 for appt.

BEAUTICIAN F/T or P/T. Exp. pref. Start immed. Call Joy. 432-4900.

Reading Vocabulary

distribution (8) payroll
entry (6) specialist (9)
machinist

Part A Answers

1) Employment or Help Wanted **2)** Accountant, Computer Operator, Machinist **3)** The job is available. **4)** approximately 40 hours a week **5)** Answers will vary. Possible responses include: health insurance, paid vacation, paid holidays, free parking, expenses. **6)** Answers will vary. Possible responses include: dependability, reliability, self-initiative, self-confidence, ability to work well with others.

Part B Answers

1) Data Distribution Specialist: pos.—position; trans.—transportation; lb.—pounds; typ.—typing
2) Bookkeeper/Payroll: w/—with; exper.—experience; immed.—immediately; sal.—salary; &—and
3) Carpet Mechanic: opp.—opportunity; &—and **4)** Book Store: F/T—full time; pos.—position; exp.—experience; appt.—appointment **5)** Beautician: F/T—full time; P/T—part time; exp.—experience; pref.—preferred; immed.—immediately

Learning Styles

Logical/Mathematical
Divide the class into groups of three. Invite each group to create a ten-question quiz on the help-wanted ads shown between pages 200 and 205. Afterward, ask the groups to exchange their quizzes and to answer the questions on the quiz they received. Discuss anything new the groups learned from this activity.

Lesson at a Glance

Chapter 7 Lesson 5

Overview This lesson explains how to use television and radio to get information.

Objective

- To demonstrate a knowledge of radio and television terms.

Student Pages 206–215

Teacher's Resource Library

Activity 27

Workbook Activity 45

Reading Vocabulary

antenna (5)	percentage
broadcast (6)	purchase (5)
channel (5)	receiver
increase (5)	satellite (5)
location (6)	transmitter
microwave	videocassette
occur (6)	videodisc

Teaching Suggestions

Introducing the Lesson

As you discuss the text, provide a diagram to reinforce the concept of how television and radio signals are transmitted and received.

Reviewing Skills

Review newspaper advertising.

Presenting Activity A

Engage students in a discussion of how television has changed in recent history. For example, how many more channels are available now then when students were children? What technology is available today that wasn't when they were born or when their parents were their ages? Following the discussion, help students complete Activity A.

Activity A Answers

1) from communications satellites; from microwave transmitters; through telephone lines; through cables and satellite dishes 2) watch movies; play video games 3) Citizens Band

Lesson 5 Television and Radio

Television and radio communications have changed the way we get information about the world. Instead of reading about important events in the newspaper after they occur, we see these events or hear about them *as they happen.*

> ***Broadcast***
> *To send radio or television signals through the air to receivers in the home, the car, or other location.*

Television and radio stations **broadcast**, or send, signals through the air to receivers in the home, the car, or wherever we are. Signals also come to us from communications satellites orbiting around the earth, microwave transmitters, and telephone lines. They also come into our homes through cables and satellite dishes.

Broadcast television is free to anyone who has a television set and an antenna. To receive information using other methods, people purchase or rent a telephone, cable box, or satellite dish. They also pay a monthly fee.

Cable television has increased the number of television channels from a few to more than 100. More than 65 percent of people have cable TV and the percentage is increasing each year.

Many people also use their television sets to watch movies on videocassettes or videodiscs. Some people use them to play video games.

Radio, too, plays a major role in people's lives. People listen to radio for music, news, weather, and traffic reports. People call in and discuss their opinions or ask questions on talk radio programs, which are very popular. People with Citizens Band (CB) receivers in their cars and homes may talk to people all over the world using radio signals.

Activity A Write on your paper your answers to these questions.

1) Name four ways that television and radio signals can reach our receivers.

2) Name at least two ways that people use television other than for watching TV programs.

3) What does CB stand for?

Television Literacy

TV viewing plays an important part in our lives. In the United States, 99% of the households have at least one color television set. If you want to use TV as an information tool, you need to understand the television industry. The goal of the next few activities is to help you become "television literate."

Did you know?

- A recent survey shows that in the average American home, a television set is on about 7 hours per day. That is nearly 30% of the 168 hours in one week.
- Women who are 18 to 24 years old watch, on average, about 4 hours more per week than men of the same age group. Throughout their lives, women watch more television than men, on average.
- On the average, male and female teenagers watch television over 20 hours per week.
- America's favorite shows are comedies, dramatic series, football games, and movies. Americans especially enjoy the Super Bowl—an annual football game that determines the year's champion football team. In fact, the 50 most popular television shows from 1964 to 1994 included 18 Super Bowl games.

Using What You Have Learned

Survey your class to find out if your group has the same tastes as average American viewers. Have each person list his or her five favorite TV programs. Beside each person's name, write the types of programs that person has listed: comedy, drama, sports, movies, news. (If your classmates are like most American viewers, their favorite programs will be situation comedies.)

Television Viewing and Advertising

Much of what we see on television is commercial advertising. Audience viewing habits are important to the TV industry and especially to companies that advertise on television. Obviously, the more people who see an advertisement the better.

Reading Vocabulary

audience (5)
comedy (7)
commercial (6)
drama (7)
dramatic (7)
industry (6)
literacy
obviously
series (5)
situation (5)
survey (5)

Using What You Have Learned

Engage students in a discussion about the results of their survey. Students can extend this activity by surveying five family members and friends. Have them collect the results of their outside survey in a second chart to compare with the results of their original class survey.

Global Connection

Students may be interested to learn how television viewing habits in America compare to television viewing habits in other countries of the world. Suggest that students do research to learn how much time teenagers in countries such as England, Spain, Italy, China, and Japan spend watching television in an average day or week. They might also find out what types of shows teens in these countries tend to watch.

Learning Styles

Body/Kinesthetic

Ask volunteers to present a charade or pantomime of their favorite television show. Encourage the other students to name the show. After each program is correctly guessed, have someone record the name of the program. Use this listing to determine which programs are most popular with the students.

Reading Vocabulary

network
population (5)
prime time
syndicate (11)

APPLICATION

At Home

The next time students sit down to watch television, ask them to keep track of the advertisements that are shown during the different programs. Ask them to record on note cards or on paper the name of the program, the type of program it is (comedy, police drama, mystery, and so on), the length of the program, the number of advertisements, and the kinds of advertisements. Invite students to share their findings with the class. What can students conclude about television advertisers from their observations?

Who cares how much TV certain people watch and what shows people like best?

Advertisers and television station owners care very much. TV programs and commercials are expensive to make. Advertisers pay high fees to have them broadcast. They want the largest audiences possible.

How much money do TV advertisers spend each year?

Advertisers spend more than 23 billion dollars each year advertising on television. That includes the amount they spend on network TV, syndicated TV, and cable TV. Businesses spend such large amounts of money because television stations promise that a certain number of people will be watching.

How do advertisers know which programs are popular? How do they know what kinds of people are watching?

The Nielsen Company reports on how many people watch each program. They choose about 1,200 families to represent the population. The families include young, old, rich, poor, and "average" people. The Nielsen sample is a small part of the entire TV viewing population.

Advertisers and TV stations are interested in what programs people watch during prime time. When is prime time?

Prime time

The hours when television is watched the most, between 8 P.M. and 11 P.M.

Prime time is between 8 P.M. and 11 P.M. each day (7 P.M. and 10 P.M. in some time zones). TV has its largest audience during these hours. TV stations charge the most for ads shown during those hours.

TV advertisers try to find out whether the viewing audience is made up of mostly men or women. They want to know as much as possible about those people. Then they advertise their products on shows with a certain kind of audience.

Activity B Write on your paper your answer to the following question. Then share and discuss your answer with the class.

How much do advertisements that you see on television affect what products you buy?

Activity C Write on your paper the kinds of products you would expect to be advertised on a show that is aimed at each of the following audiences. Then compare and discuss your answers with your class.

1) Mostly teenagers

2) Mostly men

3) Mostly women

4) Mostly children

5) Mostly older people (over 50)

6) Professionals and business people

Advertisers know that teens watch sporting events. Many products teens use are advertised on TV during these events.

Reading Vocabulary

affect (5) discuss (5)
compare (5) professional (6)

■ Presenting Activity B

Before students do Activity B, ask them if they have ever bought a product or wanted to buy a product just because of an ad that they saw on television. Ask these questions:

1. What was the product?
2. What was it about the ad that made you want the product?
3. If you bought the product, were you satisfied that the ad provided honest information about the product?
4. Did you or would buy the product again? Why or why not?

After students complete Activity B, allow time for them to share and discuss their answers with the class.

Activity B Answers

Answers will vary.

■ Presenting Activity C

Have students work in small groups to do Activity C. Suggest that group members discuss the needs and interests of each target audience and the types of television programs each audience is likely to watch before creating a list of products for that audience.

Activity C Answers

Answers will vary.

Reading Vocabulary

affiliate (12) federal (6)
airway independent (6)
college (5) portion (6)
corporation (8) **subscriber**
donation (7) value (5)
educational

Application

In the Community
The FCC requires that all television and radio stations provide a certain percentage of air time for free public service advertisements. Help students identify a community service issue. Then suggest that students work together to create a public service announcement related to that issue. If video equipment is available, students might videotape their announcement, or they could tape record an audio message. Students could play their public announcements for other classes in the school. They might even write to local radio and television stations to ask if they would consider airing their announcement.

Kinds of TV Stations

- **Network television**
A network is a large TV corporation that has member stations. It broadcasts its signal over the airways to these member stations all over the United States. Four of the largest TV networks are American Broadcasting Company (ABC), Columbia Broadcasting System (CBS), National Broadcasting Company (NBC), and Fox Broadcasting Company. Each network earns money by selling airtime to advertisers. The member stations are called **affiliates**. Each affiliate carries some of the network programming and other local programming. Affiliates provide local news, weather, sports, and other shows directed at a small portion of the country. Affiliates sell airtime to local advertisers.

Affiliate
A member station that carries some of the programs broadcast by a large television network.

- **Independent stations**
This group of small TV companies may own one or several stations. Independent stations also sell advertising time. They may produce some original programs, but they usually buy programs from syndicates. Many independent stations broadcast old movies, game shows, and reruns of shows first shown on network stations.

- **Public Broadcasting System (PBS)**
This network of educational television stations does not accept advertisements. PBS stations get much of their money from people who watch the station and send in **donations**. A donation is a gift of money or other items of value. Businesses also donate money as a public service. The federal government and some state governments also give money to public television stations. These stations offer college courses, documentaries, news, entertainment programming, and children's programming.

Donation
A gift of money or other items of value.

- **Cable networks**
These corporations send program signals by cable or satellite dish to local cable companies. The local cable company sells these programs to its customers, or **subscribers**, by providing what is called cable service. There are many cable networks.

Subscriber
A customer of a local cable television company.

210 Chapter 7 Information From the Media

Some of the most popular are the Cable News Network (CNN); the Discovery Channel; USA Network; Music Television Network (MTV); Turner Broadcasting System (TBS); Black Entertainment Television (BET); The Nashville Network (TNN); and ESPN. All of these cable networks have millions of subscribers. Most cable networks focus on one main type of programming. For example, ESPN presents sports programming; CNN is all news; and MTV has music videos. These networks sell advertising time. Advertisers and subscription fees pay for the programming.

- **Premium cable networks and pay-per-view TV**
  These networks do not have advertisements. Subscribers pay extra fees that cover the cost of this programming. Home Box Office (HBO), Showtime, Cinemax, The Disney Channel, and The Movie Channel are some of the main premium networks. These stations show mainly movies. Sometimes these channels have special features and other types of programming. On pay-per-view TV channels, people call the local cable company and order programs. They pay a fee for each program they request. Pay-per-view TV offers current movies and special sports programming.

- **Syndicates**
  A syndicate is a company or organization that sells television programs to television stations. The syndicate buys the programming from other producers. Game shows and talk shows are popular syndicated programs. You will see these programs on different channels in different cities. Syndicates also purchase old network programs and sell them to independent and local stations.

APPLICATION

In the Community

Many cable companies offer communities access to one of the free channels. Have students contact the cable service in their area to find out if there is a community access channel available; what the procedure is for getting a program aired on the community access channel; and what types of community programs have aired recently. Interested students can get together to discuss the idea of writing and producing a show for the community access channel. Students may also benefit from talking to community members who have produced programs in the past.

Information From the Media Chapter 7 **211**

Reading Vocabulary

generation (5)
personality (6)

■ Presenting Activity D

Provide students with copies of a daily television schedule from a local newspaper. Ask them to use the schedule to answer the following questions:[8]

1. What are the call letters for the major network stations in your area?
2. When are most children's shows aired?
3. When are most of the more violent or controversial shows aired?
4. Which channels show mainly movies?
5. Which channels air educational programs only?
6. At what time do the different major network stations broadcast the news?

Then encourage students to use the schedules to make up questions of their own to ask classmates. Following this activity, have students complete Activity D on their own.

Activity D Answers

1) NBC (WRC), FOX (WTTG), ABC (WJLA), CBS (WUSA) 2) WDCA, WBDC 3) WDCA broadcasts Wake, Rattle; WBDC broadcasts Video Power 4) WTTG 5) FOX

Activity D Look at the example of part of the daily television broadcast schedule in the newspaper for one city. Then answer on your paper the questions that follow.

	NBC 4 WRC	FOX 5 WTTG	ABC 7 WJLA	CBS 9 WUSA	20 WDCA	50 WBDC
6 :00	NBC News	News	ABC News	News	K. Copeland	Movie (cont.)
6 :30	News	News	News		Jetsons	Heathcliff
7 :00	Today	Fox Morning News	Good Morning America	This Morning	Flintstones	Felix the Cat
7 :30					Wake, Rattle	Video Power

1) What are four of the largest network channels?

2) Name the independent channels.

3) What does each independent channel broadcast at 7:30?

4) Name the call letters for Channel 5.

5) What major network is Channel 5 an affiliate of?

The newspaper schedule does not list every station that viewers in that area can watch. A TV program guide on sale at newsstands has a more complete listing. Below is a listing for one time slot on a certain evening.

11:30 P.M.		
	2 4	TONIGHT Host: Jay Leno
	5	PERSONALITIES
	7 45	NIGHTLINE
	9	LATE SHOW WITH DAVID LETTERMAN
	11	EVENING SHADE
	20	STAR TREK: THE NEXT GENERATION
	26	CHARLIE ROSE
	32	ITN WORLD NEWS
	50	DESIGNING WOMEN

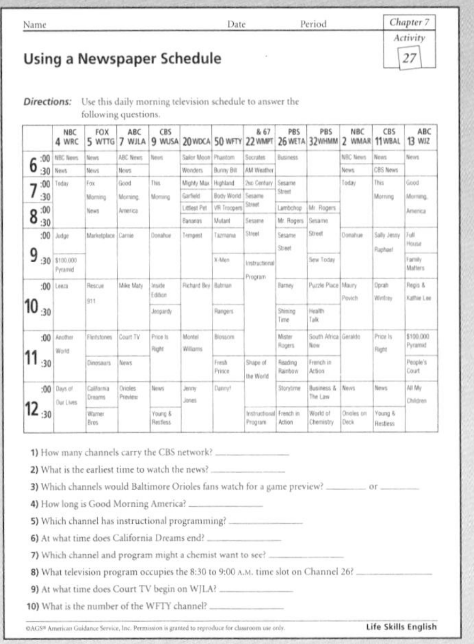

Name Date Period *Chapter 7 Activity 27*

Using a Newspaper Schedule

Directions: Use this daily morning television schedule to answer the following questions.

	NBC 4 WRC	FOX 5 WTTG	ABC 7 WJLA	CBS 9 WUSA	20 WDCA	50 WFTY	& 67 22 WMPT	PBS 26 WETA	PBS 32 WHMM	NBC 2 WMAR	CBS 11 WBAL	ABC 13 WJZ
6 :00	NBC News	News	ABC News	News	Sailor Moon	Phantom	Socrates	Business		NBC News	News	News
6 :30	News	News	News		Wonders	Bunny Bill	AM Weather			News	CBS News	
7 :00	Today	Fox Morning News	Good Morning America	This Morning	Mighty Max	Highland	2nd Century	Sesame Street		Today	This Morning	Good Morning America
7 :30					Garfield	Body World	Sesame Street					
8 :00					Littlest Pet	VR Troopers		Lambchop	Mr. Rogers			
8 :30					Bananas	Mutant	Sesame Street	Mr. Rogers	Sesame Street			
9 :00	Judge	Marketplace	Carnie	Donahue	Tempest	Tazmania		Sesame Street		Donahue	Sally Jessy Raphael	Full House
9 :30	$100,000 Pyramid					X-Men	Instructional Program		Sew Today			Family Matters
10 :00	Leeza	Rescue 911	Mike Maty	Inside Edition	Richard Bey	Batman		Barney	Puzzle Place	Maury Povich	Oprah Winfrey	Regis & Kathie Lee
10 :30				Jeopardy		Rangers		Shining Time	Health Talk			
11 :00	Another World	Flintstones	Court TV	Price Is Right	Montel Williams	Blossom		Mister Rogers	South Africa Now	Geraldo	Price Is Right	$100,000 Pyramid
11 :30		Dinosaurs	News			Fresh Prince	Shape of the World	Reading Rainbow	French in Action			People's Court
12 :00	Days of Our Lives	California Dreams	Orioles Preview	News	Jenny Jones	Danny!		Storytime	Business & The Law	News	News	All My Children
12 :30		Warner Bros		Young & Restless			Instructional Program	French in Action	World of Chemistry	Orioles on Deck	Young & Restless	

1) How many channels carry the CBS network? ______
2) What is the earliest time to watch the news? ______
3) Which channels would Baltimore Orioles fans watch for a game preview? ______ or ______
4) How long is Good Morning America? ______
5) Which channel has instructional programming? ______
6) At what time does California Dreams end? ______
7) Which channel and program might a chemist want to see? ______
8) What television program occupies the 8:30 to 9:00 A.M. time slot on Channel 26? ______
9) At what time does Court TV begin on WJLA? ______
10) What is the number of the WFTY channel? ______

 Life Skills English

Activity 27

Name Date Period *Chapter 7 Workbook Activity 45*

Using a Schedule in the Newspaper

Here is an example of a daily television schedule published in the newspaper:

	4 NBC WRC	5 WTTG	7 ABC WJLA	9 CBS WDVM	20 WDCA	26 PBS WETA
7 :00	Wings	Three's Company	Roseanne	Rescue 911	Love Boat	News Night
7 :30	News Radio	M*A*S*H	Hudson Street			Hometime
8 :00	Frasier	MOVIE: "GOING HOME"	Home Improvement	Courthouse	Cheers	Masterpiece Theater
8 :30	Pursuit		Coach		Dobie Gillis	
9 :00	Dateline NBC		College Football: UCLA at Georgia	MOVIE: "GOLD COUNTRY"	Moore	Frontline
9 :30					Newhart	
					Gunsmoke	Great

1) How many channels are listed? ______
2) What are three network channels? ______ ______ ______
3) What is the number of the PBS channel? ______
4) At what time does the program "Wings" end? ______
5) What channel carries the program "Frontline"? ______
6) At what time does the show M*A*S*H begin on Channel 5? ______
7) What programs occupy the 7:00 to 8:00 time slot on Channel 26? ______
8) How many channels feature full-length movies? ______
9) What channel carries "Courthouse"? ______
10) What college football teams can be seen on Channel 7? ______

 Life Skills English

Workbook Activity 45

Activity E Use the information in both programming guides on page 212 to answer the questions. Write your answers on your paper.

1) On which two channels is *Nightline* broadcast at 11:30 P.M.?

2) Name the program that WTTG will show at 11:30 P.M.

3) What program does channel 50 show at 11:30 P.M.?

4) Who is the host of *The Tonight Show*?

5) On which network does David Letterman appear?

6) What program does WDCA show at 11:30 P.M.?

Activity F Use the information on pages 210–212 to answer these questions. Write your answers on your paper.

1) What type of programming does each of the following cable stations show?

- **a)** ESPN
- **b)** CNN
- **c)** MTV

2) Name three kinds of programs that PBS stations offer.

3) What television network operates WUSA, Channel 9?

4) What program does WJLA show at 7 A.M. every weekday morning?

5) Which station could you tune in to see a movie at 6 A.M.?

6) How many stations are broadcasting news at 7 A.M.?

Educational TV Stations

Today, many stations besides PBS broadcast educational programs. Here are some subjects you may find on these channels:

EXAMPLES

Computer education	How to buy life insurance
Managing a business	How to invest your money
How to find a job	Sewing, cooking, and gardening

Reading Vocabulary

operate (5)

■ Presenting Activity E

After students complete Activity E, encourage them to work with a partner to create their ideal television schedule beginning at 6:00 P.M. and ending at midnight. Students should include the major network stations, a PBS station, a movie channel, and one independent station. Students can list the names of current shows, old programs, and programs that they create themselves. They should be ready, however, to explain what each of their invented shows is about. Students who have access to a computer and printer, can create their schedules on a computer and then print copies to share with the class.

Activity E Answers

1) 7 and 45 **2)** Personalities **3)** Designing Women **4)** Jay Leno **5)** CBS **6)** Star Trek: The Next Generation

■ Presenting Activity F

Before asking students to complete Activity F on their own, you might wish to point out to them that not that long ago stations such as MTV and ESPN did not even exist. Just a few decades ago, cable companies existed mainly to provide access to the networks for communities that had difficulty receiving network transmissions and that had only one or perhaps no local affiliates within broadcast range. The early cable companies made it possible for people to get more than just one station on their television sets.

Activity F Answers

1) a) sports **b)** news **c)** music videos **2)** Answers will vary. Possible responses include: college courses, documentaries, news, entertainment programming, and children's programming **3)** CBS **4)** Good Morning America **5)** WBDC (50) **6)** one—5/WTTG (FOX)

Reading Vocabulary

classical
documentary
Federal Communications Commission (FCC)
frequency
historical (6)
indicate (6)
license (5)
nonfiction
source (6)

Global Connection

Television has elevated people's awareness and understanding of the variety of cultures around the world. Invite students to share knowledge about another culture that they gained through watching a television documentary or news program. Ask students how they think television and technological advances might work to bring cultures together in the future.

Educational channels and PBS stations also have news programming that focuses on the government and the stock market. Some programs are about historical events. They are called **documentaries**. A documentary is a nonfiction film.

Documentary
A nonfiction film or television program.

Radio Broadcasting

Each radio station usually has a special type of programming, such as all news, rock and roll, or classical music.

You may like to explore the different stations on your radio. Although radio stations also belong to networks, their programs are different in each area. You can usually find more local news on the radio than on TV. Radio is also one of the most up-to-the-minute sources of news.

The Federal Communications Commission

Federal Communications Commission (FCC)
A government agency that provides licenses to people or companies to operate television and radio stations.

The **Federal Communications Commission (FCC)** is a government agency that gives licenses to people or companies that want to operate television and radio stations. The FCC also makes rules for these stations. The rules indicate how much air time stations can sell to commercial advertisers.

Radio and TV stations broadcast their signals over the air. The airways belong to the public, which is why the government controls their use. Each station must broadcast over a specific frequency. Citizens Band (CB) radio also has a certain frequency. The word *band* means a certain range of frequencies.

214 *Chapter 7 Information From the Media*

Lesson 5 Review

Lesson Review Write on your paper the answers to these questions.

1) What are two ways that radio and television signals are sent?
2) What is the name of the federal agency that makes rules for radio and television stations?
3) What do the initials "CB" mean?
4) Approximately how many hours a week is a television set on in the average American household?
5) How do the owners of TV stations and TV networks earn money?
6) Which TV viewing hours are called "prime time"?
7) Why do TV station owners charge more money to show a commercial during prime time?
8) What are the four major TV networks?
9) What do the initials "PBS" mean?
10) What are two ways that PBS stations receive money?
11) What are stations called that do not belong to a network?
12) What is a documentary?
13) How are pay-per-view TV stations different from network stations?
14) What does the Nielsen Rating Service do for the TV networks?

Reading Vocabulary

household (6) initial (6)

Lesson Review Answers

1) Answers will vary. Possible responses include: through cables, over the air, from communication satellites, through microwaves, and through telephone lines. **2)** FCC/Federal Communications Commission **3)** Citizens Band **4)** 49 hours **5)** by selling time for commercial advertising **6)** between 8 P.M. and 11 P.M. (or in certain time zones, 7 P.M. and 10 P.M.) **7)** More people watch during those hours. **8)** CBS, ABC, NBC, and FOX **9)** Public Broadcasting System **10)** from donations from people and business; from government funding **11)** independent stations **12)** a nonfiction program **13)** There are no commercials; people pay a fee to see a program. **14)** It reports how many people are watching certain programs. The networks use this information to determine whether a show is worth keeping on the air.

Chapter 7 Review

The Teacher's Resource Library includes two parallel forms of the Chapter 7 Mastery Test. The difficulty level of the two forms is equivalent. You may wish to use one form as a pretest and the other form as a posttest.

Part A Answers

1) newspapers **2)** newspaper **3)** editorial **4)** editor **5)** PBS

Part B Answers

1) Who? What? When? Where? Why? How? **2)** Answers will vary: Possible answers include: world news, local news, classified ads, help wanted ads, comics, obituaries, sports, business, arts and entertainment. **3)** Answers will vary.

Chapter 7 Review

Part A Write the best answer for each question on your paper.

1) Which are mass media?

a) newspapers

b) letters

c) telephone calls

2) Which of these media has the most facts about job openings?

a) television

b) radio

c) newspaper

3) Which section of a newspaper has opinions about current events?

a) front page

b) classified

c) editorial

4) Who decides which stories to print and how long they will be—the reporter or the editor?

5) Which TV network has educational programming without commercial advertising—HBO, PBS, or NBC?

Part B Write on your paper your answers to these questions.

1) What six questions should a news story answer?

2) What are four parts, or sections, of a newspaper?

3) What is an example of an advertising slogan?

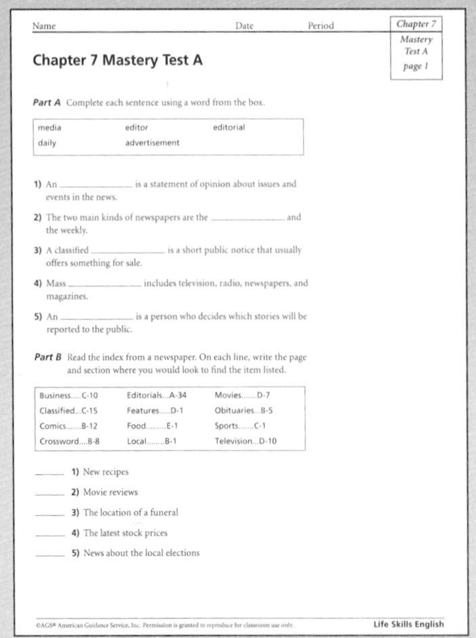

Name Date Period | *Chapter 7 Mastery Test A page 1*

Chapter 7 Mastery Test A

Part A Complete each sentence using a word from the box.

media	editor	editorial
daily	advertisement	

1) An ______________ is a statement of opinion about issues and events in the news.

2) The two main kinds of newspapers are the ______________ and the weekly.

3) A classified ______________ is a short public notice that usually offers something for sale.

4) Mass ______________ includes television, radio, newspapers, and magazines.

5) An ______________ is a person who decides which stories will be reported to the public.

Part B Read the index from a newspaper. On each line, write the page and section where you would look to find the item listed.

Business.....C-10	Editorials...A-34	Movies.......D-7
Classified...C-15	Features.....D-1	Obituaries...B-5
Comics.......B-12	Food.........E-1	Sports.......C-1
Crossword....B-8	Local........B-1	Television...D-10

______ **1)** New recipes

______ **2)** Movie reviews

______ **3)** The location of a funeral

______ **4)** The latest stock prices

______ **5)** News about the local elections

 Life Skills English

Name Date Period | *Chapter 7 Mastery Test A page 2*

Chapter 7 Mastery Test A, continued

Part C Read the classified ad index. On the lines, write where you would look to find each of these items.

100-199 Announcements	400-499 Recreation and Leisure	600-699 Notices	1000-1099 Financial
200-299 Merchandise	500-599 Personal and Business Services	700-799 Employment	1100-1199 Transportation
300-399 Pets and Animals		800-899 Rentals	
		900-999 Real Estate	

1) Town houses for sale ______________

2) Bedroom furniture for sale ______________

3) Houses for rent ______________

4) Job openings for secretaries ______________

5) Someone to take your old couch to the dump ______________

Part D Below are abbreviations commonly found in help wanted and classified ads. Write the meaning of the abbreviation on the line.

1) bdrm. ______________ **6)** am/fm ______________

2) TV ______________ **7)** pos. ______________

3) utils. ______________ **8)** F/T ______________

4) a/c ______________ **9)** sal. ______________

5) eng. ______________ **10)** pref. ______________

Part E Read the following statements. If the statement is true, write *True* on the line. If the statement is not true, write *False*.

______ **1)** The four major network television stations are TNN, PBS, ESPN, and MTV.

______ **2)** The Public Broadcasting System is a network of educational television stations that does not accept advertisements.

______ **3)** Cable networks send program signals by cable or satellite dish to local cable companies.

______ **4)** FCC stands for Federal Citizens Communication.

______ **5)** The FCC makes documentaries.

 Life Skills English

Chapter 7 Mastery Test A

4) What are the initials of the federal agency that makes rules for radio and TV stations.

5) What does the term *documentary* mean?

Part C Write on your paper all of the abbreviations in these ads. Beside each abbreviation, write its meaning.

JACKSON HEIGHTS 2 BR apt., A/C, 5 min. walk to bus. $675 + elec. 246-9871

CHEVETTE 91, 4 dr., 4 cyl., ps, pb, red w/white int. Best offer. 235-7109.

CLERK F/T, 50 wpm, exper. req. Sal. $18,000 to start. Send résumé to Daily Banner, POB 34D.

Test Taking Tip

Look over a test before you begin answering questions. See how many parts there are. See what you are being asked to do on each part.

(Part B Answers, continued)
4) FCC **5)** a nonfiction film or television program

Part C Answers

1) Jackson Heights: BR—bedroom; apt.—apartment; A/C—air conditioning; min.—minute; +—plus; elec.—electricity **2)** Chevette: 4 dr.—4 door; 4 cyl.—4 cylinders; ps—power steering; pb—power brakes; w/—with; int.—interior **3)** Clerk: F/T—full time; wpm—words per minute; exper.—experience; req.—required; Sal.—Salary; POB—Post Office Box

Name Date Period

Chapter 7 Mastery Test B page 1

Chapter 7 Mastery Test B

Part A Complete each sentence using a word from the box.

mass	editor	editorial
weekly	classified	

1) The person who decides which stories will be reported to the public is called an ______________ .

2) The two main kinds of newspapers are the daily and the ______________ .

3) A statement of opinion about issues and events in the news is called an ______________ .

4) ______________ media includes television, radio, newspapers, and magazines.

5) A ______________ advertisement is a short public notice that usually offers something for sale.

Part B Read the index from a newspaper. On each line, write the page and section where you would look to find the item listed.

Business.....C-10	Editorials...A-34	Movies.......D-7
Classified...C-15	Features.....D-1	Obituaries...B-5
Comics.......B-12	Food.........E-1	Sports.......C-1
Crossword....B-8	Local........B-1	Television...D-10

______ 1) A list of job openings

______ 2) Football scores

______ 3) Opinions on current issues

______ 4) A list of houses for sale

______ 5) "Dear Abby" column

 Life Skills English

Name Date Period

Chapter 7 Mastery Test B page 2

Chapter 7 Mastery Test B, continued

Part C Read the classified ad index. On the lines, write where you would look to find each of these items.

100-199 Announcements	400-499 Recreation and Leisure	600-699 Notices	1000-1099 Financial
200-299 Merchandise	500-599 Personal and Business Services	700-799 Employment	1100-1199 Transportation
300-399 Pets and Animals		800-899 Rentals	
		900-999 Real Estate	

1) Concert tickets ______________

2) Information on travel tours ______________

3) Horses for sale ______________

4) Someone to take care of your lawn ______________

5) Help with managing money ______________

Part D Below are abbreviations commonly found in help wanted and classified ads. Write the meaning of the abbreviation on the line.

1) BA ______________ 6) sunrf ______________

2) w/d ______________ 7) exp. ______________

3) elec. ______________ 8) P/T ______________

4) ps ______________ 9) immed. ______________

5) auto ______________ 10) WP ______________

Part E Read the following statements. If the statement is true, write *True* on the line. If the statement is not true, write *False*.

______ 1) The four major network television stations are ABC, CBS, NBC, and Fox Broadcasting Company.

______ 2) The Public Broadcasting System sells programs to subscribers.

______ 3) Cable networks get much of their money from donations.

______ 4) FCC stands for Federal Communications Commission.

______ 5) The FCC is a government agency that provides licenses to people or companies to operate television and radio stations.

 Life Skills English

Chapter 7 Mastery Test B

Chapter 8

Planning Guide

Completing Applications and Other Forms

	Student Text Lesson			
	Student Pages	Vocabulary	Practice Exercises	Lesson Review
Lesson 1 Personal Information	220-225	✔	✔	✔
Lesson 2 Job Application Forms	226-236	✔	✔	✔
Lesson 3 Filling Out a Financial Form	237-243	✔	✔	✔

Chapter Activities

Teacher's Resource Library

Putting It Together 8: Application Crossword Puzzle

Community Connection 8: Fill Out an Application Form

Assessment Options

Student Text

Chapter 8 Review

Teacher's Resource Library

Chapter 8 Mastery Tests A and B

Teaching Strategies						Language Skills			Learning Styles						Teacher's Resource Library		
Reviewing Skills	Teacher Alert	Career Application	Home Application	Global Connection	Community Application	Identification Skills	Writing Skills	Punctuation Skills	Visual/Spatial	Auditory/Verbal	Body/Kinesthetic	Logical/Mathematical	Group Learning	LEP/ESL	Activities	Workbook Activities	Self-Study Guide
220	221			221		✔	✔	✔			225						✔
226	233	229	228		230	✔	✔	✔						228	29	47-52	✔
237	242				240	✔	✔	✔				243				53	✔

Chapter at a Glance

Chapter 8: Completing Applications and Other Forms

pages 218–245

Lessons

1) **Personal Information**
   pages 220–225

2) **Job Application Forms**
   pages 226–236

3) **Filling Out a Financial Form** pages 237–243

Chapter 8 Review
pages 244–245

Teacher's Resource Library

Activities 28–29

Workbook Activities 46–53

Putting It Together 8

Community Connection 8

Chapter 8 Self-Study Guide

Chapter 8 Mastery Tests A and B

(Answer Keys for the Teacher's Resource Library begin on page 282 of this Teacher's Edition.)

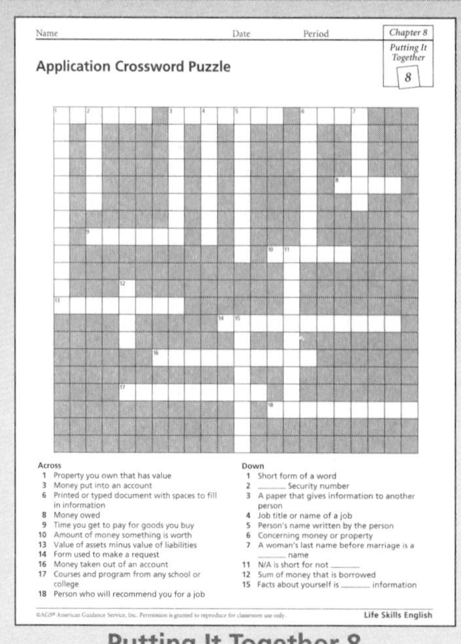

Name Date Period | Chapter 8 *Putting It Together* 8

Application Crossword Puzzle

Across
1 Property you own that has value
3 Money put into an account
6 Printed or typed document with spaces to fill in information
8 Money owed
9 Time you get to pay for goods you buy
10 Amount of money something is worth
13 Value of assets minus value of liabilities
14 Form used to make a request
16 Money taken out of an account
17 Courses and program from any school or college
18 Person who will recommend you for a job

Down
1 Short form of a word
2 ______ Security number
3 A paper that gives information to another person
4 Job title or name of a job
5 Person's name written by the person
6 Concerning money or property
7 A woman's last name before marriage is a ______ name
11 N/A is short for not ______
12 Sum of money that is borrowed
15 Facts about yourself is ______ information

 Life Skills English

Putting It Together 8

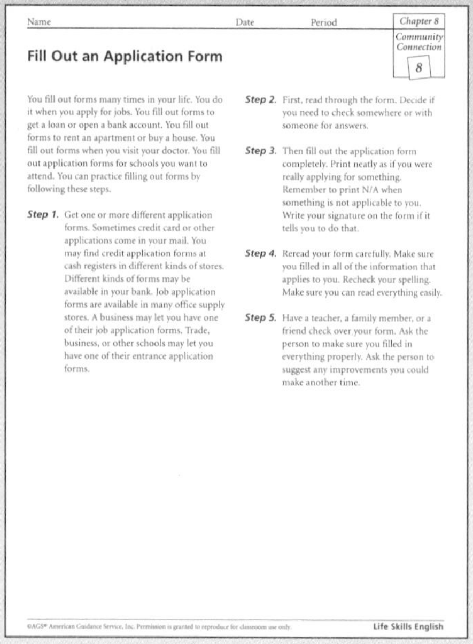

Name Date Period | Chapter 8 *Community Connection* 8

Fill Out an Application Form

You fill out forms many times in your life. You do it when you apply for jobs. You fill out forms to get a loan or open a bank account. You fill out forms to rent an apartment or buy a house. You fill out forms when you visit your doctor. You fill out application forms for schools you want to attend. You can practice filling out forms by following these steps.

Step 1. Get one or more different application forms. Sometimes credit card or other applications come in your mail. You may find credit application forms at cash registers in different kinds of stores. Different kinds of forms may be available in your bank. Job application forms are available in many office supply stores. A business may let you have one of their job application forms. Trade, business, or other schools may let you have one of their entrance application forms.

Step 2. First, read through the form. Decide if you need to check somewhere or with someone for answers.

Step 3. Then fill out the application form completely. Print neatly as if you were really applying for something. Remember to print N/A when something is not applicable to you. Write your signature on the form if it tells you to do that.

Step 4. Reread your form carefully. Make sure you filled in all of the information that applies to you. Recheck your spelling. Make sure you can read everything easily.

Step 5. Have a teacher, a family member, or a friend check over your form. Ask the person to make sure you filled in everything properly. Ask the person to suggest any improvements you could make another time.

 Life Skills English

Community Connection 8

Chapter 8

Completing Applications and Other Forms

Throughout your life, you will be asked to fill out forms. You may have to fill out a form to apply for a job, to obtain a driver's license, to rent an apartment, to open a checking account, or to travel to another country. A form is a printed or typed document with spaces to fill in information about you or someone else.

In Chapter 8, you will learn about completing different types of applications and forms. Each lesson focuses on the kinds of information you have to know to fill out forms and the different kinds of forms you may have to fill out.

Goals for Learning

- To learn how to fill out applications and other forms correctly and completely
- To learn about the kinds of personal information asked for on applications and forms
- To learn how to answer questions on job applications
- To learn about questions and vocabulary related to loans, credit, and financial forms

219

Reading Vocabulary

account (5)
apply (6)
focus (7)
license (5)
relate (6)
throughout (6)
vocabulary (7)

Introducing the Chapter

List the following items on the board in a column: driver's license, job, college degree, apartment, passport, bank account. Ask students what all the items in the list have in common. Accept all reasonable answers. Eventually, lead students to recognize that in order for people to obtain each item on the list, at some point, they must fill out a form. Then invite students to add to the list other items that require people to fill out forms. Explain to students that by the end of Chapter 8, they will know how to fill out many common forms.

SELF-STUDY GUIDE

Name ______

CHAPTER 8: Completing Applications and Other Forms

Goal 8.1 *To learn how to fill out applications and other forms correctly and completely*

Date	Assignment	Score
______	1: Read page 219.	______

Comments:

Goal 8.2 *To learn about the kinds of personal information asked for on applications and forms*

Date	Assignment	Score
______	2: Read page 220. Complete Activity A on page 220 and Activity B on page 221.	______
______	3: Read pages 221-222. Complete Activity C on page 222.	______
______	4: Complete Workbook Activity 46.	______
______	5: Read page 223. Complete Activity D on page 223.	______
______	6: Read page 224. Complete Activity E on page 224.	______
______	7: Complete the Lesson 1 Review, Parts A-C on page 225.	______

Comments:

Goal 8.3 *To learn how to answer questions on job applications*

Date	Assignment	Score
______	8: Read pages 226-227. Complete Activity A on page 227.	______
______	9: Read page 228. Complete Activity B on page 229.	______
______	10: Read page 229. Complete Activity C on page 230 and Activity D on page 231.	______
______	11: Read pages 231-232. Complete Activity E on page 232.	______
______	12: Read page 233. Complete Activity F on page 234.	______
______	13: Complete Workbook Activity 47.	______
______	14: Read page 235. Complete Activity G on page 235.	______

 Life Skills English

SELF-STUDY GUIDE

Name ______

CHAPTER 8 Completing Applications and Other Forms, continued

Goal 8.3 *To learn how to answer questions on job applications (continued)*

Date	Assignment	Score
______	15: Complete Workbook Activity 48.	______
______	16: Complete Workbook Activity 49.	______
______	17: Complete the Lesson 2 Review, Parts A-B on page 236.	______
______	18: Complete Workbook Activity 50.	______
______	19: Complete Workbook Activity 51.	______
______	20: Complete Workbook Activity 52.	______

Comments:

Goal 8.4 *To learn about questions and vocabulary related to loans, credit, and financial forms*

Date	Assignment	Score
______	21: Read page 237. Complete Activity A on page 237 and Activity B on page 238.	______
______	22: Read page 238. Complete Activity C on page 238.	______
______	23: Read page 239. Complete Activity D on page 239.	______
______	24: Read page 240. Complete Activity E on page 240.	______
______	25: Read page 241. Complete Activity F on page 241.	______
______	26: Complete Workbook Activity 53.	______
______	27: Read page 242. Complete Activity G on page 242.	______
______	28: Complete the Lesson 3 Review, Parts A-C on page 243.	______
______	29: Complete the Chapter 8 Review, Parts A-B on pages 244-245.	______

Comments:

Student's Signature ______ Date ______

Instructor's Signature ______ Date ______

 Life Skills English

Chapter 8 Self-Study Guide

Lesson at a Glance

Chapter 8 Lesson 1

Overview This lesson presents terms commonly associated with application forms and explains how to write a standard mailing address.

Objectives

- To identify the meanings of terms found on applications.
- To answer questions similar to those found on applications.
- To write a standard mailing address.

Student Pages 220–225

Teacher's Resource Library

Activity 28

Workbook Activity 46

Reading Vocabulary

abbreviation (8)
document (6)
form (3)
full name
initial (6)
legal (6)
maiden name
personal information
postal
provide (5)
require (6)
signature (6)
Social Security

Teaching Suggestions

Introducing the Lesson

Discuss the text, focusing on the terms introduced on page 220.

Reviewing Skills

Review how to follow directions.

Presenting Activity A

Read through the items with students. Students should skip any item that does not apply to them or that they do not know. If they are able to obtain the missing facts later, they can fill in any blanks they left.

Activity A Answers

Answers will vary.

Lesson 1 Personal Information

Document
A paper that gives information to another person.

Form
A printed or typed document with spaces to fill in information.

Full name
A person's whole legal name.

Maiden name
A woman's last name before she marries.

Personal information
Facts about yourself.

Signature
The name of a person written by that person.

Almost every **form** you complete asks for **personal information**. Personal information includes facts about yourself. You should know your Social Security number, date and place of birth, and telephone number. Sometimes you will be asked for the full names of your parents. You may also be asked for your mother's **maiden name**. A woman's maiden name is her last name before she marries and takes her husband's last name. Women are not required to take a husband's last name, but many women do. You may also be asked for the names and ages of your brothers and sisters.

It is important to know your **full name**, or your legal name.

Most forms must be signed with a legal **signature**. A signature is a person's name written by that person. You will use your legal signature on legal papers such as checks and other **documents**. A document is a paper that gives information to another person. You must always write, not print, your legal signature. You may also use your initials.

On most forms, you will need to provide your complete mailing address. Depending on the form, you may or may not be able to use abbreviations, or short forms of words. You will probably need to know the two-letter postal abbreviation for your state.

Activity A Write on your paper these facts about yourself.

1) Your Social Security number
2) Your date of birth (month, day, year)
3) Your place of birth (city, state, country)
4) Your home telephone number, including area code
5) Your father's full name
6) Your mother's full name
7) Your mother's maiden name
8) The names and ages of your brothers and sisters

Activity B Write on your paper the answers to these questions about yourself.

1) What is your full, legal name? Include your middle name if you have one.

2) Write your legal signature. Do not print your signature.

3) What is your complete address? Do not use any abbreviations. Use capitals and punctuation correctly. Follow the example below:

Mr. Howard Simmons
2121 48th Avenue, Apartment 101A
Seat Pleasant, Maryland 20716

4) What is the two-letter postal abbreviation of the state in which you live? For example, the abbreviation for California is CA.

5) What is your Social Security number?

6) What is your telephone number with the area code? Use this format: (301) 555-2938.

Your Name and Your Signature

You probably do not use your full, legal name all the time. People with nicknames, such as Rob for Roberto or Pam for Pamela, often sign their names that way. However, if you buy a house or rent an apartment, you will usually sign your full, legal name. When you open a checking account at a bank, you fill out a signature card. You are to sign your name on your checks exactly as you write it on that card.

Ray D. Ryan
Anna Maria DeMarco
Andy Thomas
Leon Jones-Washington

Reading Vocabulary

capital (5)
format
nickname (5)
punctuation (7)

Presenting Activity B

Have students take turns saying aloud their full legal name and nickname, if any. Invite students to share any interesting stories they have about their names. Students with nicknames may enjoy telling how they got them. Other students can explain how they were named. For example, were they named after a relative, a place, or an event?

Activity B Answers

Answers will vary.

Teacher Alert

Throughout this chapter, be sensitive to the fact that some students may not wish to share personal information, or because of family circumstances, may not know or have certain information available to them. With this in mind, you may decide to have students correct their own papers. It would also be advisable to only call upon volunteers to demonstrate activities.

Global Connection

Invite students whose names reflect their cultural heritage to share any background history they know about their first and last names. Students whose names have been Anglicized can give the comparable names in their primary languages. Students with ethnic names can provide the English version, if any.

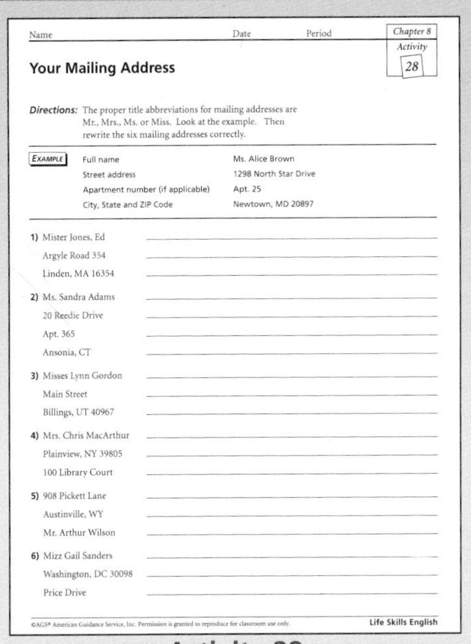

Name Date Period — Chapter 8 Activity 28

Your Mailing Address

Directions: The proper title abbreviations for mailing addresses are Mr., Mrs., Ms. or Miss. Look at the example. Then rewrite the six mailing addresses correctly.

EXAMPLE
Full name — Ms. Alice Brown
Street address — 1298 North Star Drive
Apartment number (if applicable) — Apt. 25
City, State and ZIP Code — Newtown, MD 20897

1) Mister Jones, Ed
Argyle Road 354
Linden, MA 16354

2) Ms. Sandra Adams
20 Reedie Drive
Apt. 365
Ansonia, CT

3) Misses Lynn Gordon
Main Street
Billings, UT 40967

4) Mrs. Chris MacArthur
Plainview, NY 39805
100 Library Court

5) 908 Pickett Lane
Austinville, WY
Mr. Arthur Wilson

6) Mizz Gail Sanders
Washington, DC 30098
Price Drive

 Life Skills English

Activity 28

Name Date Period — Chapter 8 Workbook Activity 46

Mailing Address

There is a special form for writing a mailing address. Study the examples below.

EXAMPLES
Full name: → Ms. Patricia Shukert
Street address: → 1611 Pond Meadow Drive
Apartment (if applicable): → Apt. 101
City, state, ZIP Code: → Fort Worth, TX 76109

Directions:
- Write your complete mailing address on the lines. Use the example as a guide.
- Use the punctuation and capitalization shown in the examples.
- Then follow the directions below.

1) Write the two-letter postal code for your state. ______
2) Write the abbreviation for your state. ______
3) If you live in an apartment, write the number exactly as you would write it on an envelope. ______
4) Circle your title. **A)** Mr. **B)** Miss **C)** Mrs. **D)** Ms.
5) Write your full name. ______
6) Write your street address. ______
7) Write your ZIP Code. ______
8) Write the name of your post office. ______
9) Sometimes the post office address is different from the subdivision you live in. Write your subdivision. ______
10) Check your name and address above. Is it exactly correct? ______ If not, make corrections.

 Life Skills English

Workbook Activity 46

Your Address

Most forms ask for your mailing address. Be sure that you can write your address in the correct form.

Mrs. Anna M. Wong
13 West Park Avenue
Apt. 102
Seattle, WA 98109

Postal Codes

The post office has its own method of abbreviating state names. The U.S. Postal Service uses a two-letter postal code. Both letters are capitalized and no periods are used. These abbreviations are used when you write addresses. In other situations, write out the full name of the state.

Activity C Write each of these state abbreviations on your paper. Next to the abbreviation, write the name of the state in full. Use a dictionary if necessary.

1) AK	**11)** HI	**21)** ME	**31)** NJ	**41)** SD
2) AL	**12)** IA	**22)** MI	**32)** NM	**42)** TN
3) AR	**13)** ID	**23)** MN	**33)** NV	**43)** TX
4) AZ	**14)** IL	**24)** MS	**34)** NY	**44)** UT
5) CA	**15)** IN	**25)** MO	**35)** OH	**45)** VA
6) CO	**16)** KS	**26)** MT	**36)** OK	**46)** VT
7) CT	**17)** KY	**27)** NC	**37)** OR	**47)** WA
8) DE	**18)** LA	**28)** ND	**38)** PA	**48)** WI
9) FL	**19)** MA	**29)** NE	**39)** RI	**49)** WV
10) GA	**20)** MD	**30)** NH	**40)** SC	**50)** WY

Reading Vocabulary

abbreviate (8)
capitalize (9)
code (5)
method (6)
situation (5)

■ Presenting Activity C

Hand out 50 index cards. Assign each student one or more states so that all 50 have been assigned. Then read each state abbreviation and have the class tell the state it stands for. The student assigned that state should print the abbreviation on one side of a card and the full state name on the other. Then divide the class into two teams. Place shuffled cards in a pile with the state name side up. Have teams take turns picking a card, reading the state name, and telling the abbreviation. If the team answers correctly, they keep the card. If not, they put the card back in the pile. When all the cards are gone, the game is over.

Activity C Answers

1) Alaska **2)** Alabama **3)** Arkansas **4)** Arizona **5)** California **6)** Colorado **7)** Connecticut **8)** Delaware **9)** Florida **10)** Georgia **11)** Hawaii **12)** Iowa **13)** Idaho **14)** Illinois **15)** Indiana **16)** Kansas **17)** Kentucky **18)** Louisiana **19)** Massachusetts **20)** Maryland **21)** Maine **22)** Michigan **23)** Minnesota **24)** Mississippi **25)** Missouri **26)** Montana **27)** North Carolina **28)** North Dakota **29)** Nebraska **30)** New Hampshire **31)** New Jersey **32)** New Mexico **33)** Nevada **34)** New York **35)** Ohio **36)** Oklahoma **37)** Oregon **38)** Pennsylvania **39)** Rhode Island **40)** South Carolina **41)** South Dakota **42)** Tennessee **43)** Texas **44)** Utah **45)** Virginia **46)** Vermont **47)** Washington **48)** Wisconsin **49)** West Virginia **50)** Wyoming

Your Social Security Number

Almost every form and application you will ever fill out will ask for your Social Security number. For example:

- A bank, when you open a savings account.
- Your employer, when you apply for a job.
- The government, when you file a tax return.
- A stockbroker, if you buy stocks or bonds.
- Colleges, if you enroll in courses.
- The Social Security Administration, if you apply for benefits.

When you apply for a Social Security card, the form asks for your full name as used in business and for the names of your parents.

Activity D In your own words, explain in one or two sentences why it is important to have a Social Security card. Write your explanation on your paper.

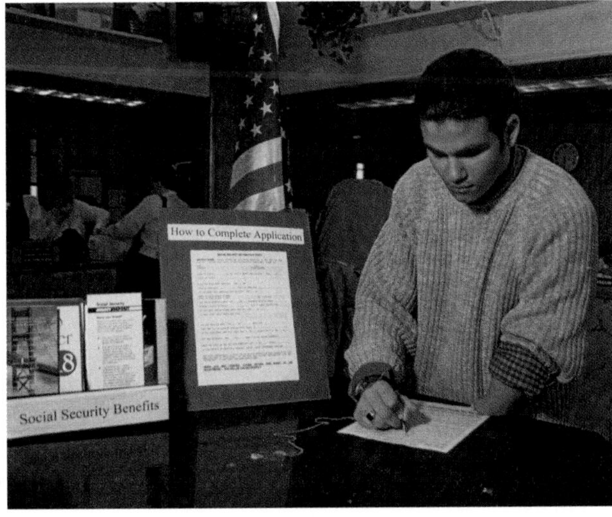

You must fill out an application to receive a Social Security card.

Reading Vocabulary

administration (7)
benefit (5)
bond (6)
college (5)
enroll (7)
stock (5)
stockbroker
tax (5)

■ Presenting Activity D

Before students write their explanations, engage them in a discussion of the importance of having a Social Security card. You might want to list students' best ideas on the board. Students can then refer to this list of ideas as they write their explanations.

Activity D Answers

Answers will vary. Students might include in their explanations some of the following: to obtain a job; to open a bank account; to file a tax return; to enroll in college; to apply for Social Security benefits.

Completing Applications and Other Forms Chapter 8 **223**

Reading Vocabulary

acceptable
alien
certificate (5)
citizenship (6)
contact (6)
fee (7)
green card
native (5)
naturalize (8)
official (5)
photocopy
register (6)
responsibility (6)

■ Presenting Activity E

If you have students in your class who are not United States citizens or who have family members who are not citizens, invite them to share their knowledge of the alien registration process and of the naturalization process. Some students and their family members may feel a stigma attached to green cards and the "alien" designation. Be sensitive to this and be sure other students in the class are as well. Remind students that the United States is a nation of immigrants. Stress that this country is enriched by the contributions of people from all cultures and backgrounds.

Activity E Answers

Some answers will vary. Possible responses are given.

1) To obtain a passport; to prove citizenship of the U.S.; to get a Social Security card **2)** To get a driver's license; to get a job **3)** green card **4)** the city and state in which you were born

Your Birth Certificate

To apply for a Social Security number, you will need an official copy of your birth certificate. An official copy of a birth certificate has a raised seal. A photocopy is not acceptable. If you don't have a copy, contact the capital of the state where you were born. Give them your full name and date of birth and ask them to send you your birth certificate. You will probably have to pay a fee.

If you were born in the United States, you are a United States citizen. If you were born in another country and one of your parents is a U.S. citizen, you are also a U.S. citizen.

A person who was not born in the United States may apply for citizenship. He or she then becomes a "naturalized" citizen and receives citizenship papers. These people have all of the rights and responsibilities of native citizens.

A person who was not born in the United States and who is not a naturalized citizen must register with the state as an alien. He or she may then apply for a green card. A green card is an official document that allows aliens to work legally in the United States. Green cards used to be the color green. They are still called green cards even though they are no longer that color.

Activity E Write on your paper your answers to these questions. Then discuss your answers with your class.

1) When might it be important to have a birth certificate that proves you were born in the United States?

2) When might you have to use your birth certificate to prove your age?

3) What does someone who is not a citizen need to work legally in the United States?

4) What city and state would you contact to get a copy of your birth certificate?

Lesson 1 Review

Part A Number your paper from 1 to 9. Write the correct letter of the definition beside the number of each word.

Terms	Meanings
1) Form	a) A printed paper with spaces to fill in information
2) Document	b) 214-45-4501
3) Social Security number	c) A woman's last name at birth
4) Signature	d) Name recorded at birth
5) Birth certificate	e) (931) 264-4592
6) Citizen	f) Your name as you write it
7) Legal name	g) Person belonging to a country
8) Maiden name	h) Official paper stating when and where a person was born
9) Telephone number	i) A paper with official information

Part B Write on your paper your answers to these questions.

1) What is your legal name?
2) What is your signature?
3) What is your mother's maiden name?
4) What is your Social Security number?
5) What do you need to know and what documents do you need when you apply for a Social Security number?

Part C Write this mailing address on your paper. Put the information in the correct order and spell it correctly.

Ms. Tara Gillan, Franklin, Pa 15222, Route 1, P.O. Box 23

Reading Vocabulary

definition (6)

Part A Answers

1) a 2) i 3) b 4) f 5) h 6) g 7) d 8) c 9) e

Part B Answers

1) Answers will vary.
2) Answers will vary.
3) Answers will vary.
4) Answers will vary.
5) You need an official copy of your birth certificate. You need to know your full name and the names of your parents.

Part C Answers

Ms. Tara Gillan
Route 1, P.O. Box 23
Franklin, PA 15222

Learning Styles

Body/Kinesthetic

On separate slips of paper, print the nine terms from Part A of the review on page 225. Call on volunteers to choose a slip and to use charades, pantomimes, riddles, hints, drawings, and so on to demonstrate the term on their slip of paper. Have the other members of the class try to guess which term the volunteer is demonstrating.

Lesson at a Glance

Chapter 8 Lesson 2

Overview This lesson explains the meaning of terms used on job application forms and how to fill in a job application form.

Objectives

- To understand how to complete job application forms.
- To understand terms associated with job application forms.

Student Pages 226–236

Teacher's Resource Library

Activity 29

Workbook Activities 47–52

Reading Vocabulary

application (8)
available (6)
consider (5)
employee (6)
employer (6)
former (6)
position (4)
previous (6)
refer (6)
request (6)
salary (5)
supervisor (7)

Teaching Suggestions

Introducing the Lesson

Focus students' attention on the blank job application form on page 226. What similarities and differences are there between the sample job application form and actual forms students have completed? Discuss any parts of the sample form that students do not understand or would have trouble completing.

Reviewing Skills Provide a review of writing one's full name and mailing address.

Lesson 2 Job Application Forms

Application
A form to make a request.

Available
Refers to when you can begin a job.

Employee
A person who works for someone else.

Employer
A person or company that pays you a salary.

Former
Refers to something that happened in the past.

Position
The name of your job.

Previous
Refers to something that happened in the past.

Salary
The amount of money you are paid for working.

Supervisor
A person who is your boss.

You will often have to complete an **application** form. An application is a form to make a request. A job application form is your request that a company consider you for a job. You will have to provide many kinds of information on application forms.

Here is a list of words you will find on many job application forms.

Words	Meanings
Position	The name of your job
Employer	The person or company that pays you a salary
Employee	A person who works for someone else
Supervisor	Your boss
Salary	Amount of money you are paid
Previous/Former	Something that happened in the past
Available	When you can begin a job

Here is part of a job application form.

Employer ____________________

Address ____________________

Phone (   ) ____________

Supervisor ____________________

Dates employed: from __/__/__ to __/__/__

Position title ____________________

No. hours worked/week ____________________

Salary: starting $______ ☐ hourly ☐ weekly ☐ monthly

ending $______ ☐ hourly ☐ weekly ☐ monthly

Description of work: ____________________

Advice for Completing Applications

Rule 1	Answer every question. Never leave a question unanswered. The employer will think you forgot to answer it or that you cannot answer it.
Rule 2	There may be some questions that are not **applicable** to you. Applicable means suitable or appropriate. You do not have to answer questions that are not applicable. Instead, you can write N/A for not applicable in those spaces. The employer will know that you read the question.
Rule 3	Always print or type your answers. Often people do not get a job because the employer can't read their application form.
Rule 4	Be sure your answers are correct. Every fact on your application must be accurate. If the employer tries to call you to offer you the job, you want the right phone number on your application. At the end of the form, you will be asked to sign it to verify that all the information is true and accurate. Any false answer that you provide could mean that you will not get the job.

Applicable

Something that is appropriate or suitable.

Activity A Answer the following questions.

1) Some employers "grade" a job application. They check the answer to every question and give the application a score. The people with the highest scores are then interviewed. What do you think a neat, complete, and correct job application tells the employer about you?

2) Why should you be very careful that your answers are correct?

3) What is the difference between a "false" answer and a mistake? Is there any way for an employer to know why the information is wrong?

Reading Vocabulary

accurate (6) interview (6)
applicable suitable (6)
appropriate (6) verify (9)
false (6)

■ Presenting Activity A

Divide students into small groups. Suggest that each group use the questions in Activity A as a basis for a group discussion about completing job applications. Before they begin, each group should choose a group leader who reads each question and makes sure the discussion stays on track. Each group can also choose a secretary, or recorder, who can write down any additional questions that might arise during the discussion as well as summaries of students' responses. Allow time for the groups to cover all three questions, then bring the groups together and invite them to share their answers.

Activity A Answers

Answers will vary. Possible responses are given.

1) A neat, complete, and correct application indicates that the person cares about the impression he or she makes, pays attention to details, and does accurate work. **2)** The potential employer reading the application does not know if you made an error or were not telling the truth. **3)** A false answer is a deliberate attempt to give inaccurate information. A mistake is inaccurate information given in error. Employers can find out that information is incorrect in a variety of ways. A few examples include checking educational records, asking questions of former employers, and talking to persons provided as references by the applicant.

Reading Vocabulary

attend (5)
career (6)
combination (6)
education (5)
item (6)
location (6)
specialty
subject (5)
university (5)

APPLICATION

At Home
Parents and other family members with work experience can offer students insight into the value employers place on a job applicant's education history. Encourage students to discuss their education and career plans with family members. Suggest that students keep questions such as the following in mind as they formulate their career goals:

- Are my expectations reasonable considering my education?
- What types of courses should I take in the future to obtain a job in my chosen field?
- What family members and friends can I turn to for advice about this type of work?

LEARNING STYLES

LEP/ESL
On the board, make two columns. In Column #1, print the following seven terms: *position, employer, employee, supervisor, salary, previous/former,* and *available.* Then ask students for whom English is a second language to translate these terms into their primary language. Ask them to write their translations in Column #2 and then to give examples of what the terms mean to them. Invite volunteers to share stories about when they have needed to know and use these terms.

Questions About Your Education

> *Education*
> *A combination of the courses and programs taken at a school or college.*

Whenever you apply for a job, you will be asked about your **education**. Education refers to the courses and programs you have taken at any school or college.

Keep your educational records in a special place. You may change jobs several times during your career. Each time you apply for a new job, you will need this information.

Here is a sample of a completed job application form. Notice how many items relate to education.

Job Application Form

Print Name Margaret Louisa Gomez

Address 9301 Watkins Ave., Apt. 101, Wilton, Delaware 19973

Home Phone (302) 217-3881 Business Phone (302) 217-2800

College or University: University of Delaware, Newark, Delaware

Major and specialty: Business Administration, Accounting

Dates attended: From 9/85 To 6/89 Degree received ☑ Yes ☐ No

If yes, give title and date B.S. 6/89

If no, give number of credit hours completed N/A Years completed: N/A

List pertinent courses completed Accounting, Marketing, Business Administration

Other Training: Wilton Business School, Wilton, Delaware
(Name and Location of School)

Subject studied: Word Processing, Computerized Bookkeeping

Dates attended: From 9/92 To 6/94 Years completed: Day __ Night 2

228 Chapter 8 Completing Applications and Other Forms

Activity B Answer these questions about yourself. Print your answers on your paper.

1) What was the name of the last high school you attended?

2) Where was this school located (city and state)?

3) When did you attend this school (From ______ To ______)?

4) On what date did you graduate or do you expect to graduate?

5) What were the chief courses that you took?

Your Job Skills

Pertinent
Applicable.

Employers want to know about your skills. When you apply for a job, list skills that are **pertinent**. That means the skills that are applicable to the job for which you are applying. Here are some machines that office workers often use. A person applying for an office job might list all or some of these on an application.

- copier
- word processor
- document binder
- FAX machine
- telephones
- calculator
- dictation machine
- switchboard
- computer
- printers
- videotape recorders and camcorders
- audiocassette players and recorders
- postage meter

Reading Vocabulary

audiocassette	meter (6)
binder (11)	**pertinent (10)**
calculator	postage (5)
camcorder	processor
computer (8)	recorder (8)
dictation	switchboard
graduate (6)	videotape

■ Presenting Activity B

Suggest that students print their responses to the questions in Activity B as if they were actually completing an application. Point out to students that when they are asked to list courses they have taken, they should consider which of those courses would help them better perform the job for which they are applying. They should list those courses first.

Activity B Answers

Answers will vary.

Application

Career Connection Although some of the machines listed on page 229 may be very familiar to students, others may not be as familiar. Arrange for the class to visit a business office where they can see many or all of these machines at work. If that is not possible, try to obtain pictures of the machines and detailed descriptions of each machine's function in an office.

Name ______ Date ______ Period ______ *Chapter 8* *Activity* *29*

Application for Employment

Directions: Complete this form. If a question does not apply to you, write "N/A."

APPLICATION FOR EMPLOYMENT

PERSONAL INFORMATION

Date ______ Social Security Number ______

Name ______ (*last* *first* *middle*) Sex ______

Present Address ______ (*street* *city* *state* *ZIP code*)

Phone No. ______ (*area code*) Age 18 or older? ______

Are you either a U.S. citizen or an alien authorized to work in the U.S.? ______

EDUCATION	Name and Location of School	Years Attended	Date Graduated	Subjects Studied
High School				
College				

FORMER EMPLOYERS List below your last two employers, starting with the last one first.

Date Month / Year	Name and Address of Employer	Salary	Position	Reason for Leaving
From To				
From To				

REFERENCES Give below the names of three persons not related to you and whom you have known at least one year.

Name	Address	Phone	Business	Years Aquainted
1.				
2.				
3.				

Position Desired ______ Salary Desired ______ Date you can start ______

Are you presently employed? ______ May we contact your present employer? ______

I certify that the above information is accurate and understand that, if employed, falsified statements on this application are grounds for dismissal. I authorize investigation of all data given and all references listed.

Date ______ Applicant's Signature ______

 Life Skills English

Activity 29

Reading Vocabulary

accounting (5), data (9), database, describe (5), desktop, entry (6), graphic (11), management, operate (5), paid, process (6), publish (6), software, specific (8), spreadsheet, system (5), volunteer (5)

Presenting Activity C

Be sure students understand all of the computer-related terms listed in item 5. A dictionary of computer terms may be helpful to have on hand. Students may actually be familiar with these types of software without being aware, for example, that a program is a database management program or a graphics program. In other words, they may be familiar with the program and its specific name, such as *Filemaker Pro,* without being aware that it's a database program.

Activity C Answers

Answers will vary.

APPLICATION

In the Community

Students with computer skills might wish to volunteer their services at the library, the school office, or any community organization that could use assistance entering data into existing programs. Students with advanced computer skills might also help set up a program that would improve office efficiency. Remind students that they can list volunteer work on job applications as experience. Not only does this indicate a level of competency in a certain area, but it also shows potential employers that the applicant has concern for and is willing to help others.

Activity C Answer these questions about yourself. Print your answers on your paper.

1) List any machines that you can operate. Describe in your own words why you think being able to operate a specific machine will help you get the job you want.

2) Can you type? If yes, give the number of words per minute (wpm). Do you think knowing how to type is a useful skill? Explain your answer.

3) Can you use a computer? What kinds of computer systems have you used?

4) Have you ever used a computer for schoolwork? If yes, describe when. Have you ever used a computer on a volunteer or paid job? If yes, describe when.

5) What kinds of software can you use? Examples are word processing, spreadsheet, database management, accounting, graphics, and desktop publishing.

6) List any other special skills that you have.

If you apply for a data entry job, you should list all of your computer skills.

230 Chapter 8 Completing Applications and Other Forms

Activity D Use the information in the sample job application form on page 228 to answer these questions. Write your answers on your paper.

1) Name the college that Margaret Louisa Gomez attended.

2) What was her major course of study?

3) Did she graduate from college? If so, when?

4) What kind of degree did she earn?

5) Which of her college courses did Margaret think were pertinent to this job?

6) What does N/A mean?

7) What other school did Margaret attend?

8) Did Margaret take any computer courses? If yes, what kind?

Questions About Your Employer and Immediate Supervisor

Your employer is the person or company that you work for. Your immediate supervisor is your boss, the person who tells you what to do. Your employer and your immediate supervisor can be the same person; however, they usually are different people.

EXAMPLES

Joseph Piña works for Howard J. Dauss, Contractors. Mr. Dauss owns the company. He pays Joseph for his work. Mr. Dauss is Joseph's employer.

Joseph is an apprentice plumber for the company. His boss is a foreman. The foreman's name is Mike Sievers. Mike is Joseph's immediate supervisor.

Reading Vocabulary

apprentice (5)
contractor
foreman (6)
immediate
major (6)
plumber (6)

■ Presenting Activity D

Do Activity A together as an oral activity. After students have answered all of the questions about the sample job application, have them suggest what kind of job Ms. Gomez might be applying for. Then have them scan the help wanted ads in the classified sections of several newspapers to identify jobs that might interest Margaret Louisa Gomez, based on the information in her application form.

Activity D Answers

1) University of Delaware
2) Business Administration, Accounting **3)** Yes; June, 1989
4) B.S. (Bachelor of Science)
5) Accounting, Business Administration, Marketing
6) Not Applicable
7) Wilton Business School
8) Yes; Word Processing and Computerized Bookkeeping

Reading Vocabulary

agent (5)
bookkeeper (5)
drafter
electrician
employment (6)
journeyman
layout
lease (8)
receptionist
secretary (5)
senior (6)
technician
temporary (8)
title (5)

■ Presenting Activity E

Before students complete Activity E, help them generate a list of job titles that are of particular interest to them. Begin by having students select titles of interest from those listed on page 232. Then distribute copies of newspaper help wanted ads, preferably from a large city Sunday paper. Have students look through the ads for additional job titles to add to the list.

Activity E Answers

1) apprentice plumber **2)** Mike Sievers **3)** Howard J. Dauss, Contractors **4)** Answers will vary.

Questions About Your Positions and Job Titles

A position is a job title. It is the name of a job. By knowing job titles, you can find jobs that interest you in the help wanted ads in the newspaper.

EXAMPLES

apprentice plumber
bookkeeper
carpenter
computer technician
electrician journeyman
layout drafter
leasing agent
receptionist
secretary
senior bus driver

Activity E Use the information above and on page 231 to answer these questions. Write your answers on your paper.

1) What is Joseph Piña's job title?

2) Who is Joseph Piña's immediate supervisor?

3) Who is Joseph Piña's employer?

4) On your own paper, make a chart of your employment history. Start with the most recent job and work back. List every job, including part-time, temporary, or volunteer positions. Use these headings to create your chart: *Dates of Employment, Position, Employer, Supervisor.*

DATES OF EMPLOYMENT	POSITION	EMPLOYER	SUPERVISOR

More About Your Work Experience

The Standard Form 171 is the name of the federal government job application form. It is also called a Personal Qualifications Statement. It is a good example of the information you need to know about your experience.

WORK EXPERIENCE *If you have no work experience, write "NONE" and go to 25 on page 3.*

23 May we ask your present employer about your character, qualifications, and work record? *A "NO" will not affect our review of your qualifications. If you answer "NO" and we need to contact your present employer before we can offer you a job, we will contact you first.* . . . . YES | NO

24 READ **WORK EXPERIENCE** IN THE INSTRUCTIONS BEFORE YOU BEGIN.

- Describe your current or most recent job in Block **A** and work backwards, describing each job you held **during the past 10 years**. If you were **unemployed** for longer than **3 months** within the past 10 years, list the dates and your address(es) in an experience block.
- You may sum up in one block work that you did **more than 10 years ago**. But if that work **is related** to the type of job you are applying for, describe each related job in a separate block.
- INCLUDE VOLUNTEER WORK *(non-paid work)*--**If the work** *(or a part of the work)* **is like the job you are applying for,** complete **all** parts of the experience block just as you would for a paying job. You may receive credit for work experience with religious, community, welfare, service, and other organizations.
- INCLUDE MILITARY SERVICE--You should complete **all** parts of the experience block just as you would for a non-military job, including all supervisory experience. Describe each major change of duties or responsibilities in a separate experience block.
- IF YOU NEED MORE SPACE TO DESCRIBE A JOB--Use sheets of paper the same size as this page (be sure to include **all** information we ask for in **A** and **B** below). On **each** sheet show your name, Social Security Number, and the announcement number or job title.
- IF YOU NEED MORE EXPERIENCE BLOCKS, use the SF 171-A or a sheet of paper.
- IF YOU NEED TO UPDATE (ADD MORE RECENT JOBS), use the SF 172 or a sheet of paper as described above.

A Name and address of employer's organization *(include ZIP Code, if known)*	Dates employed *(give month, day and year)* From: To:	Average number of hours per week	Number of employees you supervise
	Salary or earnings Starting $ per Ending $ per	Your reason for wanting to leave	
Your immediate supervisor Name Area Code Telephone No.	Exact title of your job	If Federal employment *(civilian or military)* list series, grade or rank, and, if promoted in this job, the date of your last promotion	

Description of work: Describe your specific duties, responsibilities and accomplishments in this job, **including** the job title(s) of any employees you supervise. *If you describe more than one type of work (for example, carpentry and painting, or personnel and budget), write the approximate percentage of time you spent doing each.*

For Agency Use (skill codes, etc.)

B Name and address of employer's organization *(include ZIP Code, if known)*	Dates employed *(give month, day and year)* From: To:	Average number of hours per week	Number of employees you supervised
	Salary or earnings Starting $ per Ending $ per	Your reason for leaving	
Your immediate supervisor Name Area Code Telephone No.	Exact title of your job	If Federal employment *(civilian or military)* list series, grade or rank, and, if promoted in this job, the date of your last promotion	

Description of work: Describe your specific duties, responsibilities and accomplishments in this job, **including** the job title(s) of any employees you supervised. *If you describe more than one type of work (for example, carpentry and painting, or personnel and budget), write the approximate percentage of time you spent doing each.*

For Agency Use (skill codes, etc.)

Page 2 IF YOU NEED MORE EXPERIENCE BLOCKS, USE SF 171-A *(SEE BACK OF INSTRUCTION PAGE).*

Reading Vocabulary

federal (6) standard (6)
qualification (7)

Teacher Alert

The Application for Federal Employment-SF 171 is an extensive six-page document that includes one page of detailed instructions. Completing this form would provide students with an excellent real-life opportunity to use what they have learned in Lessons 1 and 2. You can obtain copies of Standard Form 171 by contacting any federal office.

Completing Applications and Other Forms Chapter 8 **233**

Reading Vocabulary

accomplishment (6)
civilian (8)
earnings
exact (6)
manufacture (5)
military (5)
organization (7)
promotion (6)
response (6)
rank (6)
series (5)
supervise (7)

■ Presenting Activity F

Some students may have never worked; others may have limited work experience. Because of this, you may wish to do Activity F as a whole class activity. Accept several responses from different students for each item.

Activity F Answers

Answers will vary.

Activity F Here are items you would have to fill in on a Standard Form 171. Use a job you have now or one you have had in the past to complete each item. Write your responses on your paper.

1) Name, address, and phone number of employer's organization (include ZIP code and area code)

2) Dates employed (give month, day, and year)
From ______
To ______

3) Average number of hours per week

4) Salary or earnings; $ ______ per week or per hour

5) Place of employment (city and state)

6) Exact title of your position

7) Name of immediate supervisor and phone number (include area code)

8) Number and kind of employees you supervise

9) Kind of business or organization (manufacturing, accounting, social services, etc.)

10) If you worked for the federal government, give your civilian or military series, your grade or rank, and date of last promotion

11) Your reason for wanting to leave

12) Description of work (tell about your specific duties, responsibilities, and accomplishments in this job)

13) Whether your present or former employer can be contacted

234 *Chapter 8 Completing Applications and Other Forms*

Name ______ Date ______ Period ______

Chapter 8 *Workbook Activity* 47

Word Scramble for Applications

A. Directions: Unscramble these words. Then use them to fill in the missing words in the sentences below.

Scrambled Words	Unscrambled Words
1) PPIINOTAACL	1) ______
2) AIENMD	2) ______
3) ALYSRA	3) ______
4) BBNTVRAEIAIO	4) ______
5) ZTNCIIE	5) ______
6) ERUTASIGN	6) ______
7) SSBO	7) ______
8) LULF	8) ______
9) EEEEFRRCN	9) ______
10) SIITOONP	10) ______

B.

1) At the bottom of the form, please write your ______.

2) Your immediate supervisor is your ______.

3) A ______ is the same as a job title.

4) A shortened form of a word is an ______.

5) The amount of money that you earn is your ______.

6) Maria was born in New York; therefore, she is a ______ of the United States.

7) Before she was married, Rosa Gomez's name was Rosa Hernandez. Hernandez is her ______ name.

8) Before the job interview, Yolanda was asked to fill out a job ______.

9) Your whole legal name is your ______ name.

10) Martin worked for Donna Smith for three years. He gave her name as a job ______.

 Life Skills English

Workbook Activity 47

Your Job Application References

When you fill out a job application, you are asking that you be hired for a certain job. A reference is a person who will recommend you for that job. Always ask a person's permission before you use his or her name as a reference.

A reference should be

- a person who knows about your skills and past work experience.
- a person who likes and admires you and will say positive things about you.
- a person whom the new employer will believe and respect.

A reference should not be

- a relative.
- a person who did not like you or your work.

USING WHAT YOU HAVE LEARNED

Write the names, complete addresses, and phone numbers in your personal address book of the three people you added to the list in Activity G. You will need this information when you apply for jobs.

Activity G Explain why each of these people would or would not be a good reference. Write your answers on your paper. Then name three references of your own and explain why each person would be a good reference.

1) A teacher

2) A guidance counselor

3) A previous employer

4) Your present employer

5) Your best friend

6) A relative

7) A member of the clergy

8) Your next-door neighbor

Reading Vocabulary

clergy (8)
counselor
guidance (9)
member (5)
positive (6)
recommend (6)
reference (6)
relative (5)

■ Presenting Activity G

Ask students to imagine what they would say if they had to recommend themselves for a job. What character traits would make them valuable to an employer? Have students write a positive, honest reference for themselves. Then invite volunteers to share their references with the class.

Activity G Answers

Answers may vary. Possible responses are given.

1) Teacher—good because a teacher knows a person's skills and work habits. **2)** Guidance counselors—good because they know a person's school history and reputation. **3)** Previous employer—good if they liked your work. **4)** Present employer—good if they like your work. **5)** Your best friend—not good; he or she might be biased. **6)** A relative—not good; he or she might also be biased in your favor. **7)** Clergy—good because they are respected in the community. **8)** Neighbor—good because he or she has a chance to observe your behavior.

USING WHAT YOU HAVE LEARNED

Remind students that references should not be relatives or people who did not like or respect their work.

Name Date Period

Chapter 8 Workbook Activity 48

Filling Out an Application

A. Directions: Below is a list of terms that can be found on job applications. Next to each term in column A write the letter of the meaning found in column B.

A	B
_____ **1)** Position desired	**a)** people who can verify your good work habits
_____ **2)** Full name	**b)** name of job you want
_____ **3)** Education	**c)** when you can begin a job
_____ **4)** Personal information	**d)** an area of study in which a student spends the most time and effort
_____ **5)** References	**e)** your whole legal name
_____ **6)** Occupation	**f)** amount of money you expect to earn
_____ **7)** Experience	**g)** courses and programs from a school or college
_____ **8)** Major	**h)** the same kind of work that you have done before
_____ **9)** Expected salary	**i)** facts about yourself
_____ **10)** Available	**j)** a profession or vocation

B. There are two correct forms of printing for a job application. One is all capital letters.

EXAMPLE BETTY JONES

The second correct form has capital letters only at the beginning of words, and small letters everywhere else.

EXAMPLE Betty Jones

Directions: Following are some samples of the way people filled in an application. If the printing is correct, write C on the line. If the printing is incorrect, write I on the line. Then print it correctly. The first one is done.

I 1) HARoLd P. DAVIS Harold P. Davis
___ 2) 3113 CLARK LANE
___ 3) February 14
___ 4) SuN ORdeR CompAny
___ 5) Cashier
___ 6) Ms. JAne Q. DAvis
___ 7) 210 Snowhill Court
___ 8) DRAKE HIGH SCHOOL
___ 9) BUSINESS EDUCATION
___ 10) RelAtionship: MOTHER

 Life Skills English

Workbook Activity 48

Name Date Period

Chapter 8 Workbook Activity 49

Application Forms Acrostic

Directions: Read each clue. Fill in the blanks with the letter of the words that match each clue. Then solve the acrostic message.

1) A form used to make a request — 1 5 5 10 7 6 1 4 7 15 12

2) Printed document with spaces to fill in information — 3 15 9 13

3) A nine digit identification number (2 words) — 2 15 6 7 1 10   2 16 6 14 9 7 4 17

4) Person belonging to a country — 6 7 4 7 11 16 12

5) Appropriate, suitable — 1 5 5 10 7 6 1 8 10 16

6) A paper with information — 18 15 6 14 13 16 12 4

7) Your name as you write it — 2 7 19 12 1 4 14 9 16

8) Courses and programs from a school or college — 16 18 14 6 1 4 7 15 12

9) A person who will recommend you for a job — 9 16 3 16 9 16 12 6 16

10) Boss or supervisor — 16 13 5 10 15 17 16 9

Acrostic Message

1 6 6 14 9 1 6 17   6 15 14 12 4 2

 Life Skills English

Workbook Activity 49

Part A Answers

1) to request a job 2) N/A
3) so that the employer knows that you read the application carefully and does not think that you are trying to hide information 4) your signature 5) name, address, telephone number, position
6) your present or most recent position

Part B Answers

1) e 2) a 3) h 4) j 5) b 6) c
7) d 8) f 9) g 10) i

Lesson 2 Review

Part A Write the answers to these questions on your paper.

1) What is the purpose of a job application?
2) What do you write in a space if the question does not apply to you?
3) Why is it important to answer every question on a job application form?
4) You may print or type your answers on a job application. What is the one thing that you must write?
5) What information do you need about people you want to give as references?
6) When you tell about your work experience, which job do you describe first?

Part B Match the words with their meanings. Write the correct letter next to each number on your paper.

Words	Meanings
1) Job application	a) Your school experience
2) Education	b) The name of your job
3) Reference	c) Your boss
4) Work experience	d) The person or company you work for
5) Position	e) A form you fill out to ask for a job
6) Immediate supervisor	f) Your earnings
7) Employer	g) Your written legal name
8) Salary	h) A person who will recommend you for a job
9) Signature	i) Your first, middle, and last name
10) Full name	j) The jobs you have had

Name Date Period | *Chapter 8 Workbook Activity 50*

Application for Employment, Part 1

Directions: Complete this form. Answer all the questions. If a question does not apply to you, answer it with "N/A."

Date of Application ______

Position(s) Applied For ______

Name ______ LAST FIRST MIDDLE

Address ______ NUMBER STREET CITY STATE ZIP CODE

Phone No. (____) ______ AREA CODE Social Security No. ______

Are you a citizen of the United States? ☐ Yes ☐ No

If not, do you possess a green card? ☐ Yes ☐ No

If yes, give Alien Registration Number ______

Are you available to work? ☐ Full Time ☐ Part Time ☐ Shift Work

Are you on layoff and subject to recall? ☐ Yes ☐ No

Can you travel if a job requires it? ☐ Yes ☐ No

Have you been convicted of a felony within the last 7 years? ☐ No ☐ Yes

If yes, explain ______

Are you a veteran of the U.S. military service? ☐ Yes ☐ No

If yes, what branch? ______

What foreign languages do you speak, read, and/or write? ______

Do you have any physical, mental or medical, impairment or disability that would limit your job performance for the position for which you are applying? ☐ No ☐ Yes If yes, explain

List professional, trade, business, or civic activities and offices held.

Give name, address, and phone number of three references not related to you.

 Life Skills English

Workbook Activity 50

Name Date Period | *Chapter 8 Workbook Activity 51*

Application for Employment, Part 2

Employment History
List each job held. Start with your present or last job. Include military service assignments and volunteer activities.

		Dates		
1	Employer:	From	To	Work Performed
	Address:			
	Job Title:	Hrly. Rate/Salary		
	Supervisor:	Starting	Final	
	Reason for Leaving:			
2	Employer:	Dates From	To	Work Performed
	Address:			
	Job Title:	Hrly. Rate/Salary		
	Supervisor:	Starting	Final	
	Reason for Leaving:			

Education	Elementary	High	College/University	Graduate/Professional
School Name				
Years Completed: (Circle)	4 5 6 7 8	9 10 11 12	1 2 3 4	1 2 3 4
Diploma/Degree				
Describe Course of Study				
Describe Specialized Training, Apprenticeship, Skills, and Extracurricular Activities				
Honors Received:				
State any additional information you feel may be helpful to us in considering your application.				

Agreement: The information given is correct. Any misrepresentation or omission found by the company at any time will be sufficient cause to terminate my employment. I authorize the company to obtain from others information pertinent to my employment.

Signature ______ Date ______

 Life Skills English

Workbook Activity 51

Name Date Period | *Chapter 8 Workbook Activity 52*

Letter of Application

The purpose of a letter of application is to request an interview. To increase the employer's interest in your letter, you should:

A. Write neatly in blue or black ink or type.
B. Use $8^1/_2 \times 11$ inch paper
C. Address the letter using the person's name. (If you don't know it, call the company to find out what it is.)
D. Give the name of the position you are seeking.
E. Be brief, polite, and businesslike.
F. Describe your important qualifications.
G. Spell and punctuate correctly.

Read the help wanted ad below.

CLERICAL RECEPTIONIST—Busy surgeon will train receptionist interested in medical career. Accurate typing needed. Send letter of application to Dr. Susan Adams, 711 N. Main St., Union, Texas 78148. EOE

Read the letter at the right that answers the ad. Study it carefully.

687 Laurel Lane
Union, Texas 78143
March 6, 20–

Dr. Susan Adams
711 N. Main Street
Union, Texas 78148

Dear Dr. Adams:

I am interested in applying for the job of clerical receptionist that was advertised in the newspaper. I am twenty years old and a high school graduate. I have worked as a receptionist at Memorial Hospital for two years. I can type 40 words per minute. I also work as a volunteer nurse's aide in the evening at the same hospital.

My references are: Dr. Allen Carr (Internist)
217 Booker Avenue
Union, Texas 78149
488-1331

Mr. David Foster (Teacher)
913 Sudbrook Court
Union, Texas 78147
766-5591

I am available for an interview at your convenience. Please contact me at 483-3333 any time after 2 P.M. Thank you for considering me for the job.

Sincerely,
Frances Ward
Frances Ward

Directions: Write a letter of application for the job advertised at the right. Use your true personal information when writing the letter. Use your own paper for the letter.

STUDENTS—Needed to tutor people in reading or math. Part-time. We will train you in tutoring techniques. Must be responsible, dependable. Send letter of application to John Howard, Director of Personnel, Windsor School, 238 Windsor Lane. EOE

 Life Skills English

Workbook Activity 52

Lesson 3 Filling Out a Financial Form

Assets
Property you own that has value.

Debt
Money owed, or liability.

Financial
Concerning money or property with value.

Liability
The money you owe.

Net worth
The value of your assets minus the value of your liabilities.

Value
The amount of money your property is worth to a buyer.

When you borrow money or receive credit, you will be asked questions about your finances. You may need to fill out a **financial** form. Financial matters have to do with money or property with **value**.

You may need to prepare a financial statement at some time. To do this, you will need to list your **liabilities**. A liability is the money you owe to someone. **Debt** is another word for liability or money owed. Then you add up all your **assets** and all your liabilities. The value of your assets minus the value of your liabilities is your **net worth**.

Activity A Use the sample financial statement to answer the questions below. Write your answers on your paper.

Robert Thompson's Financial Statement

Assets		*Liabilities*	
Car	$2,800.00	Car loan at bank	$2,300.00
Watch	$25.00	Department store credit card	$144.32
Stereo	$200.00		
Total	$3,025.00	Total	$2,444.32

$3,025.00 Assets
– $2,444.32 Liabilities
$ 580.68 Net worth

1) Which of these two items is an asset?
   a) Things you own with value
   b) Money that you owe
2) List Robert Thompson's assets.
3) How much money does he owe?
4) If Robert sold everything he owns and paid all his debts, how much cash would he have?

Lesson at a Glance

Chapter 8 Lesson 3

Overview This lesson explains financial statements and credit applications.

Objectives

- To distinguish between credit and personal references.
- To identify the meanings of finance and credit terms.
- To prepare a financial statement.

Student Pages 237–243

Teacher's Resource Library
Workbook Activity 53

Reading Vocabulary

assets (9)	**liability (10)**
cash (6)	minus
concern (5)	**net worth**
debt (4)	sample (5)
finances (8)	stereo
financial (8)	**value (5)**

Teaching Suggestions

■ Introducing the Lesson

Invite students to share their personal experiences of opening a bank account or a charge account. Discuss the responsibilities that come with checking and charge accounts.

■ Reviewing Skills

Review what students have learned about completing an application form.

■ Presenting Activity A

Help students understand the sample financial statement. Then ask them to complete Activity A.

Activity A Answers

1) a 2) car, watch, stereo
3) $2,444.32 4) $580.68

Reading Vocabulary

column (5)	**loan (5)**
expense (6)	payment (7)
income (6)	purchase (5)
lender	subtract (5)

■ Presenting Activity B

Do Activity B as a whole class activity. Rather than ask students to give personal information, which might seem intrusive, have students create a fictional character and help them make up a financial statement for their invented character.

Activity B Answers

Answers will vary.

■ Presenting Activity C

Point out to students that there are some people who refuse to buy anything, even a car, with credit. Lead a discussion about the benefits and drawbacks of waiting until you can pay cash for something and the benefits and drawbacks of buying with credit. Ask students when it might be more practical to use credit rather than cash, and when it would make more sense to use cash.

Activity C Answers

1) Answers will vary. Two possible answers are: to buy a car; to buy a house **2)** to verify that you can repay the loan **3)** In case you can't make the payments, the bank can sell the property for the amount of the loan. **4)** asset **5)** liability **6)** value

Activity B Follow the directions below to prepare a financial statement of your own.

1) Make a list of your assets. Guess what their value is.

2) Make a list of your liabilities (debts).

3) Add up both columns.

4) Subtract your liabilities from your assets.

5) Circle your net worth.

Borrowing Money for a Car or House

> *Loan*
> *A sum of money that you borrow.*

Someday you may wish to obtain a **loan** to buy a car or a house. A loan is a sum of money you borrow. Lenders, or the people who loan money, want to be sure they can get their money back. They will want answers to these questions:

1. How much money can you pay each month? Each month you pay back part of the loan. The bank will ask you about your income and about your other expenses.
2. What is the value of your car or house? You may not be able to make your payments. The bank can sell the car or house to get the money back.

Activity C Write on your paper the answers to these questions.

1) What are two reasons you may wish to get a loan?

2) Why will a lender ask you about your income and other expenses?

3) Why is it important for a lender to know the value of the item you wish to purchase?

4) If you bought a car, how would you list it on your financial statement?

5) How would you list a loan for a car on your financial statement?

6) What do you call the amount of money your car is worth to a buyer?

Credit and Finance Charges

Credit
The time you get to pay for the goods you buy.

Finance charge
A fee you pay on money you owe to a business.

Joint
An account that is shared or owned together.

Merchandise
Goods for sale or that you buy.

Credit is the time you get to pay for goods you buy. The goods you buy are also known as **merchandise**.

Department stores offer credit cards that customers can use to purchase merchandise on credit. If you charge goods on a credit card, the store will send you a monthly bill, or statement. If you pay all of the money you owe on time, you do not have to pay any extra fees. When you pay only a part of what you owe, the store charges you a **finance charge**. A finance charge is the fee you pay for borrowing on credit from a store.

Charge accounts can be individual or **joint.** An individual account means that one person can use the card. A joint account means that two people can use the card. They are both responsible for paying the bill.

Activity D Here are some of the questions a store may ask you when you apply for a credit card. Answer as many of them as you can. Write your answers on your paper.

1) Will this be an individual or a joint account?
2) What is the name of the applicant (the person applying for the charge card)?
3) What is your Social Security number?
4) What is your date of birth?
5) What is your present address?
6) How long have you been at this address?
7) If you have been at the above address for less than four years, list your former address.
8) What is your phone number? (Include area code.)
9) Who is your current employer?
10) What is your employer's address?
11) What is your business telephone number?
12) What type of business is this?
13) What is your present position?
14) What is your monthly salary?

Reading Vocabulary

applicant (8) individual (6)
credit (5) **joint (6)**
finance charge **merchandise (7)**
include (5)

■ Presenting Activity D

Obtain the credit application forms from several local department stores as well as major credit card applications. Pass the forms around for students to look at and compare. Have students note the payment schedules and annual finance charges for the different accounts. List each account with payment terms on the board. Have students identify the store or card that offers the best terms.

Activity D Answers

Answers will vary.

Reading Vocabulary

checkbook
interest (3)
deposit (6)
withdrawal

■ Presenting Activity E

Provide students with samples of a checkbook register, checks, a savings passbook, and a loan payment book. Point out and explain, or invite volunteers to explain, the different features of each item and how to use these features.

Activity E Answers

1) checking, savings, loan **2)** savings **3)** loan **4)** by making a deposit **5)** by writing checks **6)** checking account **7)** savings account **8)** for the privilege of borrowing money; it is paid to the bank or lender

APPLICATION

In the Community
Some community banks sponsor financial education courses that prepare students for their financial future. These programs provide students with the skills and knowledge that will help them attain financial independence. Contact banks in your community to learn if they have such a program. You might also arrange a field trip to a neighboring branch office to give students an up-close look at how a bank operates.

Bank Accounts

When you ask for a loan or credit, you usually have to provide information about your bank accounts. There are several kinds of bank accounts.

Checking Accounts

You open a checking account by putting some money into the bank. The bank gives you a checkbook. You withdraw money from your account by writing checks. You can write checks to other people or to yourself. You can't write checks for more money than you have in your account. A **deposit** is money you have put into an account.

> ***Deposit***
> *The money you put into an account.*

Savings Accounts

You open a savings account by depositing money into the bank. The purpose is to save money. You should not need this money right away. The bank pays you **interest** on this money. Interest is the money a bank pays you for putting money into a savings account. You don't write checks to get your money from a savings account; you use a **withdrawal** slip. A withdrawal is the money you have taken from your account.

> ***Interest***
> *The money a bank pays you for putting money into a savings account; the fee you pay for borrowing money.*

> ***Withdrawal***
> *Money that you have taken out of your bank account.*

Loan Accounts

You open a loan account when you borrow money. Every month you make a payment to pay back part of the loan. Included in your monthly payment is interest. The interest on a loan is the fee you pay to the bank or lender for borrowing money.

Activity E Write on your paper your answers to these questions about bank accounts.

1) Name three kinds of bank accounts.

2) Which type of bank account pays you interest?

3) On which account do you pay interest?

4) How do you add money to your checking account balance?

5) How do you withdraw money from a checking account?

6) Which account would you probably use to pay bills?

7) Which account would you use to save money?

8) Why do you pay interest on a loan? To whom do you pay it?

More About Credit

A credit reference is a person or bank that will recommend you for a loan or credit. A personal reference is someone who knows you personally. The first time you borrow money or open a charge account, you are establishing credit. When you repay a loan on time, the bank becomes a solid credit reference. If you pay your bills at a department store, the store is also a good credit reference.

Good credit is a history of paying bills and loans on time. Bad credit is a history of late or skipped payments.

A credit limit is the maximum amount that a bank will let you borrow. It can also be the maximum amount a store will allow you to charge.

Credit Application please print

NAME–FIRST	MIDDLE INITIAL	LAST	AGE (MUST BE AT LEAST 18)
PRESENT ADDRESS–STREET	CITY	STATE	ZIP CODE
TIME AT THIS ADDRESS ____Yrs. ____Mos.	☐ OWN/BUYING ☐ LIVE WITH RELATIVES	☐ RENT ☐ OTHER	DRIVER'S LICENSE NUMBER & STATE
RESIDENCE TELEPHONE (AREA CODE)	SOCIAL SECURITY NO. (MUST BE PROVIDED)		
IF LESS THAN 3 YEARS AT RESIDENCE, GIVE PREVIOUS ADDRESS		NUMBER OF DEPENDENTS (EXCLUDE APPLICANT)	
EMPLOYED BY		HOW LONG ____Yrs. ____Mos.	BUSINESS PHONE (AREA CODE)
BUSINESS ADDRESS			TYPE OF BUSINESS
OCCUPATION	YEARLY SALARY	OTHER INCOME*	*Income from alimony, child support or separate maintenance payments need not be revealed if you do not choose to have it considered as a basis for repaying this obligation
☐ CHECKING ACCOUNT	ACCOUNT NUMBER	FINANCIAL INSTITUTION'S NAME AND ADDRESS	
☐ SAVINGS ACCOUNT	ACCOUNT NUMBER	FINANCIAL INSTITUTION'S NAME AND ADDRESS	
CREDIT CARD	ACCOUNT NUMBER	CREDIT CARD	ACCOUNT NUMBER
CREDIT REFERENCE	ACCOUNT NUMBER	CREDIT REFERENCE	ACCOUNT NUMBER

Activity F Write your answers to these questions on your paper.

1) Do you have a bank account? If yes, what type do you have?

2) Do you have any credit references? Name them.

3) Write the name and address of a person who knows you personally and who might help you obtain credit. Do not name a relative or any person who lives in your home.

Reading Vocabulary

alimony (11)
basis (7)
consider (5)
dependent (10)
establish (5)
institution (7)
limit (5)
maintenance (8)
maximum (8)
obligation (7)
occupation (6)
repay (5)
reveal (7)
separate (5)
solid (5)

■ Presenting Activity F

Focus students' attention on the credit application form that precedes Activity F. Ask students to follow along with you as you go over each item on the form. Encourage students to ask questions about any part of the application that they find confusing or that they would not know how to answer. Following this process, ask students to complete Activity F.

Activity F Answers

Answers will vary.

Name Date Period

Chapter 8 *Workbook Activity* 53

Charge It!

Directions: Fill out this application for a charge account. You have been a teacher for five years. Use your school's address and phone number for place of employment. You are earning $800.00 biweekly (double this for your monthly salary or divide by two for your weekly salary). You are thirty years old, married, with two children. While in college, you worked as a cook for Frank's Carryout for three years earning $50.00 a week. You have a savings account with Chester Savings and Loan at 1010 Smith Street. You own a 3-year-old Dodge Colt financed by your bank. Your license number is 558-321-7766R. Your only credit reference is Money America, 710 East Avenue. Your account number is 00221, and there is no balance.

CREDIT APPLICATION for SMITH'S DEPARTMENT STORE

Last Name | First | Initial | Birthdate | Dependents | Social Security No. | ☐ Own ☐ Rent

Present Address (Street & Number) | Payment or Rent $ | How Long | Name and Address of Landlord or Mortgage Holder

City | State | Zip | Home Telephone | Previous Address | How Long

Applicant's Employer | Business Address | How Long

Position | Salary: Wk / Mo / Yr | Business Telephone

Previous Employer | Position | Salary | How Long

Name and Address of Nearest Relative Not Living With You | Telephone

Other Source of Income (Income from alimony, child support or separate maintenance payments need not be disclosed if you do not wish to have it considered as a basis for repaying this obligation.) | Annual Amount ________ How Long ________ Source ________

Bank | Branch | ☐ Checking ☐ Savings ☐ Loan

Make of Car and Year | Financed by | Driver's License No.

CREDIT REFERENCES

Name	Address	Acct. No.	Balance

 Life Skills English

Workbook Activity 53

Completing Applications and Other Forms Chapter 8 **241**

Reading Vocabulary

guideline overdraw
minimum (8)

■ Presenting Activity G

Ask students what they think a person should do if he or she charged something at a department store but then couldn't make the minimum payment on the due date. Help students to recognize that the worst thing a person could do would be to ignore the bill. Introduce other options that the person has. For example, he or she could call the credit office and explain the situation and ask for more time. Or, the person might offer to make a smaller payment and not use the card until the bill is completely paid. By acting in good faith, the person may be able to maintain a good credit rating during a financially difficult time.

Activity G Answers

1) Get a job so that you have a regular income. **2)** checking and savings **3)** charge account **4)** the amount up to which you can charge on a charge account **5)** Make your payments on time.

Teacher Alert

As you discuss the importance of establishing a good credit rating, emphasize the risk of using credit cards and charge accounts without restraint. Explain that doing so can result in an accumulation of bills that cannot be paid on time, or in extreme cases, cannot be paid at all. When this happens, a person's good credit may be ruined.

Establishing Credit

Whenever you try to borrow money, the lender will want to know your credit history. You will probably be asked for credit references. The first time you ask for credit, you do not have a history—good or bad. Here are guidelines for establishing credit:

Step 1 You usually need a regular income before you can establish credit.

Step 2 Open a checking account and a savings account at a bank. Do not overdraw your checking account. Add to your savings account regularly. You can use your bank as a credit reference.

Step 3 Open a charge account at a department store. The store will probably give you a low credit limit. Purchase something with your charge card. When the bill comes each month, pay at least the minimum amount until the item is paid for. Don't buy things unless you need them. Always pay your bill on time. Then your charge account can be a credit reference.

Step 4 Take out a small loan at a bank. Make your payments on time. After you have repaid this loan, you will have another credit reference.

Activity G Write the answer to these questions on your paper.

1) What is the first thing you could do to establish credit so that you can borrow money to buy a car?

2) What are two kinds of accounts you can open at a bank?

3) What kind of account do you open at a department store?

4) What is a credit limit?

5) What is the most important rule when you take out a loan?

242 *Chapter 8 Completing Applications and Other Forms*

Lesson 3 Review

Part A Write on your paper your answers to these questions.

1) What are three kinds of people or businesses that would be good credit references?
2) What kind of person would be a good personal reference?
3) What are three types of bank accounts?

Part B Match the words with their meanings. Write on your paper the correct letter beside each number.

Words	Meanings
1) Asset	a) Taking money out of a bank account
2) Liability	b) Any property that you own
3) Value	c) Putting money into an account
4) Loan	d) The amount a buyer will pay
5) Interest	e) A fee for borrowing on credit
6) Credit	f) Money a bank pays on a savings account
7) Finance charge	g) Goods for sale or that you buy
8) Merchandise	h) Money you owe; a debt
9) Deposit	i) Time that you get to pay for merchandise
10) Withdrawal	j) Money that you have borrowed

Part C Write on your paper a financial statement for Harry Mays. List his assets and liabilities. Compute his net worth.

1) He has a car worth $4,200.00.
2) He has a TV set valued at $300.00
3) He owes $133.81 at Wilton's Department Store.
4) He has a savings account with a balance of $312.80.
5) He has $129.15 in his checking account.
6) He owes the bank $ 2,568.00 on a car loan.

Reading Vocabulary

compute (9)

Part A Answers

Some answers will vary. Possible responses are given.

1) banker, department store where you have an account, employer
2) teacher, former employer, clergy
3) savings, checking, loan

Part B Answers

1) b **2)** h **3)** d **4)** j **5)** f **6)** i
7) e **8)** g **9)** c **10)** a

Part C Answers

Assets

Car	$4,200.00
TV	300.00
Savings	312.80
Checking	129.15
Total	$4,941.95

Liabilities

Wilton's	$133.81
Car loan	2,568.00
Total	$2,701.81

$4,941.95	Assets
−2,701.81	Liabilities
$2,240.14	Net Worth

Learning Styles

Logical/Mathematical
Divide the class into five groups. Assign each group one aspect from this lesson's overview of finances: 1) Financial Statement—pg. 237; 2) Borrowing Money for a Car or House—pg. 238; 3) Credit and Finance Charges and More About Credit—pgs. 239 and 241; 4) Bank Accounts—pg. 240; and 5) Establishing Credit—pg. 242. Ask each group to work together to create a presentation on its section. Suggest that the students consider charts, role play, a quiz, a strip of drawings, or any other creative way to present the information in their section. Provide time for the presentations.

Chapter 8 Review

The Teacher's Resource Library includes two parallel forms of the Chapter 8 Mastery Test. The difficulty level of the two forms is equivalent. You may wish to use one form as a pretest and the other form as a posttest.

Reading Vocabulary

checklist
former (6)
residence (7)
rural (6)

Part A Answers

Answers will vary.

Chapter 8 Review

Part A Each item on this form has a number. Number your paper from 1 to 15. Beside each number, print the information asked for on the form.

1. Full name ________________________________
   Last First Middle Maiden
2. Present address ________________________________
   No. Street or Rural Route City State ZIP
3. Years at this address _____ 4. Phone (___) ___-______
5. Former address (if less than 2 years at present address)
   ____
   No. Street or Rural Route City State ZIP
6. Date of birth __/__/__ 7. Place of birth (city, state) ____________
8. U.S. Citizen? Yes ☐ No ☐ 9. If no, name country ____________
10. Social Security number ___-__-____
11. Father's full name ________________________________
    First Middle Last
12. Mother's full name at birth ________________________________
    First Middle Last
13. Your present age __ 14. Today's date __/__/__
15. Your signature ________________________________

Use the following checklist before going on.

- Did you print your answer neatly?
- Did you answer every question?
- Is the information correct?
- Did you follow the directions exactly?

Name Date Period *Chapter 8 Mastery Test A page 1*

Chapter 8 Mastery Test A

Part A Complete each sentence using a word from the box.

form	maiden	card	document	name
full	Social Security	United States	information	birth

1) Facts about yourself is called personal ____________ .
2) A ____________ is a paper that gives information to another person.
3) A person's whole legal name is called a ____________ name.
4) A document saying when and where you were born is called a ____________ certificate.
5) The ____________ of a person written by that person is called a signature.
6) Most applications ask for your ____________ number.
7) A woman's last name before she marries is her ____________ name.
8) If you were born in the ____________ , you are a United States citizen.
9) A green ____________ is an official document that allows aliens to work legally in the United States.
10) A printed or typed document with spaces to fill in information is called a ____________ .

Part B Read the following statements. If the statement is true, write *True* on the line. If the statement is not true, write *False*.

_____ 1) Debt is money owed.
_____ 2) An asset is a sum of money that you borrow.
_____ 3) A loan is property you own that has value.
_____ 4) Your net worth is the value of your assets minus the value of your liabilities.
_____ 5) Credit is the money you put into an account.

 Life Skills English

Name Date Period *Chapter 8 Mastery Test A page 2*

Chapter 8 Mastery Test A, continued

Part C Complete each part of this form. Use your own information.

APPLICATION FOR EMPLOYMENT

PERSONAL INFORMATION

DATE ____________ SOCIAL SECURITY NUMBER ____________
NAME ____________ SEX ______
last first middle
PRESENT ADDRESS ____________
street city state ZIP code
PHONE NO. ____________ AGE 18 OR OLDER? ______
DATE OF BIRTH ____________ PLACE OF BIRTH ____________

EDUCATION	NAME AND LOCATION OF SCHOOL	YEARS ATTENDED	DATE GRADUATED	SUBJECTS STUDIED
GRAMMAR				
HIGH SCHOOL				
COLLEGE				
TRADE SCHOOL				

DATE ____________ APPLICANT'S SIGNATURE ____________

 Life Skills English

Chapter 8 Mastery Test A

Part B Write on your paper the word or phrase that completes each sentence. Use the word or phrases in the list. You will not use all of the terms listed.

maiden	finance charge	salary	charge account
position	job application	loan	work experience
interest	credit history	deposit	birth certificate
value	reference	liability	signature
asset	withdrawal	education	

1) A ______ is a form you use to ask for work.
2) A ______ is a person who will recommend you for a job.
3) The money that you earn is called your ______ .
4) Your legal name is on your ______ .
5) Your mother's last name at birth is her ______ name.
6) A ______ is the name of a job.
7) Your ______ is all of your school experiences.
8) You write your ______ on a check.
9) An ______ is something that you own.
10) A ______ is a debt that you owe someone.
11) Emilio paid $2,500 for a car. He sold it a year later for $1,900. The ______ of the car was $1,900.
12) Chris put his money into a savings account. Every month the bank paid him ______ .
13) Ruby opened a charge account. When she got her bill, she made a payment. Because she still owed the store money, a ______ was added to her bill.
14) Anne had $100 in her savings account. She made a ______ of $10. Now she has $110 in her account.
15) Mrs. Chang borrowed money from the bank. Now she has a ______ account.

Test Taking Tip

When taking a matching test, match all the items that you are certain go together. Cross these items out. Then try to match the items that are left.

Reading Vocabulary

phrase (6) term (5)

Part A Answers

1) job application 2) reference 3) salary 4) birth certificate 5) maiden 6) position 7) education 8) signature 9) asset 10) liability 11) value 12) interest 13) finance charge 14) deposit 15) loan

Name ______ Date ______ Period ______

Chapter 8 Mastery Test B page 1

Chapter 8 Mastery Test B

Part A Complete each sentence using a word from the box.

legal	green	form	document	signature
applications	citizen	name	personal	certificate

1) Most ______ ask for your Social Security number.
2) A paper that gives information to another person is called a ______ .
3) A birth ______ is a document saying when and where you were born.
4) A printed or typed document with spaces to fill in information is called a ______ .
5) A ______ card is an official document that allows aliens to work legally in the United States.
6) A ______ is the name of a person written by that person.
7) A full name is a person's whole ______ name.
8) A woman's last name before she marries is her maiden ______ .
9) If you were born in the United States, you are a United States ______ .
10) ______ information is facts about yourself.

Part B Read the following statements. If the statement is true, write *True* on the line. If the statement is not true, write *False*.

______ 1) Debt is money you put into an account.

______ 2) An asset is property you own that has value.

______ 3) A loan is a sum of money that you borrow.

______ 4) Your net worth is a joint account that is shared or owned together.

______ 5) Credit is the time you get to pay for the goods you buy.

 Life Skills English

Name ______ Date ______ Period ______

Chapter 8 Mastery Test B page 2

Chapter 8 Mastery Test B, continued

Part C Complete each part of this form. Use your own information.

APPLICATION FOR EMPLOYMENT

PERSONAL INFORMATION

DATE ______ SOCIAL SECURITY NUMBER ______

NAME ______ (*last* *first* *middle*) SEX ______

PRESENT ADDRESS ______ (*street* *city* *state* *ZIP code*)

PHONE NO. ______ AGE 18 OR OLDER? ______

DATE OF BIRTH ______ PLACE OF BIRTH ______

EDUCATION	NAME AND LOCATION OF SCHOOL	YEARS ATTENDED	DATE GRADUATED	SUBJECTS STUDIED
GRAMMAR				
HIGH SCHOOL				
COLLEGE				
TRADE SCHOOL				

DATE ______ APPLICANT'S SIGNATURE ______

 Life Skills English

Chapter 8 Mastery Test B

Chapter 9

Planning Guide

Shopping by Catalog

	Student Text Lesson			
	Student Pages	Vocabulary	Practice Exercises	Lesson Review
Lesson 1 Reading Catalog Items	248-254	✔	✔	✔
Lesson 2 Ordering From a Catalog	255-259	✔	✔	✔
Lesson 3 When the Order Is Wrong	260-263		✔	✔

Chapter Activities

Teacher's Resource Library

Putting It Together 9: I've Got a Catalog Secret Wish

Community Connection 9: Place a Catalog Order

Assessment Options

Student Text

Chapter 9 Review

Teacher's Resource Library

Chapter 9 Mastery Tests A and B

Final Mastery Test

Teaching Strategies						Language Skills			Learning Styles						Teacher's Resource Library		
Reviewing Skills	Teacher Alert	Career Application	Home Application	Global Connection	Community Application	Identification Skills	Writing Skills	Punctuation Skills	Visual/Spatial	Auditory/Verbal	Body/Kinesthetic	Logical/Mathematical	Group Learning	LEP/ESL	Activities	Workbook Activities	Self-Study Guide
248		253	251			✔	✔	✔	250						30	54-55	✔
255	256			259		✔	✔	✔						257	31-32	56-58	✔
260					262-263	✔	✔	✔			261				33	59-60	✔

Chapter at a Glance

Chapter 9: Shopping By Catalog pages 246–265

Lessons

Teacher's Resource Library

- Activities 30–33
- Workbook Activities 54–60
- Putting It Together 9
- Community Connection 9
- Chapter 9 Self-Study Guide
- Chapter 9 Mastery Tests A and B
- Final Mastery Test

(Answer Keys for the Teacher's Resource Library begin on page 282 of this Teacher's Edition.)

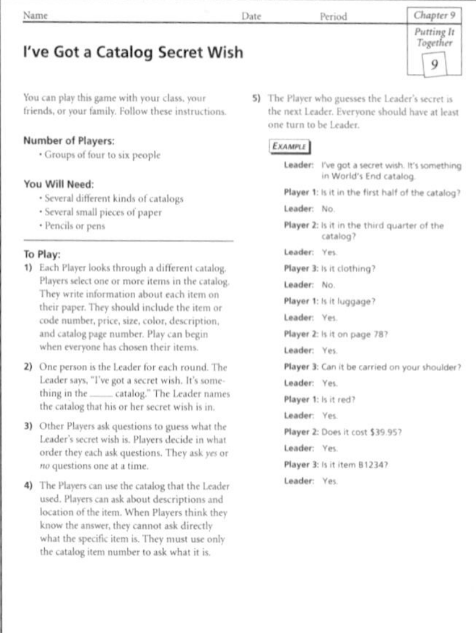

Name Date Period

Chapter 9 *Putting It Together* 9

I've Got a Catalog Secret Wish

You can play this game with your class, your friends, or your family. Follow these instructions.

Number of Players:
- Groups of four to six people

You Will Need:
- Several different kinds of catalogs
- Several small pieces of paper
- Pencils or pens

To Play:

1) Each Player looks through a different catalog. Players select one or more items in the catalog. They write information about each item on their paper. They should include the item or code number, price, size, color, description, and catalog page number. Play can begin when everyone has chosen their items.
2) One person is the Leader for each round. The Leader says, "I've got a secret wish. It's something in the ____ catalog." The Leader names the catalog that his or her secret wish is in.
3) Other Players ask questions to guess what the Leader's secret wish is. Players decide in what order they each ask questions. They ask *yes* or *no* questions one at a time.
4) The Players can use the catalog that the Leader used. Players can ask about descriptions and location of the item. When Players think they know the answer, they cannot ask directly what the specific item is. They must use only the catalog item number to ask what it is.
5) The Player who guesses the Leader's secret is the next Leader. Everyone should have at least one turn to be Leader.

EXAMPLE

Leader: I've got a secret wish. It's something in World's End catalog.
Player 1: Is it in the first half of the catalog?
Leader: No.
Player 2: Is it in the third quarter of the catalog?
Leader: Yes.
Player 3: Is it clothing?
Leader: No.
Player 1: Is it luggage?
Leader: Yes.
Player 2: Is it on page 78?
Leader: Yes.
Player 3: Can it be carried on your shoulder?
Leader: Yes.
Player 1: Is it red?
Leader: Yes.
Player 2: Does it cost $39.95?
Leader: Yes.
Player 3: Is it item B1234?
Leader: Yes.

 Life Skills English

Putting It Together 9

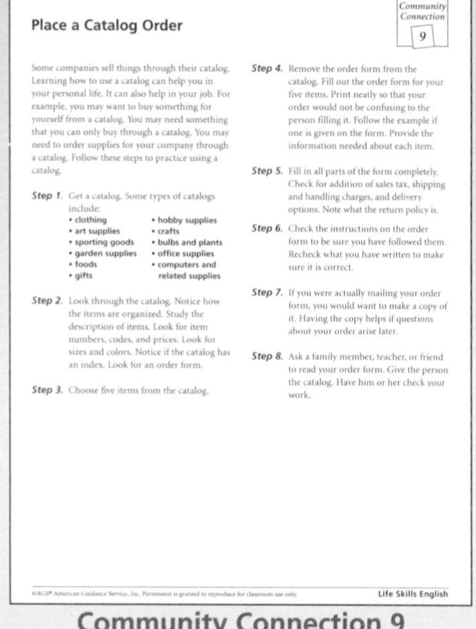

Name Date Period

Chapter 9 *Community Connection* 9

Place a Catalog Order

Some companies sell things through their catalog. Learning how to use a catalog can help you in your personal life. It can also help in your job. For example, you may want to buy something for yourself from a catalog. You may need something that you can only buy through a catalog. You may need to order supplies for your company through a catalog. Follow these steps to practice using a catalog.

Step 1. Get a catalog. Some types of catalogs include:
- clothing
- art supplies
- sporting goods
- garden supplies
- foods
- gifts
- hobby supplies
- crafts
- bulbs and plants
- office supplies
- computers and related supplies

Step 2. Look through the catalog. Notice how the items are organized. Study the description of items. Look for item numbers, codes, and prices. Look for sizes and colors. Notice if the catalog has an index. Look for an order form.

Step 3. Choose five items from the catalog.

Step 4. Remove the order form from the catalog. Fill out the order form for your five items. Print neatly so that your order would not be confusing to the person filling it. Follow the example if one is given on the form. Provide the information needed about each item.

Step 5. Fill in all parts of the form completely. Check for addition of sales tax, shipping and handling charges, and delivery options. Note what the return policy is.

Step 6. Check the instructions on the order form to be sure you have followed them. Recheck what you have written to make sure it is correct.

Step 7. If you were actually mailing your order form, you would want to make a copy of it. Having the copy helps if questions about your order arise later.

Step 8. Ask a family member, teacher, or friend to read your order form. Give the person the catalog. Have him or her check your work.

 Life Skills English

Community Connection 9

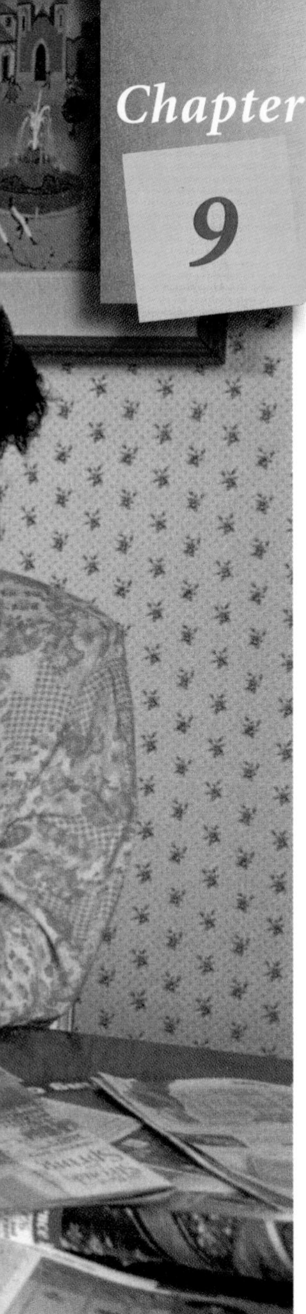

Chapter 9

Shopping by Catalog

Many businesses in the United States sell their products through the mail. Instead of selling products to a retail store, they sell them directly to the consumer. Their goods are displayed in a catalog rather than in a store. A catalog is like a reference book. It usually has pictures and descriptions of many kinds of merchandise. People use catalogs for information about products. They also use catalogs for shopping and browsing. When you browse, you read small bits of information at random.

In Chapter 9, you will learn about catalog shopping. Each lesson will help you learn how to read and understand the information in a catalog and how to order merchandise.

Goals for Learning

- To learn how to read and understand the information in a catalog
- To learn how to order merchandise from a catalog
- To learn how to solve problems related to catalog shopping

Reading Vocabulary

browse (8)	product (5)
catalog (6)	random (9)
consumer (7)	reference (6)
description (6)	relate (6)
display (6)	retail (8)
merchandise (7)	

Introducing the Chapter

Ask students to name products that people can buy through catalogs. Elicit a variety of items that include clothing, household appliances, flowers, food, office equipment, furniture, and so on. Then create a two-column chart on the board with the headings *Advantages* and *Disadvantages*. Title the chart *Catalog Shopping*. Ask students to help you complete the chart by suggesting possible advantages and disadvantages of catalog shopping. If necessary, point out that an advantage is a good point and a disadvantage is a negative point. After listing students ideas in the chart, explain that by the end of Chapter 9 students will have a clearer understanding of catalog shopping. Save the chart so that it can be used in Lesson 1 Activity A and later. At the end of the chapter, students can review the information in the chart and add any new ideas they have.

SELF-STUDY GUIDE

Name ______

CHAPTER 9: Shopping by Catalog

Goal 9.1 *To learn how to read and understand the information in a catalog*

Date	Assignment	Score
______	1: Read pages 247-248. Complete Activity A on page 248.	______
______	2: Read page 249. Complete Activity B on page 249.	______
______	3: Read page 250. Complete Activity C on page 250.	______
______	4: Read page 251. Complete Activity D on page 251.	______
______	5: Complete Workbook Activity 54.	______
______	6: Read page 252. Complete Activity E on page 252 and Activity F on page 253.	______
______	7: Complete Workbook Activity 55.	______
______	8: Complete the Lesson 1 Review, Parts A-B on page 254.	______

Comments:

Goal 9.2 *To learn how to order merchandise from a catalog*

Date	Assignment	Score
______	9: Read page 255. Complete Activity A on page 255.	______
______	10: Read page 256. Complete Activity B on page 256.	______
______	11: Read page 257. Complete Activity C on page 257.	______
______	12: Read page 258. Complete Activity D on page 258.	______
______	13: Complete Workbook Activity 56.	______
______	14: Complete the Lesson 2 Review, Parts A-B on page 259.	______
______	15: Complete Workbook Activity 57.	______
______	16: Complete Workbook Activity 58.	______

Comments:

 Life Skills English

SELF-STUDY GUIDE

Name ______

CHAPTER 9 Shopping by Catalog, continued

Goal 9.3 *To learn how to solve problems related to catalog shopping*

Date	Assignment	Score
______	17: Read pages 260-261. Complete Activity A on page 261. Read page 262.	______
______	18: Complete Workbook Activity 59.	______
______	19: Complete Workbook Activity 60.	______
______	20: Complete the Lesson 3 Review on page 263.	______
______	21: Complete the Chapter 9 Review, Parts A-D on pages 264-265.	______

Comments:

Student's Signature ______ Date ______

Instructor's Signature ______ Date ______

 Life Skills English

Chapter 9 Self-Study Guide

Lesson at a Glance

Chapter 9 Lesson 1

Overview This lesson explains how to find and understand the information in a catalog.

Objectives

- To understand terms related to catalog shopping.
- To interpret information in a catalog description.

Student Pages 248–254

Teacher's Resource Library

Activity 30

Workbook Activities 54–55

Reading Vocabulary

advantage (5)
appliance (8)
benefit (5)
compare (5)
computer (8)
dealer (7)
disadvantage
equipment (5)
feature (6)
household (6)
individual (6)
item (6)
jewelry (5)
method (6)
microwave
negative (8)
positive (6)
public (5)
purchase (5)
refer (6)
retail (8)
unfavorable
wholesale

Teaching Suggestions

Introducing the Lesson

Provide students with a variety of catalogs to examine as you discuss the terms and information presented in the text.

Reviewing Skills

Review what students have learned about filling out forms.

Presenting Activity A

Discuss the positive and negative aspects of shopping by all of the methods listed in Activity A. Students can use discussion ideas and the *Catalog Shopping* chart to complete Activity A.

Activity A Answers

Answers will vary.

Lesson 1 Reading Catalog Items

Advantage
A benefit or positive feature.

Appliance
A piece of household equipment such as a toaster, oven, dishwasher, electric mixer, or microwave oven.

Dealer
A business or individual that sells to the public.

Disadvantage
An unfavorable condition or negative feature.

Retail
Items that are for sale to the public.

Wholesale
The merchandise that is for sale to dealers.

Large department stores and mail order houses have many kinds of merchandise. They buy the merchandise **wholesale** and sell it **retail**. Wholesale refers to the merchandise that is for sale to **dealers**. A dealer is someone who sells to the public. Retail refers to items that are for sale to the public. Dealers sell clothing; **appliances** (a piece of household equipment such as a toaster, oven, dishwasher, electric mixer, or microwave oven); jewelry; furniture; machines and tools; toys and games; and other kinds of goods.

You may buy merchandise from dealers in five ways. You may

- purchase the item in the store.
- order the item by telephone.
- order the item by mail.
- order by computer through an on-line catalog.
- order by FAX.

If you order the item, you may receive it in two ways.

- You may pick up your order at the store.
- The item may be delivered to your home.

Each method of buying merchandise has **advantages** and **disadvantages**. An advantage is a benefit, or a reason, for choosing something. A disadvantage is an unfavorable condition or a reason for not choosing something.

In addition to the price of the goods, customers usually pay mailing costs. Remember to add that cost in when you are comparing prices.

Activity A Write on your paper one advantage and one disadvantage of buying

1) by phone, computer, or FAX.
2) by mail.
3) at the store.

Discount price
A price below the regular retail price.

Retail price
The price a customer pays for an item.

Sale price
A lower price on a certain item for a certain time period.

Wholesale price
The price a manufacturer charges a dealer for items bought in large amounts.

Catalog Showrooms

Department stores buy goods from manufacturers at **wholesale price**. The wholesale price is the price a manufacturer charges for items bought in large amounts. The **retail price** is what stores charge their customers. The retail price is higher than the wholesale price.

Stores will sometimes offer merchandise at a **sale price**. The sale price is lower than the retail price of a certain item. The sale price is usually for a certain period of time.

In some ways, catalog showrooms are like large department stores and mail order houses.

- They have catalogs that list their merchandise.
- They have stores where you may look at the merchandise.
- They have special sale prices on merchandise.
- You may buy goods at the store.
- You may order through the mail.

Catalog showrooms differ from department stores and mail order houses in some ways.

- Catalog showrooms sell items at a **discount price**. A discount price is below the regular retail price.
- Catalog showrooms usually do not sell as many different items.
- Catalog showrooms have different name brands. Some department stores sell only their own brand.

Activity B Write on your paper your answers to these questions.

1) Name one way that catalog showrooms are like large department stores.

2) Name one way they are different.

3) Name one advantage of ordering from a large department store catalog.

4) Name one advantage of ordering from a catalog showroom store.

Reading Vocabulary

brand (5)	**retail price**
differ (6)	**sale price**
discount price	showroom
manufacturer	**wholesale price**

■ Presenting Activity B

Discuss the similarities and differences between a department store catalog and a catalog showroom. Emphasize that a department store catalog usually highlights the store's best buys. The department store itself carries many items that are not in its catalog. When you want to purchase an item in a department store, you usually take the item from a rack or a shelf and take it to a salesperson. A catalog showroom store, on the other hand, displays samples of items sold primarily through its catalog. When you want to purchase an item, you fill out an order form using the catalog merchandise numbers. You bring the order form to a salesperson who then procures the item from a storeroom for you.

Activity B Answers

Answers may vary. Possible responses are given.

1) Items are on display. **2)** At a department store, you buy the items that are on display. At a catalog store, you fill out an order form for the item you want. **3)** You have a large variety of items to choose from. **4)** You have a large variety of brands to choose from.

Reading Vocabulary

appliance (8)	luggage (6)
automotive	personal (6)
billfold	photographic
calculator	stereo
earring	vacuum (5)
index (5)	wallet (6)

■ Presenting Activity C

Focus students' attention on the *Quick Reference Guide.* Ask students to name products that they would expect to find under each item heading. Then have students complete Activity C on their own. To extend this activity, ask students to each list five products that might be found in this catalog. Invite volunteers to read the items on their lists one at a time. Have the class identify the index heading and the pages where shoppers would look for each item.

Activity C Answers

1) 199 (floor care) **2)** 258 (luggage) **3)** 1 (jewelry) **4)** 338 (tools/hardware) **5)** 135 (giftware)

Learning Styles

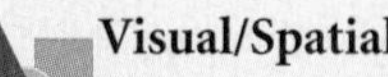

Visual/Spatial

Have students look around the classroom to discover things that someone has purchased for the school, for the students, or for themselves. Then call on volunteers to name an object they see and to name the category under which they might find it in a catalog. As the students name objects and categories, ask a volunteer to record these in a quick reference guide such as the one on page 250. Discuss synonyms for the suggested categories and add these to the listing.

Finding Items in a Catalog

Most large catalogs have an index to help you find quickly what you are looking for. Here is an example of an index with main headings.

Quick Reference Guide

appliances	173–197	jewelry	1–75
automotive	349–356	lamps	232–237
baby goods	386–396	lawn furniture	336–337
billfolds	98–101	luggage	258–266
calculators	270–273	office equipment	274–276
car stereos	355–356	personal care	206–215
clocks	96, 242–253	photographic equipment	280–290
cookware	163–175	radios	291–293
diamonds	1–22	stereo, TVs	294–329
floor care	199–201	sporting goods	347–348
giftware	135–147	tools	338–346
hardware	338–346	toys	397–444

Activity C Read each item below. Then find each item in the index above. Write on your paper the first page of the catalog where the item would be found.

EXAMPLE Jane wants a wallet. A wallet is a billfold. She would look on page 98.

1) Anita is shopping for a vacuum cleaner.
2) Richard needs a suitcase.
3) Kim is looking for some earrings.
4) Gary wants a hammer and a saw.
5) Lorie would like a pretty vase to give to her mother for her birthday.

250 *Chapter 9 Shopping by Catalog*

Comparison Shopping With Catalogs

When you compare prices at different stores, you are doing comparison shopping. You can do comparison shopping with catalogs. When you want to buy a certain item, find it in one or two catalogs. Look at the prices and the different features each product has. Decide which item is the best buy.

Activity D Use the descriptions of the three kinds of popcorn poppers to answer the questions. Write your answers on your paper.

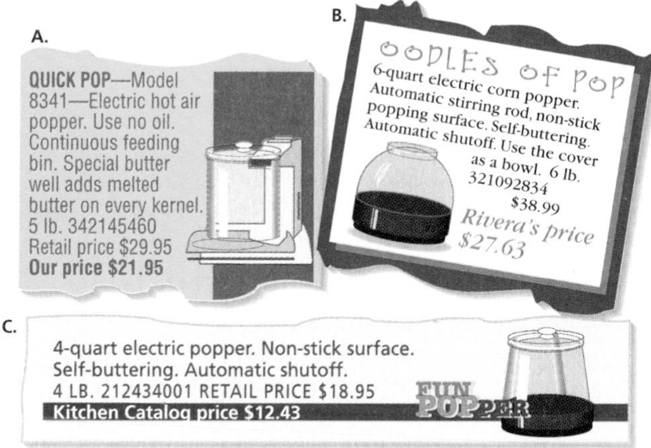

A.
QUICK POP—Model 8341—Electric hot air popper. Use no oil. Continuous feeding bin. Special butter well adds melted butter on every kernel. 5 lb. 342145460
Retail price $29.95
Our price $21.95
B.
OODLES OF POP
6-quart electric corn popper. Automatic stirring rod, non-stick popping surface. Self-buttering. Automatic shutoff. Use the cover as a bowl. 6 lb. 321092834
$38.99
Rivera's price $27.63
C.
4-quart electric popper. Non-stick surface. Self-buttering. Automatic shutoff.
4 LB. 212434001 RETAIL PRICE $18.95
Kitchen Catalog price $12.43
FUN POPPER

1) What does item A use instead of oil?

2) What is the most important difference between items B and C?

3) Which popcorn popper lets you use the cover as a bowl?

4) What is the catalog number of item A?

5) How much money will you save if you buy item A in the catalog rather than at the full retail price?

6) Which popper do you have to unplug to turn off?

7) How much does item C cost through the catalog?

Reading Vocabulary

automatic (5)
bin (5)
comparison (6)
continuous (7)
kernel (5)
rod (5)

Presenting Activity D

Divide students into small groups, and give each group two or three catalogs that carry the same type of merchandise. Ask students to first find the same product (same model and brand) in each catalog and compare prices. Then have them find different brands of the same kind of product (a portable CD player, for example) and have them compare and contrast the features and prices of the different brands. Ask students to record their findings. Then, when they have finished, invite a member of each group to share the results of their comparison shopping.

Activity D Answers

1) hot air **2)** capacity of popper—B is a 6-quart popper; C is a 4-quart popper **3)** B—Oodles of Pop **4)** 342145460 **5)** $8.00 ($29.95 minus $21.95) **6)** A-Quick Pop **7)** $12.43

APPLICATION

At Home

Most homes today receive a variety of mail-order catalogs. Encourage students to apply the comparison shopping techniques they learned in class to items found in catalogs at home. Students and family members might work together to compare the prices and features of an item they plan to purchase soon.

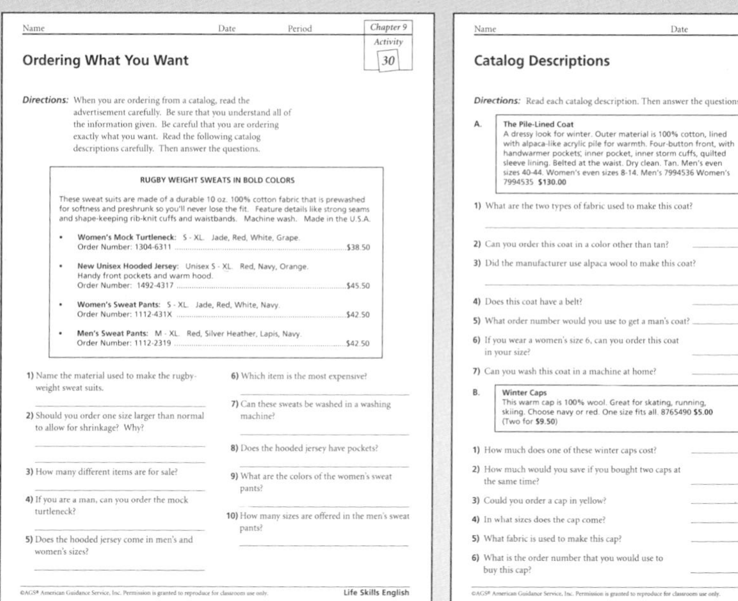

Name Date Period — *Chapter 9 Activity 30*

Ordering What You Want

Directions: When you are ordering from a catalog, read the advertisement carefully. Be sure that you understand all of the information given. Be careful that you are ordering exactly what you want. Read the following catalog descriptions carefully. Then answer the questions.

RUGBY WEIGHT SWEATS IN BOLD COLORS

These sweat suits are made of a durable 10 oz. 100% cotton fabric that is prewashed for softness and preshrunk so you'll never lose the fit. Feature details like strong seams and shape-keeping rib-knit cuffs and waistbands. Machine wash. Made in the U.S.A.

- **Women's Mock Turtleneck:** S - XL. Jade, Red, White, Grape. Order Number: 1304-6311 .... $38.50
- **New Unisex Hooded Jersey:** Unisex S - XL. Red, Navy, Orange. Handy front pockets and warm hood. Order Number: 1492-4317 .... $45.50
- **Women's Sweat Pants:** S - XL. Jade, Red, White, Navy. Order Number: 1112-431X $42.50
- **Men's Sweat Pants:** M - XL. Red, Silver Heather, Lapis, Navy. Order Number: 1112-2319 .... $42.50

1) Name the material used to make the rugby-weight sweat suits.

2) Should you order one size larger than normal to allow for shrinkage? Why?

3) How many different items are for sale?

4) If you are a man, can you order the mock turtleneck?

5) Does the hooded jersey come in men's and women's sizes?

6) Which item is the most expensive?

7) Can these sweats be washed in a washing machine?

8) Does the hooded jersey have pockets?

9) What are the colors of the women's sweat pants?

10) How many sizes are offered in the men's sweat pants?

 Life Skills English

Activity 30

Name Date Period — *Chapter 9 Workbook Activity 54*

Catalog Descriptions

Directions: Read each catalog description. Then answer the questions.

A. **The Pile-Lined Coat**
A dressy look for winter. Outer material is 100% cotton, lined with alpaca-like acrylic pile for warmth. Four-button front, with handwarmer pockets; inner pocket, inner storm cuffs, quilted sleeve lining. Belted at the waist. Dry clean. Tan. Men's even sizes 40-44. Women's even sizes 8-14. Men's 7994536 Women's 7994535 **$130.00**

1) What are the two types of fabric used to make this coat?

2) Can you order this coat in a color other than tan?

3) Did the manufacturer use alpaca wool to make this coat?

4) Does this coat have a belt?

5) What order number would you use to get a man's coat?

6) If you wear a women's size 6, can you order this coat in your size?

7) Can you wash this coat in a machine at home?

B. **Winter Caps**
This warm cap is 100% wool. Great for skating, running, skiing. Choose navy or red. One size fits all. 8765490 **$5.00** (Two for **$9.50**)

1) How much does one of these winter caps cost?

2) How much would you save if you bought two caps at the same time?

3) Could you order a cap in yellow?

4) In what sizes does the cap come?

5) What fabric is used to make this cap?

6) What is the order number that you would use to buy this cap?

 Life Skills English

Workbook Activity 54

Reading Vocabulary

advertise (6)
advertisement (6)
blouse (6)
convince (5)
crepe
enrich (8)
fabulous (5)
goal (5)
include (5)
novelty (7)
payment (7)
persuasive
rayon (7)
rebate (11)
specialty
supple (11)
total (5)

■ Presenting Activity E

Distribute several specialty catalogs to students. Ask each student to select one item from the catalog and to read the description for that item carefully. Then invite volunteers to describe the item they have selected. Does the description answer all of the questions that they have about the item? What would the total cost be to have the item delivered to their home?

Activity E Answers

1) matching skirt and blouse
2) CA4531 3) $52.00
4) 5 through 13 5) tomato red, striped with cream 6) No
7) rayon crepe 8) $56.25

Specialty Catalogs

There are many small mail order catalog businesses. They sell clothing, novelties, gift items, and other sorts of specialty items. Usually there is a picture of each item and a brief description. You must read the descriptions very carefully to be sure of what you are getting.

18D. Ripe Tomato Red, striped with cream in soft, supple rayon crepe. Here is a fabulous two-piece dress with a jewel neckline and a softly gathered skirt. Sizes 5-13.
CA4531 $52.00 (4.25—shipping and handling)

Activity E Use the catalog description to answer these questions. Write your answers on your paper.

1) What is Item 18D—a dress or a matching skirt and blouse?
2) What is the catalog number?
3) What is the price of the item?
4) What sizes of this item can you order?
5) What are the colors of this item?
6) Can you buy it in a different color?
7) What kind of material is this item?
8) What will be the total cost to have the dress delivered to you?

Catalog Descriptions

Catalog descriptions are really advertisements. They use the same type of language used in advertising. The goal of a catalog description is to convince you that your life will be enriched and improved if you buy the product.

Rebate
A return of part of a payment for a product.

Sometimes a catalog description will offer a **rebate**. A rebate is a return of part of the payment for a product or service. Check the description of the product you plan to purchase to see if it includes a rebate or any other special offers.

HOME COMPUTER — Easy to use even if you've never touched a computer before. All you need is some software and your computer is ready to teach, entertain, or help you with home finances at a touch of a button.
Order Model **4432S.**
Our price $1,624.99
Factory *rebate* $199.00
Our price $1,425.99
Monitor and keyboard extra

Activity F Use the catalog description above to answer these questions. Write your answers on your paper.

1) How much money is the store charging the customer for this computer?

2) How much money will the customer get back from the factory after purchasing the computer?

3) What does the ad say the computer can help you do?

4) What is not included in the price of the computer?

5) What is the model number of the computer?

Name Date Period

Chapter 9 *Workbook Activity* 55

Getting What You Order

Directions: Read the advertisement carefully. Then answer the questions.

Sport Shorts
(For Men)
Pull-on shorts made from the rugged, long-wearing 100% cotton you asked for! Perfect for gym workouts, hiking, and general sports use. Comfortable elasticized waist with drawstring. Side pockets. Wide-cut leg opening for freedom of movement. Excellent buy. Machine wash. Red, blue, tan, white. Men's sizes S, M, L, XL. $12.00 postpaid. 7 oz. Save more! Order 2 pairs for $23.00.
Order Number: 1213S

1) What material is used to make these shorts? ______

2) Do these shorts come in women's sizes? ______

3) How many sizes do these shorts come in? ______

4) How much money would you save if you order two pairs of these shorts. ______

5) Can you wash these shorts in your washing machine? ______

6) Do these shorts have back pockets? ______

7) Do these shorts have a zipper? ______

8) Why are these shorts comfortable for running?

______

9) What is the order number? ______

10) Do you have to add money for shipping this product? ______

 Life Skills English

Workbook Activity 55

Reading Vocabulary

entertain (5) monitor (6)
finance (8) software
keyboard

■ Presenting Activity F

Select three or four items from a catalog you have on hand. Read the description of each item aloud and ask students to identify persuasive language in each description. If necessary, explain that persuasive language includes any words and phrases that try to convince the customer that their lives will somehow be better with this product. Then ask students if they would purchase any of these products based on their descriptions. Have them explain their answers. Following this activity, have students complete Activity F on their own.

Activity F Answers

1) $1,624.99 **2)** $199.00 **3)** It can help with your home finances. **4)** the monitor and keyboard **5)** 4432S

Application

Career Connection

Students may find that the career of their choice includes some writing. They may be asked to compose letters, memos, and advertisements or to take notes at a meeting or record information about a work task. Have students discuss the requirements for these kinds of writing. Then have them think about the writing found in catalogs. What features of catalog writing are also important in the writing they might do in their careers? Have students suggest a career, the kind of writing it might require, and the features the writing should contain. Possible answers may include concise writing for a secretary taking notes, descriptions for a cafeteria worker writing about the specials of the day, and a machine operator recording the directions for using a machine. List the ideas on the board as students suggest them.

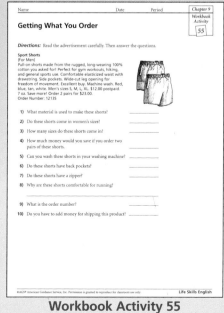

Reading Vocabulary

contents (6)
gazetteer
porcelain (6)
sip (5)
taper (6)
value (5)

Part A Answers

1) by phone or by mail 2) dealers 3) retail (b) 4) index (b) 5) Answears will vary. Possible answers include prices, sizes, type of fabric, color, specific features. 6) A rebate is a return, usually by the manufacturer, of part of the payment for a product or service.

Part B Answers

1) four 2) $3.00 3) No 4) Brazil 5) porcelain 6) Yes 7) #123-9902

Lesson 1 Review

Part A Write on your paper your answers to these questions.

1) Describe two ways to order merchandise from a catalog.
2) Who pays wholesale prices—customers or dealers?
3) Which kind of price is highest?
   a) wholesale b) retail c) discount
4) What can you use in catalogs to find a certain item quickly?
   a) table of contents b) index c) gazetteer
5) Name one kind of information about goods that you will find in a catalog. (There are several possible answers.)
6) What does it mean when a catalog offers a rebate?

Part B Read the description. Write on your paper your answers to the questions that follow.

We are happy to introduce more fine porcelain from Brazil in the form of these COFFEE MUGS. The porcelain is thick enough to keep the contents hot, but tapers to a thin rim for easy sipping. The bases are inset for stacking, and the price is designed to please. 8 oz. capac.

Set of four, #123-9902........................$12.00

1) How many cups will you receive?
2) What is the value of each cup?
3) Are customers offered a choice of colors?
4) In what country were the cups made?
5) What material was used to make these cups?
6) Can you stack these cups?
7) What is the catalog order number?

254 Chapter 9 Shopping by Catalog

Lesson 2

Ordering From a Catalog

When you order merchandise by phone or by mail, an extra charge is added because the goods are sent to your home. These charges are called either postage and handling charges or shipping charges. Shipping charges are usually found on the order form. They are computed on the total amount of the order or the weight of the items being shipped.

Shipping Charges by Cost

Amount of order:	*Include:*
Up to $9.99	$1.95
$10.00 - $19.99	$2.95
$20.00 - $29.99	$3.95
$30.00 - $39.99	$4.95
$40.00 - $49.99	$5.95
$50.00 - $74.99	$7.50
$75.00 - $99.99	$8.25
Over $100.00	$11.00

Shipping Rates by Weight

Lb.	*Charge*
1 - 5	$3.15
6 - 10	$5.07
11 - 15	$6.98
16 - 20	$8.90
21 - 25	$10.95
26 - 30	$12.78
31 - 40	$16.65
Over 40	$20.54

Activity A Figure out the total cost of each item in the two ways shown below. Write your answers as in the example.

a) Add shipping charges by cost.

b) Add shipping charges by weight.

EXAMPLE Set of 4 10-oz. mugs. Insulated plastic, 2 lb. $3.47.

a) $3.47 + $1.95 = $5.42

b) $3.47 + $3.15 = $6.62

1) PINE PAPER CUP DISPENSER. Holds about 45 5-oz. cups. 3 lb. Retail price $18.00. Our price $15.00.

2) MAPLE ROCKING CHAIR. Colonial style. 21 lb. $67.97.

3) 10-SPEED BIKE. Big, nobby tires. 26″ chrome frame. 49 lb. $134.95.

4) JOYSTICK REMOTE CONTROLS. 1 lb. Regularly $29.95. Sale price $20.00.

5) EXERCISE BENCH DELUXE MODEL. 67 lb. $109.00.

Lesson at a Glance

Chapter 9 Lesson 2

Overview This lesson explains the process of ordering from a catalog, payment options, and additional costs.

Objectives

- To answer questions about shopping by catalog.
- To complete a catalog order form.

Student Pages 255–259

Teacher's Resource Library

Activities 31–32

Workbook Activities 56–58

Reading Vocabulary

chrome
colonial (5)
compute (9)
deluxe
dispenser
insulate
joystick
maple (5)
nobby
plastic (6)
postage (5)
remote (6)

Teaching Suggestions

Introducing the Lesson

Discuss the information presented in the text. Have students look in sample catalogs to compare shipping charges. Have them also check to see which companies offer express delivery and what the charges are for this service.

Reviewing Skills

Review how to read catalog descriptions.

Presenting Activity A

Do the first item in Activity A on the board. Then depending on the needs of your class, complete Activity A together or have students work on their own.

Activity A Answers

1) a) $17.95 b) $18.15
2) a) $75.47 b) $78.92
3) a) $145.95 b) $155.49
4) a) $23.95 b) $23.15
5) a) $120.00 b) $129.54

Reading Vocabulary

applicable	optically
canteen (7)	polyurethane
credit (5)	quantity (6)
entrance (5)	reflector
expiration	retardant
fuel (5)	ripstop
insulation (8)	rustproof
lens (6)	screw (5)
multiply (5)	shatterproof
nylon (6)	

■ Presenting Activity B

You can enliven this activity by having pairs of students role play ordering the items by phone. One student can play the role of the catalog operator; the other student can play the shopper. The operator can ask questions based on the information listed at the top of page 256. The shopper should have all the necessary information on hand. Ask the class to listen carefully to make sure the shopper hasn't omitted any important details.

Activity B Answers

Answers will vary depending on the items students choose to order. Information for each item ordered should include catalog item number, name of item, description (size and color if applicable), and quantity. The shopper should have a credit card number and its expiration date ready. The shopper should also know the price of each item and the total price.

Teacher Alert

Point out to students that when ordering by phone, the operator will sometimes ask for the catalog identification number and the page number on which each item appears. The operator will usually calculate the shipping costs and inform the shopper of the total cost of the order. Shoppers should, however, calculate the total price beforehand as a double-check.

Ordering by Phone

You may want to order from a catalog store by telephone. When you order by phone, have all the information ready that you will need to place your order. Here is a list of the kind of information usually needed to place a catalog order.

1. Catalog item number
2. Name of item
3. Description (including size and color if applicable)
4. Quantity
5. Price of each item
6. Total price (multiply price of one by the number of items ordered)
7. Shipping weight
8. Credit card number and expiration date

Activity B Choose two items from the list to order by telephone. Make a list of the information you will need about each item to place the order. Write the information on your paper.

A. CAMP STOVE 3 1/2 pt. fuel tank. 22" × 13" × 6". 15 lb. #134200BC **$34.95.**

B. TWO-PERSON TENT Fire retardant–coated nylon with 3-zip screen entrance, rear screen window with storm flap. Polyurethane floor. Rope, poles, stakes. 4 lb. #134210BC **$20.00.**

C. 2 QT. DESERT CANTEEN Blanket covered for insulation. Screw cap with safety chain. Rustproof steel frame. 2 lb. #123200BC **$5.00.**

D. SLEEPING BAG 33" × 75" Ripstop nylon shell, nylon lining. 3 lb. #123400BC **$27.95.**

E. HEAVY DUTY FLASHLIGHT Optically perfect reflector with shatterproof lens. Needs two "D" batteries. 2 lb. #234540DF **$3.05.**

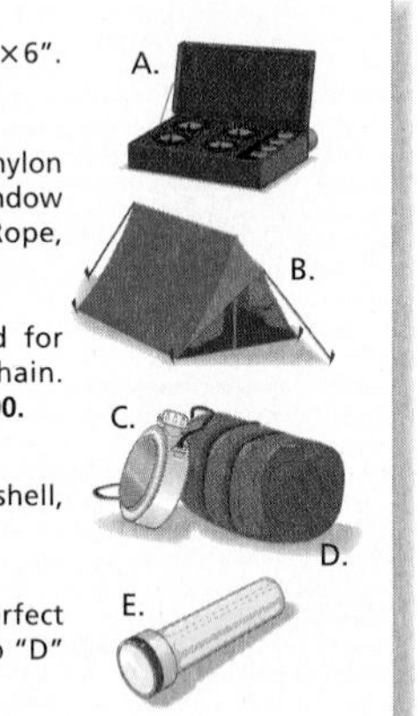

Payment Methods

There are several ways to pay for a catalog order.

Check
A draft on your bank account.

Money order
A check you purchase at the bank or post office for a certain amount of money.

Charge card
An account that allows you to charge the cost of goods to the business that issues the card.

1. **Check**—A check is a draft on your bank account. You mail a check with your order.
2. **Money Order**—You buy a money order from the bank or post office in the amount of your catalog order.
3. **Charge Card**—You may have a charge card for a certain store, or you may use a major credit card. A charge card is an account that allows you to charge the cost of goods to the company that issues the card. When you call to place your order, you give the number of your charge card. Most mail order companies accept major credit cards such as MasterCard and Visa. Large catalog stores offer their own charge accounts.

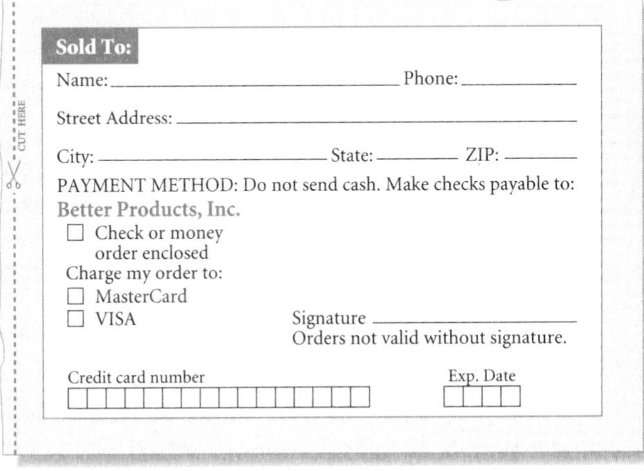
CUT HERE

Sold To:
Name: ______________ Phone: ______
Street Address: ______________
City: ________ State: ______ ZIP: ______
PAYMENT METHOD: Do not send cash. Make checks payable to:
Better Products, Inc.
☐ Check or money order enclosed
Charge my order to:
☐ MasterCard
☐ VISA
Signature ______________
Orders not valid without signature.
Credit card number ☐☐☐☐☐☐☐☐☐☐☐☐☐☐☐☐ Exp. Date ☐☐☐☐

Activity C Use the order form above to answer the following questions. Write your answers on your paper.

1) Does this company accept cash?
2) To what name do you make your check payable?
3) Will the company send your order if you do not write your signature on the form?
4) What two major credit cards may you use to pay for an order?

Reading Vocabulary

account (5)	issue (6)
cash (6)	major (6)
charge card	**money order**
check (4)	payable
draft (6)	signature (6)
enclose (5)	valid (11)

Presenting Activity C

You may wish to point out that many people prefer to use major credit cards, such as Visa, MasterCard, Discover, and American Express, when shopping by mail because often these credit card companies offer special guarantees and refunds if a product purchased with their card is lost, broken, or stolen or in any way unsatisfactory. Emphasize that as long as shoppers pay their bills in full and on time, they do not incur any added expense by using credit cards.

Activity C Answers

1) No 2) Better Products, Inc. 3) No 4) MasterCard or Visa

Learning Styles

LEP/ESL

On the board, make two columns. In Column #1, print the three following terms: *check, money order,* and *charge card.* Then ask students for whom English is a second language to translate these terms into their primary language. Ask them to write their translations in Column #2 and then to give examples of what the terms mean to them. Invite volunteers to share stories about times when they have needed to know and use these terms.

Name Date Period *Chapter 9 Activity 31*

Catalog Shopping

Directions: Read the order form. Fill in the missing information. Then answer the following questions about this order form.

Order Form
John Smith & Associates
Detach and mail check, money order, or credit card number to: **1000 Maple Street, Suite 10**
Baltimore, MD 12345

Send me the following:

No.		Each	Total
___	Fire Safety Video Kit	$99.00	___
2	Set of 10 booklets	29.00	___
___	Set of 10 post tests	10.00	___
2	Set of 10 certificates	3.00	___
		Subtotal	___
		MD residents add 5% sales tax	___
		Postage & Handling	$5.00
		Total	___

Orders placed before April 15: - $10.00

Prices are subject to change without notice. All sales final. Defective items may be exchanged. All orders must be prepaid.

We accept Visa or Mastercard!
☐ Visa ☐ Mastercard
Account # ______ Exp. Date ___
Signature ______

Send order to: 291
Name ______
Organization ______
Address ______
City ______ State ___ ZIP ___
Phone# ______ Attention ______

1) Who will receive the order form and your payment? ______
2) How many ways are there to pay for this order? List them. ______
3) How many items were ordered? ______
4) What happens to the price if you order before April 15? ______
5) What is the subtotal of your order? ______
6) Who must pay 5% sales tax? ______
7) What is the total cost of your order? ______
8) Can you return these items if you do not like them? ______
9) If paying by check or money order, what do you do with the credit card section? ______
10) Do you have to include your payment with your order? ______

 Life Skills English

Activity 31

Filling Out an Order Form

Be sure to fill out order forms very carefully. You want to be sure you get the merchandise you order. If you write the wrong catalog number, you may get the wrong item. If you write your address incorrectly, you may never receive your order.

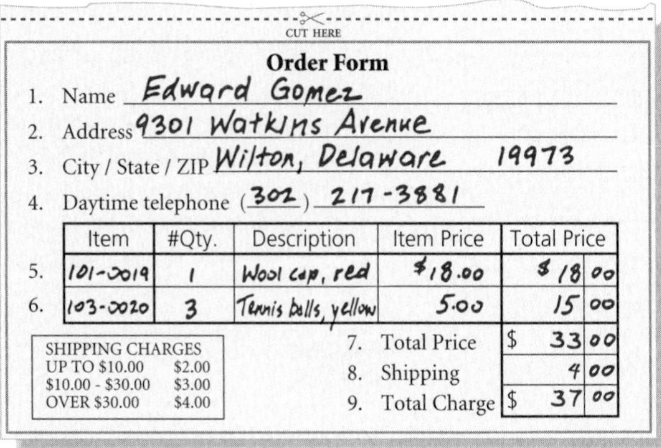

CUT HERE

Order Form

1. Name Edward Gomez
2. Address 9301 Watkins Avenue
3. City / State / ZIP Wilton, Delaware 19973
4. Daytime telephone (302) 217-3881

	Item	#Qty.	Description	Item Price	Total Price
5.	101-0019	1	Wool cap, red	$18.00	$18 00
6.	103-0020	3	Tennis balls, yellow	5.00	15 00

SHIPPING CHARGES	
UP TO $10.00	$2.00
$10.00 - $30.00	$3.00
OVER $30.00	$4.00

7. Total Price	$ 33 00
8. Shipping	4 00
9. Total Charge	$ 37 00

Activity D Number your paper from 1 to 9 as on the order form above. Choose any two items below to order. Write the information correctly as you would on the order form.

101–0019 WOOL CAPS. One size fits all. Red, blue, green. $18.00.

101–2001 WARM-UP SUIT. 100% polyester. S-M-L-XL. Blue or green. $59.95.

102–1001 BASEBALL GLOVE in fine quality leather. $49.95.

103–0020 TENNIS BALLS. Yellow or orange. Special sale price. $5.00.

104–1008 VIDEOCASSETTE RECORDER, VHS format. $195.00.

Reading Vocabulary

format, recorder (8), polyester, tennis (5), quality (5), videocassette

■ Presenting Activity D

Have students select three or four items from sample catalogs to order. Then have them fill out the order form from that catalog. If there are not enough catalog forms available for individual students, have students work in pairs or groups of three. Before students do Activity D on their own, be sure they understand what information each heading in the chart on the order form refers to. If necessary, point out the following:

Item = catalog item number

#Qty = number of items ordered

Description = name of item

Item price = cost for one

Total price = cost for number ordered

Activity D Answers

Answers will vary depending on the items and quantities chosen. Students should list information for each item they are ordering in the order listed on the chart.

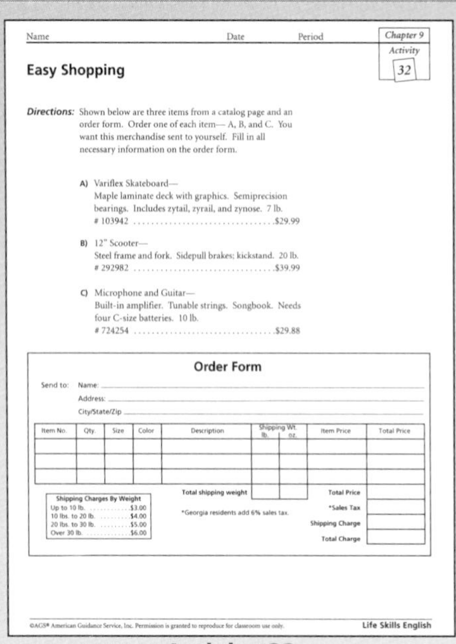

Name Date Period *Chapter 9 Activity 32*

Easy Shopping

Directions: Shown below are three items from a catalog page and an order form. Order one of each item— A, B, and C. You want this merchandise sent to yourself. Fill in all necessary information on the order form.

A) Variflex Skateboard—
Maple laminate deck with graphics. Semiprecision bearings. Includes zytail, zyrail, and zynose. 7 lb.
103942 .... $29.99

B) 12" Scooter—
Steel frame and fork. Sidepull brakes; kickstand. 20 lb.
292982 .... $39.99

C) Microphone and Guitar—
Built-in amplifier. Tunable strings. Songbook. Needs four C-size batteries. 10 lb.
724254 .... $29.88

Order Form

Send to: Name: ____ Address: ____ City/State/Zip ____

Item No.	Qty.	Size	Color	Description	Shipping Wt. lb.	oz.	Item Price	Total Price

Total shipping weight ____ Total Price ____ *Sales Tax ____ Shipping Charge ____ Total Charge ____

Shipping Charges By Weight	
Up to 10 lb.	$3.00
10 lbs. to 20 lb.	$4.00
20 lbs. to 30 lb.	$5.00
Over 30 lb.	$6.00

*Georgia residents add 6% sales tax.

 Life Skills English

Activity 32

Name Date Period *Chapter 9 Workbook Activity 56*

Catalog Shopping

A. Directions: Beside each word in Column **A** write the letter of the correct meaning found in Column **B**.

A	B
____ 1) Quantity	a) money you are charged for having items sent to you
____ 2) Item Price	b) the price for one item
____ 3) Total Price	c) number of items ordered
____ 4) Shipping Charges	d) the total amount of money owed, including total price, tax, and shipping charges
____ 5) Total Charge	e) the item price multiplied by the quantity

B. Directions: Answer the questions below about this sample order form.

Send to: Name: Robert D. Jones
Address: 345 Charter Avenue
City/State/Zip Albuquerque, New Mexico 87106

Item No.	Qty.	Size	Color	Description	Shipping Wt. lb.	oz.	Item Price	Total Price
756F	2	M	Red	Leotard	1	8	$20.00	$40.00
824G	1 Pair	10D	Black	Steel-Toe Work Boots	6	3	$61.99	61.99

Total shipping weight 7 lb. 11 oz. Total Price $101.99 *Sales Tax .00 Shipping Charge 3.00 Total Charge $104.99

Shipping Charges By Weight	
Up to 10 lb.	$3.00
10 lbs. to 20 lb.	$4.00
20 lbs. to 30 lb.	$5.00
Over 30 lb.	$6.00

Iowa residents add 6% sales tax.

1) Who will receive this order? ____
2) Where will the order be sent? ____
3) How many of each item was ordered? ____
4) What is the most expensive item ordered? ____
5) What is the total shipping weight? ____
6) Why isn't sales tax being paid? ____
7) What is the total amount owed by the customer? ____
8) What is the shipping charge? ____

 Life Skills English

Workbook Activity 56

Lesson 2 Review

Part A Write on your paper your answers to these questions.

1) Name two ways to order from a catalog.

2) Who is responsible for paying shipping charges—the catalog dealer or the customer?

3) What are two ways to pay for a catalog order?

4) Give an example of a major credit card.

CUT HERE

Order Form

1. Name ______
2. Address ______
3. City / State / ZIP ______
4. Daytime telephone (___)______

	Item	#Qty.	Description	Item Price	Total Price
5.					
6.					

SHIPPING CHARGES	
UP TO $10.00	$2.00
$10.00 - $30.00	$3.00
OVER $30.00	$4.00

7. Total Price $
8. Shipping
9. Total Charge $

Part B Number your paper from 1 to 9 as on the order form. Choose any two items below to order. Write the information as you would on the order form on your paper.

702222 RUBY PENDANT. 3 rubies and 2 diamonds in 10K gold $335.00.

34311W ELEGANT WATCH. 6-digit, displays hours, minutes, seconds, months, and days on command . . . Sale-priced $84.95.

21333A BRASS COAT TREE. Traditional hall stand in polished brass. 6′ high. $89.90 or two for $165.00.

Reading Vocabulary

digit
traditional
pendant

Part A Answers

Some answers will vary. Possible responses are given.

1) by phone or by mail
2) customer 3) check or credit card 4) Visa; accept all reasonable responses

Part B Answers

Answers will vary depending on the items and quantities chosen. Students should list information for each item they are ordering in the order listed on the chart.

Global Connection

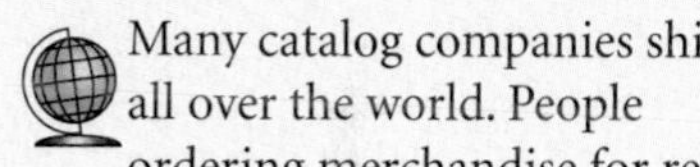

Many catalog companies ship all over the world. People ordering merchandise for relatives and friends in other countries may need additional information. Often, this information is printed on the order forms. If not, customers can ask the customer service representative such questions as:

Does the company ship all over the world, specifically does it ship to ______?

Is there any place the company does not ship?

What are the costs for shipping outside the USA?

Are there any other costs, such as import charges?

At this time, customers might also ask if the catalog is printed in any other language and if there are any bilingual customer service representatives available.

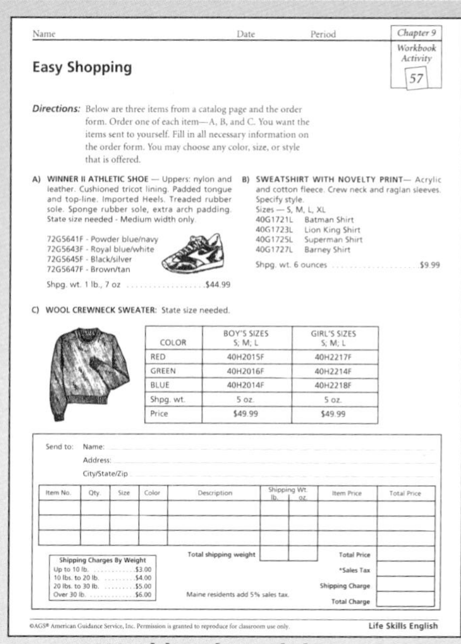

Name Date Period

Chapter 9 *Workbook Activity* 57

Easy Shopping

Directions: Below are three items from a catalog page and the order form. Order one of each item—A, B, and C. You want the items sent to yourself. Fill in all necessary information on the order form. You may choose any color, size, or style that is offered.

A) **WINNER II ATHLETIC SHOE** — Uppers: nylon and leather. Cushioned tricot lining. Padded tongue and top-line. Imported Heels. Treaded rubber sole. Sponge rubber sole, extra arch padding. State size needed - Medium width only.

72G5641F - Powder blue/navy
72G5643F - Royal blue/white
72G5645F - Black/silver
72G5647F - Brown/tan

Shpg. wt. 1 lb., 7 oz $44.99

B) **SWEATSHIRT WITH NOVELTY PRINT**— Acrylic and cotton fleece. Crew neck and raglan sleeves. Specify style.
Sizes — S, M, L, XL
40G1721L Batman Shirt
40G1723L Lion King Shirt
40G1725L Superman Shirt
40G1727L Barney Shirt

Shpg. wt. 6 ounces $9.99

C) **WOOL CREWNECK SWEATER:** State size needed.

COLOR	BOY'S SIZES S; M; L	GIRL'S SIZES S; M; L
RED	40H2015F	40H2217F
GREEN	40H2016F	40H2214F
BLUE	40H2014F	40H2218F
Shpg. wt.	5 oz.	5 oz.
Price	$49.99	$49.99

Send to: Name:
Address:
City/State/Zip

Item No.	Qty.	Size	Color	Description	Shipping Wt. lb.	oz.	Item Price	Total Price

Total shipping weight

Shipping Charges By Weight	
Up to 10 lb.	$3.00
10 lbs. to 20 lb.	$4.00
20 lbs. to 30 lb.	$5.00
Over 30 lb.	$6.00

Total Price
*Sales Tax
Shipping Charge
Total Charge

Maine residents add 5% sales tax.

 Life Skills English

Workbook Activity 57

Name Date Period

Chapter 9 *Workbook Activity* 58

Catalog Order Form

Directions: Below are sample items from a catalog page and the order form. Order at least three different items from the samples. You want the items sent to you. Fill in all necessary information on the order form.

CATALOG ENVELOPES (250 Per Box)
• Handles big jobs
• Save up to 40%
• Heavy gummed flaps
AD6-TR98 9½" x 12½" $25.79
AD6-TR99 10" x 13" 27.29
AD6-TR100 11½" x 14½" 32.87
Shipping weight .... 12 lb.

WALL CHARTS
• Save 20%
• 1 free write-on/wipe-off pen with each chart
AD4-WC201 17" x 22" $21.98
Shipping weight .... 12 oz.

BUSINESS ENVELOPES (Price Per Box of 500)
• Window style features Newglas frosted see-through panel.
• Diagonal cut
• White wove

			(4 or more boxes)
AD9-QS99	10" Plain	$10.05	$19.00
AD9-QS101	10" Window	11.95	20.70

Shipping weight .... 7 lb.

Send to: Name:
Address:
City/State/Zip

Item No.	Qty.	Size	Color	Description	Shipping Wt. lb.	oz.	Item Price	Total Price

Total shipping weight

Shipping Charges By Weight	
Up to 10 lb.	$3.00
10 lbs. to 20 lb.	$4.00
20 lbs. to 30 lb.	$5.00
Over 30 lb.	$6.00

Total Price
*Sales Tax
Shipping Charge
Total Charge

Colorado residents add 6% sales tax.

 Life Skills English

Workbook Activity 58

Lesson at a Glance

Chapter 9 Lesson 3

Overview This lesson provides suggestions for dealing with an unsatisfactory catalog order.

Objective

- To match solutions with catalog order problems.

Student Pages 260–263

Teacher's Resource Library

Activity 33

Workbook Activities 59–60

Reading Vocabulary

apply (6)
manager (6)
properly (5)
respond (6)
unsatisfactory

Teaching Suggestions

Introducing the Lesson

Discuss the information presented in the text. Invite students to share experiences they or people they know have had with an unsatisfactory catalog order. Ask students the following questions:

What was wrong with the order?

What did you (or the customer) do about it?

If a complaint was made, how did the company respond?

Was the problem resolved or fixed?

Reviewing Skills

Review what students have learned about shopping by catalog.

Lesson 3 When the Order Is Wrong

Sometimes the merchandise you order will be unsatisfactory in some way.

EXAMPLES

You may receive broken items.

The item may not work properly.

Clothing may not fit.

Merchandise may not look like the picture in the catalog.

You may not like the merchandise.

It is important to examine the merchandise carefully as soon as it arrives. You have two choices. You can

1. wrap the item up and mail it back. Explain what is wrong in a letter.
2. take it back to the store. Tell the manager what is wrong.

Whatever your choice, you should return the merchandise as quickly as possible.

What the Store Will Do

How a store responds when you return an item is partly your choice. Some stores will not return your money, especially if the item is on sale. However, a store may

1. give you another item that fits or isn't broken.
2. fix the item if it is broken.
3. return the full amount of your purchase price in cash.
4. apply a credit to your credit card if you purchased the item this way.
5. give you a store credit to use to buy something else.

A Letter of Complaint

Here is a letter that Chris Williams wrote when she returned a dress.

> 31 E. Ralston Pl.
> Wilton, DE 19999
>
> April 3, 1999
>
> Dress AMERICA
> P.O. Box 231
> Selbyville, TX 75820
>
> Attention: Customer Service
>
> Dear Sir:
> I am returning the dress #CA4531 Size 11. It is too large. Please exchange it for a size 9. Thank you for your help.
>
> Sincerely,
> *Chris Williams*
> Chris Williams

Activity A Write a letter of complaint to the following address. Use the letter above as an example. Address the letter to

Quality Products, Inc.
12 West Franklin Street
Wilkinsburg, PA 15220
Attention: Customer Service

Choose one of these problems to write about:

1) Your videotape recorder isn't working properly. It will not eject the tape.
2) A set of dishes you planned to give your sister for her new apartment arrived broken.
3) Your popcorn maker is not shutting off automatically. The popcorn is burning.

Reading Vocabulary

automatically
complaint (6)
eject (8)
sincerely (5)
videotape

Presenting Activity A

Before asking students to do Activity A, use the sample letter to review or introduce the conventions of writing a business letter, including the heading, date, inside address, greeting, body, and closing. Emphasize that the tone of a complaint letter should be polite and positive. Remind students that the purpose of the letter is to resolve the problem, not to insult someone's character. Students should use appropriate language and avoid slang. They should provide all the necessary information and state the problem quickly and clearly.

Activity A Answers

Letters will vary. One of the three problems should be addressed. Letters should follow the sample business letter format.

Learning Styles

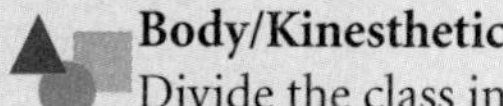

Body/Kinesthetic

Divide the class into pairs. Ask each set of partners to devise two role plays about returning or exchanging merchandise at a store. Suggest that one student be the store clerk and the other be the customer. Ask each pair to create one role play in which all goes well and both the clerk and the customer are courteous and satisfied. Then ask them to create a second role play that involves a problem with the process. Provide time for the presentation of the role plays. Afterward, discuss what the students learned from the role playing.

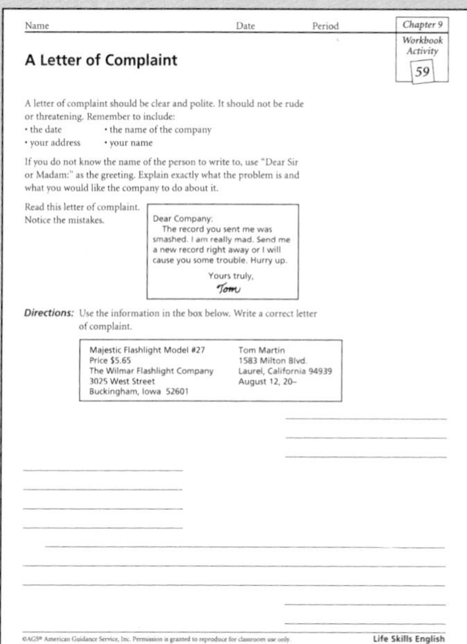

Name Date Period *Chapter 9 Workbook Activity 59*

A Letter of Complaint

A letter of complaint should be clear and polite. It should not be rude or threatening. Remember to include:
- the date
- your address
- the name of the company
- your name

If you do not know the name of the person to write to, use "Dear Sir or Madam:" as the greeting. Explain exactly what the problem is and what you would like the company to do about it.

Read this letter of complaint. Notice the mistakes.

> Dear Company:
> The record you sent me was smashed. I am really mad. Send me a new record right away or I will cause you some trouble. Hurry up.
> Yours truly,
> *Tom*

Directions: Use the information in the box below. Write a correct letter of complaint.

> Majestic Flashlight Model #27
> Price $5.65
> The Wilmar Flashlight Company
> 3025 West Street
> Buckingham, Iowa 52601
>
> Tom Martin
> 1583 Milton Blvd.
> Laurel, California 94939
> August 12, 20–

 Life Skills English

Workbook Activity 59

Name Date Period *Chapter 9 Workbook Activity 60*

Addressing an Envelope

Two addresses belong on an envelope. The name and address of the person sending the letter goes in the upper left-hand corner. The name of the address of the person receiving the letter goes in the middle of the envelope.

Directions: Look at the names and addresses below. Place them correctly on the envelope. Put a comma between the name of the city and the state. Use the Zip code abbreviation for each state. Make sure the stamp is for the correct amount for first-class postage.

The Sender:
Alice Barton
723 N. Quinn St.
Arlington Va. 22209

The Receiver:
Mrs. Edith Carlson
5489 Elk Rd.
Northfield Minn. 55057

 Life Skills English

Workbook Activity 60

Reading Vocabulary

attempt (5)
bureau (6)
contact (6)
investigate (6)
overlook (6)
persistent
supervisor (7)
toll (6)
trace (5)

Application

In the Community Bilingual students can offer to write letters or make telephone calls for family members, friends, and other members of the community who speak their same primary language and who may need assistance in resolving a problem with a catalog company.

When More Action Is Needed

Your other attempts to clear up an unsatisfactory order may not work. If that happens, here are some more steps to take when action is needed.

1. If a catalog store does not take action on your complaint within a few weeks, call them on the telephone. Use the toll-free number or call collect. Ask to speak with a manager or supervisor.
2. Contact the post office if your order was sent through the mail. Give them all the information they need to trace your letter or package. They will need to know the name of the company, the complete mailing address, the telephone number with area code, the date it was mailed, and how it was mailed.
3. Many newspapers and television stations have people who investigate consumer problems. Find out their address and write to them for help.
4. Write the store another letter. Be persistent! Don't give up until the problem is solved.
5. Contact the Better Business Bureau. Find out how they rate the company. File a complaint with them if necessary.
6. Review all of your letters and any notes from phone calls. See if you overlooked anything that would clear up the matter or would help you take more action.

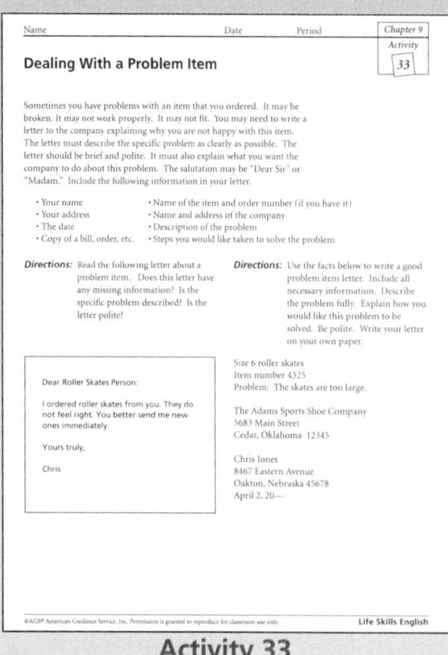

Name Date Period

Chapter 9 Activity 33

Dealing With a Problem Item

Sometimes you have problems with an item that you ordered. It may be broken. It may not work properly. It may not fit. You may need to write a letter to the company explaining why you are not happy with this item. The letter must describe the specific problem as clearly as possible. The letter should be brief and polite. It must also explain what you want the company to do about this problem. The salutation may be "Dear Sir" or "Madam." Include the following information in your letter.

- Your name
- Your address
- The date
- Copy of a bill, order, etc.
- Name of the item and order number (if you have it)
- Name and address of the company
- Description of the problem
- Steps you would like taken to solve the problem

Directions: Read the following letter about a problem item. Does this letter have any missing information? Is the specific problem described? Is the letter polite?

Dear Roller Skates Person:

I ordered roller skates from you. They do not feel right. You better send me new ones immediately.

Yours truly,

Chris

Directions: Use the facts below to write a good problem item letter. Include all necessary information. Describe the problem fully. Explain how you would like this problem to be solved. Be polite. Write your letter on your own paper.

Size 6 roller skates
Item number 4325
Problem: The skates are too large.

The Adams Sports Shoe Company
5683 Main Street
Cedar, Oklahoma 12345

Chris Jones
8467 Eastern Avenue
Oakton, Nebraska 45678
April 2, 20—

 Life Skills English

Activity 33

262 *Chapter 9 Shopping by Catalog*

Lesson 3 Review

Lesson Review Number your paper from 1 to 4. Read each problem below and choose the best solution. Write the correct letter beside each number.

Problems

1) Charles ordered a shirt from the World's Horizon catalog. When the shirt came, it was the wrong size.

2) Sandy bought a set of dishes at a catalog showroom. When she got home and opened the box, she found a broken plate.

3) Lily Collins ordered a blouse from a catalog through the mail. The blouse did not look like the one in the picture. Lily wants her money back.

4) Justin returned his computer to Quality Products, Inc. In a few weeks, they sent it back. It still did not work.

Solutions

a) Mail the merchandise back immediately. Explain what is wrong. Tell the store the size you need.

b) Mail the merchandise back at once. Tell the store you want your money refunded.

c) Call the company. Explain the problem.

d) Take the merchandise back to the store as soon as possible.

Reading Vocabulary

horizon (5) solution (6)
refund (7)

Lesson Review Answers

Answers may vary. The most likely responses are given.

1) a **2)** d **3)** b **4)** c

Application

In the Community
Point out to students that consumers with a problem that has not been resolved to their satisfaction can also contact the consumer affairs department at their state's attorney general's office.

Chapter 9 Review

The Teacher's Resource Library includes two parallel forms of the Chapter 9 Mastery Test. The difficulty level of the two forms is equivalent. You may wish to use one form as a pretest and the other form as a posttest.

Final Mastery Test

The Teacher's Resource Library includes the Final Mastery Test. This test is pictured on pages 280–281 of this Teacher's Edition. The Final Mastery Test assesses the major learning objectives of this text, with major emphasis on Chapters 5–9.

Reading Vocabulary

document (6)

Part A Answers

1) j 2) f 3) b 4) g 5) h 6) c 7) d 8) e 9) a 10) i

Part B Answers

1) retail 2) sale 3) discount 4) wholesale

Chapter 9 Review

Part A Number your paper from 1 to 10. Match the terms with their meanings. Write the correct letter next to each number.

Terms	Meanings
1) Catalog	a) VISA or MasterCard
2) Merchandise	b) A book with information
3) Reference book	c) To decide how things are different or alike
4) Advantage	d) Cost of an item in a store
5) Disadvantage	e) A draft on your bank account
6) Compare	f) Any item for sale
7) Retail price	g) A reason to choose something
8) Check	h) A reason not to choose something
9) Major credit card	i) A purchased document that is used to pay someone
10) Money order	j) Any list of items

Part B Write on your paper the word that completes each sentence. Use one of the words from the box.

discount	sale
retail	wholesale

1) Jack paid the suggested ______ price for his new coat.

2) The coat that Anna bought was on ______.

3) The catalog store sold merchandise at a ______ price.

4) The dealer paid the ______ price for her merchandise.

264 *Chapter 9 Shopping by Catalog*

Name ______ Date ______ Period ______

Chapter 9 Mastery Test A page 1

Chapter 9 Mastery Test A

Part A Complete each sentence using a word from the box.

price	dealer	money	charge	wholesale

1) A check you purchase at the bank or post office for a certain sum of money is a ______ order.

2) An account that allows you to charge the cost of goods is called a ______ card.

3) A ______ price is the price a manufacturer charges a store for items bought in large amounts.

4) A ______ is a business or individual that sells to the public.

5) A discount ______ is a price below the regular retail price.

Part B Read the catalog description. Then answer the questions.

Decorative Ribbons for Holidays and Every Day!

Use these ribbons to trim packages and to decorate dried flowers, centerpieces, wall hangings, and more. Size ⅞" wide × 25 yard rolls.

FA-3042–Tartan	FA-3043–Hearts	FA-3047–Independence Day
FA-3044–Sparkle Red	FA-3045–Sparkle Green	FA-3046–Sparkle Purple

$5.95 each. Mix and Match: Any 12 or more just **$5.45 each.**

1) List a common use for holiday ribbons. ______

2) In what size rolls is this ribbon available? ______

3) How much is one roll of ribbon? ______

4) What is the order number for Sparkle Red ribbon? ______

5) How much would it cost for each roll if you buy 6 rolls of Sparkle Purple and 6 rolls of Tartan? ______

 Life Skills English

Name ______ Date ______ Period ______

Chapter 9 Mastery Test A page 2

Chapter 9 Mastery Test A, continued

Part C Fill in the order form as if you are ordering the following item:

893-58 **TELEPHONE AND ADDRESS BOOK** Black vinyl cover, wirebound with Velcro closing. Tab indexed; 4 pages per letter…
$8.98 each/2 for $16.00

Order Form

Send to: 1. Name: ______ 2. Daytime Phone: ______
3. Address: ______
4. City, State and ZIP ______

	Item #	Qty.	Description	Item Price	Total Price
5.					
				6. Total Price	
				7. Shipping	
				8. Total Charge	

Shipping Charges	
Up to $10.00	$3.00
$10.00 to $30.00	$4.00
Over $30.00	$5.00

Part D Read the five problems. Write the letter of the best solution on the line next to each problem.

Problems

______ 1) Samantha bought a vase. When she got home, she discovered that it had a chip in it.

______ 2) John sent his watch to Compron to get it fixed. When they sent it back, it still didn't work.

______ 3) Mrs. Jones received shoes that she ordered. They are too big. Smaller sizes are not available.

______ 4) Harry ordered a large shirt. It is too big. He needs a medium.

______ 5) Vernita ordered a drill. She doesn't like it. It is too heavy and not powerful enough.

Solutions

a) Mail the merchandise back immediately. Explain what is wrong. Tell the company the size that you need.

b) Mail the merchandise back at once. Tell the company that the item won't fit and that no other sizes will work. Tell the company that you want your money refunded.

c) Call the company. Explain the problem. Discuss possible solutions.

d) Mail the merchandise back at once. Tell the company that you want your money refunded.

e) Take the merchandise back to the store for a replacement as soon as possible.

 Life Skills English

Chapter 9 Mastery Test A

Part C Read the product description below. On your paper, write the information as you would on the order form shown.

#054-9856
Telephone Answering Machine
Call from anywhere in the world and pick up messages. Built-in speaker and earphone jack.
***Sale-priced at* $125.95**

CUT HERE

Order Form

1. Name ______________________
2. Address ______________________
3. City / State / ZIP ______________________
4. Daytime telephone (____) ______________

	Item	#Qty.	Description	Item Price	Total Price
5.					
6.					
				7. Total Price	$
				8. Shipping	
				9. Total Charge	$

SHIPPING CHARGES	
UP TO $10.00	$2.00
$10.00 - $30.00	$3.00
OVER $30.00	$4.00

Part D Explain what you would do to solve the problem described below. Write your answer on your paper.

You ordered a light blue sweatshirt from a catalog to give to your brother for his birthday. You checked with the operator to be sure that you would receive the sweatshirt in time. However, it arrived late. On top of that, the sweatshirt was the wrong size *and* the wrong color.

Test Taking Tip When studying for a test, memorize only the most important points. Practice writing or saying the material out loud. Have a partner listen to check if you are right.

Reading Vocabulary

earphone	operator (5)
jack	speaker
memorize (6)	sweatshirt

Part C Answers

1) Responses will vary for individual students. **2)** Responses will vary for individual students. **3)** Responses will vary for individual students. **4)** Responses will vary for individual students. **5)** #054-9856; 1 (may vary); telephone answering machine; $125.95; $125.95 (will vary if more than one is ordered) **7)** $125.95 (will vary if more than one is ordered) **8)** $4.00 **9)** $129.95 (will vary if more than one is ordered).

Part D Answers

Answers will vary. Possible solutions are writing a letter of complaint; calling the company to explain the problem.

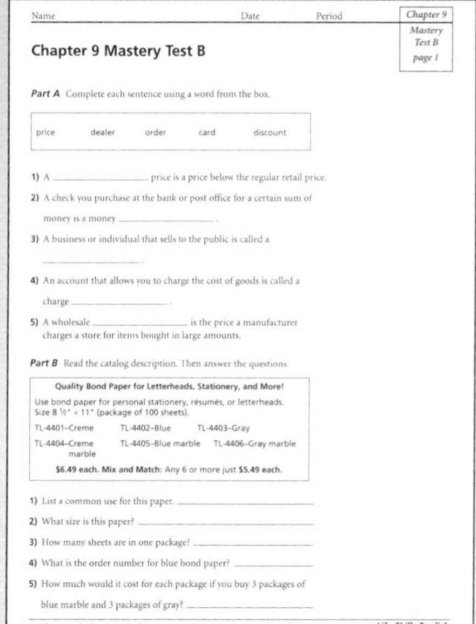

Name Date Period *Chapter 9 Mastery Test B page 1*

Chapter 9 Mastery Test B

Part A Complete each sentence using a word from the box.

price dealer order card discount

1) A ____________ price is a price below the regular retail price.

2) A check you purchase at the bank or post office for a certain sum of money is a money ____________ .

3) A business or individual that sells to the public is called a ____________ .

4) An account that allows you to charge the cost of goods is called a charge ____________ .

5) A wholesale ____________ is the price a manufacturer charges a store for items bought in large amounts.

Part B Read the catalog description. Then answer the questions.

Quality Bond Paper for Letterheads, Stationery, and More!
Use bond paper for personal stationery, résumés, or letterheads. Size 8 ½" × 11" (package of 100 sheets).
TL-4401–Creme TL-4402–Blue TL-4403–Gray
TL-4404–Creme marble TL-4405–Blue marble TL-4406–Gray marble
$6.49 each. Mix and Match: Any 6 or more just **$5.49 each.**

1) List a common use for this paper. ____________

2) What size is this paper? ____________

3) How many sheets are in one package? ____________

4) What is the order number for blue bond paper? ____________

5) How much would it cost for each package if you buy 3 packages of blue marble and 3 packages of gray? ____________

 Life Skills English

Name Date Period *Chapter 9 Mastery Test B page 2*

Chapter 9 Mastery Test B, continued

Part C Fill in the order form as if you are ordering the following item:

405-89E **CASSETTE RECORDER** Compact, lightweight, easy to use. Fits in pocket. Corrects errors fast. Includes handy edit function…
SALE PRICE $39.95

Order Form

Send to: 1. Name: ____________ 2. Daytime Phone: ____________
3. Address: ____________
4. City, State and ZIP ____________

	Item #	Qty.	Description	Item Price	Total Price
5.					
				6. Total Price	
				7. Shipping	
				8. Total Charge	

Shipping Charges	
Up to $10.00	$3.00
$10.00 to $30.00	$4.00
Over $30.00	$5.00

Part D Read the five problems. Write the letter of the best solution on the line next to each problem.

Problems

____ **1)** Cynthia ordered a sweater. It is too small, but the company doesn't have any larger sizes.

____ **2)** Mrs. Thompson ordered a radio. When it arrived, it sounded terrible and it looked nothing like the picture in the catalog.

____ **3)** Mr. Beck bought a shirt. When he brought it home, he noticed that it had a small rip in the sleeve.

____ **4)** Dwayne ordered a flashlight. When he got it, it didn't work.

____ **5)** Heng ordered a set of sheets. They are the wrong size.

Solutions

a) Mail the merchandise back at once. Tell the company that the item won't fit and that no other sizes will work. Tell the company that you want your money refunded.

b) Take the merchandise back to the store for a replacement as soon as possible.

c) Call the company. Explain the problem. Ask to be sent the correct size.

d) Mail the merchandise back immediately. Explain what is wrong. Tell the company that you would like a new one.

e) Mail the merchandise back at once. Tell the company that you want your money refunded.

 Life Skills English

Chapter 9 Mastery Test B

Glossary

A

Abbreviation (ə brē vē ā′ shən) a shortened form of a written word (p. 29)

Accent mark (ak′ sent märk) a mark that shows which part of a word to stress when pronouncing the word (p. 28)

Advantage (ad van′ tij) a benefit or positive feature (p. 248)

Advertise (ad′ vər tīz) to announce something to the public through the media (p. 192)

Advertisement (ad vər tiz′ mənt) a public notice, usually about a product or service for sale (p. 189)

Affiliate (ə fil′ ē it) a member station that carries some of the programs broadcast by a large television network (p. 210)

Alphabetical order (al fə bet′ ə kəl ôr′ dər) the order of letters of the alphabet (p. 2)

Alternative (ȯl tėr′ nə tiv) a choice between two or more possibilities (p. 109)

Antonym (an′ tə nim) a word that means the opposite of another word (p. 50)

Appliance (ə plī′ əns) a piece of household equipment such as a toaster, oven, dishwasher, electric mixer, or microwave oven (p. 248)

Applicable (ap′ lə kə bəl) something that is appropriate or suitable (p. 227)

Application (ap lə kā′ shən) a form to make a request (p. 226)

Apprentice (ə pren′ tis) a worker being trained by an experienced and skilled person (p. 167)

Assets (as′ ets) property you own that has value (p. 237)

Associate's degree (ə sō′ shē its di grē′) a degree from a two-year college or a community college (p. 158)

Atlas (at′ ləs) a book of maps and geographical facts (p. 63)

Autobiography (ȯ tə bī og′ rə fē) a story of a real person's life written by that person (p. 132)

Available (ə vā′ lə bəl) refers to when you can begin a job (p. 226)

B

Bachelor's degree (bach′ ə lərz di grē′) a degree from a four-year college or university (p. 158)

Back issue (bak ish′ ü) an issue that was published in the past (p. 148)

Benefits (ben′ ə fits) what workers receive in addition to wages, such as health insurance and vacations (p. 202)

Bibliography (bib lē og′ rə fē) a list of books and articles an author has used as references to write a book; bibliographies usually appear in the back of the book (p. 137)

Biographical dictionary (bī ə graf′ ə kəl dik′ shə ner ē) a reference book that lists famous people and facts about their lives (p. 50)

Biographical novel (bī ə graf′ ə kəl nov′ əl) a fictional account of a real person's life (p. 132)

Biography (bī og′ rə fē) a nonfiction book about a real person written by someone other than that person (p. 132)

Blue pages (blü pāj′ əs) a part of the telephone book that lists the numbers of government agencies (p. 120)

Branch (branch) one of the libraries in a system of libraries (p. 128)

Broadcast (brȯd′ kast) to send radio or television signals through the air to receivers in the home, the car, or other location (p. 206)

Bureau (byůr′ ō) a specialized group or department that focuses on one area or one main topic (p. 171)

C

Call number (kȯl num′ bər) the numbers and letters assigned to a library book; the call number determines where the book will be placed on the shelf (p. 137)

Cartoon (kär tün′) usually a single drawing that the artist uses to tell a joke or express an idea (p. 183)

Catalog (kat′ l ȯg) any list of information (p. 129)

CD-ROM (sē′ dē′ rom) a computer science term that stands for *compact disc read-only memory* (p. 58)

Chapter (chap′ tər) a part of a book (p. 18)

266 *Glossary* *Life Skills English*

Charge card (chärj kärd) an account that allows you to charge the cost of goods to the business that issues the card (p. 257)

Check (chek) a draft on your bank account (p. 257)

Circulate (sėr´ kyə lāt) can be taken out of the library (p. 147)

Classified advertisements (klas´ ə fīd ad vər tīz´ mənt) short public notices (items for sale, apartments or houses for rent, help wanted) (p. 181)

Column (kol´ əm) a regular newspaper feature about recent events, current political and social issues, and other topics of interest to readers (p. 181)

Columnist (kol´ əm nist) a person who writes from a personal point of view on events and issues and on how problems can be solved (p. 182)

Comic strip (kom´ ik strip) a series of cartoon frames that tell a story (p. 183)

Condensed (kən denst´) a shorter version of an article but with the same main idea (p. 92)

Consumer (kən sü´ mər) someone who buys and uses goods and services (p. 173)

Consumers Union (kən sü´ mərz yü´ nyən) a group that tests products and investigates businesses; the Consumers Union publishes the results of its tests in a magazine called *Consumer Reports* (p. 173)

Contractor (kon´ trak tər) a person who agrees to perform work or to provide supplies for a job (p. 167)

Credentials (kri den´ shəlz) proof that a person is an expert in a certain area of work (p. 158)

Credit (kred´ it) the time you get to pay for the goods you buy (p. 239)

Cross reference (krȯs ref´ ər əns) a related topic you can look up to find additional information on a topic; a cross reference directs you to another part or section of the book (p. 20)

Current (kėr´ ənt) up to the present (p. 180)

Current issue (kėr´ ənt ish´ ü) the most recently published issue of a magazine (p. 148)

Cycle (sī´ kəl) the period of time between events, such as the publishing of a magazine (p. 93)

D

Daily (dā´ lē) every day (p. 180)

Dealer (dē´ lər) a business or individual that sells to the public (p. 248)

Death notice (deth nō´ tis) information about a person's death and details about the funeral arrangements (p. 183)

Debt (det) money owed, or liability (p. 237)

Deposit (di poz´ it) the money you put into an account (p. 240)

Derived (di rīvd´) to come from (p. 37)

Dewey Decimal System (dü´ ē des´ ə məl sis´ təm) a system that libraries use to classify and organize books (p. 137)

Dialogue (dī´ ə lȯg) conversation (p. 132)

Dictionary (dik´ shə ner ē) a book that contains an alphabetical listing of words and their meanings (p. 26)

Digest (dī´ jest) a magazine that contains summaries or condensed articles from other magazines (p. 92)

Disadvantage (dis əd van´ tij) an unfavorable condition or negative feature (p. 248)

Discount price (dis´ kount prīs) a price below the regular retail price (p. 249)

Doctoral degree (dok´ tər əl di grē´) the highest degree awarded by a university or professional school (p. 159)

Document (dok´ yə mənt) a paper that gives information to another person (p. 220)

Documentary (dok yə men´ tər rē) a nonfiction film or television program (p. 214)

Donation (dō nā´ shən) a gift of money or other items of value (p. 210)

E

Edit (ed´ it) to get written material ready for publication (p. 145)

Editor (ed´ ə tər) a person who decides which stories will be reported to the public (p. 187)

a	hat	e	let	ī	ice	ô	order	u̇	put	sh	she	ə	a	in about
ā	age	ē	equal	o	hot	oi	oil	ü	rule	th	thin		e	in taken
ä	far	ėr	term	ō	open	ou	out	ch	child	ᴛʜ	then		i	in pencil
â	care	i	it	ȯ	saw	u	cup	ng	long	zh	measure		o	in lemon
													u	in circus

Life Skills English Glossary **267**

Editorial (ed ə tôr´ ē əl) opinion about an issue or event in the news; editorials are written by members of the newspaper staff (p. 182)

Education (ej ə kā´ shən) a combination of the courses and programs taken at a school or college (p. 228)

Employee (em ploi´ ē) a person who works for someone else (p. 226)

Employer (em ploi´ ər) a person or company that pays you a salary (p. 226)

Encyclopedia (en sī klə pē´ dē ə) a book or set of books with a collection of articles and facts on many subjects, organized in alphabetical order (p. 71)

Entry (en´ trē) a listing in a dictionary; an entry provides facts about a word (p. 26)

Equator (i kwā´ tər) an imaginary line that circles the center of the earth (p. 69)

Etymology (et ə mol´ ə jē) the study of the history of a word (p. 37)

Executive (eg zek´ yə tiv) a manager, a supervisor, or an administrator (p. 202)

Experience (ek spir´ ē əns) the same kind of work that you have done before (p. 202)

Expert (ek´ spėrt) a person with training and knowledge about a specific subject (p. 158)

F

Farmer's almanac (fär´ mərz ȯl´ mə nak) an annual calendar of days, weeks, and months with weather predictions and astronomical facts (p. 58)

Federal Communications Commission (FCC) (fed´ ər əl kə myü nə kā´ shənz kə mish´ ən) (ef sē sē) a government agency that provides licenses to people or companies to operate television and radio stations (p. 214)

Fee (fē) a charge for a service (p. 102)

Fiction (fik´ shən) an imaginary story (p. 132)

Finance charge (fī´ nans chärj) a fee you pay on money you owe to a business (p. 239)

Financial (fī nan´ shəl) concerning money or property with value (p. 237)

Foreman (fôr´ mən) a supervisor or boss (p. 167)

Form (fôrm) a printed or typed document with spaces to fill in information (p. 220)

Former (fôr´ mər) refers to something that happened in the past (p. 226)

Full name (fu̇l nām) a person's whole legal name (p. 220)

Full time (fu̇l tīm) a job that requires approximately 40 hours per week, or 8 hours a day for 5 days (p. 202)

G

Gazetteer (gaz ə tir´) a dictionary of geographical place names (p. 63)

General information almanac (jen´ ər əl in fər mā´ shən ȯl´ mə nak) an almanac that contains facts and figures about a variety of subjects from the previous year and from the past (p. 59)

Geographical dictionary (jē ə graf´ ə kəl dik´ shə ner ē) a reference book with a list of rivers, mountains, cities, and other features (p. 50)

Gimmick (gim´ ik) an important feature about something that is kept secret (p. 190)

Globe (glōb) a model of the earth; it shows the actual placement of the continents, islands, and oceans (p. 65)

Grid (grid) a network of lines on a map that makes it possible to locate specific places (p. 66)

Grid map (grid map) a map with grid lines (p. 66)

Guide words (gīd wėrdz) words at the top of a page of information given in alphabetical order; all words that come in alphabetical order between the two guide words can be found on that page (p. 6)

H

Historical novel (hi stôr´ ə kəl nov´ əl) a fictional story about real people and events (p. 132)

History (his´ tər ē) a nonfiction book about real people and events of the past (p. 132)

Homonym (hom´ ə nim) a word that sounds exactly like another word but is spelled differently and has a different meaning (p. 45)

Horizontal (hôr ə zon´ tl) a word that means going across (p. 66)

How-to books (hou tü bu̇ks) reference books that provide detailed instructions for how to complete specific tasks (p. 87)

I

Independent contractors (in di pen´ dənt kon´ trak tərz) people in business for themselves (p. 167)

268 *Glossary Life Skills English*

Index (in´ deks) an alphabetical list of main topics covered in a book (p. 18)

Interest (in´ tər ist) the money a bank pays you for putting money into a savings account; the fee you pay for borrowing money (p. 240)

Internet (in´ tər net) the largest computer network in the world; it allows people from all over the world to use computers to interact with one another and to get information on a wide variety of topics (p. 87)

Interval (in´ tər vəl) the space of time between events (p. 91)

Itemized (ī´ tə mīzd) listed one by one (p. 110)

J

Joint (joint) an account that is shared or owned together (p. 239)

Journeyman (jėr´ nē mən) a worker who has completed an apprenticeship and passed a test (p. 167)

K

Key (kē) a guide to symbols and abbreviations (p. 26)

Key word (kē wėrd) a word that names what you want to find out about (p. 13)

L

Latitude lines (lat´ ə tüd līnz) the horizontal lines on a map that indicate east to west (p. 68)

Lead (lēd) the first paragraph of a news story; summarizes the most important facts in the story and answers the questions *Who? What? Where?* and *When?* (p. 187)

Liability (lī ə bil´ ə tē) the money you owe (p. 237)

Library catalog (lī´ brer ē kat´ l òg) a catalog that lists most of the materials in a library; there are three types of listings: title, author, and subject (p. 129)

Library of Congress (lī´ brer ē ov kong´ gris) the national library of the United States (p. 130)

Loan (lōn) a sum of money that you borrow (p. 238)

Local (lō´ kəl) having to do with one certain place (p. 180)

Longitude lines (lon´ jə tüd līnz) the vertical lines on a map that indicate north to south (p. 68)

M

Magazine (mag´ ə zēn) a paperback publication with stories and articles on a variety of topics by different writers (p. 91)

Magazine catalog (mag´ ə zēn kat´ l òg) a catalog that lists all the magazines a library subscribes to and identifies the issues the library has (p. 129)

Maiden name (mād´ ən nām) a woman's last name before she marries (p. 220)

Mass media (mas mē´ dē ə) a way to communicate with the most people at one time; for example: television, radio, newspapers, and magazines (p. 180)

Master's degree (mas´ tərz di grē´) an advanced degree, beyond a bachelor's degree, from a graduate school or university (p. 159)

Master's level (mas´ tərz lev´ əl) a worker who has more experience than a journeyman and has passed another test; this worker has earned a master's license (p. 167)

Merchandise (mėr´ chən dīz) goods for sale or that you buy (p. 239)

Microfiche (mī´ krō fēsh) a film card on which many pages of reduced copy are stored (p. 129)

Money order (mun´ ē ôr´ dər) a check you purchase at the bank or post office for a certain amount of money (p. 257)

N

National (nash´ ə nəl) having to do with a whole country, or nation (p. 180)

Net worth (net wėrth) the value of your assets minus the value of your liabilities (p. 237)

Nonfiction (non fik´ shən) based on facts (p. 132)

Novel (nov´ əl) a long, complex story (p. 132)

a	hat	e	let	ī	ice	ô	order	ů	put	sh	she	ə { a	in about
ā	age	ē	equal	o	hot	oi	oil	ü	rule	th	thin	e	in taken
ä	far	ėr	term	ō	open	ou	out	ch	child	TH	then	i	in pencil
â	care	i	it	ò	saw	u	cup	ng	long	zh	measure	o	in lemon
												u	in circus

Life Skills English Glossary **269**

O

Obituary (ō bich´ ü er ē) a short article about someone who has recently died (p. 183)

Occupation (ok yə pā´ shən) the regular work or business a person does (p. 158)

Organization (ôr gə nə zā´ shən) a group of people united for a common cause (p. 171)

Origin (ôr´ ə jin) the beginning of something (p. 37)

P

Part time (pärt tīm) a job that requires less than 40 hours per week (p. 202)

Periodical (pir ē od´ ə kəl) a magazine published at regular intervals, such as daily, weekly, or monthly (p. 91)

Permanent (pėr´ mə nənt) a job that is expected to last a long time (p. 202)

Personal information (pėr´ sə nəl in fôr mā´ shən) facts about yourself (p. 220)

Pertinent (pėrt´ n ənt) applicable (p. 229)

Physical map (fiz´ ə kəl map) a map that shows the roughness of the earth's surface (p. 65)

Political map (pə lit´ ə kəl map) a map that shows the boundaries of states and countries (p. 65)

Position (pə zish´ ən) the name of your job (p. 226)

Predominance (pri dom´ ə nəns) being most frequent or common (p. 84)

Preface (pref´ is) an introduction to a book (p. 18)

Previous (prē´ vē əs) refers to something that happened in the past (p. 226)

Prime time (prīm tīm) the hours when television is watched the most, between 8 P.M. and 11 P.M. (p. 208)

Product map (prod´ əkt map) a map that has symbols that show where goods are grown or produced (p. 65)

Products (prod´ əkts) goods that you can buy (p. 112)

Profession (prə fesh´ ən) a job that requires special information and training (p. 116)

Professional (prə fesh´ ə nəl) someone who works at a specific profession (p. 116)

Publish (pub´ lish) to print and distribute magazines, books, newspapers, or other reading materials (p. 93)

Q

Qualifications (kwäl ə fə kā´ shənz) a description of your skills and work experience (p. 202)

R

The Readers' Guide to Periodical Literature (ᴛʜə rē´ dərz gīd tü pir ē od´ ə kəl lit´ ər ə chür) a magazine found in the library that lists articles from many other magazines (p. 96)

Rebate (rē´ bāt) a return of part of a payment for a product (p. 252)

Recipe (res´ ə pē) a list of ingredients and directions for the preparation of a specific food (p. 77)

Reference book (ref´ ər əns bůk) a book that contains facts about a specific topic or on several topics (p. 18)

References (ref´ ər ən səz) people who know about your work and who will recommend you for a job (p. 202)

Related topic (ri lāt´ əd top´ ik) a topic connected in some way to another topic (p. 16)

Reliable (ri lī´ ə bəl) a worker who is dependable and does what he or she is expected to do (p. 202)

Reporter (ri pôr´ tər) a person who researches facts and writes stories for a newspaper (p. 187)

Resident (rez´ ə dənt) a person who lives in a certain place (p. 102)

Retail (rē´ tāl) items that are for sale to the public (p. 248)

Retail price (rē´ tāl prīs) the price a customer pays for an item (p. 249)

Road map (rōd map) a map that shows roads, highways, towns, and other useful travel information (p. 65)

S

Salary (sal´ ər ē) the amount of money you are paid for working (p. 226)

Sale price (sāl prīs) a lower price on a certain item for a certain time period (p. 249)

Scale (skāl) the relationship shown between distances on the map and actual distances (p. 63)

Service (sėr´ vis) what a business or individual can do for you (p. 112)

270 *Glossary* *Life Skills English*

Short story (shôrt stôr´ ē) a story that can usually be read in one sitting (p. 132)

Signature (sig´ nə chər) the name of a person written by that person (p. 220)

Slogan (slō´ gən) a word or phrase that is repeated over and over again that expresses the main idea of a product, business, political group, or other organization (p. 190)

Stress (stres) to pronounce a syllable with more emphasis than the other syllables in the word (p. 28)

Subscriber (səb skrīb´ ər) a customer of a local cable television company (p. 210)

Subscription (səb skrip´ shən) a regular order for a magazine, newspaper, or other publication (p. 94)

Subtopic (sub´ top ik) a topic that is part of a larger topic (p. 13)

Supervisor (sü´ pər vī zər) a person who is your boss (p. 226)

Syllable (sil´ ə bəl) a part of a word with one vowel sound (p. 28)

Symbol (sim´ bəl) a sign or mark that stands for something else (p. 63)

Synonym (sin´ ə nim) a word with the same or nearly the same meaning as another word (p. 14)

T

Table of contents (tā´ bəl ov kon´ tents) a list of the chapters or sections of a book and the page numbers on which the chapters or sections begin (p. 18)

Temporary (tem´ pə rer ē) a job that lasts for a limited amount of time (p. 202)

Toll-free (tōl frē) a long-distance number with an 800 area code (p. 107)

Topic (subject) (top´ ik) (sub´ jikt) what you want to find out about (p. 13)

Trade (trād) an occupation that requires manual or mechanical skill (p. 167)

V

Value (val´ yü) the amount of money your property is worth to a buyer (p. 237)

Vertical (vėr´ tə kəl) a word that means going up and down (p. 66)

Vertical file (vėr´ tə kəl fīl) a file that contains pamphlets and other materials too small to put on a shelf (p. 152)

Video catalog (vid´ ē ō kat´ l ȯg) a catalog that lists films or videotapes that a library owns by title or subject (p. 129)

Volume (vol´ yəm) a single book, or one book in a set of books (p. 71)

W

White pages (wīt pāj´ əs) a part of the telephone book with residential, business, and government listings arranged in alphabetical order (p. 102)

Wholesale (hōl´ sāl) the merchandise that is for sale to dealers (p. 248)

Wholesale price (hōl´ sāl prīs) the price a manufacturer charges a dealer for items bought in large amounts (p. 249)

Withdrawal (with drȯ´ əl) money that you have taken out of your bank account (p. 240)

Y

Yellow pages (yel´ ō pāj´ əs) a part of the telephone book with business listings that are organized under subject headings arranged in alphabetical order (p. 104)

a	hat	e	let	ī	ice	ô	order	u̇	put	sh	she	ə	a in about
ā	age	ē	equal	o	hot	oi	oil	ü	rule	th	thin		e in taken
ä	far	ėr	term	ō	open	ou	out	ch	child	TH	then		i in pencil
â	care	i	it	ȯ	saw	u	cup	ng	long	zh	measure		o in lemon
													u in circus

Index

272 *Index* *Life Skills English*

Life Skills English Index **273**

E

F

274 *Index* *Life Skills English*

Life Skills English Index **275**

M

N

O

P

276 *Index Life Skills English*

Q

R

Life Skills English *Index* **277**

278 *Index Life Skills English*

Life Skills English *Index* **279**

Final Mastery Test

Name Date Period

Chapters 1-9 *Final Mastery Test* *page 1*

Final Mastery Test

Part A Read the following statements. If the statement is true, write *True* on the line. If the statement is not true, write *False*.

_______ **1)** *House cats* could be used as a related topic for the topic *buying a house.*

_______ **2)** This word is spelled correctly: *miselaneous.* (Use a dictionary to check your answer.)

_______ **3)** You could not find facts about income tax in an almanac.

_______ **4)** An encyclopedia is not arranged in a particular order.

_______ **5)** A digest is a magazine containing condensed articles from other magazines.

_______ **6)** You can find the phone number of a business in the Yellow Pages by looking up the address.

_______ **7)** The Blue Pages lists phone numbers of government agencies.

_______ **8)** If the guide words on a page are **pall—paltry**, the word **palm** would appear on that page.

_______ **9)** Libraries just have print materials.

_______ **10)** Fiction materials are organized in a library alphabetically by the author's last name.

_______ **11)** The Dewey Decimal System has fifteen main categories.

_______ **12)** A trade is an occupation that requires manual or mechanical skill.

_______ **13)** You can check the credentials of people you wish to hire by calling an organization or bureau.

_______ **14)** If you wanted to read a columnist's article, you would look in the classified section.

_______ **15)** A reporter decides which news stories will be reported to the public in a newspaper.

_______ **16)** Classified ads are abbreviated.

_______ **17)** On a job application, education refers to your job skills.

_______ **18)** When preparing a financial statement, you will not need to list your liabilities.

_______ **19)** Catalogs do not have indexes.

_______ **20)** Three ways to pay for a catalog order are by check, money order, and charge card.

Final Test Page 1

Name Date Period

Chapters 1-9 *Final Mastery Test* *page 2*

Final Mastery Test, continued

Part B Complete each sentence using a word from the box.

microfiche	benefits	subscriber	obituary	catalog
advertisement	doctoral	subtopic	biographical	form
retail	check	document	stress	grid

1) When you _______________ a syllable, you emphasize that syllable more than the other syllables in the word.

2) A _______________ dictionary lists famous people and facts about their lives.

3) A _______________ is a network of lines on a map.

4) _______________ is a film card on which many pages of reduced copy can be stored.

5) A _______________ is any list of information.

6) _______________ are what workers receive in addition to wages.

7) A _______________ is a topic that is part of a larger topic.

8) The highest degree awarded by a university or professional school is a _______________ degree.

9) An _______________ is a short article about someone who has recently died.

10) A public notice, usually about a product or service for sale is called an _______________.

11) A customer of a local cable television company is called a _______________.

12) A paper that gives information to another person is a _______________.

13) A _______________ is a printed or typed document with spaces to fill in information.

14) Items that are for sale to the public are _______________.

15) A _______________ is a draft on your bank account.

Final Test Page 2

Name Date Period

Chapters 1-9 *Final Mastery Test* *page 3*

Final Mastery Test, continued

Part C Circle the correct answer for each question.

1) If you wanted to look up information about how to get a job, which key word could you use?
a) shopping **b)** college **c)** careers

2) What is an index?
a) list of the chapters or sections of a book
b) introduction to a book
c) alphabetical list of main topics covered in a book

3) Use a dictionary to look up the word *longspur.* What does this word mean?
a) a kind of boot **b)** a kind of finch **c)** a kind of horse

4) What is the abbreviation for *pound?*
a) pd. **b)** pnd. **c)** lb.

5) Where would you find *Susana Dominguez* listed in the White Pages of a phone book?
a) between *Dodd* and *Dolan*
b) between *Donovan* and *Dorn*
c) between *Dolan* and *Donley*

6) What numbers does the Dewey Decimal System use?
a) 111-999 **b)** 1-999 **c)** 000-999

7) Which organization would be the best to contact if you want more information about a certain company?
a) The Travelers Aid **b)** The Legal Aid Society
c) The Better Business Bureau

8) What is the abbreviation for *apartment* that you will often see in classified ads?
a) a/c **b)** apt. **c)** condo.

9) Which is *not* a network television station?
a) ESPN **b)** CBS **c)** ABC

10) You ordered a pair of shoes by catalog, but you were sent the wrong size. What should you do?
a) keep the shoes anyway
b) return the shoes and ask for the correct size
c) call the company and ask for a free pair of shoes

Final Test Page 3

Name Date Period

Chapters 1-9 *Final Mastery Test* *page 4*

Final Mastery Test, continued

Part D Find the correct definition for each term. Write the letter of the definition on the line.

_______ **1)** table of contents
_______ **2)** entry
_______ **3)** synonym
_______ **4)** reference book
_______ **5)** autobiography
_______ **6)** credentials
_______ **7)** apprentice
_______ **8)** mass media
_______ **9)** references
_______ **10)** broadcast
_______ **11)** signature
_______ **12)** maiden name
_______ **13)** employer
_______ **14)** assets
_______ **15)** charge card

a) a story of a real person's life written by that person
b) people who know about your work and will recommend you for a job
c) the name of a person written by that person
d) listing in a dictionary
e) account that allows you to charge the cost of goods
f) list of the chapters or sections of a book
g) a person or company that pays you a salary
h) a woman's last name before she marries
i) proof that a person is an expert in a certain area of work
j) a book such as an encyclopedia or atlas
k) word with a similar meaning as another word
l) to send radio or television signals through the air to receivers
m) includes television, radio, newspapers, and magazines
n) property you own that has value
o) a worker being trained by an experienced and skilled person

Final Test Page 4

Final Mastery Test

Name Date Period

Chapters 1-9 *Final Mastery Test* *page 5*

Final Mastery Test, continued

Part E Write the following list of words in alphabetical order.

disgrace	discount	disinfect	discuss	disgust

1) ______ **3)** ______ **5)** ______

2) ______ **4)** ______

Part F Read the information below from a how-to book. Then answer the questions.

Using a Photocopier

To copy a document, first open the lid on the top of the copier. Place the page you want to copy face down on the glass. Use the number keypad to select the number of copies you wish to make. Select the paper size. Close the lid. Press *Copy.* The copied pages will feed out of the left side of the machine.

1) Who would use this information? ______

2) What must you do first to copy a document? ______

3) What must you do second? ______

4) What are two settings that must be selected? ______

5) What button do you press when you are ready to copy? ______

Part G Read the index from a newspaper. On the lines provided, write the section letter and number where you would look to find each of these items.

Business.....C-10	Crossword....B-8	Food.........E-1	Obituaries...B-5
Classified...C-15	Editorials...A-34	Local........B-1	Sports.......C-1
Comics.......B-12	Features.....D-1	Movies.......D-7	Television...D-10

______ **1)** Whether M*A*S*H is on tonight

______ **2)** The weather

______ **3)** What sports teams played yesterday

______ **4)** News about the stock market

______ **5)** Job opportunities

Final Test Page 5

Name Date Period

Chapters 1-9 *Final Mastery Test* *page 6*

Final Mastery Test, continued

Part H Below are abbreviations commonly found in help wanted and classified ads. Write the meaning of the abbreviation on the line.

1) carp. ______

2) dep. ______

3) firepl. ______

4) NS ______

5) cass ______

6) 4wd ______

7) conv ______

8) co. ______

9) req'd ______

10) immed. ______

Part I Read the catalog description. Then answer the questions.

Scented Candles

Use these candles for centerpieces, entertaining, holidays, and more. Size 1" wide × 8" tall. (Five candles per package.)

CA-4344—Evergreen	CA-4345—Raspberry	CA-4346—Blueberry
CA-4347—Coconut	CA-4348—Vanilla	CA-4349—Cinnamon

$4.95 each. Mix and Match: Any 3 or more just **$3.95 each.**

1) List a common use for scented candles. ______

2) In what size are the candles available? ______

3) How much is one set of candles? ______

4) What is the order number for vanilla candles? ______

5) How much would it cost for each package of candles if you buy two packages of blueberry and one evergreen? ______

Final Test Page 6

Teacher's Resource Library Answer Key

Activities

Activity 1–Alphabetizing Drills

List 1: **1)** frighten **2)** fringe **3)** frisk **4)** fritter **5)** frivolous **6)** frizzy **7)** frock **8)** frog **9)** frolic **10)** front

List 2: **1)** armor **2)** armpit **3)** army **4)** aroma **5)** around **6)** arrange **7)** arrest **8)** arrival **9)** arrive **10)** arrow

List 3: **1)** scout **2)** scramble **3)** scrap **4)** scrape **5)** scratch **6)** scream **7)** screech **8)** screen **9)** scribble **10)** script

Activity 2–Alphabetizing Place Names

A. **European Countries:** **1)** Bulgaria **2)** Denmark **3)** France **4)** Greece **5)** Iceland **6)** Italy **7)** Portugal **8)** Romania **9)** Sweden **10)** Switzerland

B. **World Capitals:** **1)** Athens (Greece) **2)** Bern (Switzerland) **3)** Bucharest (Romania) **4)** Copenhagen (Denmark) **5)** Lisbon (Portugal) **6)** Paris (France) **7)** Reykjavik (Iceland) **8)** Rome (Italy) **9)** Sofia (Bulgaria) **10)** Stockholm (Sweden)

Activity 3–Using Guide Words

1) b) seaman **c)** season **2) a)** frown **c)** frock **3) c)** fawn **d)** February **4) a)** military **d)** milk **5) a)** zoo **b)** zoology **c)** zucchini **d)** zoom **6) c)** wood **7) c)** turnaround **8) a)** super **b)** superb **c)** superman **9) c)** phobia **10) a)** Aaron **b)** abbey **c)** Abel

Activity 4–Using Synonyms

Correct answers may vary.

1) abdomen **2)** strange, odd **3)** none **4)** smart **5)** doctor **6)** nylons, hose, socks **7)** excuse **8)** rich **9)** help, assistance **10)** disease **11)** home, house **12)** attorney **13)** stream **14)** car **15)** truthfulness

Activity 5–Dictionary Entries

1) two **2)** three **3)** verb **4)** hire; or use **5)** employment **6)** Latin **7)** to fold **8)** noun **9)** 3 **10)** 1 **11)** 3 **12)** verb **13)** 2 **14)** authorize; enable

Activity 6–Sound-Alike Words

1) It's **2)** its **3)** It's **4)** It's **5)** It's **6)** your **7)** you're **8)** your **9)** your **10)** You're **11)** They're **12)** their **13)** Their **14)** they're **15)** their

Activity 7–Using a Dictionary for Spelling

1) a) ran **b)** swam **c)** taught **d)** drew **e)** sold **2) a)** geese **b)** shelves **c)** women **d)** children **e)** ladies **3) a)** stopped **b)** science **c)** tennis **d)** their **e)** forty

Activity 8–Words About Words

Part A: **1)** plural **2)** fiction **3)** abbreviation **4)** biography **5)** syllable **6)** antonyms **7)** homonyms **8)** synonym **9)** vowels

Part B: **1)** biography **2)** plural **3)** syllable **4)** synonym **5)** abbreviation **6)** vowels **7)** homonyms **8)** antonyms **9)** fiction

Activity 9–Information on Food Labels

1) a) 8.4 **b)** 25 **c)** 6.7 **d)** 20 **e)** 2.5 **f)** 25 **g)** 0 **2)** 630 calories **3)** Grade A milk, skim milk, sugar, natural coffee flavor with other natural flavors, pectin, active yogurt cultures with *L. acidophilus*

Activity 10–Finding Information in Reference Books

1) The Telephone Book **2)** *Webster's New World Dictionary* **3)** *The World Almanac and Book of Facts* **4)** *Roget's Thesaurus, New World Dictionary* **5)** *Julia Child's Home Cooking Cookbook* **6)** *The World Almanac and Book of Facts* or *The World Book Encyclopedia* **7)** *Handyman's Encyclopedia* **8)** *Hammond Contemporary World Atlas, The World Almanac and Book of Facts,* or *The World Book Encyclopedia* **9)** Telephone Book **10)** *Webster's New World Dictionary, World Book Encyclopedia, World Almanac and Book of Facts*

Activity 11–Building Vocabulary

1) E **2)** G **3)** A **4)** H **5)** B **6)** O **7)** L **8)** D **9)** C **10)** F **11)** I **12)** N **13)** M **14)** K **15)** J

Activity 12–Reference Book Word Search

Part A:

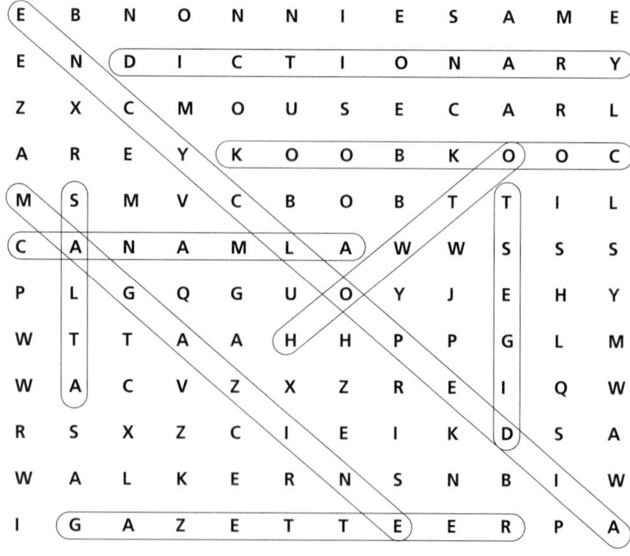

Part B: **1)** alamanac **2)** atlas **3)** gazetteer **4)** encyclopedia **5)** magazine **6)** cookbook **7)** dictionary **8)** digest **9)** how-to (book)

Activity 13–Alphabetical Order in a Telephone Directory

1) Green Landing Nursery **2)** Green Leaf The **3)** Green Life Lawn Service **4)** Greene & Associates **5)** Greene & Co **6)** Greene's Shoe Service **7)** Greenhouse The **8)** Greenleaf Landscaping **9)** Greenley's Tub & Tile Service **10)** Greens Multi-Services, Inc. **11)** Green's Variety Store **12)** Greenway Neurology Associates **13)** Greenway Village Condominiums **14)** Greenwich Group The **15)** Greenwich Woods Apartments **16)** Grey Earth Bakery **17)** Grey Pony The

Activity 14–Finding Information in the White Pages

1) Western Avenue **2)** attorney **3)** 334-8754 **4)** 599-6000 **5)** 334, 261, 599 **6)** 334-6500 **7)** Major **8)** 2341 North Street **9)** 334-1756

Activity 15–Yellow Pages Listings

List 1: **1)** Bakers Equipment **2)** Bakers–Retail **3)** Bakers Supplies **4)** Bakers–Wholesale

List 2: **1)** Automobile Alarm Systems **2)** Automobile Appraisers **3)** Automobile Auctions **4)** Automobile Body Shop Equipment & Supplies **5)** Automobile Dealers–Antique & Classic

List 3: **1)** Doll Clothing & Accessories **2)** Doll Houses & Accessories **3)** Dolls–Collectors **4)** Dolls–Repairing **5)** Dolls–Retail

List 4: **1)** Boat Builders **2)** Boat–Charter **3)** Boat Dealers **4)** Boat Equipment & Supplies **5)** Boat–Excursions

List 5: **1)** Cosmetics & Perfumes–Retail **2)** Cosmetics & Toilet Preparations–Wholesale & Manufacturers **3)** Cosmetology Schools–See Beauty Schools **4)** Costume Fabrics & Accessories

Activity 16–Which Pages Do You Use?

1) Blue Pages **2)** White Pages **3)** Yellow Pages **4)** Blue Pages **5)** White Pages **6)** Yellow Pages **7)** White Pages **8)** Blue Pages **9)** Yellow Pages **10)** White Pages **11)** Blue Pages **12)** Yellow Pages

Activity 17–Information in a Library

1) D **2)** A **3)** G **4)** H **5)** C **6)** F **7)** B **8)** E

Activity 18–Arranging Books in a Library

1) Alcott, Louisa May, *Little Women* **2)** Austen, Jane, *Pride and Prejudice* **3)** Brontë, Charlotte, *Jane Eyre* **4)** Buck, Pearl, *The Good Earth* **5)** Doctorow, E. L., *Ragtime* **6)** Fitzgerald, F. Scott, *The Great Gatsby* **7)** Hammet, Dashiell, *The Maltese Falcon* **8)** Heller, Joseph, *Catch-22* **9)** Lewis, Sinclair, *Main Street* **10)** Melville, Herman, *Moby Dick* **11)** Morrison, Toni, *Jazz* **12)** Stevenson, Robert Lewis, *Treasure Island* **13)** Wharton, Edith, *Ethan Frome* **14)** Wolfe, Thomas, *Look Homeward, Angel* **15)** Wouk, Herman, *Marjorie Morningstar*

Activity 19–The Dewey Decimal System

1) 500s **2)** 700s **3)** 100s **4)** 100s **5)** 800s **6)** 200s **7)** 600s **8)** 900s **9)** 400s/000–009 **10)** 600s **11)** 400s **12)** 000–099 **13)** 800s **14)** 900s **15)** 000–099 **16)** 300s **17)** 700s **18)** 500s **19)** 200s **20)** 300s

Activity 20–Words About Books

1) biography **2)** fiction **3)** encyclopedia **4)** almanac **5)** cookbook **6)** circulates **7)** reference book **8)** video catalog **9)** autobiography **10)** telephone directory **11)** nonfiction **12)** novel

Activity 21–Selecting Experts

1) realtor **2)** optometrist **3)** florist **4)** social worker **5)** school guidance counselor **6)** dentist **7)** nutritionist **8)** career counselor **9)** horticulturist **10)** dermatologist

Activity 22–Words About Experts

1) a **2)** b **3)** c **4)** b **5)** a **6)** b **7)** c **8)** c **9)** b **10)** b

Activity 23–Occupational Sentence Completion

1) obstetrician **2)** tailor **3)** chiropractor **4)** allergist **5)** attorney **6)** pediatrician **7)** plumber **8)** psychiatrist **9)** chef **10)** dental hygienist **11)** periodontist **12)** barber **13)** nutritionist **14)** accountant **15)** architect **16)** florist **17)** real estate agent **18)** travel agent **19)** horticulturist **20)** pharmacist

Activity 24–Abbreviations in the Classifieds

1) f **2)** d **3)** l **4)** e **5)** p **6)** g **7)** m **8)** h **9)** o **10)** i **11)** n **12)** r **13)** j **14)** q **15)** a **16)** t **17)** b **18)** k **19)** c **20)** s

Activity 25–Abbreviations in Ads

1) bedroom, bath, washer/dryer, includes, utilities **2)** bedroom apartment with, air conditioning **3)** bedroom, bath, building, equipped kitchen, fireplace, washer/dryer, parking **4)** efficiencies, washer/dryer, dishwasher, parking **5)** bedroom with hardwood floors, central air conditioning, washer/dryer **6)** bedroom, carpeted basement apartment, washer/dryer, utilities included

Activity 26–Understanding Help Wanted Ads

1) retail sales **2)** optometric technician and waiter/waitresses/ kitchen help **3)** receptionist **4)** They examine eyes and sell eyeglasses. **5)** the furniture business **6)** housekeeper/cook **7)** waiters/waitresses/kitchen help **8)** housekeeper/cook and truck washer **9)** $80.00 **10)** by going to the address listed and speaking with Christine **11)** retail sales **12)** a promotion to a management position

Activity 27–Using a Newspaper Schedule

1) Two **2)** 6:00 A.M. **3)** Channel 7 or Channel 2 **4)** Two hours **5)** Channel 22 **6)** 12:30 P.M. **7)** Channel 32, *World of Chemistry* **8)** *Mr. Rogers* **9)** 11:00 A.M. **10)** Number 50

Activity 28–Your Mailing Address

Note: Boldfaced figures may vary.

1) Mr. Ed Jones 354 Argyle Road Linden, MA 16354

2) Ms. Sandra Adams 20 Reedie Drive Apt. 365 Ansonia, CT **06483** **3)** Mrs. Lynn Gordon **67** Main Street Billings, UT 40967

4) Mrs. Chris MacArthur 100 Library Court Plainview, NY 39805

5) Mr. Arthur Wilson 908 Pickett Lane Austinville, WY **82801**

6) Ms. Gail Sanders **213** Price Drive Washington, DC 30098

Activity 29–Application for Employment

Answers will vary.

Activity 30–Ordering What You Want

1) cotton **2)** No, they have been preshrunk. **3)** four **4)** No, it is only for women. **5)** It comes in unisex sizing, which means that it can fit women or men. **6)** the hooded jersey **7)** yes **8)** yes **9)** jade, red, white, and navy **10)** three: M, L, and XL

Activity 31–Catalog Shopping

1) John Smith & Associates **2)** three ways: check, money order, or credit card **3)** four **4)** You get a discount of $10. **5)** $64.00 **6)** residents of Maryland **7)** $72.20 if you live in Maryland; $69.00 if you are not a Maryland resident **8)** No, all sales are final. **9)** Leave it blank. **10)** Yes

Activity 32–Easy Shopping

Completed forms may vary.

Activity 33–Dealing With a Problem Item

> Chris Jones
> 8467 Eastern Avenue
> Oakton, Nebraska 45678
>
> April 2, 20—
>
> The Adams Sports Shoe Company
> 5683 Main Street
> Cedar, Oklahoma 12345
>
> Dear Sir or Madam:
>
> I ordered a pair of size 6 roller skates, item number 4325, from your company. Unfortunately, they are too large for me. I would like to exchange these for a pair of size 5 roller skates. Thank you for your help in this matter.
>
> Sincerely,
>
> Chris Jones

Workbook Activities

Workbook Activity 1–Alphabetizing Drills

A. **1)** wharf **2)** what **3)** whatever **4)** whatnot **5)** whatsoever **6)** wheat **7)** wheel **8)** wheelchair **9)** when **10)** whereas

B. **1)** can **2)** candle **3)** candlestick **4)** canned **5)** canning **6)** cannon **7)** canon **8)** can't **9)** canvas **10)** canyon

C. **1)** do **2)** dodge **3)** doe **4)** does **5)** do-it-yourself **6)** dome **7)** done **8)** donor **9)** don't **10)** door

Workbook Activity 2–Alphabetical Order

A. **Common Last Names:** **1)** Hamelton **2)** Hamilton **3)** Hammel **4)** Harding **5)** Hardy **6)** Harris **7)** Harrison **8)** Henry **9)** Hewitt **10)** Howard

B. **Budget Items:** **1)** Clothing **2)** Entertainment **3)** Furniture **4)** Gasoline **5)** Groceries **6)** Insurance **7)** Rent **8)** Savings **9)** Taxes **10)** Utilities

C. **Baseball Hall of Famers:** **1)** Baker, Home Run **2)** Gehrig, Lou **3)** Goslin, Goose **4)** Koufax, Sandy **5)** Musial, Stan **6)** Paige, Satchel **7)** Ruth, Babe **8)** Stengel, Casey **9)** Wynn, Early **10)** Young, Cy

Workbook Activity 3–Alphabetizing Place Names

A. **1)** Alabama **2)** Alaska **3)** Arizona **4)** Maryland **5)** Nevada **6)** New Hampshire **7)** New York **8)** Texas **9)** Wisconsin **10)** Wyoming

B. **Alphabetical Order:** **1)** Albany New York **2)** Annapolis Maryland **3)** Austin Texas **4)** Boston Massachusetts **5)** Carson City Nevada **6)** Cheyenne Wyoming **7)** Juneau Alaska **8)** Madison Wisconsin **9)** Montgomery Alabama **10)** Phoenix Arizona

Workbook Activity 4–Putting Titles in Order

A. **Famous Novels:** **1)** *Call of the Wild, The* **2)** *Gone With the Wind* **3)** *Lonesome Dove* **4)** *Lord of the Rings, The* **5)** *Outsiders, The* **6)** *Pathfinder, The* **7)** *Robinson Crusoe* **8)** *Show Boat* **9)** *Treasure Island* **10)** *Watership Down*

B. **Oscar-Winning Movies:**
Alphabetical Order: **1)** *Ben-Hur* **2)** *Chariots of Fire* **3)** *French Connection, The* **4)** *Gandhi* **5)** *Going My Way* **6)** *Kramer vs. Kramer* **7)** *Lawrence of Arabia* **8)** *Out of Africa* **9)** *Rain Man* **10)** *Schindler's List*

Chronological Order: **1)** *Going My Way*–1944 **2)** *Ben-Hur*–1959 **3)** *Lawrence of Arabia*–1962 **4)** *The French Connection*–1971 **5)** *Kramer vs. Kramer*–1979 **6)** *Chariots of Fire*–1981 **7)** *Gandhi*–1983 **8)** *Out of Africa*–1985 **9)** *Rain Man*–1988 **10)** *Schindler's List*–1994

Workbook Activity 5–Using Guide Words

1) graduate, grain **2)** dolphin, donkey, doormat **3)** scrub, sculpture **4)** ginger, giggle **5)** mate, math **6)** well-informed, well-read, western, we're **7)** age, agency **8)** butter, but, busy **9)** frosting, front, frizzle **10)** Newton, Sir Isaac; NH, nickname, niece

Workbook Activity 6–The Name's the Same

Answers will vary. Suggested answers are given.
1) rain **2)** physicial **3)** boss **4)** village **5)** creek **6)** dinner **7)** lady **8)** couch **9)** soda **10)** well-liked **11)** high **12)** slender **13)** bathing **14)** canine **15)** subject

Workbook Activity 7–Look it Up!

Answers will vary. Suggested answers are given.
1) Auto repair **2)** Dairy cows **3)** Garden flowers **4)** Paint **5)** Beverages **6)** Solar system **7)** Astronauts **8)** Great Britain **9)** Furs **10)** Music **11)** Horses **12)** Fruits **13)** Board games **14)** College degrees **15)** Pasta

Workbook Activity 8–Understanding Indexes

1) Page 39 **2)** Page 17 **3)** Computer languages **4)** Database management **5)** Chapter 4 **6)** Page 53 **7)** Page 30 **8)** An index lists subjects in alphabetical order. A table of contents lists the chapters and pages in numerical order. **9)** At the end of a book. **10)** Pages 51–58

Workbook Activity 9–Understanding Words

1) sweet **2)** one **3)** swēt **4)** adjective **5)** The history of the word. **6)** Old English **7)** Three **8)** Something sweet, as a sweet food. Sentences will vary. **9)** Answers will vary. **10)** sweetly **11)** sweet or sweetness **12) A)** noun **B)** adverb **C)** adjective **D)** adjective **E)** noun

Workbook Activity 10–Dictionary Search

1) You would probably eat it. It is a dish made with lobster, mushrooms, and a sauce, served in a half of a lobster shell. **2)** No. Robin Hood was a legendary figure. Robin Hood is listed in the dictionary by the first name. **3)** Nelson Rockefeller was vice president from 1974 to 1977. **4)** You could expect to find one in the water or on land. A mudskipper is a fish that is able to leave the water to search for food. **5)** Yes, this is a compliment. Munificent means "to be generous." **6)** You could put it into a vase. A four-o'clock is a flower. **7)** No, he could not. A featherweight weighs between 118 and 126 pounds. **8)** Lance could wear it on his head. A fedora is a felt hat with a curved brim. **9)** Juan would show that he loved books. He might have a large collection of books. **10)** Ralph should expect a performance of sacred choral music.

Workbook Activity 11–Dictionary Abbreviations

1) noun **2)** pronoun **3)** adjective **4)** adverb **5)** verb **6)** transitive verb **7)** intransitive verb **8)** preposition **9)** conjunction **10)** interjection **11)** singular **12)** plural **13)** Latin **14)** Old English **15)** Greek **16)** Middle English **17)** French **18)** Spanish **19)** German **20)** Old French

Workbook Activity 12–The Meaning of a Word

1) a) eating **b)** ate **c)** eaten **d)** eater **e)** eat **2)** Old English **3)** etan **4) a)** 3a **b)** 2 **c)** 1 **d)** 3b **e)** 2 **5)** verb **6)** b **7)** eater

Workbook Activity 13–Dictionary Entries

A. 1) noun **2)** two **3)** Old English **4)** *is*–ice *gicel*–piece of ice **5)** A tapering, pointed, hanging piece of ice. **6)** By the freezing of dripping water. **7)** icicles

B. 1) iciness **2)** Answers will vary. **3)** two **4) a)** icy **b)** icily **c)** iciness **5) a)** 4 **b)** 1 **c)** 3

Workbook Activity 14–The Dictionary as a Reference Tool

1) 83 **2)** China **3)** 26 miles **4)** Greece **5)** Fat Tuesday **6)** The last Tuesday before Lent. **7)** New Orleans **8)** Louis XVI **9)** 38 **10)** She was guillotined. **11)** He was not born. **12)** Mars

Workbook Activity 15–A Road Map

1) 3 and 7 **2)** 301 **3)** 7 **4)** 7 and 50; or 301 and 3 **5)** Whitehall and Clinton **6)** About 90 miles **7)** 3 and 50; or 302 and 7 **8)** 302 or 50 **9)** Clinton **10)** Lewes

Workbook Activity 16–Abbreviations in Cookbooks

1) two **2)** t. or tsp. **3)** lb. **4)** two **5)** liter **6)** oz. **7)** Fahrenheit **8)** three **9)** six **10)** 90 **11)** 28 times larger **12)** a pint **13)** a teaspoon **14)** a quart **15)** 16 **16)** 32 **17)** 8

Workbook Activity 17–Reading the Information on Food Labels

1) Rolled oats **2)** Salt **3)** Granola bars **4)** Chicken broth **5)** Granola bars **6)** Chicken broth **7)** Granola bars **8)** Sodium

Workbook Activity 18–Times and Cycles: An Acrostic Puzzle

1) Semimonthly **2)** Daily **3)** Annually **4)** weekly **5)** Interval **6)** Cycle **7)** Periodical **8)** Biannually **9)** Semimonthly **10)** Digest **Acrostic phrase:** Time and time again

Workbook Activity 19–A Magazine Subscription Form

A. The box for 1 year should be checked. All other information will vary.

B. 1) e **2)** g **3)** d **4)** c **5)** b **6)** f **7)** a **8)** h

Workbook Activity 20–Reference Puzzle

1) almanac **2)** biography **3)** index **4)** statistic **5)** globe **6)** atlas **7)** gazetteer **8)** degree **9)** encyclopedia **10)** volume **11)** magazine **12)** digest **13)** recipe **14)** cookbook **15)** grid **16)** title **17)** fiction

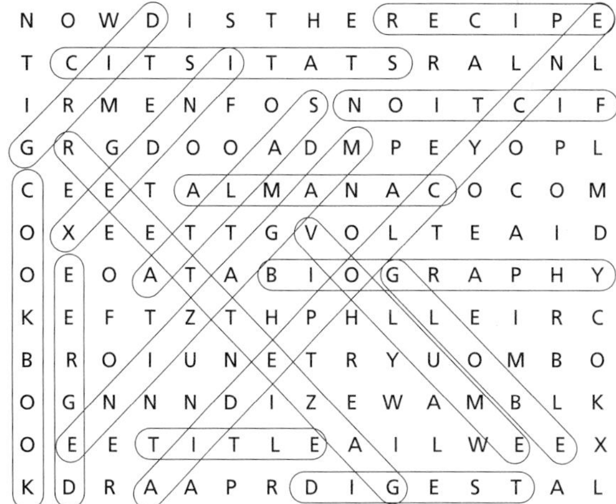

Workbook Activity 21–Alphabetical Order in a Directory

W & R Sportswear WWDC-AM 1200 WWDC-TV 6 Walker A Walker A L Walker April and Dave Walker April L Wall: Paint and Paper, The Wallpaper Inc Walton William Attorney-at-Law Wilkinson, City of Wilson Barbara R MD Wiltons Telephone Repairs Woodmore C Woodmore Carly Woodmore J Woodmore Jean and Ray Woodmore R L Woodmore Ralph Woodmore Realty

Workbook Activity 22–Spelling Names

1) L **2)** E **3)** P **4)** F **5)** N **6)** D **7)** A **8)** I **9)** J **10)** H **11)** S **12)** K **13)** Q **14)** M **15)** C **16)** T **17)** O **18)** G **19)** B **20)** R

Workbook Activity 23–Number, Please

1) Cooke–Cooper **2)** 848-7943 **3)** Five. The sixth Cooke listing is a business. **4)** 285-5594 **5)** 664-4009 **6)** 879-8627 **7)** 4222 Elmley Av. **8)** 647-0207 **9)** 490-1800 **10)** John B. Cooney, Sr. **11)** Arthur Cooper **12)** 349 **13)** 1000 Richards Rd. **14)** 744-6909 **15)** Five. Arthur Cooper is listed twice.

Workbook Activity 24–Common Last Names: Word Puzzle

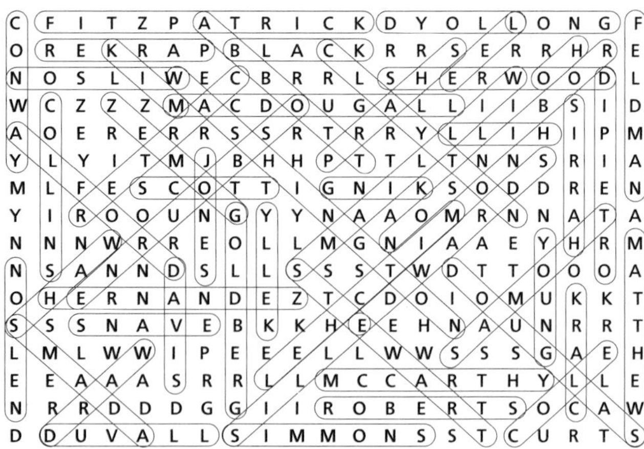

Workbook Activity 25–Alphabetical Lists

List 1: Floral Arrangements Florists Florists–Weddings Flowers–*See* Florists

List 2: Dance Instruction–*See* Dancing Schools Dancing–Clothing Dancing Schools Dancing Supplies

List 3: Baby-Sitting–*See* Day Care Child Care–*See* Day Care Day Care Day Nurseries & Schools

List 4: Physical Therapists Physicians–Allergy Physicians Clinics & Medical Groups Physicians–Dermatology Physicians–Family Practice

List 5: Real Estate Realtors–*See* Real Estate Rental Management Rental Services

Workbook Activity 26–Practice With the Yellow Pages

1) National Detective Agency, Inc. **2)** Michaels & Daniels Investigation Service **3)** National Detective Agency, Inc. **4)** The Raven Investigators **5)** Union Security Bureau, Inc. **6)** Freedom Security Investigation **7)** 969-3345 **8)** J. E. Royer **9)** Michaels & Daniels Investigation Service **10)** 13 N. Preston Ave. **11)** Blockman's Jewelry **12)** diamond jewelry

Workbook Activity 27–When to Use the Yellow Pages

1) White **2)** Yellow **3)** White **4)** White **5)** White **6)** Yellow **7)** Yellow **8)** Yellow **9)** White **10)** White **11)** White **12)** Yellow

Workbook Activity 28–Arranging Books in a Library

(In some libraries, Mark Twain's books are listed under Samuel Clemens, Twain's real name.) *Watership Down* by Richard Adams *The Clan of the Cave Bear* by Jean Auel *The Valley of the Horses* by Jean Auel *The Living Reed* by Pearl Buck *Murder at the Vicarage* by Agatha Christie *Robinson Crusoe* by Daniel Defoe *Bleak House* by Charles Dickens *A Tale of Two Cities* by Charles Dickens *Show Boat* by Edna Ferber *The Outsiders* by S. E. Hinton *Book of Lights* by Chaim Potok *Penrod* by Booth Tarkington *Tom Sawyer* by Mark Twain *Exodus* by Leon Uris *Rebecca of Sunnybrook Farm* by Kate Douglas Wiggins

Workbook Activity 29–Fiction and Nonfiction: Acrostic Puzzle

1) dialogue **2)** autobiography **3)** short story **4)** novel **5)** biography **6)** nonfiction **7)** Dewey **8)** decimals **9)** author **10)** title **Acrostic message:** Edgar Allen Poe

Workbook Activity 30–The Dewey Decimal System

1) 400s **2)** 300s **3)** 200s **4)** 900s **5)** 92 or 900s **6)** 200s **7)** 800s **8)** 600s **9)** 600s **10)** 400s **11)** 600s **12)** 800s **13)** 400s **14)** 400s **15)** 700s **16)** 900s **17)** 900s **18)** 700s **19)** 92 or 900s **20)** 800s **21)** 000–099 **22)** 500s **23)** 600s **24)** 700s **25)** 100s

Workbook Activity 31–Records in the Library Catalog

1) *My Life Story* **2)** 92 Ga **3)** Art and title **4)** Corrine Gamble **5)** Autobiography **6)** World Books Press **7)** 1985 **8)** New York **9)** 250 **10)** Yes

Workbook Activity 32–Roman Numerals

1) 8 **2)** 70 **3)** 62 **4)** 3 **5)** 14 **6)** 103 **7)** 64 **8)** 1982 **9)** 200 **10)** 1891 **11)** 11 **12)** 3,055 **13)** 1,351 **14)** 55 **15)** 654

Workbook Activity 33–References in a Library

1) C **2)** A **3)** E **4)** F **5)** B **6)** H **7)** J **8)** I **9)** G **10)** D

1) fiction, nonfiction **2)** hardback, paperback **3)** library catalog **4)** novel, short story **5)** biography, autobiography

Workbook Activity 34–Medical Professionals

1) D **2)** E **3)** I **4)** O **5)** G **6)** H **7)** C **8)** A **9)** B **10)** F **11)** J **12)** P **13)** L **14)** M **15)** K **16)** N

Workbook Activity 35–Choosing an Expert

Exercise 1: **1)** C **2)** A **3)** C **4)** B **5)** C

Exercise 2: **1)** apprentice **2)** license **3)** Better Business Bureau **4)** real estate agent or broker **5)** librarian or media specialist

Workbook Activity 36–Select an Expert

1) attorney **2)** accountant **3)** cabinetmaker **4)** veterinarian **5)** librarian **6)** architect **7)** banker **8)** plumber **9)** electrician **10)** pharmacist

Workbook Activity 37–Occupational Match

1) N **2)** P **3)** L **4)** E **5)** G **6)** F **7)** D **8)** M **9)** C **10)** H **11)** K **12)** O **13)** I **14)** Q **15)** J **16)** T **17)** S **18)** R **19)** A **20)** B

Workbook Activity 38–Organizations That Can Help

1) Travelers Assistance or Travelers Aid **2)** The Legal Aid Society **3)** Welcome Wagon or Welcome, Neighbor **4)** The Chamber of Commerce **5)** The Better Business Bureau **6)** The Medical Bureau or Medical Society

Workbook Activity 39–Word Match

1) G **2)** I **3)** A **4)** C **5)** H **6)** B **7)** E **8)** F **9)** D **10)** J **11)** L **12)** M **13)** K

Workbook Activity 40–Media Puzzle

1) Obituary **2)** Editorial **3)** Column **4)** Mass media **5)** Current **6)** Daily **7)** Reporter **8)** Editors **9)** Classified **10)** Advertisement

A	D	V	E	R	T	I	S	E	M	E	N	T	N	G
P	A	T	L	D	A	N	H	A	M	W	I	N	R	L
B	I	O	M	N	I	I	E	A	O	P	R	E	Q	T
D	L	D	W	V	Y	T	K	C	D	G	T	D	W	B
H	Y	J	K	C	C	K	O	K	S	R	R	I	R	L
J	K	E	D	X	Y	L	I	R	O	T	R	T	T	W
X	V	E	B	Z	U	K	A	P	I	Y	P	O	W	C
B	O	N	N	M	Y	Y	E	S	S	A	N	R	Y	U
N	I	I	N	Z	E	R	K	K	S	G	L	S	S	R
C	R	L	T	Y	P	D	Z	Z	M	I	H	X	B	R
A	B	Y	R	A	U	T	I	B	O	C	F	R	T	E
B	O	B	N	N	I	E	W	K	K	N	K	I	Y	N
L	K	E	R	B	A	R	B	R	J	B	C	K	E	T
M	A	S	S	M	E	D	I	A	S	T	M	A	S	D

Workbook Activity 41–Using a Newspaper Index

1) Classified; C; 18 **2)** Comics; B; 24 **3)** Television; B; 16 **4)** Food; B; 1 **5)** Movies; B; 13 **6)** Obituaries; C; 10 **7)** Editorials; A; 15 **8)** National and World; A; 1 **9)** Local; C; 1 **10)** Sports; D; 1 **11)** Classified; C; 18 **12)** National and World; A; 1

Workbook Activity 42–Reading Advertisements

1) b **2)** a **3)** a **4)** c **5)** b **6)** a

Workbook Activity 43–Abbreviations in Ads

Part A: **1)** g **2)** j **3)** k **4)** i **5)** b **6)** a **7)** e **8)** d **9)** f **10)** h **11)** c

Part B: **1)** experienced **2)** opportunity, available, established, with experience, week, weekends **3)** practice, prefer experienced **4)** experienced **5)** Immediate **6)** Saturdays, excellent salary **7)** experienced, weekdays **8)** after **9)** and, experience, and **10)** Monday, through, Friday, hours, week **11)** with, appointment, Monday, Friday, Equal Opportunity Employer **12)** K = thousand

Workbook Activity 44–Reading Help Wanted Ads

1) 10 **2)** $8.00 **3)** 20 **4)** Landscape laborer **5)** Real estate **6)** The salary will be higher for a person with greater ability. **7)** Manager, office cleaners **8)** Two **9)** $300.00 **10)** Paid vacation, sick pay, health insurance **11)** Furniture finisher: apply in person. General office worker: write to newspaper.

Workbook Activity 45–Using a Schedule in the Newspaper

1) Six **2)** WRC; WJLA; WDVM **3)** 26 **4)** 7:30 **5)** 26 **6)** 7:30 **7)** *News Night, Home Time* **8)** Two **9)** 9 **10)** UCLA and Georgia

Workbook Activity 46–Mailing Address

Answers will vary.

Workbook Activity 47–Word Scramble for Applications

Part A: **1)** application **2)** maiden **3)** salary **4)** abbreviation **5)** citizen **6)** signature **7)** boss **8)** full **9)** reference **10)** position

Part B: **1)** signature **2)** boss **3)** position **4)** abbreviation **5)** salary **6)** citizen **7)** maiden **8)** application **9)** maiden **10)** reference

Workbook Activity 48–Filling Out an Application

Part A: **1)** b **2)** e **3)** g **4)** i **5)** a **6)** j **7)** h **8)** d **9)** f **10)** c

Part B: **1)** I–Harold P. Davis **2)** I–3113 Clark Lane **3)** C **4)** I–Sun Order Company **5)** C **6)** I–Ms. Jane Q. Davis **7)** C **8)** I–Drake High School **9)** C–I–Business Education **10)** I–Relationship: Mother

Workbook Activity 49–Application Forms Acrostic

1) application **2)** form **3)** Social Security **4)** citizen **5)** applicable **6)** document **7)** signature **8)** education **9)** reference **10)** employer **Acrostic message:** accuracy counts

Workbook Activity 50–Application for Employment, Part 1

Answers will vary.

Workbook Activity 51–Application for Employment, Part 2

Answers will vary.

Workbook Activity 52–Letter of Application

Answers will vary.

Workbook Activity 53–Charge It!

Answers will vary, but the completed form should include the following information.

CREDIT APPLICATION for SMITH'S DEPARTMENT STORE

Last Name / First / Initial	Birthdate	Dependents	Social Security No.	☐ Own ☐ Rent
		2		

Present Address (Street & Number)	Payment or Rent $	How Long	Name and Address of Landlord or Mortgage Holder
City / State / Zip	Home Telephone	Previous Address	How Long
Applicant's Employer	Business Address		How Long

Position	Salary Wk	Salary Mo	Salary Yr	Business Telephone
Teacher	$400	$1,600		

Previous Employer	Position	Salary	How Long
Frank's Carryout	Cook	$50 wk.	3 yr.

Name and Address of Nearest Relative Not Living With You — Telephone

Other Source of Income (Income from alimony, child support or separate maintenance payments need not be disclosed if you do not wish to have it considered as a basis for repaying this obligation.) Annual Amount ______ How Long ______ Source ______

Bank: Chester Savings and Loan, 1010 Smith Street — Branch — ☐ Checking ☑ Savings ☐ Loan

Make of Car and Year	Financed by	Driver's License No.
19__ Dodge Colt	Chester Savings and Loan	558-321-7766R

CREDIT REFERENCES

Name	Address	Acct. No.	Balance
Money America	710 East Avenue	00221	None

Workbook Activity 54–Catalog Descriptions

Part A: **1)** Cotton and acrylic pile **2)** No **3)** No, it is lined with alpaca-like pile. **4)** Yes **5)** 7994536 **6)** No. The smallest size is 8. **7)** No. The description says that the coat must be dry cleaned.

Part B: **1)** $5.00 **2)** $.50 **3)** No. It comes in only navy or red. **4)** One size fits all. **5)** Wool **6)** 8765490

Workbook Activity 55–Getting What You Order

1) 100% cotton **2)** No **3)** 4 **4)** $1.00 **5)** Yes **6)** No **7)** No **8)** They have wide-cut leg openings for freedom of movement. **9)** 1213S **10)** No

Workbook Activity 56–Catalog Shopping

Part A: **1)** c **2)** b **3)** e **4)** a **5)** d

Part B: **1)** Robert D. Jones **2)** 345 Charter Avenue, Albuquerque, New Mexico 87106 **3)** 2 leotards, 1 pair boots **4)** The steel-toe work boots **5)** 7 lb. 11 oz. **6)** The customer doesn't live in Iowa. **7)** $104.99 **8)** $3.00

Workbook Activity 57–Easy Shopping

Answers will vary, but the completed order form should include the following information.

Send to: Name: ______
Address: ______
City/State/Zip ______

Item No.	Qty.	Size	Color	Description	Shipping Wt. lb.	Shipping Wt. oz.	Item Price	Total Price
	1				1	7	$44.99	$44.99
	1					6	$9.99	$9.99
	1					5	$49.99	$49.99
				Total shipping weight			Total Price	$104.97
							*Sales Tax	—
							Shipping Charge	$3.00
				Maine residents add 5% sales tax.			Total Charge	$107.97

Shipping Charges By Weight	
Up to 10 lb.	$3.00
10 lbs. to 20 lb.	$4.00
20 lbs. to 30 lb.	$5.00
Over 30 lb.	$6.00

Workbook Activity 58–Catalog Order Form

Answers will vary. Students should be instructed to choose one of each item.

Workbook Activity 59–A Letter of Complaint

Letters will vary.

1583 Milton Blvd.
Laurel, California 94939

August 12, 20—

The Wilmar Flashlight Co.
3025 West Street
Buckingham, Iowa 52601

Dear Sir or Madam:

The flashlight that I ordered from your company has arrived broken. It is Model #27 and costs $5.65. I am sending it back to you. Please send me a replacement as soon as possible. Thank you.

Yours truly,

Tom Martin

Workbook Activity 60–Addressing an Envelope

The amount for first-class postage should be filled in on the stamp.

Alice Barton
723 N. Quinn St.
Arlington, VA 22209

Mrs. Edith Carlson
5489 Elk Rd.
Northfield, MN 55057

Putting It Together

Putting It Together 1–Information Crossword Puzzle

Across		Down	
1	index	1	information
3	cross	2	descriptor
4	reference	3	chronological
6	synonym	5	subtopic
7	alphabetical	8	heading
11	guide	9	chapter
12	topic	10	refer
13	preface		
14	table		
15	related		

Putting It Together 8–Application Crossword Puzzle

Across		Down	
1	assets	1	abbreviation
3	deposit	2	social
6	form	3	document
8	debt	4	position
9	credit	5	signature
10	value	6	financial
13	net worth	7	maiden
14	application	11	applicable
16	withdrawal	12	loan
17	education	15	personal
18	reference		

Putting It Together 2–7 and 9

Game participation will vary for each player or team. Putting It Together activities can be completed inside or outside of the classroom. They are meant to test students' knowledge of information sources studied in *Life Skills English*. Most activities give students practice in using the sources. Assist students in following directions and in creating reasonable questions and answers.

Community Connection

Completed activities will vary for each student. Community Connection activities are real-life activities completed outside of the classroom by the students. These activities give students practical learning and practice of the skills taught in *Life Skills English*. Check completed activities to see that students have followed directions, completed each step, filled in all charts and blanks, provided reasonable answers to questions, written legibly, and used proper grammar and punctuation.

Tests

Chapter 1 Mastery Test A

Part A: **1)** cheetah **2)** chicken **3)** chipmunk **4)** eel **5)** elephant **6)** elk **7)** mongoose **8)** monkey **9)** mouse **10)** mule

Part B: **1)** a **2)** a, c **3)** a, b **4)** a, c **5)** a, b

Part C: Answers will vary. Some possible answers are listed. **1)** Oscars, best actor, acting **2)** capital, state capitals, Montana **3)** lakes, Michigan **4)** vice president, government, politics **5)** football, Super Bowl

Part D: Answers will vary. Some possible answers are listed. **1)** water sports, doing the breaststroke **2)** home repair, kinds of housepaint **3)** diets, exercise **4)** cat diseases, housebreaking pets **5)** reading music, instruments **6)** computer programs, computers **7)** arts and crafts, mending clothes **8)** exercise, marathons **9)** foreign languages, Mexico **10)** kinds of letters, parts of a business letter

Part E: **1)** a **2)** b **3)** a **4)** a **5)** b

Chapter 1 Mastery Test B

Part A: **1)** baboon **2)** bear **3)** bird **4)** buffalo **5)** giraffe **6)** goat **7)** gorilla **8)** pig **9)** pony **10)** puppy

Part B: **1)** a, b **2)** b, c **3)** a, b **4)** a, c **5)** c

Part C: Answers will vary. Some possible answers are listed below. **1)** Pulitzer Prize, authors, fiction **2)** television, popular television programs **3)** rain, Florida **4)** Tucson, Arizona, states **5)** battles, Bull Run, wars

Part D: Answers will vary. Some possible answers are listed below. **1)** popular songs, American songs **2)** foreign languages, France **3)** medical careers, dental assistants **4)** kinds of birds, outdoors **5)** plants, kinds of herbs **6)** American wars, Confederacy **7)** desserts, kinds of cookies **8)** card games, games of chance **9)** riding a bicycle, bicycle racing **10)** kinds of fish, outdoors

Part E
1) b **2)** a **3)** a **4)** b **5)** a

Chapter 2 Mastery Test A

Part A: **1)** c **2)** e **3)** d **4)** a **5)** b

Part B: **1)** 3 **2)** noun **3)** tragedies **4)** 3 **5)** yes

Part C: **1)** Their **2)** correct **3)** dipped **4)** guppies **5)** invite

Part D: **1)** a mountain system in Europe **2)** U.S. writer and humorist **3)** czar of Russia and the father of *Peter the Great* **4)** Mont Blanc **5)** Mark Twain

Chapter 2 Mastery Test B

Part A: **1)** d **2)** e **3)** a **4)** b **5)** c

Part B: **1)** 3 **2)** noun **3)** currencies **4)** 2 **5)** no

Part C: **1)** mice **2)** to **3)** different **4)** correct **5)** interesting

Part D: **1)** 2 **2)** 153,379 **3)** Egypt **4)** U.S. writer, delegate to the UN, and the wife of Franklin Delano Roosevelt **5)** 51–49 B.C. and 48–30 B.C.

Chapter 3 Mastery Test A

Part A: **1)** True **2)** False **3)** True **4)** True **5)** False

Part B: **1)** Evan **2)** Meran River and Wosco River **3)** 5 miles **4)** Meran River **5)** Sole

Part C: **1)** a **2)** c **3)** a **4)** b **5)** b

Part D: **1)** cake mix, eggs, oil, orange gelatin, water **2)** cake mix, eggs, and oil **3)** 8-inch cake pan **4)** 350° F **5)** 40 minutes

Part E: **1)** at the horse's neck **2)** rubber curry, stiff body brush, soft body brush, and hoof pick **3)** on the face or leg area **4)** to clean out the hooves **5)** Answers will vary. Someone who cares for, trains, or breeds horses might use this how-to book.

Chapter 3 Mastery Test B

Part A: **1)** False **2)** True **3)** False **4)** False **5)** True

Part B: **1)** Rio **2)** Meran River **3)** about 6 miles **4)** Sole **5)** Rio

Part C: **1)** c **2)** a **3)** b **4)** a **5)** c

Part D: **1)** blueberry muffin mix, eggs, oil **2)** blueberry muffin mix, eggs, oil **3)** muffin pan **4)** 375° F **5)** 20 minutes

Part E: **1)** face down **2)** Press 1, dial the area code, then dial the fax number. **3)** press start **4)** The fax machine will beep. **5)** The fax machine has an automatic feed that pulls the documents through.

Chapter 4 Mastery Test A

Part A: **1)** no **2)** Selby **3)** (233) 454-8912 **4)** (333) 998-4937 and (333) 998-4000 **5)** 233 **6)** (233) 454-9876 **7)** L Young is a business because it is followed by INC. **8)** 577 and 578 **9)** 743 Bagley Street, Denton **10)** (333) 998-6442 (Lynne's Pizza)

Part B: **1)** a **2)** a **3)** a **4)** b **5)** b

Part C: **1)** False **2)** True **3)** False **4)** False **5)** True **6)** True **7)** False **8)** True **9)** True **10)** False

Chapter 4 Mastery Test B

Part A: **1)** no **2)** Wallace **3)** (265) 349-4437 **4)** (225) 443-9876 and (225) 443-1000 **5)** 225 **6)** (225) 443-2587 (Sallin Apartments) **7)** three **8)** 348 and 349 **9)** 26438 Fenwick Avenue, Wallace **10)** (265) 448-2100 (Sallee's Restaurant)
Part B: **1)** a **2)** b **3)** a **4)** b **5)** b
Part C: **1)** True **2)** False **3)** True **4)** True **5)** False **6)** False **7)** False **8)** True **9)** False **10)** True

Chapter 5 Mastery Test A

Part A: **1)** media center **2)** Library of Congress **3)** nonfiction **4)** reference **5)** materials **6)** catalog **7)** subject **8)** video **9)** softcover **10)** hardcover

Part B: **1)** False **2)** True **3)** False **4)** True **5)** True

Part C: Students should have circled the following words. **1)** philosophy and psychology **2)** pure sciences **3)** history and geography **4)** literature **5)** arts and recreation **6)** general works **7)** religion **8)** technology (applied sciences) **9)** language **10)** social sciences

Part D: **1)** a **2)** c **3)** a **4)** c **5)** c

Chapter 5 Mastery Test B
Part A: **1)** media **2)** national **3)** fiction **4)** encyclopedias **5)** catalog **6)** magazine **7)** author **8)** catalog **9)** paperback **10)** hardback

Part B: **1)** True **2)** False **3)** True **4)** False **5)** False

Part C: Students should have circled the following words. **1)** general works **2)** pure sciences **3)** religion **4)** social sciences **5)** arts and recreation **6)** language **7)** history and geography **8)** technology (applied sciences) **9)** philosophy and psychology **10)** literature

Part D: **1)** b **2)** b **3)** c **4)** c **5)** a

Chapter 6 Mastery Test A
Part A: **1)** b **2)** a **3)** b **4)** c **5)** b **6)** a **7)** a **8)** b **9)** a **10)** c

Part B: **1)** auto mechanic **2)** tailor **3)** electrician **4)** insurance agent **5)** locksmith

Part C: **1)** Aid **2)** Bureau **3)** Chamber **4)** Union **5)** Welcome

Chapter 6 Mastery Test B
Part A: **1)** b **2)** a **3)** c **4)** b **5)** a **6)** c **7)** c **8)** a **9)** c **10)** b

Part B: **1)** locksmith **2)** insurance agent **3)** tailor **4)** electrician **5)** auto mechanic

Part C: **1)** Legal **2)** Business **3)** Commerce **4)** Consumers **5)** Wagon

Chapter 7 Mastery Test A
Part A: **1)** editorial **2)** daily **3)** advertisement **4)** media **5)** editor

Part B: **1)** E–1 **2)** D–7 **3)** B–5 **4)** C–10 **5)** B–1

Part C: **1)** 900–999 Real Estate **2)** 200–299 Merchandise **3)** 800–899 Rentals **4)** 700–799 Employment **5)** 500–599 Personal and Business Services

Part D: **1)** bedroom **2)** television **3)** utilities **4)** air conditioned or air conditioner **5)** engine **6)** AM/FM radio **7)** position **8)** full time **9)** salary **10)** preferred

Part E: **1)** False **2)** True **3)** True **4)** False **5)** False

Chapter 7 Mastery Test B
Part A: **1)** editor **2)** weekly **3)** editorial **4)** Mass **5)** classified

Part B: **1)** C–15 **2)** C–1 **3)** A–34 **4)** C–15 **5)** D–1

Part C: **1)** 200–299 Merchandise **2)** 1100–1199 Transportation **3)** 300–399 Pets and Animals **4)** 500–599 Personal and Business Services **5)** 1000–1099 Financial

Part D: **1)** bathroom **2)** washer and dryer **3)** electricity **4)** power steering **5)** automatic transmission **6)** sunroof **7)** experience **8)** part time **9)** immediately **10)** word processing

Part E: **1)** True **2)** False **3)** False **4)** True **5)** True

Chapter 8 Mastery Test A
Part A: **1)** information **2)** document **3)** full **4)** birth **5)** name **6)** Social Security **7)** maiden **8)** United States **9)** card **10)** form

Part B: **1)** True **2)** False **3)** False **4)** True **5)** False

Part C: Answers will vary. Check to see that each part of the application is filled out with students' personal information.

Chapter 8 Mastery Test B
Part A: **1)** applications **2)** document **3)** certificate **4)** form **5)** green **6)** signature **7)** legal **8)** name **9)** citizen **10)** Personal

Part B: **1)** False **2)** True **3)** True **4)** False **5)** True

Part C: Answers will vary. Check to see that each part of the application is filled out with students' personal information.

Chapter 9 Mastery Test A
Part A: **1)** money **2)** charge **3)** wholesale **4)** dealer **5)** price

Part B: **1)** Accept any of the following: centerpieces, wall hangings, to trim packages, or to decorate dried flowers **2)** 7/8″ wide × 25 yard rolls **3)** $5.95 each **4)** FA-3044 **5)** $5.45 each

Part C:

Order Form

Send to: 1. Name: (student's name) 2. Daytime Phone: (student's)
3. Address: (student's address)
4. City, State and ZIP (student's city, state, and ZIP)

	Item #	Qty.	Description	Item Price	Total Price
5.	893-58	1	Telephone and address book	$8.98	$8.98
				6. Total Price	$8.98
				7. Shipping	$3.00
				8. Total Charge	$11.98

Shipping Charges	
Up to $10.00	$3.00
$10.00 to $30.00	$4.00
Over $30.00	$5.00

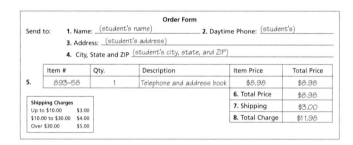

Part D: **1)** e **2)** c **3)** b **4)** a **5)** d

Chapter 9 Mastery Test B
Part A: **1)** discount **2)** order **3)** dealer **4)** card **5)** price

Part B: **1)** Accept any of the following: personal stationery, résumés, or letterheads **2)** 8 1/2″ × 11″ **3)** 100 sheets **4)** TL-4402 **5)** $5.49 each

Part C

Order Form

Send to: 1. Name: (student's name) 2. Daytime Phone: (student's)
3. Address: (student's address)
4. City, State and ZIP (student's city, state, and ZIP)

	Item #	Qty.	Description	Item Price	Total Price
5.	405-89E	1	Cassette recorder	$39.95	$39.95
				6. Total Price	$39.95
				7. Shipping	$5.00
				8. Total Charge	$44.95

Shipping Charges	
Up to $10.00	$3.00
$10.00 to $30.00	$4.00
Over $30.00	$5.00

Part D: **1)** a **2)** e **3)** b **4)** d **5)** c

Midterm Mastery Test

Part A: **1)** True **2)** True **3)** False **4)** True **5)** False **6)** True **7)** True **8)** False **9)** False **10)** True **11)** False **12)** True **13)** True **14)** True **15)** False

Part B: **1)** entry **2)** mark **3)** geographical **4)** symbol **5)** Blue Pages **6)** syllable **7)** Yellow Pages **8)** topic **9)** synonym **10)** key **11)** recipe **12)** periodical **13)** scale **14)** professional **15)** federal

Part C: **1)** c **2)** b **3)** a **4)** c **5)** a **6)** b **7)** c **8)** a **9)** c **10)** b

Part D: **1)** healthy **2)** hearing **3)** heart **4)** heat **5)** heavy

Part E: **1)** a computer how-to book **2)** to the *File* window **3)** move it to *Print Document* **4)** the user will be sent to *Printer Control* **5)** move the mouse cursor to *Print* and click once

Part F: **1)** five **2)** noun **3)** immediacies **4)** two **5)** yes

Final Mastery Test

Part A: **1)** False **2)** False **3)** False **4)** False **5)** True **6)** False **7)** True **8)** True **9)** False **10)** True **11)** False **12)** True **13)** True **14)** False **15)** False **16)** True **17)** False **18)** False **19)** False **20)** True

Part B: **1)** stress **2)** biographical **3)** grid **4)** Microfiche **5)** catalog **6)** Benefits **7)** subtopic **8)** doctoral **9)** obituary **10)** advertisement **11)** subscriber **12)** document **13)** form **14)** retail **15)** check

Part C: **1)** c **2)** c **3)** b **4)** c **5)** c **6)** c **7)** c **8)** b **9)** a **10)** b

Part D: **1)** f **2)** d **3)** k **4)** j **5)** a **6)** i **7)** o **8)** m **9)** b **10)** l **11)** c **12)** h **13)** g **14)** n **15)** e

Part E: **1)** discount **2)** discuss **3)** disgrace **4)** disgust **5)** disinfect

Part F: **1)** anyone who uses a photocopier **2)** open the lid on the copier **3)** place the page you want to copy face down on the glass **4)** paper size and number of copies **5)** the *Copy* button

Part G: **1)** D–10 **2)** B–1 **3)** C–1 **4)** C–10 **5)** C–15

Part H: **1)** carpeting **2)** deposit **3)** fireplace **4)** nonsmoker **5)** cassette tape player **6)** four-wheel drive **7)** convertible **8)** company **9)** required **10)** immediately (or immediate)

Part I: **1)** centerpieces, entertaining, and holidays **2)** 1″ wide × 8″ tall **3)** $4.95 **4)** CA-4348 **5)** $3.95 each

AGS

Teacher Questionnaire

Attention Teachers! As publishers of *Life Skills English,* we would like your help in making this textbook more valuable to you. Please take a few minutes to fill out this survey. Your feedback will help us to better serve you and your students.

1) What is your position and major area of responsibility? ____________

____

____

2) Briefly describe your setting:

___ regular education ___ special education ___ adult basic education

___ community college ___ university ___ other ____________

3) The enrollment in your classroom includes students with the following (check all that apply):

___ at-risk for failure ___ low reading ability ___ behavior problems

___ learning disabilities ___ ESL ___ other ____________

4) Grade level of your students: ____________

5) Racial/ethnic groups represented in your classes (check all that apply):

___ African-American ___ Asian ___ Caucasian ___ Hispanic

___ Native American ___ Other

6) School Location:

___ urban ___ suburban ___ rural ___ other ____________

7) What reaction did your students have to the materials? (Include comments about the cover design, lesson format, illustrations, etc.)

____

____

____

8) What features in the student text helped your students the most?

____

____

____

OVER ➤

9) What features in the student text helped your students the least? Please include suggestions for changing these to make the text more relevant.

____

____

____

10) How did you use the Teacher's Edition and support materials, and what features did you find to be the most helpful?

____

____

____

11) What activity from the program did your students benefit from the most? Please briefly explain.

____

____

____

12) Optional: Share an activity that you used to teach the materials in your classroom that enhanced the learning and motivation of your students.

____

____

____

Several activities will be selected to be included in future editions. Please include your name, address, and phone number so we may contact you for permission and possible payment to use the material. Thank you!

▼ **fold in thirds and tape shut at the top** ▼

Name: ____________________
School: ____________________
Address: ____________________
City/State/ZIP: ____________________
Phone: ____________________

NO POSTAGE NECESSARY IF MAILED IN THE UNITED STATES

BUSINESS REPLY MAIL
FIRST-CLASS MAIL PERMIT NO.12 CIRCLE PINES MN

POSTAGE WILL BE PAID BY ADDRESSEE

AGS
ATTN MARKETING SUPPORT
AMERICAN GUIDANCE SERVICE, INC.
4201 WOODLAND ROAD
PO BOX 99
CIRCLE PINES MN 55014-9923